INTRODUCTION TO ECONOMIC REASONING

The Addison-Wesley Series in Economics

Abel/Bernanke
Macroeconomics

Bade/Parkin
Foundations of Economics

Bierman/Fernandez
Game Theory with Economic Applications

Binger/Hoffman
Microeconomics with Calculus

Boyer
Principles of Transportation Economics

Branson
Macroeconomic Theory and Policy

Bruce
Public Finance and the American Economy

Burgess
The Economics of Regulation and Antitrust

Byrns/Stone
Economics

Carlton/Perloff
Modern Industrial Organization

Caves/Frankel/Jones
World Trade and Payments: An Introduction

Chapman
Environmental Economics: Theory, Application, and Policy

Cooter/Ulen
Law and Economics

Eaton/Mishkin
Online Readings to Accompany The Economics of Money, Banking, and Financial Markets

Ehrenberg/Smith
Modern Labor Economics

Ekelund/Tollison
Economics: Private Markets and Public Choice

Fusfeld
The Age of the Economist

Gerber
International Economics

Ghiara
Learning Economics: A Practical Workbook

Gordon
Macroeconomics

Gregory
Essentials of Economics

Gregory/Stuart
Russian and Soviet Economic Performance and Structure

Hartwick/Olewiler
The Economics of Natural Resource Use

Hubbard
Money, the Financial System, and the Economy

Hughes/Cain
American Economic History

Husted/Melvin
International Economics

Jehle/Reny
Advanced Microeconomic Theory

Klein
Mathematical Methods for Economics

Krugman/Obstfeld
International Economics: Theory and Policy

Laidler
The Demand for Money: Theories, Evidence, and Problems

Leeds/von Allmen
The Economics of Sports

Lesser/Dodds/Zerbe
Environmental Economics and Policy

Lipsey/Courant/Ragan
Economics

McCarty
Dollars and Sense: An Introduction to Economics

Melvin
International Money and Finance

Miller
Economics Today

Miller/Benjamin/North
The Economics of Public Issues

Mills/Hamilton
Urban Economics

Mishkin
The Economics of Money, Banking, and Financial Markets

Parkin
Economics

Parkin/Bade
Economics in Action Software

Perloff
Microeconomics

Phelps
Health Economics

Riddell/Shackelford/Stamos/Schneider
Economics: A Tool for Critically Understanding Society

Ritter/Silber/Udell
Principles of Money, Banking, and Financial Markets

Rohlf
Introduction to Economic Reasoning

Ruffin/Gregory
Principles of Economics

Sargent
Rational Expectations and Inflation

Scherer
Industry Structure, Strategy, and Public Policy

Schotter
Microeconomics

Sherman/Kolk
Business Cycles and Forecasting

Smith
Case Studies in Economic Development

Studenmund
Using Econometrics

Su
Economic Fluctuations and Forecasting

Tietenberg
Environmental and Natural Resource Economics

Tietenberg
Environmental Economics and Policy

Todaro
Economic Development

Waldman/Jensen
Industrial Organization: Theory and Practice

Williamson
Macroeconomics

Introduction to Economic Reasoning

FIFTH EDITION

WILLIAM D. ROHLF, JR.
Drury University

Addison
Wesley

Boston San Francisco New York
London Toronto Sydney Tokyo Singapore Madrid
Mexico City Munich Paris Cape Town Hong Kong Montreal

Acquisitions Editor: Victoria Warneck
Assistant Editor: Jennifer Jefferson
Managing Editor: James Rigney
Production Supervisor: Katherine Watson
Marketing Manager: Adrienne D'Ambrosio
Supplements Editor: Meredith Gertz
Project Coordination and Text Design: Electronic Publishing Services Inc., NYC
Design Manager: Regina Hagen
Cover Designer: Jeannet Leendertse
Manufacturing Manager: Hugh Crawford
Electronic Page Makeup: Electronic Publishing Services Inc., NYC

Library of Congress Cataloging-in-Publication Data

Rohlf, William D.
  Introduction to economic reasoning / William D. Rohlf, Jr. — 5th ed.
    p. cm. — (The Addison-Wesley series in economics)
  Includes index.
  ISBN 0-201-72625-4
  1. Economics, 2. United States—Economic conditions. I. Title. II. Series.

HB171.5.R73 2001
330—dc21   2001022088

Please visit our website at http://www.aw.com/rohlf

ISBN 0-201–72625-4
  4 5 6 7 8 9 10—MA—05 04 03

To my parents, who helped me learn the value of persistence.

PREFACE

Almost one hundred years ago, Alfred Marshall defined economics as "the study of mankind in the ordinary business of life." Today, the ordinary business of life has become incredibly complex. The purpose of this textbook is to help prepare students for that life.

Introduction to Economic Reasoning is intended for students taking the one-term course in introductory economics. Many of these students, perhaps a majority, will take only one course in economics. They have a variety of interests and educational objectives. Some are enrolled in pre-professional programs; others will pursue majors in areas such as business, psychology, or the liberal arts. At a number of institutions, the one-term course also enrolls first-year students in MBA programs and other graduate business programs. Many of these students pursued nonbusiness majors as undergraduates and did not elect to take an economics course. Others desire to review economics before entering the graduate program. Although the students enrolling in the one-term course have diverse objectives and interests, they can all benefit from a course that prepares them to understand economic issues better and helps them to become better decision makers.

THE FOCUS OF THE BOOK

How do we prepare students to understand economic issues and help them become better decision makers? I am convinced that we cannot accomplish these objectives by focusing solely on economic issues and short-cutting a discussion of economic concepts. This approach might provide students with ready answers to existing problems, but it would do little to prepare students for coping with new social problems and little to refine their decision-making skills. To accomplish those objectives, we must teach students something about economic reasoning.

Economists are fond of saying that economics is a way of thinking, or a way of reasoning about problems. The essence of economic reasoning is the ability to use theories or models to make sense out of the real world and devise policy solutions to economic problems. If we want students to use economic reasoning, we have to help them to learn and understand the basic economic theories. Without an understanding of economic theory, a course in economics can leave the student with little more than memorized solutions to current economic problems.

THE NEED TO MAKE CHOICES

Obviously, we can't do everything in a one-term course in introductory economics. And unless we can keep the student's interest and show the relevance of economics, we can't accomplish anything. So the instructor in a one-term course (and the author of a one-term text) must make choices. He or she must decide what to include and what to exclude, how to balance theory with application, and how to motivate the students without sounding too much like a cheerleader. This textbook attempts to bridge these extremes.

Because economists use theories or models in problem solving, the core of this text is economic theory. No essential micro or macro concept is omitted. Many refinements are omitted, however, so that more time can be devoted to the careful development of the most important concepts. This is one of the distinctive features of the text: a very careful development of the core ideas in economic theory.

MAKING ECONOMICS RELEVANT

Today's student wants to know why he or she should be studying economics. What problems or issues will it help to clarify? What decisions will it help to improve? In *Introduction to Economic Reasoning*, the relevance of economics is illustrated by the use of examples in the text and through special features entitled "Use Your Economic Reasoning." These features, which are listed in a separate table of contents on pages xxv–xxvi, contain current news articles that have been carefully selected to illustrate the relevance of the economic principles being discussed and to provide the student with an opportunity to test his or her knowledge of those principles. Each article is accompanied by a set of questions to ensure that the student gains the maximum benefit from the article, and the features themselves have been designed to make them easy to locate.

WRITING STYLE

In writing this text, my overriding objective has been to make economics accessible to the average student. I have been careful to avoid unnecessarily sophisticated vocabulary and needlessly long sentences. Most important, I have worked to ensure that my explanations of economic concepts are carefully and clearly developed. While professors may adopt a text for a wide variety of reasons, I am convinced that the most common reason for discontinuing its use is because students can't understand it. Your students will be able to read this text and understand it.

AIDS IN LEARNING

In addition to a clear writing style, the text contains a number of other learning aids:

1. Learning objectives are stated at the beginning of each chapter.
2. New terms are presented in boldface type and are always defined when they are introduced.
3. "Use Your Economic Reasoning" news article selections not only generate student interest but also give the student an opportunity to apply the concepts that have been presented and thereby reinforce learning.
4. Careful summaries highlight the contents of each chapter.
5. A glossary of new terms appears at the end of the text so that a student can easily review definitions.
6. A study guide including fill-in-the-blank and multiple choice questions (with answers) and problems and questions for discussion appears at the end of each chapter. This increases the likelihood that the study guide will be used, and encourages the student to review the chapter to correct deficiencies.

ADDITIONAL FEATURES

1. The demand and supply model (the core of micro theory) is more fully developed than in other one-semester texts, and the student is given numerous opportunities to test his or her understanding of the model.
2. The organization of the text provides for maximum flexibility in use. Instructors can choose how detailed they want to make their coverage of a given topic.
3. The importance of marginal reasoning is developed at the personal level and then extended to business decision making. Numerous illustrations make this principle come to life for the students.
4. Potentially challenging topics such as the theory of rational expectations and game theory are presented in a manner that is accessible to the beginning student.
5. The student is exposed to important areas of debate among economists (the activist–nonactivist debate in macroeconomics, for example) without being left with the impression that economic analysis is solely a matter of opinion.

FIFTH EDITION CHANGES

The fifth edition contains an all-new Chapter 5, "Economic Growth: The Importance of the Long Run." This chapter is intended to demonstrate the importance of economic growth in improving a society's standard of living. The chapter begins by introducing the *rule of seventy-two* and using that rule to illustrate how small changes in the rate of economic growth can have a significant impact on our standard of living. After establishing the importance of economic growth, the chapter proceeds to examine the sources of economic growth and how policymakers might attempt to alter an economy's growth path.

Additional changes in the fifth edition include updated coverage of economic systems and fiscal policy. Chapter 2, "Economic Systems," now contains a series of brief descriptions that illustrate important differences between existing economic systems. Chapter 12, "Fiscal Policy," has been refocused to call attention to significant trends in the federal budget—the growing importance of transfer payments, for instance—in addition to providing the traditional coverage of discretionary fiscal policy and the impact of the national debt.

Although new material has been added, the macro coverage has been streamlined. The aggregate demand–aggregate supply model serves as the framework for all macro chapters. Optional coverage of the Keynesian aggregate expenditures model has been removed from the text and is now available on the Web. Detailed coverage of the debate between Keynes and the classical economists has also been moved to the Web. Finally, the "Use Your Economic Reasoning" selections have been updated. The fifth edition contains almost thirty new selections drawn from diverse sources including the *Wall Street Journal*, the *New York Times*, the *San Francisco Chronicle*, *The Guardian (London)*, and the *New Straits Times* (Malaysia).

STRATEGIES FOR USING THE TEXT

Introduction to Economic Reasoning provides balanced coverage of microeconomics and macroeconomics. The book is divided into four parts. A two-chapter introduction (Part 1) examines the basic economic problem and economic systems. This is followed by seven chapters on microeconomics (Part 2), six chapters on macroeconomics (Part 3), and two chapters on international economics (Part 4).

The chapters in the text are arranged in micro–macro sequence, but an instructor could easily reverse this order by covering Chapters 1, 2, and 3 and then moving directly to Part 3. The remaining micro chapters and Part 4 could then be covered in sequence.

If an instructor desires to shorten the micro portion of the course, numerous options exist. Chapter 4 ("The Elasticity of Demand and Supply") can be omitted with no loss of continuity. And the discussion of market models can be tailored to provide varying degrees of coverage. For instance, instructors who do not want to emphasize the marginal principle can omit Chapter 5 ("Marginal Reasoning and Profit Maximization"). Instructors desiring still briefer coverage of market models can also omit Chapter 8 ("Industry Structure and Public Policy"). An instructor following these suggestions would be left with the core of micro theory: the model of supply and demand, the distinction between price takers and price searchers, and a discussion of market failure.

The macro coverage can also be reduced. For instance, instructors may opt to omit Chapter 14 ("The Activist–Nonactivist Debate") and/or Chapter 15 ("Economic Growth: The Importance of the Long Run"). The remaining macro chapters will identify measures of aggregate performance, introduce students to the aggregate demand–aggregate supply model, and discuss fiscal and monetary policies.

International economics is the last part of the book. This material has traditionally been the first to be omitted whenever an instructor found it necessary to shorten his or her course. Today, the growing importance of this subject matter may call for a different strategy. As a compromise course of action, an instructor might cover Chapter 16 ("International Trade") and omit Chapter 17 ("International Finance").

SUPPLEMENTARY MATERIALS

The instructor's manual that accompanies this book is intended to make the instructor's job easier. New instructors may benefit from the teaching tips provided for each chapter. The manual also contains answers to the "Use Your Economic Reasoning" questions and "Problems and Questions for Discussion." Transparency masters of all the text images are located in the back of the instructor's manual.

The test bank is also available in Test Generator Software (TestGen-EQ with QuizMaster-EQ for Windows). Fully networkable, this software is available for Windows and Macintosh. TestGen-EQ's friendly graphical interface enables instructors to easily view, edit, and add questions; transfer questions to tests; and print tests in a variety of fonts and forms. Search and sort features let the instructor quickly locate questions and arrange them in a preferred order. QuizMaster-EQ automatically grades the exams, stores results on disk, and allows the instructor to view or print a variety of reports.

To facilitate classroom presentation, PowerPoint slides of all the text images are available for Macintosh and Windows. A PowerPoint viewer is provided for use by those who do not have the full software program.

Finally, a Web page has been added. The Web page will provide instructors with materials that can be used to supplement the textbook, and it will provide students with links to important data sources and other relevant information. The Web page will also provide answers to the "Use Your Economic Reasoning" questions and "Problems and Questions For Discussion."

ACKNOWLEDGMENTS

One author is listed on the cover of this textbook, but there are many people who have helped in its preparation and to whom I owe my thanks.

First I would like to thank those who reviewed the fourth edition proposal and/or manuscript:

Vic Brajer
  California State University

Jeffrey Davis
  ITT Technical Institute

Phillip Graves
  University of Colorado

Mark Maier
  Glendale Community College

Michael Marlow
  California Polytechnic Institute

Costas Nicolaou
  University of Manitoba

Catherine O'Conner
  Bucknell University

Robert Posatko
  Shippensburg University

Geoffrey Schneider
  Bucknell University

Maurice Weinrobe
  Clark University

Michael White
  St. Cloud State University

Their comments and suggestions have been immensely helpful to me and are reflected in the content of this revision.

As with the previous editions, I owe a particular debt of thanks to Steve Mullins, my colleague at Drury University. He was often called upon to help me interpret reviewer comments and decide between conflicting opinions. His good judgment and ready assistance have made a major difference in the quality of this edition.

I would also like to thank those with whom I have worked at Addison-Wesley: Regina Hagen, Melissa Honig, Jennifer Jefferson, Diane Korta, Katherine Watson, and Victoria Warneck.

Finally, I would like to thank my wife, Bev. Without her patience and support this edition would never have been completed.

W.D.R.
Springfield, MO

BRIEF CONTENTS

CONTENTS

CHAPTER EIGHT

CHAPTER NINE

USE YOUR ECONOMIC REASONING NEWS ARTICLES

"Use Your Economic Reasoning" is a news article spread that builds critical thinking skills by illustrating and reinforcing the economic concepts of each chapter.

PART ONE

Introduction: Scarcity and the Economic System

Chapter 1 explains what the study of economics is about and how the knowledge you gain from this course may affect your thinking in many ways. Here you will be introduced to the concept of "opportunity cost"—one of the most important concepts in economics and in everyday living. You will learn about the role of economic theory in helping us make sense out of the things we observe in the world around us. In Chapter 2 you will discover what an economic system is and how economic systems differ from country to country.

With that introductory material behind you, you can begin exploring economics in more detail. Part 2 of the text examines microeconomics: the study of individual markets and individual business firms. Part 3 explores macroeconomics: the study of the economy as a whole and the factors that influence the economy's overall performance. Part 4 considers international economics: the study of economic exchanges between nations.

CHAPTER ONE

The Study of Economics

LEARNING OBJECTIVES

1. State the fundamental economic problem and provide a definition of economics.
2. Identify the categories of economic resources.
3. Explain cost-benefit analysis and the concept of opportunity cost.
4. Draw a production possibilities curve and use it to illustrate opportunity cost, economic growth, and the benefits of trade.
5. Discuss the three fundamental economic questions.
6. Identify five common goals of economic systems and illustrate how they may conflict.
7. Define economic theories and discuss their role.
8. Explain why economists sometimes disagree.

Beginning a subject you haven't explored before is something like starting out on a blind date: You always hope for the best but anticipate the worst. This time, be reassured. No course you take in college is likely to be more relevant to your future—whatever your interests—than this one. An understanding of economic principles is valuable because so many of the questions and decisions that touch our lives have an economic aspect. This is true whether you are evaluating something as personal as your decision to attend college or attempting to grapple with one of today's fundamental social issues: the debate about how to improve elementary and secondary education in the United States, for example, or how to provide adequate retirement incomes for older Americans without overburdening younger Americans, or the advisability of protecting U.S. businesses and workers from foreign competition. Each of these issues has important implications for your welfare and mine, yet they are just a few of the many complex questions that confront us as consumers, workers, and citizens. To understand and evaluate what economists, politicians, and others are saying about these issues, we need a knowledge of economics. Then we can do a better job of separating the "sense" from the "nonsense" and forming intelligent opinions.

Obviously you won't learn all there is to know about economics from one short textbook. But here is your opportunity to build a solid understanding of basic economic principles and discover how economists interpret data and analyze economic problems. That is especially important because economics is as much a way of reasoning as it is a body of knowledge. Once you have learned what it means to "consider the opportunity costs," to "compare the costs and benefits," and to "think marginally," nothing will ever look quite the same again. You'll find yourself making better decisions about everything from how to use your time more effectively to whom to support in the next presidential election. Watching the TV news and reading newspapers and magazines will become more meaningful and enjoyable. You will begin to notice the economic dimension of virtually every problem confronting society—pollution, crime, health care, higher education, and so on. Your knowledge of economics will help you understand and deal better with all these problems.

THE ECONOMIC PROBLEM

The fundamental economic problem facing individuals and societies alike is the fact that our wants exceed our capacity for satisfying those wants. Consider, for example, one of your personal economic problems: how to use your limited income—your limited financial resources. With the possible exception of the very rich, none of us can afford to buy everything we'd like to have. Each of us can think of a virtually limitless number of products we want or "need": food, shelter, clothing, membership at a health club, new tires for the car, a personal computer. Economist and social critic John Kenneth Galbraith has suggested that the satisfaction of a want through the purchase of a product not only fails to reduce our wants but in fact creates new ones. Purchase an audio system, for instance, and soon you will want compact discs, headphones, storage cabinets, and the like.

Societies face essentially the same dilemma: The wants of their members exceed the societies' capacities for satisfying those wants. In order to satisfy human wants, societies or nations require the use of **economic resources,** the scarce inputs that are used in the process of creating a good or providing a service. Traditionally economists divide these resources into four categories: land, labor, capital, and entrepreneurship. **Land** signifies more than earth or acreage;

it includes all raw materials—timber, water, minerals, and other production inputs—that are created by nature. **Labor** denotes the work—both physical and mental—that goes into the production process. **Capital** refers to physical aids to production, such as factories, machinery, and tools.[1] **Entrepreneurship** is the managerial function that combines all these economic resources in an effective way and uncovers new opportunities to earn a profit—for example, through new products or processes. Entrepreneurship is characterized by a willingness to take the risks associated with a business venture.

Every society's stock of economic resources is limited, or *scarce*, in relation to the infinite wants of its members. At any given time, even the world's richest economies have available only so much raw material, labor, equipment, and managerial talent to use in producing goods and services. Consequently, an economy's ability to produce goods and services is limited, just as an individual's ability to satisfy his or her personal wants is limited.

The inability to satisfy all our wants forces us to make choices about how we can best use our limited resources. That is what economics is all about: making wise choices about how to use scarce resources. Therefore, we define **economics** as the study of how to use our limited resources to satisfy our unlimited wants as fully as possible. When individuals, businesses, or nations try to make the most of what they have, they are "economizing."

COST-BENEFIT ANALYSIS AND OPPORTUNITY COST

In order to make wise choices, we must compare the costs and benefits associated with each alternative or option we consider. A particular decision or choice will improve our well-being only if the benefits associated with that decision exceed the costs, if what we gain is worth more to us than what we lose. Individuals, businesses, and even governments engage in **cost-benefit analysis**—a systematic comparison of costs and benefits—before deciding on a course of action.

Comparing costs and benefits probably seems like a relatively straightforward process. Sometimes that's the case, but not always. In some instances, the costs and benefits may be very subjective and hard to compare. In other instances, there may be hidden costs or benefits that are easily ignored.

---

[1] Machines and tools are also known as **physical capital** or **capital goods**. This term distinguishes these physical production aids from **human capital**, the knowledge and skills possessed by workers, and **financial capital**, or money.

One of the fundamental lessons of economics is that all our choices entail costs: There is no "free lunch." Whenever you make a decision to do or have one thing, you sacrifice the opportunity to do or have some other thing. The best, or *most valued*, alternative you must sacrifice in order to take a particular action is the **opportunity cost** of that action. What opportunity are you sacrificing by reading this chapter? Perhaps you could be studying for another class or watching your favorite TV show. The opportunity cost of reading this chapter is whatever you wanted to do most. When your city council or town meeting allocates tax dollars to install sidewalks, it may sacrifice books for the public library, streetlights for a residential area, or tennis courts for a local park. Whatever that body would have chosen to do if it hadn't installed sidewalks is the opportunity cost of the sidewalks.

When Congress debates the size of the defense budget, the outcome of that debate affects each of us. If a nation's resources are fully employed, an increase in the output of military goods and services requires a reduction in the output of something else. An increase in military spending may mean a cut in funding for job training, road construction, or aid to education; it may mean an increase in taxes which, in turn, will lead to a reduction in private consumer spending and the output of consumer goods.

Either way, more military output means less civilian output because, at any given time, there is a limit to the amount of total output the economy can produce. This doesn't necessarily mean that we shouldn't spend more on military goods if there are sound reasons for doing so. It does mean that we should be aware of what that spending costs us in terms of private goods and services or other government programs. The economist's point here is that we can't make the best decisions about how to use our scarce resources unless we know the true costs and benefits of our decisions. (See "Teen Tycoon," on page 8, to learn why one budding entrepreneur has decided that the costs of attending college outweigh the benefits.)

THE PRODUCTION POSSIBILITIES CURVE

We can illustrate the concept of opportunity cost with a simple graph called a production possibilities curve. (The appendix at the end of this chapter explains how graphs are constructed and interpreted.) A **production possibilities curve** shows the combinations of goods that the economy is capable of producing with its present stock of economic resources and its existing techniques of production. Because it outlines the boundaries, or limits, of the economy's ability to produce output, it is sometimes called a *production possibilities frontier*. Any point along or inside the frontier represents a combination of goods that the economy can produce; any point above the curve is beyond the economy's present production capacity.

Exhibit 1.1 shows the production capabilities of a hypothetical economy. The economy's output of civilian goods is measured on the vertical axis and its output of military goods on the horizontal axis. According to this exhibit, if all the economy's resources were used to produce civilian goods, 80 million units of civilian goods could be produced each year (point *A*). On the other hand, if the economy were to use all its economic resources to produce military goods, 50 million units of military goods could be produced each year (point *D*). Between these extremes lie other production possibilities—combined outputs of military and civilian goods that the economy is capable of producing. For example, the economy might choose to produce 70 million units of civilian goods and 20 million units of military goods (point *B*). Or it might choose to produce 40 million units of civilian goods and 40 million units of military goods (point *C*). We can see, then, that the curve *ABCD* outlines the boundaries of our hypothetical economy's production abilities. Point *E*, which lies above the curve, represents a combination of products that is beyond the economy's present capacity.

EXHIBIT 1.1
The Production Possibilities Curve

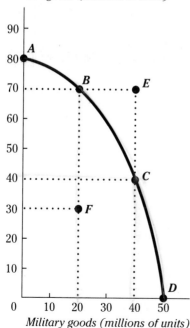

Civilian goods (millions of units)

Military goods (millions of units)

The production possibilities curve, *ABCD*, shows the combinations of civilian goods and military goods that the economy is capable of producing with its present stock of economic resources and the existing techniques of production. Any point on or below the curve is possible. Any point above the curve is ruled out (impossible).

Teen Tycoon: Who Needs to Stay in High School to Become a CEO? Not Jayson Meyer

Robert Johnson

DAYTONA BEACH, Fla.—A waitress at the Kiwanis Club luncheon plops a plate of meatloaf and peas in front of Jayson Meyer, a prospective member. She looks tempted to tell him to eat all his vegetables.

Who could blame her? Mr. Meyer is 17 years old. Even in his blazer and red tie, the president and chief executive officer of Meyer Technologies Inc. looks as if he should change into cutoff jeans and mingle with the throngs of college students enjoying spring break on the Atlantic shore nearby.

"I'll probably never go on spring break," he says, with a twinge of regret. But he adds quickly, "I'd rather be building an international business and making a lot of money."

While he may look out of place at the staid Kiwanis Club, Mr. Meyer as teenage CEO isn't exactly an anomaly these days. In a society that has produced scads of under-age technology entrepreneurs—Bill Gates, Michael Dell and Steve Jobs, just to name a few of the more famous and precocious ones—the teenage CEO seems to have little trouble being taken seriously.

Meyer Tech builds customized computers (which Mr. Meyer and his team make from hardware parts they buy); writes a variety of software programs, including customized accounting and billing programs; and designs and maintains communications systems for business clients. It's a line of business crawling with competitors — from one-person enterprises based in homes to giant corporations like IBM and Microsoft. But location, location, location favors Mr. Meyer: He has set up shop in fast-growing Central Florida, which teems with small businesses that can't afford in-house computer technicians and must rely on independent trouble-shooters.

Meyer Tech has grown rapidly in this market, but is still minuscule by high-tech standards. Revenue in 1997 was about $4,000, rose to $500,000 last year, and this year the company is on track to hit $1.5 million. "The phone hardly stops ringing," Mr. Meyer says.

Even by today's standards, Mr. Meyer seems to be in exceptionally high gear. He dropped out of high school, not college, to start his business, when he was 15 years old. He began in a booth at a flea market with $1,500 he had saved from computer trouble-shooting for neighbors and from mowing lawns. (He later received his high-school diploma through part-time study at a community college.)

Mr. Meyer got the idea of starting the company when word spread at Ormond Beach Middle School in 1996 that he could fix seemingly any computer glitch. "Teachers were always calling me out of class to work on their computers somewhere else at school." He says that one day while riding home from school with his father, 47-year-old Michael Meyer, he told his dad: "I'm working on computers all the time anyway.

Why not just start a company, call it Meyer Technologies, and see where it goes?"

So far the business—which by early 1999 had expanded beyond just weekend operations out of the flea-market booth—has allowed him to acquire some of the adult trappings of success: a new silver Lexus, a Rolex watch. Yet all this has a price: almost no semblance of a normal adolescence. Mr. Meyer typically works 80 to 100 hours a week. About once a week, he calls his parents, with whom he still lives, to say he'll just sleep on his office couch in order to get an early start the next day.

Some say all this is too much responsibility, too soon. Brien Biondi, executive of the Young Entrepreneurs Organization, a nonprofit professional group in Washington, says, "I have reservations about a 17-year-old going into business on their own. He's so alone. He can't turn to his high-school buddies for advice because they won't know what he's talking about."

Jayson's mother, Kim Meyer, encourages her son to have as normal a teenage life as possible, given his career. He has a girlfriend, a student at Spruce Creek High School in Daytona Beach, and they recently attended her school's prom. "I tell him I don't want him to miss these sorts of activities and that many of them won't come again in his life," she says. "But he keeps saying, 'Mom, work is fun for me.'"

But does the value of the professional experience outweigh starting at so young an age? One former wunderkind has mixed feelings. Geoff Allen, an erstwhile teenage entrepreneur who is now 29 and busily planning an Internet start-up, says the simple experience of running a company as a youth can be invaluable, even if the enterprise flops. "The main value of teenage entrepreneurship for me wasn't profit, it was the hard knocks," he says. "Learning from bad decisions and failure was very important." Mr. Allen ended up selling his teenage venture, a desktop-publishing company, at a loss. (He went on to other high-tech small business ventures that he says have made him wealthy.)

But Mr. Meyer will have no talk of failure. With a sense of urgency that illustrates the gulf in perspective between the young and very young entrepreneur, he says, "I'd rather learn from success. There are going to be some missteps, but I hope they'll be relatively small and I can learn from them without ruining the business."…

So far, Mr. Meyer has kept his balance sheet lean and mean by, among other things, using the widespread start-up tactic of promising future stock options to employees, instead of paying high salaries. His entire payroll is less than $300,000 a year, and he plows much of his own $50,000 salary back into the business.

His staff pitches in with him to pinch pennies when possible. Last year Mr. Meyer led late-night work crews of volunteer staffers who repainted and recarpeted their new offices in a modest tan stucco building. Mr. Meyer even persuaded his father, a residential builder, to repair damaged drywall surfaces in some offices.

The senior Mr. Meyer also does the bookkeeping at his son's company free of charge and at one point invested $15,000—which has been repaid. He says, "I offer advice, but he really doesn't need much. Jayson has never been a normal kid. He didn't just walk at eight months, he ran. When he was 10 years old he acted like he was 18. Now he's 17 and has the maturity of a 25-year-old."…

Use Your Economic Reasoning

1. Mr. Meyer appears to have it made: $50,000 a year salary, a new Lexus, etc. Is there any opportunity cost associated with becoming a teenage CEO?
2. Mr. Meyer doesn't appear to be planning on a college education. Why? Is the opportunity cost of attending college greater for Meyer than it is for the average 17-year-old?
3. Has Meyer weighed the costs and benefits of his decision to become a CEO? Support your conclusion with evidence from the article.

Unfortunately, economies do not always live up to their production capabilities. Whenever an economy is operating at a point inside its production possibilities curve, we know that economic resources are not being fully employed. For example, at point *F* in Exh. 1.1, our hypothetical economy is producing 30 million units of civilian goods and 20 million units of military goods each year. But according to the production possibilities curve, the economy could do much better. For example, it could increase its output of civilian goods to 70 million units a year without sacrificing any military goods (point *B*). Or it could expand its output of civilian goods to 40 million units while also expanding its production of military goods to 40 million units (point *C*). In short, when an economy has unemployed resources, it is not satisfying as many of the society's unlimited wants as it could if it used its full potential.

Opportunity Costs along the Curve

We have seen that the production possibilities curve graphically represents the concept of opportunity cost. When an economy's resources are fully employed—that is, when an economy is operating on the production possibilities curve rather than inside it—larger amounts of one product can be obtained only by producing smaller amounts of the other product. The production possibilities curve slopes downward to the right to illustrate opportunity cost: More of one thing means less of the other thing. We can see opportunity costs changing as we move from one point on the production possibilities curve to another. For example, suppose that the society is operating at point *A* on the production possibilities curve in Exh. 1.1, producing 80 million units of civilian goods and no military goods. If the society decides that it would prefer to operate at point *B*, the opportunity cost of acquiring the first 20 million units of military goods would be the loss of 10 million units of civilian goods. The economy can move from point *A* to point *B* only by transferring resources from the production of civilian goods to the production of military goods.

Suppose that the society would like to have even more military goods—for example, 40 million units of military goods produced each year. According to the production possibilities curve, the opportunity cost of acquiring the next 20 million units of military goods (and moving from point *B* to point *C*) would be a loss of 30 million units of civilian goods—three times what it cost the society to acquire the first 20 million units of military goods. Moving from point *C* to point *D* would be even more expensive. In order to acquire the last 10 million units of military goods, the society would have to sacrifice 40 million units of civilian goods.

The Law of Increasing Costs

Our hypothetical production possibilities curve illustrates an important principle known as the **law of increasing costs:** As more of a particular product is produced, its opportunity cost per unit will increase. How do we explain the law of increasing costs? Why does our hypothetical society have to sacrifice larger and larger amounts of civilian output in order to obtain each additional increment of military output?

The explanation is fairly simple. Not all resources are alike; some economic resources—skilled labor and specialized machinery, for instance— are better suited to the production of one product than another. In our example some resources are better suited to the production of civilian goods and services, others to the production of military products. Consequently when the society attempts to expand its output of military goods and services, it must eventually use resources that are not well suited to producing those military products.

To illustrate that problem, let's examine the process of transferring resources from the production of civilian products to the production of military products. Suppose that initially our hypothetical economy is not producing any military output. At first, it will not be difficult for the economy to increase its military output. Some of the existing capital resources, including factories, can be converted to the production of military products with relative ease, and many members of the labor force will have skills that are readily transferable to the production of military products. For example, it would be fairly simple to convert a clothing factory to the production of uniforms or to convert an awning factory to the production of tents. Since these conversions are relatively easy, the society will gain just about as much in military output as it will lose in civilian output.

But to continue expanding the output of military products, it will be necessary to use resources that are increasingly less suitable. For instance, consider the difficulty that might be encountered in converting an amusement park to a missile-manufacturing facility, or a toy factory to an explosives plant. Much of the equipment that was useful in producing civilian output will be of no use in producing military output. Therefore, although the conversion of these facilities will require society to give up a large quantity of civilian output (many rides at the amusement park and thousands of toys), it will not result in very many additional units of military output.

The point is that because some resources are better suited to the production of civilian goods than to the production of military products, increasing amounts of civilian goods and services will have to be sacrificed to obtain each additional increment of military output. It is this principle (the law of increasing costs) that causes the production possibilities frontier to have the curved shape depicted in Exhs. 1.1 and 1.2.

Economic Growth and the Benefits of Trade

As we have seen, it is important for economies to operate on, rather than inside, their production possibilities curves. But even when an economy fully employs its resources, it cannot satisfy all of a society's wants. Any point *above* the production possibilities frontier exceeds the economy's current production capabilities. For instance, point E in Exh. 1.2, which combines 70 million units of civilian goods and 40 million units of military goods, is beyond the inside production possibilities curve representing the existing capacity of this hypothetical economy. Society clearly would prefer that combination of products to the combination represented by, say, point C, but it can't obtain it.

Of course, the economy's production capacity is not permanently fixed. If the quantity of economic resources were to increase or if better production methods were discovered, the economy could produce more goods and ser-

EXHIBIT 1.2
Illustrating Economic Growth

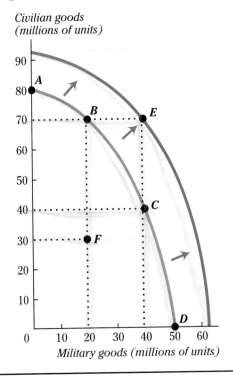

Civilian goods (millions of units)

Military goods (millions of units)

If the quantity of economic resources were to increase or better production methods were discovered, the economy's ability to produce goods and services would expand. Such economic growth can be illustrated by shifting the production possibilities curve to the right.

Like economic growth, free trade can increase the goods and services available for consumption.

vices. Such an increase in production capacity is usually described as *economic growth* and is illustrated by shifting the production possibilities curve to the right. The outside curve in Exh. 1.2 represents economic growth sufficient to take point *E* within the economy's production possibilities frontier.

Trade between nations can provide benefits that are very similar to those that result from economic growth—increased amounts of goods and services. To illustrate, suppose that our hypothetical economy is operating at point *A* on the inside production possibilities curve in Exh. 1.2, producing 80 units of civilian goods and no military goods. According to the production possibilities curve, the economy could acquire 40 million units of military goods (and move to point *C*) only if it was willing to give up 40 million units of civilian goods; the cost of acquiring each additional unit of military goods would be the sacrifice of one unit of civilian goods. But suppose that through trade with other nations, this economy could acquire a unit of military goods by sacrificing only one-fourth of a unit of civilian goods. That would permit the economy to acquire the 40 million units of military goods it desires by giving up (trading) only 10 million units of civilian goods. The economy could move to point *E*, a point well beyond its own production capabilities.[2]

---

[2] Unlike economic growth, trade does not shift an economy's production possibilities curve but instead merely permits a nation to consume a combination of products beyond its own production capabilities.

The ability to acquire goods at a lower opportunity cost (and thereby increase the total amount of goods and services available for consumption) is why **free trade**—trade that is not hindered by artificial restrictions or trade barriers—is generally supported by economists. Chapter 16 explores the theoretical basis for trade in much greater detail.

As you can see, the production possibilities curve is a useful tool for thinking about our economy. It shows that an economy with fully employed resources cannot produce more of one thing without sacrificing something else. Equally important, the production possibilities model can be used to illustrate the benefits of economic growth and free trade. Of course, neither economic growth nor free trade eliminates the need to make choices about how to use our scarce resources. The next section explores the nature of those choices in more detail.

THE THREE FUNDAMENTAL QUESTIONS

The choice between military goods and civilian goods is only one of the broad decisions that the United States and other nations face. The dilemma of unlimited wants and limited economic resources forces each society to make three basic choices, to answer the "three fundamental questions" of economics: (1) What goods and services will we produce and in what quantities? (2) How will these goods and services be produced? (3) For whom will these products be produced—that is, how will the output be distributed?

What to Produce

Because no society can produce everything its members desire, each society must sort through and assess its various wants and then decide which goods and services to produce in what quantities. Deciding the relative value of military products against civilian goods is only one part of the picture, because each society must determine precisely which civilian and military products it will produce. For example, it must decide whether to produce clothing or to conserve its scarce resources for some other use. Next, it must decide what types of clothing to produce—how many shirts, dresses, pairs of slacks, overcoats, and so on. Finally, it must decide in what sizes to produce these items of clothing and determine the quantities of each size. Only after considering all such alternatives can a society decide which goods and services to produce.

How to Produce

After deciding which products to produce, each society must also decide what materials and methods to use in their production. In most cases, a given good or service can be produced in more than one way. For instance, a shirt can be made of cotton, wool, or acrylic fibers. It can be sewn entirely by hand, partly by hand, or entirely by machine. It can be packaged in paper, cardboard, plastic, or some combination of materials. It can be shipped by truck, train, boat, or plane. In short, the producer must choose among many options with regard to materials, production methods, and means of shipment.

For Whom to Produce

Finally, each society must decide how to distribute or divide up its limited output among those who desire to receive it. Should everyone receive equal shares of society's output? Should those who produce more receive more? What about those who don't produce at all, either because they can't work or because they don't want to work? How much of society's output should *they* receive? In deciding how to distribute output—how output will be shared—different societies are influenced by their traditions and cultural values.

Whether a society is rich or poor, simple or complex, democratic or authoritarian, it must have some *economic system* through which it addresses the three fundamental questions. Chapter 2 examines a variety of economic systems and discusses how each responds to these questions.

FIVE ECONOMIC GOALS

A given economic system's answers to the three fundamental questions are not always satisfactory to either the nation's citizens or its leaders. For example, if an economy is operating inside its production possibilities curve, it is not using all its production capabilities and is therefore not satisfying as many human wants as possible. A society with unemployed resources may want to take steps to improve the economy's performance so that it does a better job of fulfilling citizens' expectations or, in some cases, the expectations of those in power.

What should a society expect from its economic system? Before a society can attempt to improve its economic performance, it must have a set of goals, objectives, or standards by which to judge that performance. Although there is room for debate about precisely what constitutes "good performance" from an economic system, many societies recognize five essential goals:

1. *Full employment of economic resources.* If a society is to obtain maximum benefit from its scarce resources, it must utilize them fully. Whenever resources are unemployed—when factories stand idle, laborers lack work,

or farmland lies untilled—the society is sacrificing the goods and services that those resources could have produced. Therefore, it is doing a less than optimal job of satisfying the unlimited wants of its members.

2. *Efficiency.* Economic efficiency means getting the most benefit out of limited resources. This goal has two separate elements: (a) production of the goods and services that consumers desire the most and (b) realization of this production at the lowest cost in terms of scarce resources. Economic efficiency is the very essence of economics. If an economic system fully employs its resources but uses them to produce relatively unwanted products, the society cannot hope to achieve maximum satisfaction from its resources. By the same token, if an economy does not minimize the amount of resources used in producing *each* product, it will not be able to produce as many products; consequently, fewer wants will be satisfied.

3. *Economic growth.* Because most people want and expect their standard of living to improve continually, economic growth—expansion in the economy's capacity to produce goods and services—is an important objective. If population is increasing, some economic growth is necessary just to maintain the existing standard of material welfare. When a nation's population is stable or is increasing less rapidly than output,

When labor or other economic resources are unemployed, society must do without the goods and services those resources could have produced.

economic growth results in more goods and services per person, contributing to a higher standard of living.

4. *A fair distribution of income.* Distribution of income means the way income is divided among the members of a society. In modern economies the income distribution is the primary factor determining how output will be shared. (In primitive economies, such as Ethiopia or Burundi, custom or tradition plays a major role in deciding how output is divided.) People with larger incomes receive larger shares of their economy's output. Is this a fair distribution of output? Some contend that it is. Others call for redistribution of income to eliminate poverty in the society. Still others argue that nothing less than an equal distribution is truly fair.

5. *A stable price level.* A major goal of most economies is a stable price level. Societies fear inflation—that is, a rise in the general level of prices. Inflation redistributes income arbitrarily: Some people's incomes rise more rapidly than inflation, whereas other people find that their incomes can't keep pace. The former group emerges with a larger share of the economy's output, while the latter group must make do with less than before. The demoralizing effect of this redistribution can lead to social unrest.

In pursuing the five economic goals, societies strive to maintain compatibility with their noneconomic, or sociopolitical, objectives. Americans, for example, want to achieve these economic goals without harming the environment or sacrificing the rights of people to select their occupations, own property, and spend their incomes as they choose. Societies that place high value on tradition, such as Japan, may strive to pursue these economic goals without violating the customs of the past. Insofar as the cultural, political, religious, and other noneconomic values of societies differ, the relative importance of each of the five economic goals and the methods of meeting those goals will also differ.

CONFLICTS AND TRADE-OFFS

Defining economic goals is only the first step in attempting to improve our economy's performance. The next step is to decide how to achieve these goals. Often the pursuit of one goal forces us to sacrifice at least part of some other economic or noneconomic goal. That is what economists call a *trade-off*—society gets more of one thing only by giving up, or trading off, something else. This is another way of stating the problem of opportunity cost. The opportunity cost of achieving a particular goal is whatever other goal has to be sacrificed or compromised. Let's consider three problems societies face in pursuing economic goals.

Full Employment versus Stable Prices

The goal of achieving full employment may conflict with the goal of maintaining a stable price level. Experience has taught us that attempting to reduce unemployment generally results in a higher rate of inflation. By the same token, attempts to reduce the rate of inflation often lead to higher unemployment. Frequently it becomes necessary to sacrifice part of one goal in favor of the other. For instance, society may accept some unemployment to maintain a lower inflation rate. The trade-off each society makes depends partly on economic analysis but is also influenced by societal values.[3]

Economic Growth versus Environmental Protection

Conflict frequently occurs between the goals of economic growth and a clean environment. Although most Americans support these two goals, it has become apparent that expansion of the economy's output takes a toll on the environment. For instance, our attempts to expand agricultural output by using pesticides and chemical fertilizers have been partially responsible for the pollution of our rivers and streams. We make trade-offs between economic growth and environmental preservation, trade-offs that reflect prevailing national values.

Equality versus Efficiency

Consider now the potential conflict between income equality and economic efficiency. Suppose that a society decided that fair income distribution demanded greater equality of income than currently exists. Many economists would point out that efforts to achieve greater equality tend to have a negative impact on economic efficiency. Remember, efficiency means producing the most-wanted products in the least costly way. To accomplish this, the economy must be able to direct labor to the areas where it is most needed, often by making wages and salaries in these areas more attractive than those in other areas. For example, if a society needs to increase its number of computer programmers more rapidly than its number of teachers or nurses, it can encourage people to become computer programmers by making that occupation more rewarding financially than teaching or nursing.[4] If pay differentials are reduced in order to meet the goal of equality, a society will sacrifice economic efficiency because it will be more difficult to direct the flow of labor.

---

[3] Most economists agree that there is a short-run trade-off between unemployment and inflation that may not exist in the long run. This issue is discussed in Chapter 11.

[4] In some economic systems these adjustments in wages and salaries would occur automatically; in others deliberate action would be required. Chapter 2 has more to say about how specific economic systems direct or allocate labor.

Choosing between Objectives

When our society's goals conflict and demand that we choose between them, it is not the function of economists to decide which is the more important. The choice between objectives such as more rapid economic growth and a cleaner environment, or between greater equality and enhanced efficiency, is not solely a matter of objective cost-benefit analysis. Rather, it involves "**normative judgments**"—judgments about what *should be* rather than what *is*. This is a realm in which economists have no more expertise than anyone else. Setting goals is the job of the society or its representatives. The function of the economist is to make sure that those in charge of setting goals (or devising policies to achieve goals) are aware of the alternatives available to them and the sacrifices each alternative requires—in other words, the costs and benefits of their actions.

ECONOMIC THEORY AND POLICY

Before economists can recommend policies for dealing with economic problems or achieving goals, they must understand thoroughly how the economic system operates. This is where economic theory comes into play.

Theories are generalizations about causal relationships between facts, or variables; they help us to understand how events are connected or what causes what in the world around us. Theories are also referred to as laws, principles, and models. When in later chapters you encounter the *law* of demand, the *principle* of comparative advantage, and the *model* of command socialism, bear in mind that each of these tools is a theory.

Theory in Everyday Life

You probably think of theory as something exotic; something you would not normally encounter or use. But nothing could be further from the truth. We each use theory in our daily life. If you don't recognize the role of theory in your life, it's because many of the theories you use were learned informally and are applied unconsciously. To illustrate, consider the following problem. You roll out of bed in the morning and crawl to the TV to turn it on. But instead of seeing your favorite morning program, all you see is a black screen—no picture, no sound, nothing. What is the *first* thing you will do to try to get the TV to work? You won't call the cable company, not at first anyway, and you won't throw the TV out the window—yet. Take some time to think about what you would do before reading further.

In response to this question, a common answer is, "I'd check to see if it's plugged in." Most people agree that that's a sensible response, but why do we agree on this sensible answer? Why don't people say, "I'd look outside to see

USE YOUR ECONOMIC REASONING

Children Smart Enough to Get into Elite Schools May Not Need to Bother

By Alan B. Krueger

YOUR SON or daughter has just been accepted to both the University of Pennsylvania and to Penn State. The deadline for decision is May 1. Where should he or she go?

Many factors should be considered, of course, but lots of parents and students are particularly interested in the potential economic payoff from higher education. Until recently, there was a consensus among economists that students who attend more selective colleges—ones with tougher admissions standards—land better paying jobs as a result. Having smart, motivated classmates and a prestigious degree were thought to enhance learning and give students access to job networks.

But is it true?

A study that I conducted with Stacy Dale of the Andrew W. Mellon Foundation, "Estimating the Payoff to At-

tending a More Selective College"... has unintentionally undermined this consensus.

It is easy to see how one could think that elite colleges enhance their graduates' earnings. According to the College and Beyond Survey, data collected by the Mellon Foundation, the average student who entered a highly selective college like Yale, Swarthmore or the University of Pennsylvania in 1976, earned $92,000 in 1995. The average student from a moderately selective college, like Penn State, Denison or Tulane, earned $22,000 less.

The problem with this comparison is that students who attend more selective colleges are likely to have higher earnings regardless of where they attend college for the very reasons that they were admitted to the more selective colleges in the first place.

Trying to address the problem, earlier studies compared students with similar

standardized test scores and grade point averages who attended more and less selective schools. But this approach takes account of much less information than admissions committees see. There is no guarantee that all the relevant differences among students have been held constant.

This problem is known as selection bias. More selective schools accept students with greater earnings potential, and students with greater earnings potential are more likely to apply to more selective schools.

To overcome the problem, Ms. Dale and I restricted the comparison to students who applied to and were accepted by comparable colleges. Some students chose more selective schools; some less selective ones....

Our research found that earnings were unrelated to the selectivity of the college that students had attended among those who had com-

Source: The New York Times, April 27, 2000, Page C2

if it's snowing," or "I'd run to my car to see if it has gas in it." They don't select these answers because we all know they have nothing to do with getting a picture on our TV. And, more importantly, we know that electricity *does* have something to do with getting a picture. In short, we all have theories about how TVs work,

parable options. For example, the average earnings for the 519 students who were accepted by both moderately selective (average College Board scores of 1,000 to 1,099) and highly selective schools (average scores greater than 1,275), varied little, no matter which type of college they attended.

One group of students, however, clearly benefited from attending a highly selective college: those from lower-income families—defined approximately as the bottom quarter of families who send children to college. For them, attending a more selective school increased earnings significantly.

Restricting the comparison to those with similar choices helps solve the selection bias problem because these students were equivalent in the eyes of the admissions committees.

More important, students who applied to equally selective schools revealed that they had similar aspiration levels and self-confidence. If the comparison is restricted to students who applied to equally selective schools—regardless of whether they were admitted—attending a more selective school is still unrelated to earnings.

Although the selectivity of a school does not appear to influence the typical student's economic success, our analysis finds that the resources schools devote to instruction, which are related to tuition costs, do influence it....

There are several reasons that college selectivity might have little impact on post-college careers. First, even elite colleges have diverse student bodies, and it is possible for apathetic students at elite schools to find other apathetic students with whom to play Nintendo and guzzle beer. By contrast, a good student can get a good education almost anywhere.

Second, about a third of college graduates earn higher degrees, whose prestige is often more relevant to professional or business success than undergraduate degrees.

Third, a student who goes to Penn State instead of the University of Pennsylvania, is more likely to end up near the top of the class. Employers and graduate schools may not adequately adjust for the competition.

My advice to students ... Recognize that your own motivation, ambition and talents will determine your success more than the college name on your diploma.

My advice to elite colleges: Recognize that the most disadvantaged students benefit most from your instruction. Set financial aid and admission policies accordingly.

Use Your Economic Reasoning

1. The typical graduate of an elite college earns more than the typical graduate of a less-selective school. Doesn't this *prove* that attending an elite school boosts earnings?
2. To determine if an education at an elite school results in higher earnings, we must compare students with equal test scores and GPAs. What other factors should we attempt to hold constant?
3. Dale and Krugman attempted to hold constant hard-to-quantify success factors (like personality and motivation) by focusing their study only on students who were accepted to selective schools. Some these students went on to attend the selective school, others went elsewhere. They then tracked and compared their earnings. What does this approach accomplish?
4. Suppose we found out that the graduates of elite schools did in fact earn more than the graduates of less-selective schools, ceteris paribus. Would that be sufficient evidence to opt for an elite school? (Hint: Remember our cost-benefit model!)

and all those theories involve electricity. Your theory may be fairly elaborate—if you've had a physics course—or it may be fairly simple, if you've learned it informally by repeated observations. Here's a simple theory of how TVs work:

electricity → causes → pictures.

Note that this theory does not fully describe the way TVs work; theories never do. Theories help us understand the real world by simplifying reality. In fact, theories or models are sometimes described as simplified pictures of the real world. By leaving out extraneous details and complexities, theories help us see the essential relationships more clearly, much as a map clarifies the shape and layout of a city by excluding unnecessary detail.

Lessons from the Production Possibilities Model

The production possibilities curve introduced earlier in the chapter is a simple model of an economy. It certainly doesn't tell us everything we would like to know about an economy; in fact, it leaves out a host of details. But it points out very clearly that every economy's production capacity is limited, so that attempts to produce more of one thing mean producing less of something else.

The production possibilities model also points out another important feature of models or theories: They are based on assumptions. The production possibilities model assumes that resources are limited and that some resources are better suited to producing one product than another.[5] Those assumptions give us a production possibilities curve that slopes downward and is concave. If we make different assumptions, we end up with a different model and different conclusions. For example, if an economy had *unlimited* resources, its production possibilities curve would slope upward because it could produce more of both products simultaneously; that is, it would not be necessary to give up some military products to produce more civilian products. (What would the production possibilities curve look like if resources were fixed but were equally well suited to producing either product?)[6] The objective is to start with assumptions that are sufficiently realistic so that the resulting model allows us to explain and predict the real world. Otherwise, we end up with a model of little or no practical value.

A Theory of Cigarette Consumption

Theories are absolutely essential to solving problems and making sense out of the world we live in. Without a theory of how the TV works, we don't know what to do when it doesn't work; we don't know how to solve the problem. The same is true of economic problems. When you read the evening newspaper or tune in the evening news on television, you are exposed to a deluge of facts and figures about everything from housing construction to foreign trade.

---

[5] The production possibilities model also assumes the existing techniques of production. In other words, it assumes that technology does not change.

[6] Under these assumptions, the production possibilities curve would slope downward (since producing more of one thing would still require the sacrifice of some of the other thing), but it would be a straight line rather than curving outward.

Without theories to help you interpret them, however, these data are of little value because you don't know what facts are relevant to the problem at hand.

In the early 1990s, researchers noted that cigarette consumption in the United States was no longer declining as rapidly as it had in the previous decade. In other words, smokers were not "kicking the habit" as readily as before. Health experts wanted to understand why the trend toward quitting smoking was slowing down. Without a theory explaining cigarette consumption, researchers wouldn't know where to begin looking for an explanation because they wouldn't know what facts were relevant.

On the other hand, suppose that over time we have developed a tentative theory, a hypothesis, that lower cigarette prices cause higher cigarette consumption. That would pinpoint certain relevant facts that might explain the increase in cigarette consumption. We could test our theory by gathering data for a number of different time periods to see if, in fact, cigarette consumption has increased and decreased consistently in accordance with changes in price.

Testing economic theories is more difficult than it might seem. For example, to determine whether cigarette consumption is, in fact, related to the price of cigarettes, economists have to be able to eliminate the impact of changes in personal income and other nonprice factors that might affect the quantity of cigarettes consumed. After all, even if the price of cigarettes is a major factor influencing the amount consumed, it is clearly not the only factor.[7] Unfortunately, economists cannot control these factors as precisely as chemists or physicists can control variables in their experiments. So economists do the next best thing; that is, they assume that other factors, such as personal incomes, remain constant. This is the assumption of **ceteris paribus**, which literally means "other things being equal." In a sense, what economists are doing is stating the conditions under which they expect a theory to be valid. To illustrate, our theory about cigarette consumption might be restated this way: "Consumers will buy more cigarettes at lower prices than at higher prices, ceteris paribus—other things being equal or held constant." Economists then compare what actually happens to what, on the basis of theory, they expected. If the facts are not consistent with the theory, we must determine whether it is because the theory is invalid or because the assumption of ceteris paribus has been violated (that is, because something other than the price of cigarettes has changed). Of course, if the theory is found to be invalid—if its predictions are not consistent with reality—it's back to the drawing board; more work will be required to devise a better theory. (Test your understanding of the ceteris paribus concept by reading " Is Harvard Worth It?" on page 20.)

---

[7] For example, it seems likely that over a given period, personal income also affects cigarette consumption. If the incomes of smokers remain constant while cigarette prices fall, cigarette consumption may well increase. But if incomes fall during the same period, offsetting the reduction in cigarette prices, cigarette consumption will probably remain the same or may even decrease.

Policies and Predictions

Once a theory has been tested and accepted, it can be used as a basis for making predictions and as a guide for formulating economic policy. On the basis of our cigarette-price theory, for example, we would predict that if cigarette prices go up, consumption will decline, and if prices fall, consumption will increase. We could also use this theory as the basis for devising policies for influencing the level of cigarette consumption. In order to reduce cigarette consumption, for instance, we might recommend an increase in the federal tax on cigarettes. This higher tax would make the retail price to consumers higher and thereby reduce consumption.

ECONOMISTS AND CONCLUSIONS

The formulation of policies for dealing with economic problems is the most important use of economic theory and the most important function of economists. But if you listen to TV news or read the newspaper, you know that economists do not always agree on matters of economic policy. Laypersons may therefore be skeptical about the contribution that economics can make to solving society's problems. Because you are going to spend that next few months studying economics, it seems appropriate to take a few minutes now to consider the two reasons that economists disagree. Economists may disagree either because they have different views of what *should be* or because they have different views about what *is*.

We've already explained that economists possess no special expertise in choosing goals, in deciding how things ought to be. Yet like all thinking people, economists have individual values and opinions about which of society's economic goals are most important. Consider the issue of smoking. Many economists support higher taxes on cigarettes in an effort to deter smoking, particularly among young smokers who have yet to become addicted. But others argue that such a policy would impose a financial hardship on older smokers who are, on average, poorer than nonsmokers and who are unlikely to change their behavior because of the higher taxes. Here the disagreement is about goals. Which is more important, reducing smoking by young people or protecting the living standards of older smokers? Obviously, economists with different philosophies about what the society should be attempting to achieve will have different recommendations with regard to economic policy.

Economists may also disagree about economic policies because they disagree about how things are—about how the economy works or how a particular policy would work. For example, even economists who support higher cigarette taxes to stem teenage smoking may disagree about the amount of the tax hike. Here the source of disagreement is likely to be conflicting statistical evidence regarding the responsiveness of consumers to changes in cigarette prices. For instance, some studies suggest that a tax hike of about $1.05 per pack would be sufficient to cut teenage smoking in half, while other studies suggest that the tax increase would need to be $1.50 or more to accomplish that objective.[8] Because of these conflicting results, economists may make different recommendations about how much to increase cigarette taxes—recommendations that reflect their different conclusions about how teens would respond to the tax hike.

In summary, economists can disagree either because they have different views about what should be or because they have different views about how the economy works. Of course, these areas of dispute are more likely to be reported than areas of agreement. But the fact that economists, like all social scientists, are intensely interested in exploring and debating issues on which they disagree does not mean that they can never reach a conclusion. There are many issues and answers on which economists are in general agreement, so don't let the disagreements about particular policy questions mislead you. The study of economics has a great deal to contribute to your understanding of the world and its many social problems. Approach that study with an open mind, and it will help you to make sense out of facts and events you never before understood.

THE ORGANIZATION OF THE TEXT

Now that you have some sense of what the study of economics is about, let's take a brief look at the organization of this book. It is composed of four major parts. Part 1 forms the introduction and lays the conceptual groundwork for the rest of the text. Part 2 takes up **microeconomics,** the study of the individual units of the economy. These chapters examine how the prices of particular goods and services are determined and how individual consumers and businesses function. True to its name, microeconomics looks at the small units that make up the whole economy. Part 3 examines **macroeconomics,** the study of the economy's overall performance and the factors influencing that performance. These chapters address such problems as unemployment and inflation and examine the role of government in combating these economic ills. Through macroeconomics you will begin to view the economy in terms of the big picture. Part 4 turns to **international economics,** the study of international trade and finance. These chapters explore the reasons for trade and how transactions between nations are financed.

---

[8] Studies suggest that each 1 percent increase in the price of a pack of cigarettes will reduce teenage consumption by 1 to 1.4 percent. Therefore, if the current price of a pack of cigarettes is $3.00, it would need to be raised to between $4.07 and $4.50 to reduce teen consumption by 50 percent.

As you can see, economics embraces several specialized areas. Because these areas are interrelated, what you learn in Part 1 will help you understand problems taken up in Part 4. In fact, to a large extent, the chapters in this text build on one another. So please take the time to understand each one thoroughly for an easier and more rewarding trip through economic theory and practice.

SUMMARY

The fundamental economic problem facing both individuals and societies is that our wants exceed our capacity for satisfying those wants. No society has enough *economic resources* (*land, labor, capital,* and *entrepreneurship*) to satisfy its members fully. Consequently, individuals and societies must make choices about how best to use their limited resources. *Economics* is the study of how to use our limited resources to satisfy our unlimited wants as fully as possible.

Making wise choices requires *cost-benefit analysis*—a systematic comparison of costs and benefits. A decision will only improve our well-being if the benefits associated with that decision exceed the costs.

One of the principal lessons of economics is that all choices entail costs, that there is no "free lunch." Whenever you make a decision to do or have one thing, you are sacrificing the opportunity to do or have some other thing. The most valued alternative you must sacrifice in order to take a given action is the *opportunity cost* of that action.

A *production possibilities curve* illustrates the concept of opportunity cost by showing the combinations of goods that an economy is capable of producing with its present stock of economic resources and existing techniques of production. It shows that unless there are unemployed resources, producing more of one thing means producing less of something else.

The dilemma of unlimited wants and limited resources forces each society to make three basic choices, to answer the three fundamental questions of economics: (1) What goods and services will the society produce and in what quantities? (2) How will these goods and services be produced? (3) For whom will these products be produced?

In order to determine how well it is answering the three fundamental questions, a society must establish goals or objectives against which it compares its performance. Full employment, economic efficiency, economic growth, a fair distribution of income, and a stable price level are widely accepted goals. When these goals are in conflict, as they often are, the pursuit of one goal commonly requires a trade-off, some sacrifice in terms of fulfilling another goal.

Before economists can recommend policies for dealing with economic problems or achieving specific objectives, they must develop *economic theories,* generalizations about causal relationships between economic facts, or variables. Testing economic theories can be tricky because the assumption of *ceteris paribus* ("other things being equal") is often violated. This makes it difficult to determine when a theory is flawed, since the results of an experiment could be biased by changes in uncontrolled factors.

Once a theory has been tested and accepted, it can be used as a basis for making predictions and as a guide to formulating economic policy. When it comes to making policy recommendations, economists do not always agree. They may disagree for one or both of two distinct reasons: because they have different views about what *should be* or because they have have different views about what *is.*

KEY TERMS

Capital	Entrepreneurship	Macroeconomics
Ceteris paribus	Free trade	Microeconomics
Cost-benefit analysis	International economics	Normative issue
Economics	Labor	Opportunity cost
Economic resources	Land	Production possibilities curve
Economic theories	Law of increasing costs	Theories

STUDY QUESTIONS

Fill in the Blanks

1. Land, labor, and capital are examples of

   Economic Resources

2. The dilemma of _Unlimited_ wants and _limited_ resources is referred to as the economic problem.

3. _Entrepreneurship_ are combiners, innovators, and risk takers.

4. The term _Land_ is used by economists to describe the economic resources created by nature.

5. When we sacrifice one alternative for another, the alternative forgone is called the

   Opportunity Cost of that action.

6. A _Production Possibility Curve_ shows the combinations of goods that an economy is capable of producing.

7. Economists use economic _Theories_ to make sense out of the facts they observe.

8. When the pursuit of one objective forces society to sacrifice or compromise some other objective, economists say that a

   trade off exists.

9. Issues involving what "should be" rather than what "is" are referred to as _normative_ issues.

10. Because economists cannot conduct controlled experiments, they often make the assumption of _Celeris Parbues_ to state the conditions under which they expect their theory to hold.

Multiple Choice

1. Economics is the study of how to
   a) distribute output fairly.
   b) do the best we can with what we have.
   c) reduce our unlimited wants.
   d) expand our stock of economic resources.

2. The opportunity cost of attending summer school is
   a) whatever you could have purchased with the money spent for tuition and books.
   b) negative, because you will finish college more rapidly by attending summer school.
   c) the income you could have earned over the summer.
   d) the products, income, and recreational opportunities that must be forgone.

3. If something has an opportunity cost, we should
   a) avoid that action.
   b) take that action.
   c) be sure that the benefit of the action exceeds the cost.
   d) be sure that the cost of the action exceeds the benefit.

4. Producing the most-wanted products in the least costly way is
   a) full employment.
   b) economic growth.
   c) a fair income distribution.
   d) economic efficiency.

5. Economists have trouble testing their theories because
   a) people are unpredictable.

b) the real world is too complicated to be explained.
   c) they can't hold constant the "other factors" that might influence the outcome of the experiment.
   d) the necessary economic data are almost never available.

6. Economists should not be permitted to
   a) devise policies to achieve economic goals.
   b) determine society's economic goals.
   c) explain how the economy works.
   d) explain how particular economic goals conflict.

7. Economists sometimes reach different conclusions on a given issue because
   a) they disagree about goals.
   b) they disagree about the way the economy works.
   c) a and b
   d) neither a nor b

8. Macroeconomics deals with the study of
   a) international trade.
   b) individual economic units.
   c) production possibilities.
   d) the economy's overall performance.

9. Of the three fundamental questions, the "distribution" question has to do with
   a) who will receive the output.
   b) how the output will be shipped from the place of production to the consumer.
   c) how economic resources are distributed to producers.
   d) what products will be produced.

10. Suppose that you have just found $10 on the street and are thinking of using it to buy a ticket to the movies. The opportunity cost of going to the show would be
    a) nothing—since you found the money, you are sacrificing nothing to spend it.
    b) whatever you would have bought with the money if you hadn't used it to go to the show.
    c) the other activities you would have to sacrifice to attend the show.
    d) b and c

11. The production possibilities curve slopes downward because
    a) some resources are better suited to the production of one product than another.
    b) economic resources are limited.
    c) economic wants are unlimited.
    d) All of the above

    Use the production possibilities curve at the end of this section in answering questions 12 through 14.

12. If the economy is operating at point C, the opportunity cost of producing an additional 10,000 automobiles will be
    a) 10 million bushels of wheat.
    b) 20 million bushels of wheat.
    c) 30 million bushels of wheat.
    d) 40 million bushels of wheat.

13. Point G on the diagram represents
    a) an optimal use of the society's resources.
    b) a combination of outputs beyond the economy's productive capacity.
    c) a situation in which some of the economy's resources are unemployed.
    d) the same output combination as point B.

14. The production possibilities curve might shift outward to include G if
    a) the economy put all unemployed resources to work.
    b) the economy experienced more rapid price inflation.
    c) improved training increased the productivity of workers.
    d) the nation's population declined.

15. Foreign trade permits an economy to
    a) eliminate the problem of scarcity.
    b) operate inside its production possibilities curve.
    c) shift its production possibilities curve outward.
    d) consume a combination of products beyond its own production possibilities.

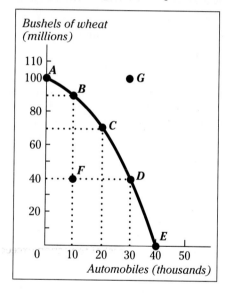

Problems and Questions for Discussion

1. List the four categories of economic resources and explain each.

2. Define *economics*. Why is economics sometimes called the "study of choice"?

3. List and explain the three fundamental choices that each society is forced to make.

4. What is meant when we say that a secretary is efficient? What about a salesclerk? Why is

economic efficiency an important performance objective for an economy?

5. Airline personnel are often allowed to make a certain number of free flights each year. How would you compute the opportunity cost to the airlines of these free trips? Might this cost vary from route to route? Might the cost be different at different times of the year? Explain.

6. List and briefly explain the economic objectives recognized as worthwhile by many societies.

7. What are trade-offs? Give some examples.

8. A theory that has been around for quite some time says, "Better-educated people earn higher incomes than less-educated people, ceteris paribus." If we know a high school dropout who earns $200,000 a year, does this mean that we should discard the theory? Explain.

9. Suppose that we accept the theory given in problem 8 and decide to use it to formulate policies for reducing poverty. Apply this theory by suggesting three policies to reduce poverty.

10. Why is it important to separate the process of setting economic goals from the process of devising policies for achieving these goals? In which process is the economist more expert? Explain.

11. How would you go about using cost-benefit analysis to decide whether or not to attend college? What factors would complicate this analysis?

12. Foreign immigration into the United States normally shifts the U.S. production possibilities curve to the right. Why? If it has this impact, why do some citizens oppose immigration? Is foreign immigration a normative issue?

ANSWER KEY

Fill in the Blanks

1. economic resources
2. unlimited, limited
3. Entrepreneurs
4. land
5. opportunity cost
6. production possibilities curve
7. theories (or models)
8. trade-off
9. normative
10. ceteris paribus

Multiple Choice

1. b
2. d
3. c
4. d
5. c
6. b
7. c
8. d
9. a
10. d
11. b
12. c
13. b
14. c
15. d

Appendix: WORKING WITH GRAPHS

Economists frequently use graphs to illustrate economic concepts. This appendix provides a brief review of graphing and offers some practice problems to help you become more comfortable working with graphs.

The Purpose of Graphs

The basic purpose of a graph is to represent the relationship between two variables. A *variable* is any quantity that can take on different numeric values. Suppose, for example, that a university has conducted a survey to determine the relationship between two variables: the number of hours its students study and their grade-point averages. The results of that hypothetical survey could be shown in table, or schedule, form, as in panel (a) of Exh. A.1, or they could be represented graphically, as in panel (b) of Exh. A.1. Notice the difference: The graph reveals the relationship between the variables at a glance; you don't have to compare data as you do when reading the table.

Constructing a Graph

The first step in constructing a graph is to draw two perpendicular lines. These lines are called *axes*. In our example the vertical axis is used to measure the first variable, the grade-point average; the horizontal axis is used to measure the second variable, hours of study. The place where the two axes meet is called the *origin* because it is the starting point for measuring each of the variables; in our example the origin is zero. Once the axes are in place, we are ready to draw, or *plot*, the points that represent the relationship between the variables. Let's begin with the students who study 32 hours a week. According to the table in panel (a), these students typically earn a grade-point average of 4.0. To show this relationship graphically, we find the point on the horizontal axis that represents 32 hours of study per week. Next, we move directly upward from that point until we reach a height of 4.0 grade points. This point, which we will label *A*, represents a combination of two values; it tells us at a glance that the typical student who studies 32 hours a week will earn a 4.0 grade-point average.

We plot the rest of the information found in panel (a) in the same way. To represent the typical, or average, grade of the student who studies 24 hours a week, all we need to do is locate the number 24 on the horizontal axis and then move up vertically from that point to a distance of 3.0 grade points (point *B*). We plot all the remaining points on the graph in the same way.

Once we have plotted all the points, we can connect them to form a curve. Economists use the term *curve* to describe any graphical relationship between two variables, so don't be surprised when you discover a straight line referred to as a curve. You can see that the resulting curve slopes upward and to the right. This indicates that there is a positive, or *direct*, relationship between the two variables—as one variable (study time) increases, the other (grade-point average) also increases. If the resulting curve had sloped downward and to the right, it would have indicated a negative, or *inverse*, relationship between the two variables—as one variable increased, the other would decrease. We would be surprised to find an inverse relationship between these particular variables; that would suggest the unlikely possibility that increased study time lowers the grade-point average!

EXHIBIT A.1
The Hypothetical Relationship between Grades and Study Time

HOURS OF STUDY (per week)	GRADE-POINT AVERAGE
32	4.0
28	3.5
24	3.0
20	2.5
16	2.0
12	1.5
8	1.0
4	0.5
0	0.0

(a) Relationship with Table

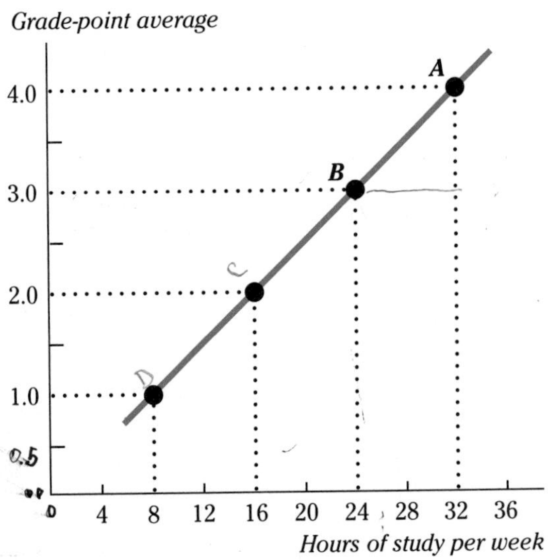

(b) Relationship with Graph

Panels (a) and (b) both illustrate the relationship between hours of study and grades. Panel (a) uses a table to show this relationship; panel (b), a graph. Both illustrations show that the relationship between the two variables is direct; more hours of study tend to be associated with a higher grade-point average.

Practice in Graphing

All graphs are basically the same, so if you understand the one we just considered, you should be able to master all the graphs in this textbook and in library sources. If you want some practice, take a few minutes to graph the three sets of data at the end of this appendix.

The first step is to draw and label the vertical and horizontal axes and mark them off in units that are convenient to work with. As you probably know, mathematicians always measure the *independent* variable (the variable that causes the other to change) along the horizontal axis and the *dependent* variable (the variable that responds to changes) along the vertical axis. Economists are less strict in deciding which variable to place on which axis, so don't be alarmed if occasionally you see the dependent variable on the horizontal axis.

Once you have decided which variable to place on which axis, the next step is to plot the information from the table as points and connect them. Then see if you can interpret your graph. What does it tell you about the relationship between the two variables? Are they directly or inversely related? (It's possible that they are not related at all. For example, there is probably no relationship between a student's weight and his or her grade-point average.) Does the relationship change somewhere along the graph? The way to become comfortable with graphs is to work with them. Try drawing these graphs to see how easy it is.

1. Graph the relationship between the hourly wage rate paid by the school and the number of students desiring to work in the school cafeteria. Is the relationship direct or inverse?

POINT	WAGE RATE (per hour)	NUMBER OF STUDENT WORKERS
A	$6.50	5
B	7.00	10
C	7.50	15
D	8.00	20
E	8.50	25
F	9.00	30

2. Graph the relationship between the average daily temperature and the average number of students playing tennis on the school tennis courts. How does this relationship change?

POINT	TEMPERATURE (in degrees Fahrenheit)	NUMBER OF TENNIS PLAYERS
A	60	20
B	70	30
C	80	40
D	90	30
E	100	20

3. Graph the relationship between the price of gasoline and the quantity of gasoline purchased by consumers. Is the relationship direct or inverse?

POINT	PRICE (per gallon)	QUANTITY PURCHASED (in gallons)
A	$ 1.00	15 million
B	1.50	12 million
C	2.00	9 million
D	2.50	6 million
E	3.00	3 million

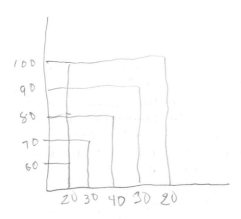

Economic Systems

1. Explain the concept of an economic system.
2. Describe how economic systems differ from one another.
3. Identify the elements of pure capitalism.
4. Draw and explain the circular-flow model of pure capitalism.
5. Explain how pure capitalism answers the three fundamental questions.
6. Discuss the strengths and weaknesses of pure capitalism.
7. Identify the elements of command socialism.
8. Draw and explain the pyramid model of command socialism.
9. Explain how command socialism answers the three fundamental questions.
10. Discuss the strengths and weaknesses of command socialism.
11. Explain why all real-world economies are mixed economies.

Every nation, from the richest to the poorest, faces the same economic dilemma: how to satisfy people's unlimited wants with its limited economic resources. Each society must decide which goods and services to produce, how to produce them, and for whom to produce them; in other words, it must establish an economic system. An **economic system** is a set of institutions and mechanisms for answering the three fundamental questions of economics—what, how, and for whom to produce.

In describing economic systems, it is helpful to ask two questions: (1) Who owns the means of production—the factories, farms, mines, and other resources used to produce goods and services? (2) Who makes the economic decisions; that is, who answers the three fundamental economic questions? The variety of real-world economic systems is probably as great as the number of world nations, but all economic systems combine elements of two divergent models. At one extreme, the means of production are privately owned, and individual buyers and sellers interacting in markets make the economic decisions. At the other extreme, the means of production are publicly owned, and a central authority makes the fundamental economic choices.

This chapter will begin by providing you with an overview of these two divergent models—the models of pure capitalism and pure command socialism. Recall from Chapter 1 that models simplify reality, making it possible to see more clearly how the parts of a system function and interact. Once we have become familiar with how "pure" capitalism and "pure" command socialism would function, we can compare the U.S. economy and other selected economies against these theoretical models to discover how these real-world economic systems conform and how they deviate from the models.

THE MODEL OF PURE CAPITALISM

The American Heritage Dictionary defines something as *pure* if it is "free from impurities or contaminants." So pure capitalism is a hypothetical economic system that is totally or completely capitalist, one without traces of anything else. In this section we examine the elements of such a system, diagram its operation or functioning, see how it answers the three fundamental questions, and conclude by assessing its strengths and weaknesses.

Elements of Capitalism

We define **capitalism** as an economic system in which the means of production are privately owned and fundamental economic choices are made by individual buyers and sellers interacting in markets. The model of pure capitalism is entirely consistent with our definition and contains five basic elements, which we will describe briefly.

Private Property and Freedom of Choice

One of the principal features of capitalism is private property. In a capitalist economy, private individuals and groups are the owners of the **means of production:** the raw materials, factories, farms, and other economic resources used to produce goods and services. These resource owners may sell or use their resources, including their own labor, as they see fit. Businesses are free to decide what products they will produce and to purchase the necessary economic resources from whomever they choose. Consumers, in turn, are free to spend their incomes any way they like. They can purchase whatever products they choose, and they can decide what fraction of their incomes to save and what fraction to spend.

Self-Interest

The driving force of capitalism is self-interest. In 1776 Adam Smith, the founder of economics, described a capitalist economy as one in which the primary concern of each player—of each producer, worker, and consumer—was to promote his or her own welfare.[1]

Smith introduced the **invisible hand** doctrine, which held that as individuals pursued their own interests, they would be led as if by an invisible hand to promote the good of the society as a whole. In order to earn the highest profits, predicted Smith, producers would generate the products consumers wanted most. Workers would offer their services where they were most needed because wages would be highest in those sectors. Consumers would favor producers who offered superior products and/or lower prices because they would seek the best value for their money. The result would be an economy that produced the goods and services desired by the society without the need for any central direction by government.

Markets and Prices

Capitalism is often described as a market system. This is because a capitalist economy contains numerous interdependent markets through which the functioning of the economy is coordinated and directed. A **market** consists of all actual or potential buyers and sellers of a particular item and can be local, regional, national, or international. For example, there are numerous local and regional markets for used automobiles, each consisting of all buyers and sellers of such vehicles in that particular area. Similar markets exist for all other goods and services and for all economic resources as well.

Market prices are determined by the interaction of buyers and sellers and serve two important functions. First, prices help to divide up, or ration, the society's limited output of goods and services among those who desire to receive it. Only those who are willing and able to pay the market price receive the product. Second, prices motivate businesses to produce more of some products and less of others. Businesses generally want to supply products that yield the highest profits, the ones with the highest prices in relation to their costs of production. These products tend to be those most desired by consumers. So, by motivating suppliers, price changes help to ensure that society's scarce resources are used to produce the goods and services most highly valued by consumers.

Competition

Adam Smith recognized that for the invisible hand to work—for individuals seeking their own interests to promote the good of all—the pursuit of

---

[1] Adam Smith's description of the functioning of a capitalist economy appeared in *An Inquiry into the Nature and Causes of the Wealth of Nations*, published in 1776.

self-interest had to be guided and restrained by competition. Competition ensures that producers remain responsive to consumers and that prices remain reasonable.

Pure capitalism requires **pure competition,** a situation in which a large number of relatively small buyers and sellers interact to determine prices.[2] Under conditions of pure competition, no individual buyer or seller can set— or even significantly influence—the prevailing price of a product or resource. Prices are thus determined by market forces, not by powerful buyers or sellers, and change only when market conditions change.

Limited Government Intervention

Pure capitalism is above all a **laissez-faire economy.** (*Laissez-faire* is a French phrase that in this context means "let the people do as they choose.") The model describes no role for government in making economic decisions. Through pricing, the market makes all production and distribution decisions—what, how, and for whom to produce—and competition ensures that consumers will be charged reasonable prices. The only role of government is to provide the kind of environment in which a market economy can function well. For example, government must define and enforce the private-property rights that enable individuals to own and use property.

The Circular-Flow Model

We can represent the operation of a capitalist economy in a diagram called the circular-flow model. Exhibit 2.1 models an economy composed of only two sectors: households and businesses. You can see that these two sectors are connected through transactions, or flows, that occur continuously between them. We'll examine how each sector processes the flow it receives and returns it to the other sector.

The Household and Business Sectors

The household sector is shown at the right in Exh. 2.1. A **household** is defined as one or more people living in the same dwelling. Whether it consists of a single person or many people, each household will have a source of income and will spend that income. The household sector is composed of all the individual households in the economy. Because households own the land, labor, capital, and entrepreneurship that businesses need to produce goods and services, this sector is the source of all economic resources in the model of pure capitalism. It is also the source of consumer spending for the goods and services produced.

---

[2] Chapter 6 describes further assumptions relating to pure competition.

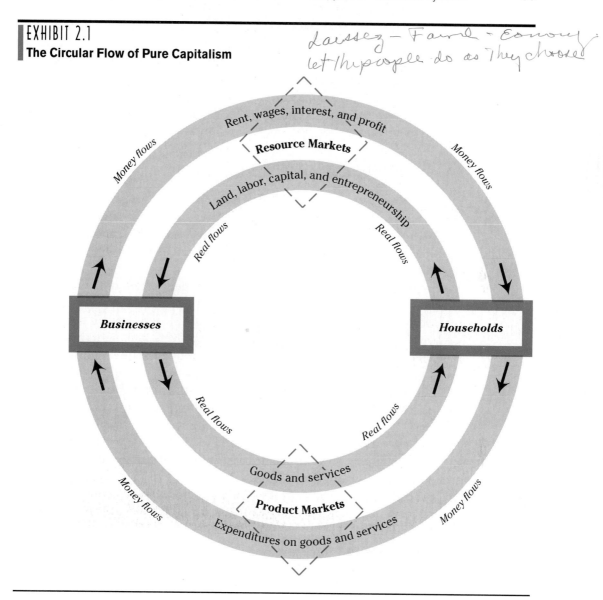

EXHIBIT 2.1
The Circular Flow of Pure Capitalism

Laissez - Faire - Economy:
let the people do as They choose

The business sector, on the left, is composed of all the businesses in the economy. The business sector purchases economic resources from households, converts those resources into products, and sells the products to the households.

Real Flows and Money Flows
You can see in the diagram that two types of flows circle in opposite directions. In the outside circle *money flows*, in the form of rent, wages, interest,

and profit, go from businesses to households to pay for economic resources. These flows return to businesses as households pay for products. *Real flows* involve the physical movement of the resources and products. The inner flow in the diagram shows economic resources in the form of land, labor, capital, and entrepreneurship flowing from the household sector to the business sector, where they are used to produce goods and services. The unbroken arrows in the diagram show that these circular flows are endless.

The Resource and Product Markets

Markets are the key to the operation of a capitalist system because they hold together its decentralized economy of millions of individual buyers and sellers. The interaction of these buyers and sellers ensures that the right products (the ones desired by consumers) are produced and that economic resources flow to the right producers (the ones producing the most-wanted products at the lowest prices).

In the resource markets, depicted in the upper portion of Exh. 2.1, the interaction of buyers and sellers determines the prices of the various economic resources. For example, in the labor market for accountants, an accountant's salary is determined by the interaction of employers seeking to hire accountants (the buyers) and accountants seeking employment (the sellers). Changes in resource prices guide and motivate resource suppliers to provide the type and quantity of resources producers need most. Using our example of labor, suppose that the number of businesses desiring accountants is expanding more rapidly than new accountants are being trained. What will happen to the salaries of accountants? They will tend to increase. As a result, we can expect more people in the household sector to invest the time and money necessary to become accountants. You can see how the price mechanism ensures that (1) the types of labor, equipment, and other resources most needed by businesses will be supplied and (2) these resources will be supplied in the proper quantities.

In the product markets, depicted in the lower portion of Exh. 2.1, the prices of all products—from eggs and overcoats to haircuts and airline tickets—again are determined by the interaction of buyers and sellers. Prices serve the same function here as they do in the resource market: They make it possible to divide up, or ration, the limited amount of output among all those who wish to receive it. Only those consumers who are willing and able to pay the market price can obtain the product. When prices change, this informs producers about desired changes in the amount they are producing and motivates them to supply the new quantity. For example, when consumers want more of a product than is available, they tend to bid up its price. Producers, getting a clear signal that consumers like that item, thus have an incentive to supply more of it.

How Capitalism Answers the Three Fundamental Questions

Now that we have discussed the elements of pure capitalism and have a general idea of the role of markets in such an economy, we can determine more easily how this system answers the three fundamental questions.

What to Produce

One feature of pure capitalism is **consumer sovereignty,** an economic condition in which consumers dictate which goods and services businesses will produce. Because producers are motivated by profits and because the most profitable products tend to be the ones consumers desire most, producers must be responsive to consumer preferences. To illustrate consumer sovereignty in action, let's consider how automobile manufacturers in a pure capitalist economy would respond if consumer preferences suddenly took a dramatic turn away from sport-utility vehicles (SUVs) in favor of mid-sized cars. If people began to buy more mid-sized automobiles and fewer SUVs, the price of mid-size cars would rise and they would become more profitable, whereas SUVs would decline in price and become less profitable. Therefore, automobile manufacturers would produce more mid-size vehicles and fewer SUVs—just what consumers want.

Because consumers are free to spend their incomes as they choose, producers who wish to earn profits must be responsive to consumers' desires. As a result, pure capitalism might be described as a system in which the consumer is the ruler and the producer an obedient servant.

How to Produce

Automobile producers have a number of options available for manufacturing compact cars and other vehicles that consumers desire. They can produce these automobiles through highly mechanized techniques, or they can rely primarily on skilled labor and simpler tools. They can manufacture car bodies from steel, aluminum, fiberglass, or some combination of the three. In selecting which production technique and combination of resources to use, capitalist manufacturers will minimize the cost of production; they will adopt the *least-cost* approach because lower costs contribute to higher profits.

The search for the least-cost approach is guided by the market prices of the various economic resources. Because the scarcest resources cost the most, producers use them only when they cannot substitute less expensive resources. For example, if steel is very expensive, automobile makers will tend to use it only where other materials would be inadequate, perhaps in the frame or in other parts of the car that require great strength. And if skilled labor is expensive, as it is in Japan and the United States, robots will be used to perform as many jobs as possible. Thus, the prices of resources help to ensure that resources are used to

In a capitalist economy, highly mechanized production methods—such as those utilizing robots—may be selected if labor is expensive.

their best advantage in a capitalist economy. Abundant, cheaper resources are used when they will suffice; scarcer, more costly resources are conserved.

For Whom to Produce

Finally, we consider the task of distributing our hypothetical economy's output of automobiles. We know that only those who can afford to buy automobiles will receive them. The ability to pay, however, is only half the picture; the other half is willingness to purchase, which takes into account consumer preferences. Some of those who can afford a new car will prefer to spend their money elsewhere: remodeling their homes perhaps or sending their children to college. Some who seemingly cannot afford a new car may be able to purchase one by doing without other things—new clothes or a larger apartment, for example. Of course, consumers with low incomes will face less attractive choices than those earning high incomes. A low-income consumer may sacrifice basic necessities in order to afford an automobile, whereas a wealthy consumer need choose only between the new car and some luxury item, such as a sailboat or a winter vacation. In the final analysis those with higher incomes will always have more choices than those with lower incomes and will receive a larger share of the economy's total output.

Capitalism: Strengths and Weaknesses

Before moving on from our discussion of pure capitalism, we will describe briefly some of the strengths and weaknesses inherent in such a system. One of the major strengths of pure capitalism is *economic efficiency.* In a market economy, businesses are encouraged to produce the products that consumers want most and to produce those products at the lowest cost in terms of scarce resources. A system that accomplishes those objectives goes a long way toward ensuring that a society achieves the maximum benefit possible from its limited resources.

A second positive feature of capitalism is *economic freedom.* Under pure capitalism, consumers, workers, and producers are free to make decisions based on self-interest. To many people this economic freedom is the overwhelming virtue of the capitalist model.

Economist Milton Friedman, a vocal advocate of competitive capitalism, notes a third strength of the system: It promotes *political freedom* by separating economic and political power. The existence of private ownership of the means of production ensures that government officials are not in a position to deny jobs or goods and services to individuals whose political views conflict with their own.[3]

Pure capitalism also has some shortcomings. First, people are not uniformly equal in ability, and some will succeed to a greater extent than others. In a capitalist system the result is the unequal distribution of income and output. This inequality tends to be perpetuated because the children of the rich usually have access to better educational opportunities and often inherit the income-producing assets of their parents. Such inequality weakens capitalism's claim that it produces the goods and services that the *society* wants the most. It is more the case that capitalism produces the products that the *consumers who have the money* want most.

A second, closely related criticism was voiced by the late Arthur Okun, chairman of the Council of Economic Advisors during the Johnson administration. In a capitalist economy, observed Okun, money can buy a great many things that are not supposed to be for sale:

> Money buys legal services that can obtain preferred treatment before the law; it buys platforms that give extra weight to the owner's freedom of speech; it buys influence with elected officials and thus compromises the principle of one person, one vote. . . . Even though money generally cannot buy extra helpings of rights directly, it can buy services that, in effect, produce more or better rights.[4]

Third, pure capitalism may be criticized for encouraging the destruction of the environment. Because air, rivers, lakes, and streams are **common-property resources** belonging to the society as a whole, they tend to be seen as free—available to be used or abused without charge or concern. The pursuit of self-interest would cause producers to dump their wastes into nearby rivers to avoid the cost of disposing of those wastes in an environmentally acceptable

---

[3] Milton Friedman, *Capitalism and Freedom* (Chicago: The University of Chicago Press, 1962), p. 9.
[4] Arthur M. Okun, *Equality and Efficiency: The Big Tradeoff* (Washington: The Brookings Institution, 1975), p. 22.

manner. Farmers would select pesticides according to their favorable impact on output and without regard to their undesirable effects on wildlife and water supplies. In this case, Adam Smith's invisible hand fails. The pursuit of self-interest by individuals may not promote the good of all but may instead lead to environmental destruction.[5]

THE MODEL OF PURE COMMAND SOCIALISM

The opposite of the model of pure capitalism is the model of pure command socialism. The socialist command economy described in this section represents no existing economic system. Like the model of pure capitalism, the model of pure command socialism is simply a tool to help us understand how command economies operate. Again, we will examine the basic elements of the model, diagram how the hypothetical economy operates, and see how the system decides what, how, and for whom to produce. Then we will examine the strengths and weaknesses of pure command socialism.

Elements of Command Socialism

We define **command socialism** as an economic system in which the means of production are publicly owned and the fundamental economic choices are made by a central authority. Four basic elements of command socialism support this definition.

Public Ownership

A socialist economy is characterized by state, or public, ownership of the means of production. In the model of pure command socialism, state ownership is complete. The factories, farms, mines, hospitals, and other forms of capital are publicly owned. Even labor is publicly owned in the sense that workers and managers do not select their own employment but are assigned their jobs by the state.

Centralized Decision Making

One of the most distinctive features of command socialism is that economic choices are made by a central authority. This central authority may be either responsive to the feelings of the people (democratic socialism) or unresponsive to their wishes (authoritarian socialism or communism). In either case, this authority makes the fundamental production and distribution decisions and then takes the necessary actions to see that these decisions are carried out.

---

[5] It can be argued that the problem here is not capitalism, but too little capitalism. If someone were assigned the ownership of these common-property resources, that party would have both the ability and the incentive to protect those resources from abuse.

Economic Planning

In the model of command socialism, economic planning replaces the market as the method for coordinating economic decisions. The central authority, or central planning board, gathers information about existing production capacities, supplies of raw materials, and labor force capabilities. It then draws up a master plan specifying production objectives for each sector or industry in the economy. Industrywide objectives are translated into specific production targets for each factory, farm, mine, or other kind of producing unit. Central planning ensures that specific production objectives agree so that automobile manufacturers will not produce 1 million cars, for example, while tire manufacturers produce only 2 million tires.

Allocation by Command

In command socialism, resources and products are allocated by directive, or command, and the central authority uses its power to enforce these decisions. Once it determines production and distribution objectives, the central planning board dictates to each producing unit the quantity and assortment of goods the unit is to produce and the combination of resources it is to use. Commands are also issued to producers of raw materials and other production inputs to supply these inputs to the producing units that need them. Further commands direct individuals to places of employment—wherever the central planning board determines that their services are needed—and dictate distribution of the economy's output of goods and services. All the allocative functions that a capitalist economy leaves to the market and the pursuit of self-interest are accomplished in pure command socialism through planning and allocation by directive.

The Pyramid Model

Exhibit 2.2 represents a socialist command economy as a pyramid, with the central planning board at the top and the various producing and consuming units below it. This diagram emphasizes the primary feature of a command economy: centralization of economic decision making.

 The outer arrow at the right in Exh. 2.2 shows how information about production capacities, raw materials supplies, and labor capabilities flows up from the producing units in the middle of the pyramid to the central planning board at the top. Information, if requested, about which goods and services consumers desire also flows up from the consuming units at the base of the pyramid (outer left arrow). Production objectives, or targets, are transmitted back to the individual producing units, which then supply the targeted quantity and assortment of products and produce them as specified. Finally, the output is distributed to consumers in accordance with the plan.

EXHIBIT 2.2
The Command Pyramid

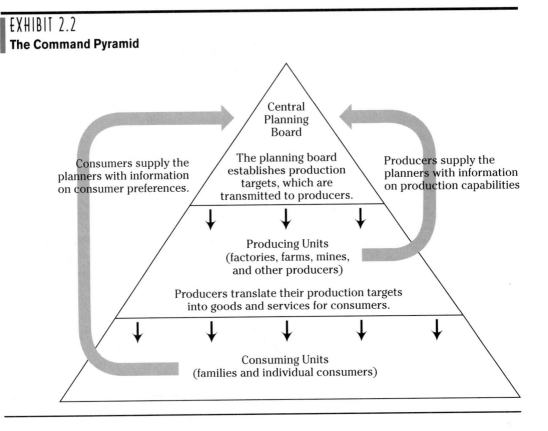

Central
Planning
Board

The planning board establishes production targets, which are transmitted to producers.

Consumers supply the planners with information on consumer preferences.

Producers supply the planners with information on production capabilities

Producing Units
(factories, farms, mines, and other producers)

Producers translate their production targets into goods and services for consumers.

Consuming Units
(families and individual consumers)

How Command Socialism Answers the Three Fundamental Questions

In many respects the operation of a socialist command economy is easier to understand than the functioning of a capitalist economy. The answers to the three fundamental questions are decided by the central planning board, which then uses its authority to ensure that all directives are carried out.

The central planners can select any output targets, any mix of products within the limits set by the economy's production capacity. Of course, the planners will have to gather an abundance of information before they have a good picture of the economy's capabilities. They must determine the size of the labor force and the skills it possesses, for example, as well as how many factories exist and what they are capable of producing. Until the central planners have this kind of information, they cannot establish realistic output targets. And, even then, they will face some tough decisions because, as you already know, more of one thing means less of something else. So if they decide to produce more automobiles, they won't be able to manufacture as many refrigerators and military weapons and other products.

In deciding how to produce each product, central planners must try to stretch the economy's limited resources as far as possible. This requires that each resource be used efficiently—where it makes the greatest contribution to the economy's output. If some resource is particularly scarce, planners must be careful to use it only where no other input will suffice; otherwise they won't be able to maximize the economy's output.

Even with the best planning, an economy's resources will stretch only so far. The central planning board can allocate the economy's limited output in accordance with any objective it has set. If the planning board's primary objective is equality, it can develop a method of rationing, dividing up the society's output in equal shares to each member. If it wants to promote loyalty to the government, the central authority can give supporters extra shares while penalizing dissenters. Whatever its objectives, the central planning board can use distribution as a method to further them.

Command Socialism: Strengths and Weaknesses

Like pure capitalism, the economy of pure command socialism has certain strengths and certain weaknesses. Some people argue that a major strength of command socialism is its ability to promote a high degree of equality in the distribution of income and output. Because the central planners control the distribution of goods and services, they can elect to distribute output in ways that achieve whatever degree of equality in living standard they consider appropriate. Thus, it is theoretically possible for command socialism to avoid the extremely unequal income and output distribution that characterizes pure capitalism.

Another major strength of command socialism is its potential for achieving economic objectives in a relatively short period of time. As an example, consider the power of the planners to foster more rapid economic growth. If a society wants to increase its capacity for producing goods and services, it must devote more of its resources to producing capital goods (factories and equipment) and fewer resources to producing consumer goods. In other words, society must consume less *now* in order to be able to produce and consume more *later.* Because the central authority has the power to dictate the fraction of the society's resources that will be devoted to capital goods production, in effect, it can force the society to make the sacrifices necessary to increase the rate of economic growth.

You probably recognize that the power to bring about rapid economic changes is not necessarily a good thing. The major shortcoming of command socialism, in fact, is the possibility that the central planning board may pursue goals that do not reflect the needs or desires of the majority. If the socialist government is not democratically elected, its goals may bear no relationship to the wants of the general population.

A second weakness in the model of command socialism is its inefficient information network. The system we have described needs more information than it can reasonably expect to acquire and process to ensure efficient use of the economy's resources. The system must not only have a substantial organizational network to acquire information about consumer preferences and production capabilities but must also use that network to transmit the decisions of central planners to millions of economic units. Moreover, the central planners have to be able to process all the acquired information and return it in the form of a consistent plan—a staggering task, considering that the output of one industry is often the production input required by some other industry. Finally, they must see that each product is produced efficiently. This complex and cumbersome process is bound to result in breakdowns in communication and decision making. When these occur, the wrong products may be produced or the right ones produced using the wrong combinations of resources. In either case, inefficiency means that the society does not achieve maximum benefit from its limited resources.

MIXED ECONOMIES: THE REAL-WORLD SOLUTION

No existing economic system adheres strictly to either pure capitalism or pure command socialism. All real-world economies are **mixed economies;** they represent a blending of the two models. To illustrate this point, we look next at the U.S. economy. Then we highlight the diversity of economic systems by taking a brief tour of several of the world's economies.

The U.S. Economic System

Because the U.S. economic system is marked by such a high degree of private ownership and individual decision making, American children learn early from their teachers, the news media, and others that they live in a capitalist economy. And certainly there is ample evidence to support that viewpoint. Most U.S. businesses, from industrial giants like General Motors and IBM to small firms like your neighborhood barbershop or hair salon, are private operations, not government-owned enterprises. The U.S. economy is coordinated and directed largely by the market mechanism, the interaction of buyers and sellers in thousands of interdependent markets. Each of those buyers and sellers is guided by self-interest, which among producers takes the form of profit seeking. Fortunately for consumers, the drive for profits is usually kept in check by another feature of pure capitalism: competition. In most American industries, competition, though not pure, is adequate to keep prices reasonable and to ensure that consumers receive fair treatment.

Given these elements of pure capitalism, why do we call the United States a *mixed economy*? In part, that label stems from the degree of public ownership that exists in our economy. A second, perhaps more important, reason is the extent to which the government makes or influences the fundamental economic choices. Let's briefly consider each of these reasons.

Public Ownership of the Means of Production

Pure capitalism requires private ownership of the means of production. The U.S. economy does not fully meet that requirement. Although most American businesses are privately owned, some very important and visible producers are publicly owned enterprises. For example, the electricity on which we rely to heat and cool our homes and to run our appliances is supplied in part by municipal, state, or county power companies. The vast majority of our school children—almost 90 percent—attend public elementary and secondary schools. When we apply for admission to college, we mail those applications via the U.S. Postal Service, often to state universities. If we ride the bus in the morning, that vehicle is probably the property of a public transit system. In short, although public ownership is by no means the dominant feature of the American economy, it cannot be ignored.

Government Decision Making

Although government decision making is the hallmark of a socialist command economy, some government intervention is unavoidable, even in a capitalism economy. The most basic function of government is to establish a *legal framework*—the rules by which citizens must deal with one another. A capitalist economy requires rules to protect private property—from theft, damage, etc. These rules must be maintained and enforced by legal institutions—police and a court system. Without these institutions, the concept of private property has little meaning and a capitalist economy could not exist. The U.S. economy has a highly developed legal system, with well-established principles of law.

Government's role in establishing a legal framework clearly is consistent with the model of pure capitalism. But government does much more than this in the U.S. economy. Consider the following functions of government and decide for yourself which are consistent with pure capitalism and which are not.

1. *Maintaining competition.* Competition helps to channel the profit-seeking motives of producers into socially desirable outcomes. When competition is inadequate, consumers may be forced to pay higher prices or accept inferior products. In the U.S. economy, the federal government uses *antitrust laws* to discourage anticompetitive behavior and to promote competition. One highly visible use of the antitrust laws was the Justice Department's recent

A capitalist economy requires rules to protect private property.

case against the Microsoft Corporation. In November 1999, Judge Thomas Penfield Jackson found that Microsoft had monopoly control over PC operating systems and that it used that power in ways that harm consumers. In June 2000, he agreed with federal antitrust enforcers that the software giant should be split into two companies in order to reduce its power and to promote competition. As this text goes to press, the case is on appeal. Antitrust laws are discussed in greater detail in Chapter 8.

2. *Correcting for externalities.* Buyers and sellers make decisions based on costs and benefits. If an individual judges that the benefits of an action exceed the costs incurred, he or she will perform that action. If, on the other hand, the person determines the costs of the action exceed its benefits, he or she will refrain from that action. This behavior commonly leads to an efficient use of society's scarce resources. But when an action creates *externalities*—costs or benefits that spill over into third parties—the resulting decision may not be optimal for society. For instance, the managers of electricity-generating power plants may use more high-sulfur coal than is socially desirable because they ignore the damage that this variety of coal inflicts on the environment. And dog owners may opt *not* to have their pets inoculated against rabies because they ignore the benefits that this protection provides to others. The U.S. government attempts to adjust for

these and other externalities by establishing laws—laws requiring rabies inoculations and limiting waste emissions, for example—and by using taxes and subsidies to alter the behavior of firms and individuals. Chapter 9 further explores the topic of externalities.

3. *Providing public goods.* Some important products cannot be profitably produced by private businesses; they must be provided by government if they are to be available. In the United States, government uses its taxing authority to pay for public goods such as national defense, flood-control dams, and tornado-warning systems. A wide variety of quasi-public goods such as fire and police protection are also financed in this manner. Public goods are discussed in more detail in Chapter 9.

4. *Redistributing income.* As we saw earlier, total reliance on the market mechanism can produce substantial income inequality. In the United States, government has assumed responsibility for reducing income inequality. This is accomplished in a variety of ways. The federal income tax is somewhat "progressive"—that is, it is intended to take a greater proportion of the incomes of the rich than the poor. Those with very low incomes qualify for an "earned income tax credit." In effect, rather than receiving taxes from them, the government pays these people. Some government programs attempt to bolster the incomes of the poor by providing them with subsidized job training. Other programs attempt to reduce poverty directly. For example, Social Security provides financial assistance to the old, the disabled, and those that are experiencing financial distress due to the death of a breadwinner. In addition, state unemployment compensation provides financial assistance to workers who are temporarily unemployed. In spite of these efforts, however, there is still substantial income inequality in the U.S. economy. Chapter 9 covers this topic in greater detail .

5. *Stabilizing the economy.* Many economists argue that capitalist economies are inherently unstable—subject to periodic bouts of unemployment or inflation. The Employment Act of 1946 requires Congress to pursue policies aimed at achieving high employment, economic growth, and price stability. In addition, the Federal Reserve—the governmental agency that regulates the nation's money supply—attempts to guide the economy's overall performance. Later chapters will discuss the factors that influence the macroeconomic performance of our economy and examine how policymakers attempt to manage that performance.

6. *Regulating health and safety.* In addition to the preceding functions, government regulates businesses to assure product quality and the safety of working conditions. It bans certain goods and services (fully automatic weapons, prostitution, illicit drugs, and child pornography, for example) and certain ingredients (lead in gasoline, for instance, and red dye number two). Government also mandates the purchase of certain products such as seatbelts and airbags in automobiles, smoke detectors in apartments, and

lifejackets on boats. Clearly, government's role in attempting to maintain health and safety is not insignificant.

As you can see, there are many decisions that the United States does not leave to the impersonal dictates of the market. And even this relatively lengthy list is not exhaustive! Is all this government intervention a good thing? Does it allow markets to function more efficiently or more humanely? Does it succeed in making our economy more stable? This is open to debate. Succeeding chapters will examine elements of this debate further.

THE REST OF THE WORLD

As we've seen, the U.S. economy does not conform to the model of pure capitalism. A number of important enterprises are publicly owned, and the visible hand of government influences many of our economic decisions. And yet the U.S. economy is probably as close to pure capitalism as any economy in existence. The rest of the world's economies represent an even more thorough blending of public and private ownership, of market and government decision making.

Consider some of the major European countries. **France** has extensive state ownership of the means of production, substantial government regulation, and a long history of using "indicative" planning to influence business decisions. Under a system of indicative planning, the planning agency collects and disseminates information, but does not command that specific production targets be achieved. Instead, it uses indirect means, such as tax incentives, to influence business decisions. In 1995, France elected a conservative president, Jacques Chirac. Under Chirac, France has turned away from planning and has focused more attention on privatization of the French economy—that is, on converting public enterprises to private enterprises. While many in France continue to proclaim their loyalty to planning, the reality appears to be increasingly more in tune with the capitalist model.

Great Britain, prior to the long Conservative rule of Margaret Thatcher and John Majors (1979–1997), was often described as a socialist economic system. This description stemmed from the size of the government's budget, the extent of publicly owned enterprises, and the nation's reliance on economic planning. The socialist label was never completely accurate, but it has grown increasingly inaccurate. While publicly owned firms are still visible in some key industries, their overall importance is relatively low. Economic planning, which was never practiced to the same extent as in France, has been largely abandoned. What remains is clearly a mixed economy, though one that is more highly regulated than the U.S. economy.

The **German** economy is, in some ways, closer to the U.S. economy than it is to either the British or French economies. Privately owned enterprises dominate

German industry, and markets dictate most decisions. There is, however, extensive government intervention to achieve social objectives. For example, there is a state-run system of health insurance, extensive public housing for the poor, and a variety of regulations to protect workers and consumers. All of these can be found in other industrialized nations, but the German programs are among the most comprehensive. In addition, the government pursues a policy known as "codetermination." Codetermination means that corporations must have worker representatives on their boards of directors. In effect, this forces corporations to consider worker interests when formulating business policy. The Germans describe their economic system as a "social market economy."

The **Swedish** economy is similar, in many respects, to the German economy. Private ownership is the norm, and markets dictate most outcomes. The state, however, goes to great lengths to maintain an egalitarian income distribution. For instance, it provides very generous benefits for retirement, medical care, education, and the like. These programs, coupled with higher income taxes on those earning higher incomes, lead to a substantial redistribution of income. This may be at least part of the reason that the income distribution in Sweden is significantly more equal than that found in the United States.

When we consider Eastern Europe and Asia, we find a number of economic systems in transition. For most of the last century, the **Soviet Union** was held up as a nearly perfect example of command socialism. Most factories, farms, and other enterprises were owned and operated by the state, and the fundamental choices about what, how, and for whom to produce were made by the State Planning Committee (GOSPLAN). **China**, which patterned its economy after the Soviet Union, also relied heavily on state ownership and central direction, as did **Poland, Hungary, Romania,** and **Bulgaria.**

In the late 1970s things began to change, largely due to dissatisfaction with the performance of these centrally directed economies. China, while retaining state ownership of heavy industry and other important activities, began permitting significant private ownership in agriculture, trade, and small-scale industry. That trend has continued, but the Chinese leadership shows no signs of privatizing heavy industry and continues to rely heavily on planning and central direction. (For a more detailed look at the Chinese economy, see "Private Business in China" on page 54.) More significant changes are occurring in the former Soviet Union and its satellite countries. In **Russia**, Poland, Hungary, Romania, and Bulgaria, for example, the governments appear to be abandoning both state ownership and planning. Unfortunately, these nations are finding that the transition to freer markets is not painless. Consider the situation in Russia, for example. Russia began closing and privatizing state enterprises in 1991. By 1996 approximately 60 percent of Russia's output was produced in privately owned enterprises. But while the share of output coming from the private sector rose, the total output of the Russian economy fell every year until 1997, when output began increasing modestly. In short, the growth of the private sector has not been

USE YOUR ECONOMIC REASONING

Private Business in China: A Tough, Tortuous Road

By Craig S. Smith

YU XIANGLIN wants to build a blimp. He has notebooks filled with drawings of airships that recall his boyhood fantasies of 50 years ago. He has regulatory specifications and a business plan. But after two years of hard work, Mr. Yu, 60, remains grounded because he is a private businessman, something not quite as scarce as a zeppelin in this officially socialist country, but still rare where "capitalist" is a dirty word.

His most pressing problem is getting a bank loan. The bank requires a guarantor, almost impossible for a private businessman to find in China. Even if a private company has a guarantor, most loans are for only three or four months—18 months in exceptional cases. "That's not long enough to get a business off the ground," said Mr. Yu, a portly man dressed in a black Hugo Boss shirt that matched his jet-black hair. "It's really, really tough for private companies in China," he added.

Though this country has been marching famously on the road toward economic change for more than two decades now, it is far from the evolving capitalist society that many people in the West imagine. The private sector, concentrated on the country's southeastern coast, remains a small slice of an economy that is still dominated by government-owned enterprises. Even China's 800 million ostensibly independent farmers grow crops on state-owned land and sell grain to state-owned grain companies. Private companies, excluding those controlled by foreigners, accounted last year for less than 20 percent of China's economic output, and employed fewer than 50 million people in a country of 1.25 billion. While a sizable gray economy accounts for much hidden private activity, barriers to raising money keep most private businesses from providing more than a handful of jobs.

There is growing pressure to change that. Allowing private companies to absorb the state's excess workers is an obvious way to improve the Chinese economy, locked in a cycle of bank lending to the money-losing state-owned enterprises that sustain those workers. And officials are beginning to realize that they need people like Mr. Yu for an even more pressing reason rooted in Chinese nationalism: with World Trade Organization membership expected to open the domestic market wider to foreign companies in the next five years, foreigners could take over a huge part of the economy unless China unleashes private entrepreneurs soon. "If state-owned enterprises can't perform and there isn't a viable domestic private sector, the economy will by default become mostly foreign-owned," warned Andy Xie, an economist for Morgan Stanley Dean Witter in Hong Kong.

Yet entrepreneurs like Mr. Yu are systematically shunned by China's banks, often discriminated against by government regulators and barred from entering many industries. In a conference room above the auto repair shop that has already made him relatively wealthy, Mr. Yu said he could sell as

Source: New York Times, July 12, 2000.

many as 90 blimps immediately if he had the money to make them…. He envisions blimps used for advertising, geological surveys, even heavy lifting in the country's mountainous west, where the government plans to build dozens of dams in the next few years. If he does not start soon, foreign blimp makers will take the market once the country joins the W.T.O.…

China's president, Jiang Zemin, laid new foundations for privatization nearly three years ago by officially redefining state ownership, the central tenet of China's economy, to include minority stakes in otherwise private enterprises. Private property was given constitutional protection the next year. But ideological inertia still stands in the way. Allowing capitalists to accumulate capital is anathema to the country's hard-line Marxists, who fear that a powerful private sector would erode the Communist Party's power. "The government doesn't want to develop the private sector; they just want to use it to help the state-owned economy," said Chen Rong, one of Shanghai's largest private entrepreneurs, who exudes a seen-it-all air….

Because relationships with officials are still so crucial, many private business owners are really just opportunists exploiting their party connections. The resulting corruption has not helped improve the private sector's image. One of the most celebrated entrepreneurs, Mou Qizhong, was recently sentenced to life in prison for fraud. Other businesses disguise themselves as government-owned entities to survive. Guo Hongnian and four friends pooled $72,000 in 1992 to establish a liquefied cooking gas factory in Shanghai. But as a private company, they could not get the proper license to sell their gas. They paid a city-owned cooking gas supplier $30,000 in return for registering them as a collective enterprise, and their business took off. Its assets are worth about $12 million today.

Much of China's economic growth in the last 20 years has come from such variants of private enterprise. But the fuzzy ownership structure has limited their growth into bigger companies. Banks and outside inventors are reluctant to finance the collectives because it is not clear to whom the enterprises belong….

Despite all the problems, there is a growing sense in China that the private sector is an idling dynamo about to shudder to life. All that is needed is a mechanism to give private owners access to capital. The government is already talking about expanding the two stock exchanges to make it easier for fledgling companies, including private ones, to raise money. And it is talking about letting foreign-owned companies list shares for buying and selling by Chinese. That would encourage foreigners to pump money into young companies because it would give investors an easy way to get their money out later….

Given the current harsh environment, those private companies that do play by the rules and survive end up remarkably healthy, with resilient streams of revenue. Mr. Yu quit a state-owned machine tool factory to start repairing trucks in 1977. The business grew along with traffic on the roads and he never needed to borrow. Having beaten the system once, he is confident his new venture will succeed even though he has never been up in a blimp. "When we build one, I'll be the first passenger," he said.

Use Your Economic Reasoning

1. Why is Yu Xianglin finding it difficult to obtain a bank loan? What other barriers do entrepreneurs face in China?
2. According to the article, "Allowing capitalists to accumulate capital is anathema to the country's hard-line Marxists." Why?
3. Private businesses are disguising themselves as government-owned enterprises. How does the author explain this behavior? Why are banks and other investors reluctant to finance such enterprises?
4. The article says that "many private business owners are really just opportunists." How is this likely to influence the country's willingness to accept capitalist reforms?

rapid enough to offset the decline in output resulting from the closing of state enterprises. As a result, the average Russian's standard of living has dropped substantially, and unemployment has been a major social problem. This has caused critics to call for a return to the old command economy. Although most experts expect Russia to continue along the path toward a more market-oriented economy, it is too early to tell what mixture of market and command will ultimately emerge. The same can be said of the economies of many other Eastern European countries—Hungary and Romania, for example. Although these nations have abandoned centralized planning, they may well maintain a more substantial role for government than is found in either the United States or Western Europe. Only time will tell if this forecast is accurate.

If we venture to Southeast Asia, we encounter mixed economies that appear to have a strong capitalist flavor. In the **Japanese** economy, there is little public ownership, and most decisions are market driven. But Japan pursues an "industrial policy" in which state bureaucrats attempt to promote what they deem to be key sectors of the economy and phase out other, less-promising sectors. Some have described this approach as midway between planning and free markets. Similar approaches appear to characterize the economies of **South Korea** and **Taiwan**. In these nations the government has routinely targeted specific industries (and specific companies) for assistance.

What can we make of this brief tour of a few of the world's economies? First, it should be apparent that all real-world economies combine elements of capitalism and socialism. Even the economies of the United States and **Hong Kong**, which rely heavily on markets, reserve some role for government.[6] And markets are apparent even in the most centrally directed of the world's economies—the Chinese economy, for example. Second, it should be apparent that interest in the command model is waning. Only a few countries—China, **Cuba**, and **North Korea**—maintain any commitment to planning, and even here the market mechanism is becoming increasingly evident. Of course, the economies of the new millennium will continue to blend elements of capitalism and command socialism. It's just that the blend is one in which markets play an increasingly important role.

The preceding section provided some appreciation of the diversity of existing economic systems. But our primary interest is in the U.S. economy. In the remaining chapters of this text, we will examine the operation of the U.S. economy in more detail. To better understand our economy, we need to know more about how markets work and how government influences economic choices in our system. In Chapter 3 we begin to broaden our understanding of markets.

---

[6] Since 1998 Hong Kong has been under the rule of mainland China. The impact of this change on Hong Kong's economy remains to be seen.

SUMMARY

An *economic system* is a set of institutions and mechanisms for answering the three fundamental questions of economics—what, how, and for whom to produce. In describing economic systems, it is helpful to ask two questions: (1) Who owns the means of production? (2) Who makes the economic decisions?

Economists commonly use theoretical models to explain the operation of economic systems. *Capitalism* describes an economic system in which the *means of production* are privately owned and fundamental economic choices are made by individual buyers and sellers interacting in markets. The principal features of pure capitalism include private property and freedom of choice, with self-interest as the driving force (held in check by *pure competition*); price determination through markets; and a minimum of government intervention—a *laissez-faire economy*.

In a capitalist economy, *consumer sovereignty* dictates which goods and services will be produced. If consumers want more of a particular product, its price will tend to rise, encouraging profit-seeking businesses to produce more of it. To produce these products, businesses buy economic resources (e.g., labor) from *households*, thereby providing households with the money needed to purchase the output of businesses. The circular-flow model of capitalism diagrams this process by showing how the flows of money (money flows) and resources and products (real flows) circulate between the household and business sectors and operate through product and resource markets.

At the other extreme, the model of *command socialism* describes an economic system in which the means of production are owned by the public, or the state, and the fundamental economic choices are made by a central authority. The principal features of command socialism include public ownership, centralized decision making, economic planning, and allocation by command.

In command socialism the central planning authority gathers information on production capabilities and consumer preferences (if the latter is a concern) and establishes production targets for the producing units, such as factories and farms. These units are required to produce the products dictated by the central authority in the manner specified. Output is then distributed according to the central authority's goals. Command socialism is depicted as a pyramid, with the central planning board at the top and the producing and consuming units below. The producing and consuming units supply information to the central planners, who use this information to develop production targets and decide how the limited output will be distributed among the potential customers.

No existing economic system fits neatly into either model. All real-world economic systems are *mixed economies* because they represent some blending of the two models. For example, the U.S. economy, commonly described as a capitalist system, contains some elements of a socialist economy. Public ownership is not uncommon in the United States, and government influences many of our fundamental economic choices. And markets are important even in the most centrally directed of the world's economies—China and North Korea, for example.

KEY TERMS

Capitalism
Command socialism
Common-property resources
Consumer sovereignty

Economic system
Household
Invisible hand
Laissez-faire economy

Market
Means of production
Mixed economies
Pure competition

STUDY QUESTIONS

Fill in the Blanks

1. The driving force or engine of capitalism is _Self interest_ .

2. The functioning of a capitalist economy is coordinated and directed through _Market_ in which _Prices_ are determined by the interaction of buyers and sellers.

3. In the model of pure capitalism, the pursuit of self-interest by producers is kept in check by _Competition_. The model of pure capitalism requires _Pure Competition_, a situation in which there are a large number of buyers and sellers of each product.

4. Because businesspeople in a capitalist economy are motivated by self-interest, they want to produce the goods and services that will allow them to earn the highest _Profits_ . Those products tend to be the ones that are most desired by _Consumers_ .

5. According to Milton Friedman, competitive capitalism promotes _Political Freedom_ by separating economic and political power.

6. In pure command socialism the fundamental economic decisions are made by the _Central Authority_ and implemented through _Command_.

7. In pure command socialism _Economies_ replaces the market as the method of coordinating the various economic _Planning_ decisions.

8. It is possible to represent a socialist command economy as a _Pyramid_ with the _Planning board_ at the top and producing and consuming units at the bottom.

9. One weakness of command socialism is its inefficient _Information_ network.

10. The United States and China are both examples of _Mixed_ economies.

Multiple Choice

1. Which of the following is *not* a characteristic of pure capitalism?
   a) Public ownership of the means of production
   b) The pursuit of self-interest
   c) Markets and prices
   d) Pure competition
   e) Limited government

2. In a market economy the scarcest resources will be used very conservatively because
   a) central planners will allocate such resources only where they are most needed.
   b) the scarcest resources will tend to have the highest prices.
   c) government officials will not permit their use.
   d) the scarcest resources will tend to have the lowest prices.

3. In a capitalist economy
   a) businesses are free to produce whatever products they choose.
   b) consumers are free to utilize their incomes as they see fit.
   c) resource owners have the freedom to sell their resources to whomever they choose.
   d) All of the above
   e) None of the above

4. Consumer sovereignty means that
   a) consumers dictate which goods and services will be produced by the way they spend their money.
   b) central planners allocate a major share of society's resources to the production of consumer goods.
   c) the role of government in the economy is very limited.
   d) all economic resources are used efficiently.

5. According to the "invisible hand" doctrine,
   a) as individuals pursue their own interests, they tend to promote the interests of society as a whole.
   b) the actions of individuals often have unanticipated and undesirable effects on society.

   c) individuals should put the interests of society first.
   d) when individuals attempt to promote the best interests of the entire society, they also further their own personal interests.

6. Adam Smith recognized that the "invisible hand" would function as he envisioned only if
   a) individuals unconsciously considered the welfare of others in making their decisions.
   b) government regulations forced businesses to behave in an ethical manner.
   c) a high degree of competition existed in the economy.
   d) individuals lived in accordance with the golden rule.

7. In a market economy, if consumers suddenly stop buying 10-speed bikes and start buying 21-speed bikes,
   a) the price of 10-speeds will tend to fall and more of them will be produced.
   b) the price of 21-speeds will tend to rise, making them less profitable to produce and encouraging producers to supply more of them.
   c) resources will tend to be shifted from the production of 10-speeds to the production of 21-speeds.
   d) the price of 10-speeds will tend to rise, making them more profitable to produce and encouraging producers to supply more of them.

8. Which of the following best describes command socialism?
   a) An economic system characterized by private ownership of the means of production, centralized decision making, and command implementation.
   b) An economic system characterized by public ownership of the means of production, centralized decision making, and market implementation.

c) An economic system characterized by public ownership of the means of production, individual decision making, and command implementation.

d) An economic system characterized by public ownership of the means of production, centralized decision making, and command implementation.

9. Which of the following is correct?
   a) In command socialism, the basic economic choices are made by individuals.
   b) In pure capitalism, powerful economic units have a substantial impact on the way economic choices are made.
   c) In command socialism, producers are required to produce whatever products central planners dictate.
   d) In pure capitalism, economic planning ensures that the various production decisions will be consistent with one another.

10. In deciding what products to produce, the central planners in a socialist command economy need not consider
    a) the size of the economy's labor force.
    b) the production capabilities of the economy's factories.
    c) consumer preferences.
    d) the economy's stock of raw materials.

11. In order to get the most output from society's limited resources, the scarcest resources must be used only where no other input will suffice.
    a) In command socialism this function is performed by planners; in pure capitalism it is performed by the central government.
    b) In pure capitalism this function is performed by input prices; in command socialism it is performed by planners.
    c) In command socialism this function is performed by the producing units; in pure capitalism it is performed by planners.

d) In pure capitalism this function is performed by government regulations, in command socialism it is performed by output targets.

12. In a comparison of command socialism and pure capitalism, which of the following is true?
    a) Prices play a larger role in command socialism than in pure capitalism.
    b) Resources are likely to be used more efficiently in command socialism than in pure capitalism.
    c) Economic planning plays a larger role in pure capitalism than in command socialism.
    d) Decision making is more decentralized in pure capitalism than in command socialism.

13. Which of the following is *not* a function of government in the U.S. economy?
    a) Providing public goods
    b) Economic planning
    c) Redistributing income
    d) Maintaining competition

14. One reason the United States is not an example of pure capitalism is that
    a) most producing units are publicly owned.
    b) commands are used to implement some economic decisions.
    c) the pursuit of self-interest is a powerful force.
    d) markets are used to coordinate most economic decisions.

15. Codetermination is a feature of which of the following economies?
    a) France
    b) Russia
    c) Germany
    d) Great Britain

Problems and Questions for Discussion

1. What is an economic system? Why is it valid to say that no two real-world economic systems are exactly alike?

2. List the characteristics or elements of pure capitalism and explain each. Are any of these elements absent from the U.S. economy? Explain.

3. How would a socialist command economy answer the three fundamental questions? What elements of command socialism exist in the U.S. economy?

4. Explain the role of economic planning in command socialism. Who is in charge of economic planning in a capitalist economy?

5. Try to draw the circular-flow diagram without looking back at the diagram in the text. Now, label all the parts of the diagram, and indicate which flows are money flows and which are real flows. Use the diagram to explain how a capitalist economy works.

6. Draw the command pyramid and label the parts. What does the command pyramid tell us about the way a socialist economy functions?

7. Milton Friedman suggests that competitive capitalism promotes political freedom. Explain.

8. What functions does the government perform in the U.S. economy? Which of these functions is consistent with the model of pure capitalism?

9. Why can't capitalism exist without a well-developed legal system?

10. Japan, South Korea, and Taiwan all pursue an "industrial policy." Explain what is meant by an industrial policy and why this policy is inconsistent with pure capitalism.

11. How are the objectives of government intervention in Japan and Taiwan different from the objectives of government intervention in Germany and Sweden?

12. Government intervention in Germany appears to have a single, overriding focus. Does government intervention in the U.S. economy have a single focus or objective?

ANSWER KEY

Fill in the Blanks

1. self-interest
2. markets, prices
3. competition, pure competition
4. profits, consumers
5. political freedom
6. central authority, commands
7. economic planning
8. pyramid, planning board
9. information
10. mixed

Multiple Choice

1. a	4. a	7. c	10. c	13. b
2. b	5. a	8. d	11. b	14. b
3. d	6. c	9. c	12. d	15. c

PART TWO

Microeconomics: Markets, Prices, and the Role of Competition

In Chapter 3 we begin our study of microeconomics by investigating how prices are determined in competitive markets. You will learn the precise meaning of "supply" and "demand" and how the interaction of these forces determines prices. You will examine how prices can change and will learn the functions that price changes perform in a market economy. In Chapter 4 you will investigate the degree of consumer and producer responsiveness to price changes.

Chapter 5 explores the idea that human beings are rational decision makers who are motivated by self-interest. You will find that rational decision making involves a careful comparison of costs and benefits and that the relevant costs and benefits are always "marginal." Chapter 6 examines the behavior of the purely competitive firm and explores how firms use marginal reasoning to determine the profit-maximizing output. You will discover the characteristics of a competitive industry and see why competition is beneficial for consumers. Chapter 7 examines how firms acquire pricing discretion, or market power, and how the behavior of firms that possess market power differs from that of purely competitive firms. An appendix to the chapter examines the pricing techniques actually employed by businesses and compares them with the theoretical techniques suggested by economists. Chapter 8 considers the "degrees" of competition that exist in different industry structures and explores the impact of those different industry structures on the well-being of consumers. Chapter 9 looks at some of the inherent limitations of a market economy by examining the origin of problems such as pollution.

CHAPTER THREE

Demand and Supply:
Price Determination in Competitive Markets

LEARNING OBJECTIVES

1. Define demand and supply and represent these concepts graphically.
2. State the "laws" of demand and supply.
3. Identify the determinants of demand and supply.
4. Recognize the difference between a change in demand (supply) and a change in the quantity demanded (supplied).
5. Explain and illustrate graphically how the equilibrium price and quantity are determined.
6. Describe the rationing, signaling, and motivating functions of prices.
7. Identify the factors that can cause the equilibrium price to change.
8. Use demand and supply curves to predict changes in the equilibrium price and quantity.
9. Discuss the impact of government-established maximum and minimum prices.

How do markets work? A market economy is governed by the interaction of buyers and sellers in thousands of different product and resource markets. This interaction—what you might describe as bargaining or negotiating—determines prices. The prevailing prices of goods and services tell producers which products consumers want the most. Resource prices tell producers which resources to use to produce those products profitably. Because resource prices affect consumers' incomes, they also influence the distribution of goods and services. For example, workers whose skills are particularly scarce can command higher salaries and thereby claim a larger share of the society's limited output. In short, prices play a very important role in the functioning of all mixed economies.

This chapter introduces the model of demand and supply, the model intended to illustrate how buyers and sellers interact to determine prices in competitive markets. Competitive markets are composed of many independent buyers and sellers, each too small to be able to influence the market price significantly. We'll explore the meaning of competitive markets in greater detail later in the text. For now, just remember that in competitive markets, prices are determined by the impersonal forces of demand and supply, not by manipulations of powerful buyers or sellers.

After you study this chapter, you will have a better understanding of how prices are determined and a greater appreciation of the role that prices play in a market economy. You'll understand why the price of gold fluctuates and why salaries are higher in some occupations than in others. You'll understand why antique cars often command higher prices than this year's models and why a poor wheat harvest in Canada or Ukraine can mean higher bread prices in the United States. You will also understand how prices both direct the actions of producers and determine the distribution of society's limited output of goods and services. In summary, the material in this chapter will give you a clearer comprehension of the role of markets and prices in our economy.

DEMAND

In a market economy, consumers are sovereign; that is, consumers dictate which goods and services will be produced. But it is consumer *demand* rather than consumer wants or desires that actually directs the market. We have already noted that human wants are unlimited. Wanting an item, however, and being willing and able to pay for it are two distinctly different things. If the item we want carries a price tag, we may do without it: We may lack the money to pay or we may prefer to spend that money on something else.

People who are both *willing and able* to make purchases are the consumers who determine which products a market economy will produce. When consumers lack either the willingness or the ability to spend their dollars, producers do not respond. Thus, the concept of demand includes the willingness and ability of potential buyers to purchase a product. We define **demand** as a schedule (or table) showing the quantities of a good or service that consumers are willing and able to purchase at various prices during a given time period, when all factors other than the product's price remain unchanged.

Exhibit 3.1 illustrates the concept of demand through a simple example. The schedule shows the yearly demand for jogging shoes of a given quality in the hypothetical community of Hometown, U.S.A. You can see that the number of pairs of jogging shoes that Hometown consumers are willing and able to purchase each year depends on the selling price. If jogging shoes sell for $100 a pair, Hometowners will purchase 2,000 pairs a year, assuming that other factors remain the same—their incomes, for example, and their present jogging routines.

EXHIBIT 3.1

Hometown Demand for Jogging Shoes

PRICE (per pair)	QUANTITY (pairs per year)
$100	2,000
80	4,000
60	6,000
40	8,000
20	10,000

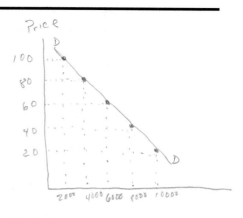

Demand Curves

Economists usually represent schedules in the form of graphs. To graph the demand for jogging shoes, we first plot the information in Exh. 3.1 and then connect the points to form a demand curve, as shown in Exh. 3.2. A **demand curve** is simply a graphical representation of demand. By convention we measure price on the vertical axis and quantity on the horizontal axis. Each point on the curve represents a price and the quantity that consumers would demand per year at that price. For example, we can see in Exh. 3.2 that at a

EXHIBIT 3.2

The Demand Curve for Jogging Shoes in Hometown, U.S.A.

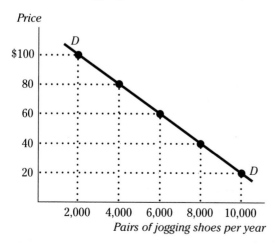

A demand curve is a graphical representation of demand. It demonstrates the inverse relationship between price and quantity demanded.

price of $80, Hometown joggers would demand 4,000 pairs; at a price of $60, the quantity demanded would increase to 6,000 pairs.

THE LAW OF DEMAND

Our hypothetical demand schedule and demand curve for jogging shoes demonstrate clearly what economists call the **law of demand,** which holds that the quantity demanded of a product is *negatively, or inversely, related* to its price. This simply means that consumers will purchase more of a product at lower prices than at higher prices. That's why demand curves always slope downward and to the right.

Economists believe that two factors explain the inverse relationship between price and quantity demanded:

1. When prices are lower, consumers can afford to purchase a larger quantity of the product out of any given income. Economists refer to this *ability* to purchase more as the **income effect** of a price reduction.
2. At lower prices the product becomes more attractive relative to other items serving the same function. This **substitution effect** explains the *willingness* of consumers to substitute for other products the product that has declined in price.

To illustrate the income and substitution effects, let's return to our Hometown consumers. Why will they purchase more jogging shoes at $20 than at $100? Because of the income effect, their incomes will now buy more: If the price of jogging shoes declines and other prices don't change, consumers will be able to buy more goods and services with their fixed incomes. It's almost as though each consumer had received a raise. And because of the substitution effect, consumers will buy jogging shoes instead of tennis shoes, sandals, or moccasins because jogging shoes have become a better footwear buy. Because of both the income effect and the substitution effect, we all, like these hypothetical consumers, tend to purchase more of a product at a lower price than at a higher price.

DETERMINANTS OF DEMAND

The demand curve and the law of demand emphasize the relationship between the price of a product and the quantity demanded. But price is not the only factor that determines how much of a product consumers will buy. A variety of other factors underlie the demand schedule and determine the precise position of the demand curve. These **determinants of demand** include income, tastes and preferences, expectations regarding future prices, the price of related goods, and the number of buyers in the market. Any demand curve is based on the assumption that these factors are held constant. Changes in one or more of these determinants cause the entire demand curve to shift to a new position.

Income

The most obvious determinant of demand is income. Consumers' incomes influence their *ability* to purchase goods and services. For what economists call **normal goods,** an increase in income will cause consumers to purchase more of a product than before at each possible price. For example, an increase in per capita income (income per person) will probably cause consumers to buy more steak than before at whatever price exists. We would show this by shifting the demand curve to the right, as illustrated in Exh. 3.3.

Not all products are normal goods, however. An increase in income will cause consumers to purchase less of an **inferior good,** thus shifting the demand curve to the left. Powdered milk, generic macaroni and cheese, and cheap wine are examples of products that might be inferior goods. When

---

EXHIBIT 3.3
Income as a Determinant of Demand

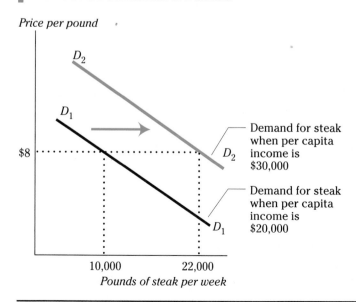

Price per pound

D_2

D_1

$8

— Demand for steak when per capita income is $30,000 D_2

— Demand for steak when per capita income is $20,000 D_1

10,000   22,000
Pounds of steak per week

An increase in per capita income will shift the demand curve for a normal good to the right. Consumers will purchase more of the product at each price.

consumers' incomes increase, they may choose to buy less of these products in favor of more appetizing grocery items.

Tastes and Preferences

Consumers' tastes and preferences—how well they like the product relative to other products—are also important determinants of demand. A change in tastes and preferences will affect the demand for products. For example, the desire to limit cholesterol intake has altered consumer tastes and preferences for various food products. Today consumers demand less red meat and fewer eggs than in times past but demand more fish and chicken. In other words, this change in tastes and preferences has caused the demand curves for red meat and eggs to shift to the left and the demand curves for fish and chicken to shift to the right.

Expectations about Prices

Expectations may also influence consumer behavior. For example, the expectation that the price of an item will rise in the future usually encourages consumers to buy it now. We would represent this by shifting the entire demand curve to the right to show that more would be demanded now at whatever price prevailed. Similarly, the expectation that a product will decline in price is a good incentive to postpone buying it; the present demand curve for the product would shift to the left.

Price of Related Goods

A somewhat less obvious determinant of demand is the price of related goods. Although all goods compete for a consumer's income, the price of substitutes and complements may be particularly important in explaining consumer behavior. **Substitutes** are simply products that can be used in place of other products because, to a greater or lesser extent, they satisfy the same consumer wants. Hot dogs are a typical substitute for hamburgers, and tennis shoes may substitute for jogging shoes unless one is a serious jogger. **Complements** are products normally purchased along with or in conjunction with another product. For example, pickle relish and hot dogs are complements, as are lettuce and salad dressing.

If the price of hamburgers increased and the price of hot dogs remained unchanged, consumers might be expected to buy fewer hamburgers and more hot dogs. The demand curve for hot dogs would shift to the right. By the same token, an increase in the price of lettuce is likely to have an adverse effect on the sale of salad dressing. Because people buy salad dressing as a complement to salad vegetables, anything that causes consumers to eat fewer salads causes them to demand less salad dressing. The demand curve for salad dressing would shift to the left.

The Number of Consumers in the Market

The final determinant of demand is the number of consumers in the market. The more consumers who demand a particular product, the greater the total demand for the product. When the number of consumers increases, the demand curve for the product shifts to the right to show that a greater quantity is now demanded at each price. If the number of consumers declines, the demand curve shifts to the left.

As we think about the demand for a particular product, we need to remember the five determinants we have listed and how changes in these factors will affect the demand curve. We also need to recognize that more and more U.S. firms are selling their products to consumers in Mexico, Europe, and other locations outside the United States. As a consequence, the position of the demand curve for many products is determined not solely by local or national factors but by international factors as well. For instance, rising incomes in Mexico are certain to shift the demand curve for American-made computers and software to the right, whereas the availability of cheap Chilean wines will probably shift the demand curve for many California wines to the left. The point is that markets are often international in scope, so that we need to look beyond national boundaries to determine the level of demand.

CHANGE IN QUANTITY DEMANDED VERSUS CHANGE IN DEMAND

In analyzing the factors that cause consumers to increase or decrease their purchases of a particular product, it is helpful to distinguish between the impact of a change (1) in the price of the product and (2) in one or more of the determinants of demand.

A change in the price of the product results in a **change in quantity demanded** and is represented graphically by movement along a stationary demand curve. For example, if the price of steak declines from $8 a pound to $6 a pound, consumers will move from point A to point B on demand curve D_1 in Exh. 3.4. Note that the consumers will now choose to purchase a greater quantity of the product because its price is lower. This is an increase in the quantity demanded. If, on the other hand, the price rises from $4 a pound to $6 a pound, the consumers will move from point C to point B on the demand curve. Here a price increase will cause a reduction in the quantity demanded.

EXHIBIT 3.4
Distinguishing Change in Demand from Change in Quantity Demanded

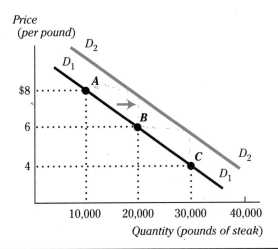

A change in the price of steak will cause a *change in the quantity demanded.* When the price of steak declines from $8 to $4 a pound, the quantity demanded increases from 10,000 to 30,000 pounds; consumers move from *A* to *C* along demand curve *D*₁.

A change in a determinant of demand will cause a *change in demand:* the entire curve will shift. The movement from *D*₁ to *D*₂ is an increase in demand.

When any determinant of demand changes, the result is a **change in demand**—an entirely new demand schedule represented graphically by a shift of the demand curve to a new position. If consumers develop a stronger preference for steak, for instance, or if the prices of substitutes for steak rise, the entire demand curve for steak will shift to the right—an increase in demand. Exhibit 3.4 depicts this shift. An entire demand curve shift to the left would denote a decrease in demand. (See "Auto Sales May Be Feeling First Pinch of Higher Rates," on page 74, to test your understanding of the difference between a change in demand and a change in the quantity demanded.)

SUPPLY

A knowledge of demand is essential to an understanding of how prices are determined, but it is only half the picture. Now we turn to the supply side of the market.

When we use the term "supply" in our everyday language, we are usually referring to a fixed quantity. That's what the owner of the local sporting-goods store means when advertising a *limited supply* of Fleet Feet tennis shoes or SuperFit swimsuits. But that's not what economists mean when they talk about supply. To economists, supply is a schedule—just as demand is. **Supply** is a schedule (or table) showing the quantities of a good or service that producers

EXHIBIT 3.5
Hometown Supply of Jogging Shoes

PRICE (per pair)	QUANTITY (pairs per year)
$100	10,000
80	8,000
60	6,000
40	4,000
20	2,000

are willing and able to offer for sale at various prices during a given time period, when all factors other than the product's price remain unchanged.

Exhibit 3.5 represents the annual supply of jogging shoes in the Hometown market area. As the schedule shows, the number of pairs of jogging shoes that suppliers will make available for sale depends on the price of jogging shoes. At a price of $100 a pair, suppliers are willing to produce 10,000 pairs of jogging shoes a year; at a price of $60, they would offer only 6,000 pairs. Because supply is a schedule, we can't determine the quantity supplied unless we know the selling price.

EXHIBIT 3.6
The Supply Curve of Jogging Shoes in Hometown, U.S.A.

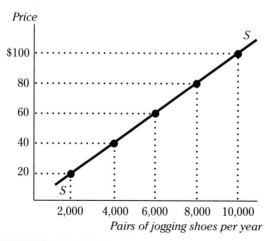

A supply curve is a graphical representation of supply. It demonstrates the direct relationship between price and quantity supplied.

USE YOUR ECONOMIC REASONING

Auto Sales May Be Feeling First Pinch of Higher Rates

By Keith Bradsher

AUTOMAKERS say that despite recent deep discounts, auto sales have not picked up in June from the relatively subdued pace of May, providing evidence to the Federal Reserve that recent interest-rate increases may be slowing the American economy.

Auto executives and dealers say sales of luxury cars and luxury sport utility vehicles remain extremely strong.

But the mass market for more affordable cars, minivans, sport utility vehicles and pickup trucks has clearly softened as middle-class families have become leery of borrowing money at ever-steeper rates, they said....

Automakers, especially Daimler-Chrysler A.G., have been stepping up their rebates, with Dodge now offering discounts on every model except the Viper sports car. But the manufacturers have also been quietly raising the subsidized interest rates they offer on car loans. They have concluded that it has become too costly to continue offer-

ing loans at 1.9 percent and subsidizing the difference compared with market rates on auto loans, which are approaching 10 percent for a three-year loan....

High gasoline prices appear to have had surprisingly little effect so far on the types of vehicles being sold, industry officials said. Even in the Midwest, where gasoline prices are highest, the biggest gas-guzzlers, mainly large sport utilities, are selling well because they are being purchased by households so affluent that they are not especially worried about the cost of fuel, they noted.

The auto industry sold cars and light trucks at a tor-

rid seasonally adjusted annual rate of 18 million vehicles in the six-month period that ended on April 30. That pace cooled to a rate of 17.1 million vehicles in May, and both Ford and General Motors are predicting virtually the same rate—17 million—for June.

The auto industry sold 17 million vehicles in all of last year, its best year ever, so the pace in the last two months does not represent a significant slowdown. But it still shows a contrast with the brisk pace last winter, as small and midsize cars, sport utility vehicles, minivans and pickup trucks are now beginning to clog some dealerships' lots....

Use Your Economic Reasoning

1. Rising interest rates appear to be reducing auto sales. Does this represent a decrease in demand or a decrease in the quantity demanded?
2. Automakers are trying to stimulate sales offering discounts on the slow-sell-

ing models. Are they attempting to increase demand or the quantity demanded?
3. What impact would you expect falling new car prices to have on the used car market? How would you represent this graphically?

Source: New York Times, June 24, 2000, p. C2.

The Supply Curve

To transform our supply schedule into a supply curve, we follow the same procedure we used in constructing a demand curve. Here we graph the information in Exh. 3.5, measuring price on the vertical axis and quantity on the horizontal axis. When we've finished graphing the points from the schedule, we connect them to get a **supply curve**—a graphical representation of supply (Exh. 3.6, see p. 73).

Interpreting a supply curve is basically the same as interpreting a demand curve. Each point on the curve represents a price and the quantity of jogging shoes that producers will supply at that price. You can see, for example, that producers will supply 4,000 pairs of shoes at a price of $40 per pair or 8,000 pairs at a price of $80 per pair.

THE LAW OF SUPPLY

You've probably noticed that the supply curve slopes upward and to the right. The supply curve slopes upward because the **law of supply** holds that price and quantity supplied are *positively*, or *directly*, *related*. Producers will supply a larger quantity at higher prices than at lower prices.

Why would producers supply more jogging shoes at a higher price than at a lower price? The major reason is that the higher price allows them to cover the higher unit costs associated with producing the additional output. It probably costs more to produce the thousandth pair of jogging shoes than it did to produce the five hundredth pair. It's also likely that it would cost even more to produce the two thousandth pair, and so on. Producers are willing to supply a greater quantity at a higher price because the higher price enables businesses to cover the higher cost of producing the additional units—units that would not have been profitable at lower prices.

Costs per unit tend to increase with output because some of a business's resources, such as its production plant and equipment, cannot be expanded in a short period of time. Therefore, as the business increases output by hiring more labor and employing more raw materials, it eventually begins to overutilize its factory and equipment. This leads to congestion, workers waiting to use equipment, more frequent breakdowns of equipment, and production bottlenecks—situations in which one stage of the production process is slowing down the entire operation. These problems increase the cost of producing additional units. Producers will supply the additional units only if they can obtain a price high enough to justify paying the higher costs. Thus, the supply curve slopes upward because a higher price is *necessary* to call forth additional output from suppliers.

DETERMINANTS OF SUPPLY

The supply curve shows the relationship between the price of a product and the quantity supplied when other factors remain unchanged. However, price is not the only factor that influences the amount producers will offer for sale. Three major **determinants of supply** underlie the supply schedule and determine the position of the supply curve: technology, prices of the resources used in producing the product, and the number of producers in the market. Each supply curve is based on the assumption that these factors are held constant. Changes in any of the determinants will shift the entire supply curve to a new position.

Technology

Each supply curve is based on the existing technology. **Technology** is our state of knowledge about how to produce products. It influences the types of machines we use and the combinations of other resources we select to produce goods and services. A **technological advance** is the discovery of a better way to produce a product—a method that uses fewer resources to produce each unit of output or that produces more output from a given amount of resources. Because a technological advance allows producers to supply a higher quantity at any given price, it is represented by shifting the supply curve to the right, as depicted in Exh. 3.7. As you can see, the development of a better method for producing personal computers will allow computer producers to supply a higher quantity at each price.

Resource Prices

Businesses must purchase economic resources in order to produce their products. Each supply curve assumes that the prices of resources remain unchanged. An increase in the price of labor, materials, or some other production input will increase producers' costs and cause them to supply less at any given price. The supply curve will shift to the left. A reduction in resource prices will have the opposite effect; the supply curve will shift to the right because producers will be able to supply a higher quantity at each price.

The Number of Producers in the Market

A third determinant of supply is the number of producers in the particular market: the more producers, the greater the supply. Each supply curve assumes that the number of producers is unchanged. If additional producers en-

EXHIBIT 3.7
The Impact of a Technological Advance on the Supply of Personal Computers

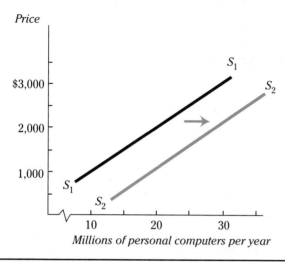

A technological advance will allow producers to supply a higher quantity at any given price.

ter the market, the supply curve will shift to the right; if some producers leave, the supply curve will shift left.

Many other changes have essentially the same impact on supply as an increase or decrease in the number of producers. A severe frost destroys half the orange crop, decreasing supply; a good growing season enlarges the wheat harvest, increasing supply; trade barriers are lowered and additional beef enters the United States, increasing supply. With each of these changes, the supply curve shifts as it would if the number of suppliers had increased or decreased.

As with demand, we need to recognize that the three determinants of supply—technology, resource prices, and the number of producers in the market—may be subject to international influences. For instance, the need to compete with foreign rivals has been a major factor spurring U.S. producers to search for and implement cost-reducing technological advances. In the furniture industry, for example, pressure from foreign producers has resulted in innovations that increase the amount of furniture produced from a given amount of wood. These innovations will cause the supply curve for furniture to shift to the right. At the same time, the supply curve of aluminum has shifted to the right for a very different reason. In the wake of the collapse of the Soviet Union, Russia has been supplying the world with massive amounts of aluminum—aluminum that once would have gone to military uses in the USSR. As you can see, we cannot ignore international factors as we attempt to determine the level of supply.

CHANGE IN SUPPLY VERSUS CHANGE IN QUANTITY SUPPLIED

Earlier in this chapter you learned the difference between a change in demand and a change in *quantity* demanded. Economists make the same distinction for supply. A **change in the quantity supplied** results from a change in the price of the product, with factors other than price held constant. It is represented graphically by movement along a stationary supply curve. According to Exh. 3.8, if the price of personal computers declines from $2,000 to $1,000, the quantity supplied will decrease from 20 million units to only 10 million units a year, as suppliers move from point *B* to point *A* along supply curve S_1. But if the price of computers increases from $2,000 to $3,000, producers will move from point *B* to point *C*, and the quantity supplied will expand from 20 million to 30 million computers a year.

A **change in supply** is an increase or decrease in the amount of a product supplied at each and every price. A change in supply is caused by a change in

EXHIBIT 3.8
Distinguishing Change in Supply from Change in Quantity Supplied

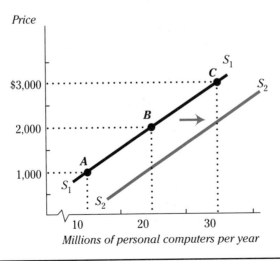

A change in the price of computers will cause a *change in the quantity supplied.* When price increases from $1,000 to $3,000, the quantity supplied increases from 10 million to 30 million computers per year; we move from *A* to *C* along supply curve S_1.

A change in a determinant of supply will cause a *change in supply:* the entire curve will shift. The movement from S_1 to S_2 is an increase in supply.

one of the determinants of supply and is represented graphically by a shift of the entire supply curve, as depicted in Exh. 3.8. If the supply curve shifts to the right (from S_1 to S_2), it denotes an increase in supply; a shift to the left indicates a decrease in supply. (To test your ability to distinguish between a change in supply and a change in the quantity supplied, read the article "Price Is Right," on page 80, and answer the questions.)

THE PROCESS OF PRICE DETERMINATION

Now that you understand the basics of demand and supply, let's put those two pieces of the puzzle together and examine how prices are determined. To do that, we'll consider again the market for jogging shoes. Exhibit 3.9 displays hypothetical demand and supply schedules for that product. As you already know, the demand schedule shows the quantities of jogging shoes that will be demanded at various prices, and the supply schedule reveals the quantities that will be supplied at those prices. But which of these possible prices will prevail in the market? And what quantity of jogging shoes will be exchanged between buyers and sellers? To answer those questions, let's compare the reactions of buyers and sellers to each possible price.

What would happen in the market if jogging shoes were selling for $20 a pair? Because the $20 price would be attractive to consumers but not to producers, 10,000 pairs of jogging shoes would be demanded, but only 2,000 pairs would be supplied. At the $20 price there would be a **shortage**—an

---

EXHIBIT 3.9

The Demand and Supply of Jogging Shoes in Hometown, U.S.A.

PRICE (per pair)	QUANTITY DEMANDED (pairs per year)	QUANTITY SUPPLIED (pairs per year)
$100	2,000	10,000
80	4,000	8,000
60	6,000	6,000
40	8,000	4,000
20	10,000	2,000

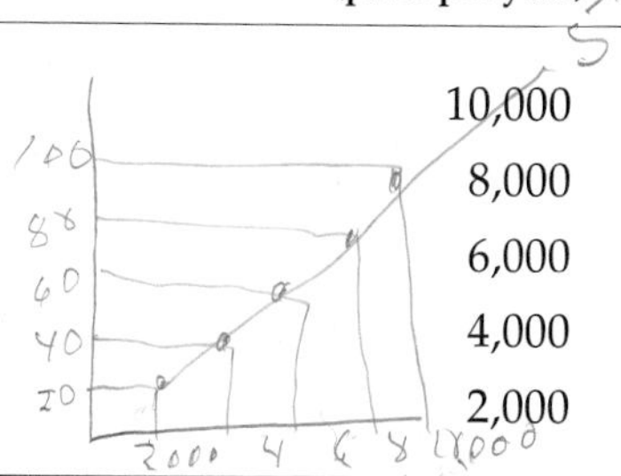

USE YOUR ECONOMIC REASONING

Price is Right

By Bruce Gottlieb

EIGHT YEARS AGO, an article appeared in an obscure Israeli medical journal, *Medicine and Law*, arguing that American citizens should be permitted to sell their kidneys. This would require changing federal law, which since 1984 has made selling any organ, even one's own, a felony punishable by up to five years in jail. The author of the article was a Michigan pathologist named Jack Kevorkian.

Kevorkian's argument was that the current system of accepting kidneys only from dead patients and Good Samaritan donors provides too few kidneys. While this was true even then, the situation is worse today. As of April 30, there were 44,989 people on the waiting list for a kidney transplant. About 2,300 of them will die this year while waiting. If kidney sales were permitted, Kevorkian ar-gued, these lives would almost certainly be saved.

He may be right. In recent years, economists and economically minded lawyers at the University of Chicago and Yale Law School have made similar arguments. The idea was endorsed two years ago in the pages of *The Lancet* by a group of prominent transplant surgeons from Harvard Medical School and hospitals in Canada and England. Of course, legalizing kidney sales remains a fringe view, both within the medical profession and outside it. But that needs to change....

There are several familiar arguments against legalizing kidney sales, beginning with the idea that giving up a kidney is too dangerous for the donor. But, popular though this argument is, the statistics don't bear it out—at least relative to other risks people are legally permitted to assume. In terms of effect on life expectancy, donating one of your two kidneys is more or less equivalent to driving an additional 16 miles to work each day. No one objects to the fact that ordinary jobs—like construction or driving a delivery van—carry roughly similar risks.

Another common objection is that government ought to encourage altruism, not profit seeking. But, from the perspective that matters—the recipient's—this distinction is irrelevant, so long as the donated kidney works.... Moreover, kidneys from cadavers function for eight years, on average, whereas those from live donors last 17 years. (The reason is that kidneys can be "harvested" from live donors in circumstances less hectic than death and that donors and recipients can be better matched.)

This brings us to the most powerful objection to the sale of kidneys—that, in practice, it would result in the poor selling parts of their bodies to the rich. But in today's health care economy, that

Source: Reprinted by permission of *The New Republic*, May 22, 2000, p. 16, © 2000, The New Republic, Inc.

probably wouldn't be the case. For several decades, Congress has mandated that Medicare pay the medical bills of any patient—of any age—who requires dialysis. Transplant surgery and post-surgical drug treatment are expensive, yes, but they're nothing compared to dialysis, which costs about $40,000 per year. That's a savings of $40,000 per year for the 17 years or so during which a transplanted kidney will function. In other words, insurers and the federal government would probably be happy to buy a kidney for anyone who needs one. They'd even be willing to pay donors considerable sums—$50,000, $100,000, or more. (Indeed, according to one estimate, if kidneys could be found for all the patients now on dialysis, Medicare would break even after just two years.)

At these prices, there would be no shortage of sellers.... And, given the amount of money involved, it seems downright contradictory to argue that the poor should be prevented from taking the deal on the grounds that poverty is unfair. The solution to poverty is anyone's guess, but restricting poor people's economic opportunities definitely isn't the answer....

Sure, critics will say that allowing kidney sales is the beginning of a slippery slope toward selling other, more essential organs. This, of course, would be a moral disaster, since it would mean legalizing serious maiming (selling eyes) or even murder (selling hearts or lungs).... But it's easy for legislators to draft a law that clearly allows kidney selling but forbids other forms of organ selling. (Kidneys are fairly unique in that, while everybody has two, somebody with just one can lead an almost entirely normal life.) And it seems implausible that a member of Congress would mistake public approval of kidney sales for approval of economic transactions that leave sellers dead or partially blind.

Nicholas L. Tilney, a Harvard Medical School professor and transplant surgeon, wrote a paper in 1989 against kidney selling.... But in 1998—as the kidney shortage became more acute—he coauthored, along with other surgeons, lawyers, and philosophers, the provocative *Lancet* paper that argued for legalizing kidney sales. "We debated this question for about two years before writing that piece," says Tilney. " All of us transplanters, and I'm sure the public, have this tremendous gut reaction against it. That was sort of our initial reaction. And then, when we all got around and really thought about this and talked about it, our thinking began to change."

The prospect of someone going under the knife to earn a down payment on a new house or to pay for college is far from pleasant. But neither is the reality of someone dying because a suitable kidney can't be found. The free market may be the worst way to allocate kidneys. The worst, that is, except for all the other alternatives.

BRUCE GOTTLIEB is a student at Harvard Law School.

Use Your Economic Reasoning

1. What economic theory suggests that paying people for kidneys will increase the number of kidneys available for transplant?
2. If it becomes legal to buy and sell kidneys, will this increase the supply of kidneys or the quantity supplied? Defend your answer.
3. What are the normative issues involved in the debate about buying and selling kidneys?
4. Suppose it became possible to transplant, say, pig kidneys into humans. Would that represent an increase in supply or an increase in the quantity supplied?

excess of quantity demanded over quantity supplied—of 8,000 pairs of jogging shoes. Therefore, some potential buyers would offer to pay a higher price in order to obtain the product. Competition among these buyers would tend to push the price to a higher level, and the higher price of jogging shoes would tend to reduce the quantity demanded while encouraging producers to expand the quantity supplied. In this way price increases would tend to reduce the shortage of jogging shoes.

Suppose that the price of jogging shoes rose to $40 a pair. At that price 8,000 pairs of jogging shoes would be demanded and 4,000 pairs supplied. Once again there would be a shortage, but this time it would amount to only 4,000 pairs of jogging shoes (8,000 pairs demanded minus 4,000 pairs supplied). Competition among potential buyers again would bid up the price of jogging shoes. The higher price would lead to a reduction in the quantity demanded and an increase in the quantity supplied, which would reduce the shortage still further.

You can probably see what happens as we move from lower to higher prices. Now let's reverse the process, beginning with the highest price in Exh. 3.9. A price of $100 would tend to encourage production and discourage consumption. Producers would be willing to supply 10,000 pairs of jogging shoes a year, but consumers would demand only 2,000 pairs. The result would be a **surplus**—an excess of quantity supplied over quantity demanded—of 8,000 pairs of jogging shoes a year. How do producers react to a surplus? They begin to cut the price of the product in order to compete for existing customers and lure additional customers into the market. The lower price of jogging shoes tends to increase the quantity demanded and decrease the quantity supplied, thus reducing the surplus. If the price fell to $80, there would still be a surplus of 4,000 pairs of jogging shoes (8,000 pairs supplied minus the 4,000 pairs demanded). Price cutting would then continue, and the surplus would continue to shrink.

Equilibrium Price and Quantity

In our example $60 is the market-clearing, or equilibrium, price, and 6,000 units is the equilibrium quantity. The **equilibrium price** is the price that brings about an equality between the quantity demanded and the quantity supplied. The **equilibrium quantity** is the quantity demanded and supplied at the equilibrium price. Equilibrium essentially means stability; once established, the equilibrium price will be maintained so long as the basic supply and demand conditions remain unchanged.

In a competitive market the actual, or prevailing, price will tend toward equilibrium. As you saw in Exh. 3.9, when the price of jogging shoes is above or below equilibrium, market pressures tend to push it down or up toward the

EXHIBIT 3.10
Demand and Supply Curves for Jogging Shoes in Hometown, U.S.A.

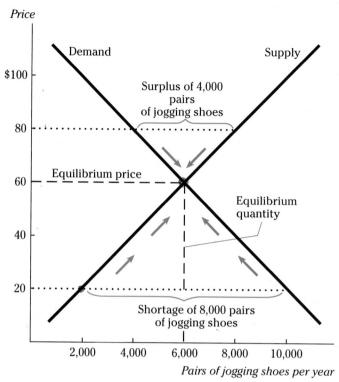

Price

The equilibrium price is the price that equates the quantity supplied and the quantity demanded. In our example the equilibrium price is $60. Whenever the existing price is above or below equilibrium, pressure exists to push it toward the equilibrium level. For example, at a price of $80, there would be a surplus, and price cutting would take place. At a price of $20, there would be a shortage, and the price would tend to rise in order to eliminate the shortage. The arrows indicate the direction of the adjustments in price and quantity.

equilibrium level. Only when the existing price is at the equilibrium level will there be neither a shortage nor a surplus and no pressure for price to change.

We use supply and demand curves to represent the process of price determination. By graphing the demand and supply schedules in Exh. 3.9, we can construct the demand and supply curves found in Exh. 3.10. These curves intersect at the equilibrium price ($60) and the equilibrium quantity (6,000 pairs of jogging shoes). At any price *above* equilibrium (say, $80), we can measure the amount of the surplus as the horizontal distance between the demand curve and the supply curve. For any price *below* equilibrium ($20, for example), the horizontal distance between the curves tells us the amount of the shortage. As we noted earlier, the shortage or surplus tends to shrink as price approaches the equilibrium level. The graph visually represents these shrinking amounts in the diminishing distance between the demand curve and the supply curve. When price finally achieves equilibrium, the curves intersect. At that point quantity demanded equals quantity supplied, and there is neither shortage nor surplus.

The Rationing and Motivating Functions of Prices

In the preceding example the equilibrium price succeeds in matching up the quantity supplied and the quantity demanded because it performs two important functions. First, the equilibrium price rations jogging shoes perfectly among the various users; at a price of $60, 6,000 pairs of jogging shoes are demanded—exactly the quantity made available by producers. Second, the $60 price motivates producers to supply the correct quantity, the quantity consumers are willing to purchase at $60. Let's consider these important functions in greater detail.

You may recall from Chapter 2 that because every society faces the basic economic problem of unlimited wants and limited resources, some system must exist for **rationing**—that is, dividing up or allocating the scarce items among those who want them. In the United States and other economies that rely heavily on markets, price is the dominant rationing device. Rationing in a market economy works hand in hand with **motivating**—providing incentives to produce the desired output. Let's use Exh. 3.10 to examine this process further, first from the perspective of the consumers demanding jogging shoes and then from the perspective of the producers supplying them.

How does the price of a product ration the supply of it among users? Prices ration because they influence our ability and willingness to purchase the product. The higher the price of jogging shoes, the more of our income it takes to buy them (which means a greater sacrifice in terms of other goods and services we must do without), and the less attractive jogging shoes become in relation to substitute products (tennis shoes, for instance).

To illustrate how price rations, let's begin with a relatively low price for jogging shoes—$20. If jogging shoes were selling for $20 (a price well below equilibrium), consumers would be willing and able to purchase a relatively high quantity—10,000 pairs. But as we learned earlier, producers are willing to supply only 2,000 pairs at that price, and so there will be a shortage, and price will tend to rise. As the price of jogging shoes rises toward its equilibrium level, the quantity demanded is reduced—fewer consumers are willing and able to pay the higher price. By discouraging consumers from purchasing the product, the higher price of jogging shoes helps to bring the quantity demanded into line with the number of jogging shoes available; it *rations* jogging shoes. By the same token, at a price initially above equilibrium—for example, $80—the quantity demanded would be too low. But price will tend to decline, and the falling price will encourage consumers to purchase more of the product. Thus, higher prices ration by reducing the quantity demanded, and lower prices ration by increasing it.

But changing prices do more than reduce or increase the quantity demanded: They also motivate producers to expand or contract production. We know from the law of supply that more will be supplied at higher prices than at lower prices. Thus, when the price of jogging shoes increases from $20 to $60, the quantity of jogging shoes supplied will increase from 2,000 pairs to 6,000 pairs. At the same time, the quantity of jogging shoes is being rationed among consumers; the quantity demanded is declining from 10,000 pairs to 6,000 pairs. This is how the rationing and motivating functions of price work together to balance the desires of consumers and producers and prevent a shortage or surplus. Every consumer who values jogging shoes enough to pay $60 will have them, and every producer that is willing to supply jogging shoes at that price will be able to sell its entire output.

CHANGES IN THE EQUILIBRIUM PRICE

You have seen that in the absence of artificial restrictions, prices in competitive markets tend toward equilibrium. Once established, the equilibrium price will hold as long as the underlying demand and supply conditions remain unchanged. Of course, such conditions don't remain unchanged forever, often not even for a short time. Anything that causes a change in either demand or supply will bring about a new equilibrium price.

The Impact of a Change in Demand

Recall from earlier in this chapter that the determinants of demand are all the factors that underlie the demand schedule and determine the precise position of the demand curve. These include consumer tastes and preferences, consumer income, the prices of substitutes and complements, expectations regarding future prices, and the number of buyers in the market. Changes in any of these factors will cause a change in demand—a shift of the entire demand curve.

The housing market provides a good example. Increased demand for new houses in your city or town could result from any of several factors: heightened desire for single-family dwellings instead of apartments, an increase in residents' incomes, rent hikes in the area, expectations of higher housing prices in the near future, or a local population expansion. Any of these changes will cause the demand curve for new homes to shift to the right, as depicted in Exh. 3.11.

You can see that 8,000 new houses are demanded and supplied at the initial equilibrium price of $120,000. However, as demand increases from D_1 to D_2, perhaps because of an increased number of buyers in the market, there is a shortage of 4,000 houses (12,000 minus 8,000) at the $120,000 price. This shortage will lead to competition among prospective home buyers, which in turn will push the average price upward toward the new equilibrium level of $130,000. The higher price will ration new houses by reducing

EXHIBIT 3.11

The Effect of an Increase in Demand on the Equilibrium Price

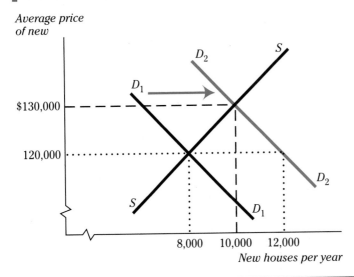

Average price of new

$130,000

120,000

8,000   10,000   12,000

New houses per year

An increase in the demand for new houses will cause the equilibrium price of new homes to rise.

the quantity demanded and will motivate builders to increase the quantity supplied from 8,000 to 10,000. Note here that the increase in demand (the shift of the entire demand curve) causes an increase in the *quantity* supplied (movement along the stationary supply curve). In other words, a *shift* in one curve causes movement *along* the other curve. Thus, an increase in demand leads to a higher equilibrium in both price ($130,000) and quantity (10,000 new homes per year).

Now, suppose that any of the conditions that might have increased the demand for new houses is reversed, causing demand to decline. As shown in Exh. 3.12, the demand curve will shift to the left, from D_1 to D_2. As demand declines, a surplus of houses develops at the old price of $120,000 (only 4,000 homes will be demanded, but 8,000 will be supplied). This surplus will lead to price cutting as builders compete for buyers and as customers shop around for the best buys. Once again, the price change performs two functions. The falling price convinces home buyers to purchase more than 4,000 homes per year, and it motivates builders to supply fewer than 8,000 homes. Price will continue to decline until the quantity of new houses demanded is exactly equal to the quantity supplied at that price. In our example the new equilibrium price is $110,000, and the new equilibrium quantity is 6,000 new homes per year.

EXHIBIT 3.12
The Effect of a Decrease in Demand on the Equilibrium Price

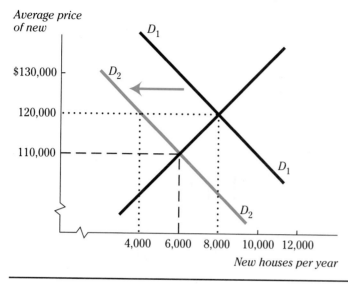

A decrease in the demand for new houses will cause the equilibrium price of new homes to fall.

The Impact of a Change in Supply

Price changes also can be initiated on the supply side. Recall the three determinants of supply: technology, prices of economic resources, and the number of suppliers in the market. Changes in any of these factors that underlie the supply schedule will cause a change in supply. In our example the supply of housing might be increased by any of the following: (1) the development of new construction methods that enable builders to produce more houses from a given amount of resources; (2) decreases in the cost of land, labor, or materials used in home construction; (3) an increase in the number of builders, enabling the market to produce more houses than before at each possible price.

An increase in the supply of new houses is represented by shifting the supply curve to the right, as shown in Exh. 3.13. When the supply of housing increases from S_1 to S_2, 12,000 new homes will be supplied at a price of $120,000, but only 8,000 will be demanded. As before, the surplus will lead to price cutting downward toward the new equilibrium level of $110,000. Note that here the increase in supply (the shift of the entire supply curve) causes an increase in the *quantity* demanded (movement along the stationary demand curve). As we saw earlier, a shift in one curve causes movement *along* the other. This is the process that results in the lower price and

EXHIBIT 3.13

Effect of an Increase in Supply on Equilibrium Price

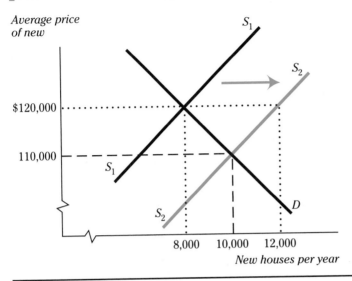

An increase in the supply of new houses will cause the equilibrium price of new homes to fall.

the higher equilibrium quantity. A *decrease* in the supply of housing would have the opposite effect; it would raise the equilibrium price and lower the equilibrium quantity.

The Impact of Simultaneous Changes in Demand and Supply

All the price changes we have explored so far have resulted from a single cause: either a change in demand while supply remained constant or a change in supply while demand remained constant. But in many real-world situations simultaneous changes occur in demand and supply. Let's consider two examples in the housing market. In the first case we find an area undergoing a population expansion (a source of increased demand for new houses) at the same time that building-material costs are rising (causing a decrease in supply). In the second case a period of high unemployment is causing the incomes of area residents to decline (less demand for new houses) while new production methods are reducing the cost of new-home construction (increased supply).

In these two examples the forces of demand and supply are pulling in opposite directions—the demand curve is shifting one way while the supply

EXHIBIT 3.14

Effect of Simultaneous Increases in Demand and Supply on Equilibrium Price

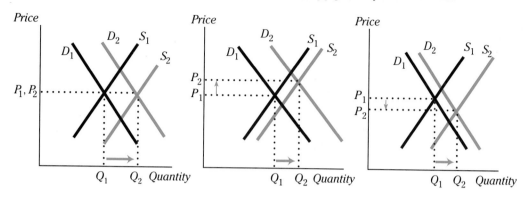

(a) Demand and supply increase by equal amounts; quantity increases but price does not change.

(b) Demand increases by more than supply; both price and quantity increase.

(c) Supply increases by more than demand; quantity increases, but price falls.

curve is shifting the other way. Under these conditions it is relatively easy to determine what will happen to the equilibrium price. In the first example demand increases while supply decreases, so that the equilibrium price tends to rise. In the second example demand decreases while supply increases, so that the equilibrium price tends to fall. Take a minute to draw the diagrams and convince yourself of these results.

Predicting the impact of simultaneous changes in demand and supply becomes a little trickier when both the demand curve and the supply curve are shifting in the same direction. As you can see from Exh. 3.14, when demand and supply are both increasing, we can be certain that the equilibrium quantity will also increase. But the impact on the equilibrium price is uncertain; it depends on how much demand increases relative to supply. If demand and supply increase by the same amounts, the equilibrium price will not change. If demand increases more than supply, the equilibrium price will rise. If supply increases more than demand, the equilibrium price will fall. (If demand decreases and supply increases, the equilibrium price is certain to decrease. But in this instance, the impact on equilibrium quantity will be indeterminate. See if you can predict what will happen to the equilibrium quantity if demand and supply both decrease by the same

USE YOUR ECONOMIC REASONING

Reversing Course, Home-PC Prices Head Higher

By Gary McWilliams

For the first time in years, the cheapest home computers are getting more expensive.

Hewlett-Packard Co.'s lowest-priced Pavilion today costs $100 more than an equivalent did four months ago. Compaq Computer Corp.'s lowest-priced Presario desktop now costs $200 more than its predecessor did last fall.

All together, average personal-computer selling prices rose in November and December, according to market researcher PC Data Inc. After dipping below $800 from August through October, the average price for consumer computers reached a six-month high of $844 in December, the market research company said.

Driving the price hikes are a huge drop-off in competition, a healthy economy and the PC's growing role in home entertainment. The increases are particularly unusual for January, a month when computer makers routinely cut prices to generate new sales. What's more, newer business PCs are cheaper than their home counterparts, due to a more-competitive corporate market. Compaq's new iPaq business PC costs less than its consumer version.

International Business Machines Co, Packard Bell NEC Inc. and Acer Inc. each pulled out of retail stores last year, leaving much more shelf space to Compaq and Hewlett Packard. The three who pulled out accounted for a total of 33.2% of retail sales in the fourth quarter of 1998, according to researcher NPD Intelect Inc....

Component shortages that hit the PC industry last year are not behind the current shift. While higher

amount, if demand decreases more than supply, and if supply decreases more than demand.)

In summary the price of a product can change because of a change in demand, a change in supply, or simultaneous changes in demand and supply. In all cases the basic principle is the same: Whenever demand increases in relation to supply, the equilibrium price will rise; whenever supply increases relative to demand, the equilibrium price will fall. By keeping that

memory-chip prices were blamed for higher PC prices in November, chip costs have already returned to August's lower levels.

The ability to push prices up offers PC makers their first real break since Packard Bell NEC launched a bloody price war three years ago with a multimedia PC priced at $999. Prices for name-brand machines fell as low as $499 last year. But now, coming full circle, the newest home PC lines from Dell Computer Corp. and Compaq start at the old $999 price.

Can it last? Probably not. Hewlett-Packard marketing executive Robert Wait says falling prices may well return soon. "It's dangerous to bet a trend on just two quarters. What we know is there are two things stopping people from buying a PC today. The first is price. The second is it's too complex. Frankly, the company that manages to make lower-cost product that's simpler to use can still have a huge share in the consumer market."

Several companies are starting to roll out cheap stripped-down PCs de-signed for hooking up to the Internet. They should keep the lid on PC price increases as computer makers try to keep the new gadgets from winning over buyers. "This will be the first year that we have an important contribution from low-cost, Web-access devices," says Merrill Lynch & Co. analyst Steven M. Fortuna. "It'll behoove the PC vendors to keep entry prices low."

Still, consumers who were expecting a selection of below-$500 PCs from big-name brands should forget it. Mark Bates, senior analyst at PC Data, says the new pricing aims to put the bulk of home PC sales at between $700 and $900 this year....

For now, it appears demand is strong enough to support the price hikes. Barbara Canetti, a Houston college professor, just spent $2,000 on a new high-powered PC. "I bought a Cadillac—19-inch monitor, DVD, and CD-Writer," says Ms. Canetti. Having put off replacing her old clunker, "I figured I might as well get everything," she said....

Use Your Economic Reasoning

1. In part, the hike in computer prices is due to a "huge drop-off in competition." How would you represent that graphically? What other factors are leading to higher computer prices?
2. According to the article, higher memory chip prices were responsible for earlier increases in PC prices. How would you represent this graphically?
3. Why are business computers now cheaper than comparable home PCs? Try to represent this graphically.
4. The author expects the appearance of new, Web-access devices to help hold down computer prices. Why? (Hint: What impact will these devices have on the PC market?)

principle in mind, we can predict what is going to happen to the price of cattle, wheat, or any other product whose price is determined in a competitive market. (The market for home computers is not as competitive as the market for cattle or wheat, but the supply and demand model can help us to understand that market as well. Read "Reversing Course, Home-PC Prices Head Higher," on page 90, and see if you can explain why home computer prices are rising.)

INTERVENTION IN PRICE DETERMINATION: SUPPORTS AND CEILINGS

Sometimes the prices that result from the interaction of demand and supply may cause hardship for producers or consumers and may therefore be perceived as "unfair" by the injured group. Producers may feel that prevailing market prices are too low to provide them with adequate incomes. Consumers may believe that market prices are too high and thus place an unreasonable burden on households—particularly low-income households. To protect their various interests, both consumers and producers form pressure groups and lobby the government to intervene in the process of price determination. Agricultural price supports, minimum-wage laws, interest rate ceilings, and rent controls are just a few examples that illustrate the success of these campaigns.

Price Supports

Government usually intervenes in pricing by establishing maximum or minimum prices. A **price support** is a legally established minimum price above the equilibrium price.[1] In the 1930s, for example, the federal government initiated a program of agricultural price supports designed to raise the income of farmers. Under this program the government "supported" the price of the product by agreeing to purchase, at the legally established price, whatever output the farmer was unable to sell at that price.

Exhibit 3.15 shows a hypothetical situation in which the government has established a price support (or support price) for corn at $4, which is $1 above the equilibrium price of $3 per bushel. At $4 a bushel, customers are willing to purchase only 10 billion bushels a year, but producers are eager to supply 20 billion bushels. We know that in a free or unregulated market, sellers of corn would deal with the surplus of 10 billion bushels by cutting prices down to the equilibrium level of $3, at which the equilibrium quantity of 15 billion bushels would be supplied. Once the government establishes a price support of $4, however, the market remains in disequilibrium, with surpluses continuing to accumulate. The government is then required

---

[1] When established, price supports are usually above the equilibrium price. Over time, however, the equilibrium price may rise above the support level, causing the price support to be ineffective. For example, in 2000 the minimum wage (a form of support price) of $5.15 was probably below the equilibrium wage for unskilled labor in most parts of the country.

EXHIBIT 3.15
Price Supports and Surpluses

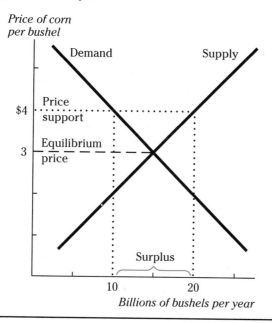

to buy the surplus corn, store it, and dispose of it (through donations to poor nations, for example), all at the expense of taxpayers. In April of 1996, this expense caused Congress to pass the Federal Agricultural Improvement and Reform Act (FAIR), legislation ending price supports for wheat, feed grains, cotton, and rice. To ease the transition to a free market, the bill replaces traditional price supports with fixed but declining payments every year until 2002, regardless of market prices or how much is planted. While some are hailing this legislation (also known as the Freedom to Farm Act) as the end of government intervention in farming, that assessment is probably premature. In the first place, FAIR legislation expires in 2002, and it is unclear what will happen after that. A return to price supports is a real possibility. In addition, the Reform Act did nothing to eliminate a variety of indirect subsidies that have the same effect as price supports. For instance, the federal government still regulates the price of milk at an artificially high level, and it continues to tax imported peanuts and sugar in an effort to restrict supply and prop up the domestic price of those products. In short, even if agricultural price supports are a thing of the past, other government efforts to prop up agricultural prices remain in effect.[2]

When we look beyond agricultural markets, the minimum wage provides another example of a price support. By law most employers are required to pay their employees at least the government-established minimum wage ($5.15 an hour in 2000). Because this wage is generally above the equilibrium wage for unskilled labor, there are more people willing to work at that wage than employers are willing to hire at that wage. Of course, those who can find jobs are better off because of the minimum wage. But some unskilled workers who would have been able to find jobs at the equilibrium wage will be unemployed at the minimum wage. This occurs because employers simply do not believe that these workers will be able to contribute enough to the production process to justify that high a wage. Just as the price support for corn created a surplus of that product, the minimum wage creates a surplus of workers. To the extent that the minimum wage increases unemployment, it conflicts with our objective of raising the incomes of low-income Americans.

Price Ceilings

Government may also intervene in the pricing process when it is convinced that prevailing prices are either too high or are increasing too rapidly. In such cases the government will set **price ceilings,** maximum prices that are established below the equilibrium price. During World War II, for example, price ceilings were placed on most nonfarm prices in order to prevent them from being pushed to exorbitant levels by the demands of the war effort. Price ceilings (or ceiling prices) also have been used during peacetime as a technique both for combating inflation (a general rise in the level of prices) and for controlling specific prices. For instance, in 1971 President Nixon "froze" virtually all wages and prices for a period of 90 days in an attempt to slow the rate of inflation. In the same decade the federal government

---

[2] While Exhibit 3.15 captures the most important elements of the price support program, it is not completely accurate. Under federal price support legislation, customers would pay the market price, not the support price, as depicted in the graph. The difference is made up by the federal government in a **deficiency payment** ($1 a bushel, in this example) paid directly to the farmer. As a result, the actual shortage will be somewhat smaller than that depicted in the exhibit. Because consumers are responding to the market price, they will want to purchase 15 million bushels. On the other hand, since suppliers are responding to the support price, they will want to supply 20 million bushels. The result will be a surplus of 5 billion bushels, which must be purchased by the government (at $4 a bushel).

used price ceilings selectively to limit the prices of beef, pork, gasoline, and natural gas, among other products.

One form of price ceiling that was initiated in World War II still survives today. **Rent ceilings** (or rent controls) are maximum rents that are established below the equilibrium level. They were initially instituted in World War II to prevent transient wartime workers (who were typically well paid) from out-bidding local residents for apartments in industrial cities. After the war, these ceilings were abolished everywhere except in New York. Then in the infla-tionary 1970s, rent-control laws spread to cities in Massachusetts, to much of suburban Long Island and New Jersey, to Washington, and to about half the population of California.

Although rent ceilings may seem to be in the best interest of consumers, they frequently create problems for prospective renters. Because the rent is fixed at an artificially low level, more people will want to rent in that city (or the rent-controlled portions of the city) than would desire to do so at the equilib-rium rent. In addition, the low rent will make renting apartments less attractive

EXHIBIT 3.16
Price Ceilings and Shortages

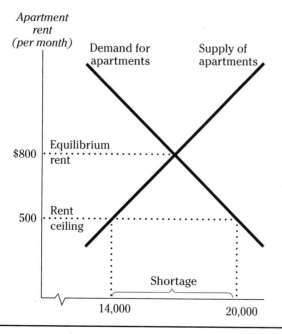

A price ceiling will tend to produce a shortage since price is legally fixed below the equilibrium level. In this example a rent ceiling of $400 leads to a shortage of 6,000 apartments.

to owners, who consequently will make fewer apartments available than would be provided at the equilibrium rent. The result will be a shortage of apartments and a number of unsatisfied customers.

Exhibit 3.16, p. 95, represents the plight of consumers in a rent-controlled city. As you can see from the exhibit, $800 is the equilibrium rent, the rent at which the number of apartments consumers desire to rent is equal to the number that apartment owners want to make available. At the $500 rent ceiling (or ceiling rent), consumers want to rent 20,000 apartments, but owners are willing to supply only 14,000 units. There is a shortage of 6,000 apartments. We know that in unregulated markets a shortage of apartments, or any other item, will lead to a price increase, which motivates businesses to supply more of the item and which rations some consumers out of the market. A ceiling prevents the rent from rising to its equilibrium level, so that landlords are faced with more potential renters than they can satisfy. Consequently, they must use some secondary rationing device to decide which consumers will get apartments.

A **secondary rationing device** is a nonprice condition that supplements the primary rationing device, price. The prospective apartment renter in our example must not only be willing to pay the $500 rent but must also be able to satisfy some supplementary requirement imposed by landlords. Perhaps landlords will grant apartments only on the basis of first-come-first-served. Or perhaps they will choose to rent only to applicants without children and pets or only to those with the best jobs (and therefore the greatest likelihood of making timely rent payments). Perhaps they will rent only to retired persons or to those with verifiable references. Whether the use of a secondary, nonprice rationing device is preferable to higher rents is a matter for you to decide. It is clear, however, that rent ceilings do not eliminate the need to ration; they simply force sellers to use secondary rationing devices.

In New York City, where 70,000 units are under strict rent controls and an additional 900,000 units are subject to more modest rent regulations, finding an apartment is a major problem. Because rents are kept below their equilibrium level, New Yorkers face a perpetual housing shortage. To some extent, existing housing is rationed on a first-come-first-serve basis, and would-be renters spend countless hours in a vain attempt to find a vacant apartment. Some frustrated searchers resort to checking obituaries in hope of zeroing in on a newly available rental before anyone else hears of it; others make secret payments to landlords for the privilege of a new lease. Of course, landlords know how to play the system too. A few years ago, a New

York real estate executive was found guilty of requiring tenants to make political contributions in order to obtain leases on rent-regulated apartments.[3] Other forms of "under-the-table" payment undoubtedly exist.

Low rents not only produce a shortage but also prevent the supply of housing from expanding. In fact, landlords may allow some rental units to deteriorate. If rental income cannot rise, owners cannot profit from money spent on improvements or even break even on money invested in maintenance. In summary, although rent ceilings succeed in maintaining low rents for those lucky enough to find apartments, they create shortages and prevent expansion, problems that would be eliminated if rents were allowed to rise to their equilibrium level.

Recent initiatives have abolished or weakened rent-control ordinances in a number of U.S. cities. For example, in 1994, Massachusetts voters abolished rent controls, and in 1999 California made it illegal for cities to limit the rent that landlords can charge for vacant apartments. New York rent-control ordinances, however, survived the challenge; in 1997 they were renewed for another six years.

ECONOMIC EFFICIENCY AND THE ROLE OF PRICES

The automatic response of price changes to changes in demand and supply conditions is an important feature of a market economy. As increasing consumer demand pushes the price of a product upward, the higher price rations some consumers out of the market and simultaneously motivates producers to expand their production of the product. Because these producers are receiving a higher price for their product, they will be able to outbid producers of less-valued items for the resources needed to expand production. In this way price changes help to ensure that businesses produce the goods and services that consumers value the most, in the quantities they desire.

Price changes also help ensure that each product is produced with as few of society's scarce resources as possible. As a particular resource becomes scarcer (because of increased demand or reduced supply), its price tends to rise. This higher cost encourages producers to economize on its use

---

[3] "Landlord Guilty of Asking Tenants for Political Gifts," by John Sullivan, *New York Times,* Nov. 23, 1996, page 23.

by substituting cheaper resources whenever possible. The end result is the efficient use of society's scarce resources: Producers supply the most-wanted products in the least-costly way in terms of scarce resources.[4] The way competitive markets promote the efficient use of resources is explored in greater detail in Chapter 6. Later chapters examine how such factors as inadequate competition and the ability of firms to ignore the "cost" of the pollution they create can interfere with the ability of markets to achieve this optimal result.

SUMMARY

In a competitive market, prices are determined by the interaction of demand and supply. *Demand* is a schedule showing the quantities of a good or service that consumers are willing and able to purchase at various prices during some given time period, when all factors other than the product's price remain unchanged. Demand may be represented graphically in a *demand curve*, which slopes downward and to the right because the *law of demand* holds that consumers will purchase more of a product at a lower price than at a higher price. *Supply* is a schedule showing the quantities of a good or service that producers are willing and able to offer for sale at various prices during a given time period, when all factors other than the product's price remain unchanged. Supply may be represented graphically as a *supply curve.* The supply curve slopes upward and to the right because the *law of supply* states that price and quantity supplied are positively related; that is, a greater quantity will be supplied at higher prices than at lower prices.

The demand curve will shift to a new position if there is a change in any of the *determinants of demand:* consumer income, tastes and preferences, expectations regarding future prices, the prices of substitute and complementary goods, and the number of consumers in the market. By the same token, the supply curve will shift if there is a change in one or more of the *determinants of supply:* technology, the prices of resources, or the number of producers in the market.

Economists are careful to distinguish between a change in the quantity demanded and a change in demand. A change in the amount purchased as a result of a change in the price of the product while other factors are held constant is a *change in the quantity demanded* and is represented by movement up or down a stationary demand curve. A change in any of the determinants of demand while price is held constant will cause consumers to purchase more or less of a product at each possible price. This is described as a *change in de-*

---

[4] Note that the fewer the resources an economy needs to produce each product, the more goods and services it can produce with its limited resource stock. Thus, an economy that is operating efficiently is producing the goods and services that consumers value the most *and* producing as many of those goods and services as possible from the society's scarce resources.

mand and is represented by a shift of the entire demand curve to the right (in the case of increased demand) or to the left (in the case of decreased demand).

A similar distinction is necessary on the supply side of the market. A *change in the quantity supplied* results from a change in the price of the product and is represented graphically by a movement along a stationary supply curve. A *change in supply* results from a change in one of the determinants of supply and is represented by a shift of the entire supply curve to a new position.

The *equilibrium price* is the price that brings about an equality between the quantity demanded and the quantity supplied, which we call the *equilibrium quantity.* The equilibrium price can be identified by the intersection of the demand and supply curves. If the prevailing price is above equilibrium, a *surplus*—an excess of quantity supplied over quantity demanded—will occur, and sellers will be forced to reduce price to eliminate the surplus. If the prevailing price is below equilibrium, a *shortage*—an excess of quantity demanded over quantity supplied—occurs, and buyers will bid up the price as they compete for the product. Only when the existing price is at the equilibrium level will there be neither a shortage nor a surplus and no pressure for price to change.

Prices perform two important functions: They (1) *ration*, or divide, the limited amount of available output among possible buyers; and (2) *motivate* producers to supply the desired quantity. Higher prices ration by discouraging consumers from purchasing a product; they also motivate producers to increase the quantity supplied. Lower prices have the opposite effect. They encourage consumers to purchase more of the product and simultaneously motivate producers to reduce the quantity supplied. The equilibrium price succeeds in matching the quantity demanded with the quantity supplied because it balances the desires of consumers and producers. Every consumer who values the product enough to pay the equilibrium price will have it, and every producer willing to supply the product at that price will be able to sell its entire output.

In the absence of artificial restrictions, prices will rise and fall in response to changes in demand and supply. Whenever demand increases in relation to supply, the equilibrium price will tend to rise; whenever supply increases in relation to demand, the equilibrium price will fall. These price changes help to ensure that producers not only supply the goods and services consumers value the most but also use as few scarce resources as possible in the production of those goods and services.

Price supports (minimum prices above the equilibrium price) and *price ceilings* (maximum prices below the equilibrium price) prevent price from reaching its equilibrium level in the market. Because these restrictions interfere with the rationing and motivating functions of price, they give rise to surpluses (supports) and shortages (ceilings). Price ceilings also create the need for *secondary rationing devices*—nonprice conditions that supplement the primary rationing device, which is price.

KEY TERMS

Change in demand
Change in quantity demanded
Change in quantity supplied
Change in supply
Complement
Deficiency payment
Demand
Demand curve
Determinants of demand
Determinants of supply
Equilibrium price

Equilibrium quantity
Income effect
Inferior good
Law of demand
Law of supply
Motivating
Normal good
Price ceiling
Price support
Rationing
Rent ceiling

Rent control
Secondary rationing device
Shortage
Substitute
Substitution effect
Supply
Supply curve
Surplus
Technology
Technological advance

STUDY QUESTIONS

Fill in the Blanks

1. If the entire demand curve shifts to a new position, we describe this as a change in

   demand.

2. If a product is a normal good, an increase in income will cause the demand curve for the product to shift to the _Right_.

3. Movement along a stationary supply curve due to a change in price is called a change in _Quantity Supply_

4. The function of dividing up or allocating scarce items among those who desire to receive them is called _Rationing_.

5. The price that exactly clears the market is called the _Equilibrium_ price.

6. Whenever the prevailing price is above equilibrium, a _surpless_ will exist.

7. Prices perform two important functions: They ration scarce items among the consumers who desire to receive them; and they _Motivate_ producers to supply that quantity.

8. If supply rises and demand declines, we would expect the equilibrium price to _fall_.

9. If supply increases more than demand, the equilibrium price will _Fall_.

10. We would expect a price ceiling to lead to a _Shortage_.

Multiple Choice

1. If the price of automobiles increases and all other factors remain unchanged, it will be reasonable to expect
   a) an increase in the demand for automobiles.
   b) a decrease in the demand for automobiles.
   c) an increase in the quantity of automobiles demanded.
   d) a decrease in the quantity of automobiles demanded.

2. If the demand curve for Brock's Heavy Beer shifts to the left, this could be due to
   a) an increase in the price of Brock's Heavy Beer.
   b) an increase in consumer income.
   c) an increase in the price of other beers.
   d) a shift in tastes and preferences to light beers.

3. An increase in the price of apples is likely to cause
   a) a decrease in the demand for apples.
   b) an increase in the quantity demanded of apples.
   c) an increase in the demand for other types of fruit.
   d) an increase in the quantity demanded of other types of fruit.

4. If the price of black walnuts increases and other factors remain unchanged, it is reasonable to expect
   a) a decrease in the demand for black walnuts.
   b) an increase in the supply of black walnuts.
   c) an increase in the quantity of black walnuts supplied.
   d) a decrease in the demand for pecans and other walnut substitutes.

5. A new labor settlement that increases the cost of producing computers will probably cause
   a) a decrease in supply of computers.
   b) a reduction in the demand for computers.
   c) a reduction in the quantity of computers supplied.
   d) the supply curve of computers to shift to the right.

6. If grasshoppers destroy half of the wheat crop, the result will be
   a) an increase in the demand for wheat.
   b) a decrease in the demand for wheat.
   c) a decrease in the quantity of wheat supplied.
   d) a leftward shift of the supply curve for wheat.

7. If demand increases and supply declines,

   a) the equilibrium price and quantity will both increase.
   b) the equilibrium price will rise, but the quantity will fall.
   c) the equilibrium price will fall, but the quantity will rise.
   d) the equilibrium price and quantity will both fall.
   e) the equilibrium price will rise; quantity will be indeterminate.

8. If the U.S. government were to artificially restrict the price of beef below the equilibrium level, the result would be
   a) a shortage.
   b) a surplus.
   c) an excess of quantity supplied over quantity demanded.
   d) none of the above

9. If the demand for used cars declines, the likely result will be
   a) an increase in the supply of used cars.
   b) a reduction in the equilibrium price of used cars.
   c) an increase in the equilibrium price of used cars.
   d) a temporary shortage of used cars at the old price.

10. If the price of cattle feed increases, the result will probably be
   a) an increase in the supply of cattle and lower cattle prices.
   b) a decrease in the supply of cattle and higher cattle prices.
   c) an increase in the demand for cattle and higher cattle prices.
   d) a decrease in the demand for cattle and lower cattle prices.

11. If a shortage exists, it indicates that the existing price is
   a) the equilibrium price.
   b) below the equilibrium price.
   c) above the equilibrium price.

12. Consider the market for mobile homes. If personal incomes in the United States rise, we would expect to see

a) a decline in mobile home prices if mobile homes are a normal good.

b) an increase in the demand for mobile homes if mobile homes are an inferior good.

c) a decrease in mobile home prices if mobile homes are an inferior good.

d) a decrease in the demand for mobile homes if mobile homes are a normal good.

13. If the price of coffee increases, the probable result will be
   a) a decrease in the demand for coffee.
   b) a decrease in the price of substitutes for coffee.
   c) an increase in the price of substitutes for coffee.
   d) a decrease in the supply of coffee.

14. Which of the following statements is *incorrect*?
   a) If demand increases and supply remains constant, the equilibrium price will rise.
   b) If supply rises and demand remains constant, the equilibrium price will fall.
   c) If demand rises and supply falls, the equilibrium price will rise.
   d) If supply increases and demand decreases, the equilibrium price will rise.

15. If additional farmers enter the hog-producing industry, the result will be
   a) lower prices but a higher equilibrium quantity.
   b) higher prices but a lower equilibrium quantity.
   c) lower prices but the same equilibrium quantity.
   d) lower prices and a lower equilibrium quantity.

16. If the supply of cattle is increasing more rapidly than the demand,
   a) cattle prices will rise.
   b) cattle prices will fall.
   c) cattle prices will not change.
   d) each of the above is possible.

Problems and Questions for Discussion

1. My eldest daughter says that she really "needs" a new sweatshirt, but she won't use her allowance to buy it. ("I don't need it *that* badly.") How can a "need" evaporate like that? What is the difference between *need* and *demand?*

2. Podunk College experienced a substantial drop in enrollment last year. What possible explanations can you, as an economist, offer for what happened? Try to list all possibilities.

3. Why does the supply curve slope upward and to the right? In other words, why will producers supply a higher quantity at higher prices?

4. Which of the following events would cause movement along a stationary supply curve for wheat, and which would cause the supply curve to shift? Explain each situation from the producer's point of view.
   a) The price of wheat declines.
   b) The cost of fertilizer rises.
   c) Wheat blight destroys half the wheat crop.
   d) New combines make it possible for one person to do the work of three.

5. Explain the economic reasoning behind the following newspaper headlines:
   a) "Weather Slows Fishing: Seafood Prices Double"
   b) "Sugar: Crisis of Plenty"
   c) "Minimum Wage Costs Jobs"
   d) "Bountiful Wheat Crop Is Hurting Growers"

6. If the supply of oranges in a competitive market decreases as a result of severe weather, will there be a shortage of oranges? Why or why not? (*Hint:* Use graphs to help answer this question.)

7. Suppose that your local tennis courts are very crowded and your city is considering charging a fee to ration their use. Who would like to have a fee charged? Would

only wealthy individuals feel this way? Why might someone be in favor of a fee?

8. People, including news reporters, often use the terms *supply* and *demand* incorrectly. For example, you will often read "Supply exceeds demand" or "Demand exceeds supply." What is wrong with these statements? What does the writer probably mean to say?

9. Why is it important that prices in a market economy be allowed to change in response to changing demand and supply condi-

tions? What functions do these changing prices perform?

10. Assume that consumers are buying equal numbers of hamburgers and hot dogs when these products are selling at the same price. If the supply of hamburger declines, what will happen to the price of hamburgers? What about the price of hot dogs? Graph your conclusions.

ANSWER KEY

Fill in the Blanks

1. demand
2. right
3. quantity supplied
4. rationing
5. equilibrium
6. surplus
7. motivate
8. fall
9. fall
10. shortage

Multiple Choice

1. d
2. d
3. c
4. c
5. a
6. d
7. e
8. a
9. b
10. b
11. b
12. c
13. c
14. d
15. a
16. b

CHAPTER FOUR

The Elasticity of Demand and Supply

In Chapter 3 we considered how demand and supply interact to determine prices, and we discovered how changes in demand or supply cause prices to change. In this chapter we investigate the degree of consumer and producer responsiveness to increases or decreases in prices. Economists refer to this degree of responsiveness as the price "elasticity." As you will see, the concept of price elasticity is extremely important and has many applications in the world around you.

ELASTICITY OF DEMAND

The law of demand tells producers that if they raise their prices, consumers will buy less and that if producers lower their prices, consumers will buy more. But the law of demand doesn't tell them anything about the size of the response to a given change in price. If a professional football team decides to raise the price of season tickets by $100, how many fewer tickets will fans buy? If a local health club doubles its rates, how many customers will it lose? To answer these questions, we need some knowledge of how responsive consumers are to changes in the price of a particular product—we need to know something about the price elasticity of demand.

The **price elasticity of demand** is a measure of the responsiveness of the quantity demanded of a product to a change in its price. If the quantity demanded expands or contracts a great deal in response to a price change, demand is said to be very responsive, or *elastic*; if the quantity demanded doesn't change very much, demand is described as not very responsive, or *inelastic*.

As a gauge of the responsiveness of consumers, the absolute size of the changes in price and quantity means very little. Suppose that a $5 price reduction causes consumers to demand an additional 1,000 units of some product. Should we describe the demand for this product as elastic or inelastic? We can't tell unless we know the starting point, the initial price and quantity. To illustrate, suppose the firm had cut price from $10 to $5 and this price reduction caused the quantity demanded to increase from 100,000 units to 101,000 units. Would you describe demand as elastic (very responsive to the price change) under those conditions? Probably not; a 50 percent price reduction led to only a 1 percent increase in the quantity demanded! But if the price had been reduced from $100 to $95 (the same $5 but in this case only 5 percent of the original price) and the quantity demanded had increased from 1,000 to 2,000 units (100 percent), you would probably agree that consumers were quite responsive to the change in price; demand is elastic.

The point is that when we describe the responsiveness of consumers, we need to think in terms of percentages—the percent change in price and the percent change in the quantity demanded. This approach adjusts for the initial prices and quantities and gives us a much more meaningful comparison.

The Coefficient of Demand Elasticity

We can measure the degree of elasticity or inelasticity by calculating a value called the **coefficient of demand elasticity.** We compute the coefficient of elasticity by dividing the percentage change in quantity demanded by the percentage change in price:

$$\text{Coefficient of elasticity} = \frac{\dfrac{\Delta Q}{Q}}{\dfrac{\Delta P}{P}} = \frac{\text{Percentage change in quantity demanded}}{\text{Percentage change in price}}$$

In this formula for the coefficient, Q stands for quantity, P for price, and the Greek letter delta (Δ) for "change in." $\Delta Q/Q$ is the percentage change in quantity demanded, and $\Delta P/P$ is the percentage change in price.

Let's apply this formula to the elasticity of demand for Fantastic Cola after a price hike. We'll say that after the price per six-pack rises from $2.50 to $3, weekly sales decline from 1,000 six-packs to 900. What is the price elasticity of demand for Fantastic Cola? If the change in quantity demanded (ΔQ) is 100 fewer six-packs per week and the original quantity demanded (Q) is 1,000 six-packs, the percentage change in quantity demanded ($-100/1,000$) is -10 percent. And if the change in price (ΔP) is $.50 and the original price (P) is $2.50, the percentage change in price ($.50/$2.50) is 20 percent. If we divide the 10 percent reduction in quantity by the 20 percent increase in price, we arrive at an elasticity coefficient of $-.5$:[1]

$$\text{Coefficient of elasticity} = \frac{\dfrac{-100}{1000}}{\dfrac{\$.50}{\$2.50}} = \frac{-10\%}{20\%} = -.5$$

An elasticity coefficient of .5 means that for every 1 percent change in price, the quantity demanded will change by 0.5 percent. Thus, if the price of Fantastic Cola goes up by 10 percent, we would expect a 5 percent reduction in the quantity demanded. If it increases by 20 percent, we would expect a 10 percent reduction in quantity demanded. However, if the elasticity coefficient were 2.0 instead of .5, each 1 percent change in price would cause a 2 percent change in quantity demanded. For example, a 10 percent increase in price would cause a 20 percent decrease in quantity demanded.

You will note that in our formula the elasticity coefficient ($-.5$) carries a negative sign. We know from the law of demand that changes in price normally cause the quantity demanded to change in the opposite direction. Thus, price

---

[1] The simple formula we are using to compute the elasticity coefficient produces somewhat ambiguous results. If the sellers of Fantastic Cola raise the price from $2.50 to $3, the value of the elasticity coefficient is .5. But if the sellers lower their price from $3 to $2.50, the coefficient will be .67 because the initial price and quantity are different.

Economic theory does not suggest any reason that these two coefficients should be different, so we might argue that they should be the same. This can be accomplished by using the average of the two prices and the average of the two quantities as the base values for computing percentages. When this approach is used, the value of the coefficient will be the same regardless of whether the initial price is the higher price or the lower price. In the Fantastic Cola example the value of the elasticity coefficient would be .58. In the modified formula below, we add the two quantities Q_1 and Q_2 and divide by 2 to arrive at the average quantity. Average price is determined the same way:

$$\frac{\Delta Q/[(Q_1 + Q_2)/2]}{\Delta P/[(P_1 + P_2)/2]} = \frac{100/(1,900/2)}{\$.50/(\$5.50/2)} = \frac{100/950}{\$.50/\$2.75} = \frac{10.5\%}{18.2\%} = .58$$

increases cause reductions in the quantity demanded, whereas price reductions cause increases in the quantity demanded. In either case the sign is negative and is usually ignored in referring to price elasticity values.

Degrees of Elasticity

Economists use the coefficient of elasticity to define precisely the terms *elastic* and *inelastic*. Elastic demand exists when the coefficient of elasticity is greater than 1, when a given percentage change in price brings about a larger percentage change in the quantity demanded. When the elasticity coefficient is less than 1, demand is inelastic; a given percentage change in price brings about a smaller percentage change in the quantity demanded. If the coefficient is exactly 1, *unitary elasticity* prevails; a given percentage change in price results in an identical percentage change in quantity demanded. The elasticity coefficient can vary from zero to infinity, where zero represents the least elastic demand imaginable and infinity represents the most elastic demand imaginable.

If the coefficient of elasticity is zero, a change in price brings no change at all in the quantity demanded. Demand is described as *perfectly inelastic,* and the demand curve is a vertical straight line. For example, over some range of prices, the demand for lifesaving drugs, such as insulin, may be perfectly inelastic. Another example is the demand for dialysis treatment by those suffering from kidney failure.

If the coefficient of elasticity approaches infinity, a very small change in price leads to an enormous change in the quantity demanded. Demand is said to be *perfectly elastic* and is graphed as a horizontal straight line. Perfectly inelastic and perfectly elastic demand curves are depicted in Exh. 4.1. The individual apple farmer faces a situation that illustrates perfectly elastic demand. If the market price of apples is $10 a bushel, the farmer can sell as much as desired at that price. But a farmer who attempts to charge more than $10 will sell nothing; consumers will simply buy their apples from someone else. This is the type of situation we represent with a perfectly elastic demand curve. In Chapter 6 we will have much more to say about perfectly elastic demand curves. (The president of Continental Airlines thinks he knows what the demand curve for Continental tickets looks like. Read "Continental Ticket Sales Remain Robust...," on page 110 and see if you can understand his company's pricing strategy.)

Elasticity along a Straight-Line Demand Curve

In most instances demand curves do not show just one degree of elasticity; they show several. All linear, downward-sloping demand curves show unitary elasticity midway on the curve, with elastic demand above the midpoint and inelastic demand below it. Exhibit 4.2 depicts such a demand curve.

EXHIBIT 4.1
Perfectly Inelastic and Perfectly Elastic Demand Curves

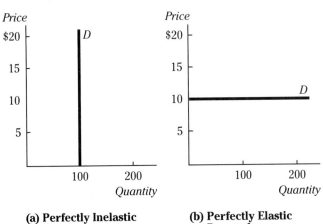

(a) Despite an increase or decrease in price, consumers buy exactly the same quantity. The demand curve for insulin may look like this over some price range. (b) A very small increase in price would cause consumers to reduce their purchases to zero. The individual apple farmer may face a demand curve like this one.

(a) Perfectly Inelastic Demand

(b) Perfectly Elastic Demand

In Exh. 4.2, note that because the demand curve is a straight line, it has a constant inclination, or "slope." Therefore, a price change of a given size will always bring the same quantity change. In this hypothetical example each $.60 drop in price brings an increase of 60 million gallons in the quantity demanded, regardless of whether we are at the upper or the lower end of the curve. (Look, for example, at what happens to the quantity demanded when price declines from $2.40 to $1.80 or from $1.80 to $1.20; in both instances quantity increases by 60 million gallons.) That would seem to suggest that consumers are equally responsive to price changes at either end of the curve. But that's not true! We have to remember that the responsiveness, or elasticity of demand, deals with percentage changes, not with absolute quantities.

If you remember that fact, you will recognize that the responsiveness of consumers changes quite dramatically as we move along this demand curve. For instance, when price drops from $3 to $2.40 (a 20 percent decline), quantity demanded increases from 60 million to 120 million gallons (a 100 percent increase). Since the percentage change in quantity is greater than the percentage change in price, demand is elastic at this upper end of the curve. At the other end the same *absolute* changes in price and quantity represent different percentage changes and consequently produce different elasticities. For instance, when price declines from $1.20 to $.60 (a 50 percent change), the quantity demanded increases from 240 million to 300 million gallons (a 25 percent change). The coefficient of elasticity is .5; demand is inelastic. We want to remember, then, that the slope of a demand curve is not

EXHIBIT 4.2

How Elasticity Changes along a Hypothetical Demand Curve for Gasoline

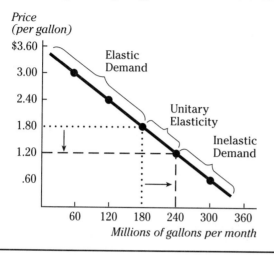

Every straight-line demand curve that is downward sloping displays unitary elasticity at its midpoint, elastic demand above it, and inelastic demand below it.

the same as its elasticity. A linear demand curve has a constant slope, but it displays many different degrees of elasticity.

Elasticity and Total Revenue

Knowing how responsive consumers will be to price changes is of vital interest to businesses. The elasticity of demand determines what happens to a business's **total revenue**—the total receipts from the sale of its product—when it alters the price of the product it is selling. (Total revenue is equal to the price of the product multiplied by the quantity sold: $TR = P \times Q$.)

To better understand total revenue and the importance of the degree of elasticity, put yourself in the place of the seller making a pricing decision. Suppose that you're a college president contemplating an increase in tuition from, say, $2,500 to $2,700 a semester. The basic question you face is whether the gain in revenue due to the higher tuition per student will be offset by the loss in revenue due to the smaller number of students who are willing and able to pay that higher tuition. To answer that question, you must know how responsive students will be to changes in tuition. In other words, you must have some estimate of the elasticity of demand for an education at your college.[2]

_____

[2] In reality the question faced by a college president or a businessperson would be somewhat more complicated because any pricing decision may also have an indirect impact on the firm's costs. For example, because a higher price will cause a firm to sell less of its product, the firm may also incur lower costs since it will not need to produce as much output. Before making any pricing decision, a wise entrepreneur considers its impact on costs as well as on revenues. (The nature and behavior of a firm's costs are discussed in Chapter 6.)

Continental Ticket Sales Remain Robust Despite Airfare Rises to Offset Fuel Costs

By Scott McCartney

NEW YORK—Airfare increases, including a recent doubling of a fuel surcharge to $40 per round trip ticket, haven't dampened the demand for seats, Continental Airlines executives told a meeting of security analysts yesterday.

"It's a very strong revenue environment," said Gregory Brenneman, Continental's president and chief operating office. "We see almost no elasticity when we increase fares."

Mr. Brenneman noted that Continental was charging business travelers $2,000 for a round-trip, last-minute trip between New York and Houston, and travelers were paying it. "Get your tickets now before it goes to $3,000," he joked.

Higher fares have helped carriers to offset the sharp run-up in jet-fuel prices. Across the industry, Chief Financial Officer Larry Kellner said, airlines "have shown good ability to respond to this. We can make money in this environment."

Use Your Economic Reasoning

1. What do you think Mr. Brenneman means when he says, "We see almost no elasticity when we increase fares"?
2. If Brenneman is correct, what is the coefficient of demand elasticity over this range of ticket prices?* What terminology is used to describe a demand curve of that elasticity?
3. If Continental is able to raise fares without losing any customers, what will happen to the firm's total revenue—its receipts from selling tickets?
4. Mr. Brenneman appears to be describing the reaction of business travelers. Would you expect leisure travelers (vacationers) to have more or less elastic demand than business travelers? Defend your conclusion. (Stumped? Come back to this question after finishing the chapter.)

*Brenneman's comment that "It's a very strong revenue environment…" indicates that the demand for airline transportation may be increasing. If that's true, the demand for airline travel is actually more elastic than it appears, since the shifting demand curve is helping to make up for travelers lost due to higher fares.

Case 1: Elastic Demand

Suppose that demand is highly elastic, that is, very responsive to price changes. If tuition is increased, the college will receive more money from each student, but it will enroll considerably fewer students; the percentage change downward in quantity demanded will be greater than the percentage change upward in price. As a result, the college will take in less total revenue than it did before the tuition hike. In the face of elastic demand, the logical action for the college to take—assuming there are vacant dormitory rooms and unfilled classes—would be to lower, not raise, tuition. The college will receive less from each student who enrolls, but it will enroll many more students, and total revenue will increase.

Case 2: Inelastic Demand

Suppose that demand for an education at your college is inelastic, that is, not very responsive to price changes. If the college increases tuition, it will lose some students but not very many, and the percentage change in quantity demanded will be less than the percentage change in price. Because each student will pay more than before, the result will be an increase in total revenue. If you decided to reduce tuition under these inelastic conditions, you would probably be fired. The tuition reduction wouldn't attract many new students, and all the students would pay a lower rate than before. As a result, total revenue would be lower than it was before the tuition reduction.

Case 3: Unitary Elasticity

If the demand for an education at your college is of unitary elasticity, any change in price will be offset exactly by a proportional change in the quantity demanded (enrollment). If you institute a 10 percent tuition increase, 10 percent fewer students will enroll, and total revenue will be unchanged. If you put into effect a 5 percent tuition reduction, 5 percent more students will enroll, and total revenue will be unchanged. As long as demand is of unitary elasticity, total revenue is unaffected by the seller's pricing decision.

The relationship among price changes, elasticity, and total revenue (*TR*) for each of the three cases is summarized in Exh. 4.3. Before continuing, take the time to work through the exhibit. You will see that if demand is inelastic, a price reduction will lead to a decline in total revenue, and a price increase will cause total revenue to increase. If demand is elastic, a price reduction will lead to an increase in total revenue, and a price increase will cause total revenue to decline. With unitary elasticity, a price change up or down is offset by a proportional change in quantity demanded, and total revenue remains unchanged.

EXHIBIT 4.3
Elasticity and Total Revenue

DEGREE OF ELASTICITY	PRICE INCREASE	PRICE DECREASE
Case 1: Elastic demand. (The coefficient of elasticity is greater than 1.)	$\uparrow \downarrow \quad \downarrow$ $P \times Q = TR$	$\downarrow \uparrow \quad \uparrow$ $P \times Q = TR$
Case 2: Inelastic demand. (The coefficient of elasticity is less than 1.)	$\uparrow \downarrow \quad \uparrow$ $P \times Q = TR$	$\downarrow \uparrow \quad \downarrow$ $P \times Q = TR$
Case 3: Unitary elasticity (The coefficient of elasticity is equal to 1.)	No change $\uparrow \downarrow$ $P \times Q = TR$	No change $\downarrow \uparrow$ $P \times Q = TR$

Symbols: ↑ increase, ↓ decrease. Length of arrow indicates relative size of increase or decrease.

The elasticity of demand for a firm's product dictates what will happen to total revenue (price × quantity) when the firm alters price. When demand is elastic, a price increase results in a *significantly lower* quantity demanded and, therefore, in lower total revenue, whereas a price decrease leads to a *significantly higher* quantity demanded and, therefore, results in higher total revenue. When demand is inelastic, a price increase results in a lower quantity demanded *but not much lower,* so that total revenue increases; a price decrease results in a higher quantity demanded *but not much higher,* so that total revenue decreases. If demand is of unitary elasticity, any change in price will be exactly offset by the change in quantity demanded, so that total revenue will not change.

The Determinants of Elasticity

As you saw in the preceding discussion, producers need to know whether the demand for their services and products is elastic or inelastic before they can make intelligent pricing decisions. But how can sellers know? Often they can gain insight into the elasticity of demand by considering two major factors that dictate the degree of elasticity: the number of good substitutes available and the importance of the product in consumers' budgets. As you examine these factors, recall our earlier discussion of the *income* and *substitution effects* that underlie the law of demand.

The Number of Available Substitutes for the Product

The primary factor in determining the price elasticity of demand is the number of good substitutes available. Recall that a substitute is a product that can be used in place of another product because, to a greater or lesser extent, it satisfies the same consumer wants. Some people consider chicken a good substitute for fish, for example; many people would acknowledge that a Ford automobile is an acceptable substitute for a Chevrolet with the same features.

When a large number of good substitutes exist, demand for a product tends to be elastic because consumers have alternatives—they can buy something else if the price of the product becomes too high. But if a product has few good substitutes, demand tends to be inelastic because consumers have few options; they must buy the product even at the higher price. Movie tickets, pond-raised catfish, and women's hats have elastic demand because there are a large number of substitutes for each of these items. Cigarettes, electricity, local telephone service, and gasoline tend to have relatively inelastic demand because of the limited options available to consumers.[3]

The Importance of the Product in Consumers' Budgets

The second factor influencing the elasticity of demand for a product is the importance of the product in consumers' budgets. If consumers are spending a significant portion of their income on a particular item (rent or long-distance phone service, for example), a price hike for that item will force a vigorous search for less-expensive substitutes. Demand will tend to be elastic. But if expenditures on the product are relatively small (the average family's annual outlay for lemon juice or soy sauce, for instance), consumers are more likely to ignore the price increase. Demand will tend to be inelastic.

Some major budget items persist in having relatively inelastic demand. For example, even though many smokers spend a significant fraction of their incomes on cigarettes, statistical research shows that the demand for cigarettes by adults is quite inelastic. In this case demand is inelastic because the more important determinant of elasticity is the number of good substitutes. If, like cigarettes, a product has few good substitutes, the fact that it is a major expense item is generally less important to consumers. The article on page 114, "Satcher Details Plan to Lower Smoking Rates," looks at efforts to reduce smoking. Read the article to discover the role of the elasticity of demand in determining the success of these efforts.

---

[3] The elasticity of demand for a product tends to increase over time. When the price of a product increases, consumers may not be aware of substitutes for that product, and so demand initially may be inelastic. But the more time that elapses after the price change, the more opportunities consumers have to discover substitutes and to develop new tastes and new habits. As consumers discover more substitutes, demand tends to become more elastic.

USE YOUR ECONOMIC REASONING

Satcher Details Plan to Lower Smoking Rates

By Gordon Fairclough

CHICAGO—Surgeon General David Satcher said the U.S. can cut smoking rates in half over the next 10 years with a comprehensive antitobacco program that includes health education, mass-media campaigns, stronger warning labels and sharp cigarette-tax increases.

"The sobering reality is that smoking remains the leading cause of preventable death and disease in the United States and the world," said Dr. Satcher, who unveiled a 460-page report at an international tobacco-control conference here, laying out a blueprint for aggressively curbing cigarette consumption.

The surgeon general's report, "Reducing Tobacco Use," says, among other things, that "substantial increases in the excise taxes on cigarettes would have considerable impact on the prevalence of smoking."

Dr. Satcher said that for every 10% rise in the price of cigarettes, consumption drops between 3% and 5%. He said he would like to see the combined level of state and federal cigarette taxes increased to at least $2 a pack.

The federal excise tax on cigarettes is 34 cents a pack, and is set to rise to 39 cents in 2002. As of May 1, state excise taxes ranged from 2.5 cents a pack in Virginia to $1.11 in New York, according to the surgeon general's report.

Dr. Satcher called on Congress to give the Food and Drug Administration

Source: Wall Street Journal, August 10, 2000, p. A3. Central Edition [Staff Produced Copy Only] by Gordon Fairclough. Copyright 2000 by Dow Jones & Co Inc. Reproduced with permission of Dow Jones & Co Inc. in the format Textbook via Copyright Clearance Center.

ELASTICITY OF SUPPLY

Thus far we have considered only how the quantity demanded responds to price changes. Now we explore the supply side of the market. The price elasticity of supply describes the responsiveness of producers to price changes. More precisely, the **price elasticity of supply** is a measure of the responsiveness of the quantity supplied of a product to a change in its price.

The Coefficient of Supply Elasticity

Individual producers of goods and services display varying degrees of response when the price of a product changes. Some are able to expand or contract their supply of the product significantly in a short period of time; others

authority to regulate the tobacco industry and to enact legislation requiring more effective warning labels on cigarettes.

"Our warning labels should be much stronger. The message should be much clearer," Dr. Satcher said. He said new warnings should be comparable to those used in Canada, where new regulations mandate labels with hard-hitting graphics, including pictures of diseased mouths.

The Canadian labels also are getting larger, covering 50% of the front of a pack. The nation's top doctor urged more regulation of tobacco advertising and more bans on indoor smoking.

"Our lack of greater progress in tobacco control is more the result of failure to implement proven strategies than it is the lack of knowledge about what to do," Dr. Satcher said.

Underscoring that point, Dr. Satcher noted that just 5% of schools in the country follow the federal Center for Disease Control and Prevention's antismoking guidelines—even though health-education programs can postpone or prevent tobacco use in 20% to 40% of teen-agers, according to the report.

Brendan J. McCormick, a spokesman for Philip Morris Cos., the nation's largest tobacco company, said "There's a lot in that report we agree with," including the emphasis on reducing youth smoking and improving the public's understanding of the health risks of cigarettes. "But," he said, "we don't think higher taxes should be used to control adult behavior...."

Use Your Economic Reasoning

1. According to Dr. Satcher, strong warning labels and cigarette taxes both reduce smoking. Does a warning label reduce the demand for cigarettes or the quantity demanded? What about a tax that raises the price of cigarettes? Review Chapter 3 if you are uncertain.

2. Dr. Satcher provides sufficient data to compute the price elasticity of demand for cigarettes. What is the value of the coefficient? Is demand elastic or inelastic?

3. Suppose policymakers decide they want to cut smoking in half. How much (in percentage terms) will they need to hike the price of cigarettes through taxes?

4. Most studies show that young smokers have more elastic demand than older smokers. How would you explain this difference? Does this difference make price hikes a more effective strategy for reducing teen smoking or a less effective strategy?

are able to make only minimal adjustments. The more responsive producers are to a change in price, the more elastic their supply.

We measure the elasticity of supply by calculating the **coefficient of supply elasticity,** a value that indicates the degree to which the quantity supplied will change in response to a price change. The coefficient of supply elasticity is computed by dividing the percentage change in quantity supplied by the percentage change in price:

$$\text{Coefficient of elasticity} = \frac{\frac{\Delta Q}{Q}}{\frac{\Delta P}{P}} = \frac{\text{Percentage change in quantity supplied}}{\text{Percentage change in price}}$$

Suppose that the price of coal rises from $40 to $50 a ton and that coal production in the United States therefore increases from 600 to 900 million tons a year. To compute the coefficient of supply elasticity, we first determine the percentage change in quantity supplied: If the change in quantity supplied (ΔQ) is 300 million tons and the original quantity supplied (Q) is 600 million tons, the percentage change in quantity supplied (300/600) is 50 percent. Next, we take the percentage change in price: If the change in price (ΔP) is $10 and the original price is $40, the percentage change in price ($10/$40) is 25 percent. When we divide the 50 percent increase in quantity supplied by the 25 percent increase in price, we arrive at an elasticity coefficient of 2.[4]

$$\text{Coefficient of elasticity} = \dfrac{\dfrac{300}{600}}{\dfrac{\$10}{\$40}} = \dfrac{50\%}{25\%} = 2$$

Note that whereas the coefficient of demand elasticity is negative, the coefficient of supply elasticity usually is positive: Because of the law of supply, an increase in price leads to an increase in the quantity supplied.

Interpreting the Elasticity Coefficient

We interpret coefficients of supply elasticity in essentially the same way we interpret coefficients of demand elasticity. A supply elasticity of 2 means that for every 1 percent change in price, the quantity supplied will change by 2 percent. For example, a 10 percent increase in price would lead to a 20 percent increase in the quantity supplied, and a 20 percent increase in price would lead to a 40 percent increase in the quantity supplied. Of course, reductions in price will have the opposite effect. A 10 percent decrease in price would lead to a 20 percent reduction in the quantity supplied.

An elasticity coefficient greater than 1 means that supply is elastic, or very responsive to price changes; a given percentage change in price results in a larger percentage change in quantity supplied. When the elasticity coefficient is less than 1, supply is inelastic; a given percentage change in price results in a smaller percentage change in quantity supplied. If the coefficient is exactly 1, supply is of unitary elasticity; a given percentage change in price results in an identical percentage change in the quantity supplied.

Using Supply Elasticity in Policy Decisions

An understanding of the elasticity of supply can be useful to government policymakers and others seeking solutions to economic problems. Consider, for example, the energy-policy debate that occurred in the late 1970s, a time when the

---

[4] As with the elasticity of demand, the more precise formula for calculating the elasticity of supply involves using the average of the two prices and the average of the two quantities as the base values for computing percentages.

United States was even more heavily dependent on foreign oil than it is today. During this period the price of domestically produced oil was regulated; it could not rise above the government-dictated price. Imported oil was beyond government control, however, and in the mid-1970s it skyrocketed in price. To reduce dependence on foreign oil, some politicians and policymakers began to argue for the deregulation of domestic oil prices so that U.S. producers would have incentives for increased exploration and production. Deregulation began in 1978–79 and, in conjunction with consumer conservation (brought about by higher prices), helped to reduce our dependence on foreign oil.

Today, we are once again facing higher prices for imported oil. And, once again, we would like to reduce our dependence on foreign sources. Suppose that the United States would like to increase domestic oil production by 50 percent to reduce its dependence on foreign oil. How much would the price of domestic oil have to rise to make that possible? Since the supply elasticity of oil is about 1 (actually it's slightly less than 1), the price of oil would have to rise by 50 percent. (Remember, when the coefficient is 1, each 1 percent change in price brings a 1 percent change in quantity supplied.) Of course, if supply were more elastic—if producers were more sensitive to price changes—a smaller price hike would accomplish the same result. For example, if the coefficient were 2, the price of oil would have to rise by only 25 percent in order to increase the quantity supplied by 50 percent.

As you can see, the elasticity of supply allows us to determine how much price has to rise to convince suppliers to increase their output by a given amount. That kind of information is very important in making sound decisions about energy policy and addressing a host of other questions.

Time and the Elasticity of Supply

The responsiveness of suppliers to a change in the price of their product depends on the amount of time they are given to adjust their output to the new price. As a general rule, the longer producers are given to adapt to a price change, the greater the elasticity of supply. We can see the importance of time as a determinant of elasticity by comparing the kinds of adjustments suppliers facing a price change can make in the short run with the changes they can make in the long run.

The Short Run

In economics the **short run** is defined as the period of time during which at least one of a business's inputs (usually plant and equipment) is fixed—that is, incapable of being changed. Therefore, short-run adjustments to a change in price are limited. Producers must use their existing plants and equipment more or less intensively, adding or eliminating a work shift or using a larger or smaller workforce on existing shifts.

The short-run supply curve in Exh. 4.4 shows an increase in the price of oil from $20 to $25 a barrel ($5 equals a 25 percent increase) bringing an increase in the quantity of oil supplied from 800 to 900 million barrels (100 million barrels equals an increase of 12.5 percent). Thus, the coefficient of supply elasticity is .50 (12.5%/25%); supply is quite inelastic in the short run.

The Long Run

The **long run** is defined as the period of time during which all of a business's inputs, including plant and equipment, can be changed. The long run provides sufficient time for firms to build new production facilities and to expand or contract existing facilities. New firms can enter the industry and existing firms can leave. These kinds of adjustments make it possible to alter output significantly in response to a price change.

Note that the long-run response to an increase in the price of oil from $20 to $25 a barrel (a 25 percent increase) is an increase in the quantity of oil supplied from 800 million to 1 billion barrels (200 million barrels equals a 25 percent increase). The coefficient of supply elasticity in this case is 1.0 (25%/25%), and so supply is of unitary elasticity in the long run.

EXHIBIT 4.4
The Effect of Time on the Elasticity of Supply

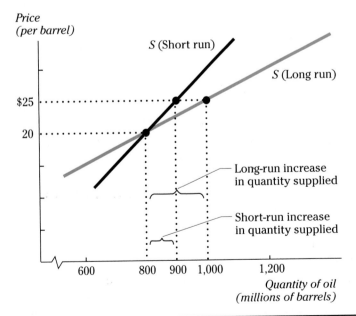

Price (per barrel)

Quantity of oil (millions of barrels)

The more time a firm or industry is given to respond to a change in price, the larger the increase or decrease in the quantity supplied and the greater the elasticity of supply. Suppose, for example, that the price of oil rises from $20 to $25 a barrel. In the short run the quantity supplied can be increased from 800 million barrels per year to 900 million barrels; in the long run it is possible to increase the quantity supplied from 800 million barrels to 1 billion barrels per year.

As you can see from our example, the elasticity of supply may vary substantially from the short run to the long run for a given product. Both the short-run and the long-run elasticities of supply also vary from industry to industry and even from firm to firm. What is certain for any particular firm or industry, however, is that the elasticity of supply will increase directly in relation to the length of time that a firm or an industry is given to adjust to the price change. The response of petroleum producers to higher oil prices illustrates the important role that price changes can play in motivating producers.

SUMMARY

To know how much more consumers will purchase at lower prices or how much less they will purchase at higher prices, we need to know how responsive consumers are to price changes. The *price elasticity of demand* is a measure of the responsiveness of the quantity demanded to a change in price. If a given percentage change in price brings about a larger percentage change in quantity demanded (a coefficient of elasticity greater than 1), demand is described as elastic. If a given percentage change in price brings about a smaller percentage change in quantity demanded (a coefficient less than 1), demand is said to be inelastic. If a given percentage change in price brings an equal percentage change in quantity demanded (a coefficient equal to 1), unitary elasticity prevails.

If demand is perfectly inelastic (the coefficient of elasticity is zero), a very large change in price will bring no change in the quantity demanded; the demand curve will be a vertical straight line. If demand is perfectly elastic (the coefficient approaches infinity), a very small change in price will bring an extremely large change in the quantity demanded; the demand curve will be a horizontal straight line. Most demand curves, however, do not show just one degree of elasticity; they show several. All linear, downward-sloping demand curves will show unitary elasticity in the middle, elastic demand at the upper end, and inelastic demand at the lower end.

The degree of elasticity is important to businesses because it determines what happens to *total revenue*, or total receipts from sales, when a business alters the price of its product. If demand is elastic, a price reduction will lead to an increase in total revenue, and a price increase will cause total revenue to decline. If demand is inelastic, a price reduction will lead to a decline in total revenue, and a price hike will cause total revenue to increase. With unitary elastic demand, any change in price will be offset exactly by a proportional change in the quantity demanded, and total revenue will be unchanged.

The major determinants of the elasticity of demand are the number of good substitutes that exist and the importance of the product in consumers' budgets.

The greater the number of substitutes for a product and the more important the item in the budgets of consumers, the greater the elasticity of demand for the product.

Suppliers as well as consumers respond to price changes. The measure of suppliers' responsiveness to a change in the price of their product is called the *price elasticity of supply*. Economists use the *coefficient of supply elasticity* to determine the degree of responsiveness. The formula for the coefficient is the percentage change in quantity supplied divided by the percentage change in price. Supply is elastic if the coefficient is greater than 1, inelastic if it is less than 1, and unitary if it is equal to 1.

As a general rule, the more time a firm or industry is given to adapt to a specified price change, the larger the change in quantity supplied and the greater the elasticity of supply. The *short run* is a time during which at least one input is fixed. In the short run, output can be expanded by employing additional units of labor and raw materials, but time does not permit plant and equipment expansion. Producers have additional options in the *long run*, a period of time sufficient to change all inputs. In the long run, new production facilities can be built and existing facilities can be expanded. As a consequence, output can be increased much more in the long run than in the short run.

KEY TERMS

Coefficient of demand elasticity	Long run	Short run
Coefficient of supply elasticity	Price elasticity of demand	Total revenue
	Price elasticity of supply	

STUDY QUESTIONS

Fill in the Blanks

1. If a decrease in the price of the product leads to a decrease in total revenue, demand must be (elastic/inelastic/unitary) ___Inelastic___ .

2. If a 10 percent reduction in price leads to a 20 percent increase in quantity demanded, the coefficient of elasticity would be equal to ___2___ .

3. If the coefficient of elasticity is greater than 1, demand is ___elastic___ ; if it is less than 1, demand is ___inelastic___ ; if it is equal to 1, demand is ___unitary___ .

4. The major determinant of the elasticity of demand for a product is the number of good ___substitutes___ that exist for the product.

5. The greater the fraction of the family budget spent for a particular product, the

   (greater/smaller) _greater_ the elasticity of demand for that product.

6. A perfectly inelastic demand curve would

   be a (vertical/horizontal) _Vertical_ straight line.

7. Along a downward-sloping linear demand curve, the elasticity of demand is the

   greatest at the (upper/lower) _upper_ end of the curve.

Multiple Choice

1. If a seller reduces the price of a product and this leads to an increase in the quantity sold, what can be concluded?
   a) Demand is elastic.
   b) Demand is inelastic.
   c) Demand is of unitary elasticity.
   d) Nothing can be concluded about the degree of elasticity.

2. If the demand curve for a product is a vertical straight line, the coefficient of elasticity would be
   a) zero.
   b) 1.
   c) infinity.
   d) different between any two points on the curve.

3. If an increase in price causes total revenue to fall, what can be concluded?
   a) Demand is elastic.
   b) Demand is inelastic.
   c) Unitary elasticity prevails.

4. On a downward-sloping demand curve, demand is more elastic
   a) at the upper end.
   b) at the lower end.
   c) in the middle.

5. In general, demand for a product is more elastic

8. The degree of responsiveness of suppliers to a price change depends in part on the

   amount of _time_ they are given to adapt to the change.

9. The time period during which all resources or inputs are variable is called

   the _long run_.

10. In general, the greater the period of time producers are given to adjust to a change in price, the (greater/smaller)

    Greater the elasticity of supply.

   a) the fewer the substitutes and the larger the fraction of the family budget spent on that product.
   b) the greater the number of substitutes and the larger the fraction of the family budget spent on that product.
   c) the fewer the substitutes and the smaller the fraction of the family budget spent on that product.
   d) the greater the number of substitutes and the smaller the fraction of the family budget spent on that product.

6. The local transit company is contemplating an increase in bus fares in order to expand revenues. A local senior-citizens group, Seniors for Fair Fares, argues that a rate increase would lead to lower revenues. This disagreement suggests that
   a) the transit company does not believe that the rate increase would reduce the number of riders, but the SFF believes that it would.
   b) the transit company believes that the demand for bus service is elastic, but the SFF believes that it is inelastic.
   c) the transit company believes that the demand for bus service is inelastic, but the SFF believes that it is elastic.

7. If the supply curve for a product was a vertical straight line,

a) the quantity supplied would not depend on price.
b) supply would be a fixed quantity.
c) supply would be perfectly inelastic; that is, the elasticity coefficient would be equal to zero.
d) All of the above

8. Which of the following is *not* a short-run adjustment?
   a) The purchase of additional raw materials
   b) The construction of a new factory building
   c) The hiring of additional workers
   d) The addition of a second production shift

9. If the coefficient of supply elasticity for widgets is equal to 4, a 20 percent increase in the price of widgets would cause the quantity supplied to expand by
   a) 80 percent.
   b) 5 percent.
   c) 40 percent.
   d) 4 percent.

10. In general, we can say that supply is more elastic
    a) in the short run than in the long run.
    b) in the long run than in the short run.

Problems and Questions for Discussion

1. If a college increases tuition as a method of increasing total revenue, what assumption is it making about the elasticity of demand for its service? Do you think that assumption is valid for your college? Why or why not?

2. If the price of Wrinkled jeans is reduced from $10 to $8 a pair and the quantity demanded increases from 5,000 to 10,000 pairs a month, what is the coefficient of demand elasticity?

3. According to Mark Moore, of Harvard's Kennedy School of Government, the ideal demand-side drug policy would make illegal drugs cheap for addicts and expensive for neophytes. What logic can you see for such a policy, and how would it relate to the elasticity of demand for illegal drugs?

4. Which would tend to be more elastic, the demand for automobiles or the demand for Ford automobiles? Why?

5. Suppose that the price elasticity of demand for water is 2.0 and that the government wants to reduce the quantity of water demanded by 40 percent. By how much must the price of water be raised to accomplish this objective?

6. Sales taxes are a major source of revenue for many state governments. But higher taxes mean higher prices, which mean lower quantities sold by merchants. If the government wants to expand its tax revenue yet inflict minimum damage on the sales of merchants, should it tax products with elastic demand or inelastic demand? Why? Can you see any drawbacks to focusing taxes on these products?

7. Suppose that the coefficient of supply elasticity is equal to 2.5 for a particular product. If the price of that product increases by 10 percent, how much will the quantity supplied increase?

8. If price declines by 5 percent and quantity supplied declines by 20 percent, what is the coefficient of supply elasticity?

9. Why do we expect supply to be more elastic in the long run than in the short run?

10. Suppose that the coefficient of supply elasticity for housing was equal to 1.5. How much would the price of housing need to rise in order to expand the quantity of housing supplied by 30 percent?

ANSWER KEY

Fill in the Blanks

1. inelastic
2. 2.0
3. elastic, inelastic, unitary
4. substitutes
5. greater
6. vertical
7. upper
8. time
9. long run
10. greater

Multiple Choice

1. d
2. a
3. a
4. a
5. b
6. c
7. d
8. b
9. a
10. b

CHAPTER FIVE

Marginal Reasoning and Profit Maximization

1. State the assumptions that economists make about human beings.
2. Describe how individuals and businesses use cost-benefit analysis to guide their decision making.
3. Discuss some of the pitfalls in decision making.
4. Explain what is meant by marginal reasoning.
5. Explain how marginal reasoning can improve both personal and business decision making.
6. Describe how a business selects the profit-maximizing level of output.

As we learned in Chapter 1, we all use models to help us understand the world around us. The past four chapters have introduced you to some economic models: the production possibilities model, the model of supply and demand, and the model of elasticity, for example. You will be introduced to many more theories or models in this book because, as we've already discovered, it is only through models that we can begin to explain the real world and solve real-world problems. But economics is more than a haphazard collection of theories or models with no unifying theme. Underlying all the models in economics is the assumption that human beings are motivated by self-interest and that they make rational decisions based on self-interest. We begin this chapter by examining those assumptions. We'll see that rational decision making involves a comparison of costs and benefits and that the appropriate costs and benefits for comparison are marginal costs and benefits. After that we examine some of the pitfalls in decision making and see how they can be avoided. The chapter concludes by exploring the similarity between individual and business decision making, and by examining how businesses select the profit-maximizing level of output.

EXPLAINING HUMAN BEHAVIOR: THE ROLE OF ASSUMPTIONS

As we noted in Chapter 1, models are always based on assumptions; the more realistic the assumptions, the greater the likelihood that the resulting model will be useful in understanding the real world. In attempting to explain and predict the behavior of individuals, economists make the assumption that men and women are motivated primarily by self-interest and pursue self-interest through a rational comparison of costs and benefits.

The Pursuit of Self-Interest

Assuming that people are motivated by self-interest is clearly an over-simplification. The factors that motivate human beings are very complex and include empathy, a sense of duty or obligation, and many others. But following the lead of Adam Smith, the father of economics, economists argue that foremost among these motivations is the pursuit of self-interest.

The role of self-interest in motivating men and women may seem self-evident to you. But the fact is that we sometimes forget this fundamental characteristic of human nature. And forgetting it may cause us to make errors in judgment. Consider, for example, the automobile salesman who promises to be your friend and "give you a good deal." If self-interest is the primary factor motivating salespeople, your first response when confronted by such a pledge should be to question it. After all, a salesperson who is motivated by self-interest won't be concerned about promoting yours—at least no more than the competition demands. And when an advertisement offers "free" products or "unbelievable bargains," don't rush down to the store. Read the fine print; that's where you will generally discover the true cost.

Remembering that people are driven by self-interest will do more than help you make good decisions; it will also help you understand behavior that may seem strange if you forget this fundamental motivation. For example, why is it that college students make it a point to call their distant grandmother while they are visiting their parents but never manage a call from the pay phone in their dormitory? And why do customers eat (and waste) more food at the "All You Can Eat For $9.99" buffet than they do when they pay by the item? And how is it that some people leave large tips in restaurants they visit regularly and smaller ones when they are out of town? Economists will argue that none of this behavior is random or accidental; it simply results from the pursuit of self-interest.

Comparing Costs and Benefits

How do individuals pursue their self-interest; how do they make certain that their decisions improve their own well-being? They do so by always comparing the costs and benefits of a contemplated action rather than acting impulsively. Consider, for example, the decision that confronts you in the morning when your alarm goes off. Do you get out of bed and go to class or stay in bed and get a couple more hours of sleep? Economists assume that rather than just hitting the alarm and going back to sleep (an impulsive reaction), you weigh the costs and benefits of getting up. In other words, you consider what you would learn in class and the likelihood of a quiz (the benefits of getting up) against the lost sleep (the cost of getting up) and make a decision. If the value of going to class exceeds the cost, you get up. If not, you make the rational decision and stay in bed.

There are several important things to note about this decision-making process. First, self-interest seeking individuals consider only the costs and benefits that affect them personally. They don't consider the benefits that their presence might convey to others in the class—better class discussion, for example—or the costs that their absence might impose on others, provoking a quiz from the professor, for instance. Second, this cost-benefit comparison may be performed unconsciously, without any real deliberation. Through experience you may know that there are substantial costs associated with missing class, and so you get up automatically, without much consideration of alternatives. It's only on mornings following a particularly short night that the cost-benefit comparison really kicks in.[1] Third, this comparison is based on expected costs and benefits; you won't know the true costs and benefits until after the fact. You may jump out of bed expecting an exhilarating class period—and not get it. Or you may stay in bed expecting to miss very little, only to find out that Brad Pitt and Melanie Griffith were team-teaching class that day, or—perhaps more realistically—you missed a 20-point quiz.

THE IMPORTANCE OF MARGINAL ANALYSIS

When costs and benefits are compared, the relevant costs and benefits for comparison are the *marginal* costs and benefits. **Marginal** means extra, or additional; the marginal costs and benefits are the additional costs and benefits

---

[1] Many cost-benefit comparisons are performed instinctively or unconsciously because you've performed them many times before. For instance, do the additional benefits provided by designer jeans justify the premium prices they generally command? You probably had to reflect on that question the first few times you went shopping. But after that, the decision became much simpler. Now, all you have to hear is the price differential and you know what you want to buy.

resulting from the decision. It may appear obvious that it's marginal costs and benefits that matter, but it's easy to confuse marginal and total values if you're not careful. And that can result in poor decision making (or in good decisions that are misunderstood).

To illustrate, consider once again that morning debate, "Do I stay in bed or get up and go to class?" Suppose that, one morning, you decide to skip class and sleep in. The next day, you tell the prof the truth—"I needed the sleep." What response might you expect from the prof? There are a number of possibilities, but one is something like this: "You mean you value sleep more than my class?" Hearing that reaction might cause you to regret missing class, but your morning's decision has actually been misrepresented. If you had to choose between sleep and, say, accounting, accounting would lose hands down. So would literature and physics and probably even the psychology of human sexuality! But that's not really the choice that most of us have to make, and it's not the choice you were trying to communicate to the prof. The choice is really not between accounting and sleep; it is between an *additional* or marginal hour of accounting and an *additional* or marginal hour of sleep. That's where decisions are always made, on the margin, between a little more of this and a little more of that.

As you can see, failing to recognize the difference between total and marginal values can lead to poor decisions, or it can get you into trouble for making good decisions that you can't defend. Consider the following additional examples:

1. Your boss asks you to work late in order to finish an important job. Your husband (wife) calls at work to find out why you're not home. He asks, "Is your job more important to you than I am?"

2. You have an 85 average in accounting and a 79 average in literature. Each course requires 80 percent to earn a B grade. Final exam week finds you spending most of your time studying literature. Is literature more important to you than accounting?

3. At the family picnic you've had three helpings of Mom's potato salad, and one helping of Aunt Mildred's cole slaw. Mom sees you reach for the cole slaw and says, "Do you like the cole slaw better than my potato salad?"

In each of these instances, the failure to recognize the difference between total and marginal values is the source of the misunderstanding. Even though you value your husband more than your job, there may be situations in which an additional evening at work is more important to you than an additional evening with him. And even if you love accounting and loathe literature, you still may value an additional weekend studying literature more highly than an additional weekend studying accounting. Finally, even if you prefer Mom's potato salad to Aunt Mildred's cole slaw and virtually every other food on the face of the earth, there is nothing irrational about preferring one *more* scoop of cole slaw, especially after already having three scoops of potato salad.

THE IMPROPER ESTIMATION OF COSTS

Even people who understand the difference between marginal and total values sometimes make bad decisions. More often than not, these poor decisions are the result of a mistaken estimate of the cost of the decision in question. Sometimes people forget to consider important costs, and sometimes they see costs where there are none. Let's consider these problems in turn.

Ignoring Opportunity Costs

Economists are fond of telling us that all decisions have costs, that there is no such thing as a "free lunch." This was part of the message of Chapter 1. Any time we make a decision to do or to have one thing, we sacrifice the opportunity to do or to have some other thing. The most-valued alternative we sacrifice to take an action is the opportunity cost of that action.

The opportunity cost concept holds that costs exist whether or not money changes hands. In fact, the money you pay for a product is just a veil; the true cost of that product is the other things you could have purchased with the same money. If you spend $200 on a CD player, the real cost of the CD player is the pizzas, movie tickets, and jeans you could have bought with the same money.

Otto's Garage, Inc

Sometimes we forget that the true cost of any decision is the opportunity cost, and that can lead to poor decisions. Consider the case of Otto Run, a recent graduate of Smalltown Technical College. Otto and his brother, Will, decided to start their own auto-repair business. So they visited their banker to arrange financing for the building they want to construct. When the banker asked them where the new business would be located, Otto reported that the location would be the corner of Main and First Streets, a longtime vacant lot in a prime location. That seemed to the banker like an expensive piece of real estate for an auto-repair shop; so she asked the brothers why they had chosen that location. Otto's response was, "Because we own the land and it won't cost us anything to use it." His answer illustrates a common problem in making decisions—failing to consider opportunity costs. Because these budding entrepreneurs were not required to make a dollar payment to buy or lease the land, they assumed that it was free; they ignored the opportunity cost.

In this instance the piece of land that was going to be used for the auto-repair business was in a good location and quite valuable. It could easily have been sold to a land developer as a building site for a bank or some other facility requiring good customer access. The true cost of using that land was whatever money the brothers sacrificed by using the land themselves.

Professor Noslack and the New York Yankees

The message of opportunity cost can also be helpful in reminding us that costs exist even if they are not easily reducible to money. To illustrate: A student walked into Professor Noslack's office to discuss his plans to attend an upcoming New York Yankees baseball game instead of his chemistry class. "My brother said he'll pick me up, drive me to the game, and pay for everything. I can't pass up this opportunity; it won't cost me anything." When Professor Noslack asked the student his average in the course, there was a moment's pause; he wasn't doing very well. And the class he was planning to miss was scheduled to be a review for the upcoming exam—an exam he really needed to pass. The point here is not that the student made a poor decision by deciding to skip class; rather, it is that the student failed to consider all the relevant costs, including the (nonmonetary) opportunity costs of missing class. (The failure to consider opportunity costs may help to explain why patients request unneeded antibiotics. Read the article on page 130 to discover the opportunity cost of this behavior, and learn how economic reasoning may ultimately save the day.)

A trip to a baseball game isn't free, even if someone else agrees to buy the tickets and pay for the snacks.

USE YOUR ECONOMIC REASONING

This Winter, Try to Avoid Taking Unneeded Antibiotics

SEPTEMBER brings the promise of another cold and flu season. When a cold strikes on the eve of a business trip, or a school-age child contracts a sore throat, how many of us phone for the quick fix of an antibiotic?

This year should be different.

After failed attempts to curb antibiotics abuse, the U.S. Centers for Disease Control and Prevention and its allies are switching tactics this month. Backed by the American Academy of Pediatrics, the American Society of Microbiology and others, CDCP is warning that misuse of the drugs isn't just a problem in hospitals but a personal threat to everyone who takes unnecessary drugs.

Thousands of doctors and clinics will receive pamphlets from the CDCP asking them to return to classic practices: Get cultures, prescribe antibiotics only for confirmed bacterial infections and treat viral cold symptoms with comfort care.

"We estimate that 50 million prescriptions for oral antibiotics are written unnecessarily every year," says Benjamin Schwartz, epidemiologist at the CDCP in Atlanta. "That's a third of the total."

Using antibiotics doesn't hasten recovery from viral colds. Instead, it wipes out all stray sensitive bacteria, leaving behind superstrains that are impervious to drugs. When these take hold in the throat, the ear, or on the skin, the next infection may be drug-resistant.

Rampant antibiotics abuse happens through the collusion of lazy physicians writing prescriptions against good medical judgment, with patients who are too busy to come in for a throat swab but desirous that the doctor "do something."

Doctors too often cave in to time pressures, or attempts to save patients the cost of a lab test. All are potential accomplices in a process that fosters superbugs and depletes the medical tool kit.

The result: pneumococcus—the leading cause of bacterial meningitis, bloodstream infections and ear infections—is already resistant to penicillin in 20% of cases, and resistant to certain sulfa drugs in 25% of cases nationwide. Since last month, researchers have reported the first two cases of vancomycin-resistant *Istaphylococcus aureus* in Michigan and New Jersey.

Failing to Ignore Fixed Costs

Ignoring opportunity costs is not the only source of poor decision making. Another problem is mistaking fixed costs for marginal costs.

All the costs that confront us in our personal lives and in business can be categorized as either *fixed costs* or *variable costs*. **Fixed costs** are costs that do

But the summer has brought hopeful medical news on resistance. In Finland, where drug-resistant group A streptococcus had risen alarmingly, researchers imposed restricted antibiotic use. After the curbs, the incidence of resistance dropped sharply. The Finnish study gives U.S. researchers hope that they can emulate this success.

To tighten U.S. doctors' prescribing antibiotics on demand, CDCP and its partners are promoting "a new paradigm" from common-cold care. If your doctor diagnoses a viral cold that needs no antibiotic, you won't be sent away empty-handed. You'll get a pamphlet detailing how and why unneeded antibiotics hurt you, plus a written "prescription" with suggestions for over-the-counter medicine and symptomatic relief while your immune system fights off the virus.

Patients would forgo antibiotics if they had better communication, Dr. Schwartz believes. But these days, pressured patients and over-scheduled physicians find the illusory quick fix of a prescription easier than sweating out the cycle of a virus. CDCP's educational materials could help, but the transition will make demands on everyone's time and patience if it's to succeed....

The key is convincing consumers of their personal stakes in this battle. "Our big mistake was telling people they were screwing up the globe," says Michael Marcy of Kaiser Permanente California Healthcare Program in Panorama City, Calif. "Now we're saying you're harming yourself and you're harming your child."

Kaiser, he says, aims to educate cold-sufferers that it's normal for a virus to last more than a week, and for coughs to persist two weeks (longer in smokers). Fevers are a natural defense mechanism treatable with acetaminophen or ibuprofen, he adds....

If CDCP's campaign can break the cycle of overuse,

more powerful bacteria-fighting drugs, now hurtling toward obsolescence, may get a new lease on life. "If you are circumspect about use, you'll without a doubt prolong the useful life of an antibiotic," predicts Anthony Fauci, director of the National Institute of Allergy and Infectious diseases.

The CDCP brochure offers a primer on antibiotics, stressing that viral infections run their course in time. Until you're well, it offers a "prescription" for relief: drink lots of fluids, use a cool-mist vaporizer and soothe sore throats with sprays and lozenges.

Use Your Economic Reasoning

1. Patients often request antibiotics inappropriately because they over-estimate the benefits and under–estimate the costs of doing so. Discuss.
2. What is the opportunity cost (to patients) of taking antibiotics when they don't really need them?
3. Use cost-benefit analysis to explain why doctors might find it in their self-interest to overprescribe antibiotics.
4. Health officials initially tried to stem inappropriate antibiotic use by "telling people they were screwing up the globe." Why was that a "big mistake"? What was wrong with their model of human behavior?
5. How have health officials modified their message to patients in order to gain greater support for reducing unnecessary antibiotic use? Is this new approach more or less consistent with the economist's model of what motivates human beings?

not vary with the level of the activity engaged in, whether that activity is driving a car, owning a home, or (in the case of a business) producing output. **Variable costs,** as the name implies, vary with the level of activity. They go up when you engage in more of the activity (drive more, spend more time at home, produce more output) and down when you engage in less. Fixed costs and variable costs can also be thought of as unavoidable and avoidable costs, respectively. Because fixed costs don't vary with the level of activity, they can't be avoided by doing less of the activity. Variable costs, on the other hand, are avoidable; do less of an activity and you reduce your variable costs.

Consider, for example, the costs of driving a car. Some of those costs are fixed—the monthly payment, for example, and the cost of insurance. Whether you drive one mile or a thousand, the amount of your fixed costs will be unchanged. Other costs, the cost of gasoline and oil, for example, vary with the amount you drive; the more you drive, the more you spend for gas and oil.

The Flying Smiths

The distinction between fixed and variable costs is an important one for decision making. To illustrate, consider the following problem. Bob Smith and his wife, Robin, are planning a two-week ski trip. They've been given free use of a condo once they arrive, so the major expense of the ski holiday is the transportation to and from the resort. They're trying to decide whether to take a plane or drive their car. They realize that driving will use up some of their skiing time, but they think the beauty of the drive will compensate for that loss. The round-trip plane fare for the couple is $400. Robin, who is an accountant, has estimated the cost of making the trip by car as follows:

$150	gas
160	one night's motel lodging each way
200	half a month's car payment
20	half a month's car insurance
10	estimated wear on tires
$540	Total Cost of transportation

Because the cost of taking the car exceeds the cost of taking the plane, the Smiths decide to take the plane. Do you agree with their decision?

As you may have noticed, the problem with Robin's estimate of the driving costs is that it fails to distinguish between fixed and variable costs. More precisely, this estimate fails to isolate the *marginal cost* of taking the trip. The car payment and the monthly payment for insurance are fixed costs; those payments have to be made whether the Smiths drive or fly. The true cost of driving to Colorado is only $320—the extra or additional variable cost of operating the automobile and the added cost of lodging. If the Smiths compare that cost to the cost of airfare, driving is the clear choice.

Note that the decision-making process used to decide between taking a plane and driving a car is really no different than the cost-benefit analysis discussed earlier. The benefit of driving the car is the $400 you save by not having to take the plane. If the cost of driving the car is less than the benefit, you drive the car; otherwise, you take the plane. But if you get your estimate of costs wrong—if you include fixed costs that don't belong—you make the wrong decision and spend money needlessly.

One more note before we proceed. Even though the car payment and the insurance payment are fixed costs in this instance, they might be marginal costs under other circumstances. Suppose, for example, that you've just moved to New York City and you're trying to decide whether to buy a car or rely on mass transit to get to work and travel about the city. Under those circumstances, the car and insurance payments are marginal costs of owning an automobile. They need to be considered along with the cost of gas, parking fees, and so forth, in deciding whether it's cheaper to travel by mass transit or purchase a car. But if you decide to purchase the car and have it insured, the insurance and car payments immediately become fixed costs in determining the cost of any trip you intend to make. The point is that insurance and car payments become fixed costs only after you've made a commitment to pay them; up to that point, they are avoidable and need to be considered along with any other marginal costs and benefits. If you're confused, read on; the case of Peggy and Sue should shed additional light on the distinction between fixed and marginal costs.

Peggy, Sue, and the One-Year Lease

Peggy and Sue live in an apartment near Ivy College. They've both decided to return home for the summer and would like to sublet their apartment for the three months of summer vacation. Peggy and Sue signed a one-year lease that obligates them to pay $500 a month, including utilities. They have been advertising their apartment for the past three weeks but have found no takers. Several new apartments have been erected in the city, and apartment rents have fallen dramatically since they have signed their lease. Two friends have hinted that they might be willing to rent the apartment if Peggy and Sue would accept substantially less than $500. Peggy and Sue would like to be able to cover their $500 monthly payment, and they're reluctant to accept less than that amount. What advice would you offer them?

Peggy and Sue need to seriously consider any offer that is made. Obviously they want to rent the apartment for as much as possible; $600 would be great if they could get it. But if the best offer they get is $300, or even $200, they should take it. After all, the $500 rent they are obliged to pay is a fixed cost; they have to pay it whether they sublet the apartment or not. If they can get $300 by subletting, they have to come up with only another $200 on their own. If they reject that offer, they have to pay the entire $500 themselves.

Of course, there are some intangibles here. There is always some risk that the people who sublet the apartment may damage it or destroy Peggy and Sue's relationship with the landlord or in some other way impose costs on them. These intangibles are worth something and may establish a "floor" or minimum rent that Peggy and Sue are willing to accept. That's fine; there's nothing wrong with that logic. The important point is that the $500 rent is a fixed cost and is irrelevant in deciding how much to accept when subletting.

The Travels of Bonnie and Claude

As we've seen, the irrelevance of fixed costs doesn't prevent them from creeping into all kinds of decisions. As a final example, consider the trials of a young married couple, Bonnie and Claude Jones, who have been shopping for a new sofa. The couple recently found a sofa they like at a local furniture store, but it is selling for $800, somewhat more than they want to pay. A neighbor has suggested that they drive to Furnitureville—a 100-mile trip—because she's heard that the prices there are 25 percent lower. If they make the trip, Susan will have to miss half a day's work at a cost of about $50 in forgone income. In addition, Claude estimates that they will spend another $25 for gas. After discussion, the couple decides that the expected benefits of the trip (the $200 they anticipate saving on the sofa) justify the expense.

When they arrive, they discover that furniture prices are indeed lower than at home—but not much lower. The sofa that sold at home for $800 sells there for $775 (including delivery). Mr. Jones is very disappointed. He wants to turn around and head back home. "If we include the money we've lost because of the trip, these sofas cost $850; that's even more than the $800 they're asking back home." Mrs. Jones isn't so sure. "I don't think we should count the cost of the trip; we've already lost that money. I think we should go ahead and buy the sofa here since it's $25 less than back home." Who do you think is correct?

If you sided with Mrs. Jones, you're on the right track. The cost of the trip is a fixed cost; it can't be avoided after the trip is made and shouldn't affect the sofa-buying decision in any way. If the Joneses had known the sofa prices in Furnitureville before they made the trip, they would have stayed home. But once they've made the trip, they have to pay for it whether or not they buy the sofa. The correct decision is to buy the sofa in Furnitureville because the additional cost of the sofa there ($775) is less than the additional cost of the sofa back home ($800). The cost of the trip is fixed or "sunk" and irrelevant; it's water under the bridge or spilt milk. (Fixed costs are sometimes referred to as **sunk costs**, a label that conveys the notion that fixed costs are unavoidable.)

Before moving on to the next example, let's consider another possible outcome from the trip to Furnitureville. Suppose that on arrival, the Joneses had discovered that the sofa they were interested in was selling for $850, $50 more than back home. Under those circumstances, the correct decision would be to buy the sofa in their hometown. But the Joneses may fall into the trap of believing that it is necessary to buy the sofa in Furnitureville to justify the cost of the trip. In other words, "We've paid for this trip and we need to have something to show for it." But as we've already noted, the cost of the trip is sunk; it cannot be avoided. If the Joneses insist on buying the sofa in Furnitureville, all they will have to show for the trip is thinner wallets.

As the foregoing examples illustrate, there are many pitfalls in wise decision making. It's easy to ignore some relevant costs and equally easy to see costs where there are none. The key to avoiding these pitfalls is remembering to think marginally and to consider the opportunity costs. By applying these rules you can make better personal decisions about everything from how to spend your money to what to do next Saturday night. (Many Internet users *do* understand what it means to "think marginally." Read the article on page 136 to learn how marginal reasoning has slowed the use of the Internet in the United Kingdom.)

BUSINESS DECISION MAKING AND PROFIT MAXIMIZATION

Now that we have introduced the marginal principle and have seen how it can improve personal decision making, we shift the emphasis to business decision making. Much of this text focuses on the behavior of businesses rather than that of individuals. That's because businesses are at the center of the productive activity in our economy. They not only produce the goods and services that consumers demand, they also provide the employment opportunities that make it possible for consumers to purchase those goods and services. Business decision making is really no different than personal decision making; it involves a comparison of costs and benefits. The only real distinction between business and personal decision making is the goals involved. Economists generally assume that self-interest-seeking individuals attempt to maximize personal satisfaction, or **utility**. Businesses, on the other hand, are generally assumed to be **profit maximizers;** they are attempting to make decisions that will allow them to earn as much profit as possible.

Profit is the excess of a business firm's total revenue over its total costs. Businesses pursue profits by producing and selling products. **Total revenue** represents the total receipts of the business, that is, the amount of money it takes in from the sale of its product. Total revenue is calculated by multiplying the selling price of the product by the number of units sold. For example, if you sell five pens for $2 each, your total revenue is $10. **Total cost** refers to the sum of all the fixed and variable costs incurred by a business in producing its product and making it available for sale. As long as a business's total revenue exceeds its total costs, it is earning a profit. When total costs exceed total revenue, the business is incurring a **loss**. (Profit and loss are simple accounting terms; we'll see later why economists need special terms for different kinds of profits.)

Freeing the Internet: Unmetered Calls Would Promote Use

THE MAIN reason the US is so far ahead of the rest of the world in internet usage is that they have flat-rate telephone calls. Users pay a monthly rental then surf as long as they like. Because they don't feel they are "on the clock" with charges mounting up all the time they spend much more time learning, chatting and visiting e-commerce sites. A report by Durlacher this week claims that the UK internet economy is being "dramatically held back" by the absence of unmetered calls. The research shows that average residential users could triple their use from 130 to 386 hours per year if unmetered access were introduced.

In the US the driving force for cheap access was fierce competition whereas in the UK (and, to be fair, most other countries) domestic telephone monopolies were left largely unaffected by privatization. It was never in their interest to risk something that might dent their revenues. But now the market is changing fast as BT [British Telecom] faces new competition from cable companies. In the domestic market Telewest, the UK's largest cable company, is to introduce unlimited web access for a flat monthly fee of £ 10 [about $14.50]. This makes BT's plans (from £ 6.99 a month for free weekend access to £ 34.99 for unlimited access all the time) look expensive.

In the business market, the American company Metromedia Fibre Network is laying high capacity fibre-optic cables (each hair thread of which can carry 4m phone calls at once) in central London. These will, for the first time, be tariff-free after rental payments. BT argues that, until recently, there wasn't the demand for unlimited access to the web. But in the internet world supply generates its own demand. And in the internet world delays of even a few months can be fatal. In the national and corporate interest BT should introduce affordable unmetered access now. Then it can sit back and watch demand booming.

Use Your Economic Reasoning

1. Under a flat-rate pricing scheme, where customers pay a monthly fee for unlimited use, what is the marginal cost of an additional hour of internet use once you've become a subscriber?
2. How much benefit (in monetary terms) must users anticipate from an additional hour of Internet use in order to justify the added expense of staying connected for that hour?
3. Use cost-benefit analysis to explain why flat rates encourage internet use.

Source: © *The Guardian* (London), February 15, 2000, p. 21.

SELECTING THE PROFIT-MAXIMIZING LEVEL OF OUTPUT

The most fundamental decision that a business makes is selecting the optimal level of output, the output that will maximize its profits or minimize its losses. Managers attempt to locate that output by repeatedly asking themselves the same question: "Will the marginal benefit from producing this additional unit of output exceed the marginal cost?" As long as the answer is yes, they continue to expand production. When the answer is no, they stop; they've found the optimal level of output.

Marginal Revenue Is the Marginal Benefit

The benefit that a firm receives from producing and selling its product is the money it takes in—the revenue it receives. As we've already noted, the amount of revenue the firm generates depends on two things: the selling price of the product and the quantity of the product sold. For the sake of illustration, imagine that you own a small sawmill producing pine lumber for home building. Suppose, also, that the prevailing price of pine lumber is $270 per thousand feet and that this price is set by market forces and is largely beyond your control. (The next chapter will examine this assumption in some detail.) Under these circumstances, what is the marginal benefit to your sawmill of selling an additional thousand feet of lumber? If you answered $270, you've got the right idea. That $270 is the price the firm receives for each unit of output (each thousand feet of lumber) it sells. It also represents the mill's marginal revenue—the additional revenue from selling one more unit of output.

Exhibit 5.1 illustrates how the sawmill's total revenue and marginal revenue change as the mill expands production. As you can see from column 2, total revenue (the result of multiplying the selling price times the number of units sold) climbs steadily upward as output is increased. On the other hand, the marginal revenue values in column 3 remain constant. Because marginal revenue represents the additional revenue from selling another unit of output, we compute marginal revenue by finding the change in total revenue from one output level to the next. For example, we can see from the exhibit that the mill's total revenue is $540 if it sells two units of output and $810 if it sells three units. The $270 difference between these values ($810 − $540 = $270) represents the marginal revenue from selling the third unit of output. Because the mill receives an additional $270 each time it sells another unit, total revenue rises by an additional $270 with each unit sold, and marginal revenue remains constant at that amount.

EXHIBIT 5.1

Marginal Revenue from Selling Pine Lumber

OUTPUT PER DAY	TOTAL REVENUE	MARGINAL REVENUE
0	0	—
1	$ 270	$270
2	540	270
3	810	270
4	1,080	270
5	1,350	270
6	1,620	270
7	1,890	270
8	2,160	270
9	2,430	270
10	2,700	270

If each additional unit produced and sold adds $270 to the firm's revenue, how many units should the firm produce? That depends on marginal cost. Remember the decision-making rule: Engage in an activity as long as the marginal benefit (marginal revenue) exceeds the marginal cost.

Computing Marginal Cost

Marginal cost is the cost of producing an additional unit of output; so it is the change in total cost from one unit of output to another. Consider, for example, the marginal cost of the first unit of output in Exh. 5.2. If it costs the firm $180 to produce zero output (remember fixed costs) and $445 to produce one unit of output, the marginal cost of the first unit of lumber is $265. The marginal cost of the second thousand feet of lumber is $240, the difference between the total cost of $445 and the total cost of $685. Take a few moments to compute the marginal costs for the remaining units of output, using the total cost column in Exh. 5.2. Then, check your answers against the marginal cost column in that exhibit.

If you examine the marginal cost column closely, you will notice that marginal cost declines initially and then increases as output expands further. Why

EXHIBIT 5.2

The Marginal Cost of Manufacturing Pine Lumber

OUTPUT PER DAY	TOTAL COST	MARGINAL COST
0	$ 180	—
1	445	$265
2	685	240
3	895	210
4	1,075	180
5	1,285	210
6	1,525	240
7	1,795	270
8	2,125	330
9	2,515	390
10	2,965	450

does it behave this way? The behavior of marginal cost is related to the productivity of the factors of production (or economic resources) used in producing the product.

When inputs are more productive, they produce more—they add more to the firm's output. This, in turn, means lower costs for the business. In small sawmills, for example, labor costs can be a major cost of doing business. The labor cost of producing an additional unit of output depends on the amount of labor time it takes to produce that unit. If our mill is paying its workers $10 an hour and it takes eight hours to produce the additional unit, the labor cost of that unit is $80. If the additional unit could be produced in only six hours, the labor cost of that unit could be reduced to $60.

The amount of labor time it takes to produce each additional unit of output is not constant. It depends on the degree of *specialization* of labor: the extent to which workers perform a single task rather than several. Workers who specialize tend to do their jobs better and more quickly, which means lower marginal cost.

When a firm is producing relatively little output, the labor cost of producing an additional unit tends to be high because the low volume permits little specialization. To illustrate, think about the variety of tasks you would need to perform if you wanted to run our hypothetical sawmill alone. You would be required to roll the logs onto the saws and cut them into lumber. Then, to smooth the rough surfaces of the boards, you would have to set up and operate the planer. Next, you would need to stack the lumber for drying. And, of course, you'd be the one who cleaned and serviced the equipment so that it continued to operate properly.

Many additional tasks would be required, but by now you probably get the point. If you were trying to run the mill by yourself, you would spend a great deal of time moving from one task to the next, and it's likely that you wouldn't become very proficient at any of them. As a consequence, more hours would be required to accomplish each task than would be needed if you were allowed to specialize in one job (or a few jobs) and become more skilled. This is why the marginal cost of producing the first unit of lumber is relatively high ($265).

As output expands, opportunities for specialization increase. For example, if the lumber mill needs to hire two workers to keep up with demand, one of them might do all the sawing while the other planes the boards and stacks them for drying. This greater specialization permits workers to become better at their jobs and reduces the time wasted in moving from one task to another. The result is a lower marginal cost for the second unit of output ($240) and an even lower cost for the third ($210) and fourth ($180) because the amount of labor time required to produce these additional units of output is reduced. Remember, this is a hypothetical example; the numbers are not precise but are meant only to illustrate a principle. In some businesses, specialization can result in significant reductions in marginal cost; in others, the savings may be minimal.

Marginal cost will not decline indefinitely. If the firm continues to expand output, it will eventually start to overutilize its plant and equipment, causing marginal cost to rise. In the short run, each business firm must operate with a fixed amount of plant and equipment. If the firm continues to hire additional workers in order to increase output, at some point it will experience congestion and workers waiting to use equipment. Of course, if workers are standing idle, they are not producing output but they are being paid. This causes the marginal cost of producing an additional unit of output to rise, as it does in our example when the output is expanded from four to five units of lumber.

In summary, if a firm continues to expand output in the short run, it will eventually overutilize its fixed plant and equipment, causing marginal cost to rise. This principle is simply an extension of the law of increasing costs introduced in Chapter 1.

Using the Decision Rule

Once we've computed marginal revenue (*MR*) and marginal cost (*MC*) at each level of output, selecting the optimal level of output is a relatively simple matter. We just apply the decision rule we've been using throughout the chapter: *Continue to produce as long as the marginal benefit exceeds the marginal cost.*

A note of caution before we proceed. Even if businesses consistently apply the decision rule, they are not assured of profits. Sometimes weak demand or high costs make it impossible for them to earn a profit. But even under these conditions, marginal reasoning is important. By comparing marginal costs and marginal benefits, the firm can minimize its loss and perhaps survive until business conditions improve. In short, while marginal reasoning doesn't ensure profits, it does ensure that you will do as well as possible under the existing circumstances.

Having noted that point of clarification, let's return to the hypothetical sawmill. The first three columns of Exh. 5.3 summarize the relationship between output, marginal revenue, and marginal cost that we discovered earlier. The fourth column adds another interesting bit of information, the mill's profit (or loss) at each level of output. As we've already discovered, profit is the difference between total revenue and total cost; this column simply performs that comparison for each level of output. If the $180 loss at zero output mystifies you, remember fixed costs. Even if production ceases and revenue drops to zero, some costs will remain to be paid.

EXHIBIT 5.3
Selecting the Profit-Maximizing Level of Output

OUTPUT PER DAY	MARGINAL REVENUE	MARGINAL COST	PROFIT
0	—	—	$−180
1	$270	$265	−175
2	270	240	−145
3	270	210	− 85
4	270	180	+ 5
5	270	210	+ 65
6	270	240	+ 95
7	270	270	+ 95
8	270	330	+ 35
9	270	390	− 85
10	270	450	−265

Even without column 4, the information contained in Exh. 5.3 can be used to determine the optimal (profit-maximizing/loss-minimizing) level of output. As we noted earlier, production managers attempt to locate the optimal output by repeatedly asking themselves the same question: "Will the marginal revenue from producing this additional unit of output exceed the marginal cost?" As long as the answer is yes, they continue to expand production.

Let's start with the first unit of output and ask that question. As you can see from the exhibit, the marginal revenue from the sale of the first unit of output ($270) exceeds the marginal cost of producing that unit ($265). The first unit of output should be produced because it makes the mill $5 better off than it would be if it produced nothing. (Note that the mill's loss drops from $180 to $175.) What about the second unit of output; should it be produced? According to the exhibit, the answer is yes. That unit adds another $270 to the firm's revenue but only $240 to the mill's costs; it makes the business $30 better off (the mill's loss declines from $175 to $145).

How long should the mill continue expanding production? Marginal reasoning tells us to produce each unit for which *MR* exceeds *MC* but no units for which *MC* exceeds *MR*. If the mill's manager follows that logic, he or she will expand production right up to the point at which marginal revenue is equal to marginal cost, at seven units of output. Note that the mill's profit is maximized at that point. By employing marginal reasoning, we have located the profit-maximizing output.

You may have noted that the mill's profit is actually maximized at either six or seven units of output. To eliminate any ambiguity, we will assume that businesses go ahead and produce the unit where $MC = MR$. As we will see in a moment, that makes it a relatively easy matter to locate the profit-maximizing output graphically. In some situations, there will be no (nonfractional) level of output at which *MR* and *MC* are exactly equal. In such instances the firm should continue to produce each unit of output whose *MR* exceeds its *MC*. Our complete rule for profit maximization, then, is to expand production as long as marginal revenue is greater than or equal to marginal cost.

Graphing and Profit Maximization

Graphing the marginal revenue and marginal cost curves is an alternative method of determining the optimal level of output. This approach is represented in Exh. 5.4. Since the mill receives an additional $270 for each and every unit of lumber it sells, its marginal revenue curve is a horizontal straight line at a height of $270. On the other hand, the mill's marginal cost curve is U-shaped; it dips and then rises. As noted earlier, this shape stems from the changing productivity of the mill's inputs. At low output levels, few opportunities for specialization lead to high marginal costs. As output ex-

EXHIBIT 5.4

Finding the Profit-Maximizing Output Graphically

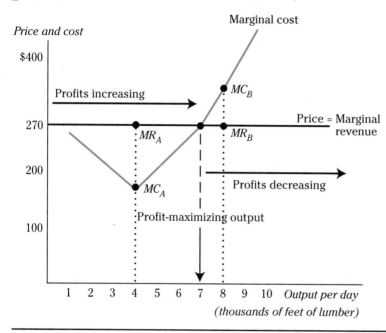

Profit is maximized at the output where marginal revenue is equal to marginal cost. As long as MR>MC, the firm can enlarge its profit (or reduce its loss) by expanding output. When MC>MR, additional units reduce the firm's profit (or increase its loss).

pands, increased opportunities for specialization bring lower marginal costs. Ultimately, the overutilization of the mill forces workers to wait to use the equipment, driving marginal cost back up and explaining the U-shaped marginal cost curve in the exhibit.

As long as the marginal revenue curve is above the marginal cost curve, *MR* exceeds *MC*, and it makes sense for the firm to expand output. For example, the marginal revenue from the sale of the fourth unit of output (represented by the point labeled MR_A on the marginal revenue curve) exceeds the marginal cost of producing it (represented by point MC_A on the marginal cost curve); so the mill will be better off producing that unit. The same is true of all additional units up to the seventh. At that point the marginal revenue curve intersects the marginal cost curve, so that *MR* = *MC*; the additional cost of producing the unit is exactly equal to the additional revenue derived from its sale. If the mill produced more than seven units of output, the marginal cost of producing those units would exceed the marginal revenue, making the firm worse off. For example, the marginal cost of producing the eighth unit of output (represented by MC_B on the marginal cost curve) is $330, well in excess of the $270 marginal revenue derived from that unit (point MR_B on the marginal revenue curve). It stands to reason, then, that output should be expanded right up to the point at which marginal revenue equals marginal cost, but not beyond. That gives us a simple way of isolating the profit-maximizing rate of output graphically: Produce at the output for which the marginal cost curve intersects the marginal revenue curve (where $MR = MC$).

Wise Decisions Don't Always Lead to Profits

As we noted earlier, the best decision making in the world can't guarantee profits. Sometimes market conditions are depressed, and the very best a firm can do is to minimize its loss. Consider, for example, a situation in which the demand for pine lumber has declined, reducing its market price from $270 to only $250. What should the mill do under these circumstances? It should use marginal reasoning, just as before. Look at Exh. 5.5 and see if you can find the loss-minimizing output without using column 4. (For simplicity, the table has been slightly abbreviated.)

Note that in this instance there is no output for which marginal revenue is exactly equal to marginal cost. Therefore, the mill should expand production, as long as $MR > MC$, to six units per day. Column 4 confirms that six units is indeed the loss-minimizing output; once again, marginal reasoning has served us well.

EXHIBIT 5.5
Selecting the Loss-Minimizing Level of Output

OUTPUT PER DAY	MARGINAL REVENUE	MARGINAL COST	PROFIT
⋮	⋮	⋮	⋮
2	$250	$240	$–190
3	250	210	–150
4	250	180	– 80
5	250	210	– 40
6	250	240	– 30
7	250	270	– 50
8	250	330	–130

There are rare but realistic circumstances in which the business will not find it desirable to expand production up to the output at which $MR = MC$. Suppose, for example, that the price of lumber became really depressed and the mill could predict that, at the output at which $MR = MC$, it would incur a loss of, say, $225. What would it do? Under these circumstances the mill would minimize its loss by shutting down or ceasing operations until market conditions improve and it can get a better price for its product. If a mill shuts down, the loss it incurs is equal to its fixed costs—the costs that continue even at zero production. Recall that in our example the mill's fixed costs total $180 a day, substantially less than the $225 a day the business would lose by continuing to operate. The next chapter will discuss in greater detail the possibility of shutting down. For now, focus your attention on the profit-maximization rule (expand production up to the point at which $MR = MC$); it's the rule that guides business decision making in the vast majority of cases.

GAS STATIONS, FAST FOOD, AND THE ALL-NIGHT GROCERY STORE

Thus far we've concentrated on the role of marginal reasoning in helping businesses select the optimal level of output. But the role of marginal reasoning is much broader than that. It permeates every aspect of business. And knowing what it means to "think marginally" can help you understand business decisions that baffle others.

Whatever Happened to Gas Stations?

There are plenty of mysteries in life, and economics won't help you to unravel all of them. But it can help to clarify one that may bug your parents: Whatever happened to gas stations? At one time there were thousands of genuine gas stations in the United States, stations that sold almost nothing but gas. And convenience stores sold quick groceries but not gas. Now, in many areas, gasoline stations are rarities, and every convenience store has gas pumps. What happened? Part of the story is the introduction of self-service gasoline; that made it possible for convenience stores to sell gas. And the increase in the number of working mothers made a difference, too; that change put greater emphasis on convenience—the ability to buy a carton of milk without trudging to the grocery store. But much of the answer lies in the marginal principle, and that's what we want to discuss here.

Imagine yourself as the owner of one of the few remaining genuine, honest-to-goodness gas stations in the United States. On the way home from work, you need a carton of milk and a few other groceries, and so you run into a convenience store and pick them up. You notice that the price you pay is somewhat higher than what you'd pay in a grocery store, but you don't complain; the convenience is worth it. But that starts you thinking. Why can't *you* sell those items and make that money? (Notice competition rearing its head; more about that in the next chapter.) So you sit down with a pad of paper and a calculator and do some figuring. How much would it cost to rent a cooler for milk and soda pop, and a display rack for bread and snack items? Not much. What about the extra electrical cost of running the cooler? Not much. And how many extra people would you have to hire to collect money from customers buying groceries? None. Pretty soon you've cleared the junk out of your gas station, installed the cooler and display racks, and another gas station has given way to a mini convenience store; the marginal principle rides again.

Owners of early convenience stores also understood marginal reasoning, and they tended to view gasoline as a marginal item. But adding gas pumps to a convenience store probably required more thought than adding coolers to gas stations. Although the additional cost of pumping gas is minimal once the pumps are in place (and that cost is fixed, or "sunk"), the cost of adding the pumps is not trivial. So, before that decision was made, the convenience store owners needed to determine whether the additional revenue that the pumps would generate would pay for the cost of the pumps, the additional electricity to run them, and the wholesale cost of the gasoline.

The answer must generally be yes because gas pumps are everywhere. The difference between gas stations and convenience stores has largely disappeared. (Note that once some convenience stores begin adding gas pumps, it puts pressure on other convenience stores in the area to do the same. If you can buy gas *and* groceries at Bob's Quick Mart, you won't stop at Joan's Fast Stop if it sells only groceries. So the option of not selling gasoline has now been largely eliminated for convenience store owners.)

Why Is Breakfast Everywhere?

If you want more evidence that businesses understand marginal reasoning, consider the ease with which you can find a cheap, quick breakfast. Even though lunch is clearly the main meal at McDonald's and Burger King, managers at these franchises understand that they can enlarge their profits by serving breakfast. That's because once the restaurant is in place, there is little added cost to serving the morning meal. The big expense items, rent and the cost of the franchise, are fixed costs; they have to be paid whether or not breakfast is served. So the restaurants do a quick cost-benefit analysis and compare the additional revenue they can generate by offering breakfast to the additional cost of serving breakfast (the cost of the food items, the additional labor time, the higher electric bill, etc.). On that basis, it appears that the breakfast meal must generally pay for itself. That's why there are so many places where you can grab a quick breakfast as you dash to class or to work.

Sale! Buy Below Cost!

Marginal reasoning even helps to explain those end-of-season sales. If you've ever found yourself looking through the sale merchandise, you've probably noticed that you can save quite a bit on the normal retail price. In fact, if you're patient and wait for the final reductions, those prices can be below even the wholesale prices paid by the stores. Does that make sense? Does it make sense to sell a designer sweater for $25 if it cost the store $50? Sure it does! Remember the rules: Sunk costs are sunk; compare marginal costs and marginal benefits.

The amount the store paid for the sweater is irrelevant in the decision about how much to sell it for. The question is: Does the marginal benefit of selling it to you for $25 exceed the marginal cost? But what's the marginal cost of selling it to you? If the sweater hasn't sold all season, the store's next course of action will be selling it to one of those chains that sell close-out merchandise. That may net the store only $5 or $10. If that's the case, the marginal revenue from selling that sweater to you ($25) exceeds the marginal cost (the $5–$10 it could get elsewhere). The store's not being silly; it's using marginal reasoning.

What a store paid for an item is irrelevant when it comes to determining closeout prices.

Late-Night Movies and Empty Airplanes

Before we close our discussion of marginal reasoning, consider the following examples for just a moment. Have you ever attended one of those late-night movies or flown home on a nearly empty airplane or visited an all-night grocery store at 2 A.M.? If you have, the limited number of customers may have had you wondering, "How can they afford to do this?" Before you feel too much sympathy for the businesses involved, remember the marginal principle; it provides the answer.

Let's take a closer look at the example of the movie theater. Once the rent on the building and the movie has been paid (both fixed costs), the marginal cost of showing the film one more time can be very low, the wages of a ticket taker and someone to run the concession stand (sometimes the same person), and a little more for utilities. So the movie theater doesn't have to attract many customers to its late-night showing to make it profitable. That's why you may find yourself attending a showing with only a dozen other people. The same thing is true of the late-night grocery store, perhaps to an even greater extent. Grocery stores tend to restock their shelves in the evening, so that the lights are still on and there are still personnel in the stores. If those employees can take a moment to check out customers, the marginal cost of serving those customers is very low. So the stores can advertise 24-hour service at very little added cost.

Even airlines find themselves in this situation, though not to the same extent. A major cost of running an airline is renting or buying the airplane. Once that expense is paid, the marginal cost of additional flights can be low enough to justify flying planes that are less than one-third full.

Of course, there are factors that can complicate marginal decision making. For instance, the movie theaters are not always able to rent films for a fixed fee; sometimes they are required to pay the film company a certain percentage of the ticket price. That would increase the theater's marginal cost and make it more difficult to justify late-night movies that might be sparsely attended. Another factor is the possibility of the theater's stealing its own customers. If the theater customers who decide to attend the midnight movie would have attended an earlier show (if the midnight show were not available), all the theater has done by offering the additional showing is to increase its costs and reduce its profits. The same is true of the airline. There is no point in offering additional flights if there is space on the earlier flights and the airline is convinced that the customers will have to fly with it anyway.

One more thought before closing this chapter. Although marginal costs (and revenues) are the key to good decision making in the preceding examples, firms must *ultimately* cover all their costs—including fixed costs—to remain in business. Consider the movie theater example once again. As we've seen, the theater owner should ignore fixed costs such as rent and insurance in deciding whether to remain open for an additional late-night showing. Those costs already exist, once the decision had been made to open a movie theater. But if the theater's total operations (afternoon, evening, and late-night showings) are unable to generate enough revenue to cover all costs, including those fixed costs, it will eventually be forced to close its doors. After all, landlords and insurance companies expect to be paid. If they aren't, they will stop providing their services, and the theater will be history. We'll have much more to say about this in the next chapter. But as you can see, there is more to running a business than understanding marginal reasoning. And there's more to economics as well. In the next chapter we will take a closer look at the behavior of business firms and explore the meaning of competitive markets.

SUMMARY

Economic models assume that men and women are motivated by self-interest and that they pursue self-interest through a rational comparison of costs and benefits. The relevant costs and benefits for comparison are marginal costs and benefits. The *marginal* costs and benefits are the extra or additional costs and benefits resulting from a decision. A decision will improve one's well-being only if the marginal benefits from that decision exceed the marginal costs.

Even rational people sometimes make bad decisions. Poor decisions stem from mistaking marginal and total values and from improperly estimating the costs of a decision. It is important to remember that all decisions have opportunity costs. In some instances these opportunity costs can easily be stated in monetary terms; in other instances they cannot. In either case failure to consider all opportunity costs can lead to poor decisions. Poor decisions can also result from mistaking relevant and irrelevant costs. The only costs that are relevant for decision making are *marginal costs*, the additional costs that result from making a decision. Costs are irrelevant if they are unaffected by a decision. Irrelevant costs include fixed, or "sunk," costs. *Fixed costs* are costs that do not vary with the level of activity engaged in and that cannot be avoided.

Business decision making also involves a comparison of costs and benefits. The only major difference between business decision making and personal decision making is the goals involved. According to economic theory, individuals attempt to maximize personal satisfaction or *utility*, while businesses attempt to maximize profits.

Profit is the excess of a business's total revenue over its total costs. Total revenue represents the total receipts of a business and can be calculated by multiplying the selling price of the product times the number of units sold. *Total cost* represents the sum of all the business's fixed costs (those costs that do not vary with the level of output) and *variable costs* (those costs that do vary with the level of output). As long as a business's total revenue exceeds its total costs, it will earn a profit. When total costs exceed total revenue, the business will incur a *loss*.

The fundamental decision that a business makes is selecting the level of output that maximizes its profits or minimizes its loss. In order to select this output, businesses compare marginal revenue and marginal cost. Output should be expanded up to the point at which marginal revenue is equal to marginal cost ($MR = MC$) but not beyond. Graphically, the profit-maximizing output can be determined by locating the output at which the marginal revenue curve intersects the marginal cost curve. Although producing where $MR = MC$ does not ensure a profit, it generally allows the firm to do as well as possible under existing market conditions. In other words, producing at the output where $MR = MC$ will generally allow the firm either to maximize its profit or to minimize its loss.

In addition to using marginal reasoning to select the profit-maximizing/loss-minimizing level of output, firms use marginal reasoning in making other business decisions. For instance, fast-food restaurants use marginal reasoning in deciding whether to serve breakfast, and airlines use marginal reasoning in deciding whether to run an additional flight between two cities. While fixed costs are irrelevant in such decisions, firms must ultimately generate enough revenue to cover all costs if they are to remain in business.

KEY TERMS

Fixed costs	Profit maximizer	Total revenue
Loss	Sunk cost	Utility
Marginal	Total cost	Variable costs
Profit		

STUDY QUESTIONS

Fill in the Blanks

1. Economists argue that individuals are motivated primarily by the pursuit of *Self Interest*.

2. Rational people make decisions by comparing *Marginal cost* and *marginal Benefits*.

3. _Fix_ costs are costs that do not vary with output and cannot be avoided.

4. Total cost is the sum of _total fixed_ cost and _total variable_ cost.

5. _Marginal_ means extra or additional.

6. Economists generally assume that individuals seek to maximize _utility_ and that businesses seek to maximize

Profit .

7. Economists argue that profits are generally maximized (or losses minimized) at the output for which _MR_ is equal to _MC_ .

8. A business would be better off shutting down (producing no output) than producing, if the loss it would incur by operating would be greater than its _Fix_ costs.

9. Marginal costs may initially decline as output is expanded and more workers are hired because higher levels of production permit greater _specialization_.

10. The statement "There's no such thing as a free lunch" means that every decision has an _Opportunity Cost_.

Multiple Choice

1. Economists assume that individuals
   a) are motivated primarily by concern for others.
   b) act impulsively.
   c) pursue their own self-interest.
   d) use their intuition to make wise decisions.

2. According to economists, when people make decisions, they
   a) are primarily concerned about the costs and benefits that their decisions impose on others.
   b) base their decisions on expected costs and benefits rather than true costs and benefits.
   c) must consciously weigh costs and marginal benefits in order to make wise decisions.
   d) must carefully compare sunk costs and marginal benefits in order to make wise choices.

3. Economic models may not accurately predict the behavior of individuals if those individuals
   a) fail to consider the interests of others.
   b) act selfishly.
   c) behave in an impulsive manner.
   d) always consider the opportunity costs of their decisions.

4. Bob walked into the clothing store and, without a moment's hesitation, bought the first shirt he saw that was his size. His behavior
   a) is clearly consistent with the assumption of rationality.
   b) might be rational if he has very little time to shop.
   c) is clearly impulsive and is therefore inconsistent with the assumption of rationality.
   d) might be impulsive if he had previously considered the alternative shirts in the store and their prices.

5. Which of the following behaviors is inconsistent with the way economists assume individuals will act?
   a) Susie selected her car by reading reports, test-driving several models, and comparing their features and prices.

b) Alex wanted to go to the concert but considered the likely impact on his calculus grade and decided to study instead.

c) Fran really wanted the red dress but thought it was too expensive; so she bought the green one instead.

d) The salesman offered to let John use the store phone, but because John didn't want to interfere with business calls, he used the pay phone.

6. If we use the cost-benefit model, which of the following high school students is most likely to attend college?

a) A student with an aptitude for auto mechanics

b) A student with a decent job and opportunities for advancement

c) A student who values present income much more highly than future income

d) A student who qualifies for several scholarships

7. Suppose that a rational person decides to spend an evening watching TV instead of studying. That person must

a) be a poor student.

b) have ignored the opportunity cost of studying.

c) value TV more highly than studying.

d) value a marginal evening of TV more highly than an marginal evening of studying.

8. Julie is 25 years old and living in an apartment. She is thinking about quitting her job and returning to college. Which of the following is least likely to be relevant to that decision?

a) The salary she is currently earning

b) Tuition at the college she is considering

c) The cost of meals while she attends college

d) The cost of books and supplies

9. Profits are maximized (or losses minimized) at the output level where

a) marginal revenue exceeds marginal cost by the largest amount.

b) fixed costs are minimized.

c) marginal revenue is equal to marginal cost.

d) marginal cost is at a minimum.

10. If the marginal cost of producing an additional unit of output is $50 and the marginal revenue from selling that unit is $60,

a) the unit should not be produced since it will make the business worse off.

b) the unit should be produced since it will make the business $60 better off.

c) the unit should not be produced since the business is already maximizing its profit.

d) the unit should be produced since it will make the business $10 better off.

Use the following information in answering questions 11–13.

Data for John's Cabinet Company

OUTPUT PER WEEK	MARGINAL REVENUE	MARGINAL COST
0	—	—
1	$440	$350
2	440	325
3	440	350
4	440	375
5	440	400
6	440	450
7	440	525
8	440	625
9	440	750
10	440	900

11. John's Cabinet Company will maximize its profit (or minimize its loss) by producing

a) 2 cabinets a week.

b) 5 cabinets a week.

c) 7 cabinets a week.

d) 10 cabinets a week.

12. If John's Cabinet Company could sell each cabinet for $525 instead of $440, the profit-maximizing level of output would be

a) 2 cabinets a week.

b) 5 cabinets a week.

c) 7 cabinets a week.
d) 10 cabinets a week.

13. John's Cabinet Company
    a) is earning a profit.
    b) is incurring a loss.
    c) cannot determine profit or loss from the information given.

Use the following information in answering questions 14–18.

Data for Apex Golf Cart Company

OUTPUT PER DAY	TOTAL COST
0	$ 200
1	500
2	700
3	1,000
4	1,400
5	1,900
6	2,500
7	3,300
8	4,300
9	5,500
10	7,000

14. The Apex Golf Cart Company faces fixed costs
    a) of $200 per day.
    b) of $300 per day.
    c) of $7,000 per day.
    d) that cannot be determined from the information given.

15. The marginal cost of producing the fourth golf cart each day is
    a) $1,400.
    b) $300.
    c) $400.
    d) $350.

16. If Apex can sell additional golf carts for $800 each, the profit-maximizing (loss-minimizing) level of output is
    a) 2 carts per day.
    b) 5 carts per day.
    c) 7 carts per day.
    d) 8 carts per day.

17. If the price Apex can get for its carts increases to $950, the profit-maximizing (loss-minimizing) output will be
    a) 2 carts per day.
    b) 5 carts per day.
    c) 7 carts per day.
    d) 8 carts per day.

18. Assume that the price Apex can get for its carts remains at $950 but that the company's fixed costs increase to $500 a day. Under those conditions, the profit-maximizing (loss-minimizing) output will be
    a) 2 carts per day.
    b) 5 carts per day.
    c) 7 carts per day.
    d) 8 carts per day.

Problems and Questions for Discussion

1. Bobby Goodguy volunteers for several local charities and is a member of several service organizations. Is it possible that such behavior is in his (financial) self-interest?

2. Why do individuals base their decisions on expected costs and benefits rather than true costs and benefits?

3. Studies tell us that students who have a difficult time in high school are less likely to attend college than students who find high school easy. Use the cost-benefit model to explain this finding.

4. Edith decided that her $100,000 a year job at Gord Motors wasn't fulfilling. So she invested savings of $20,000 (which had been earning 10% a year) in starting her own travel agency. At the end of the year, the accountants gave her the following report. After examining the report, explain why

economists might criticize it and how they would be likely to amend it.

Total Revenue
from Customers......................................$225,000
Salaries of John, Joan, and Bob.............$ 75,000
Salary of Edith. 35,000
Rent...60,000
Office supplies..10,000
Phone and utilities 15,000
Total Costs..**$195,000**
Profit...**$ 30,000**

5. Susie absolutely must drive home for Christmas. She would like a rider to share the cost of the two-day trip. Her monthly car payment is $210, and car insurance costs her another $30 monthly. In addition, she estimates that gas will cost her $100. The only student who has responded to her advertisement for a rider is willing to pay $40. Should she take the rider? Defend your answer.

6. Consider your answer to question 5. Suppose that Susie could take the bus home at a cost of $120. Should she take the bus or drive? Defend your answer.

7. (Warning: Extra tough question; uses ideas not fully discussed in the chapter. Try it only if you like a challenge.) Highflyer Corporation manufactures kites, which are being sold throughout the United States. It is currently producing 100,000 kites a year and operating its factory at 70 percent of capacity. At that output the average cost of manufacturing a kite is about $2 (average cost is computed by dividing total cost by the number of units

sold). Experience has shown that average cost drops somewhat as output is expanded beyond 100,000 units but rises again if output is increased above 125,000 units.

The Highflyer Corporation normally sells its kites for $2.50 each. It recently received an order for an additional 10,000 kites from a foreign buyer, but the buyer specified that it would pay no more then $1.50 a kite. Highflyer executives want to accept the order, but the firm's accountants estimate that at 110,000 units a year, the average cost of producing a kite would be $1.90, more than the $1.50 price being offered. Should Highflyer accept the offer?

8. Bill paid $50 for an old record album at an estate sale because he thought it was a rare Elvis recording. He was wrong; the album is worth only about $10. Bill won't sell at that price because he can't stand the thought of losing $40. What's wrong with his reasoning?

9. (Another toughie; Proceed at your own risk.) Bonnie believes that it is possible to calculate the total cost of producing x units of output by summing (adding up) the marginal cost of producing all units of output from 1 through x. Is she correct? Why or why not?

10. The amount of money that a firm loses by shutting down and producing no output is its fixed costs. Why? Under what circumstances would it make more sense to shut down than to produce at the output at which $MR = MC$?

ANSWER KEY

Fill in the blanks

1. self-interest
2. marginal costs and marginal benefits
3. fixed
4. total fixed, total variable
5. Marginal
6. utility, profit
7. *MR, MC*
8. fixed
9. specialization
10. opportunity cost

Multiple Choice

1. c
2. b
3. c
4. b
5. d
6. d
7. d
8. c
9. c
10. d
11. b
12. c
13. c
14. a
15. c
16. c
17. c
18. c

CHAPTER SIX

Price Taking: The Purely Competitive Firm

LEARNING OBJECTIVES

1. Identify the characteristics of a purely competitive industry.
2. Explain why a purely competitive firm is described as a "price taker."
3. Describe the demand and marginal revenue curves of the price taker.
4. Describe how a price taker determines the profit-maximizing level of output.
5. Distinguish between the long run and the short run.
6. Identify the different types of production costs: fixed, variable, total, average, and marginal.
7. Describe how each type of production cost is related to changes in the level of output.
8. Distinguish between an economic profit and a normal profit.
9. Evaluate graphically the extent of a price taker's profit or loss.
10. Discuss the distinction between production efficiency and allocative efficiency.
11. Explain how long-run price, profitability, and efficiency are related to the absence of barriers to entry.

In Chapter 3 we discussed how demand and supply interact to determine prices in competitive markets. To fully understand the operation of competitive markets, we need to step behind the scenes and examine the decision-making processes of the individual supplier, commonly known as the *firm*.

The **firm** is the basic producing unit in a market economy. It buys economic resources—land, labor, capital, and entrepreneurship—and combines them to produce goods and services. A group of firms that produce identical or similar products is called an **industry.** Exxon, Phillips Petroleum, and Texaco are firms in the petroleum industry; McDonald's, KFC (Kentucky Fried Chicken), and your local pizzeria are firms in the fast-food industry.

Economists argue that the performance of firms—how effectively they serve consumers—depends on the degree of competition within the industry; the greater the competition, the better the performance. As we have seen in earlier chapters, performing well in a market economy means producing the goods and services that consumers desire most and selling those goods and services at the lowest possible prices. We begin this chapter by examining the assumptions that underlie the model of pure competition. Then we investigate the types of production costs the firm incurs and discover how it decides on the level of output that will maximize its profits. Finally, we examine the factors that cause firms to enter or leave an industry, explaining why this behavior is thought to be in the best interest of consumers.

THE NATURE OF PURE COMPETITION

Since the time of Adam Smith, economists have recognized that a market economy will serve consumers well only if competition exists to protect their interests. The competition economists have in mind, however, is more than mere rivalry among a few sellers. By definition, pure competition must satisfy three basic assumptions:

1. *There must be a large number of sellers, each producing a relatively small fraction of the total industry supply.* This rules out the possibility that a single firm could affect price by altering its level of output.
2. *The firms in the industry must sell identical products.* This condition excludes the possibility of any product differences, including those created through advertising, and ensures that consumers will view the products of different firms as perfect substitutes.
3. *There can be no substantial barriers (obstacles) to entering or leaving the industry.* Examples of barriers to entry include patent restrictions, large investment requirements, and restrictive licensing regulations.

The assumptions of pure competition may sound unrealistic, but there are industries that conform reasonably well to the conditions of the model. For instance, wheat farming, cattle ranching, fish farming (aquaculture), and many other segments of agriculture are consistent with the model.[1] In addition, the

---

[1] Although most agricultural industries conform reasonably well to the competitive model, price supports and other forms of government intervention in agriculture limit the usefulness of the model in describing the performance of agricultural producers. To the extent that the Federal Agricultural Improvement and Reform Act (1996) reduces that intervention, the model's usefulness has been enhanced.

competitive model offers insights into the behavior of industries that don't meet all of the assumptions, but come reasonably close. For instance, used-car retailing, the home-repair industry, and the fast-food industry are not fully consistent with the model of pure competition because the firms sell somewhat different products. But because these industries are characterized by a relatively large number of firms and modest entry barriers, the competitive model has proved very valuable in analyzing their behavior.

While the model of pure competition has proved to be a useful tool for analyzing the behavior of existing industries, economists value it for an additional reason as well. In fact, the most important function of the competitive model is in allowing us to see how an industry would function if it conformed to the assumptions of pure competition. By using the benefits of pure competition as our standard, or yardstick, we can better understand the problems that may emerge when industries are less competitive. In later chapters we will relax these assumptions and see how the performance of industries will change when these conditions are no longer satisfied.

THE FIRM UNDER PURE COMPETITION

In a purely competitive industry the individual firm is best described as a **price taker;** it must accept price as a given that is beyond its control. This description follows from two of the basic assumptions of our model. First, because each firm produces such a small fraction of the total industry's supply, no single firm can influence the market price by altering its level of production. Even if a firm withheld its entire output from the market, the industry supply curve would not shift significantly to the left, and the equilibrium price would be essentially unchanged. Second, because all firms sell identical products, no one firm can charge a higher price for its product without losing all its customers; consumers would simply buy cheaper identical products from other firms. As a consequence of both these conditions, the firm must accept, or *take*, the price that is determined by the impersonal forces of supply and demand.

To illustrate how a firm operates under pure competition, we'll return to an example introduced in Chapter 5, a hypothetical producer of pine lumber. (Readers who skipped the preceding chapter need not be concerned. This chapter complements Chapter 5 but is not dependent on it.) Pine lumber is an important component in the construction of new homes. It is produced by several thousand sawmills in the United States, and the lumber produced by one mill is virtually identical to the lumber produced by another. We will assume that the individual lumber producer is such a small part of the total industry that it cannot influence the market price. Whether that price means a profit or a loss, the firm can do nothing to alter it. The firm can't charge more than the prevailing price because its product is identical to that of all other

EXHIBIT 6.1
The Firm as a Price Taker

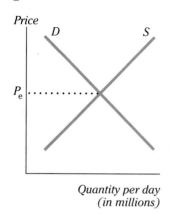

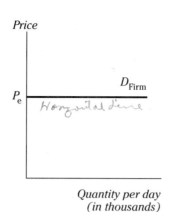

Price

Quantity per day
(in millions)

(a) The Industry

Price

D_{Firm}

Horizontal dime

Quantity per day
(in thousands)

(b) The Firm

In a purely competitive industry, market forces determine the equilibrium price, and the individual firm is unable to influence that price. The demand curve facing the firm is a horizontal line at the height of the market price because the firm can sell as much output as it desires at the prevailing price but nothing at a higher price. Note that the industry's quantity is measured in millions, whereas the firm's is measured in thousands.

producers. Withholding the firm's output from the market in an attempt to drive up prices would be fruitless because its output is just a drop in the bucket and would never be missed.

The price the firm receives for its product can change, of course, but price changes under pure competition are due to changes in *industry* demand and supply conditions, not to any actions the firm may take. Price is a given, and the demand curve facing the individual firm is therefore a horizontal line at the equilibrium price. A horizontal demand curve in Exh. 6.1 indicates that the firm can sell as much output as it wishes at the market price but no output at a higher price. Under conditions of pure competition, a firm's demand curve is perfectly, or infinitely, elastic. Recall from Chapter 4 that a high degree of elasticity means that a small change in price will lead to a large change in the quantity demanded. Here a very small change in price leads to an infinitely large change in the quantity demanded because our lumber mill would lose *all* its customers if it raised its price even slightly.

PROFIT MAXIMIZATION AND PRICE TAKERS

The model of pure competition assumes that firms are *profit maximizers;* that is, they are always attempting to earn the most profit possible. *Profit* is the excess of a firm's total revenue over its total costs. When a firm's total costs exceed its total revenue, the firm is incurring a *loss.* (Profit and loss are simple accounting terms; the next section explains why economists need special terms for different kinds of profits.)

A firm's **total revenue (TR)** is the amount of money it takes in from the sale of its product; *TR* is calculated by multiplying the selling price of the product by the number of units sold. **Total cost (TC)** refers to the sum of all the costs incurred by a business in producing its product and making it available for sale. The behavior of total cost—how rapidly it increases when output is expanded—helps to determine which level of output will maximize a firm's profit. If producing an additional unit of output adds more to a firm's revenue than it adds to cost, the additional unit should be produced. If the unit adds more to cost than it adds to revenue, it should not be produced. In other words, if an extra unit of output is profitable, it should be produced. We'll explore this profit-maximizing rule in greater detail after we discuss the types of costs a firm incurs and how they vary with output.

SHORT-RUN COSTS OF PRODUCTION

All firms must incur costs in order to produce the goods or services that they offer in the marketplace. Although this chapter concentrates on the purely competitive firm, the discussion of production costs that is presented here applies to all firms, regardless of the competitive setting in which they operate.

Our discussion of production costs will focus on the short run. The short run, as you learned in Chapter 4, is a time period during which at least one of a business's inputs (usually its plant and equipment) is incapable of being changed. In the short run a business must expand output by using its fixed production plant more intensively, since it does not have sufficient time to build a new plant or expand its existing facilities. In the long run, you will recall, all inputs can be varied, including plant and equipment. Firms have sufficient time to build new production facilities and to expand or contract existing ones. We'll have more to say about the firm's long-run adjustments later in the chapter.

Total Costs: Fixed and Variable

Short-run production costs can be classified as either fixed or variable. Total cost (*TC*) is simply the sum of the fixed and variable costs incurred by the firm.

Fixed Costs

Costs that do not vary with the level of output are called **fixed costs**. They neither increase when the firm produces more nor decrease when the firm produces less. Fixed costs are often referred to as *overhead* and include such expenditures as insurance payments, rent on the production plant, fees for business licenses, salaries of managers, and property taxes.

The distinguishing feature of fixed costs is that they have to be paid whether or not the firm is producing anything. If our hypothetical sawmill was forced to shut down because of a strike, the firm would still have to pay the salaries of its managers in order to avoid losing them to other companies. It would still have to make interest payments on loans it had taken to purchase the production plant and equipment. It would continue making payments for damage and accident insurance, and it would still require the services of security guards (an expense that might even increase).

Economists also include a normal profit as a fixed cost. **Normal profit** is the amount that the owners of a business could have earned if the money, time, and other resources they have invested in the business were invested elsewhere, in the next-best alternative. In other words, normal profit is the opportunity cost of owner-supplied resources. As an example, suppose that the owner of our sawmill had been earning $30,000 a year working for another lumber producer before he decided to buy his own mill. When he quit his job, he withdrew $20,000 from his savings account, which had been earning 10 percent interest per year, and used the money as a down payment to buy the sawmill. Since the earnings he gave up to launch this venture are his $30,000 supervisor's salary plus $2,000 interest (10 percent of $20,000) on his savings, he would have to make $32,000 in his business (after subtracting all other costs) in order to earn a normal profit.

The salaries of security guards are fixed costs because they must be paid even if a firm decides not to produce any output.

A normal profit is a fixed cost of keeping a business going. In fact, a firm that is earning a normal profit is said to be *breaking even.* Although some individuals may be willing to work for less than normal profit—perhaps because of the sense of independence they gain by being their own bosses—most owners will keep their resources employed only where they can expect at least a normal return.

Any profit above a normal profit is called an **economic profit.** If, for example, our lumber mill has total revenues of $75,000 and total costs of $57,000 (including $32,000 normal profit), the remaining $18,000 is economic profit. Economic profit is not considered a cost because the owners would remain in the business even at zero economic profit, where the firm would be breaking even.

Variable Costs

Costs that change with the level of output are termed **variable costs.** They tend to increase when the level of output increases and to decline when output declines. Many of a business's costs are variable costs: payments for raw materials, such as timber, iron ore, and crude oil, and the manufactured inputs transformed from such materials (lumber, sheet steel, paint); wages and salaries of production workers; payments for electricity and water; and shipping expenses.

In many instances a specific element of cost may be partly a fixed cost and partly a variable cost. For example, although a firm's electricity bill increases as production expands, some fraction of that bill should be considered a fixed cost because it relates to security lights, running the air conditioners in administrative offices, and other functions that are independent of the rate of output.

Total Cost

Each firm's total cost (*TC*) of production is the sum of its total fixed cost (*TFC*) and its total variable cost (*TVC*). The first four columns of Exh. 6.2 illustrate how these costs respond to changes in the level of output. The figures in column 2 show that the firm's total fixed cost (the sum of its expenditures for insurance payments, management salaries, and other fixed expenses) is constant, whereas column 3 shows the firm's total variable cost (total expenditures for gasoline, oil, labor, and other variable expenses) increasing as the level of output increases. Because total cost (column 4) includes this variable cost component, it also increases with the level of production.

Average Costs: Fixed, Variable, and Total

Producers are often more interested in the average cost of producing a unit of output than they are in any of the total cost concepts we've examined. By comparing average, or per unit, costs with those of other firms in the industry, a producer can judge how efficient (or inefficient) its own operation is.

Average cost functions are of three types: average fixed cost, average variable cost, and average total cost. **Average fixed cost (AFC)** is computed

EXHIBIT 6.2
Daily Costs of Manufacturing Pine Lumber

OUTPUT (thousands of feet of lumber)*	TOTAL FIXED COST (TFC)	TOTAL VARIABLE COST (TVC)	TOTAL COST (TC)	AVERAGE FIXED COST (AFC)	AVERAGE VARIABLE COST (AVC)	AVERAGE TOTAL COST (ATC)
0	$180	$ 0	$ 180	—	—	—
1	180	270	450	$180.00	$270.00	$450.00
2	180	510	690	90.00	255.00	345.00
3	180	720	900	60.00	240.00	300.00
4	180	900	1,080	45.00	225.00	270.00
5	180	1,110	1,290	36.00	222.00	258.00
6	180	1,350	1,530	30.00	225.00	255.00
7	180	1,620	1,800	25.71	231.43	257.14
8	180	1,950	2,130	22.50	243.75	266.25
9	180	2,340	2,520	20.00	260.00	280.00
10	180	2,790	2,970	18.00	279.00	297.00

*Large quantities of lumber are generally sold in increments of 1000 *board feet;* a board foot measures 12 × 12 × 1 inches.

by dividing total fixed cost by the firm's output. For example, if the firm was producing seven units of output, the AFC would be $180/7 = $25.71. As you can see in column 5 of Exh. 6.2, average fixed cost declines as output expands. This must be true because we are dividing a constant—total fixed cost—by larger and larger amounts of output. The decline in AFC is what a business means when it talks about "spreading its overhead" over more units of output.

The figures in column 6 describe the behavior of the firm's average variable cost. **Average variable cost** (AVC) is calculated by dividing the total variable cost at a given output level by the amount of output produced. For instance, if our lumber mill was producing six units of output (6,000 feet of lumber), its AVC would be $1,350/6 = $225. As you can see from the table, average variable cost declines initially and then rises as output continues to expand. The reason for this behavior will be provided a little later.

Average total cost (ATC) is always equal to average fixed cost plus average variable cost. For instance, the average total cost of producing four units of output is equal to the average fixed cost of $45 *plus* the average variable cost of $225; that means that *ATC* is equal to $270. Average total cost can also be computed by dividing the total cost at a particular level of output by the number of units of output. Using that technique, we find that the average total cost of producing four units of output is $1,080/4 = $270, the same answer as before. As you can see from column 7, average total cost declines initially and then rises.

Marginal Cost

Average total cost is useful in gauging a firm's efficiency in production, but the concept of marginal cost plays the more important role in guiding production decisions. As we learned in Chapter 5, the term *marginal* means "extra" or "additional." Thus, **marginal cost (MC)** is the additional cost of producing one more unit of output. It is equal to the change in total cost from one unit of output to the next. Consider, for example, the marginal cost of the first unit of output—the first thousand feet of lumber—in Exh. 6.3. If it costs the firm $180

EXHIBIT 6.3
The Marginal Cost of Manufacturing Pine Lumber

OUTPUT PER DAY (thousands of feet of lumber)	TOTAL COST (TC)	MARGINAL COST (MC)
0	$ 180	—
1	450	$270
2	690	240
3	900	210
4	1,080	180
5	1,290	210
6	1,530	240
7	1,800	270
8	2,130	330
9	2,520	390
10	2,970	450

Marginal cost is the additional cost of producing one more unit of output. For example, if it costs the firm $1,290 to produce five units of lumber and $1,530 to produce six units of lumber, the marginal cost of the sixth unit of lumber is $240.

to produce zero output (remember fixed costs) and $450 to produce one unit of output, the marginal cost of the first unit of lumber is $270. The *MC* of the second unit of output is $240, the difference between *TC* $450 and *TC* $690. Take a few moments to compute the marginal costs for the remaining units of output, using the total cost column in Exh. 6.3. Then, check your answers against the marginal cost column in that exhibit.

THE COST CURVES

The information scheduled in Exhs. 6.2 and 6.3 is depicted as cost curves in Exh. 6.4. We read cost curves in much the same way we read the demand and supply curves presented in Chapter 3. If we are interested in knowing the average total cost of producing three units of output, for example, we find three units on the horizontal axis, move directly up from that quantity to the *ATC* curve (point *A*), move across to the vertical axis, and read $300. The *ATC* of producing three units of output is $300 per unit. To determine the *AVC* when six units are being produced, we find that quantity on the horizontal axis, move directly up to the *AVC* curve (point *B*), move across to the vertical axis, -

EXHIBIT 6.4
A Graphic Look at Costs

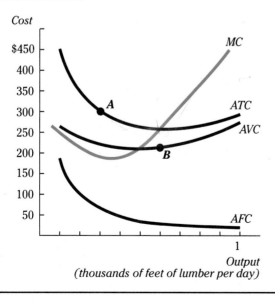

Cost curves show the way a particular type of cost is related to the level of output. Average fixed cost (*AFC*) declines as output increases. Marginal cost (*MC*), average variable cost (*AVC*), and average total cost (*ATC*) graph as U-shaped curves; that is, these types of costs decline initially and then rise.

and read $225. The *AVC* of producing six units of output is $225. The other cost curves are read in the same way.

Cost curves help us see how a particular cost behaves as the level of output changes. Note that *AFC* declines as output increases, reflecting the spreading of fixed costs over more units of output. The marginal cost curve and the average cost curves (*AVC* and *ATC*) decline initially and then begin to increase as output expands, giving them a U shape. As you read the following sections, you will see why the curves behave this way.

The Marginal Cost Curve

Why does marginal cost first decline and then increase? As you've already learned, marginal cost is the additional cost of producing one more unit of output. It is a variable cost because it changes as output changes. The shape of the marginal cost curve, therefore, must be related to some specific variable cost—often the cost of labor.

Let's see how changing labor costs can account for the U-shaped curve in Exh. 6.4. The labor cost of producing an additional unit of output depends on the amount of labor time it takes to produce that unit. If our firm is paying its workers $10 per hour and it takes eight hours of labor to produce the additional unit, the labor cost of that unit is $80. Keep in mind that the amount of labor time it takes to produce each additional unit of output is not constant. It depends on the degree of *specialization* of labor, the extent to which workers perform a single task rather than several. Workers who specialize do their jobs better, which means lower *MC*.

When a firm is producing relatively little output, the labor cost of producing an additional unit tends to be high. Because output is low, the few workers employed are required to perform a variety of diverse tasks. But the diversity of the tasks prevents workers from becoming proficient at any of them, and so a substantial amount of labor time is required to complete each task, and the cost of producing additional units is high. For instance, if you were attempting to run our hypothetical sawmill alone, you would be required to saw the logs, plane the boards to smooth them, stack the lumber for drying, and clean and service the equipment. With all these tasks to perform, you probably wouldn't become very proficient at any of them. As a consequence, the time required to accomplish each task would be relatively high. In addition, time would be wasted in moving from task to task. These factors result in a high marginal cost ($270) for the first unit of lumber.

As output expands and more workers are hired, workers can specialize in one or a few jobs and thereby become better at them. For instance, if the lumber mill needs to hire two workers to keep up with demand, one of them might do all the sawing while the other planes the boards and stacks them for drying. This greater specialization permits workers to become more proficient at their jobs and reduces the time wasted in moving between jobs. The result is a lower marginal cost for the second unit of output ($240) and an even lower cost for the third ($210) and fourth ($180) because the amount of labor time required to produce these additional units of output is reduced.

As long as the advantages of increased specialization allow our mill to expand output more rapidly than employment (and labor cost), marginal cost will continue to fall. But that won't happen indefinitely. Remember: In the short run the mill must operate with a fixed amount of plant and equipment. This restriction limits the degree of specialization possible. At some point the mill's equipment will be fully utilized, and the major advantages of specialization will be exhausted. Once the sawmill has someone working full-time on the sawing machine, the planing machine, and the forklift, further gains from specialization may be difficult to achieve. Additional workers will still allow the firm to expand output (by bringing materials to the saw operator, for example, or filling in while she takes lunch breaks), but the gain in output will be smaller than before. Workers will sometimes find themselves idle because they are waiting to use equipment. And the space limitations of a fixed plant may ultimately lead to congestion and reduce output gains even further. For these reasons the marginal cost of producing an additional unit of output will ultimately rise, as it does in our example when output is expanded from four to five units of lumber.[2]

In summary, if a firm continues to expand output in the short run, eventually it will overutilize its fixed plant and equipment, causing marginal cost to rise. This principle is simply an extension of the law of increasing costs introduced in Chapter 1.

The Relationship between Marginal and Average Costs

Marginal cost is related to average variable cost and average total cost in a very precise way. In Exh. 6.4 you'll notice that the *MC* curve intersects the *AVC* curve at the lowest point, or minimum, of the *AVC* curve. This point is not a chance intersection but is due to the relationship between marginal

---

[2] The fixed factor need not be plant and equipment; in agriculture it might be land. As a farmer adds units of fertilizer (or some other variable input such as labor, irrigation water, or insecticide) to a fixed plot of land, the second unit of fertilizer may increase the output of corn by more than the first unit, and the third unit of fertilizer may increase output by more than the second. Thus, the cost of producing each additional bushel of corn declines initially because it takes less fertilizer (and therefore less expenditure on fertilizer) to produce it.

Again, this process can't continue indefinitely. Eventually it will reach the point at which the fixed land is being overutilized, the point at which the next unit of fertilizer applied to the land will yield less additional output than the unit before it. When that happens, the marginal cost of producing the next bushel of corn will rise. In other words, the marginal cost curve will turn upward.

and average cost values. A simple example will help clarify this relationship. Let's assume that you want to know the average weight of the students in your class. To determine the class average, you coax each student onto the scales, add up the individual weights, and then divide by the number of students in the class. If an additional (marginal) student who weighs more than the average joins the class, the average will be pulled up. If the additional student weighs less than the previous class average, the average will be pulled down. As you can see, the marginal value determines what happens to the average.

Essentially the same logic applies to the cost curves. Notice that so long as the MC curve is below the AVC curve, the AVC is falling; the marginal value is pulling down the average just as the thin student pulled down the class average. However, when MC is above AVC, AVC is rising; the marginal value is pulling the average up. When MC = AVC—that is, when MC and AVC intersect—the average will remain unchanged. As you can see, the shape of the AVC curve depends largely on the behavior of marginal cost. Thus, if MC declines initially and then increases as output continues to expand, AVC must display the same general behavior.

The shape of the ATC curve is also influenced by marginal cost but in a somewhat more complex manner. Recall that average total cost is the sum of average fixed cost and average variable cost. Initially both AVC and AFC decline, and so ATC declines as well. But note that ATC continues to decline after AVC has turned upward. This occurs because AFC is continuing to decline, and for a while the downward pull of AFC outweighs the upward pull of AVC. Eventually the increase in AVC will more than offset the decrease in AFC, and ATC will begin to rise. Thus, ATC will have the same basic shape as AVC, but the minimum point on the curve will occur at a somewhat higher output. (An increase in the cost of inputs—higher wage rates or raw materials prices, for instance—would shift the cost curves upward without altering the basic relationship between the curves. A reduction in input costs would have the opposite effect; it would shift the curves downward.)

In summary, the marginal cost curve plays a major role in determining the shape of both the average variable and average total cost curves. As you will see in a moment, marginal cost also plays a major role in guiding the production decisions of the competitive firm.

PROFIT MAXIMIZATION IN THE SHORT RUN

Because the purely competitive firm is a price taker, in effect bound to the price determined by the market, the only variable it can control to maximize its profit (when market conditions permit a profit) or minimize its loss (when a loss is unavoidable) is the level of output.

In the short run the purely competitive firm can produce any level of output within the capacity of its existing plant and equipment. It adjusts its output by altering the amount of variable resources (labor and raw materials, for example) that it employs in conjunction with its fixed plant and equipment. In the long run, of course, the firm has additional options for expanding or contracting production.

Determining the Profit-Maximizing Output

How do firms go about selecting the profit-maximizing level of output? They behave as you and I do when making a decision about how to spend our time and money: They compare costs and benefits. In fact, the process of selecting the profit-maximizing (loss-minimizing) level of output can be likened to a series of cost-benefit comparisons. Imagine a production manager repeatedly asking the same question: Does the benefit from producing one more unit of output exceed the cost? As long as the answer is yes, it is sensible for the firm to continue expanding output. When the answer is no, the firm should go no further.

For a business the benefit from producing and selling output is the revenue it takes in. **Marginal revenue** (*MR*) is the additional revenue to be gained by selling one more unit of output. When firms are price takers, *MR* is always equal to price because the additional revenue to be gained by selling one more unit is exactly the market price (*MR* = *P*). This price must be compared with marginal cost, the cost of producing one more unit of output. A firm seeking to achieve the profit-maximizing output will continue to increase production as long as price or marginal revenue exceeds marginal cost. When price exceeds marginal cost (*P* > *MC*), each additional unit produced makes the firm better off because it adds more to the firm's revenue than to its cost.

Exhibit 6.5 illustrates this decision-making process in action. The market price in this example is $270, so that each additional unit produced will add $270 to revenue. If we begin our cost-benefit comparison with the fifth unit of output, we can see that the $270 the firm gains from producing this unit is more than the $210 marginal cost of that unit. In short, the firm will be $60 better off for producing that unit. The firm should produce the sixth unit as well. Although marginal cost rises to $240 for that unit, it is still less than the $270 selling price, leaving the firm $30 better off. (It is important to recognize that although the sixth unit adds less to profit than the fifth unit, it continues to enlarge the firm's total profit, and so it should be produced.)[3]

---

[3] With the information provided thus far, we cannot determine whether this firm is earning a profit or incurring a loss. But we can say that by producing the sixth unit, the firm will either enlarge its total profit or reduce its total loss. You'll see how to determine the profit or loss in just a moment.

The seventh unit of output is a little trickier to evaluate. It brings in no more revenue ($270) than it costs to produce ($270), so the firm should be neutral or indifferent toward its production. Economists generally assume, however, that the firm will go ahead and produce that unit. As we noted in Chapter 5, this assumption provides us with a simple rule for selecting the profit-maximizing output: Produce the level of output at which $MR = MC$, the output that corresponds to the point where the MR and MC curves intersect. In instances when there is no whole-number unit of output for which MR is exactly equal to MC, the firm should produce all the units for which $MR > MC$ but no unit for which $MC > MR$.

Marginal Cost and Firm Supply

Because the purely competitive firm determines the profit-maximizing output by equating price and marginal cost, any change in the prevailing market price will alter the amount of output it will choose to produce. Suppose, for example, that the existing market price was $330 instead of $270. You can see from Exh. 6.5 that if the firm's demand curve was horizontal at that price, the firm would expand output to eight units per day (the output at which the demand curve would intersect the MC curve). Alternatively, a price of $240 would

EXHIBIT 6.5
The Profit-Maximizing Output

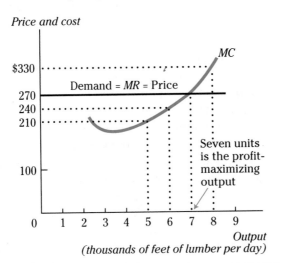

The profit-maximizing firm should continue to expand output until $MR = MC$. In this case profit maximization (or loss minimization) occurs at an output of seven units (7,000 feet) of lumber per day.

cause the firm to produce less; the demand curve would intersect the *MC* curve at six units. As you can see, the competitive firm always operates along its marginal cost curve, supplying whatever output is dictated by its intersection with the prevailing market price (the firm's demand curve). For that reason, the marginal cost curve can be thought of as the firm's supply curve because it indicates how much the firm will produce or "supply" at any given price. (Actually, the firm's supply curve is only the portion of the marginal cost curve lying above the average variable cost curve—look back at Exh. 6.4 to see what that means. That's because if price falls below average variable cost, the firm won't produce any output. More about that in a moment.)

Evaluating Profit or Loss

By producing where marginal revenue is equal to marginal cost, the purely competitive firm is doing the best it can; it is either maximizing its profit or minimizing its loss. Marginal values alone, however, will not tell us exactly how well the firm is doing; they will not tell us whether the firm is earning a profit or incurring a loss, and they will not tell us the amount of the profit or loss. To answer those questions, we need to calculate and compare the firm's total revenue and total cost. You already know that total revenue is computed by multiplying the selling price of the product by the number of units sold. To compute total cost, we need the information provided by the average total cost curve. Multiplying the *ATC* by the number of units of output produced gives us the total cost of producing the output level. (Recall that we get our per unit cost, or *ATC*, by performing the reverse operation: dividing *TC* at a particular level of output by the number of units.) By comparing total revenue with total cost, we can determine the profit or loss of the firm. Some examples should help clarify this procedure.

Profits, Losses, and Breaking Even

Exhibit 6.6 shows a purely competitive firm in three different short-run situations. As you study the three cases, keep in mind that market price equals *MR* under conditions of pure competition. And the *MR* = *P* curve is the demand curve for the purely competitive firm. In each case the firm is producing where the *MC* curve intersects the demand curve, where *MC* = *MR*, but it is experiencing different degrees of success in these three situations. In part (a), the firm is enjoying an above-normal, or economic, profit. The amount of this profit can be determined by comparing total revenue with total cost. Total revenue is equal to $1,890 (the $270 selling price × 7 units), whereas total cost is only $1,799 (*ATC* of $257 × 7 units). Therefore, the firm is earning an economic profit of $91. (Alternatively, we could determine the firm's profit by multiplying the average, or per-unit, profit by the number of units sold.

EXHIBIT 6.6
Finding the Profit or Loss

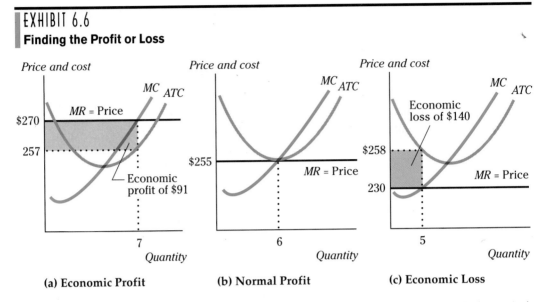

(a) Economic Profit   **(b) Normal Profit**   **(c) Economic Loss**

All firms maximize their profits or minimize their losses by producing the level of output at which marginal revenue is equal to marginal cost. In some instances a firm will be able to earn an above-normal, or *economic*, profit. In other instances only a normal profit–zero economic profit–will be possible. Finally, in some cases an economic loss–less than a normal profit–will be the best the firm can do.

Here the firm is earning a profit of $13 per unit [$270 − $257 = $13] and selling seven units; total profit is $13 × 7 = $91.)

In part (b) the firm isn't doing as well. Its total revenue of $1,530 ($255 × 6 units) exactly matches its total cost, so that the firm is breaking even; it is earning zero economic profit. Remember, zero economic profit is the same as normal profit, the amount the owners of the business could expect to earn if they invested their resources elsewhere. In part (c) the firm has fallen on hard times. Price is now so low that it will no longer cover average total cost. Indeed, the firm will be earning less than a normal profit and therefore facing an **economic loss:** total cost, including all opportunity cost, will exceed total revenue. In our example the total cost is $1,290 ($258 × 5 units), whereas its total revenue is only $1,150 (*ATC* of $230 × 5 units), a loss of $140. (Note that if we multiply the per-unit loss of $28 × 5 units, we arrive at the same $140 figure for the firm's total loss.)

Operating with a Loss

Why would the company continue to produce in part (c)? Why not simply close down the business and not reopen until conditions improve? The an-

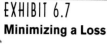

EXHIBIT 6.7

Minimizing a Loss

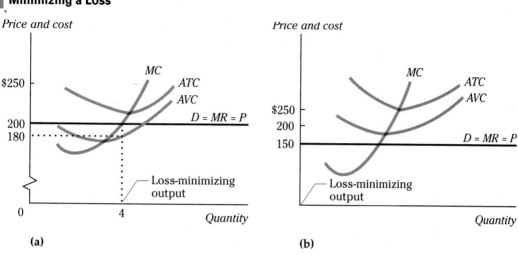

Whenever price exceeds average variable cost (P > AVC), the firm will minimize its loss by continuing to operate. This is the situation represented in part (a), where the firm will continue to produce despite an economic loss. When price is less than average variable cost (P < AVC), the firm will minimize its loss by shutting down. This situation is represented in part (b).

swer has to do with fixed costs, or overhead, which must be paid whether or not any output is produced. If a firm shuts down temporarily—if it stays in the industry but stops producing output—its loss will equal its total fixed costs. But if the price the firm can get for its product is high enough to allow the firm to cover its variable costs (costs that would not exist if the firm shut down) and pay *some* of its fixed costs, the firm will be better off if it continues to operate. This is why U.S. wheat farmers continued to produce in the mid-1980s despite substantial losses, and why cattle ranchers kept raising cattle in the mid-1990s, even though prices were at a 10-year low and well below average total cost. In both cases, continuing to operate resulted in smaller losses than would have been incurred by shutting down. When price dips so low that the firm can no longer recover even the variable cost of production, it will shut down and wait for better times.

Exhibit 6.7 illustrates these two situations. In part (a) the selling price of $200 is greater than the average variable cost of $180, so that each unit the firm produces (up to the point at which MR = MC) provides it with $20 ($200 − $180 = $20) to help pay its fixed costs. Although the firm will still incur

USE YOUR ECONOMIC REASONING

Fishermen in Alaska, Awash in Salmon, Strive to Stay Afloat

By Bill Richards
Staff reporter of The Wall Street Journal

ROCKY POINT, Alaska—
Hundreds of silvery salmon thrash and flash as they pour out of the net and into the hold of Michael Meint's 42-foot fishing boat, Jimani. In the background, clouds boil against steep, rocky hillsides and chunks of blue glacial ice drift across Prince William Sound.

It is a picture-postcard scene of a dying industry.

Alaska is awash in salmon. Huge fish runs have been building here. Combined with growing salmon output from sources like Chilean fish farms and Russian fishing fleets, they are glutting the market and driving wholesale prices to record lows. As a result, the fishing industry—Alaska's biggest employer and second-largest revenue producer, after oil—is choking on its own bounty....

Anywhere else that would be an elementary lesson in supply and demand. But Alaska's $1 billion salmon industry is different. In an era of computer-run corporate farms and genetically engineered crops, salmon fishing here still operates on romance as much as on economics. Fisherman sneer at foreign fish farms and boast they are "the last hunter-gatherers." In the small salmon-fishing ports tucked along Prince William Sound's serrated shoreline, pickup trucks bear bumper stickers that say, "Real salmon don't eat pellets."

"If you're in the beef or chicken business, you set up to produce according to market demand," says Kenneth Roemhildt, who manages a cannery in Cordova for North

a loss, continued operation will make the loss smaller than it would be if the firm shut down and paid its fixed costs. In part (b) the $150 price is less than the *AVC* of $175, and so each unit the firm produces increases its total loss by $25. This firm would be better off to shut down, accept its fixed-cost loss, and wait for business conditions to improve. Of course, if losses continue for an extended period, eventually the firm will be forced out of business. In summary, when $P > AVC$, the firm will minimize its loss by continuing to operate; when $P < AVC$, the firm should shut down. (The above article , "Fisherman in Alaska ... Strive to Stay Afloat," illustrates how market conditions can lead to losses and how firms attempt to make the best of the situation.)

Pacific Processors Inc., one of four salmon processors on the city's waterfront. "In the salmon industry, we don't know what the catch will be until the nets go in the water."

That strategy worked fine in the past, when Alaska's salmon had no real competition....But Alaska can't control fish farms springing up in Norway, Chile, Canada and states like Washington and Maine. Farm-raised fish account for about half the world's salmon sales, up from 7% a decade ago. Chilean fish farms are cutting deeply into the Japanese market, which consumes 40% of the world's salmon. Last year, sales of farmed salmon for the first time exceeded sales of Alaska's wild salmon.

"The hunter-gatherers are trying to compete with the farmers, and, just like everywhere else, the hunter-gatherers are losing," says William Gilbert, who operates Norquest Seafoods Inc.'s cannery in Cordova....

At the Fishermen United storefront headquarters in Cordova, posters on the wall tout salmon cheeseburgers, salmon sandwiches and other salmon dishes. But Executive Director Dorne Hawxhurst says many of her group's 300 members have given up fishing for pinks. "The ones that haven't are fishing their brains out and going broke," she says.

Mr. Meints falls in the latter category. On a recent three-day trip, he and his crew spent 20-hour days pulling a total of 80,000 pounds of pinks out of Prince William Sound. That kind of catch would have grossed nearly $64,000 for the Jimani and its crew in the past. But this year, Mr. Meints says, watching another load of fish come up over the side of the boat, "at five cents a pound, its hardly worth the effort." Mr Meints says that even though he is losing money, he needs to keep fishing to generate cash flow to pay bills. But if he hits his million-pound target this summer, the boat will gross only $80,000, even after he gets an additional three cents a pound for storing his catch in freezing brine....

Use Your Economic Reasoning

1. Why had the market price of salmon fallen so low?
2. How do you explain the fact that some fishermen have stopped fishing but others continue even though they are losing money? Represent each situation graphically.
3. Do you think that any "hunter-gatherers" will still be fishing for salmon 20 years from now? If they can't make money today, is that situation likely to change in the future? (*Hint*: You may want to read the discussion of the long run and return to this question later.)
4. Recall that solving the economic problem means addressing three fundamental questions: What to produce? How to produce? For whom to produce? Which of these questions do you think the article most clearly illustrates? Defend your conclusion.

PROFIT MAXIMIZATION IN THE LONG RUN

In the short run the purely competitive firm must do the best it can with fixed plant and equipment, but in the long run the firm has many more options; all costs are variable in the long run. If the industry has been profitable, the firm may decide to expand the size of its production plant or otherwise increase its productive capacity. If losses have been common, it can sell out and invest in another industry, one in which the prospects for profits appear brighter. In the short run the number of firms in an industry remains constant—time is inadequate for firms to enter or leave. But in the long run there is time for these adjustments to occur, and the industry can expand or contract. In this section we examine how firms in a purely competitive industry adjust to the presence or absence of short-run profits and how this adjustment process eventually leads to long-run equilibrium for the industry. **Long-run equilibrium** is a situation in which the size of an industry is stable: There is no incentive for additional firms to enter the industry and no pressure for existing firms to leave.

Setting the Stage: The Short-Run Picture

In Exh. 6.8 we follow the path by which a purely competitive firm and industry arrive at long-run equilibrium. Each panel shows the demand and supply curves for the industry on the left and the diagram for a representative firm on the right. In part (a) the industry demand and supply curves establish a price of $300. The representative firm takes that price as a given and maximizes its profit by producing where $MC = MR$. Because the representative firm is earning an economic profit in the short run, additional firms will be attracted to this industry in the long run.

The Entrance of Firms: Attraction of Profits

The entrance of additional firms is made possible by one of the assumptions of the purely competitive model—the absence of significant barriers to entry. As additional firms enter the industry, they will increase industry supply and depress the market price. The increase in industry supply occurs because the industry supply curve is the sum of all the firms' supply curves and is found by adding together those curves.[4] If additional firms enter the industry, the curves of those firms must be added, shifting the industry curve to the right. This adjustment is represented in the left-hand graph of Exh. 6.8(b), where supply has increased to S_1 and intersects the demand curve to establish a new price of $270. Note that at the new price the firms in the industry are still able to earn economic profits; ATC is still below $MR = P$. As a consequence, firms will continue to enter the industry until the price falls to $255, where the demand curve and S_2 intersect in part (c), and price is consistent with normal profits.

---

[4] Summing the supply curves of all the firms is relatively easy (remember, each firm's supply curve is its marginal cost curve above average variable cost). We simply add up the quantities that the firms will supply at each market price. For simplicity, suppose that there are only two firms in our industry. If firm A supplies 5 units at $300 and firm B supplies 7 units at the same price, the industry supply curve would show 12 units being supplied at $300. The amount supplied by the industry at other prices would be determined in the same manner.

EXHIBIT 6.8
The Long-Run Adjustment Process

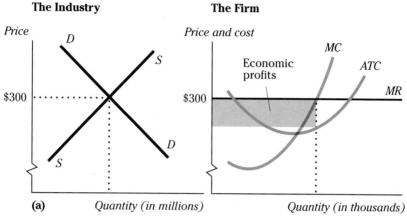

The Industry   **The Firm**

(a) At a price of $300, the firms in the industry will be able to earn an economic profit. Since above-normal profits are being earned, additional firms will be attracted to the industry. This development is reflected in (b).

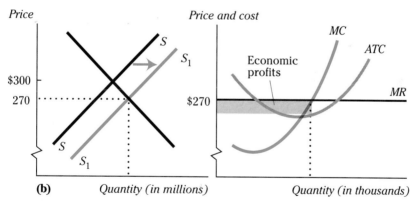

(b) As additional firms enter the industry, the industry supply curve will shift from S to S_1 and price will be forced down to $270. However, since that price still permits an economic profit to be earned, additional firms will enter the industry, as revealed in (c), on the next page.

Once the price of $255 is established, both the firm and the industry are in long-run equilibrium: they have achieved a state of balance, a situation in which there is no tendency for further change. The industry is in long-run equilibrium because at zero profit there is no incentive for additional firms to

EXHIBIT 6.8 (CONT.)

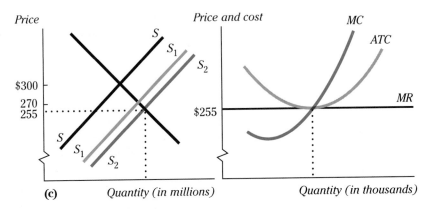

(c) The entrance of additional firms will shift the supply curve to S_2 and depress market price to $255. At that price the firms in the industry will be able to earn only a normal profit. There will be no incentive for additional firms to enter the industry, and the industry will be in long-run equilibrium.

enter it and no incentive for established firms to leave it. The individual firms are in equilibrium because they have no incentive to alter their level of output so long as the market price remains at $255. (An Internet ad offers to show you how to turn 25 cents into a $20 bill. Sound too good to be true? Read "Rare Air," on page 180, and decide for yourself.)

The Exit of Firms: Looking for Greener Pastures

If a purely competitive industry undergoes short-run economic losses, a similar adjustment process is likely to result. In the long run some firms will respond to the short-run losses (less than normal profits) by leaving the industry to search for a better opportunity elsewhere. As these firms exit, industry supply decreases and the market price rises. Firms will continue to leave the industry until the market price has risen sufficiently to afford the remaining firms exactly a normal profit. When that happens, the exodus will cease; the firms and the industry will be in long-run equilibrium.

THE BENEFITS OF PURE COMPETITION

As we noted at the beginning of this chapter, economists often use the model of pure competition as an ideal by which to judge other, less competitive industry structures. Economists hold pure competition in such high esteem primarily because it would lead to an efficient use of our scarce resources.

Production Efficiency

One of the most important features of pure competition is its tendency to promote **production efficiency:** production at the lowest possible average total cost, or minimum *ATC*. As you look at Exh. 6.9, you'll see that the purely competitive firm is in long-run equilibrium when it is producing at the output level where its *ATC* curve is tangent to, or barely touching, its demand curve. This tangency occurs at the lowest point on the firm's *ATC* curve, showing that the firm is producing at the lowest possible average cost. In essence, this means that the product is being produced with as few scarce resources as possible. Production efficiency is a benefit of pure competition; it allows us to spread our scarce resources across more products, and in so doing it enables us to satisfy more of society's unlimited wants.

Note also that in long-run equilibrium, consumers are able to purchase the product at a price equal to this minimum *ATC*. This must be true because at the tangency point in Exh. 6.9, Price (*MR*) = *ATC*. Thus, we can see that the

---

EXHIBIT 6.9

The Competitive Firm in Long-Run Equilibrium

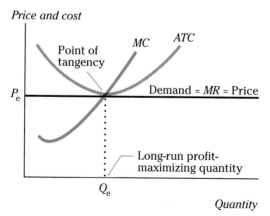

In long-run equilibrium the competitive firm will earn only a normal profit. This is indicated in the graph by the tangency between the demand curve, or price line, and the ATC curve at the profit-maximizing output (where *MR(P)* = *MC*). The equality of price and minimum *ATC* indicates that the firm is achieving *production efficiency*.

USE YOUR ECONOMIC REASONING

Rare Air

By Steve Rubenstein

PEOPLE were breathing on Valencia Street the other night, and it only cost $10.

Breathing is hot. Breathing is the latest thing. Breathing cannot be recommended too highly.

And the $10 price includes a stylish plastic tube to stick up your nose, just like in the finest emergency rooms.

"It's silly," said Tracy Burt, a San Francisco teacher who said it was the first time she had ever paid to breathe. "That's part of the ambience."

Burt was among a dozen ambience-hungry folks who dropped by the other night at 22 O 2, the brand new oxygen bar in San Francisco where customers sit on barstools and inhale oxygen-enriched air, which is supposed to be good for what ails you.

Oxygen bars have popped up in Tokyo, New York and Hollywood, but the modest nightspot at 19th and Valencia streets, which opened for business last month, is the first one in the Bay Area.

"Every cell in the body needs oxygen," said proprietor Kim Passeneau, a San Francisco nurse who sank her life savings into the enterprise. "Without oxygen, the body will shut down and perish."

No such thing was happening to the paying clientele, a testament to the power of air. A half-dozen folks were belly up to the bar, using each of the six available connections to the oxygen machine. That meant you had to wait in line to breathe.

The machine, a beige contraption with glowing lights that sat beneath the counter, converts regular air, which is 20 percent oxygen, into superduper air, which is 85 percent oxygen, Passeneau said.

At the new oxygen bar, breathing is within the means of every customer. The longer you breathe, Passeneau said, the more you save. The first 10 minutes costs $1 a minute, but after that the cost of breathing drops to 50 cents a minute.

Source: © San Francisco Chronicle, October 9, 2000, p. A17. Reprinted with permission.

benefits of production efficiency are passed on to consumers. They receive the lowest possible price, given the cost conditions that exist in the industry.

Allocative Efficiency

If pure competition resulted in the efficient production of millions of buggy whips or other products not in much demand, consumers obviously would not be pleased. However, pure competition also leads to **allocative efficiency:** Producers use society's scarce resources to provide consumers with the proper quantities of the goods and services they desire most. Economists ar-

Each customer chooses one of six flavors of oxygen from the menu. "Relax" is lavender-scented oxygen, "Aphrodisiac" is sandalwood-scented and "Euphoric" is lemon-scented.

No alcohol is served. Instead, customers may sip a $6 "herbal elixir" of ginseng, deer antlers and crushed red and black ants.

"This is the first time I've ever paid for air," said Massachia Giovanni, an actress who was sniffing 10 minutes of Aphrodisiac. "I guess that means that anything is possible."

Karen Solomon paid for 20 minutes of air and said she would have liked to go longer but she had only so much breathing money.

"I can't afford much more," she said. Passeneau let her breathe 10 additional minutes free of charge, as an opening week special, then reluctantly cut her off by yanking her hose.

"I don't like to kick anyone out," [said] Passeneau, "but you can't let it go on forever."

Passeneau bought her oxygen "enricher" machine from the same outfit that supplied actor Woody Harrelson's famous oxygen bar in Hollywood. That place shut down months ago, because in Los Angeles even breathing can fall out of fashion.

All is not lost for customers who cannot afford the $10 for oxygen or $6 for red-ant elixir. Behind the bar is a Life Energy Amplification machine, a shiny chrome gizmo that spews out a "bioenergetic energy field" of blissful vibrations into the entire bar, to paying and non-paying customers alike.

"That one's on the house," said the barkeep.

Use Your Economic Reasoning

1. There are relatively low barriers to entering the oxygen bar industry. All that is required is a modest investment and some instructions on how to obtain and handle oxygen. Does that mean it's a purely competitive industry? Defend your answer.

2. In an Internet ad, the National Oxygen Bar Association (NOBA) offered to teach you how "Oxygen bars turn 25 cents of pure oxygen into $20 bills with hundreds of customers daily." What reaction is this advertisement attempting to elicit from readers? Would that be your reaction? Why or why not?

3. Kim Passeneau, the proprietor of the 22 O 2 oxygen bar, has customers waiting in line to buy oxygen. That sounds like she may be earning economic profits. Try to represent that situation graphically. Do you think Ms. Passeneau is in long-run equilibrium? Explain.

4. According to the article, Woody Harrelson's oxygen bar closed because oxygen bars became less fashionable in Hollywood. Is that the only long-run threat that Kim Passeneau needs to be concerned about? Try to represent your concerns graphically.

gue that if pure competition prevailed throughout the economy, all our scarce resources would be allocated or distributed so as to produce the precise mix of products that consumers desire most.

Allocative efficiency requires that each product be produced up to the point at which the benefit its consumption provides to society (*marginal social benefit*) is exactly equal to the cost its production imposes on society (*marginal social cost*). In most instances, the benefits that a product provides to society are simply the benefits received by those who purchase the product. The value of these benefits is reflected in the price that consumers are willing to pay; the greater the benefit, the higher the price. This, in turn, can be determined from the industry demand curve. For instance, if consumers are willing to purchase 1,000 units of lumber at $300 and 1,001 units of lumber at $299, then the maximum price that consumers are willing to pay for the 1,001st unit of output must be $299 (since they were unwilling to purchase that unit at $300).[5]

Marginal social cost represents what society must give up to produce an additional unit of the product; in other words, it represents opportunity cost. Opportunity cost is generally reflected in the costs that the businesses incur to produce the product. In the case of pure competition, this can be determined from the industry supply curve. Because the industry supply curve is the sum of the firms' supply curves, it can be thought of as the marginal cost curve of the industry. (Remember: Under conditions of pure competition, the individual firm's supply curve is its marginal cost curve; so the industry supply curve is simply the sum of those curves.) By turning to the marginal cost curve (the industry supply curve), we can determine the sacrifice that society must make to produce an additional unit of the product in question. For instance, if the marginal cost of an additional unit of lumber is $200, that means that society must do without $200 worth of alternative goods—whatever products the same amount of raw materials, labor, and capital could have produced—in order to obtain this unit of lumber.[6]

As long as the marginal social benefit from an additional unit of output exceeds the marginal social cost, it is in society's interest to continue expanding production. This point is illustrated in Exh. 6.10. Suppose the industry chose to produce Q_A units of output. As you can see from the diagram, the marginal social benefit of the last unit of output is $300, while the marginal social cost is only $270; clearly, output should be expanded since consumers value additional units of lumber more than the alternative products they could receive instead. If the industry chose to produce Q_B units, it would have carried production too far. The marginal social benefit of the last unit produced is equal to only $270, while the marginal social cost is equal to $300. Society would be better off if more resources were allocated to the production of other things and fewer to the production of lumber.

The optimal, or allocatively efficient, level of production occurs where the marginal social benefit and marginal social cost intersect, Q_E in our example. At that output the value of the benefit consumers receive from the last unit produced

---

[5] In some instances the consumption of a product conveys benefits to individuals in addition to those who purchased the product. For instance, when you purchase a flu shot, you benefit, but so do others (who will not get the flu from you). These *external benefits* are not reflected in the industry demand curve. Chapter 9 will discuss the impact of external benefits on the efficient allocation of resources.
[6] In some instances the costs incurred by a business do not reflect all the costs associated with the production of a product. For instance, if a firm disposes of wastes by dumping them into a river in order to minimize its disposal costs, that action may kill fish and impose cleanup costs on other parties. These *external costs* are not reflected in the firm's cost curves. Chapter 9 will examine the impact of external costs on the allocation of scarce resources.

EXHIBIT 6.10
Pure Competition and Allocation Efficiency

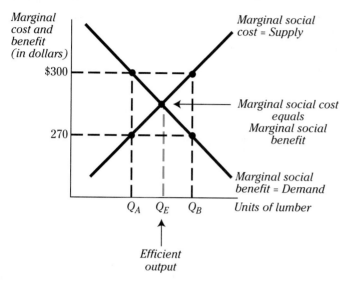

Allocative efficiency requires that each product be produced up to the point at which the marginal social benefit of the last unit produced is equal to the marginal social cost. That output is found where the demand and supply curves intersect, at Q_E in this example.

is exactly equal to the value of the alternative goods that must be sacrificed for its production. Pure competition ensures this outcome. Purely competitive industries always produce at the output level where the demand (marginal social benefit) and supply (marginal social cost) curves intersect. Therefore, pure competition ensures the efficient allocation of society's scarce resources.[7]

Let's synthesize what we have just discussed: Under conditions of pure competition, self-interest-seeking producers are guided by the presence or absence of profits to produce the right amounts of the products that consumers desire most. The forces of competition also lead to long-run equilibrium, whereby all firms in the industry operate at the lowest possible average cost (minimum *ATC*) and receive a price just equal to that cost. Thus, in the long run, consumers are able to purchase their most-desired products at the lowest possible prices.

---

[7] This conclusion assumes that there are no external costs or benefits associated with the production or consumption of the product. (See footnotes 5 and 6 for examples of external costs and benefits.) When *externalities* (external costs or benefits) exist, the industry supply and demand curves will not fully reflect social costs and benefits, and resources will be allocated inefficiently. This possibility will be considered in Chapter 9.

SUMMARY

A *firm* is the basic producing unit in a market economy, and an *industry* is a group of firms that produce similar or identical products. A purely competitive industry is one in which (1) a large number of sellers (firms) each produce a small fraction of the total industry supply; (2) the products offered by the different sellers are identical in the minds of consumers; and (3) no substantial barriers exist to prevent firms from entering or leaving the industry.

The purely competitive model is useful in analyzing the behavior of any industry that comes reasonably close to meeting the assumptions of the model. In addition, it provides a standard by which to judge the performance of less competitive industries.

The model of pure competition assumes that firms are profit maximizers; that is, they are always attempting to earn the most profit possible. *Profit* is the excess of a firm's total revenue over its total cost. When a firm's total costs exceed its total revenue, the firm is incurring a *loss*.

All costs can be classified as either fixed or variable. *Fixed costs* are costs that do not vary with the level of output. *Variable costs* are costs that change with the level of output. *Total cost* is simply the sum of the fixed and variable costs incurred by the firm.

The purely competitive firm may be described as a *price taker;* it accepts the price determined by market forces. The only variable that a purely competitive firm can control in order to influence its profit position is the level of output. In order to reach its profit-maximizing level of output, a firm should produce at the point where marginal revenue equals marginal cost. For the purely competitive firm, the price taker, *marginal revenue (MR)* is equal to price, or average revenue per unit sold; *MR* is the revenue earned from selling one more unit of output. *Marginal cost (MC)* is the additional cost of producing one more unit and is a more important concept than *average total cost (ATC)* because it determines the level of output that earns maximum profit.

In the long run, firms in a purely competitive industry tend to earn a *normal profit*, the amount that the owners' resources could earn elsewhere; earning normal profit means breaking even. Above-normal profits are called *economic profits*, and below-normal profits are called *economic losses*. If economic profits exist in the short run, the entrance of additional firms will cause an increase in supply and drive down the market price to the level of zero economic profits, where all firms are breaking even at normal profit. If losses exist, firms will exit the industry until price has risen to a level consistent with normal profits.

When *long-run equilibrium* is finally established, the purely competitive firm will be producing at minimum *ATC*, the point at which its *ATC* curve is tangent to its demand curve. When firms operate at minimum *ATC*, *production efficiency* exists. This is a desirable outcome because it indicates that the fewest possible scarce resources are being used to produce the product and that, therefore, more of society's unlimited wants are being met. In addition to production efficiency, pure competition leads to *allocative efficiency:* the production of the goods and services consumers want most in the quantities they desire. An efficient allocation of resources requires that each product be produced up to the point at which the *marginal social benefit* is equal to the *marginal social cost*. Pure competition ensures this outcome. Thus, we can say that pure competition achieves both production efficiency and allocative efficiency in long-run equilibrium.

KEY TERMS

Allocative efficiency	Firm	Marginal social cost
Average fixed cost (*AFC*)	Fixed costs	Normal profit
Average total cost (*ATC*)	Industry	Price taker
Average variable cost (*AVC*)	Long-run equilibrium	Production efficiency
Barriers to entry	Marginal cost (*MC*)	Total cost (*TC*)
Economic loss	Marginal revenue (*MR*)	Total revenue (*TR*)
Economic profit	Marginal social benefit	Variable costs

STUDY QUESTIONS

Fill in the Blanks

1. A purely competitive firm is sometimes described as a *Price taker* because it must accept the price dictated by the market.

2. The demand curve of the purely competitive firm is a *Horizontal* line at the price determined in the market.

3. Costs that don't vary with output are called *Fixed* costs; costs that vary with output are called *variable* costs.

4. A business that has no output must still pay its *Fixed* costs.

5. *Marginal* cost is the additional cost of producing one more unit of output.

6. Average total cost, *average variable* cost, and *Marginal* cost all graph as U-shaped curves.

7. If a competitive firm wants to maximize its profits, it should continue to produce additional units so long as *Marginal revenue* is greater than or equal to *Marginal cost*.

8. If economic profits exist in the short run, they will tend to be _Eliminated_ in the long run as firms _enter_ the industry and depress market price.

9. If losses exist in the short run, firms will tend to _Exit_ the industry in the long run. This will reduce market _Supply_ and help to push price back up.

10. When $P = MC$, _allocative_ efficiency exists; when a firm produces its product at minimum ATC, _Production_ efficiency exists.

Multiple Choice

1. Which of the following is not characteristic of a purely competitive industry?
   a) A large number of sellers
   b) Identical products
   c) Substantial barriers to entry
   d) Relatively small firms

2. Which of the following is the best example of a price taker?
   a) General Motors
   b) Big Bob's Burger Barn
   c) IBM
   d) An average wheat farmer

   Answer questions 3–5 on the basis of the following information:

QUANTITY	TOTAL COST
0	$10
1	18
2	23
3	30
4	42

3. The firm's fixed cost is
   a) $5.
   b) $42.
   c) $23.
   d) $10.

4. The marginal cost of the third unit would be
   a) $30.
   b) $7.
   c) $10.
   d) $5.

5. If the firm produced three units, average total cost would be
   a) $10.
   b) $30.
   c) $7.
   d) None of the above

6. Which of the following is least likely to be a variable cost?
   a) The cost of raw materials
   b) Insurance payments
   c) The wages of production workers
   d) Shipping expenses

7.

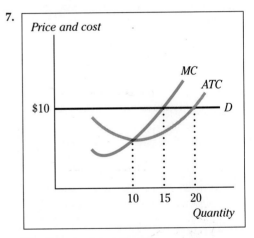

The firm depicted should
   a) produce 10 units and maximize its profits.
   b) produce 15 units and maximize its profits.
   c) produce 10 units and minimize its losses.
   d) produce 15 units and minimize its losses.
   e) shut down.

8.

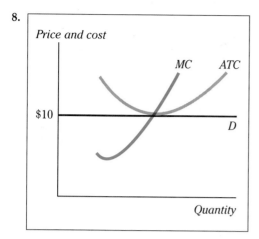

The firm depicted is
a) facing a loss.
b) making an economic profit.
c) making a normal profit.
d) about to go out of business.

9.

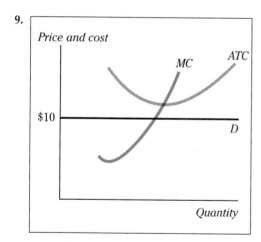

The firm represented is
a) earning a profit.
b) facing a loss.
c) not a competitive firm.
d) breaking even.

10. If the firms in an industry are earning economic profits,
a) additional firms will enter the industry, and the supply curve will shift to the left.

b) some firms will decide to leave the industry, and the supply curve will shift to the left.
c) additional firms will enter the industry, and the supply curve will shift to the right.
d) some firms will leave the industry, and the supply curve will shift to the right.

11. The Lazy Z Ranch is a purely competitive firm producing hogs. Its owner anticipates that at the output where $MR = MC$, the firm's total costs will be $500,000, its total variable costs will be $300,000, and the firm will earn $250,000 in revenue. This firm should
a) raise the price of its hogs.
b) shut down to minimize its loss.
c) continue to produce the present output to minimize its loss.
d) expand its output.

12. Suppose the firms in a purely competitive industry are in a long-run equilibrium when the industry experiences a reduction in demand. Which of the following will occur?
a) In the short run, firms will earn profits and will expand output; in the long run, additional firms will enter the industry until only a normal profit is earned.
b) In the short run, firms will incur losses but will continue to produce the same output; in the long run, firms will leave the industry until only a normal profit is earned.
c) In the short run, firms will earn profits and will contract output; in the long run, firms will leave the industry until the remaining firms can earn an economic profit.
d) In the short run, firms will incur losses and will contract output; in the long run, firms will leave the industry until the remaining firms can earn a normal profit.

13. If the firms in an industry are experiencing short-run losses, they should
a) leave the industry and enter a different, more profitable industry.
b) continue to operate provided that the prevailing market price is higher than the firm's average variable cost.

c) shut down and wait for market conditions to improve.

d) shut down provided that the prevailing market price is less than the firm's average total cost.

14. Suppose that a firm experienced a doubling of its total fixed costs while prevailing market price did not change. Under those conditions the firm would
   a) produce less output and experience lower profits or larger losses.
   b) produce more output and experience higher profits or smaller losses.
   c) produce the same output but experience higher profits or smaller losses.
   d) produce the same output but experience lower profits or larger losses.

15. Which of the following would not cause a competitive firm to increase its output?
   a) An increase in industry demand
   b) A downward shift of the marginal cost curve
   c) An increase in the market price
   d) A wage hike that shifted the marginal cost curve upward

Problems and Questions for Discussion

1. Even when an industry does not meet the first two requirements of pure competition, consumers will still benefit if barriers to entry are low. Why?

2. Complete the following:

QUANTITY	TC	TVC	TFC	MC	ATC
0	$ 50				
1	100				
2	130				
3	180				
4	260				
5	380				

3. One reason for the declining prices of hand-held calculators may be the fat profits earned by early producers. Explain.

4. Can you think of any undesirable aspects of pure competition? From the consumer's standpoint? From the producer's standpoint?

5. Why would a firm continue to operate even though it is incurring a loss? When should it decide to shut down?

6.
QUANTITY	TOTAL COST
0	$ 50
1	100
2	130
3	180
4	260
5	380

If the prevailing price of this firm's product is $50, how many units of output should it produce? Would it earn a profit or incur a loss? How much profit or loss?

7.
QUANTITY	MARGINAL COST
1	$20
2	10
3	30
4	40
5	50

If the prevailing price of our product is $35 and our total fixed costs are $15, how many units of output should we produce? What will be the amount of our profit or loss?

8. Draw the diagrams necessary to show a purely competitive firm and industry in long-run equilibrium.

9. In long-run equilibrium the purely competitive firm is forced to produce where price

equals minimum *ATC*. Why is that good news for consumers?

10. What is meant by allocative efficiency? Why must an industry produce at the output where supply is equal to demand for resources to be allocated efficiently?

ANSWER KEY

Fill in the Blanks

1. price taker
2. horizontal
3. fixed, variable
4. fixed

5. Marginal
6. average variable, marginal
7. marginal revenue, marginal cost

8. eliminated, enter
9. exit, supply
10. allocative, production

Multiple Choice

1. c	4. b	7. b	10. c	13. b
2. d	5. a	8. c	11. b	14. d
3. d	6. b	9. b	12. d	15. d

CHAPTER SEVEN

Price Searching: The Firm with Market Power

LEARNING OBJECTIVES

1. Define market power and discuss its sources.
2. Distinguish between a price searcher and a price taker.
3. Describe a price searcher's demand and marginal revenue curves.
4. Describe how a price searcher determines the profit-maximizing price and output.
5. Define price discrimination, and explain why some firms employ the practice while others do not.
6. Evaluate graphically the extent of a price searcher's profit or loss.
7. Discuss the impact of barriers to entry on the long-run profitability of price searchers.
8. Explain why price searchers distort the allocation of scarce resources.
9. Explain what is meant by economies/diseconomies of scale and how they may influence the number of sellers that survive in a particular industry.

In the world of pure competition the individual firm is a price taker—it has no pricing discretion of its own because price is determined by the impersonal forces of supply and demand. The individual seller manipulates only production output, deciding how much or how little to offer for sale at the given price.

We saw in Chapter 6 that wheat farmers, cattle ranchers, and many other agricultural producers are price takers. But there are few examples of true price takers outside of agriculture. In fact, most sellers in the U.S. economy possess a degree of pricing discretion or **market power**, some ability to influence the market price of their products. In Chapter 7, we examine how firms acquire market power and how these firms select the prices they will charge for their products. We'll explore the circumstances under which firms find it profitable to charge different prices to different customers and discuss why this practice is not universal. We'll discover why some firms with market power are able to earn long-run profits while others are not, and we'll consider how the existence of market power can distort the allocation of scarce resources. The appendix to this chapter goes on to explore some pricing techniques employed by businesses and to evaluate the extent to which these techniques make use of economic theory.

THE ACQUISITION OF MARKET POWER

Recalling the plight of the purely competitive firm can help us understand the sources of market power. Consider the situation facing a Kansas wheat farmer. If farmer Brown wants a higher price for wheat, there is little he can do. If he attempts to charge more than the market price, he will sell nothing because his wheat is identical to that offered by other sellers. And he can't drive up wheat prices by planting less (and thereby reducing supply) because his output is only a drop in the bucket and would never be missed.

Most firms are not like Kansas wheat farmers; most firms *are* able to influence price in one or both of these ways. A firm may acquire market power (1) through **product differentiation**, distinguishing its product from similar products offered by other sellers, and/or (2) by gaining control of a significant fraction of total industry output. Sellers with either or both of these abilities can exert some influence on the market price of their product; sellers that possess neither ability are powerless to influence price.

Product Differentiation as a Source of Market Power

Product differentiation promotes market power by convincing buyers that a particular firm's product is unique or superior and therefore worth a higher price than the products offered by competitors. By claiming superiority, manufacturers of brand-name aspirin tablets manage to obtain prices that are substantially higher than those charged by sellers of generic and store-brand analgesics. By associating uniqueness with status, the makers of designer-label jeans are able to sell their product at prices much higher than nameless jeans can command.

Sellers can differentiate their products in a wide variety of ways. Some product differentiation is based on real, albeit sometimes slight, product differences; in other cases the essential differentiation is created by advertising and promotional efforts. Both types of product differentiation allow the seller to distinguish its product from the competition and thereby acquire pricing discretion that is not available to the purely competitive firm.

Control over Supply
as a Source of Market Power

Firms that cannot differentiate their products successfully must turn elsewhere to acquire market power. Sellers of standardized commodities such as oil and steel can gain pricing discretion by controlling a significant share of the industry output of that product. As you already know, whenever supply is reduced, price tends to rise. When a firm produces a significant share of the total industry output, it may be able to restrict supply and thereby drive up price.

Controlling supply is a relatively easy matter when an industry is made up of a single firm, a **monopoly**. Under these circumstances, the monopolist's decision alone determines the amount of output for sale. That's the situation, for example, in the case of AZT, the primary drug used in combating AIDS; Glaxo Wellcome's patent on that product gives it a monopoly and the sole right to determine the level of output. Microsoft Corporation is in a similar situation; its Windows operating system has become standard for computer users and is also protected by patents. But most products are produced by more than one firm, and that makes the task of controlling output more difficult. One firm's decision to supply less (and thereby drive up price) can be offset by another firm's decision to supply more.

Firms that are determined to restrict supply can sometimes avoid these offsetting output decisions through an arrangement known as a *cartel*. A **cartel** is a group of producers acting together to control output (supply) and the price of their product. Although cartels are illegal in the United States (and therefore must be kept secret to avoid prosecution), several international cartels exist and operate in a relatively open manner. Perhaps the best known of these is the Organization of Petroleum Exporting Countries (OPEC). This group of primarily Middle Eastern oil-producing nations attempts to control the output of its members in order to influence the price of oil and maximize their joint profits.[1] In the 1970s the cartel controlled a substantial fraction of the world's oil production and was able to increase prices substantially (from about $2 a barrel to more than $30) by simply cutting back on production. In the early 1980s the cartel's control over price began to slip as conservation reduced the demand for oil and additional supplies were discovered. This, in turn, led to a breakdown in cooperation among OPEC members, a breakdown that has resulted in additional supplies of oil and still lower oil prices. Although OPEC tried to regain control of oil prices throughout the 1980s and 1990s, they were unsuccessful. But in 1998, that began to change. And by 2000, the OPEC cartel was once again firmly in

---

[1] OPEC was established in 1960 by Iran, Iraq, Kuwait, Saudi Arabia, and Venezuela. Six more countries have joined the cartel since then: Qatar, Indonesia, Libya, Algeria, Nigeria, and the United Arab Emirates.

charge of oil prices. The article on page 196, "OPEC Is Humming Again," looks at how the cartel managed to regain control of oil prices.[2]

Cartels are not the only method by which groups of firms attempt to limit supply and maintain high prices. In fact, when an industry is composed of just a few firms, an **oligopoly**, the mere recognition that the firms have a joint interest in limiting output may be all that is necessary to promote that behavior. (This possibility is discussed in Chapter 8.) When cartels and voluntary cooperation fail, firms can sometimes elicit government help to control the supply of a product. For instance, U.S. automakers successfully lobbied Congress for restrictions limiting the number of new foreign automobiles permitted into the United States. By limiting supply, these restrictions help domestic producers maintain high prices. Similar campaigns have been responsible for limiting the imports of shoes, peanuts, lumber, and numerous other products, all leading to higher prices for U.S. consumers.

Degrees of Market Power

It stands to reason that all firms would like to possess as much market power as possible. But some firms succeed to a greater extent than others. If your college or university is served by a single bookstore, that seller may have significant market power. Many communities are served by a single producer of electric power, or a single newspaper, or perhaps a single airline.[3] In each of these instances, the firm is the entire industry, giving it complete control over the industry's output and significant market power.

Few firms possess the potential market power enjoyed by a monopolist utility company or the single airline serving a small community. The neighborhood dry-cleaning establishment and the nearby pizzeria also have market power, but not very much. These establishments can charge somewhat higher prices than their competitors because they offer convenient locations and/or slightly different products; but their prices cannot be much higher because their products are very similar. In Chapter 8 we'll take a closer look at the degrees of market power that exist in different types of industries. For now, the important thing to remember is that most firms possess at least some pricing discretion; they are not price takers.

---

[2] While OPEC is probably the best-known example of a cartel, there are others. For instance, the DeBeers diamond cartel controls more than 75% of the world's rough (uncut) diamonds and has used that control to limit supply and maintain high diamond prices. And the Trans-Atlantic Conference—a little-known shipping cartel—sets rates on the tens of billions of dollars of cargo transported by ships. While these cartels have lasted for decades, they are now threatened by new suppliers and defections by the membership. It remains to be seen how they will withstand the pressures

[3] In the past, virtually all local utility companies enjoyed monopoly status, since consumers had to buy their power from local utility. But that's changing. Consumers in some communities can now choose their provider of electric power. This is discussed more fully in the next chapter.

When a local utility company is the sole source of a community's electricity, that firm will possess substantial market power.

PRICE SEARCHING

Firms with pricing discretion are sometimes described as **price searchers,** which means that although they have some freedom in setting prices, they still must search for the profit-maximizing price. A price searcher may possess substantial market power (as does the local utility company) or very little (as does the local pizzeria), but all price searchers have one thing in common: Unlike price takers, which will lose all their customers if they raise their prices, price searchers can charge more and still retain some customers. Conversely, although price takers can sell any quantity they desire at the market price, price searchers must reduce price to sell more.

Consider as a hypothetical example High Tech Inc., a small manufacturer of computer desks. Although a number of firms produce such furniture, we can be sure that if High Tech raises the price of its desks, it won't lose all its customers so long as it keeps its price within reason. Some customers will prefer the quality or design of the High Tech desks to those offered by other sellers. Other customers may be swayed by the firm's product warranty or by its record for prompt delivery. Still others may be influenced by the firm's policy of accepting old desks in trade or by the variety of payment plans it offers. For all these reasons and others, High Tech will still sell some desks despite the price increase. But it won't be able to sell the same quantity; it will have to choose between selling more desks at a lower price or fewer desks at a higher price. That's the fundamental dilemma faced by all price searchers.

The Price Searcher's Demand Curve

Since price searchers have to reduce their prices in order to sell a higher quantity, they must face downward-sloping demand curves, not the horizontal demand curves confronting price takers. Exhibit 7.1 depicts the demand curve facing our hypothetical desk manufacturer. It shows that at $900 a desk, High Tech will sell only three desks each week. At $600 it will sell nine desks a week. Of course, at $200 a desk, sales will be even higher—seventeen desks a week. Although the price searcher can select any price it wants, it cannot choose a high price ($900 a desk) and expect to sell a high quantity (such as seventeen desks a week) because that combination is not a point on the demand curve. Thus, even a price searcher finds that its actions are constrained by its demand curve; it cannot choose a price without being locked into a quantity. The firm's task, then, is to decide which of the price-quantity combinations it prefers in order to maximize its profit.

EXHIBIT 7.1
The Price Searcher's Demand Curve

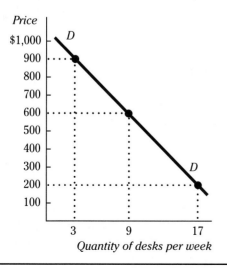

A price searcher can select any price it wants, but it must accept the quantity that results from that price. For example, High Tech can charge $900 per desk and sell three desks each week; it can charge $600 per desk and sell nine desks a week; or it can charge $200 and sell seventeen desks a week.

USE YOUR ECONOMIC REASONING

OPEC Is Humming Again: Unity, Discipline, Deals Help Oil Cartel Regain Its Influence

*Martha M. Hamilton and
William Drozdiak*

THE ORGANIZATION of Petroleum Exporting Countries is back in the driver's seat.

The cartel of major crude oil producers has regained its clout over world oil markets in the past year by showing uncharacteristic discipline in adhering to its own production quotas and by broadening its influence through deals with nonmember exporting nations.

Aided by a warming of relations between key members Saudi Arabia and Iran, OPEC has set aside for now the internal quarrels and cheating on pacts that eroded its power for years following its glory days in the 1970s, according to OPEC analysts and industry consultants.

OPEC's new solidarity has arisen in large part because the exporters were desperate after suffering a sharp loss of revenue when prices plunged in 1998. The cartel's 11 members responded by honoring their promises to pump less oil and thus help shore up prices. The cartel also bolstered its position by making fresh deals with Norway, Mexico and Russia, which are not OPEC members but produce significant amounts of oil.

The trend was reinforced by political developments including the new mood of cooperation between Saudi Arabia and Iran, long-standing Persian Gulf rivals. New leaders emerged in both countries, and the Saudis wanted to encourage better relations between Iran and the West. A new populist president in Venezuela, one of OPEC's founding members, pressured the government oil company to work more closely with the cartel.

Then, just as OPEC was getting its act together internally in early 1999, demand for oil surged with an economic recovery in Asia and the continuing boom in the United States.

As a result, the price of crude oil tripled in a year, rising well above $30 a barrel earlier this month, and some forecasts say Americans will be paying $2 a gallon for regular, self-serve gasoline by summer. With global demand running about 2.5 million barrels a day above output and gasoline inventories at historic lows, the United States and other industrialized countries are begging OPEC to open the taps. Energy Secretary Bill Richardson has been touring major oil producers since last month urging a production increase....

In the view of many Persian Gulf experts, the 1997 election of Iran's reform-minded President Mohammed Khatemi at a time of economic desperation among major oil producers helped

Source: © *Washington Post*, March 25, 2000, p. A1. Reprinted with permission.

revive cooperation within OPEC. After years of tension with Saudi Arabia, which feared that Iran's Islamic hard-liners wanted to export their revolution across the gulf, Khatemi made it clear he wanted to work with Riyadh to halt a decline in oil prices that threatened to undermine the economies of all gulf oil producers....

In addition, Venezuela's new president, Hugo Chavez, demonstrated he was more willing than his predecessors to curtail oil production to boost prices. Under his stewardship, Venezuela has stopped producing more than its allotted quota and cut output by 650,000 barrels a day despite its extreme economic difficulties. "There is no doubt that we are the OPEC member that has sacrificed the most," said Venezuelan Energy and Mines Minister Ali Rodriguez.

The new leadership in those... countries quickly demonstrated their resolve to revive OPEC's control of the market. The first step came on March 22, 1998, when Saudi Arabia, Venezuela and non-OPEC member Mexico declared that they and other oil producers would cut output by as much as 2 million barrels a day, or about 2.7 percent of world production....

The March 1998 agreement was undercut, however, when the economic downturn in Asia and warm weather in the United States and Western Europe kept demand for oil weak, said Vahan Zanoyan of the Petroleum Finance Co. Meanwhile, Iraq, which is allowed to sell oil under U.N. control but is known to engage in large sales on the black market, was rapidly increasing production.

It wasn't until March 1999, when Iran joined with Saudi Arabia, Mexico and Venezuela to design a new cutback agreement, that the production cuts began to have a major impact on oil markets.

At that meeting, the Saudis made two major concessions. They agreed to reduce their production below the 8-million-barrel-a-day level established after the Gulf War. The Saudis also accepted a formula that allowed Iran to produce 300,000 barrels a day more than the Saudis and other OPEC members preferred.

Saudi Arabia's enormous production capacity—up to 11 million barrels a day—makes it the key swing producer that can compel others to follow its wishes. But the Saudis have learned that unilateral pressure often backfires, fostering resentment that can undermine agreements.

"The Saudis have learned a painful lesson," said a senior Western oil executive whose company has large interests in the kingdom. "They now realize they must work with Iran in order to avoid the kind of open conflict that led to low oil prices and a sick economy."...

Use Your Economic Reasoning

1. How does the OPEC cartel drive up oil prices? Illustrate graphically.
2. To restrict total output to some target level, each OPEC country is given an output quota (limit) that it is expected to honor. Why does cheating (not honoring quotas) create problems for the cartel?
3. According to the article, OPEC has regained its clout because of a "new solidarity" among members. Why is solidarity necessary for the cartel to be effective? What is responsible for this new solidarity?
4. The Venezuelan energy minister talked about the "sacrifice" his country made for the sake of the cartel. What did the country sacrifice, and why did the country's leaders agree to make that sacrifice?
5. Suppose Iran insists on producing 300,000 more barrels of oil a day than other OPEC countries would prefer. How can the cartel maintain its target output level?

THE PROFIT-MAXIMIZATION RULE

For a price searcher the profit-maximization rule is essentially the same as it is for a price taker: Produce where marginal revenue equals marginal cost. The difference between a price searcher and a price taker is not in the logic used to maximize profits but in the environment confronting the seller. The price taker has no control over price, and so it uses the profit-maximization rule solely to determine the optimal level of output. The price searcher, on the other hand, uses this rule to determine both output and price.

Calculating Marginal Revenue

The first step in determining the profit-maximizing price and quantity is finding the price searcher's marginal revenue curve. Because a price searcher faces a downward-sloping demand curve, it must reduce price to sell more. Consequently, the marginal revenue that the price searcher gains by selling an additional unit of output will always be *less* than the selling price of the product (not equal to the price, as under pure competition), and the firm's marginal revenue curve will lie inside its demand curve. Since this idea is conveyed best with an example, let's consider Exh. 7.2.

The first two columns of Exh. 7.2 represent the demand schedule for desks that was graphed in Exh. 7.1. You can see that at a price of $1,000, only one desk will be sold each week. At a price of $950, two desks will be sold each week, and total revenue would increase to $1,900. What will be the marginal revenue from selling a second desk? (Remember, marginal revenue is the additional revenue gained by selling one more unit.) The correct answer is $900 ($1,900 − $1,000 = $900), $50 less than the $950 selling price. This relationship—marginal revenue being less than price—holds at all price levels.[4] To understand why, we need to consider the price reduction in more detail.

When High Tech reduces the price of executive desks from $1,000 to $950, it allows the first customer—the one who would have paid $1,000—to acquire the product for $950. In return the seller manages to attract an additional customer who is willing to pay $950 but wouldn't pay $1,000. The marginal revenue from the second desk is $900—the $950 the firm gains by selling one more unit *minus* the $50 lost by having to reduce the price on the first unit. Because marginal revenue is less than price, a price searcher's marginal revenue curve will always lie inside, or below, its demand curve (Exh. 7.3).

---

[4] Note that marginal revenue will always be equal to price for the first unit of output. For all subsequent units, marginal revenue will be less than price.

EXHIBIT 7.2
Marginal Revenue **for a Price Searcher**

PRICE PER UNIT	QUANTITY DEMANDED	TOTAL REVENUE	MARGINAL REVENUE
$1,050	0	$ 0	
1,000	1	1,000	$1,000
950	2	1,900	900
900	3	2,700	800
850	4	3,400	700
800	5	4,000	600
750	6	4,500	500
700	7	4,900	400
650	8	5,200	300
600	9	5,400	200
550	10	5,500	100
500	11	5,500	0
450	12	5,400	–100

The Profit-Maximizing Price and Quantity

To maximize its profit (or minimize its loss), High Tech must produce at the output where marginal revenue is equal to marginal cost. This rule permits the firm to continue producing additional units only so long as those units add more to revenue than to costs. Exhibit 7.3 graphs High Tech's demand and marginal revenue curves along with its marginal cost curve. Note that the marginal cost curve has the U shape introduced in Chapter 6; marginal cost declines initially and then rises as output is increased.

How many desks should High Tech produce and sell in order to maximize its profits? You can tell by studying the graph (or the table accompanying it) that the profit-maximizing (loss-minimizing) output is seven units per week. When output is less than seven units a week, marginal revenue exceeds marginal cost. For instance, the marginal revenue from the fifth unit of output is $600, and the marginal cost of that unit is only $300. Thus, High Tech will be $300 better off if it produces and sells that unit. The sixth unit doesn't make as great a contribution to the firm, but the marginal revenue of $500 still exceeds

EXHIBIT 7.3
Determining the Profit-Maximizing Price

PRICE PER UNIT	QUANTITY OF DESKS	MARGINAL REVENUE	MARGINAL COST
$800	5	$600	$300
750	6	500	340
700	7	400	400
650	8	300	480
600	9	200	580

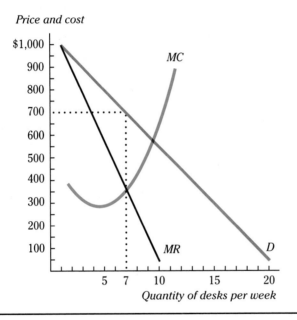

All firms maximize their profits (or minimize their losses) by producing the output at which marginal revenue is equal to marginal cost. In this example the profit-maximizing output is seven units. Once the profit-maximizing output has been determined, the profit-maximizing price can be discovered by drawing a line directly up to the firm's demand curve and over to the vertical axis. In our example the profit-maximizing price is $700 per desk.

the marginal cost of $340, and so the unit should be produced. The seventh unit adds $400 to revenue and $400 to cost; thus, seven units represents the profit-maximizing (loss-minimizing) output: the output at which $MR = MC$. Because all subsequent units would add more to cost than to revenue, their sale would either reduce the firm's profit or increase its loss.[5]

---

[5] In this example the firm will earn the same profit (or incur the same loss) whether it sells six or seven units of output. The firm wants to operate where $MR = MC$, not because it benefits from the last unit sold but because it benefits from each unit up to that point.

Once the profit-maximizing output has been determined, the profit-maximizing price can be discovered by drawing a line directly up to the firm's demand curve and over to the vertical axis. Remember, the demand curve shows the amount that consumers are willing to purchase at various prices. If we know the price, we can tell how much will be purchased. Conversely, if we know the quantity (output), we can use the demand curve to determine the maximum price the firm can charge and still sell that amount of output. In our example High Tech should charge a price of $700 per desk; that's the firm's profit-maximizing price.[6]

A Digression on Price Discrimination

In the preceding example we have assumed that there is a single profit-maximizing price, and we'll return to that assumption in just a moment. But in some instances there is more than one profit-maximizing price. **Price discrimination** exists when firms charge different consumers different prices for the same product.

Surgeons and lawyers and car dealers often practice "individual" price discrimination. They charge virtually every customer a different price, a price based largely on the customer's ability to pay (but limited, at least in the case of automobiles, by how much that customer has "shopped around" and become informed about the prices charged elsewhere). To illustrate, suppose that Honest John's Autos is selling the Rampage automobile. Assume also that the following represents a portion of the demand schedule for Honest John's automobiles.

PRICE	QUANTITY
$20,000	1
19,000	2
18,000	3
17,000	4
16,000	5

As you can see, only one consumer is willing to pay Honest John $20,000 for a Rampage. A second consumer won't pay $20,000 but is willing to pay $19,000. (Note that two consumers are willing to buy automobiles at a price of $19,000; one is the first consumer, who would pay $20,000.[7]) A third consumer won't pay $19,000 but will pay $18,000.

---

[6] In many real-world situations, firms do not possess precise information about their demand and marginal cost curves, and so they find it difficult to employ the $MC = MR$ pricing rule in precisely the manner described here. The appendix to this chapter, "Pricing in Practice," examines the pricing techniques employed by these firms.

[7] This assumes that each consumer buys only one automobile.

Car dealers that practice price discrimination want their sales personnel to obtain the highest price that each consumer will pay. So the salesperson would try to extract $20,000 from the first customer, $19,000 from the second, $18,000 from the third, and so on. Honest John would be willing to continue selling additional units as long as the price he could obtain was at least equal to the marginal cost of an additional vehicle. (Notice that when firms discriminate, the marginal revenue the firm receives from the sale of an additional unit is *equal* to its selling price, not less than its selling price as it was for the nondiscriminating price searcher.) For instance, if the marginal cost of an additional Rampage is $16,500, Honest John would be willing to sell the fourth vehicle (which adds $17,000 to his revenue) but not the fifth (which contributes only $16,000).

It is unlikely that the salesperson would actually be able to obtain the maximum price a consumer would be willing to pay. But effective sales personnel may come close. Sales reps who started at the sticker price on the vehicle and then haggle, giving in only when necessary, might approximate this solution. And, of course, that would mean more profit for the dealer than could be obtained by selling all four of these vehicles at a price low enough to convince the fourth buyer to participate.

Another form of price discrimination is "group" price discrimination. This is a situation in which a firm charges different prices to different *categories* of consumers. For example, movie theaters commonly charge different ticket prices to adults, students, and senior citizens. And we'd all like to order from the children's menu when we're short on cash. Even some telephone companies practice price discrimination, charging one price for long-distance service during the day (when most calls are business-related) and a lower price in the evening (when we make our personal calls).

The purpose of group price discrimination is similar to the purpose of individual price discrimination—to obtain the highest price possible from each category of consumer. Consider, for instance, the different ticket prices that airlines charge business and vacation travelers. The airlines recognize that business travelers usually *must* travel by air; they cannot afford the time involved in a lengthy automobile trip. In addition, many of these trips arise on short notice, so the business executive has no other alternative. These factors mean that the business traveler's demand curve for plane travel is less elastic—less price-sensitive—than the vacation traveler, who usually has a more flexible time schedule. By charging business travelers higher fares, the airlines maximize their profits from that group without discouraging travel by vacationers.[8] (Amazon.com and other e-businesses

---

[8] Airlines separate business and vacation travelers by requiring that the lower-priced tickets (intended for vacationers) be purchased well in advance and/or that the traveler stay over at least one Saturday night before returning. These are requirements that most business travelers are unable or unwilling to meet.

may be uniquely positioned to practice price discrimination. Read "What Price Fairness," on page 206, to find out why.)

Why doesn't everyone practice price discrimination? There are two primary reasons. First, it takes time, and time is money. Think about our car dealer again. It can take hours for the salesperson to negotiate with a customer and arrive at the price that particular customer will pay. That time expenditure makes sense in the case of big-ticket items such as cars and motor homes and boats. But it doesn't make sense for milk and clothing and most of the items we buy every day.

A second reason firms may not practice price discrimination is that they may be unable to prevent consumers from reselling items that they can buy more cheaply than other customers. For instance, suppose that the Ajax TV Center was charging regular customers $300 for a TV set but allowing senior citizens to buy the same set for $250. Under these circumstances we might expect to see some seniors buying TV sets in large quantities and reselling them at a profit. That would be a nice way for those senior citizens to earn extra cash, but it would make it very difficult for Ajax to sell any television sets at the higher price. The point is that when we can't prevent a product's resale, we generally offer that product at the same price to everyone. Because most markets are characterized by uniform pricing, we will now return to our single-price model.

EVALUATING THE SHORT-RUN PROFIT OR LOSS

As we discovered in Chapter 6, producing where $MR = MC$ does not ensure a profit. It ensures only that the firm will do as well as possible in any short-run situation. Recall that we find profits by subtracting total costs from total revenue. In our present example we can't tell whether High Tech Inc. is earning a profit or incurring a loss because we've focused entirely on marginal values.

To compute High Tech's short-run profit or loss, we need to know the firm's total revenue and its total costs. Exhibit 7.4 shows our hypothetical price searcher in three different situations. In case (a) the firm is earning a profit. As in the previous chapter, the amount of the profit can be determined by comparing total revenue with total cost. Total revenue is equal to $4,900 (the $700 selling price × 7 units—the profit-maximizing output). Total cost is equal to $4,200 (the ATC of $600 × 7 units). This leaves the firm with an economic profit of $700 ($4,900 − $4,200 = $700).

Case (b) finds our price searcher earning only a normal profit. You can see in the diagram that the MC curve intersects the MR curve at an output of six

EXHIBIT 7.4
Calculating the Short-Run Profit or Loss

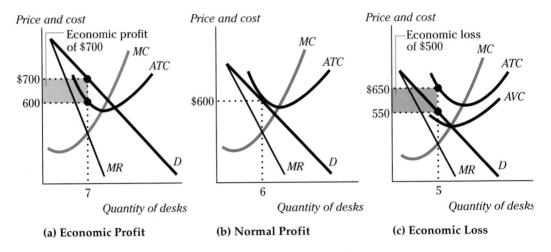

(a) Economic Profit   **(b) Normal Profit**   **(c) Economic Loss**

Case (a): When the profit-maximizing price is above *ATC*, the price searcher will earn an economic profit. Case (b): When the price is exactly equal to *ATC*, the price searcher will earn a zero economic profit, or a normal profit. Case (c): When the price is less than *ATC*, the firm will incur an economic loss—it will earn less than a normal profit.

desks. At that output the profit-maximizing price would be $600, so that total revenue would be $3,600 ($600 × 6 units). Since the *ATC* curve is tangent to the demand curve at $600, *ATC* must also be $600 when the firm is producing six desks. Therefore, the firm's total cost is $3,600 (the *ATC* of $600 × 6 units). This means that the firm is earning zero economic profit ($3,600 − $3,600 = $0), or a normal profit. Recall that a normal profit is acceptable; the owners of the business are earning as much as they could expect to earn if they invested their time and money elsewhere.

Case (c) depicts the price searcher facing a short-run economic loss (earning less than a normal profit). At the profit-maximizing (loss-minimizing) output of five desks, the firm's total cost of $3,250 (*ATC* of $650 × 5 units) exceeds its total revenue of $2,750 (the $550 selling price × 5 units). This results in a loss of $500 ($3,250 − $2,750 = $500). Note, however, that the selling price of $550 exceeds the firm's average variable cost of approximately $500, and so the firm should continue to operate rather than shut down. Since *P* exceeds *AVC* by $50, each of the five units produced will contribute $50 toward paying the firm's fixed costs. Through continued operation, the firm reduces its loss by $250. Of course, if *AVC* exceeded price (for example, if the average variable cost curve were positioned where the *ATC* curve is located at present), the firm would minimize its loss by shutting down.

BARRIERS TO ENTRY AND LONG-RUN PROFITS

We've seen that in the short run, price searchers may gain economic profits, may earn a normal profit, or may even sustain a loss. But how do they do in the long run? Is it possible for price searchers to earn economic profits in the long run, or is a normal profit the best that can be expected? (All firms, whether price searchers or price takers, must earn at least a normal profit in the long run, or the owners will sell out and reinvest their money where a normal return is possible.)

If a price searcher is earning an economic profit in the short run, its ability to continue earning that profit in the long run depends on the extent of the barriers to entering that industry. Recall from Chapter 6 that barriers to entry are obstacles that discourage or prevent firms from entering an industry. These obstacles include patent restrictions, large investments requirements, and restrictive licensing regulations.

Some price searchers exist in industries with substantial entry barriers—prescription medicine and aircraft manufacturing, for example. Others exist in industries with very modest barriers—shoe retailing, fast photo processing, and dry-cleaning establishments, to cite a few. Because entry barriers differ from industry to industry, we can't generalize about the long-run fate of price searchers as we could about the fate of price takers. (Recall that a normal profit is the *best* that a price taker can expect in the long run. Because there are no significant barriers to entering purely competitive industries, any short-run profits will be eliminated in the long run, as additional firms enter and drive down prices.)

If price searchers are protected by substantial barriers to entry, short-run profits can turn into long-run profits. For instance, it is estimated that Hoffman-La Roche of Switzerland earned multi*billion* dollar profits from the worldwide sale of its Valium and Librium tranquilizers, drugs that were protected by patents and therefore could not be duplicated by competitors.[9] Although profits of this magnitude are clearly exceptional, they

---

[9] F. M. Scherer, *Industrial Market Structure and Economic Performance*, 2d ed. (Chicago: Rand McNally, 1980), p. 449.

USE YOUR ECONOMIC REASONING

| What Price Fairness?

By Paul Krugman

WHY DO I buy books from Amazon.com? Location, location, location.

Not Amazon's—mine. The bookstores of central New Jersey are actually better than you might expect, but London it's not.

Browsing in a physical bookstore is still the best way to find books you weren't looking for. But if there's a specific book I want, I go online. Convenience, not price, is the selling point: I would buy those books from Amazon even if I were charged a couple of dollars extra.

And maybe Amazon will charge me a few dollars extra.

Recently it came to light that Amazon has been charging different customers different prices (for movies, not books). The company insists

that the price differentials were random, a way of testing the market. But many buyers accused the online retailer of tailoring its price to the consumer's characteristics. And even if Amazon's prices really were random, the outrage of those who had paid a few dollars extra suggests that "dynamic pricing" is about to become a major consumer issue, maybe even a political issue.

You see, despite that outrage, dynamic pricing won't go away. Both the nature of e-commerce—the ease with which sellers can figure out who you are and what you want—and the nature of "new economy" business in general make it almost irresistible. The only thing that is likely to stop it is government action.

Dynamic pricing is a new version of an old practice:

price discrimination. It uses a potential buyer's electronic fingerprint—his record of previous purchases, his address, maybe the other sites he has visited—to size up how likely he is to balk if the price is high. If the customer looks price-sensitive, he gets a bargain; if he doesn't he pays a premium.

To see why this is not just attractive to sellers but arguably good for the economy, look at how the publishing business works now. Books must be sold at a price well above the actual cost of producing one more copy. Otherwise the publisher couldn't cover costs that don't depend on how many books are sold—editing, typesetting and, yes, writing. But by charging, say, $25 for a book that costs only $3 to produce the publisher

Source: New York Times, Oct. 4, 2000, p. 35.

indicate the impact of entry barriers. In the absence of substantial barriers, we expect economic profits to attract additional sellers into the market. This leads to price cutting and other forms of competition that have the potential to eliminate economic profits in the long run.

loses some potential profitable sales.

So publishers try to sort customers indirectly. Most books are offered first in hardcover, then some time later in paperback. The paperback is cheaper to produce; but mainly its lower price is a way of pulling in price-sensitive customers after the juice has been squeezed out of the well heeled and impatient.

But in the world of e-commerce, such crude market segmentation isn't necessary. When I log on to Amazon, the site offers me quite accurate recommendations—not just for books but for music, which is spooky considering that I've never bought music online. In other words, Amazon's computers have got my tastes pretty well pegged. So I'm sure similar algorithms would have no trouble figuring out which customers are likely to be repelled by a high price and which are likely to ignore it—and tailoring the prices customers are actually offered accordingly.

This would obviously be good for Amazon. But it would also be good for the overall book business. Publishers would be willing to publish more titles, book buyers who would other-

wise have delayed their purchase until the thing came out in paper would be spared the wait. And it would be good for any other business with high fixed costs (it's expensive to offer the thing at all) but low marginal costs (it's cheap to satisfy one more customer) — a combination that has become ever more common as we have moved from an

economy that mainly made physical things to one that increasingly deals in digital embodiments of ideas.

But dynamic pricing is also undeniably unfair: some people pay more just because of who they are....

One thing is clear: The next battle in the eternal conflict between equity and efficiency may well be in cyberspace.

Use Your Economic Reasoning

1. If Amazon.com or any other e-business is attempting to figure out how price-sensitive you are as a consumer, what kind of information would it seek? Would your income be of interest to them? What about your age and education? Have you filled out any questionnaires (online) that would make this information available?

2. As we travel from one site on the Web to another, we leave a record of our travel. Suppose an e-business—for instance, a car dealership selling on the Web—gains access to that information. How would such data be useful to the company in pricing its product to you? (*Hint*:

Who do you think pays more, customers who comparison shop or those who do not?)

3. Do you think Amazon.com is attempting to practice individual price discrimination or group price discrimination? Defend your conclusion.

4. If Amazon were able to practice individual price discrimination, it would continue to sell to customers up to the point where the last customer was charged a price just equal to marginal cost. As a result, more customers would be able to buy books than if Amazon charged a single price to all customers. How could anyone object to that outcome?

Thus, the fact that a price searcher earns above-normal profits in the short run is no assurance that it will be able to do so in the long run. Unless entry barriers exist, the entrance of additional firms will result in added competition for consumers' dollars and subsequent elimination of all economic profits.

PRICE SEARCHERS AND RESOURCE ALLOCATION

Consumers are obviously better off when low entry barriers ensure low prices and low profits. But the profits earned by Hoffman-La Roche and other price searchers are not the primary social concern of economists. After all, high prices harm consumers, but they benefit stockholders and others who own businesses. So, we can't say that the entire society is harmed by barriers to entry. A more serious concern is the inefficient allocation of resources that results from the presence of market power.

Recall from Chapter 6 that an efficient allocation of resources requires that each product be produced up to the point at which the marginal social benefit that the product provides is exactly equal to its marginal social cost. Marginal social benefit can be determined from the industry demand curve, and marginal social cost from the marginal cost curve. If all production is continued up to the point at which the demand curve is intersected by the marginal cost curve, we can be assured that society's scarce resources are being used to produce the mix of products that consumers value most.[10]

When pure competition exists, production is automatically expanded to the allocatively efficient level. But that's not the case when firms possess market power. Price searchers distort the allocation of scarce resources because they do not allow production to continue up to the point at which the marginal social benefit (*MSB*) is equal to the marginal social cost (*MSC*). To do so would cause these firms to earn a smaller profit. Consider Exh. 7.5. The profit-maximizing price searcher will produce where *MR* intersects *MC*, at seven units in this example. At that output, marginal revenue and marginal cost are equal. But if you move upward in the exhibit from seven units of output to the demand (or marginal benefit) curve, you find that price is equal to $700. This tells us that consumers derive $700 worth of benefit from the seventh unit of output, even though its marginal cost is only $400. In short, consumers value this unit of output more highly than the alternative products that could be produced with the same resources. The same is true of the eighth and ninth units of output; marginal benefit exceeds marginal cost for each of those units.

An efficient allocation of resources would require the price searcher to produce at the output where the marginal cost curve intersects the demand (marginal benefit) curve (see point *A* in Exh. 7.5). If our hypothetical price searcher produced ten units of output and charged a price of $550 (so that *P* = *MC*), resources would be allocated efficiently. But that won't happen because expanding output in this manner would cause the firm to earn a smaller profit. Note

---

[10] As we noted in Chapter 6, this conclusion assumes no spillover costs or benefits associated with the production or consumption of the products in question.

EXHIBIT 7.5
Price Searchers and Resource Misallocation

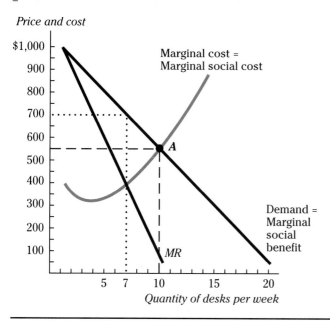

Price and cost

Marginal cost =
Marginal social cost

Demand =
Marginal
social
benefit

MR

A

Quantity of desks per week

Allocative efficiency requires that production take place at the output where the demand curve intersects the marginal cost curve, an output of ten units in this example. But the profit-maximizing price searcher will produce where *MR* = *MC*, an output of seven units. By restricting output, price searchers fail to provide consumers with the optimal quantity of this product and misdirect resources to the production of less-valued goods and services.

---

that for each unit beyond seven (the profit-maximizing output), marginal cost *exceeds* marginal revenue. Production of these additional units would be allocatively efficient but would lower the firm's total profit. And since it is the pursuit of profits that drives businesses (and not the goal of allocative efficiency), we can be sure that output will be expanded only to the profit-maximizing level.

In summary, price searchers distort the allocation of scarce resources by producing too little output and thereby forcing resources to be used in the production of less-valued products. In response to this resource misallocation, the government has employed a variety of means to encourage competition or correct for the negative impact of market power.

PRICE SEARCHERS AND ECONOMIES OF SCALE

Although price searchers do not achieve allocative efficiency, there may be instances in which this shortcoming is counterbalanced by lower production costs than could be achieved by price takers. This possibility exists when *economies of scale* occur in the production process.

Economies of scale are reductions in the average cost of production that occur as a firm expands its size of plant and scale of output. As you learned in Chapter 4, all inputs are variable in the long run; firms can build larger (or smaller) production facilities and can enter or leave an industry. In some instances the construction of larger production facilities can lead to lower average production cost (average total cost). When this is the case, the long-run average total cost (*LRATC*) curve of the firm slopes downward as in Exh. 7.6. Under these circumstances "bigger is better." Larger firms, producing larger quantities of output per period, will be able to achieve lower average costs than smaller firms.

Larger firms may be able to achieve lower costs for a variety of reasons. As firms build larger facilities and expand output, they can justify specialized equipment and personnel that would not make sense for a smaller firm producing less output. For instance, large manufacturers of men's shirts can justify million-dollar pieces of equipment that do nothing but sew collars. They can justify this expense because the machine sews collars very quickly and with few errors. This saves on the labor cost of performing this operation when compared with the less-sophisticated equipment and more labor-intensive technique that would be employed by a smaller firm. Of course, this sav-

---

EXHIBIT 7.6
Economies of Scale

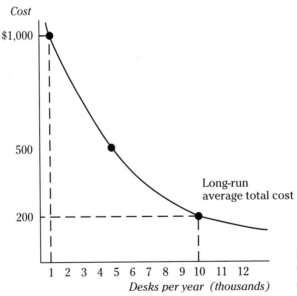

Economies of scale cause the firm's long-run average total cost curve to slope downward.

ing occurs only if the machine can be kept busy so that its cost can be spread over millions of shirts. That's why only larger firms opt for this approach. Smaller firms are forced to stick with more labor-intensive processes that generally mean higher average costs. High volume also allows firms to achieve greater specialization of labor than firms producing less output. For example, our large shirt manufacturer may be able to justify employing a crew of workers whose sole job is the maintenance of equipment, and a different crew whose sole task is stocking the factory with supplies. By allowing these workers to concentrate on a single task, the firm enables them to become better at their jobs, which results in fewer errors and reduces the time necessary to perform each task. In short, more specialized equipment and greater specialization of labor may allow larger firms to produce their products at lower average costs than smaller firms, whose size makes these options uneconomical.

The importance of economies of scale varies from industry to industry. In some industries large firms have substantially lower average costs than small firms; in others the difference is insignificant. Similarly, there are industries in which the advantages of size continue indefinitely and others in which they are quickly exhausted. When the long-run average total cost curve declines indefinitely, as it does in Exh. 7.6, it is always cheaper for a single firm (a monopolist) to serve the industry. Note that a single firm can produce an industry output of 10,000 desks at an average cost of $200, whereas if there were ten firms sharing the same market, average cost would rise to $1,000. When a market is most cheaply served by a single firm, it is described as a **natural monopoly**. This is a situation in which the benefits to society of lower production costs may outweigh the harm caused by a price searcher's tendency to restrict output below the allocatively efficient level.

If the cost curve depicted in Exh. 7.6 were commonplace, the U.S. economy would be largely populated by monopolies. But that's not the case; monopoly is relatively rare in our economy. That's because most long-run average cost curves don't decline indefinitely; they eventually turn up. The cost curve depicted in Exh 7.7 displays economies of scale up to point *A* (an output of 1,000 units) and *diseconomies of scale* beyond that point. **Diseconomies of scale** are increases in the average cost of production stemming from larger plant size and scale of output; they cause the long-run average total cost curve to turn upward, as it does to the right of point *A*. The major source of diseconomies of scale is the difficulty of managing a large enterprise. When organizations become very large, it becomes difficult to maintain the communication and information flows necessary to coordinate such enterprises. This results in long delays and inappropriate decisions, which raise the average cost of production, causing the long-run average total cost curve to turn upward.

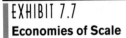

EXHIBIT 7.7
Economies of Scale

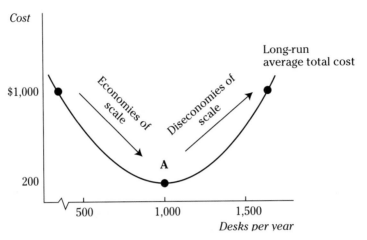

Long-run average costs decline as a result of economies of scale and increase as a result of diseconomies of scale.

When a firm experiences both economies and diseconomies of scale, bigger is better but only up to a point. The firm's *LRATC* curve will have the U shape depicted in Exh. 7.7. Under these conditions the degree of competition that is likely to emerge in the industry depends on both the optimal size of the firm (the output at which the *LRATC* curve is at a minimum) and the total demand for the industry's product. In our hypothetical example, for instance, if consumers are willing to purchase 100,000 desks at $200 (a price that would provide a normal profit), this industry could support 100 optimal-sized firms (100,000/1,000 = 100), and so it would tend to be highly competitive. But if consumers were willing to purchase only 3,000 desks at that price, the industry could supply only three optimal-sized firms and would be likely to develop into an oligopoly. Although more competition is generally preferred to less, under these circumstances oligopoly would probably be preferable to a more competitive industry structure because insisting on a large number of firms would require each firm to be too small to achieve significant scale economies.[11]

In summary, when firms must be relatively large in order to achieve economies of scale, consumers may be better off with one firm or a few large

---

[11] If the oligopolists enjoy substantial economies of scale, they may be able to earn economic profits and still charge a lower price than would prevail if the industry were composed of a large number of firms, each too small to achieve significant economies of scale.

firms, even though this means an absence of competition. Under these circumstances the advantages of lower production costs (and lower prices) may more than compensate for any allocative inefficiency resulting from the limited number of competitors.

SUMMARY

In most U.S. industries, individual firms have some pricing discretion, or *market power.* A firm may acquire market power either through *product differentiation*—distinguishing its product from similar products offered by other sellers—or by gaining control of a significant fraction of total industry output. Firms with either or both of these abilities can exert some influence on the market price of their product.

Sellers with pricing discretion are described as *price searchers* because they must search for the profit-maximizing price. All price searchers face demand curves that slope downward and to the right. Unlike the price taker, which can sell as much as it desires at the market price, the price searcher has to reduce price to sell more. Therefore, the price searcher is forced to choose between selling a lower quantity at a higher price or selling a higher quantity at a lower price.

Because price must be reduced to sell more, the marginal revenue the price searcher obtains from selling an additional unit of output is always less than the unit's selling price, and the price searcher's marginal revenue curve lies inside its demand curve. The price searcher can determine the profit-maximizing (loss-minimizing) level of output by equating marginal revenue and marginal cost. The profit-maximizing price can then be discovered by drawing a line directly up from the quantity to the firm's demand curve and over to the vertical (price) axis.

Some price searchers are able to enlarge their profits by practicing price discrimination. *Price discrimination* is charging different consumers different prices for the same product. When firms engage in individual price discrimination, they attempt to charge each consumer the maximum price he or she will pay. Group price discrimination results when firms charge different prices to different categories of consumers.

Like price takers, price searchers must determine the amount of their profit or loss by comparing total revenue and total cost. If total revenue exceeds total cost, the price searcher is earning an economic profit; if total cost exceeds total revenue, the firm is incurring an economic loss. When total revenue is exactly equal to total cost, the firm is earning a normal profit.

Although a normal profit is the most a price taker can hope to earn in the long run, a price searcher may be able to do better. When price searchers are protected by substantial barriers to entry, they may continue to earn long-run economic profits.

The possibility of long-run profits is not the only outcome that distinguishes price searchers from price takers. In addition, price searchers fail to achieve allocative efficiency. Allocative efficiency requires that producers expand output up to the point at which the marginal social benefit of the last unit produced is exactly equal to its marginal social cost. Price searchers stop short of that point; that is, they produce less output than is socially desirable.

Although price searchers fail to achieve allocative efficiency, there may be instances in which this shortcoming is counterbalanced by the ability to achieve *economies of scale.* Economies of scale are reductions in the average cost of production that occur when a firm expands its plant size and the scale of its output. When economies of scale continue indefinitely, the market will always be most cheaply served by a single firm. This situation is termed a *natural monopoly.* Natural monopolies are rare. In most instances, long-run costs decline initially but eventually turn up as a result of *diseconomies of scale.*

When a production process exhibits both economies and diseconomies of scale, the firm's long-run average total cost curve will be U-shaped; it will decline initially but will eventually turn upward. Under these circumstances the degree of competition that is likely to emerge in the industry depends on both the optimal size of the firm and the total demand for the industry's product. When the optimal size of the firm is relatively large, consumers may be better off with a few large firms that are able to achieve all economies of scale, even though this means less competition.

KEY TERMS

Cartel
Cost-plus pricing
Cost of goods sold
Depreciation
Diseconomies of scale

Economies of scale
Market power
Monopoly
Natural monopoly
Oligopoly

Price discrimination
Price searcher
Product differentiation

STUDY QUESTIONS

Fill in the Blanks

1. Firms that possess pricing discretion are

   sometimes described as _____ .

2. _____
   creates market power by convincing buyers

that a particular product is unique and superior.

3. A price searcher maximizes profit by

   equating _____ and

   _____ .

4. For a price searcher, marginal revenue is

   (greater/less) _____ than price.

5. In the short run, a price searcher that is incurring a loss will continue to operate rather than shut down, provided that price

   is greater than _____ cost.

6. A price searcher will not be able to earn economic profits in the long run unless

   _____ exist.

7. A price searcher would achieve allocative efficiency if it produced at the output

   where the _____ curve intersects the marginal cost curve.

8. Price searchers will not choose to produce the allocatively efficient level of output because doing so would reduce their

   _____ .

9. A _____ is a situation in which a market is most cheaply served by a single firm.

10. If the long-run average cost curve of a firm is U-shaped, we know that the firm initially

    experiences _____ of scale, and ultimately experiences

    _____ of scale.

Multiple Choice

1. Which of the following would probably *not* be a price searcher?
   a) The local utility company
   b) A Kansas wheat farmer
   c) General Motors
   d) A local movie theater

2. All price searchers
   a) face downward-sloping demand curves.
   b) must reduce price to sell more.
   c) can raise their prices without losing all their customers.
   d) possess some pricing discretion.
   e) All of the above

3. Both price searchers and price takers
   a) must produce homogeneous products.
   b) produce where *MR* = *MC* to maximize profits.
   c) face horizontal demand curves.
   d) must earn normal profits in the long run.

4. If a price searcher is operating where *MR* exceeds *MC*,
   a) it is producing the profit-maximizing output.
   b) it is producing too much to maximize profits.

   c) it is producing too little to maximize profits.
   d) None of the above is true.

   Use the exhibit following question 7 to answer questions 5–7.

5. To maximize its profit or minimize its loss, this price searcher should
   a) produce six units and charge a price of $50.
   b) produce six units and charge a price of $110.
   c) produce eight units and charge a price of $90.
   d) produce nine units and charge a price of $80.

6. This price searcher is
   a) incurring a loss of $180.
   b) earning a normal profit.
   c) earning a profit of $360.
   d) earning a profit of $180.

7. Allocative efficiency would require this firm to
   a) produce seven and one-half units of output and charge a price of $78.
   b) produce eight units and charge a price of $90.

c) produce six units and charge a price of $50.

d) None of the above

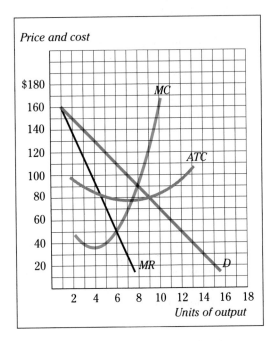

8. If a price searcher's fixed costs have increased,
   a) the firm's profit-maximizing quantity will increase.
   b) the firm's profit-maximizing quantity will not change.
   c) the firm's profit-maximizing quantity will decline.
   d) the firm will operate at a loss.

9. Sonic Waterbeds faces a traditional downward-sloping demand curve (included below), but its marginal cost curve is a horizontal straight line at a height of $600. In other words, marginal costs are constant at $600. How many units should Sonic sell, and what price should it charge to maximize profit?

PRICE (per bed)	QUANTITY (per day)
$1,000	1
900	2
800	3
700	4
600	5
500	6

a) One unit at $1,000
b) Two units at $900
c) Three units at $800
d) Four units at $700
e) Five units at $600

10. If the waterbed retailer described in question 9 was able to practice individual price discrimination, it would sell _____ waterbeds and earn a profit of _____ dollars on the last waterbed sold.
   a) 3,   200
   b) 4,   200
   c) 5,   0
   d) 6,   0

11. When firms practice group price discrimination, they tend to charge higher prices to consumers
   a) whose demand is more elastic.
   b) who are more price-sensitive.
   c) whose demand is less elastic.
   d) who do comparison shopping.

12. When a price searcher produces the output level at which marginal revenue is equal to marginal cost, it is
   a) maximizing its profit and producing the allocatively efficient level of output.
   b) maximizing its profit but producing more than the allocatively efficient level of output.
   c) maximizing its profit but producing less than the allocatively efficient level of output.

d) producing less than the profit-maximizing output.

13. Imagine a situation in which a firm experienced diseconomies of scale immediately. The long-run average total cost curve would be
a) U-shaped.
b) downward-sloping.
ⓒ upward-sloping.
d) a horizontal straight line.

14. Imagine a long-run average cost curve that is U-shaped and has its minimum at 5,000 units of output and an average cost of $10. Under those conditions this industry would be

a) a natural monopoly if only 5,000 units were demanded at $10 but highly competitive if 10,000 units were demanded at that price.
b) an oligopoly if only 5,000 units were demanded at $10 but highly competitive if 10,000 units were demanded at that price.
c) highly competitive if 10,000 units were demanded at $10.
ⓓ a natural monopoly if only 5,000 units were demanded at $10 but highly competitive if 500,000 units were demanded at that price.

Problems and Questions for Discussion

1. The price searcher's price and output decisions are one and the same. Explain.

2. Explain how product differentiation conveys market power.

3. Why is marginal revenue less than price for a price searcher? Illustrate with an example.

4. From time to time, farmers have attempted to form organizations to restrict the amount of corn and other grains being planted. What is the real intent of these organizations, and why do you think they have been largely ineffective in achieving their objective?

5. Why do cartels need cooperation of their members to ensure high prices? How can cheating—selling more output than permitted, for example—undermine a cartel?

6. Why should consumers be concerned about barriers to entry?

7. Both price searchers and price takers produce at the output where $MR = MC$. Yet price takers achieve allocative efficiency, whereas price searchers do not. Explain.

8. Suppose that a price searcher finds itself incurring a short-run loss. How should it decide whether to shut down or continue to operate? What would the price searcher's graph look like if it was in a shut-down situation?

9. If the long-run average total cost curve always slopes downward, bigger is better and the industry will probably develop into a monopoly. What do you suppose it would mean if the firm's long-run cost curve was horizontal? Would big firms be able to drive the small ones out of business? Would large firms be at a disadvantage?

10. If the firm's long-run average total cost curve is U-shaped the industry could be a monopoly or purely competitive or even an oligopoly. We can't tell from the information given. What additional information is needed, and how would we use it to determine the degree of competition in this industry?

11. The local newspaper offers the following rates for placing classified advertisements:

    $3.00 for three lines for three days (for items totaling under $100)

    $6.00 for three lines for three days (for items totaling $100–$499)

    $9.00 for three lines for five days (for items totaling $500–$3,999) $20.00 for three lines for eight days (for items totaling $4,000–$35,000)

    a) Is the newspaper practicing price discrimination? If so, which type of price discrimination is it practicing, individual or group?

    b) What is the logic behind the pricing scheme contained in these ad rates?

12. Suppose your college or university wanted to charge different tuition rates to different categories of students. In the following pairs, who do you think would pay the higher rates? Why?

    a) Students interested in premed or students interested in the humanities?

    b) Students who apply for early admission or those who apply later?

    c) Students who came for on-campus visits or those who did not?

    d) Entering freshmen or students beginning their senior year?

ANSWER KEY

Fill in the Blanks

1. price searchers
2. product differentiation
3. Marginal cost, marginal revenue
4. less
5. average variable
6. barriers to entry
7. demand
8. profit
9. natural monopoly
10. economies, diseconomies

Multiple Choice

1. b
2. c
3. b
4. c
5. b
6. d
7. b
8. b
9. c
10. c
11. c
12. c
13. c
14. d

Appendix: PRICING IN PRACTICE

A firm's day-to-day pricing techniques may differ somewhat from the theoretically correct pricing practices that we have discussed thus far. This difference stems in part from the fact that firms are frequently guided by motives other than profit maximization. Ethical considerations, for example, may result in the pursuit of a "satisfactory" profit rather than a maximum profit. The quest for prestige is another motive that may cause the firm or its managers to maximize sales or market share, subject to some minimum profit constraint.[12] Firms pursuing objectives such as these will not select the price at which $MR = MC$. For instance, if a firm wants to maximize sales, it will choose a lower price than the one that maximizes profit to encourage additional customers to buy the product.

Even those firms motivated by the pursuit of maximum profit may find it difficult to employ the $MR = MC$ rule in precisely the manner we've described. In most real-world situations, pricing takes place in an environment beset with uncertainty. Firms seldom possess precise information about their demand and cost curves. These deficiencies force sellers to rely on other methods for determining price.

Cost-Plus Pricing

The most common technique for determining selling price is probably **cost-plus pricing** (or full-cost pricing, as it is sometimes called). In its simplest form the cost-plus method involves adding some percentage, or markup, to the cost of the goods acquired for sale. For example, a furniture store may pay $100 for a chair, mark it up 150 percent, and attempt to sell it for $250.

Firms using this method do not consider all their costs in arriving at the selling price. They assume that the markup on the **cost of goods sold** (the cost of the items they buy for resale) will be sufficient to cover all other costs—rent, utilities, wages, and salaries—and leave something for profit.

A more sophisticated version of the cost-plus technique attempts to ensure that *all* costs are recovered by building them into the price. Here the seller arrives at a price by determining first the average total cost (ATC) of producing the product or offering the service and then adding some margin for profit.

---

[12] Although firms may choose to pursue objectives other than profit maximization, they must strive to achieve at least a normal profit in the long run. Otherwise they won't be able to attract the economic resources they need in order to remain in business. Thus, although some firms may not choose to pursue profit *maximization*, no firm can ignore profitability entirely.

A Cost-Plus Example: Building a Boat. Let's assume that we have just purchased a boat-manufacturing facility for $200,000. It has an expected useful life of 20 years and was designed with a production capacity of 1,000 boats per year. The estimated cost of materials is $150 per boat, and estimated direct labor cost (the cost of the labor directly involved in the manufacture of the boat) is $200 per boat. Besides these variable costs, we have a variety of fixed costs—everything from utility payments to the salaries of security guards— which amount to $125,000 per year. Since our factory cost $200,000 and has a useful life of 20 years, we must also add $10,000 per year ($200,000/20 years) for **depreciation**—the reduction in the value of the production plant due to wear and tear and obsolescence.

Assuming that we expect to sell 1,000 boats this year, which would mean that we would be able to operate the plant at its designed capacity, we arrive at the following costs per boat:

Direct labor	$200.00
Materials	150.00
Depreciation on plant and equipment ($10,000 per year, or $10 per boat—i.e., $10,000 divided by 1,000 boats)	10.00
Fixed costs ($125,000 per year, or $125 per boat—i.e., $125,000 divided by 1,000 boats)	125.00
Total cost per boat (average total cost)	**$485.00**

Now that we have the average total cost of producing a boat, the final step in determining the selling price is adding on the markup that provides our profit margin. A number of factors seem to influence the size of the markup that firms strive to achieve. For instance, executives commonly mention the firm's assessment of what is a "fair" or "reasonable" profit margin.

Custom is another factor that seems to play a major role in some industries. Retailers, for example, often use a particular percentage markup simply because they have always used it or because it is the accepted, therefore "normal," markup in the industry. Obviously a markup that endures long enough to become customary must be somewhat successful in allowing firms to meet their profit objectives. In fact, it may indicate that these firms have discovered through informal means the price and output levels that would have emerged if they had applied the theoretical $MR = MC$ rule.

A final factor influencing the size of the markup is the impact of competition. Although a firm may desire high profit margins, ultimately the degree of actual and potential competition determines what margins the firm will be able to achieve. The more competitive the industry, the lower the profit margin.

Let's assume that we've considered all these factors and have decided to use a 10 percent markup on cost in determining our selling price. Our final step, then, is to add the 10 percent markup to the average total cost calculated earlier. The resulting value is the firm's selling price as determined by the cost-plus technique:

Total cost per boat (average total cost)	$485.00
Markup on cost (10 percent × $485)	48.50
Selling price	**$533.50**

Cost-Plus Pricing in Action.   Cost-plus pricing has been criticized by economists as a naive pricing technique that ignores demand and competition and bases price solely on cost considerations. When the cost-plus technique is used in a mechanical or unthinking way, these criticisms are certainly valid. But that's seldom the case. Most businesses consider carefully the strength of demand and the degree of competition before selecting their markup or profit margin. In addition, the cost-plus price generally is viewed as a preliminary estimate, or starting point, rather than as the final price. Since demand and competition can seldom be measured precisely, the firm must be willing to adjust its price if it has misjudged market conditions. It is through these subjective adjustments that the firm gropes its way closer to the profit-maximizing price. A few examples may help to illustrate this point.

Example 1: The Department Store.   A local department store receives its shipment of Nifty Popcorn Poppers just in time for the Christmas gift-buying season. It prices the item at $19.50 in order to earn a 30 percent markup on the popper's cost.

Two weeks later the store has sold 50 percent of the shipment, and Christmas is still six weeks away. The manager realizes that he has a "hot" selling item and that he won't be able to get any more from the manufacturer in time for Christmas. He decides to increase his markup (and consequently the product's selling price) in order to take advantage of the product's strong demand.

Example 2: The Car Dealer.   A car dealer in a large metropolitan area has found that in the past several years she has been able to average a 15 percent profit margin on the cost of the automobiles she sells. Her experience has taught her that it is much easier to sell a car at a high markup early in the season, when people will pay to be among the first to own the new model, than later, when the next year's model is about to be announced. So the dealer instructs her sales personnel to strive for a 20–25 percent markup early in the year and to settle for a 5–10 percent margin toward the end of the season.

Example 3: The Appliance Manufacturer. Acme Appliance manufactures refrigerators for sale to a regional market. In response to consumers' different budgets and "needs" in terms of optional features, the company offers two models: a basic model that is available only in white and a deluxe model that offers additional features and comes in a variety of colors.

In pricing its product, Acme feels that a 10 percent markup on average cost will produce the desired rate of return on its investment. Rather than use a single markup percentage, however, Acme has decided to apply a 5 percent markup to the basic model and a 15 percent markup to the deluxe model, for an average markup of 10 percent. This decision was made because previous sales experience indicated that low-income customers are substantially more sensitive to price than are intermediate- and high-income customers.

Although the cost-plus technique is essentially straightforward, its application requires management personnel to make subjective judgments about the strength of demand and the degree of competition, as these examples illustrate. Both factors are difficult to evaluate and impossible to quantify. As a consequence, pricing remains more an art than a science.

Marginal Analysis and Managerial Decisions

As the foregoing examples indicate, firms that desire to maximize profits must adjust their cost-plus prices to reflect market conditions; they cannot use the technique mechanically. Learning to "think marginally" can also lead to better decisions and greater profits.

The major limitation of the cost-plus technique is that it doesn't rely on the *marginal analysis* introduced in Chapter 5. It concentrates instead on average values, stressing the need to recover all costs plus some markup. That can lead to smaller profits (or larger losses) than necessary since (as we discovered in Chapter 5) marginal costs are the only relevant costs for many business decisions.

Although firms commonly lack the information required to use the $MR = MC$ approach to price determination, they generally have some knowledge of marginal values. For instance, even though a firm probably does not know the marginal cost of producing the 200,000th unit of output, it can usually determine the additional cost of producing some block of units—another 10,000 cars, for example. And it can probably discover the additional cost of some contemplated course of action, such as adding or discontinuing a product line. This information will allow a firm to improve the quality of its decisions.

To illustrate, suppose that you own a chain of fast-food restaurants that has traditionally opened for business at 11 A.M. What costs would you consider in deciding whether it would be profitable to open earlier in order to serve breakfast?

The cost-plus approach implies that the decision should be based on the full cost (or *fully allocated cost,* as it is sometimes called) of the new project—on the project's share of the firm's total costs. In other words, the breakfast meal would be expected to generate enough revenue to pay for the labor, utilities, and food used in the morning meal, plus a share of the firm's overhead costs (rent, insurance, equipment depreciation) and some profit margin. If you anticipate enough business to achieve that objective, you should open for business. Otherwise you would remain closed.

Marginal analysis yields a different conclusion. According to marginal analysis, the only costs relevant to a decision are those that are influenced by the decision. In deciding whether to open for breakfast, you should *ignore* such costs as rent and insurance because these fixed costs will have to be paid whether or not the restaurants are open for breakfast. The only true cost of serving breakfast is the marginal cost: the increase in the restaurant's total cost that results from the breakfast meal. If the marginal revenue derived from serving breakfast is expected to exceed the marginal cost, you should open earlier. If not, you should continue to serve only the noon and evening meals.

Marginal analysis can often improve the quality of managerial decisions. Many projects that don't appear to be profitable when evaluated on the basis of their fully allocated costs look quite appealing when analyzed in terms of their marginal costs and revenues. By using marginal analysis and applying judgment to cost-plus prices, firms may be able to approximate the profit levels that would be achieved by using the $MR = MC$ rule.

Test your understanding of the material contained in this appendix by answering the following questions:

1. Explain the cost-plus pricing technique.
2. Why is it often necessary to modify the result determined by the cost-plus method?
3. If a firm includes all its costs in its price by using the cost-plus method, will it ever show a loss? Explain.
4. What determines the markup used in the cost-plus pricing technique?
5. A major limitation of the cost-plus technique is that it does not utilize marginal analysis. Discuss.
6. The Springfield Bouncers, a new professional basketball team, want to rent the high school gymnasium on Sunday afternoons. How would

determine an appropriate rent? If they reject your first offer, how would you determine the *minimum* acceptable rate?

7. Bland Manufacturing Company manufactures men's suits for sale throughout the Midwest. For the past five years Bland has operated with about 20 percent unused capacity. Last month a retailer on the West Coast offered to buy as many suits as Bland could supply as long as the price did not exceed $45 per suit. This price is substantially below the price Bland charges its regular customers. Given the information presented below, should Bland accept the offer? Why or why not?

   ATC at present output level (80,000 units) = $55

   ATC at capacity output (100,000 units) = $50

   Normal markup = 40% on *ATC*

CHAPTER EIGHT

Industry Structure and Public Policy

LEARNING OBJECTIVES

1. Explain the meaning of "industry structure."
2. Describe how market power is related to industry structure.
3. Identify the characteristics of the four industry structures.
4. Discuss the sources of the pricing discretion enjoyed by monopolistically competitive firms, oligopolists, and monopolists and the limits of that discretion.
5. Explain why monopolists and oligopolists may be able to earn long-run profits while monopolistically competitive and purely competitive firms cannot.
6. Define "interdependence," and explain how it influences the actions of oligopolists.
7. Describe the content and purpose of game theory.
8. Explain how monopolists and oligopolists may distort the allocation of scarce resources and alter the income distribution.
9. Identify the three major antitrust statutes and their content.
10. Explain the objectives and limitations of antitrust enforcement and industry regulation.

Nearly all the firms in our economy enjoy some pricing discretion, or market power. In Chapter 7 we saw how these firms determine their prices, and we considered the impact of market power on the allocation of scarce resources. Chapter 8 takes a closer look at the degrees of market power that exist in different industries and considers how the makeup, or structure, of an industry influences the amount of pricing discretion enjoyed by its individual firms. This chapter also explores the impact of market power on consumer welfare and examines the role of antitrust enforcement and government regulation in limiting that power.

INDUSTRY STRUCTURE AND MARKET POWER

You have learned that a firm may acquire market power either through product differentiation—distinguishing its product from similar products offered by other sellers—or by gaining control of a significant fraction of total industry output. The degree of product differentiation and the extent to which a firm is able to control industry output are related to the structure of the industry in which the firm operates. **Industry structure** is the makeup of an industry as determined by certain factors: (1) the number of sellers and their size distribution (all sellers approximately the same size as opposed to some much larger than others); (2) the nature of the product; (3) the extent of barriers to entering or leaving the industry. Note that these factors correspond to the three assumptions of the competitive model discussed early in Chapter 6.

There are four basic industry structures: pure competition, monopolistic competition, oligopoly, and pure monopoly. Their characteristics are summarized in Exh. 8.1. You are already familiar with pure competition, so we will use that model to open our discussion of the relationship between industry structure and market power.

EXHIBIT 8.1
Industry Structure: A Preview

PURE COMPETITION (No pricing discretion)	MONOPOLISTIC COMPETITION (Modest pricing discretion)	OLIGOPOLY (Modest to substantial pricing discretion)	PURE MONOPOLY (Substantial pricing discretion)
1. Many sellers, each small in relation to the industry	1. Many sellers, each small in relation to the industry	1. Few sellers, large in relation to the industry	1. One firm the sole supplier
2. Identical products	2. Somewhat differentiated products	2. Identical or differentiated products	2. Unique product; no close substitutes
3. No substantial barriers to entry	3. No substantial barriers to entry	3. Substantial barriers to entry	3. Substantial barriers to entry
Examples: Wheat farming, cattle ranching, fish farming, and other agricultural industries	*Examples:* Retail trade (hair salons, restaurants, gas stations) and a few manufacturing industries (men's suits and women's dresses)	*Examples:* Steel and aluminum manufacturing (identical products); automobile and cigarette manufacturing (differentiated products)	*Examples:* Microsoft, developer of the Windows operating system; some local utility companies; the single campus bookstore

PURE COMPETITION

As you learned in Chapter 6, firms that operate in a purely competitive industry are price takers and lack market power for two reasons. First, because they produce and sell identical products, no one firm can expect consumers to pay a higher price than they would pay elsewhere. Such firms must be content with the price dictated by the market. Second, because the purely competitive firm is quite small in relation to the industry, it cannot affect the total industry supply enough to alter the market price. It cannot, for instance, push up prices as do the OPEC oil cartel and the DeBeers diamond cartel.

That cannot happen in wheat or corn production or any other industry that approximates pure competition. In these industries the individual seller supplies such a small fraction of total industry output that the firm is not in a position to alter the market price by reducing production. Once again, the purely competitive firm has no choice but to accept the price that is dictated by the market.

MONOPOLISTIC COMPETITION

Few industries in the U.S. economy approximate pure competition. Monopolistic competition is a much more common industry structure. Most of the retailers with which you do business regularly are firms in monopolistically competitive industries: restaurants, day-care centers, grocery stores, hair salons, and photo processors, to name just a few examples. In addition, some manufacturers, such as those making wooden furniture, women's dresses, and men's suits, operate in monopolistically competitive industries.

Like pure competition, **monopolistic competition** is characterized by a large number of relatively small sellers and by modest barriers to entering the industry. The feature that distinguishes monopolistic competition from pure competition is product differentiation. Each monopolistically competitive firm sells a product that is slightly different from those of other firms in the industry. Firms compete on price *and* through product differentiation. Products are differentiated by style, quality, packaging, the location of the seller, advertising, the services offered by the firm (free delivery, for example), and other real or imagined characteristics.

As the term suggests, a monopolistically competitive firm is part monopolist and part competitor. It is a monopolist because it is the only firm selling its unique product; it is competitive because of the large number of firms selling products that are close substitutes. We all have a favorite pizza parlor. It is a monopolist in the limited sense that no other restaurant offers exactly the same food, service, atmosphere, and location. On the other hand, our pizza parlor is in competition with dozens, perhaps hundreds, of other restaurants that sell pizza and substitutes for pizza as well. Your neighborhood eyeglass retailer and clothing store are in a similar situation. They may have convenient locations and offer some brands that are not available elsewhere, but they face substantial competition from other sellers of similar products.

Monopolistic Competition and Market Power

Insofar as it sells a unique product, each monopolistically competitive firm has some pricing discretion. In other words, it is a price searcher rather than a price taker. If a monopolistic competitor raises the price of its product, it will lose some customers but not all of them. Some will still prefer the product because they believe it to be superior to that of competitors. We can infer, then, that the firm faces a downward-sloping demand curve, not the horizontal or perfectly elastic demand curve facing competitive firms. However, with many substitute products available, the demand for the monopolistically competitive firm's product will be quite elastic, so that consumers will be very responsive to price changes. As a consequence, the market power of the firm is limited; no monopolistically competitive firm can raise its price very much without losing an injuriously large number of customers.

The low entry barriers also function as a check on market power. Additional firms can easily enter a monopolistically competitive industry to take advantage of short-run economic profits. Consider the monopolistically competitive firm represented in Exh. 8.2. In case (a) the firm is earning a short-run profit (price exceeds ATC at the output where $MR = MC$). In the long run, however, this profit will be eliminated by the entrance of additional firms selling similar but slightly differentiated products. As the new firms enter the industry, the demand curve facing our hypothetical firm will begin to shift to the left because each firm's share of total industry demand will become smaller. If there are now 20 pizza restaurants instead of 10, the typical restaurant will have fewer customers than before. Additional firms will continue to enter the industry (and the individual firm's demand curve will continue to shift leftward) until the typical firm is earning just a normal profit. This situation is depicted in case (b). In long-run equilibrium, then, the monopolistically competitive firm will do no better than a purely competitive firm: it will just break even. (Do microbreweries fit the model of monopolistic competition? Read "Specialty Beers No Longer Fill Nation's Thirst" on page 230, and decide for yourself.)

EXHIBIT 8.2
The Long-Run Adjustment Process in Monopolistic Competition

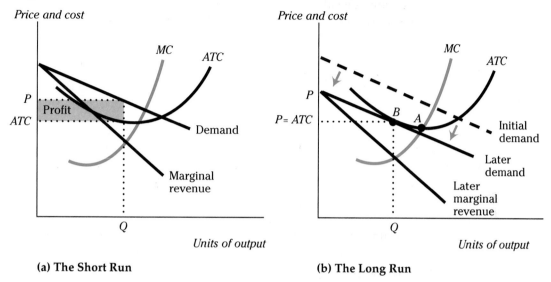

(a) The Short Run

(b) The Long Run

In the short run a monopolistically competitive firm may earn an economic profit, as represented in case (a). In the long run, however, the presence of the above-normal profit will cause additional firms to enter the industry, reducing each firm's share of the industry demand and eventually eliminating all economic profit, as in case (b). In long-run equilibrium the typical monopolistically competitive firm will earn just a normal profit.

Evaluating Monopolistic Competition

We discovered in Chapter 6 that price searchers misallocate resources because they fail to expand output up to the point at which the marginal social benefit equals the marginal social cost. An examination of Exh. 8.2 confirms that monopolistically competitive firms behave this way. Note that in long-run equilibrium, as shown in case (b), the firm maximizes profit at an output of Q. But at that output the price (which reflects the marginal benefit from consuming that unit) exceeds marginal cost. This tells us that society values the last unit of *this* product more highly than the other products that could be produced with the same resources. Allocative efficiency would require the firm to expand output until the marginal social benefit equals the marginal social cost, until the demand curve intersects the marginal cost curve. (Why won't

USE YOUR ECONOMIC REASONING

Specialty Beers No Longer Fill Nation's Thirst—Over 300 Small Breweries Have Closed Since 1996, on Flat Sales, Clutter

PORTLAND, Maine (AP) — Just a few years ago, connoisseurs thought small breweries and their tasty pale ales, amber lagers and dark stouts were going to transform the beer industry.

But the country's thirst for specialty beers has never fulfilled expectations and many small breweries are cutting back after an industry shakeout. Nationwide, more than 300 brewpubs and breweries have shut down since 1996 — the year sales peaked for four of the largest specialty brewers, Boston Beer Co., Pete's Brewing Co., Redhook Ale Brewery Inc. and Pyramid Breweries Inc.

The latest casualties include Vermont's oldest brewery, the Catamount Brewing Co., which shut down last month. Also, the Miller Brewing Co. has given up its stake in Maine's largest brewer, the Shipyard Brewing Co., after distribution was scaled back in the Midwest and the Middle Atlantic states.

Some brewers learned the hard way that they should have focused on their local audiences instead of trying to grow too fast.

"The lesson is: Devote your time, your money and your effort to your core market, and you'll be fine," said David Geary, who opened D.L. Geary's Brewing Co. in Portland in 1986.

But some closings were inevitable because the market couldn't support the entry of more than 900 brewpubs and microbreweries over a three-year period leading up to 1998, when sales went flat, said David Edgar of the Institute for Brewing Studies in Colorado.

Back then, observers thought specialty or craft beers could obtain as much as 10% of the national beer market, but the market

the firm be willing to do that?[1]) If output must be increased to achieve allocative efficiency, we know that at present the firm must be producing less than the efficient level. In summary, monopolistically competitive firms produce less output than is socially desirable.

---

[1] The firm won't be willing to expand output because that behavior is not consistent with profit maximization; MC exceeds MR for each unit beyond Q. In fact, if the firm chose to produce at the output where the demand curve intersects the MC curve, it would incur a loss since the ATC curve is above the demand curve at that point.

share of these beers remains below 3%.

"I think what you're finding in this segment of the beer market was more of a flash in the pan," said Skip Carpenter, an analyst at Donaldson, Lufkin and Jenrette in New York.

What exactly constitutes a craft beer is murky, but connoisseurs say they know it when they taste it.

Mr. Geary defines it as traditional beer brewed by traditional methods with traditional ingredients. Edgar says craft beer is produced with 100% malted barley instead of the 30% to 40% rice or corn found in the nation's top-selling brands. Another difference is price, about $6 to $7 for a six-pack of craft beer, compared with about $4.50 or $5 for a six-pack of traditional American brews in 12-ounce bottles.

The cluttered marketplace was one of several problems facing the new entrants. Analysts said some of the companies lacked a hands-on knowledge of the industry; they didn't have a good handle on large-scale transportation and distribution issues, and the quality of the beer suffered.

Meanwhile, some fair-weather beer drinkers moved to the next fad, flavored drinks such as "Hooper's Hooch" and "Bodean's Twisted Tea" that are filling shelf space to the detriment of brews.

For breweries, it was a case of the survival of the fittest, and that is not necessarily a bad thing for the 1,447 brewpubs, microbreweries and regional specialty brewers still in business, analysts said. Scaling back means many of the breweries are getting back to their original goal of producing local beer for local people, according to Mr. Geary.

"It's fairly clear that when people get excited about something being good, they think, `If some is good, more is better,'" he said. "That's not the case."…

Use Your Economic Reasoning

1. Do microbreweries represent a purely competitive, monopolistically competitive, or oligopolistic industry? Do they represent a separate industry or should they be lumped in with the larger producers— Anheuser-Busch, Miller Brewing, etc.? Defend your conclusions.

2. Imagine a community containing only one microbrewery or brewpub. Would that firm enjoy substantial market power? Why or why not?

3. More than 900 brewpubs and microbreweries entered the industry in the three years prior to 1998. Why do you think they chose to enter this industry? Draw a graph representing the situation of the average microbrewery in 1995 that may have prompted this entry.

4. According to the article, there has been an industry "shakeout" and only the "fittest" breweries will survive. Is this consistent with our economic model? In other words, should this outcome have been anticipated? Support your conclusion with the appropriate graphs.

In addition to distorting the allocation of resources, monopolistically competitive firms are somewhat less efficient at producing their products and charge slightly higher prices than purely competitive firms with the same costs. These outcomes are at least in part the result of the overcrowding that characterizes most monopolistically competitive industries.

The crowded nature of monopolistically competitive industries is illustrated by the large number of clothing stores, video-rental establishments, convenience groceries, and fast-food restaurants in your city or town. By differentiating its product, each of these firms is able to capture a small share of the market. But often so many firms share that market that it is difficult for any one of them to attract enough customers to use its facilities efficiently—to permit it to operate at minimum *ATC*.

Because the monopolistically competitive firm underutilizes its production facilities, its average cost of production will be higher than the *ATC* of a purely competitive firm with identical cost curves.[2] For example, consider the *ATC* curve in case (b) of Exh. 8.2. In long-run equilibrium a purely competitive firm would earn zero economic profit and produce its product at minimum *ATC* (point *A*), whereas we've seen that monopolistically competitive firms will operate at a somewhat higher *ATC* (point *B*). As a consequence, the monopolistically competitive firm must charge a higher price than the purely competitive firm in order to earn a normal profit in the long run.

Fortunately for consumers, the difference in price is probably not substantial. Furthermore, consumers gain something for the additional dollars they pay. Remember, purely competitive firms sell products that are identical in the minds of consumers, whereas monopolistic competitors aim for product differentiation. Many of us are willing to pay a little more to obtain the product variety that monopolistic competition provides.

OLIGOPOLY

Millions of firms in hundreds of U.S. retail industries match the model of monopolistic competition reasonably well. However, most manufacturing industries—steel, aluminum, automobiles, and prescription drugs, for example—are more accurately described as oligopolistic. An **oligopoly** is an industry dominated by a few relatively large sellers that are protected by substantial barriers to entry. The distinguishing feature of all oligopolistic industries is the high degree of interdependence among the sellers and the very personal nature of the rivalry that results from that interdependence.

Oligopolists and Market Power

Because oligopolistic firms enjoy a large share of their market, their production decisions have a significant impact on market price. A substantial increase in production by any one of them would cause downward pressure on

---

[2] This analysis assumes that the monopolistic competitor has cost curves that are identical to those of the pure competitor. In fact, the monopolistic competitor probably has higher costs due to advertising expense and other product differentiation efforts. Thus, there are two reasons to expect its selling price to be higher: It does not operate at the minimum on its *ATC* curve (whereas a pure competitor does), *and* its ATC curve is higher than that of a pure competitor.

price; a significant decrease would tend to push price upward. Suppose, for instance, that the Aluminum Company of America (Alcoa) decided to increase production by 50 percent. Since Alcoa is a major producer, this increase in output would expand industry supply significantly and thereby depress the industry price. A substantial reduction in Alcoa's output would tend to have the opposite effect; it would push price upward.

We have seen that soybean farmers, hog producers, and others in purely competitive industries cannot influence price by manipulating industry output: They're not big enough; that is, they don't control a large enough share of the market. In addition, the large number of firms in these competitive industries makes it virtually impossible for them to coordinate their actions— to agree to limit production, for example. As a consequence, changes in the output of a competitive industry are always the unplanned result of independent actions by thousands of producers. Output in an oligopolistic industry, on the other hand, is often carefully controlled by the few large firms that dominate production. This control is one of the keys to the pricing discretion of the oligopolists.

Some oligopolists also acquire market power through product differentiation. Although producers of such commodities as aluminum ingots, steel sheet, and heating oil sell virtually identical products, many oligopolists sell differentiated products. Producers of automobiles, pet foods, video-game machines, greeting cards, cigarettes, breakfast cereals, and washers and dryers belong in this category. Oligopolistic sellers of differentiated products possess market power both because they are large in relation to the total industry *and* because their product is in some way unique.

Mutual Interdependence and Game Theory

Since oligopolistic firms have pricing discretion, they are price searchers rather than price takers. But the high degree of interdependence among oligopolists tends to restrict the pricing discretion of the individual firm and complicate its search for the profit-maximizing price.

Because there are only a few large sellers, each firm must consider the reactions of its rivals before taking any action. For instance, before altering the price of its product, Ford Motor Company must consider the reactions of General Motors, Toyota, and the other firms in the industry. And Coca-Cola must weigh the likely reactions of Pepsi-Cola and other soft-drink suppliers before contemplating any price change. In both instances, raising prices may be ill-advised unless the other firms can be counted on to match the price hike. Price reductions may be an equally poor strategy if rivals respond with matching price cuts or with deeper cuts that lead to continuing price warfare.

One tool that economists use to understand and predict the behavior of oligopolists such as Ford and Coca-Cola is *game theory*. **Game theory** is the study of the strategies employed by interdependent players involved in some form of competition, or game. The "players" can be individuals, sport teams, nations, or business firms. And the "games" involved can be true games of chance or sporting events or struggles between armies on a battlefield or business rivalries.

All games involve strategy and a payoff matrix. A strategy is simply a plan for accomplishing an objective: winning a battle or earning as much profit as possible, for example. And a payoff matrix is a grid showing the outcomes for the various combinations of strategies employed by the players. The following examples will help to illustrate these terms and will also reveal some of the important conclusions of the game theory model.

Games with Dominant Strategies

Consider the rivalry between Coca-Cola and Pepsi-Cola, the most important firms in the soft-drink industry. Let's assume that these two firms are trying to decide whether to charge $10 or $12 for each case of their soft drinks; these are the alternative strategies under consideration. In making this decision, each firm recognizes that its profit (the payoff from its strategy) depends not only on the price it selects but also on the price selected by its rival. The different possible outcomes are contained in the payoff matrix presented in Exh. 8.3.

According to the matrix, if Coke charges $12 a case and Pepsi chooses the same price, each firm will earn a profit of $300 million (see the cell in the upper left-hand corner of the matrix). The problem with this strategy is that neither firm can be certain that its rival will decide to charge $12. In fact, as the matrix reveals, each firm has incentive to undercut its rival. For example, if Coke selects the $12 price and Pepsi counters with a $10 price, Pepsi will earn a profit of $400 million (see the lower left-hand cell), while Coke will earn only $100 million. If Pepsi charges $12 and Coke opts to charge $10, the outcome will be reversed; Coke will earn a $400 million profit, and Pepsi will earn only $100 million (see the upper right-hand cell).

The remaining possibility is that both firms will decide to charge $10. In that case each firm will earn a profit of $200 million. While this is not the best the firms could do, it is not the worst either since it avoids the possibility of earning a profit of only $100 million. According to game theorists, both oligopolists will see the $10 price as particularly attractive. There are two reasons for this attraction: First, if one firm decides to charge $10 and its rival opts to charge $12, the firm charging the lower ($10) price will earn a $400 million profit, the highest amount possible. Second, charging $10 eliminates the possibility that a firm will be undercut by its

EXHIBIT 8.3

A Game with Two Dominant Strategies

Coke's price strategies

		$12	$10
Pepsi's price strategies	$12	Each firm earns a profit of $300 million.	Coke earns $400 million. Pepsi earns $100 million.
	$10	Coke earns $100 million. Pepsi earns $400 million.	Each firm earns a profit of $200 million.

The payoffs matrix shows that each firm's profits depend not only on its actions but also on the actions of its rival. For instance, if Coke charges $12, it will earn a profit of $300 million if Pepsi matches that price but only $100 million if Pepsi opts to charge $10.

In this example each firm has a *dominant strategy*, a strategy that should be pursued regardless of the strategy selected by its rival. The dominant strategy for both Coke and Pepsi is to charge $10; that strategy leads to higher profits regardless of the strategy selected by the other firm.

rival and find itself able to earn a profit of only $100 million (the lowest outcome in the matrix).

In the preceding example the decision to select the $10 price is the *dominant strategy* for both firms. A **dominant strategy** is one that should be pursued regardless of the strategy selected by the rival. In our example, for instance, Coke is better off charging the $10 price regardless of whether Pepsi opts to match that price or to charge $12 instead. The same is true for Pepsi. As a result the equilibrium solution occurs in the lower right-hand cell, with both firms charging $10. As long as these firms act independently, neither firm has any incentive to modify its strategy.

Games without Dominant Strategies

Not all games have dominant strategies. Others have dominant strategies for one rival but not the other. To illustrate, suppose that Coke and Pepsi are trying to decide whether to utilize both television and newspaper advertising or to limit their campaigns to newspaper advertising. As in the earlier example, the payoff for each strategy depends on the reaction of the rival. These payoffs

EXHIBIT 8.4
A Game with Only One Dominant Strategy

Coke's advertising strategies

		TV and newspaper	Newspaper only
Pepsi's advertising strategies	TV and newspaper	Coke earns $300 million. Pepsi earns $200 million.	Coke earns $200 million. Pepsi earns $300 million.
	Newspaper only	Coke earns $500 million. Pepsi earns $100 million.	Coke earns $400 million. Pepsi earns $350 million.

In this example Coke's dominant strategy is to engage in both TV and newspaper advertising. Pepsi does not have a dominant strategy; its optimal strategy depends on the strategy adopted by Coke.

are represented in Exh. 8.4. Take a moment to examine the matrix before reading further. Can you determine the strategy that will be selected by each firm? Does each firm have a dominant strategy?

In this case Pepsi does *not* have a dominant strategy; its optimal strategy depends on the strategy adopted by Coke. If Coke decides to pursue both TV and newspaper advertising, Pepsi's optimal strategy is to use both TV and newspaper advertising as well (a profit of $200 million rather than $100 million). On the other hand, if Coke decides to limit its advertising to newspapers, Pepsi's best strategy is to do the same (a profit of $350 million rather than $300 million). As you can see, Pepsi does not have a dominant strategy; its best strategy depends on what Coke does.

Before Pepsi can decide on a strategy, it must predict what Coke is likely to do. In this instance that's not too difficult because Coke *does* have a dominant strategy. Here Coke's dominant strategy is to engage in both TV and newspaper advertising; that yields the most profit regardless of the strategy pursued by Pepsi.[3] Once Pepsi recognizes that Coke's dominant strategy is to advertise in both media, it knows that its own best strategy is to follow suit.

---

[3] Note that if Pepsi engages in TV and newspaper advertising and Coke does the same, Coke earns a profit of $300 million rather than the $200 million it would earn if it chose only newspaper advertising. On the other hand, if Pepsi limits its campaign to newspaper advertising, Coke will earn a profit of $400 million if it matches that strategy or $500 million if it uses both media. As you can see, Coke is always better off to pursue a strategy of both TV and newspaper advertising.

The equilibrium solution, then, is in the upper left-hand cell, with both firms advertising in both media.[4]

One interesting point about the equilibrium solution is that neither firm earns as much profit as it could if both firms decided to avoid TV advertising. But each firm is reluctant to select this strategy for fear that the other firm *will* run TV ads. A similar problem existed in the initial example. (See Exh. 8.3 to refresh your memory.) Even though the dominant strategy was to select the $10 price, each firm could earn more profit if both firms decided to charge $12. But, as in the advertising example, neither firm was willing to pursue that strategy for fear of being undercut by its rival. This points to the incentive that oligopolists have to cooperate (rather than compete). We turn next to the methods that they might employ to facilitate cooperation.

Tactics for Cooperating

Oligopolists may respond to their interdependence by employing tactics that allow them to cooperate and make mutually advantageous decisions. One tactic is **collusion**, agreement among sellers to fix prices, divide up the market, or in some other way limit competition. For instance, in our earlier example (see Exh. 8.3), suppose that Pepsi and Coke secretly agreed to charge $12 (rather than $10). That action would allow each firm to earn more profit. An agreement to avoid TV advertising (see Exh. 8.4) would have a similar impact.

Collusive agreements result in cartels, such as the OPEC oil cartel and the DeBeers diamond cartel. Although collusive agreements are legal in some countries, they are illegal in the United States and are punishable by fine and imprisonment. (As a consequence, firms attempt to keep them secret.) In spite of the penalties, some U.S. firms continue to engage in collusion. Dozens of violators are prosecuted each year, and many others probably go undetected. That business executives are willing to risk prison sentences to engage in collusion is testimony both to the potential financial gains and to the problems posed by interdependence.

A more subtle form of cooperation (and communication) is price leadership. **Price leadership** is much like a game of follow-the-leader. One firm—perhaps the biggest, the most efficient, or simply the most trusted—initiates all increases or decreases in prices. The remaining firms in the industry follow the leader. This leader–follower behavior is generally reinforced by indirect

---

[4] If both firms decide to advertise, they will have reached a **Nash equilibrium** (named for John Nash, the 1997 Nobel prize–winning economist who discovered the concept). A Nash equilibrium exists when each firm's strategy is the best it can choose, given the strategy chosen by the other firm. There is more than one way to achieve a Nash equilibrium. For example, when both firms have a dominant strategy, the result is a Nash equilibrium. But, as this example illustrates, a Nash equilibrium does not *require* that both players have dominant strategies.

forms of communication (rather than the direct communication involved in collusion). For example, price leaders usually signal their intent to raise prices through press releases or through public speeches. This lets the follower firms know that a price increase is coming so that they will not be taken by surprise. (If the price leader hikes its price and no one follows, it will probably have to back down, creating confusion for the industry.) This tactic allows the firms in the industry to accomplish price changes legally, without collusion.

Neither collusive agreements nor price leadership may be necessary when an industry is dominated by firms that recognize their interdependence. **Conscious parallelism** occurs when, without any communication whatsoever, firms adopt similar policies. For instance, even without meeting or signaling each other, firms may come to recognize that price cutting, because it invites retaliation, leaves all firms worse off. They may therefore shun this practice as long as their rivals reciprocate. Conscious parallelism may also explain why all firms in an industry provide the same discounts to larger buyers and why they all raise prices at the same time of year.

Collusion, price leadership, and conscious parallelism all tend to result in an avoidance of price competition. Instead, oligopolists channel their competitive drive into *nonprice competition*—advertising, packaging, and new product development. This form of rivalry has two significant advantages over price competition. First, a new product or a successful advertising cam-

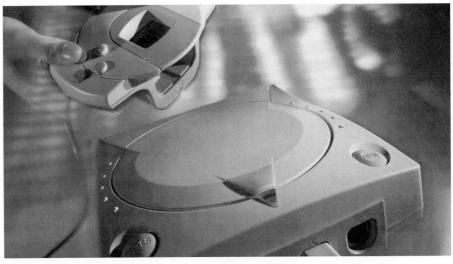

Oligopolists often channel their competitive instincts into nonprice competition: advertising, packaging, and new product development.

paign is more difficult for a competitor to match than a price cut is, and so an oligopolist may gain a more lasting advantage over its rivals. Second, rivalry through product differentiation or new product development is less likely than price competition to get out of control and severely damage the profits of all firms in the industry. Thus, nonprice competition is seen as a more promising strategy than price competition.

Factors Limiting Cooperation

Although oligopolists strive to avoid price warfare and confine their rivalry to nonprice competition, these efforts are not always successful. Collusion and price leadership often break down because of the strong temptation to cheat (price-cut) in order to win customers. Even conscious parallelism can give way to price cutting if firms believe their actions may be undetected. To understand this temptation, look back at Exh. 8.3 for a moment. Suppose that Coke and Pepsi have agreed, either informally or through collusion, to charge a price of $12. Each firm recognizes that if it undercuts the other firm by charging $10, it can expand its profits. And if the firm is not too greedy—if the price cutting is limited to a small fraction of industry sales, for example—the practice may go undiscovered and the rival may not retaliate.

The likelihood of cheating is greatest in markets in which prices tend to be secret (so that price cutting may go undetected) and in which long contracts may delay the impact of retaliation. Cheating also becomes more commonplace as the number of firms in the industry increases since it becomes more difficult for the firms to agree on the best price. In addition, the state of the economy clearly influences the likelihood of cheating. History shows that price cutting is particularly common in periods of weak demand, when firms have substantial excess capacity that they would like to put to work. During such periods, firms will be tempted to undercut their rivals in order to expand sales.

In truth, the success of oligopolists in avoiding price competition varies significantly from industry to industry. Some industries—the breakfast cereal and cigarette manufacturing industries, for example—have demonstrated a marked ability to avoid price competition; others—steel manufacturing, for instance—experience recurring bouts of price warfare.[5] Because the behavior of oligopolists is so varied, it is difficult to generalize about the impact of oligopoly on social welfare. We will attempt some cautious observations after discussing the final industry structure, pure monopoly.

---

[5] Although cereal producers have a long history of avoiding price warfare, even their discipline can break down. In 1996 Kellogg and Philip Morris (which owns Post and Nabisco cereals) announced price cuts averaging about 20 percent. This led to price cutting by other manufacturers.

MONOPOLY

Although both monopolistic competitors and oligopolists have some pricing discretion, the classic example of a firm with market power is the monopolist.

Monopoly is an industry structure in which a single firm sells a product for which there are no close substitutes. (Monopoly is sometimes called *pure monopoly* to emphasize that it is the industry structure farthest removed from pure competition.) A firm can become a monopolist in a variety of ways but can remain a monopolist only if barriers prevent other firms from entering the industry. One barrier to entry is exclusive control of some critical input—a basic raw material needed in the production process, for instance. A second way a firm may enjoy a monopoly is through sheer size, when larger size brings with it greater efficiency and lower production costs. Entry into the industry is effectively blocked by the large capital investment a rival would require to begin operating at competitive size. A possible third source of monopoly is government policies. For instance, the U.S. government issues patents that provide a firm with the exclusive right to control a new product for a period of twenty years. The government franchise is another example of government policies promoting monopoly. A **government franchise** is an exclusive license to provide a product or service. Government franchises account for the presence of only one restaurant chain on the interstate highway and the single boat-rental establishment in a state park. National governments can also create or preserve monopolies through their trade policies. By erecting trade barriers, governments can prevent foreign products from entering their countries, thereby reserving the market for domestic firms.

Monopoly and Market Power

Monopolists enjoy substantial pricing discretion because they are the sole suppliers of their products. This enables the monopolist to manipulate industry output and thereby alter the market price. The monopolist's control over output does not provide it with complete or unlimited pricing discretion, however. Complete pricing discretion would result in a vertical, perfectly inelastic demand curve, signifying the ability to increase price without losing *any* customers. This condition would represent the true opposite of the purely competitive firm, which possesses no market power and faces a horizontal, perfectly elastic demand curve.

But a monopolist does stand to lose some customers when it raises its price, because monopolists face a certain amount of competition from rivals in *other* industries. To illustrate, think about a community served by a single newspaper and a single provider of electric power. These sellers fit the description of a monopolist, but neither is without competition. If the newspaper charges a high subscription rate, residents can turn to their local TV or radio station for their news. If it charges high prices for its classified ads, residents can buy cardboard signs and post them around town. Or they can turn to the Internet and try to reach customers that way. Residents face tougher choices when it comes to dealing with the local electric company, but even here they have options. If the utility company effects a drastic rate increase for electricity, residents can begin by reducing their use of electricity. They can insulate their homes and install energy-saving appliances; ultimately, they can even purchase their own electricity generators. The point is that the availability of substitutes, however imperfect, constrains the monopolist's pricing discretion.[6]

Monopoly and Profit Maximization

Because a monopolist stands to lose some customers when it raises its price, the demand curve it faces must slope downward just as those of other price searchers do. This tells us that the monopolist must restrict output to charge a high price; conversely, it must reduce price to sell more. The monopolist will select the profit-maximizing output and price in exactly the same way other price searchers do; it will produce the output at which $MR = MC$ and find its price by going up to the demand curve. The difference between a monopolist and other price searchers is found not in the rules used to determine their price but in the competitive situation. Monopolistically competitive firms and oligopolists face some degree of competition from other firms in the industry. The monopolist *is* the industry, and so its only competition comes from firms in other industries.

Because monopolists enjoy substantial pricing discretion, it is commonly believed that they must earn economic profits. But that need not be the case. In the short run, monopolists, like other producers, may experience economic profits, normal profits, or even losses. How well a monopolist will fare depends on the demand and cost conditions that it faces. Imagine, for instance, a firm that has patented a medicine for a very rare disease—with an average diagnosis of ten cases a year. This monopolist has substantial pricing discretion with these unfortunate victims, but the demand is so limited that the product probably will be unprofitable to produce. Or consider the boat-rental concession at an isolated state park. The owner enjoys a government-granted monopoly, but if few vacationers frequent the lake, it won't be a very profitable monopoly. The point is that even a monopolist can't earn a profit if the demand

---

[6] Although many communities are still served by a single provider of electric power, technological advances and regulatory changes are undermining these monopolies. Perhaps someday, in the not-too-distant future, most consumers will have choices about where to buy their power. But don't hold your breath! California's efforts at deregulation have not had the desired impact, so other states are likely to proceed with caution.

for its product is very limited. High production costs can signal a similar problem. Exhibit 8.5 depicts a monopolist incurring a short-run economic loss.

When monopolists are able to earn short-run profits, substantial entry barriers help them to continue earning those profits in the long run. But the long run does not mean forever! Ultimately the development of new products, the introduction of new technologies, and/or the elimination of legal barriers to entry tend to undermine the monopolist's position. For example, at one time Atlantic Telephone and Telegraph (AT&T) enjoyed a monopoly in providing long-distance telephone service. But new technology ultimately destroyed its monopoly status (this will be discussed in greater detail in a moment). A similar fate seems in store for your provider of local phone service. Cell phone companies now provide consumers with an alternative to the wired service offered by these former monopolists. Moreover, the deregulation of this industry carries the promise of additional competition for wired service as well.

While technological change has played a critical role in undermining the telephone monopolies, it's not the only thing that monopolists have to fear. Consider the monopoly currently enjoyed by Glaxo Wellcome in the manufacture of AZT, a major drug used to treat AIDS patients. Glaxo Wellcome obtained

EXHIBIT 8.5
A Monopolist Incurring a Loss

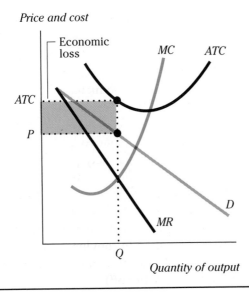

Even a monopolist can incur a loss if there is little demand for its product or if its costs are high.

a monopoly in AZT by developing the drug and then obtaining a patent to prevent other firms from duplicating it. But the substantial profits the firm is earning from the drug ensure that other companies will go to great lengths to develop a substitute. And even if they are not successful, patent protection will ultimately expire and consumers will be flooded with generic forms of AZT, which will substantially lower its price and Glaxo Wellcome's profits.

None of this is intended to make you feel sorry for monopolists. Technological progress is hard to predict and generally occurs slowly. And patent protection is currently granted for a period of twenty years. The point is that change is inevitable and eventually most monopolists find their status eroded by forces that are largely beyond their control.

THE CONSEQUENCES OF MONOPOLY OR OLIGOPOLY

The presence of monopolies can have a significant effect on consumer well-being. Monopolists tend to produce too little output and sometimes charge prices that are inflated by economic profits. These negative effects may be partially offset by lower production costs or greater innovation. Oligopoly can have a similar impact on consumer welfare, though it is much more difficult to generalize about the consequences of this industry structure.

The Problems of Misallocation of Resources and Redistribution of Income

Economists generally agree that monopolists distort the allocation of scarce resources. Like monopolistically competitive firms, monopolists fail to produce up to the point where marginal social benefit equals marginal social cost—the point at which resources would be allocated efficiently. As a consequence, too few resources are devoted to the production of the goods and services produced by monopolists, and too many resources are left over to be used in the more competitive sectors of the economy. For example, if there were only two industries in the economy, a monopolized computer industry and a purely competitive farming industry, society probably would receive too few computers and too many agricultural products.

The redistribution of income is another problem caused by monopolies. Because entrance into these industries is blocked, consumers may be required to pay higher prices than necessary, prices that include economic profits on top of the normal profits that are necessary to convince firms to continue operation. These higher prices redistribute income from consumers (who will be worse off) to monopolists (who will be better off).

Although economists are fairly confident in generalizing about the consequences of monopoly, they find it more difficult to make blanket statements regarding the impact of oligopoly. This is primarily because the behavior of oligopolists is so varied. To the extent that oligopolists cooperate and avoid price competition, the welfare effects of oligopoly probably are very similar to the effects of pure monopoly. When cooperation breaks down, consumer welfare is enhanced and the negative effects of oligopoly are reduced. Since it is clear that oligopolists do not always succeed in avoiding price competition, the impact of oligopoly on consumer well-being probably lies somewhere between the impacts of monopoly and pure competition.

The Possible Benefits of Size

Although monopoly and oligopoly often have undesirable effects on consumer welfare, this is not always the case. Under certain conditions these structures may benefit society. For example, if a monopolist's/oligopolist's greater size leads to economies of scale (lower long-run average costs), it may be able to charge a lower price than a competitive firm even as it earns an economic profit. And because monopolists and oligopolists are often able to earn economic profits in the long run, they can afford the investment necessary to develop new products and cost-reducing production techniques. Thus, in the long run, society may receive better products and lower prices from monopolists and oligopolists than from competitive firms.

Studies of the U.S. economy provide limited support for these arguments. For example, in the refrigerator-manufacturing industry a firm needs 15–20 percent of the market in order to achieve production efficiency, or minimum *ATC*. This means that for optimal efficiency, room exists for only five or six firms in that industry. The efficient manufacture and distribution of beer requires a somewhat smaller but nevertheless substantial market share: 10–14 percent. (Plant economies of scale appeared to become more important in the 1970s and early 80s, but the emergence of many microbreweries shows that small firms can still survive—albeit with higher average costs—if they are successful in differentiating their products and charging premium prices.) But in the majority of the manufacturing industries surveyed, firms with 3 percent of the market or less were large enough to operate at minimum *ATC*. Thus, it is not generally necessary for industries to be dominated by one or a few firms in order to achieve efficiency in production and distribution.[7]

Evidence on business research and development efforts leads to a similar conclusion. Firms in highly competitive industries are not particularly innov-

---

[7] F. M. Scherer and David Ross, *Industrial Market Structure and Economic Performance*, 3d ed. (Houghton Mifflin, 1990), p. 140.

ative, perhaps because they are unable to earn the profits necessary to finance research and development efforts. But firms in "tightly" oligopolistic industries (in which a very few firms closely coordinate their actions) don't tend to be innovative either. These firms often have the money but seem to lack the incentive, which stems from competitive pressure, to invest in research and development. The most innovative tend to be medium-sized firms in "loosely" oligopolistic industries—industries composed of several firms (perhaps ten or twenty) with no single dominant firm. Because some competitive pressure exists, it may be harder for the firms in these industries to coordinate their actions, but because they have some pricing discretion, such firms often earn the economic profits necessary to support research and development efforts.[8]

In summary, economies of scale and greater innovation may sometimes compensate for the resource misallocation and income redistribution caused by oligopolists and monopolists. In some cases we may even be able to justify a "natural" monopoly on the basis of greater production efficiency or technical considerations, a possibility that was discussed in the last chapter. Even when we take these benefits into consideration, however, we find that manufacturing industries have fewer and larger firms than necessary to achieve the advantages of production efficiency and increased innovation. In general, U.S. consumers would be better off if the existing industry structure were more, not less, competitive.

ANTITRUST AND REGULATION

Because the exercise of market power by monopolists and oligopolists can distort the allocation of scarce resources and redistribute income, the federal and state governments pursue policies designed to promote competition and restrict the actions of firms with market power. The primary weapons used in the battle against market power are antitrust laws and industry regulation. As you will see, these two approaches to the problem differ significantly in both their philosophies and the remedies they propose.

Antitrust Enforcement

Antitrust laws have as their objective the maintenance and promotion of competition. These laws (1) outlaw collusion, (2) make it illegal for a firm to attempt to achieve a monopoly, and (3) ban **mergers,** the union of two or more companies into a single firm, when such mergers are likely to result in substantially less competition.

---

[8] Douglas F. Greer, *Industrial Organization and Public Policy* (New York: Macmillan, 1980), p. 598.

Virtually all antitrust enforcement in the United States is based on three fundamental statutes: the Sherman Antitrust Act of 1890, the Clayton Antitrust Act of 1914, and the Federal Trade Commission Act, also passed in 1914. Exhibit 8.6 offers a brief comparison of these laws.

The Sherman Antitrust Act

The Sherman Act, the first of the big three, was a response to the monopolistic exploitation that occurred in the latter half of the nineteenth century, when trusts had become commonplace. **Trusts** are combinations of firms organized for the purpose of restraining price competition and thereby gaining economic profit. (For our purposes, a trust is the same thing as a cartel.) So many companies were merging at this time that competitors were disappearing at an alarming rate. Du Pont, for example, achieved a near monopoly in the manufacture of explosives by either merging with or acquiring some 100 rival firms between 1872 and 1912.[9] Monopolies and monopolistic practices translated into higher

---

[9] F. M. Scherer, *Industrial Market Structure and Economic Performance*, 2d ed. (Chicago: Rand McNally, 1980), p. 121.

EXHIBIT 8.6
The Antitrust Laws and What They Do

The Sherman Antitrust Act (1890)	Outlawed agreements to fix prices, limit output, or share the market. Also declared that monopolies and attempts to monopolize are illegal.
The Clayton Antitrust Act (1914)	Forbade competitors to merge if the impact of merger would be to lessen competition substantially. Also outlawed certain practices, such as tying contracts.
The Federal Trade Commission Act (1914)	Created the Federal Trade Commission and empowered it to initiate and decide cases involving "unfair competition." Also declared that deceptive practices and unfair methods of competition are illegal.

prices for consumers and inspired a strong political movement that led to the passage of the Sherman Antitrust Act in 1890.

The Sherman Act declared illegal all agreements between competing firms to fix prices, limit output, or otherwise restrict the forces of competition. It also declared illegal all monopolies or "attempts to monopolize any part of trade or commerce among the several states, or with foreign nations." In 1911, the law became the basis for the antitrust suit that resulted in the breakup of Standard Oil, a trust that controlled some 90 percent of the petroleum industry.

In deciding the Standard Oil case, the Supreme Court applied a principle known as the "rule of reason." According to this interpretation, possessing a monopoly is not, by itself, a violation of the law. Rather, it must be shown that the firm deliberately sought to obtain a monopoly or engaged in conduct intended to preserve its monopoly. This principle was evident in Judge Penfield Jackson's findings in the recent antitrust case involving the Microsoft Corporation. On April 3, 2000, Judge Jackson found that Microsoft had violated the Sherman Act because it had illegally protected its Windows monopoly against competitors and had attempted to monopolize the market for browsers used to navigate the World Wide Web. The judge went on to order that Microsoft be split into two companies, one company that sells the Windows operating system and another that sells all other Microsoft products. As this text goes to

Microsoft chairman, Bill Gates, maintains that his company is a tough, but fair competitor that has not violated antitrust laws.

press, the case is on appeal. (Is the Sherman Act still relevant in the New Economy? Might monopoly be a good thing? To consider these issues, read "For Policy Makers, Microsoft Suggests Need to Recast Models," on page 250.)

As a result of the limits laid down by the courts in the Standard Oil case, businesses became somewhat less aggressive in their monopolistic practices. Rather than strive for monopoly, they were content to become the dominant firms in their respective oligopolistic industries. However, many firms gained dominion not by abandoning such practices but by pursuing them in disguised and subtle ways. This led Congress in 1914 to pass two more bills aimed at curbing anticompetitive practices: the Clayton Antitrust Act and the Federal Trade Commission Act.

The Clayton Antitrust Act

The Clayton Act was designed primarily to stem the tide of mergers that had already reduced competition significantly in a number of important industries, such as steel production, petroleum refining, and electrical equipment manufacture. The act prohibited mergers between competing firms if the impact of their union would be to "substantially lessen competition or to tend to create a monopoly." The act also outlawed other practices if they lessened competition. "Other practices" included **tying contracts**—agreements specifying that the purchaser would, as a condition of sale for a given product, also buy some other product offered by the seller. Once again, enforcement was a problem because the courts interpreted this law in ways that permitted mergers between competing firms to continue. Finally, in 1950, the Cellar-Kefauver Act amended the Clayton Act by closing a major loophole, thus effectively eliminating the possibility of mergers involving major competitors.

During the Reagan and Bush administrations, the government relaxed its restrictions against mergers involving major competitors. The Clinton administration, with a few exceptions, also tended to be consenting in its attitude toward mergers. The result was a wave of merger activity beginning in the 1980s and continuing through the 1990s. This trend shows every indication that it will continue into the new millennium, though with a new twist. The new twist is cross-border mergers, like the recent merger between German auto producer, Daimler-Benz, and U.S. producer, Chrysler Motors.

The Federal Trade Commission Act

The last of the three major antitrust statutes, the Federal Trade Commission Act, was also passed in 1914. Its primary purpose was to establish a special agency, the Federal Trade Commission (FTC), empowered to investigate allegations of "unfair methods of competition" and to command businesses in violation of FTC regulations to cease those practices. Although the FTC Act did not specify the precise meaning of "unfair methods of competition," the phrase has been interpreted by the commission to include practices prohibited under the Sherman and Clayton Acts—price fixing and tying contracts, for example—and any other practices that can be shown to limit competition or damage the consuming public. For instance, the FTC has deemed it unfair for a funeral home to fail to provide, in advance, an itemized price list for funeral services and merchandise or to furnish embalming without first informing customers about alternatives.

The Federal Trade Commission is one of the two federal agencies charged with the enforcement of the antitrust statutes. The other agency is the Antitrust Division of the Justice Department. The Antitrust Division is responsible for enforcing the Sherman and Clayton Acts and lesser pieces of antitrust legislation. The FTC is also charged with antitrust enforcement, including civil actions against violators of either the Sherman or Clayton Acts, but its responsibilities are somewhat broader. About half its resources are devoted to combating deception and misrepresentation: improper labeling and misleading advertisements, for example. The overlapping responsibilities of the FTC and the Antitrust Division have posed some problems of coordination, but these are at least partially offset by the likelihood that one agency's oversights may be picked up by the other.

Criticisms of Antitrust

Some economists argue that antitrust should be discarded because it is based on the outmoded perception that bigness (being large in relation to the size of the market) is bad. These economists believe that the ability of large firms to achieve economies of scale and rapid development of new products more than compensates for any reduction in competition. This is particularly true, they argue, in an era of increased foreign competition. Lester Thurow of MIT points out that firms that seem large relative to the U.S. economy are not so large when viewed in the context of the world economy; therefore, they possess less market power than is commonly assumed. According to Thurow, even some of the largest U.S. firms are now in danger of being driven out of business by foreign rivals: "Think, for example, about General Motors. For many years it was the largest industrial firm in the world. Today, even if it were the only American auto manufacturer, it would still be in a competitive fight for its life."[10]

According to these economists, U.S. antitrust laws handicap domestic producers in this competitive struggle. Consider, for example, the Japanese *keiretsu*, or "group of companies." This arrangement joins together rival producers, along with their suppliers, banks, and government agencies, in order to share knowledge and gain efficiency. These structures, although legal in Japan, would probably be illegal in the United States under present antitrust laws. Antitrust critics argue that by prohibiting such joint ventures, we tie the

---

[10] Lester C. Thurow, "An Era of New Competition," *Newsweek*, Jan. 18, 1982, p. 63.

For Policy Makers, Microsoft Signals Need to Recast Models

By Alan Murray

WASHINGTON—The Microsoft case is just the beginning.

As government policy makers grapple with a rapidly changing American marketplace, they are increasingly struck by this fact: In the New Economy, monopoly is becoming the rule, not the exception.

Whether today's hot companies deal in Web services, business-to-business exchanges or MP3 songs, many have the look of what economics textbooks...call "natural monopolies." The products and services often involve a relatively big upfront investment. But they cost little or nothing to manufacture and distribute....

In such a business, it's inexpensive to expand rapidly into a dominant position, and

dangerous not to. Competition of the traditional variety, with multiple firms offering nearly identical products and services, can quickly push prices to zero. But how, if at all, should the government respond to these new monopoly-like businesses?...

In the world described by Scottish economist Adam Smith more than two centuries ago, monopolies tended to stifle competition. Freed from direct competition, the monopolist would raise prices and harm consumers.

But in today's world, many New Economy enthusiasts argue, the quest for monopoly can actually prompt competition. At the Fed meeting in April, business theorist Hal Varian referred to it as "hypercompetition." Like purchasers of lottery tickets, companies seem even more eager to

compete when they know the winner will take all. Instead of competing on price, they compete by innovating, and trying to leapfrog old technologies.

"When there is a big prize at the end of the day, you will see this hypercompetitive struggle to catch the brass ring," says Mr. Varian, a professor at the University of California at Berkeley....

Does that mean the government's antitrust forces will have to get more active, doing to other companies what they have done to Microsoft Corp.? The Clinton administration's top economist, Treasury Secretary Lawrence Summers, steadfastly refuses to comment on the Microsoft case, as do other administration officials. But he gave an intriguing speech in San Francisco last month, titled "The New

hands of our domestic producers and put them at a competitive disadvantage relative to their foreign rivals.[11]

---

[11] Patrick M. Boarman, "Antitrust Laws in a Global Market," *Challenge*, Jan.–Feb. 1993, pp.30–36.

Wealth of Nations," that suggested the proliferation of natural monopolies is more good than bad.

In an information-based economy, he said, "the only incentive to produce anything is the possession of temporary monopoly power—because without that power the price will be bid down to the marginal cost and the high initial fixed costs cannot be recouped." (The "marginal cost" is the cost of producing and distributing, say, one more widget.) Mr. Summers went on: "So the constant pursuit of that monopoly power becomes the central driving thrust of the New Economy. And the creative destruction that results from all that striving becomes the essential spur of economic growth."...

The relentless push toward monopoly in today's economy is increased by something economists call "network effects." In information businesses, the desire for everyone to be part of the same network is intense. Schoolchildren like to use America Online Inc.'s instant-messaging service because their friends use it. Computer users like Microsoft's Word software because it makes it easier to trade files with their colleagues, who also use Word. In his speech in San Francisco, Mr. Summers used the fax machine to describe this network effect. If there is only one, it "is best used as a doorstop." But if there are 100,000, "that is 10 billion possible connections."...

[I]n a network world, the monopolist faces incentives different from those of the Old Economy. Jeremy Bulow, who directs the Bureau of Economics at the Federal Trade Commission, notes that the diamond monopoly of DeBeers Consolidated Mines Ltd. works to keep its product scarce, so prices stay high and consumers suffer.

But for software makers, the scarcity principle is turned upside down. Like Microsoft, such companies have every incentive to try to make their product ubiquitous. The more users they find for their software, the more value it will have for each user, and the more incentive there is for software makers to write related software. In such a situation, consumers may reap the benefits.

Joel Klein, the assistant attorney general for antitrust who brought the Microsoft case, argues that all the talk about the New Economy misses the point. Microsoft's crime lay not in having a monopoly, but in using illegal tactics to both protect that monopoly and extend it into new markets.

"While technology changes," he told a technology forum at the University of California at Berkeley last month, "human nature does not." The anticompetitive techniques "used to protect and extend monopoly power in the New Economy are essentially no different from those used throughout history.... When it comes to antitrust enforcement, the new, new thing isn't so new after all."...

Use Your Economic Reasoning

1. What are "network effects" and how do they increase the tendency toward monopoly?
2. What does the author mean when he says that monopoly can "actually prompt competition"? Isn't monopoly the opposite of competition?
3. Mr. Summers doesn't seem too concerned about monopoly harming consumers. How would you explain that attitude?
4. Joel Klein, the assistant attorney general for antitrust at the time of the Microsoft trial, says that all the talk about the New Economy misses the point. What is the point—why was the antitrust case filed?

Supporters of antitrust laws point out that while bigness is not always bad, it is not always good either. So, they argue, the correct response is not to discard antitrust enforcement but to apply it on a case-by-case basis. For example, some mergers and cooperative ventures may be in the best interests of consumers because they lower costs or create more effective competitors. But others may reduce competition without achieving offsetting efficiencies. And while competition from foreign firms has changed the economic environment for many U.S. businesses, other industries do not face significant competitive pressure from abroad. Furthermore, statistical evidence suggests that most U.S. firms are large enough to compete effectively with foreign rivals. And while there may be exceptions to this generalization—the *keiretsu* and similar foreign alliances may require that similar alliances be permitted in the United States—the existence of these exceptions does not justify abandoning our antitrust statutes.

Industry Regulation

Government regulation of industry approaches the problem of market power from a different perspective and therefore provides a different solution.[12] The basic assumption is that certain industries cannot or should not be made competitive. Hence, the role of government is to provide a framework whereby the actions of these less than competitive firms can be constrained in a manner consistent with the public interest. This is accomplished by establishing regulatory agencies empowered to control the prices such firms can charge, the quality of service they must provide, and the conditions under which additional firms will be allowed to enter the industry.

The reason that certain industries should not be made competitive is that they are *natural monopolies*. As we learned in the last chapter, a natural monopoly exists when a single firm can supply the entire market at a lower average cost than two or more firms could. In essence, natural monopolies are situations in which we don't want to permit competition between firms because it would interfere with our ability to achieve the lowest possible production costs. The provision of local phone service has traditionally been regarded as a natural monopoly, as has the provision of electric power. To understand why, think about your local phone company for a moment. Providing local phone service requires a very large initial investment in switching equipment, telephone poles, wires, and other hardware. These fixed costs are the major costs of doing business as a phone company; the variable cost of providing phone service is relatively low. Of course, the more customers the phone company serves, the lower the firm's average fixed cost. And since most of the phone company's costs are fixed costs, as average fixed cost falls, so does average total cost.

Because average cost declines with output, society is better off with one big firm rather than several smaller firms. At least it is if the monopolist passes on its cost savings to consumers. That's where regulation comes in.

---

[12] Regulation designed to deal with the problems posed by market power is sometimes described as "price and entry regulation" to distinguish it from "health and safety regulation."

Natural monopolies like the local telephone and utility companies are generally subject to rate regulation by state regulatory commissions. The logic is straightforward. Government allows these firms to operate as monopolists to gain the benefits associated with size—low average cost. But it regulates these monopolists to ensure that some of those benefits are passed on to consumers in the form of lower prices.

Although the logic for regulating natural monopolies is straightforward, regulation has not been confined to natural monopolies. Over the years, numerous industries—including airlines, trucking, radio and television, and water carriers (ships and barges)—have been thought to be sufficiently "clothed with the public interest" to justify regulation, even though none of these would be described as natural monopolies. In the last two decades, this questionable regulation has come under increasing attack and virtually all of these industries have been deregulated. Today, deregulation is even stalking industries long-regarded as natural monopolies. For instance, while electric utility companies have long been viewed as natural monopolies, that viewpoint is changing as technological advances make it possible for smaller plants to produce electricity economically.[13] As a consequence, twenty-four states have already deregulated their electric utilities to some extent and many more are in the process. Even the natural monopoly status of the local phone company has been questioned, given the inroads made by cell phones and potential competition from cable TV companies and electric utilities, who often own fiber optic cable networks that could carry phone calls. (For now, local phone rates remain regulated, but that is likely to change in the near future.) In summary, regulation is playing a smaller and smaller role in our economy as policymakers recognize the benefits of competition and technological changes undermine natural monopolies.

SUMMARY

In the U.S. economy, most firms have some market power, or pricing discretion. Market power is exercised through product differentiation or by altering total industry output. The extent of the firm's market power depends on the structure, or makeup, of the industry in which it operates. The definitive characteristics of *industry structure* are the number of sellers in the industry and their size distribution, the nature of the product, and the extent of barriers to

---

[13] The electricity industry can be separated into three distinct services: power generation, transmission, and retail distribution. There is general agreement that generation and retailing are not natural monopolies, but transmission—which involves a large investment in poles and lines—probably still qualifies and is likely to remain regulated.

entry. The four basic industry structures are pure competition, monopolistic competition, oligopoly, and pure monopoly.

At one end of the spectrum lie purely competitive firms, which are totally without market power. Because the competitive industry is characterized by a large number of relatively small firms selling undifferentiated products, each firm is powerless to influence price. The absence of significant barriers to entry prevents purely competitive firms from earning economic profits in the long run.

Monopolistic competition is the market structure most closely resembling pure competition; the difference is that monopolistically competitive firms sell differentiated products. The ability to differentiate its product allows the monopolistically competitive firm some pricing discretion, although that discretion is limited by the availability of close substitutes offered by competing firms. Monopolistically competitive firms misallocate resources because they fail to produce up to the point at which marginal social benefits equal marginal social costs. They also are somewhat less efficient at producing their products than are purely competitive firms with identical cost curves. These disadvantages are at least partially offset by the product variety offered by these sellers.

The third market structure, *oligopoly,* is characterized by a small number of relatively large firms that are protected by significant barriers to entry. Although these firms may enjoy substantial pricing discretion, their market power is constrained by the high degree of interdependence that exists among oligopolistic firms. *Game theory* is one of the tools used to understand and predict the behavior of these interdependent rivals.

Oligopolists sometime use *collusion,* secret agreements to fix prices, and *price leadership,* informal agreements to follow the price changes of one firm, as tactics to reduce competition. Even in the absence of collusion or price leadership, oligopolists may choose to avoid price competition because it tends to invite retaliation. Instead these firms tend to channel their competitive instincts into *nonprice competition*—advertising, packaging, and new product development.

The market structure farthest removed from pure competition is monopoly, or *pure monopoly.* The monopolist enjoys substantial pricing discretion and dictates the level of output. The monopoly *is* the industry because it is the sole seller of a product for which there are no close substitutes. Unlike that of the purely competitive firm, the monopolist's position is protected by substantial barriers to entry, which may enable monopolistic firms to earn economic profits in the long run.

Like monopolistically competitive firms, monopolists tend to distort the allocation of resources by halting production short of the point at which marginal social benefit equals marginal social cost. Monopolists may charge higher prices than necessary—prices that include economic profits. These higher prices redistribute income from consumers to the monopolists. Oligopoly can have a similar impact on consumer welfare, but it is more difficult to generalize about the consequences of that market structure. In some industries the negative consequences of monopoly or oligopoly may be offset by the lower production costs that result from their greater size or by greater innovation due to their ability to invest economic profits in research and development.

Because monopolists and oligopolists may misallocate resources and redistribute income, the U.S. Congress has passed antitrust laws and created regulatory agencies. Enacted in response to the formation of *trusts* (combinations of firms organized to restrain competition), *antitrust laws* prohibit certain kinds of behavior: price fixing, *tying contracts*, and *mergers* entered into for the purpose of limiting competition. The major antitrust statutes are the Sherman Antitrust Act of 1890, the Clayton Antitrust Act of 1914, and the Federal Trade Commission Act, also passed in 1914.

Critics of antitrust argue that it should be discarded because it is based on the misperception that bigness is bad. According to this view, the ability of large firms to achieve economies of scale and more rapid new-product development more than compensates for any reduction in competition. Moreover, in an era of increased foreign competition, even relatively large U.S. firms may be small in comparison with the world market. In fact, cooperative ventures between U.S. firms may be necessary in order to compete effectively with foreign rivals.

Supporters of antitrust respond by pointing out that size does not always confer advantages such as economies of scale or more rapid new product development. In addition, available evidence suggests that most U.S. firms are large enough to compete effectively with their foreign rivals.

Industry regulation, the other approach to dealing with potentially exploitive market power, is designed to establish and police rules of behavior for *natural monopolies*, industries in which competition cannot or should not develop because of technical or cost considerations. In addition, regulation was once extended to some industries where there is little evidence of natural monopoly status—transportation, for example. Today, virtually all of this questionable regulation has been eliminated, and technological changes are undermining some long-standing natural monopolies.

KEY TERMS

Antitrust laws
Collusion
Conscious parallelism
Dominant strategy
Game theory

Government franchise
Industry structure
Merger
Monopolistic competition
Monopoly

Nash equilibrium
Oligopoly
Price leadership
Trusts
Tying contract

STUDY QUESTIONS

Fill in the Blanks

1. Firms that can influence the price of their product are said to possess *Market Power*.

2. An industry dominated by a few relatively large sellers is an *Oligapoly*.

3. The closest market structure to pure competition is *Monopolistic Competition*.

4. In long-run equilibrium, purely competitive firms and *Monopolstic dealer* firms can earn only a normal profit.

5. The distinguishing feature of oligopoly is the high degree of *Interdependance* that exists among sellers.

6. *A Monopoly* is the sole seller of a product for which there are no good substitutes.

7. *Collusion* is agreement between sellers to fix prices or limit competition.

8. Monopolists distort the allocation of scarce resources because they produce (more/less) *less* of their product than is socially desirable.

9. The first major antitrust law, the *Sherman* Act, was passed in 1890.

10. Both oligopolists and monopolists may earn economic profits in the long run because they are protected by substantial *Barriers to entry*.

11. The study of the strategies employed by interdependent firms is known as *game Theory*.

12. *Conscious Parallelism* refers to oligopolists adopting similar policies without any communication whatsoever.

Multiple Choice

1. Which of the following is *not* an element of industry structure?
   a) The number of sellers in the industry
   b) The extent of barriers to entry
   c) The existence of economic profits
   d) The size distribution of sellers

2. Which of the following statements about unregulated monopolists is *false*?
   a) They may incur an economic loss in the short run.
   b) They maximize their profit (or minimize their loss) by producing the output at which $MR = MC$.
   c) They sell their product at a price equal to marginal cost.

   d) They face competition from rivals in other industries.

3. Which of the following is *not* a characteristic of monopolistic competition?
   a) Substantial barriers to entry
   b) Differentiated products
   c) A large number of sellers
   d) Small firms

4. Which of the following is probably *not* a monopolistically competitive firm?
   a) A barber shop
   b) A wheat farm
   c) A hardware store
   d) A furniture store

5. American Airlines will not raise prices without first considering how United will behave. This is probably evidence of their
    a) cutthroat competition.
    b) collusion.
    c) interdependence.
    d) price fixing.

6. Which of the following is *not* a characteristic of oligopolistic industries?
    a) Mutual interdependence
    b) Substantial barriers to entry
    c) Relatively large sellers
    d) Fierce price competition

7. Which of the following do monopolistically competitive firms, oligopolists, and monopolists have in common?
    a) All are relatively large.
    b) All have some market power.
    c) All are protected by substantial barriers to entry.
    d) All are concerned about the reactions of rivals to any actions they take.

8. Which of the following statutes outlawed mergers that would substantially lessen competition?
    a) The Sherman Act
    b) The Clayton Act
    c) The Merger Act
    d) The Federal Trade Commission Act

9. What is the primary difference between antitrust enforcement and industry regulation?
    a) Antitrust enforcement attempts to promote competition; industry regulation does not.

b) Antitrust enforcement has some critics; industry regulation does not.
    c) Antitrust enforcement is concerned about the public interest; industry regulation attempts to protect the regulated firms.
    d) Industry regulation deals only with natural monopolies; antitrust does not.

10. The concept of conscious parallelism suggests that oligopolists
    a) will always collude.
    b) can adopt similar policies without any communication.
    c) use price leadership to coordinate their pricing policies.
    d) prefer price competition to nonprice competition.

Use the payoff matrix at the bottom of this page in answering questions 11 and 12.

11. Which of the following is true?
    a) X's dominant strategy is to charge $15; Y doesn't have a dominant strategy.
    b) The dominant strategy for both X and Y is to charge $15.
    c) Y's dominant strategy is to charge $20; X doesn't have a dominant strategy.
    d) The dominant strategy for both X and Y is to charge $20.

12. If both firms charge $15,
    a) each firm will earn a profit of $30,000.
    b) there will be incentive to collude and raise the price to $20.
    c) firm X will earn $40,000.
    d) firm Y will earn $40,000.

Firm X's price strategies

		$15	$20
Firm Y's price strategies	$15	Each firm earns a $20,000 profit.	X earns $10,000. Y earns $40,000.
	$20	X earns $40,000. Y earns $10,000.	Each firm earns a $30,000 profit.

13. Cheating on collusive agreements is more likely when
    a) there are very few firms in the industry.
    b) the economy is weak and firms have excess capacity.
    c) each firm's prices are readily known.
    d) cheaters can expect swift retaliation.

14. Which of the following is *not* an example of a barrier to entry?
    a) A government franchise
    b) Exclusive control of a critical input
    c) The presence of a small number of firms in the industry
    d) The requirement of a large investment to begin production

15. Firms that are monopolists
    a) always earn economic profits in the short run.
    b) always earn economic profits in the long run.
    c) can see their monopoly status eroded by technological progress.
    d) All of the above

16. When a monopolistically competitive firm is in long-run equilibriums,
    a) price equals marginal cost.
    b) the demand curve is tangent to the marginal cost curve.
    c) price equals average total cost.
    d) the firm earns an economic profit.

17. If the firms in a monopolistically competitive industry are earning economic profits,
    a) additional firms will enter the industry, shifting each firm's demand curve to the right.

    b) firms will tend to leave the industry until a normal profit is earned.
    c) firms will enter the industry, reducing the demand for each firm's product.
    d) firms will enter the industry until each firm's demand curve is tangent to its marginal cost curve.

Use the payoff matrix below in answering questions 18–20.

18. Which if the following is true?
    a) A's dominant strategy is to advertise.
    b) B's dominant strategy is to not to advertise.
    c) A does not have a dominant strategy.
    d) B's dominant strategy is to advertise.

19. If A decides not to advertise, B's best strategy is
    a) not to advertise, in which case it will earn $40,000.
    b) to advertise, in which case it will earn $40,000.
    c) not to advertise, in which case it will earn $80,000.
    d) to advertise, in which case it will earn $80,000.

20. Because B knows that A's dominant strategy is
    a) to advertise, B's best strategy is to advertise also.
    b) not to advertise, B will also opt not to advertise.
    c) to advertise, B's best strategy is not to advertise.
    d) not to advertise, B's best strategy is to advertise.

Firm A's advertising strategies

		Don't advertise	Advertise
	Don't advertise	A earns $100,000. B earns $80,000.	A earns $150,000. B earns $0 profit.
Firm B's advertising strategies	*Advertise*	A earns $0 profit. B earns $60,000.	A earns $60,000. B earns $40,000.

Problems and Questions for Discussion

1. What constrains a monopolist's pricing discretion?

2. What problems might be associated with monopolistic or oligopolistic market structures? That is, how might they harm consumer well-being?

3. How do firms acquire market power? What impact do barriers to entry have on a firm's market power?

4. Why would we expect prices to be somewhat higher under monopolistic competition than under pure competition?

5. Suppose that there is only one grocery store in your neighborhood. What limits its market power? If your neighborhood were more isolated, would that increase or decrease the grocery store's market power?

6. In some communities, grocery stores may act as oligopolists, whereas in other communities, they may act as monopolistically competitive firms. How is this possible? How would you distinguish the first situation from the second?

7. Under what circumstances might consumers be better off with monopoly or oligopoly than with a competitive structure?

8. What is meant by a *natural monopoly,* and how can its existence justify regulation?

9. Some economists argue that antitrust is an outmoded policy that should be discarded. Discuss the basis for this conclusion, and summarize the opposing view.

10. Explain what is meant by a dominant strategy.

ANSWER KEY

Fill in the Blanks

1. market power
2. oligopoly
3. monopolistic competition
4. monopolistically competitive
5. interdependence
6. monopoly
7. Collusion
8. less
9. Sherman
10. barriers to entry
11. game theory
12. Conscious parallelism

Multiple Choice

1. c
2. c
3. a
4. b
5. c
6. d
7. b
8. b
9. a
10. b
11. b
12. b
13. b
14. c
15. c
16. c
17. c
18. a
19. c
20. a

CHAPTER NINE

figure

Market Failure

LEARNING OBJECTIVES

1. Define market failure and identify its sources.
2. Distinguish between internal and external costs (and benefits).
3. Describe how externalities distort the allocation of scarce resources.
4. Explain pollution as the result of poorly defined property rights.
5. Discuss why pollution taxes are superior to direct controls.
6. Explain why government should encourage the production of products yielding significant external benefits.
7. Distinguish between private and public goods.
8. Explain the free-rider problem and its consequences.
9. Describe the income distribution and the extent of poverty in the U.S. economy.
10. Discuss the views of public-choice economists and the concept of government failure.

At times a market economy may produce too much or too little of certain products and thus fail to make the most efficient use of society's limited resources. This, as you might expect, is referred to as **market failure.** In *The Affluent Society,* John Kenneth Galbraith describes numerous instances of market failure:

> ...The family which takes its...automobile out for a tour passes through cities that are badly paved, made hideous by litter, blighted buildings, billboards, and posts for wires that should long since have been put underground. They pass on into a countryside that has been rendered largely invisible by commercial art....They picnic on exquisitely packaged food from a portable icebox by a polluted stream and go on to spend the night at a park which is a menace to public health and morals. Just before dozing off on an air mattress, beneath a

nylon tent, amid the stench of decaying refuse, they may reflect vaguely on the curious unevenness of their blessings. Is this, indeed, the American genius?[1]

In Galbraith's view the American economy has produced an abundance of consumer goods—automobiles, appliances, sporting goods, and numerous other items—but far too little of other goods that Americans desire: clean air and water, parks, and well-paved roads, for example. Why do such market failures occur? As you will learn in this chapter, there are three major sources of market failure: market power, externalities, and public goods. The passage from Professor Galbraith's book points at two of these: externalities and public goods. In this chapter we explore those two sources of market failure in some detail. Because the impact of market power has been examined at length in Chapters 7 and 8, we will review it only briefly here.

MARKET POWER REVISITED

As you've already discovered, resources are allocated efficiently when they are used to produce the goods and services that consumers value most. This, in turn, requires that each product be produced up to the point at which the benefit its consumption provides to society (the marginal social benefit) is exactly equal to the cost its production imposes on society (the marginal social cost). This occurs under pure competition, but it doesn't happen when firms possess market power.[2] Consequently, the existence of market power constitutes the first source of market failure.

Firms with market power tend to restrict output in order to force up prices. As a consequence they halt production short of the output at which marginal social benefit equals marginal social cost, causing too few of society's resources to be allocated to the goods and services they produce. In simplified terms this means that because firms such as Ford Motor Company and General Electric have market power, fewer of society's resources are devoted to producing new motor vehicles and appliances, and too few Americans will be able to own these products. Instead, these resources will flow to the production of products that consumers value less. Markets are "failing" in the sense that they are not allocating resources in the most efficient way, that is, to the production of the goods and services that consumers value most.

---

[1] John Kenneth Galbraith, *The Affluent Society* (New York: New American Library, 1958), pp. 199–200.
[2] The conclusion that pure competition leads to an efficient allocation of resources rests on the assumption that there are no externalities. *Externalities* are costs or benefits that are not borne by either buyers or sellers but that spill over onto third parties. They are the next topic in this chapter.

Although virtually all economists agree that this form of market failure exists, clearly it is not what Galbraith was describing when he wrote the words we quoted. Galbraith seems to believe that Americans have done quite well in the area of consumer goods. How, then, do we explain his criticism of our economy's performance? The answer lies beyond the problems caused by market power, in some shortcomings of the market mechanism itself.

EXTERNALITIES AS A SOURCE OF MARKET FAILURE

A second source of resource misallocation is the failure of markets to take into account all the costs and benefits associated with the production and consumption of a good or service.

Consider for a moment the information that guides producers and consumers in their decision making. When businesses are deciding what production techniques to use and what resources to purchase, they consider only **private costs**, or **internal costs**—the costs borne by the firm. They do not take into account any external costs that are borne by (or spill over onto) other parties. Consumers behave in a similar manner: They tend to consider only **private benefits**, or **internal benefits**—the benefits that accrue to the person or persons purchasing the product—and to ignore any external benefits that might be received by others.

If businesses and consumers are permitted to ignore these external costs and benefits, or **externalities**, the result will be an inefficient use of our scarce resources. We will produce too much of some items because we do not consider the full costs; we will produce too little of others because we do not consider the full benefits.

Externalities: The Case of External Costs

It's not difficult to think of personal situations in which external costs have come into play. Perhaps you've planned to savor a quiet dinner at your favorite restaurant, only to have a shrieking baby seated with its harried parents at the next table. Think about the movie you might have enjoyed if that rambunctious five-year-old hadn't been using the back of your seat as a bongo drum. Why do parents bring young children to these places, knowing that they will probably disturb the people around them? According to the teachings of Adam Smith, they are pursuing their own self-interest—in this case by minimizing the monetary cost of an evening's entertainment. But their actions are imposing different kinds of costs on everyone around them.

The frazzled nerves, poorly digested meals, and generally spoiled evenings experienced by you and your fellow diners or moviegoers are examples of **external costs**: the costs created by one party or group and imposed on, or *spilled over onto*, some other (nonconsenting) party or group.

Pollution as an External Cost

The classic example of external costs is pollution: the contamination of our land, air, and water caused by the litter that lines our streets and highways, the noxious fumes emitted into our atmosphere, and the wastes dumped into our rivers, lakes, and streams. Why does pollution exist? The answer is really quite obvious. It's less expensive for a manufacturer to dispose of its wastes in a nearby river, for example, than to haul that material to a so-called safe area. But it is a low-cost method of disposal only in terms of the private costs borne by the manufacturing firm. If we consider the social cost, there may well be a cheaper method of disposal.

Social cost refers to the full cost to society of producing a product. It represents the sum of private costs plus external costs. In situations where there are no external costs, private costs and social costs will be the same. But when external costs are present, social costs will be higher than private costs. That's

Dumping wastes into a river may minimize private costs, but it can create substantial external costs.

the case in our example of the polluting manufacturing firm. The private cost of manufacturing the firm's product includes the payments made for materials, labor, rent, and everything else it takes to run a business. But it does not include a payment for the damage done when the river is used for waste disposal. Because the firm is able to ignore this cost, it is described as an external cost; it is external to the firm's decision making.

To understand why pollution is a cost, think of the damage it does. Polluted water means fewer fish and fewer people enjoying water sports. It also means less income for people who rent boats and cottages and sell fishing bait, for example. It further affects the people living downstream, who need water for drinking and bathing; they will have to pay—through taxes—to purify the water. Finally, it may have a deadly effect on the birds and animals that live off the fish and other creatures in the water. Thus, water pollution may create numerous costs for society, costs that are ignored by polluters.

External Costs and Resource Misallocation

When the act of producing or consuming a product creates external costs, an exclusive reliance on private markets and the pursuit of self-interest will result in a misallocation of society's resources. We can illustrate why this is so by investigating a single, hypothetical, purely competitive industry.

For the purpose of our investigation, let's assume that the paint industry is purely competitive. Under those circumstances, the equilibrium price and quantity will be determined by the interaction of the industry demand and supply curves. In Exh. 9.1, demand curve D shows the quantity of paint that would be demanded at each possible price. Recall from Chapter 6 that the demand curve is a product's marginal benefit curve because it tells us the value that consumers place on an additional unit of the product. For example, the 100,000th can of paint provides benefits worth $10, and the 120,000th can of paint provides benefits worth $8.

The other important element in the diagram is the supply curve. As you already know, when an industry is purely competitive, the supply curve can be thought of as the marginal cost curve for the industry because it is found by summing the marginal cost curves of the firms in the industry. The first supply curve, S_1, shows the quantity of paint the industry would supply if each firm in the industry considered only its private costs and disposed of its wastes by dumping them into local rivers. As you can see, under these conditions the demand and supply curves reveal an equilibrium price of $8 per can of paint and an equilibrium quantity of 120,000 cans per year.

The equilibrium output of 120,000 cans is labeled the "market output" because that is the output that will be produced in the absence of government intervention. Remember, businesses respond only to private costs; they tend to ignore external costs unless they are required to take them into consideration.

EXHIBIT 9.1
The Impact of External Costs

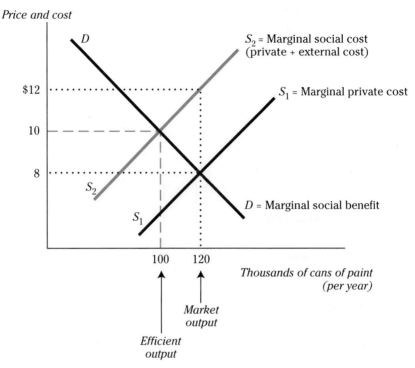

Because paint producers consider only private costs, they produce 120,000 units, more than the optimal, or allocatively efficient, output of 100,000 units.

Suppose that we find a way to require the firms in the industry to consider the external costs they have been ignoring. Under those conditions the supply curve would shift to S_2, the curve reflecting the full social cost of production. (Recall that whenever there is an increase in resource prices or anything else that increases the cost of production, the supply curve will shift left, or upward.) As you can see from the diagram, the result of this reduction supply is an increase in the price of paint to $10 a can and a reduction in the equilibrium quantity to 100,000 cans. Note that 100,000 cans is the allocatively efficient level of output, the output for which the marginal social benefit equals the marginal social cost. Consumers receive $10 worth of benefits from the 100,000th can of paint, exactly enough to justify the $10 marginal cost of producing that can.

If 100,000 units is the optimal or efficient level of output, 120,000 must have been too much! So long as paint producers were allowed to shift some of their production costs to society as a whole (or to some portion of society), the price of paint was artificially low; that is, it did not reflect the true social cost of producing paint. Consumers responded to this low price by purchasing an artificially high quantity of paint—more than they would have purchased if the price reflected the true social cost of production. As a consequence more of society's scarce resources were allocated to the production of paint than was socially optimal. (Note that consumers receive marginal benefits worth $8 from the 120,000th can of paint, but the marginal social cost of producing that unit is $12; production has been carried too far.) In summary, when businesses fail to consider external costs, they produce too much of their product from society's point of view.

Correcting for External Costs

How do we force businesses and individuals to consider all the costs of their actions, to treat external costs as if they were private or internal costs? (This process is sometimes referred to as forcing firms to **internalize costs**.) One possibility is for government to assign property rights to unowned resources such as lakes and rivers so that some individual will be in a position to charge for their use. Another possibility is for Congress to pass laws that forbid (or limit) activities that impose external costs (such as dumping wastes into lakes and streams). A third possibility is for government agencies to harness market incentives in an effort to compensate for external costs. Let's consider those alternatives.

Assigning Property Rights   Our paint example points out that when manufacturers create external costs, the private market does not record the true costs of production and thereby fails to provide the proper signals to ensure that our resources are used optimally. Why is the private market unable to communicate the true cost of production? In many instances the problem is poorly defined property rights. **Property rights** are the legal rights to use goods, services, or resources. For example, you have the right to use your car and lawnmower and barbeque grill; your neighbor does not. But who owns the Mississippi River and the Atlantic Ocean and the air we breathe? Of course, no one owns these natural resources. And that's the problem. Because no one owns these resources, no one has the right to charge for their use. And because no one has the right to charge for their use, individuals assume that they are available to be used (and abused) for free. Remember, individuals and businesses respond to private costs and benefits; if private markets don't register the cost, people may act as if there is none.

Because the source of the pollution problem is poorly defined property rights, one possible solution is for government to clarify the ownership of the resources being abused. Think about our hypothetical example involving the polluting paint company. Suppose that the state legislature gives the legal ownership of the river to the paint company. Suppose also that the only use of the river has been as the water supply for a small city downstream. Once the ownership of the river is established, we might expect the city to attempt to bargain with the paint company to stop dumping its wastes into the river. Assume, for example, that the next-cheapest disposal technique would cost the company $100,000 a year. Suppose also that it would cost the city $200,000 a year to purchase water from a neighboring community. Since the river is worth more as a source of drinking water than as a method of waste disposal, the city should be able to negotiate with the paint company to stop dumping its wastes in the river. For example, if the city offers the paint company $150,000 to stop discharging its wastes, the paint company would probably agree. The paint company would stop dumping its wastes into the river because it would no longer see the use of the river as free. If it dumps its wastes into the river, it would have to forgo the $150,000 payment from the city. Since the cost of alternative disposal is only $100,000, the firm would choose the alternative method and pocket the $50,000 difference.

Suppose that the legislature assigns the ownership of the river to the city. Would the outcome be different? This time the company would need to approach the city to get permission to dump into the river. The company would be willing to pay up to $100,000 a year to use the river since that is the cost of alternative disposal. But since an alternative water supply would cost the city $200,000, it would not be willing to deal; the river would again be used as a water supply.

The preceding example illustrates two important points. First, when property rights are clearly defined, resources are put to their most valued use; that is, they are used efficiently. In this case the river will be used as a water supply, but in some instances its most valued use might be for waste disposal.[3] Second, the resources will be used efficiently regardless of who is assigned their ownership. (Note that, either way, the river is used as a water supply.) The idea of solving externality problems by assigning property rights and encouraging negotiation is based on the work of Nobel prize–winning economist Ronald Coase. In our society many cases involving externalities are resolved by negotiation after the courts have clarified property rights.[4] However, as Professor Coase has recognized, this solution works only in situations in which the transactions costs—the costs of striking a bargain between the

---

[3] Suppose, for example, that alternative disposal would cost the paint company $250,000 a year. In that case the paint company would be willing to bid up to $250,000 to use the river for waste disposal. If it offered the city $225,000, the city would probably agree (since it can purchase water for $200,000 a year), and the river would be used for waste disposal.

[4] For instance, New York City agreed to pay neighboring Catskill communities and farms approximately $700 million to follow practices that will preserve the water quality in the Catskill Mountain region—the region from which the city obtains its drinking water (Duane Chapman, *Environmental Economics: Theory, Application, and Policy*, Addison-Wesley, 2000, p. 75).

parties—are relatively low and in which the number of people involved is relatively small. When the assignment of property rights does not work, another method must be sought to solve the problem.

Direct Controls

The United States has attempted to limit pollution primarily by imposing direct government controls. The emissions standards imposed on automobile manufacturers are an example of direct controls, as are the leaf-burning ordinances in your local community.

Under a system of direct controls, firms and individuals are told how much pollution they will be allowed to emit into the environment, and they are often told what *specific* technique they must use to meet the standard. (For instance, prior to the Clean Air Act of 1990, coal-burning electric power plants were generally required to meet their air-quality standards by installing devices known as scrubbers.)

As firms take steps to reduce their emissions to the mandated level, their cost of production tends to increase. This, in turn, leads to higher product prices. When consumers are required to pay a price that more fully reflects the true cost of production, they purchase fewer units of the formerly underpriced items. Therefore, resources can be reallocated to the production of other items whose prices more accurately reflect the full social cost of production.

Although direct controls have helped to reduce pollution, they have been criticized as needlessly expensive. There are two reasons for this criticism. First, because government often specifies precisely how the environmental standard is to be met, businesses have no incentive to seek out less-expensive methods of reducing their pollution. Second, this approach requires that all firms meet the same environmental standard, even though some firms find it much more expensive to meet that standard than others. (Remember, these firms come from a wide range of industries and employ vastly different production techniques.) While this approach may appear to be "fair," it increases the total cost to society of achieving any given level of environmental quality.

Pollution Taxes Many economists contend that it would be less expensive to create a *pollution tax*, which firms would be required to pay on any waste they discharge into the air or water. Under a system of pollution taxes, firms could discharge as much waste into the environment as they chose, but they would have to pay a specified levy—say, $50—for each unit emitted. Ideally this tax would bring about the desired reduction in pollution. If not, it would be raised to whatever dollar amount would convince firms to reduce pollution to acceptable levels.

A major advantage of a pollution tax is that it would allow the firms themselves to decide which ones could cut back on emissions (the discharges of wastes) at the lowest cost. For example, given a fee of $50 for each ton of wastes emitted into the environment, those firms that could reduce their emissions for less than $50 per ton would do so; other firms would continue to pollute and pay the tax. As a result, pollution would be reduced by the firms that could do so most easily and at the lowest cost. Society would then have achieved a given level of environmental quality at the lowest cost in terms of its scarce resources.

A simple example may help to illustrate why the pollution tax is a less expensive approach. Assume that the economy is made up of firms A and B and that each firm is discharging 4 tons of waste a year. Assume also that it costs firm A $30 per ton to reduce emissions and firm B $160 per ton.

Suppose that society wants to reduce the discharge of wastes by 4 tons a year. An emissions standard that required each firm to limit its emissions to 2 tons a year would cost society $380 ($60 for firm A and $320 for firm B). A pollution tax of $50 a ton would accomplish the same objective at a cost of $120 since it would cause firm A to reduce its emissions from 4 tons to zero. (Firm A would opt to reduce its emissions because this approach is less costly than paying the pollution tax. If the firm pays the pollution tax, it will be billed $50 × 4 tons = $200. But it can reduce emissions at a cost of $30 × 4 tons = $120. Thus, it would prefer to reduce its emissions rather than pay the pollution tax.) Note that firm B will prefer to pay the tax; thus, government will receive $200 in pollution tax revenue. This $200 should not be considered a cost of reducing pollution, since it can be used to build roads or schools or be spent in any other way society chooses.

Tradable Emission Permits

As we noted earlier, the United States has relied primarily on direct controls to reduce pollution. With the passage of the federal Clean Air Act, that began to change. The 1990 law contains provisions that, like pollution taxes, encourage businesses to reduce pollution in the least costly way. As before, firms are told how much pollution they will be permitted to emit into the environment. That portion of the law is consistent with direct controls. But there are new twists in the 1990 law. First, firms are given more flexibility in deciding how to meet the standard; the technique is not strictly mandated. Second, if firms exceed the standard—if they reduce their pollution below the permitted amount—they may sell the residual to other firms. In effect, these firms are selling their unused right to pollute. These rights are known as *tradable emission permits* (or credits); they are the marketable right to discharge a specified amount of a pollutant.

Who would want to buy emissions permits? The buyers will be other businesses that find it very costly to reduce their emissions. By giving firms the option of either buying permits or reducing their own emissions, the act aims to achieve its air-quality standards at the lowest possible cost. (To see how this system has worked in Southern California, see "Cost of Clean Air Credits Soars in Southland," on page 270.)

USE YOUR ECONOMIC REASONING

Cost of Clean Air Credits Soars in Southland

By Gary Polakovic

OVER the last five years, business has tripled at Custom Alloy Light Metals, a company…that turns scrap aluminum into ingots for auto makers. As the company has grown, so has the volume of air pollutants its factory emits. To stay within Southern California's strict emission limits, the company in the past turned to a pioneering program allowing firms that pollute more than the law allows to buy credits from other companies that are cleaner than the law requires.

Not now. As the air in Southern California has gotten cleaner, and as the economy has boomed, the laws of supply and demand have sent the price of such legal pollution soaring. Last year, a credit that carries the right to emit one pound of nitrogen oxide gas went for as little as 13 cents. By January, the price was up to $1.14. In July, the same credit sold for $37, according to the Automated Credit Exchange in Pasadena, which has processed more than two-thirds of the credits traded in Southern California. By last week, prices had settled to about $13 per pound—100 times what they were a year ago.

Those increases, and other problems, have some Southern California businesses fuming as they scramble for credits in a booming economy and a deregulated energy market…. Companies that cannot buy enough credits to cover their actual emissions must reduce production or face strict regulations and possible penalties….

In August, the Los Angeles Department of Water and Power agreed to pay a record $14 million penalty and install extensive new control technologies at power plants because its emissions will exceed its pollution allocation by the end of the year.

The new equipment that the department agreed to install, beginning in January, is expected to slash emissions by at least 90%, said S. David Freeman, general manager at DWP. Although the price is high—about $40 million—it is cheaper than trying to buy credits on the market, he said. "We tried to buy the credits, but we reached the point where there weren't any more to be bought," Freeman said. "The program is teetering and in shaky shape," he added….

But air quality officials say the trading program is working as intended. When the program was started in 1994, businesses demanded it as a flexible, cheaper alternative to edicts that the government used traditionally to fight pollution. It is the primary strategy for squeezing smokestack emissions from 340 sources, including power plants, oil refineries and manufacturers, to help the Los Angeles region meet federal clean-air goals.

The idea was that businesses would get flexibility in how they cleaned the air, but the amount of allowable pollution would still shrink

Source: Los Angeles Times; Sept. 5, 2000, p. B1.

270

each year. At the time, with the economy in recession, businesses focused on the lower compliance costs, not on the inevitable crunch that would come as the allowable amount of emissions shrank.

The reduction in the number of credits is about 8% a year for nitrogen oxides and 7% for sulfur oxides. As a result, the total amount of pollution allowed now under the credit program is only half of that allowed at the start. By 2003, emissions from all sources will have been sliced by 75%, according to the South Coast Air Quality Management District, which administers the program.

"Under this trading program, there is a ceiling on the amount of pollution, and that ceiling gets lowered each and every year until 2003," said Barry R. Wallerstein, executive officer at the air quality district. "That's a benefit to the breathing public," Wallerstein said. "What the companies get in return is flexibility in how to choose ways to stay under that ceiling. It's a win for the environment and a win for the businesses."

The pollution credit crunch peaked this summer when about 170 companies entered the market simultaneously to buy and sell smog credits. Their entry coincided with a heat wave that sent power companies into the market looking for ways to offset emissions for power plants that were working overtime. "Companies didn't think about what would happen to the market when they all jump into it together," said Jane Hall, an economist at Cal State Fullerton. "People expected there would be a crunch. It was inevitable. But it's come sooner than people thought."

Companies that planned ahead, however, were able to sell credits for high prices and pocket a handsome windfall. Libbey Glass Co., for example, employs 250 people at a plant making champagne glasses and other products. A few years ago, the company installed low-polluting burners at its factory in Walnut. Those burners lowered the plant's emissions far below what the law required, freeing up nearly half its smog credits, which Libbey sold on the open market, said Kimberly Lagormarsino, the company's environmental health and safety manager.

"It's simple supply and demand, like the stock market," Lagormarsino said. "A lot of facilities at the outset of [the program] didn't plan ahead, but Libbey from the very beginning started looking at ways to fine-tune the process. Our pollution has turned into a commodity, and I think it's great. If you allow the companies with low cost to control [pollution] and sell the benefit to someone else, then you do it and it saves money," she said.

Robert Wyman, an attorney for the Regulatory Flexibility Group, a business organization that led the push to establish the program, estimates that the free market trading has saved his clients about $400 million in compliance costs since it began. Among the companies that have taken advantage of the program are Disneyland, Hughes Aircraft Co., TRW Inc. and Anheuser-Busch Inc. The program "is experiencing stress, but on the whole this program has been a resounding success," Wyman said.

Use Your Economic Reasoning

1. At one time, Custom Alloy Light Metals preferred to buy emission credits rather than to reduce its own emissions. Now it has apparently decided to reduce its emissions. How do you explain this behavior? Is it consistent with the goal of reducing pollution at least cost?

2. Why did Libbey Glass decide to lower its plant's emissions below what the law required? How did it profit from this decision?

3. How can a system of tradable emission permits (credits) minimize the cost of achieving air-quality standards?

271

Tradable emission permits have helped to significantly reduce sulfur emissions in the United States. Moreover, U.S. policymakers have been touting them as an important element of any concerted effort to reduce air pollution worldwide. In November of 2000, delegates from 160 nations met in the Netherlands to attempt to finish the 1997 Kyoto Protocol on global warming. If the protocol is ratified, industrial nations will be required to cut their combined emissions of greenhouse gases by more than 5 percent below their 1990 levels. The extent to which countries will be permitted to rely on emissions trading to achieve their goals has been a sticking point in the negotiations. The United States, Japan, and Canada favor extensive use of emissions-trading—allowing industrialized nations to buy permits from countries whose emissions already fall below 1990 levels. The European Union prefers less reliance on this approach. In the end, this disagreement helped to scuttle the 2000 talks, keeping the Kyoto Protocol in limbo. Talks are scheduled to resume in May of 2001.

The Optimal Level of Pollution

Although emissions standards and pollution taxes are both designed to reduce pollution, neither system is designed to eliminate pollution entirely. The total elimination of pollution would not be in society's best interest since it requires the use of scarce resources that have alternative uses. Economists support reducing pollution only so long as the benefits of added pollution controls exceed their costs. For example, it makes no sense to force firms to pay an additional $30 million to reduce pollution if the added benefits to society amount to only $10 million. For that reason, any rational system of pollution control—whether based on emissions standards or pollution taxes—will permit some level of pollution. Unfortunately, because it is difficult to measure the costs and benefits of pollution control in an exact manner, it is also difficult to determine whether efforts to control pollution have been carried too far or not far enough.

Externalities: The Case of External Benefits

Not all externalities are harmful. Sometimes the actions of individuals or businesses create **external benefits**—benefits that are paid for by one party but spill over to other parties. One example is the flowers your neighbors plant in their yard each year. You can enjoy their beauty without contributing to the cost of their planting and upkeep. Another example is flu shots. You pay for them, and they help protect you from the flu. But they also help protect everyone else; if you don't come down with the flu, you can't pass it on to others.

Businesses also can create external benefits. For example, most firms put their workers—particularly their young and/or inexperienced workers—through some sort of training program. Of course, the sponsoring firm gains a more productive, more valuable employee. But most people do not stay with one employer for their entire working careers; when trained employees decide to move on, other employers will benefit from the training they have received.

External Benefits and Resource Allocation

In a pure market economy, individuals would tend to demand too small a quantity of those products that generate external benefits. To understand why this is so, consider your own consumption decisions for a moment. When you are deciding whether to purchase a product (or how much of a product to purchase), you compare the product's benefits with its price. If you value a unit of the product more than the other items you could purchase with the same money, you buy it. If not, you spend your money on the product you value more highly. In effect, you are deciding which product delivers the most benefits for the money. But whose benefits are you considering? Your own, of course! In other words, you respond to private rather than external benefits. Most consumption decisions are made this way. As a result, consumers purchase too small a quantity of the products that create external benefits, and our scarce resources are misallocated. That is to say, fewer resources are devoted to producing these products than are justified by their **social benefits**—the sum of the private benefits received by those who purchase the product and the external benefits received by others.[5]

Adjusting for External Benefits

To illustrate the underproduction of products that carry external benefits, let's examine what would happen if elementary education were left to the discretion of the private market. Reading, writing, and arithmetic are basic skills that have obvious benefits for the individual, but they also benefit society as a whole. In his prize-winning book *Capitalism and Freedom*, economist Milton Friedman makes the case as follows:

> A stable and democratic society is impossible without a minimum amount of literacy and knowledge on the part of most citizens and without widespread acceptance of some common set of values. Education can contribute to both. In consequence, the gain from the education of a child accrues not only to the child or to his parents but also to other members of the society. . . .[6]

For the sake of our example, let's suppose that all elementary education in the United States is provided through private schools on a voluntary basis. In such a situation the number of children enrolled in these schools would be

---

[5] As we learned earlier, when property rights are clearly defined, the existence of external benefits need not lead to resource misallocation. To illustrate, suppose that a restaurant owner notices higher sales on weekends when a neighboring pub has live entertainment. The restaurant owner may entice the pub into more frequent entertainment by agreeing to share its cost. This bargaining solution can lead to an optimal level of entertainment.

[6] Milton Friedman, *Capitalism and Freedom* (Chicago: University of Chicago Press, 1962), p. 86.

determined by the forces of demand and supply. As shown in Exh. 9.2 the market would establish a price of $500 per student, and at that price 3 million students would attend elementary school each year. The market demand curve (D_1) provides an incomplete picture, however. It considers marginal private benefits—the benefits received by the students and their parents—but ignores external benefits. If we include the external benefits of education, society would want even more children educated. Demand curve D_2 shows that society would choose to educate 5 million students a year if it considered the full social benefits (private plus external benefits) of education, leading to an equilibrium price of $700 per student.

As you can see from Exh. 9.2, individuals pursuing their own self-interest would choose to purchase less education than is justified on the basis of the full social benefits. (To confirm this conclusion, note that the marginal *social*

EXHIBIT 9.2
The Impact of External Benefits

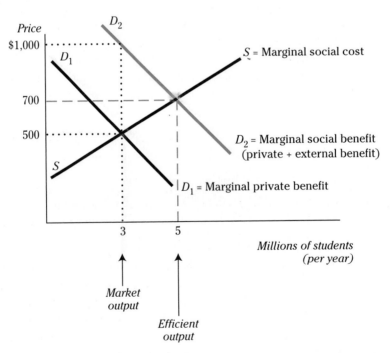

When individuals consider only the private benefits of education, they choose to educate only 3 million students per year, less than the optimal, or allocatively efficient, level of 5 million students per year.

benefit derived from the education of the 3 millionth student is $1,000, well in excess of the $500 marginal social cost of providing that education. Too few students are being educated, from society's point of view.) An obvious solution to this problem would be to require that each child attend school for some minimum number of years, allowing the family to select the school and find the money to pay for it. The U.S. government has taken a different approach, however. That is, most elementary and secondary schools are operated by local governments and financed through taxes rather than through fees charged to parents. This spreads the financial burden for education among all taxpayers rather than just the parents of school-age children. In effect, taxpayers without children "subsidize" taxpayers with children. The rationale for this approach is fairly clear-cut. Since all taxpayers share in the benefits of education (the external benefits, at least), they should share in the costs as well.

In a variety of circumstances, subsidies can be used to encourage the consumption of products that carry external benefits. Consider the flu shots again. They protect not only the people inoculated but also those in contact with them. Still, many people will not pay to receive a flu shot. So if we want more people to get flu shots (but we don't want to pass laws requiring such shots), we could have the government subsidize all or part of the cost. The lower the price of flu shots, the more people who will agree to get them.

There is no reason that subsidized flu shots would have to be provided by government doctors; the government could simply agree to pay private doctors for each flu shot administered. It is precisely this approach that Milton Friedman would like to see implemented in education. Rather than continuing to subsidize public schools, Friedman would prefer a system that permitted students to select their own privately run schools.

> Government could require a minimum level of schooling financed by giving parents vouchers redeemable for a specified maximum sum per child per year if spent on "approved" educational services. Parents would then be free to spend this sum and any additional sum they themselves provided on purchasing educational services from an "approved" institution of their own choice. . . . The role of government would be limited to insuring that the schools met certain minimum standards. . . .[7]

Whether or not you agree with Friedman's particular approach, it should be clear to you by now that subsidies can be useful in correcting for market failure. By encouraging the production and consumption of products yielding external benefits, subsidies help ensure that society's resources are used to produce the optimal assortment of goods and services. (Should government subsidize meningitis inoculations for college freshmen? Read "Lining Up for a Shot for Meningitis," on page 276, and decide for yourself.)

---

[7] Milton Friedman, *Capitalism and Freedom* (Chicago: University of Chicago Press, 1962), p. 86.

USE YOUR ECONOMIC REASONING

Lining Up for a Shot for Meningitis

By Robert Worth

LIKE most 18-year-olds, Heather Lynn had scarcely heard of meningitis when she applied to college last fall. But after being accepted at the University of Massachusetts, she received a letter from the school recommending that she be vaccinated for the disease. And when she discovered that all her college-bound friends in New Rochelle were getting the vaccination, she went to the Sound Shore Medical Center and got one herself.

Ms. Lynn and her cohorts have the unusual distinction of being the first class to enter college since the federal Centers for Disease Control and Prevention in Atlanta recommended late last year that college students be educated about the disease, which can be fatal and strikes freshmen living in dormitories at six times the rate of the general population.

A result, said several Westchester medical practices, has been a vastly increased demand for the vaccine as students prepare to leave home.

In July and August, the Westchester Medical Group of White Plains administered between 180 and 200 meningitis vaccinations, said Dr. Barbara Coven, one of the group's four practitioners. Last year the figure was 15....

Meningitis is caused by meningococcal bacteria and is spread through the air in droplets from coughs and sneezes, or through direct contact—kissing, for example, or sharing drinking glasses. One of the mysteries of the disease is that many people carry meningococci in their throats without becoming ill.

No one knows why the disease is so much more common among freshman dorm residents, said Dr. James Turner, the director of student health at the University of Virginia and chairman of the Preventable Diseases Task Force at the American College Health Association.

But, he said, meningitis appears to have something to do with groups of people from different backgrounds living in close proximity. Meningitis rates were very high in the United States military, particularly in training camps where recruits were housed together until 1971, when the services began performing routine immunizations.

A spokesman for Aventis Pasteur, the only licensed maker of the meningitis vaccine in the United States, said that private-sector sales over the last four months—the period when college freshmen are most likely to be immunized—had nearly tripled compared with the same period last year.

Colleges and universities in Westchester have also made the vaccine available, at the urging of the state Board of Health....

Source: New York Times; Sept. 10, 2000, p. 5.

Nationwide, about 470 schools are making the vaccine available, compared with 10 in 1997, Dr. Turner said.

In addition to the federal agency's recommendations, the demand for vaccines has been fueled by news coverage of meningitis cases and scares. In late August a student at the University of Delaware became seriously ill with the disease. And during the same week 1,000 people who attended a "rave" in Michigan and allegedly shared a pacifier dipped in the drug Ecstasy were urged to see a doctor after meningitis was diagnosed in one of them.

Even among freshman dormitory residents the disease is extremely rare, striking only 3.8 of every 100,000, according to the disease control centers. But it has triggered anxiety and sensational news coverage well beyond its case numbers because of its deadliness and because it is difficult to diagnose.

Meningitis starts out like a mild flu, with symptoms like fever, sore throat, headache, rash, muscle aches and nausea, but if it is not treated quickly with antibiotics the victim can go into a coma and die within hours. It is fatal in 13 percent of those who catch it, a rate rivaled by few other types of infection. And about 15 percent of those who survive develop permanent brain damage.

The response by school authorities has varied. Some have pursued immunization aggressively, bringing in private companies to help administer the shots. The University of Virginia, for instance, administered 3,800 meningitis shots over two days in the student union ballroom last November....

But some students have been reluctant to get the vaccine because of the cost, which is about $75 when bought at a campus health center, said Dr. Audrey Sheehy, the director of student health services at Purchase College. At private clinics like Sound Shore, the cost is about $125, Dr. [Jeffrey] Lederman said. Some insurance companies cover the expense, but many do not. In some cases, because the meningitis shot is a new recommendation, insurance companies have not had time to integrate it into their compensation package.

In addition, Dr. Sheehy said, some doctors doubt that mass immunizations are necessary for such a rare disease. There are deadlier diseases that are more common, she said, like hepatitis B, for which there has been no equivalent vaccination campaign.

It may be the mystery of the disease's transmission, she said, that has resulted in the widespread anxiety and consequent publicity of the past few years.

"It's interesting because it gets to the heart of what people are afraid of," she said. "It's the same as the West Nile virus. People are much more afraid of things they don't have any control over. It's the things that fall out of heaven on the innocent that really spark our imagination."...

Use Your Economic Reasoning

1. Heather Lynn decided to get a meningitis shot before heading off to college. How do you think she arrived at that decision? Did she (or her parents) consider the cost of the shot? Did she consider the benefits that the shot would convey to others?

2. Do meningitis shots confer external benefits? What passages in the article support your conclusion?

3. Suppose policymakers wanted to encourage college students to obtain meningitis shots. What policies might they employ?

4. Many childhood inoculations are mandated—required by law. Meningitis inoculations are not. How do you think public health officials decide which inoculations to require? How would an economist decide?

MARKET FAILURE AND THE PROVISION OF PUBLIC GOODS

Market power and the existence of externalities are not the only sources of market failure. Markets may also fail to produce optimal results because some products are simply not well suited to sale by private firms. These products must be provided by government or they will not be provided at all.

Private Goods versus Public Goods

To understand this problem, we must think first about the types of goods and services our economy produces. Those goods and services fall into three categories: pure private goods, private goods that yield external benefits, and public goods.

Pure private goods are products that convey their benefits only to the purchaser.[8] The hamburger you had for lunch falls in that category, as does the jacket you wore to class. Most of the products we purchase in the marketplace are pure private goods.

Some products convey most of their benefits to the person making the purchase but also create substantial external benefits for others. These are **private goods that yield significant external benefits.** We have talked about education and flu shots, but there are numerous other examples—fire protection, police protection, and driver's training, to name just a few.

The third category, **public goods,** consists of products that convey their benefits equally to paying and nonpaying members of society. National defense is probably the best example of a public good. If a business attempted to sell "units" of national defense through the marketplace, what problems would arise? The major problem would be that nonpayers would receive virtually the same protection from foreign invasion as those who paid for the protection. There's no way to protect your house from foreign invasion without simultaneously protecting your neighbor's. The inability to exclude nonpayers from receiving the same benefits as those who have paid for the product is what economists call the *free-rider problem.*

---

[8] Note that although pure private goods convey their benefits only to the purchaser, the purchaser may *choose* to share those benefits with others. For instance, you may decide to share your hamburger with another person or allow someone else to wear your jacket. But if others share in the benefits of a pure private good, it is because the purchaser allows them to share those benefits, not because the benefits automatically spilled over onto them.

The Free-Rider Problem

Why does the inability to exclude certain individuals from receiving benefits constitute a problem? Think about national defense for just a moment. How would you feel if you were paying for national defense and your neighbor received exactly the same protection for nothing? Very likely, you would decide to become a free rider yourself, as would many other people. Products such as national defense, flood-control dams, and tornado warning systems cannot be offered so as to restrict their benefits to payers alone. Therefore, no private business can expect to earn a profit by offering such goods and services, and private markets cannot be relied on to produce these products, no matter how important they are for the well-being of the society. Unless the government intervenes, they simply will not be provided at all.

Of course, we're not willing to let that happen. That's why a substantial amount of our tax money pays for national defense and other public goods. (Not all publicly *provided* goods are public goods. Our tax dollars are used to pay for education and public swimming pools and a host of other goods and services that do not meet the characteristics of public goods.) As we have emphasized, the ultimate objective of government intervention is to improve the allocation of society's scarce resources so that the economy will do a better job of satisfying our unlimited wants. To the extent that government intervention contributes to that result, it succeeds in correcting for market failure and in improving our social welfare.

POVERTY, EQUALITY, AND TRENDS IN THE INCOME DISTRIBUTION

As we've seen, market failure results when a market economy fails to use its scarce resources in an optimal way; when it produces too much or too little of certain products. But even if a market system were able to achieve an optimal allocation of resources, if it distributed income in a way that a majority of the population saw as inequitable or unfair, we might judge that to be a shortcoming of the system.

In a market system, a person's income depends on what he or she has to sell. Those with greater innate abilities and more assets (land and capital) earn higher incomes; those with fewer abilities and fewer assets earn lower incomes. These differences are often compounded by differences in training and education and by differences in the levels of inherited wealth. As a consequence, a total reliance on the market mechanism can produce substantial inequality in the income distribution. Some people have less while others have much more.

How unequal is the income distribution in the United States? As you can see from Exhibit 9.3, there is a significant amount of inequality. In 1999 the households in the lowest quintile (the lowest fifth) of the income distribution received less than 4 percent of total money income in the United States, while the households in the upper fifth received more than 49 percent of total income. In fact, the households in the upper fifth of the income distribution received almost as much total income as all the households in the bottom four-fifths of the distribution. Moreover, the income distribution in the United States seems to be growing somewhat less equal. As you can see in the exhibit, the fraction of aggregate income going to the richest fifth of U.S. households has increased over the last 20 years, while the share going to the remaining four-fifths of households has declined.

The existence of inequality may not concern us very much if everyone—including the households in the bottom fifth of the income distribution—is earning enough income to live comfortably. What most of us are really concerned about is households that are living in poverty—those with incomes that are insufficient to provide for their basic needs (according to some standard established by society).

In the United States we have adopted income standards by which we judge the extent of poverty. For example, in 1999 a family of four was classified as "poor" if it had an annual income of less than $17,029. By that definition there were 32.3 million poor people in the United States in 1999—11.8 percent of the population. Most people would probably agree that if almost 12 percent

---

EXHIBIT 9.3

Percent of Aggregate Income Received by Each Fifth of Households in the United States*

	1979	1989	1999
Lowest fifth	4.2%	3.8%	3.6%
Second fifth	10.3	9.5	8.9
Third fifth	16.9	15.8	14.9
Fourth fifth	24.7	24.0	23.2
Highest fifth	44.0	46.8	49.4

* Current Population Reports, pp. 60–209, *Money Income in the United States: 1999*, U.S. Government Printing Office, Washington, DC, 2000.

of our population is living in poverty, we have some cause for concern. The U.S. government has attempted to address the problem of poverty in a variety of ways, primarily by enacting programs designed to address the source of poverty: the inability of the family to earn an adequate income. Examples include government-subsidized training programs for unemployed workers and policies designed to reduce discrimination in hiring. In addition, the minimum wage is intended to lift the earnings of unskilled workers.

Other government programs are designed to reduce the misery of the poor, even if they do not address the cause of poverty. Social Security, for example, provides financial assistance to the old, the disabled, the unemployed, and families that are experiencing financial difficulty because of the death of a breadwinner. Temporary Assistance for Needy Families (TANF) is a federal program that provides money to the states that may be used to aid poor families.[9] In addition to these cash-assistance programs, there are a variety of in-kind assistance programs that provide the poor with some type of good or service. Food stamps and subsidized public housing are two examples. All of these programs are designed to improve the status of the poor and in this way moderate the income distribution dictated by the market.

While there is widespread agreement with the objective of helping the poor, economists are quick to point out that government intervention does not always achieve the intended effects. For instance, many economists believe that the minimum wage does more harm than good, since it tends to reduce employment (at the higher wage, employers hire fewer workers). And attempts to aid poor families can have unintended effect of discouraging work. As these examples suggest, government intervention may not always improve market outcomes. The next section explores that possibility.

GOVERNMENT FAILURE: THE THEORY OF PUBLIC CHOICE

The existence of market failures and poverty suggests that market economies do not always use resources efficiently or distribute income fairly. But whether government can be relied upon to improve either the allocation of scarce resources or the income distribution is open to debate. In fact, public-choice economists point out that **government failure**—the enactment of government policies that produce inefficient or inequitable results, or both—is also a possibility.

---

[9] The TANF program replaces Aid to Families with Dependent Children (AFDC), the old "welfare" program that was widely criticized for discouraging work. Under program guidelines, adult family members must begin doing some work (or community service) within two years of beginning the program. In addition, benefits are limited to five years. Both the work requirement and the limitation on benefits are intended to encourage work.

Public choice is the study of how government makes economic decisions. This area of economics was developed by James Buchanan, a professor at Virginia Polytechnic Institute and the 1986 recipient of the Nobel Prize in economics. Although many of us would like to think of government as an altruistic body concerned with the public interest, public-choice economists advise us to think of government as a collection of individuals each pursuing his or her own self-interest. Just as business executives are interested in maximizing profits, politicians are interested in maximizing their ability to get votes. And government bureaucrats are interested in maximizing their income, power, and longevity. In short, the people who make up government are no different than the rest of us, and we need to remember that if we want to understand their behavior.

Recognizing that politicians are merely "vote maximizers" can help us to understand why special-interest groups exert a disproportionate influence on political outcomes. Consider, for example, the efforts of farmers to maintain price supports, land set-asides (payments to farmers for not raising crops on certain acreage), and other forms of aid to agriculture. The farm lobby represents a relatively small group of people who are intensely interested in the fate of these programs. If this aid is eliminated, each of these individuals will be significantly harmed. So farm lobbyists make it clear that their primary interest in selecting a senator or representative is his or her position on this one issue. And they reward those who support their position with significant financial contributions. The rewards for opposing agricultural subsidies are likely to be nonexistent! Because the cost of farm subsidies to any one consumer is relatively small, few voters are likely to choose their next senator or representative on the basis of how they voted on this issue. As a consequence, public-choice theory predicts that the members of Congress will vote in favor of agricultural subsidies even though they lead to the overproduction of agricultural products (are inefficient) and benefit people with incomes greater than the national average (are inequitable).

It is not just special-interest groups that can distort the spending decisions of government. The voting mechanism itself may lead to inefficient outcomes. One problem is that there is no way for voters to reflect the strength of their preferences. They can vote in favor of an issue, or against it, but they cannot indicate the strength of their favor or opposition. Consider, for example, a vote regarding the building of a flood-control dam. Even if the benefits of the dam vastly outweigh its costs, majority voting may prevent its construction. While voters living near the dam stand to benefit in a major way from its construction, most voters will see little reason to help pay for it. As a consequence, the project is likely to be rejected even though it represents an efficient use of society's resources.

Another problem stems from the logrolling efforts that are commonplace in Congress. **Logrolling** is trading votes to gain support for a proposal; politicians agree to vote for a project they oppose in order to gain votes for a project they support. For example, a senator from Missouri might agree to vote in favor of a bill that would expand the federal highway system in Florida in return for a Florida senator's favorable vote on a bill appropriating more money for Missouri's military bases. In many instances, logrolling can lead to efficient outcomes. But in others, it can lead to the approval of projects or programs whose costs exceed their benefits.

In addition to the problems posed by special-interest groups and the voting process itself, public-choice economists point to the problems posed by government bureaucrats. Many of the spending decisions that are made by our local, state, and federal governments are not made by elected officials; they are made by the bureaucrats who run our various government agencies. Public-choice economists argue that these individuals, like the rest of us, pursue their own self-interest. In other words, they seek to increase their salaries, their longevity, and their influence. Rather than attempting to run lean, efficient agencies, their goal is to expand their power and resist all efforts to restrict their agencies' growth or influence. As a consequence, these agencies may become unjustifiably larger and require tax support in excess of the benefits they provide to citizens.

As you can see, public-choice economists are not optimistic that government will make decisions that improve either efficiency or equity. Instead, they see politicians and bureaucrats making decisions intended largely to benefit themselves. While-public choice economists make important observations, they may overstate their case. In recent years significant strides have been made in reducing trade barriers and some agricultural subsidies, despite howls of protest from those adversely affected.[10] These reforms indicate that government action can lead to a more efficient use of society's scarce resources. In addition, while majority voting can lead to inefficient results, it can also lead to outcomes that are more efficient than those produced by private markets. This is likely to be true, for example, in the case of public goods, where private markets may fail to provide the product at all.

The real message of public-choice economics is not that government action always leads to inefficiency or inequity. Rather, it is that we need to be just as alert to the possibility of government failure as we are to the possibility of market failure.

---

[10] Although the 1996 Freedom to Farm Act did eliminate deficiency payments, which rise when commodity prices fall, other price-sensitive payments went into effect in response to sagging prices in the late 1990s. As a result, government is expected to pay farmers almost $23 billion in 2000, more than three times the 1996 outlay. While farm lobbyists may have lost the 1996 battle, they have yet to lose the war.

SUMMARY

Market failure occurs when a market economy produces too much or too little of certain products and thus fails to make the most efficient use of society's limited resources.

There are three major sources of market failure: market power, externalities, and public goods. The exercise of market power can lead to a misuse of society's resources because firms with market power tend to restrict output in order to force up prices. Consequently, too few of society's resources will be allocated to the production of the goods and services provided by firms with market power.

Another source of market failure is the market's inability to reflect all costs and benefits. In some instances the act of producing or consuming a product creates *externalities*—costs or benefits that are not borne by either buyers or sellers but that spill over onto third parties. When this happens, the market has no way of taking those costs and benefits into account and adjusting production and consumption decisions accordingly. As a consequence, the market fails to give us optimal results; our resources are not used as well as they could be. We produce too much of some things because we do not consider all costs; we produce too little of other things because we do not consider all benefits. To correct these problems, government must pursue policies that force firms to pay the full *social cost* of the products they create and encourage the production and consumption of products with *external benefits*.

Markets may also fail to produce optimal results simply because some products are not well suited for sale by private firms. Public goods fall into that category. *Public goods* are products that convey their benefits equally to all members of society, whether or not all members have paid for those products. National defense is probably the best example. It is virtually impossible to sell national defense through markets because there is no way to exclude nonpayers from receiving the same benefits as payers. Since there is no way for a private businessperson to earn a profit by selling such products, private markets cannot be relied on to produce these goods or services, no matter how important they are to the well-being of the society.

Even if a market system uses its resources efficiently, if income is distributed unfairly, we may judge that to be a shortcoming of the system. There is significant income inequality in the U.S. economy. In 1999 the lowest quintile of the income distribution received less than 4 percent of total money income, while the highest quintile received more than 49 percent of total income. In addition, almost 12 percent of the population were living in poverty. A variety of programs have been adopted to attack the problem of poverty and moderate the income distribution. These include training programs for the unemployed and programs to provide direct financial assistance to the poor: Temporary Assistance for Needy Families, for example.

Although market economies may fail to use resources efficiently and distribute income fairly, public-choice economists are not convinced that government can be counted on to improve either of these outcomes. *Public choice* is the study of how government makes economic decisions. According to public-choice economists, government is a collection of individuals each pursuing his or her own self-interest. Because politicians and government bureaucrats make decisions largely to benefit themselves, we cannot count on them to pursue policies that further the public interest. In fact, *government failure*— the enactment of government policies that produce inefficient or inequitable results, or both—is also a possible consequence.

KEY TERMS

External benefits
External costs
Externalities
Government failure
Internal benefits
Internal costs
Internalize costs

Logrolling
Market failure
Private benefits
Private costs
Private goods that yield signif-
    icant external benefits
Property rights

Public choice
Public goods
Pure private goods
Social benefit
Social cost

STUDY QUESTIONS

Fill in the Blanks

1. _Market failures_ are instances in which a market economy fails to make the most efficient use of society's limited resources.

2. The term _Externalities_ is used to describe costs borne or benefits received by parties other than those involved in the transaction.

3. Social costs are the sum of _Private Cost_ and _External Cost_.

4. One way to encourage the consumption of products with external benefits would be to _Subsidize_ their purchase.

5. _Private goods_ are products that convey their benefits only to the buyer.

6. National defense is an example of a _Public good_.

7. Another word for private costs and benefits is _Internal_ costs and benefits.

8. _External benefits_ are benefits that are paid for by one party but that spill over to other parties.

9. The major reason our rivers and streams have been used as disposal sites is that this approach minimized the firm's _Private or Internal_ costs of production.

10. If an action creates no external costs or benefits, private costs will equal

_Social_____ costs.

11. _Public choice_____ is the study of how government makes economic decisions.

12. When politicians trade votes to gain support for a proposal, they are engaging

in _Logrolling_____ .

Multiple Choice

1. A market economy will tend to underproduce products that create
   a) social benefits.
   b) social costs.
   ✓ c) external benefits.
   d) external costs.

2. Which of the following is an example of a pure private good?
   ✓ a) A desk
   b) Education
   c) A fence between neighbors
   d) A park

3. Which of the following is most likely to produce external costs?
   ✓ a) Liquor
   b) A steak
   c) A flower garden
   d) A storm warning system

4. Suppose that chicken-processing plants create external costs. Then, in the absence of government intervention, it is likely that
   a) too few chickens will be processed, from a social point of view, and the price of a processed chicken will be artificially low.
   b) too many chickens will be processed, from a social point of view, and the price of a processed chicken will be artificially high.
   c) too few chickens will be processed, from a social point of view, and the price of a processed chicken will be artificially high.

   d) too many chickens will be processed, from a social point of view, and the price of a processed chicken will be artificially low.

5. If the firms in an industry have been creating pollution and are forced to find a method of waste disposal that does not damage the environment, the result will probably be
   a) a lower price for the product offered by the firms.
   b) a higher product price and a higher equilibrium quantity.
   c) a lower product price and a higher equilibrium quantity.
   ✓ d) a higher product price and a lower equilibrium quantity.

6. Which of the following is the best example of a pure public good?
   a) A cigarette
   b) A bus
   ✓ c) A lighthouse
   d) An automobile

7. Suppose that an AIDS vaccine is developed. In the absence of government intervention, it is likely that
   a) too few AIDS shots will be administered because individuals will fail to consider the private benefits provided by the shots.
   b) too many AIDS shots will be administered because individuals will consider only the private cost of the shots.

c) too few AIDS shots will be administered because individuals will consider only the private benefits provided by the shots.

d) too many AIDS shots will be administered because individuals will ignore the external benefits associated with the shots.

8. If a product creates external benefits, the demand curve that reflects all social benefits
   a) will be to the left of the demand curve that reflects only private benefits.
   b) will be to the right of the demand curve that reflects only private benefits.
   c) will not slope downward.
   d) will be the same as the demand curve that reflects private benefits.

9. Public goods can lead to market failure because they
   a) create external costs.
   b) create social costs.
   c) cannot be sold easily in markets.
   d) cannot be paid for through taxes.

10. Banning all pollution may not be the optimal strategy, because
    a) the costs may exceed the benefits.
    b) the benefits of this approach are probably limited.
    c) the harm caused by pollution is generally overestimated.
    d) the benefits of a clean environment are generally overestimated.

11. Which of the following is *not* true?
    a) If social costs exceed private costs, external costs are present.
    b) If a product creates external costs, society should devote fewer resources to its production.
    c) If a society fails to consider externalities, it will not use its resources optimally.

d) Consumers tend to purchase too much of products that create external benefits.

12. Which of the following best describes the free-rider problem?
    a) Your brother always rides home with you but never pays for the gas.
    b) Some private goods create external benefits for those who have not paid.
    c) Some people think that the environment is a free resource and therefore abuse it.
    d) Some goods cannot be sold in markets because the benefits they confer are available to all—whether they have paid or not.

13. Public-choice economists argue that
    a) majority voting always leads to efficient outcomes.
    b) government bureaucrats tend to act in the public interest.
    c) politicians generally find it in their self-interest to oppose special-interest groups.
    d) self-interest is the motivation of both business executives and politicians.

14. Suppose that a proposed government project would cost $50,000 and convey benefits worth $100 to 1,000 people, and benefits worth $5 to the remaining 9,000 people in the community. If each person was assessed a $50 tax to pay for this project, the theory of public choice predicts that it would be
    a) rejected because the project's total costs exceed its total benefits.
    b) approved because the project's total benefits exceed its total costs.
    c) rejected because voters are unable to reflect the strength of their preferences.
    d) approved because voters recognize that it is an efficient use of society's limited resources.

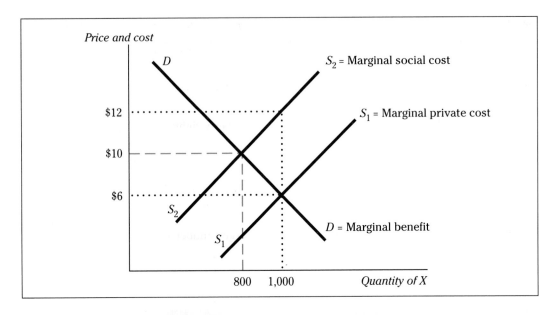

Use the diagram above in answering questions 15 and 16.

15. Suppose that production of product X creates external costs. In the absence of government intervention, this industry would tend to produce
   a) 800 units of output, which is less than the allocatively efficient output of 1,000 units.
   b) 1,000 units of output, which is more than the allocatively efficient output of 800 units.
   c) 800 units, which is the allocatively efficient output.
   d) 1,000 units, which is the allocatively efficient output.

16. At 1,000 units of output, the marginal benefit from consuming the last unit of X is equal to
   a) $6, but the marginal social cost is equal to about $12, and so, from a social point of view, too little output is being produced.
   b) $12, but the marginal social cost is equal to about $6, and so, from a social point of view, too little output is being produced.
   c) $6, but the marginal social cost is equal to about $12, and so, from a social point of view, too much output is being produced.
   d) $12, but the marginal social cost is equal to about $6, and so, from a social point of view, too much output is being produced.

Problems and Questions for Discussion

1. Why should you and I be concerned about whether our society's resources are used optimally?

2. What is market failure, and what are the sources of this problem?

3. How can fines and subsidies be used to correct market failure?

4. Most businesses are concerned about our environment, but they may be reluctant to stop polluting unless all other firms in their industry are also forced to stop. Why?

5. If we force firms to stop polluting, the result will probably be higher product prices. Is that good or bad? Why?

6. Why is it important (from society's viewpoint) to encourage the production and consumption of products that yield external benefits?

7. If we're really concerned about external costs, there would be some logic in fining any spectator who insisted on standing up to cheer at football games. What would be the logic? What practical considerations make this an impractical solution?

8. Why is a tornado warning system a public good? What about a flood-control dam? Why does it fall into that category?

9. Milton Friedman suggests that although it makes sense to subsidize a general education in the liberal arts, it makes much less

sense to subsidize purely vocational training. What do you suppose is the logic behind that distinction?

10. Explain how the free-rider problem leads to market failure.

11. How can the absence of clearly defined property rights lead to the abuse or misuse of a resource?

12. According to Ronald Coase, the assignment of property rights can help to resolve externality problems if the number of parties involved is relatively small. Why is this solution unworkable when a large number of people are involved, as when a firm's pollution affects thousands of people?

ANSWER KEY

Fill in the Blanks

1. Market failures
2. externalities or spillovers
3. private costs, external costs
4. subsidize
5. Private goods
6. public good
7. internal
8. External benefits
9. private or internal
10. social
11. Public choice
12. logrolling

Multiple Choice

1. c	5. d	8. b	11. d	14. c
2. a	6. c	9. c	12. d	15. b
3. a	7. c	10. a	13. d	16. c
4. d				

PART THREE

Macroeconomics: The Economy as a Whole

Macroeconomics is the study of the economy as a whole and the factors that influence the economy's overall performance. (If you have a hard time remembering the difference between microeconomics and macroeconomics, just remember that *micro* means "small"—microcomputer, microfilm, microsurgery—whereas *macro* means "large.") Macroeconomics addresses a number of important questions: What determines the level of total output and total employment in the economy? What causes unemployment? What causes inflation? What can be done to eliminate these problems or at least to reduce their severity? These and many other considerations relating to the economy's overall performance are the domain of macroeconomics.

In Chapter 10 we begin our study of macroeconomics by examining some indicators, or measures, that economists watch to gauge how well the economy is performing. Chapter 11 introduces aggregate demand and aggregate supply and considers how these twin forces interact to determine the overall price level and the levels of output and employment in the economy. The chapter then uses the aggregate demand and supply framework to examine the possibility that the economy is self-correcting in the long run. Chapter 12 deals with fiscal policy—government spending and taxation policy designed to combat unemployment or inflation. It also considers the limitations of fiscal policy and examines the sources and consequences of federal budget deficits and the public debt.

Chapter 13 explains how depository institutions, such as commercial banks and savings and loan associations, "create" money and how the Federal Reserve attempts to control the money supply in order to guide the economy's performance. Chapter 14 explores the debate between "activists" who believe that government should attempt to manage the economy's overall performance, and "nonactivists," who believe that such attempts are ill-advised. Chapter 15 concludes the macroeconomics section of the textbook by considering economic growth. The chapter examines the sources of growth, the impact of growth on our standard of living, and reservations regarding the pursuit of economic growth as an objective.

CHAPTER TEN

Measuring Aggregate Performance

What economic problems have the potential to really excite Americans? Do Americans lose sleep over the market power of large corporations? Do they have nightmares about agricultural subsidies, minimum wage laws, or environmental pollution?

Although each of these issues gains the attention of some Americans, national surveys tell us that none of them can hold a candle to two problems that can hit closer to home: unemployment and inflation. In the next few chapters we'll be examining the factors that influence the economy's *aggregate*, or overall, performance and how problems such as unemployment and inflation arise. We will also consider policies to combat unemployment and inflation and the difficulties that may be encountered in applying these policies.

This chapter sets the stage for that discussion by examining some **economic indicators**—signals, or measures, that tell us how well the economy is performing. After all, policymakers can't take actions that lead to better performance unless they know when problems exist. Economic indicators provide that information. The economic indicators we will discuss in this chapter include the unemployment rate, the Consumer Price Index, and the gross domestic product (GDP)—the indicator that many economists believe is the most important single measure of the economy's performance.

MEASURING UNEMPLOYMENT

One dimension of our economy's performance is its ability to provide jobs for those who want to work. For most of us, that's an extremely important aspect of the economy's performance because we value work not only as a source of income but also as a basis for our sense of personal worth. The most highly publicized indicator of performance in this area is the unemployment rate. The **unemployment rate** traditionally reported is the percentage of the civilian labor force that is unemployed. The **civilian labor force** is made up of all persons over the age of sixteen who are not in the armed forces and who are either employed or actively seeking employment. The Bureau of Labor Statistics (BLS), the agency responsible for gathering and analyzing labor force and employment data, surveys some 60,000 households throughout the United States monthly to determine the employment status of the residents. It uses the statistics gathered from this sample (which is scientifically designed to be representative of the entire U.S. population) to estimate the total size of the labor force and the rate of unemployment.

Counting the Unemployed

How does the Bureau of Labor Statistics decide whether a person should be classified as unemployed? First, it determines whether the person has a job. As far as the BLS is concerned, you are employed if you did *any* work for pay in the week of the survey. It doesn't matter how long you worked, provided that you worked for pay. You are also counted as employed if you worked fifteen hours or more (during the survey week) as an unpaid worker in a family-operated business.

Even if you didn't have a job during the survey week, you are not recognized as unemployed unless you were actively seeking employment. To be "actively seeking employment," you must have done something to try to find a job—filled out applications, responded to want ads, or at least registered at an employment agency. If you did any of those things and failed to find a job, you are officially unemployed. If you didn't look for work, you're considered as "not participating" in the civilian labor force, and consequently you won't be counted as unemployed.

The purpose of the BLS monthly survey is to estimate the size of the civilian labor force (the number employed plus those actively seeking employment) and the number of unemployed. Then the bureau computes the unemployment rate by dividing the total number of unemployed persons by the total number of people in the civilian labor force. In 2000, for example, there were 140.9 million people in the civilian labor force; 5.7 million were unemployed. These figures represent averages—the average number of people in the civilian labor force and the average number of people unemployed—for 2000. This means that the average **civilian unemployment rate** for 2000 was 4 percent:

$$\text{Unemployment rate} = \frac{\text{Total number of unemployed persons}}{\substack{\text{Total number of persons} \\ \text{in the civilian labor force}}}$$

$$\text{Unemployment rate (2000)} = \frac{\text{5.7 million unemployed persons}}{\substack{\text{140.9 million persons in} \\ \text{the civilian labor force}}}$$

$$= 4.0 \text{ percent}$$

As you can see from Exh. 10.1, our unemployment rate compares quite favorably with those of other industrialized nations. In 2000 the average unemployment rate in the seven nations surveyed was 7 percent, well above

---

EXHIBIT 10.1
Unemployment Rates in Major Industrialized Countries

	UNITED STATES	CANADA	JAPAN	FRANCE	GERMANY	ITALY	UNITED KINGDOM	7-NATION AVERAGE
Unemploy- ment rate 2000	4.0%	5.8%	4.8%	9.7%	8.3%	10.7%	5.6%	7.0%
Average unemploy- ment rate 1991–2000	5.6%	8.6%	3.3%	11.4%	8.2%	10.5%	8.1%	8.0%

Source: Bureau of Labor Statistics, U.S. Department of Labor.

our 4 percent. When we look at the figures for the last decade, our performance still looks relatively good; the seven-nation average was 8 percent, whereas our average unemployment rate was 5.6 percent. But is 5.6 percent the best the U.S. economy can hope to achieve, or can we do better still? Let's turn to that question.

Types of Unemployment

In general, a high unemployment rate is interpreted as a sign of a weak economy, whereas a low rate is seen as a sign of strength. But in order to recognize a low rate of unemployment when we see it, we have to know what we are aiming for, what is possible or realistic. That, in turn, requires knowledge of the three basic types of unemployment—frictional, cyclical, and structural—and the extent to which these types of unemployment are unavoidable.

Frictional Unemployment

Even when plenty of jobs are available, there are always some people out of work because they are changing jobs or searching for their first job. Economists call this **frictional unemployment** to distinguish a type of labor-market adjustment involving time lags, or "friction." A certain amount of frictional unemployment is unavoidable and probably even desirable. It is a sign that employers are looking for the most-qualified workers and that workers are searching for the best jobs. Neither party is willing to settle for the first thing that comes along. That's good for the economy because it means that the right people are more likely to be matched to the right jobs. But it takes time for workers and employers to find each other, and meanwhile the job seekers are adding to the nation's unemployment rate.

Cyclical Unemployment

Joblessness caused by a reduction in the economy's total demand for goods and services is termed **cyclical unemployment**. When such a reduction occurs, perhaps because consumers have decided to save more and spend less, businesses that are not able to sell as much output as before usually must cut back on production. This means that some of their workers will become unemployed. We call this unemployment cyclical because we recognize that the economy goes through cycles of economic activity. For awhile the economy expands and unemployment declines; then economic activity slows and unemployment rises. These recurring ups and downs in the level of economic activity are known as the **business cycle**. A period of rising output and employment is called an *expansion*; a period of declining output and employment is called a *recession*. The impact of the business cycle on the unemployment rate is evident in Exh. 10.2.

EXHIBIT 10.2
The Unemployment Rate: 1929–2000

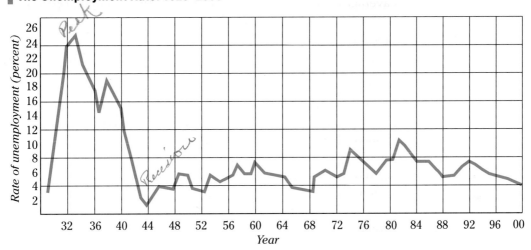

This exhibit shows that the unemployment rate varies significantly from year to year. But even though the unemployment rate is not a constant, there is a pattern to that variation, an up-and-down cycle that keeps repeating itself. For example, we can see that the unemployment rate dropped from a high of about 25 percent in 1933 to approximately 14 percent in 1937. Then the unemployment rate jumped back up to 19 percent in 1938 and started a steady decline that continued until 1944. The same sort of pattern is evident over other time periods although the magnitude of the changes certainly is not as great.

The rate reported is the civilian unemployment rate. Older data was drawn from *Historical Statistics of the United States,* published by the United States Bureau of the Census. Recent data is from the Bureau of Labor Statistics, U.S. Department of Labor.

When people are cyclically unemployed, the economy is losing the output these workers could have produced, and, of course, the workers are losing the income they could have earned. Many economists argue that it is possible to reduce the amount of cyclical unemployment by using government policies to stimulate the total demand for goods and services.

Structural Unemployment
Changes in the makeup, or structure, of the economy that render certain skills obsolete or in less demand result in **structural unemployment**. The economy is always changing. New products are introduced and old ones are dropped; businesses continually develop new production methods. These kinds of changes can have a profound effect on the demand for labor. Skills that were very much in demand ten or twenty years ago may be

virtually obsolete today. Computerized photocomposition machines have virtually eliminated the need for newspaper typesetters, for example, and robots have begun to replace semiskilled workers in automobile manufacturing plants. Further automation will signal a similar fate for workers in many other manufacturing industries.

The Bureau of Labor Statistics reports that more than 500,000 manufacturing jobs were eliminated over the last ten years. Many of the displaced manufacturing workers found employment in the service sector—which added more than 20 million jobs over the same period. But the transition was probably difficult. The skills required in the service sector are often quite different from those required in manufacturing. Displaced manufacturing workers may need to be retrained before they can find employment in the service sector. In the interim, they will be structurally unemployed.

The changing skill requirements for the workplace are not the only source of structural unemployment. Some people cannot hold a job in the modern economy because they never received much education or training in the first place. This is the case with many members of inner-city minorities, who often are educated in second-rate school systems that have a high

Structurally unemployed workers may need to be retrained before they can find jobs.

Companies Try Dipping Deeper into Labor Pool

By Louis Ochitelle

UNABLE to find enough workers in the booming economy, American corporations are trying to expand the labor pool.

Until recently, employers had met their labor needs by hiring people who were already employed or at least wanted to work. But as this pool shrinks, they are increasingly recruiting from among the 36 million working-age people in the United States who had not sought a job, or even thought about taking one.

Conrad Bell is one of these new workers. Mr. Bell, a college junior, did not need a job. Living at home, he had enough pocket money, and the first payments on his school loans were still in the future. But when a notice went up on a campus bulletin board that H & R Block was hiring students skilled in computers to trouble-shoot problems called in from Block offices around the country, Mr. Bell applied and got one of the jobs. "Most of my friends now work," he explained.

The company has gone out of its way to accommodate the 23-year-old student, juggling schedules so that he can carry four courses at the DeVry Institute of Technology and still work 25 hours a week....

In addition to students like Mr. Bell, companies are stepping up recruiting of the urban poor, retirees, homemakers, men and women mustering out of military service, the handicapped, women coming off welfare and illegal immigrants not already counted in the labor force. People with jobs are being recruited to moonlight in second jobs, and part-timers are adding hours more easily than in the past. To get workers, some companies even relocate to pockets of relatively high unemployment.

(Continued)

Source: New York Times, March 26, 2000, p. 1.

dropout rate. It is also possible for people to be structurally unemployed even though they have marketable skills. For example, unemployed construction workers in Fresno, California, may have skills that are very much in demand. But if the available jobs are on the East Coast, the Fresno workers remain structurally unemployed.

All structurally unemployed workers have one thing in common: If they are to find jobs, they must make drastic changes. They will have to acquire

(Companies Try Dipping into
Labor Pool *Continued*)

The recruiting poster and
the promise of flexible hours
were what landed Mr. Bell
despite his mother's resistance. "She does not want me
to work while I'm in school,"
he said. Aside from flexible
hours, companies are offering subsidized transportation, child care, store
discounts, free meals, family
outings, tuition subsidies,...
everything, but significantly
higher pay.

"We really are in uncharted
territory," said Lawrence
Katz, a labor economist at
Harvard University. "The last
time we had such tight labor
markets, in the 1960's, the
baby boomers were beginning
to take jobs, and they fed the
labor pool. We don't have
them today, and we really
don't know how many people
we can draw."

The economy may ride, or
fall, on the answer. Alan
Greenspan, chairman of the
Federal Reserve Board, argues that the pool of people
still available to take jobs has
dwindled to the point that
employers will have to pay
higher wages to compete for
workers and then will push
up prices to cover the higher
labor costs. Citing this inflationary danger as one reason
for their actions, the Fed's
policy makers have moved
interest rates up a quarter
percentage point five times
since last June to slow the
economy, with the latest increase coming last Tuesday.

But Mr. Greenspan's esti-
mate of the number of people still available for jobs
relies on the Labor Department's monthly employ-
ment surveys, which do not
count as available the people who say they are not interested in working. Many
of these people are now being recruited, including Mr.
Bell, who was busy being a
student until he saw the H &
R Block poster and popped
into the labor force....

Certainly inflationary
wage increases are not evident in national wage statistics or in the Kansas City
metropolitan area, where the
unemployment rate of 3.2
percent is nearly a percentage point less than the nation's 4.1 percent and
employers are offering all the
new lures, short of big raises.

That is especially the case
at Block's recently opened
technology center. A quarter
of the 800 people working
there in the tax season are
students like Mr. Bell, who is
earning $11.54 an hour,
barely up from last year's
rate. Another 200 are low-
skilled customer call-center
operators, some of whom
commute by municipal bus
from an impoverished neighborhood nearby. H & R Block
has put the new center, and
its jobs, near enough for the
operators to get to a job, one
that pays $8 to $9 an hour,
good pay in their world.

"We have not been pres-
sured to raise wages because
of the labor shortage," said
Frank L. Salizzoni, the company's chief executive.

Even some officials in the
Clinton administration, despite its hands-off policy

new skills or move to a different part of the country. They may even find it necessary to do both. Since such changes cannot be made overnight, economists
see structural unemployment as a more serious and longer-term problem than
frictional or cyclical unemployment. (The low unemployment the United
States has experienced in recent years has made even structural unemployment less painful. That's because the difficulty in finding workers makes employers more willing to foot the bill for retraining. In 2000, employers were
reaching out for workers in other ways as well. Read "Companies Try Dipping
Deeper into Labor Pool," on page 299, to see how.)

vis-a-vis the Federal Reserve, are challenging the Fed's view that an inflationary labor shortage is developing. Martin Bailey, chairman of the president's Council of Economic Advisers, said, "We don't see wage pressure coming from the labor market at this time." More bluntly, the labor secretary, Alexis M. Herman, declared in a recent interview: "I tell everybody Alan Greenspan is a wise man, and I don't comment on Fed policy. But this is a balanced economy that can continue to perform at a very solid and steady pace."

Part of the difference lies in how the experts tally the number of available workers. Ms. Herman counts at least 13 million people across the nation available for jobs, including 3 million part-time workers who have told surveyors from the Bureau of Labor Statistics that they would take more hours if they could get them.

Mr. Greenspan's more conservative estimate of 10 million people available for jobs leaves out the part-timers. He focuses on the nearly 6 million people who are listed as officially unemployed because they are actively looking for work, as well as 4 million others who tell the bureau's surveyors that they have not looked for work lately but would like a job or might like one in the right circumstances....

But both his estimate and Ms. Herman's miss those who are not thinking about working but can be lured into jobs. Most of them are among the 36.3 million civilians between 16 and 64 who are busy in other activities and see themselves as not available for work, unless, like Mr. Bell, a company is able to change their minds....

Use Your Economic Reasoning

1. Before Conrad Bell accepted a job with H&R Block, would he have been classified as unemployed?
2. Suppose a person has a part-time job but wants a full-time job. Would he or she be classified as unemployed?
3. The article discusses three categories of potential workers: those who are actively seeking work but unable to find it, those who have not looked for work lately but would like a job, and those who are not thinking about work but might be lured into working. Which of these groups would be officially classified as unemployed?
4. Why is Alan Greenspan, chairman of the Federal Reserve Board, concerned about the dwindling pool of available workers? Why do you suppose he chooses to ignore the third category of potential workers mentioned in question 3?

Full Employment versus Zero Unemployment

Since a certain amount of frictional and structural unemployment is unavoidable, economists consider zero unemployment an unattainable goal. Although no one knows precisely how much unemployment is of the frictional and structural varieties, a common estimate is 5 percent.[1] This is con-

---

[1] Some economists believe that the natural rate may be significantly less than 5 percent. For instance, three economists at the Brookings Institution—a Washington think tank—argue that the natural rate has fallen to 4.5 percent. See "New Study Stirs Federal Reserve Debate," *Wall Street Journal*, June 28, 2000, Section A; Page 2, By Yochi J. Dreazen.

sidered to be the **natural rate of unemployment**—the minimum level of unemployment that our economy can achieve in normal times.[2] (Note that this is the rate that would exist in the absence of cyclical unemployment.) When the actual rate of unemployment is equal to the natural rate, the economy has achieved **full employment**.

A Closer Look at Unemployment Rates

Recognizing that full employment doesn't mean zero unemployment is an important step in learning how to interpret unemployment statistics. The next step is learning to look beyond the overall unemployment rate to see how various groups in our society are being affected. Although we all talk about "the" unemployment rate, in reality the rate of unemployment varies substantially among the different subcategories of the American labor force. Historically, blacks have been about twice as likely to be unemployed as whites, in part because, on the whole, they have lower levels of education and training. Teenagers, who are often unskilled and lacking in good work habits, generally have unemployment rates about two and a half to three times the overall rate for their racial group.

Exhibit 10.3 shows the unemployment rates for 2000. Note that in 2000 the overall unemployment rate for all civilian workers—that is "the" unemployment rate—was 4 percent. During the same period the overall rate for blacks (7.6 percent) was more than twice the rate for white workers (3.5 percent), and this relationship held for each of the subcategories: men, women, and teenagers. The rates for teens were also within the expected range: black and white teens had unemployment rates about three times the overall rate for their racial group.

As you can see, the overall unemployment rate conceals a great deal of variation across particular groups. Even when the overall rate is low, the unemployment rate among certain subcategories of our population may be unacceptably high. For that reason, those who rely on unemployment statistics for devising policies to combat unemployment or for helping the unemployed in other ways must be willing to look beyond the overall rate to gain a clearer picture of the nature and severity of the unemployment problem.

Unemployment Rates: A Word of Caution

Before we leave this section on unemployment statistics, a few words of caution are appropriate. Watching the unemployment rate can help you understand whether the economy is growing weaker or stronger. But changes in the

---

[2] While there is disagreement about how low the natural rate may be, very few economists believe it is as low as 4 percent, the rate that prevailed in the United States in 2000. In other words, the levels of frictional and structural unemployment we experienced were due to special circumstances and were below those we would expect to sustain.

EXHIBIT 10.3
Unemployment Rates for 2000

WORKER CATEGORY	RATE	WORKER CATEGORY	RATE	WORKER CATEGORY	RATE
All civilian workers	4.0%	*White*	3.5%	*Black*	7.6%
Men (20 and over)	3.3	Men (20 and over)	2.8	Men (20 and over)	7.0
Women (20 and over)	3.6	Women (20 and over)	3.1	Women (20 and over)	6.3
Teenagers (16–19)	13.1	Teenagers (16–19)	11.4	Teenagers (16–19)	24.7

Source: Bureau of Labor Statistics, U.S. Department of Labor.

---

unemployment rate from one month to the next may not be very meaningful and, in fact, can sometimes send misleading signals about the state of the economy.

To illustrate that point, suppose that the economy is in the midst of a deep recession when the Bureau of Labor Statistics reports a small drop in the unemployment rate. Should that drop be taken as a sign that the economy is growing stronger? Not necessarily. When the economy has been in a recession for quite a while, some unemployed workers become discouraged in their search for jobs and stop looking. Since these "discouraged workers" are no longer actively seeking employment, they are no longer counted as unemployed. That makes the unemployment rate look better, but it's not really a sign that the economy has improved. In fact, it may be a sign that labor-market conditions have become even worse.

Of course, we can be misled in the other direction just as easily. Suppose that the economy has begun to recover from a recession and that the unemployment rate is falling. Suddenly the monthly survey shows an increase. Does that mean that the economy is headed back toward recession? It may, but a more likely interpretation is that the economy's improved condition has attracted a lot of additional job seekers who have swelled the labor force and pushed up the unemployment rate. Here the unemployment rate has risen not because the economy is worse but because it is better: People are more confident about their prospects for finding jobs.

Because changes in the unemployment rate can send misleading signals about the strength of the economy, they should be interpreted with caution.

But even when the unemployment rate seems to be sending clear signals (for instance, when it has risen for several consecutive months), we must be careful not to base our evaluation of the economy's health solely on this statistic. After all, the unemployment rate looks at only one dimension of the economy's performance—its ability to provide jobs for the growing labor force. Other dimensions are equally important. To obtain an accurate picture of our economy's performance, we must consider each of these dimensions by examining several different economic indicators.

MEASURING INFLATION

Another important dimension of our economy's performance is its success or failure in avoiding inflation. **Inflation** is defined as a rise in the general level of prices. (The existence of inflation does not necessarily mean that *all* prices are rising but rather that *more* prices are going up than are coming down.) Inflation means that our dollars won't buy as much as they used to. In general, this means that it will take more money to pay the grocery bill, buy clothes, go out for an evening, or do almost anything else.

Unanticipated Inflation and Income Redistribution

Each of us tends to believe that we are being hurt by inflation, but that is not necessarily the case. We forget that at the same time that prices are rising, our money incomes are also likely to be rising, sometimes at a faster rate than the increase in prices. Instead of focusing solely on prices, then, we ought to be concerned about what economists call real income. **Real income** is the purchasing power of your income—the amount of goods and services it will buy. Economists argue that unanticipated inflation is essentially an income redistribution problem: It takes real income away from some people and gives it to others. (As you will see later, when people anticipate inflation, they tend to prepare for it and thereby reduce its redistributive effects.)

Keeping Pace with Inflation

The people hurt by unanticipated inflation are those whose money incomes (the number of *dollars* they earn) don't keep pace with rising prices. If prices rise by 10 percent but your money income increases by only 5 percent, your real income will have fallen. The amount of goods and services that you can buy with your income will be 5 percent less than before.

Whether your money income keeps pace with inflation depends on a variety of factors. The most important is how flexible your income is, that is, how easily it can be adjusted. Professional people—doctors, lawyers, dentists, and so on—often can adjust the prices they charge their customers and thereby stay abreast (or ahead) of inflation. People who own their own businesses— their own hardware store or motel or janitorial service—may be able to adjust their prices similarly. Of course, whether professional people and businesses can successfully increase prices and stay abreast of inflation depends on the degree of the market power they possess. If a seller faces very little competition and therefore has significant market power, it may be able to increase its prices to offset inflation. If it operates in a highly competitive environment, it may not be able to do so.

Workers who are represented by strong unions also may do reasonably well during periods of inflation. Often these unions are able to negotiate cost-of-living adjustment (COLA) clauses, which provide for automatic wage and salary adjustments to compensate for inflation. Other workers may have the forces of demand and supply operating to their advantage. When the demand for workers with a particular skill is strong relative to their supply, those workers often are able to obtain wage or salary increases that more than offset the impact of inflation. Unskilled workers and others in oversupplied fields—those in which there are several prospective employees for each job opening—usually find it more difficult to gain wage increases that match the rate of inflation.

Savers and People on Fixed Incomes

Hardest hit by inflation are people on fixed incomes, whose incomes are by definition inflexible. The classic example is a retired person living on a fixed pension or perhaps on his or her accumulated savings. (Of course, many retired persons are not dependent on fixed pensions. For example, Social Security payments are automatically adjusted for increases in the cost of living.)

Savers can also be hurt by inflation. Whether you are relying on your savings to provide retirement income, to make a down payment on a home someday, or to buy a car next summer, inflation can eat away at the value of your savings account and make your objective more difficult to achieve. For example, if your savings account is paying 6 percent interest and the inflation rate is 10 percent, the purchasing power of your savings is declining by 4 percent a year. After you pay taxes on the interest, you're even further behind.

Creditors versus Debtors

Unanticipated inflation can also hurt banks and other creditors since borrowers will be able to repay their loans with dollars that are worth less than those that were borrowed. As the largest debtor of all, the federal government is probably the biggest gainer from such inflation. Other gainers include families with home mortgages and businesses that borrowed money to purchase factories or equipment.

When Inflation Is Anticipated

The redistributive effects of inflation occur because inflation is unforeseen or unanticipated. To the extent that inflation is anticipated, the redistributive effects will tend to be reduced because individuals and businesses will take actions to protect themselves from inflation.

COLA clauses are one way in which we attempt to insulate ourselves from inflation, but there are others. For example, banks try to protect themselves from anticipated inflation by working the inflation rate into the interest rates they set for loans. If a bank wants to earn 5 percent interest on a loan and expects the inflation rate to be 4 percent, the bank will charge 9 percent interest to get the desired return. If the inflation rate turns out to be 4 percent, neither the bank nor the customer will be harmed by inflation. Of course, the bank's inflation forecast won't always be correct. Forecasting inflation has proved very difficult, and bankers and others will make mistakes. As a consequence, inflation is likely to benefit some and hurt others.

Consequences of inflation extend beyond its effect on the income distribution. When inflation is anticipated, individuals and businesses waste resources in their attempts to protect themselves from its impact. Labor time and energy are expended shopping around and shifting money from one financial institution to another in pursuit of the highest interest rate. Restaurant menus and business price lists must be continually revised, and sales personnel must be kept informed of the most recent price information. In short, efforts to stay ahead of inflation use up resources that could be used to produce other things.

In addition to wasting resources, inflation (whether anticipated or unanticipated) can lead to inefficiency through its tendency to distort the information provided by the price system. To illustrate, suppose that the price of laptop computers increases. Does the higher price indicate greater demand for the product, or does it merely reflect an increase in the overall price level? Because computer manufacturers are uncertain, they may be reluctant to invest in new production capacity. Thus, inflation may slow investment spending and retard the economy's rate of growth.

In summary, inflation, both anticipated and unanticipated, imposes costs on society. Unanticipated inflation causes income redistribution; anticipated inflation causes scarce resources to be wasted and used inefficiently.

Calculating a Price Index

Bankers, union leaders, business executives, and most other people in our society are keenly interested in changes in the general level of prices because they want to try to compensate for those changes; they'd like to build them into the prices they charge their customers and the wages they negotiate with their employers. Government policymakers also want to know what is happening to the price level in order to know when inflation-fighting policies may be necessary.

Economists attempt to measure inflation by using a **price index.** A price index is really nothing more than a ratio of two prices: the price of an item in a base period that serves as a reference point divided into the price of that item in a period we wish to compare with the base period. For example, if the price of steak was $3.75 a pound in 1995 and $6.00 a pound in 2000, the price index for steak in 2000 would be 160 if 1995 was used as the base year:

$$\text{Price index} = \frac{\text{Price in any given period}}{\text{Price in the base period}}$$
$$= \frac{\$6.00}{\$3.75}$$
$$= 1.60 \text{ or } 160 \text{ percent or } 160$$

(Note that although the price index is in fact a percentage, by convention it is written without the percent sign.)

The price index tells us how much the price of the item in question has increased or decreased since the base period. Since the price index in the base period is always 100, an index of 160 means that a price has increased by 60 percent since the base period.[3] By the same logic, an index of 75 would indicate that a price had decreased by 25 percent since the base period. Although price indexes can be used to determine how much prices have risen or fallen since the base period, their most common use is to determine the annual rate of inflation for a particular product or group of products. The **annual inflation rate** is the percent change in a price index from one year to the next. For example, if the price index for steak increased from 160 in 2000 to 170 in 2001, the rate of inflation for steak between 2000 and 2001 would be 6.3 percent (10/160 = 0.063). Exhibit 10.4 provides another example of how to compute the annual inflation rate.

Three basic price indexes are used in the United States: the Consumer Price Index, the Producer Price Index, and the Implicit Price Deflator. Each index surveys a particular range of goods and services in order to determine the rate of inflation among those items. Each computes an overall index showing the average rate of price change for its assortment (or "basket") of commodities and

---

[3] The price index in the base period is always 100 because the numbers in the numerator and denominator of the price-index formula must be the same. For example, if we want to calculate the price index for steak in 1995 using 1995 as the base period, we would have $3.75/$3.75 = 1.00 or 100 percent.

EXHIBIT 10.4
Computing the Annual Rate of Inflation for College Tuition

The price index for college tuition was 318.7 in 1999 and 331.9 in 2000, using 1984 as the base year. Thus, the price of attending college increased by 231.9 percent between 1984 and 2000. But what was the rate of inflation in college tuition in 2000?

$$\text{Annual rate of inflation} = \frac{\text{Change in the price index from one year to the next}}{\text{Price index in the initial year}}$$

$$= \frac{331.9 - 318.7}{318.7}$$

$$= \frac{13.2}{318.7}$$

$$= .041 \text{ or } 4.1 \text{ percent}$$

---

presents individual price indexes for each major class of items in the survey. This makes it possible to determine which products are most responsible for any change in the overall index.

The Consumer Price Index

The best-known index is the Consumer Price Index (CPI). The CPI looks at the prices of some 400 goods and services that have been chosen to represent the kinds of products typically purchased by urban consumers. The CPI measures the purchasing power of consumers' dollars by comparing the current cost of this so-called basket of goods and services to the cost of the same basket at an earlier date.

Exhibit 10.5 shows the kinds of items that are included in the Consumer Price Index survey. You can see how the rate of inflation differs from one class of items to another. The top line—the all-items index—is the CPI usually referred to by economists and the media. It tells us the average rate of price increase for all the items in the market basket. According to the exhibit, the all-items index stood at 172.2 in 2000. Because the most recent CPI uses the average level of prices between 1982 and 1984 as the base, prices increased approximately 72 percent between the period 1982–1984 and 2000. More precisely, in 2000 it cost $172.20 to purchase a basket of goods and services that sold for $100 in 1982–1984. As you can see, some items increased even more

EXHIBIT 10.5
Consumer Price Indexes, 2000 (1982–1984 = 100)

ALL ITEMS	172.2		
Food and beverages	168.4	Apparel and upkeep	129.6
Housing	169.6	Transportation	153.3
Shelter	193.4	Medical care	260.8
Fuel & other utilities	137.9	Education*	112.5
Household furnishings & operation	128.2	Other goods and services	260.8

*Education index based on December, 1997 = 100

Source: Bureau of Labor Statistics, U.S. Department of Labor.

than that. For example, medical care rose to an index of 260.8; the cost of medical care increased more than 160 percent between 1982–1984 and 2000.

Because consumers spend greater percentages of their incomes on certain index items—more, say, on food and beverages than on apparel and upkeep—merely averaging all the indexes at face value to arrive at the all-items index would be misleading. Therefore, the all-items index is computed as a *weighted average* of the individual indexes. That is, the things for which consumers spend more of their incomes are counted more heavily in determining the all-items index. For example, if consumers spend twice as much on food and beverages as they do on apparel and upkeep, food and beverage prices will be twice as important in computing the all-items index.[4]

By comparing the 1999 and 2000 consumer price indexes, we can compute the annual inflation rate for consumer goods. Recall that the annual inflation rate is the percent change in the price index from one year to the next. The CPI was 166.6 in 1999 and 172.2 in 2000, so the rate of inflation in 2000 was 3.4 percent (5.6/166.6 = .034).

---

[4] The CPI has been criticized for overstating the rise in the cost of living. In 1999, the Bureau of Labor Statistics completed a series of changes intended to make the CPI a more-accurate gauge. The new formula, called the geometric mean, attempts to capture the tendency of consumers to substitute among similar items in response to price rises (for instance, buying catfish if the price of trout rises). Some critics argue that, even after this and other changes, the CPI still overstates the rise in the cost of living by about 0.8 percent per year. In response, the Federal Reserve (the agency charged with regulating the nation's money supply) has adopted something called the personal consumption expenditures index, or PCE, as its prime measure of inflation. The PCE index is released quarterly by the Commerce Department.

How does our 3.4% inflation rate compare with the rates experienced by other major industrialized nations? As you can see from Exh. 10.6, our 2000 inflation rate was somewhat higher than most of the other nations surveyed. When we look at inflation over the last decade, a similar picture emerges. Only Italy had a higher average inflation rate than the United States.

The rates of inflation reported in this table reflect inflation on consumer goods; the U.S. rates are based on the CPI, and the foreign rates are based on similar indexes. But in some instances we may be more interested in inflation at the wholesale level, or the rate of inflation in government services or capital goods (factories and equipment). For these purposes we need to turn to other price indexes.

The Producer Price Index and the Implicit Price Deflator

The Producer Price Index (PPI) and the Implicit Price Deflator (IPD) don't receive as much publicity as the Consumer Price Index, which is closely watched because it is used for cost-of-living adjustments in labor contracts and Social Security payments. Nevertheless, they have their particular uses and advantages. The PPI and the IPD are interpreted in precisely the same way as the CPI; that is, an index of 170 means that prices have risen by 70 percent since the base period.

The Producer Price Index is sometimes called the Wholesale Price Index.[5] It reflects the rate of inflation in the wholesale prices of finished prod-

---

[5] Actually, there are three separate Producer Price Indexes: one for finished goods, one for semi-finished goods, and one for raw materials. The index for finished goods is the one referred to as the Wholesale Price Index. It's also the one commonly referred to in the news.

EXHIBIT 10.6

Inflation Rates in Major Industrialized Countries

	UNITED STATES	CANADA	JAPAN	FRANCE	GERMANY	ITALY	UNITED KINGDOM	7-NATION AVERAGE
Inflation rate, 2000	3.4%	2.7%	-.7%	.9%	1.0%	3.0%	.9%	1.6%
Average inflation rate, 1991–2000	2.8%	2.0%	.8%	1.6%	2.3%	3.7%	2.8%	2.3%

Sources: Economic Report of the President, 2000; Bureau of Labor Statistics (United States), Statistics Canada, Japanese Statistics Bureau, National Institute of Statistics and Economic Studies (France), Federal Statistical Office (Germany), National Institute of Statistics (Italy), Office For National Statistics (United Kingdom).

ucts—both consumer goods and capital goods. Economists pay particular attention to the PPI because they think that it provides an indication of what will happen to consumer prices in the months to come. The logic here is fairly simple. Any increases in wholesale prices are eventually going to be passed on to consumers.

The broadest measure of inflation is the Implicit Price Deflator. This index examines the rate of increase in prices for all the different items included in the gross domestic product (GDP). This includes the prices of consumer goods, but it also includes the prices of items produced for business and government use and for export to foreign buyers. The range of products covered by the Implicit Price Deflator will be more apparent after you have completed the next section.

MEASURING TOTAL OUTPUT

The fundamental purpose of every economic system is to produce output in order to satisfy human wants. Therefore, many economists argue that gross domestic product (GDP) is the most important single indicator of our economy's performance. **Gross domestic product** is the total monetary value of all final goods and services produced within a nation in one year. In other words, it is a measure of the economy's annual production or output.

Calculating GDP: A Sneak Preview

Because GDP is measured in monetary units rather than units of output, we can add apples and oranges, so to speak; we can sum the economy's output of eggs, stereos, houses, tractors, and other products to produce a meaningful statistic. The procedure is quite simple: The output of each product is valued at its selling price, and these values are added to arrive at a figure for GDP.

Although GDP is a measure of output, you should note that only the output of final goods and services is permitted to enter the GDP calculation. *Final goods* are those that are purchased for final use rather than for further processing or resale. For example, a new pair of jeans is a final good, but the thread, cloth, zippers, and snaps that are used in manufacturing the jeans are *intermediate goods*. Since the value of the jeans already includes the value of the thread and other intermediate goods, only the value of the jeans should count in GDP. If the value of intermediate goods were to be included in the calculation, the result would be double counting, which would overstate the value of the economy's annual production.

The cloth and thread used in manufacturing clothing are intermediate goods, whereas the finished garment is a final good.

GDP and the Circular Flow

There are two ways to measure gross domestic product: the expenditures approach and the income approach. The *expenditures approach* measures how much money is spent in purchasing final goods and services; the *income approach* measures the income that is created in producing these goods and services. Since one person's expenditure becomes another person's income, the two approaches must arrive at the same amount. In dollar terms, total output *must* equal total income.

The equality between total output and total income is reflected in the circular-flow diagram in Exh. 10.7, which is simplified to show the interaction of only the household and business sectors. The expenditures approach measures GDP by summing the various expenditures that make up the flow depicted at the bottom of the diagram. The income approach computes GDP

)

EXHIBIT 10.7
Total Output = GDP = Total Income

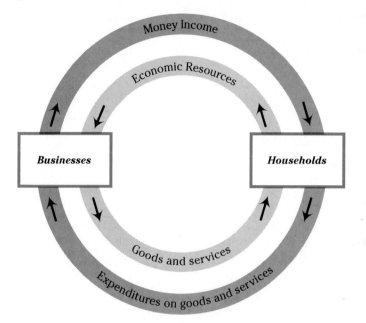

This simplified model of the economy (which ignores government and foreign trade) illustrates that there are two ways to calculate gross domestic product. The total expenditures made by households on final goods and services (the bottom flow) must equal the sum of the income received by the various economic resources (rent + wages + interest + profits)—the uppermost flow in the diagram. Both the total income received by the economic resources and the total household expenditures must equal GDP.

by adding the various categories of income contained in the flow at the top of the diagram. The circular nature of the diagram indicates that all income spent on final goods and services must be received by someone as income; thus, total output must equal total income.

The Expenditures Approach

As you know, the U.S. economy is much more complex than the system depicted in Exh. 10.7. In our economy it's not only households that make expenditures for goods and services but also businesses, various levels of government, and foreign consumers. The categories of expenditures made by these groups are as follows:

1. *Personal consumption expenditures.* The total amount spent by consumers for goods and services includes both the purchase of consumer *durables,* such as automobiles, refrigerators, and stereos, and the purchase of *nondurables,*

such as food, clothing, and entertainment. This is the largest category of expenditures, accounting for approximately two-thirds of GDP.

2. *Gross private domestic investment.*[6] This category includes all types of expenditures on capital goods, including business expenditures for new factories and equipment and household expenditures for new homes and major home improvements. (For accounting purposes, new homes are classified as an investment.) This category also includes changes in firms' inventories.[7]

3. *Government purchases.* This category covers federal, state, and local governments' purchases of all kinds of goods and services—for example, purchases of government vehicles, office supplies, weapons, concrete for roads, and even the consulting services of private firms hired to advise various government departments. This category excludes transfer payments such as welfare and Social Security, which do not represent the purchase of newly produced goods and services.

4. *Net exports.* Some of the output of American businesses is sold in foreign countries, and so it doesn't show up in our domestic sales. At the same time, some of the final goods and services sold in the United States were produced in foreign countries. To adjust for this situation, we subtract the value of imported goods from the value of our exports. The resulting figure, called *net exports,* is then added to our domestic sales. The formula for net exports is

Net exports = Total exports – Total imports

The net exports total will be positive when exports exceed imports and negative when imports exceed exports.

To calculate gross domestic product by the expenditure approach, we add these four categories of expenditures. This procedure is illustrated in Exh. 10.8, which shows the U.S. GDP for 2000 as measured by both the expenditures approach and the income approach.

---

[6] The term *domestic* means "limited to our own country"; for example, domestic investment takes place within the boundaries of the United States.

[7] Counting changes in inventories as part of investment also ensures that total expenditures will equal the value of total output. If a business produces something this year but doesn't sell it this year, that production goes into inventory and is not recorded in total expenditures. So if we just add up the various types of expenditures, we'll miss the portion of GDP that was not sold. To adjust for this problem, we add any additions to inventory that occur from one year to the next in order to make sure that all production is counted. (Decreases in inventories represent the sale of items produced in previous years. Since those items were included in GDP figures for previous years, they must be subtracted from this year's total expenditures if GDP is to reflect current production accurately.)

EXHIBIT 10.8

Gross Domestic Product in 2000 (in billions)

EXPENDITURES APPROACH		INCOME APPROACH	
Personal consumption expenditures	$6,757.3	Employee compensation	$5,638.2
		Rental income	140.0
Gross private domestic investment	1,832.7	Net interest	567.2
		Corporate profits	946.2
Government purchases of goods and services	1,743.7	Proprietors' income	710.4
		Indirect business taxes	704.0
Net exports of goods and services	-370.6	Capital consumption allowances	1,257.1
Gross domestic product	**$9,963.1**	**Gross domestic product**	**$9,963.1**

Source: Developed from the April, 2000 edition of the *Survey of Current Business,* published by the U.S. Department of Commerce.

The Income Approach

Calculating GDP by the income approach is somewhat more complicated than the circular-flow diagram would make it appear. In addition to the various forms of income that are created in the process of producing final goods and services (wages and salaries, rent, interest, and profits), two *nonincome payments* (indirect business taxes and capital consumption allowances) account for a portion of the money received by businesses. The categories of income received by the economic resources and the types of nonincome payments are as follows:

1. *Compensation of employees.* In addition to wages and salaries, this income category includes such things as payroll taxes and employer contributions to health plans.
2. *Rental income.* This is the income earned by households from the rental of property, such as buildings and land.
3. *Net interest.* This category includes the interest earned by households on the money they lend to businesses to finance inventories, build plant additions, and purchase new machinery.
4. *Corporate profits.* The before-tax profit of corporations, this category has three components, representing the three things that corporations can do

USE YOUR ECONOMIC REASONING

What Price for the Environment?

By Yong Tiam Kui

THE CONCEPT of Gross Domestic Product was first introduced in Europe after the Second World War as a means to measure a country's total production of goods and services. It has since been accepted worldwide as a standard tool of economic measurement.

But in recent times, green economists have pointed out that GDP does not necessarily provide an accurate picture of a country's economy because it does not take account of the rapid erosion of natural resources or damage to the environment.

In fact, the negative social and environmental results of economic activities are often added to the GDP as a gain, when they should logically be subtracted as a loss to produce an accurate picture of the country's well-being.

For instance, the felling of a forest would be counted positively as an increase in timber exports or the open-

ing up of new land for agriculture, rather than as the reduction of water catchment capacity and loss of flood protection, destruction of natural resources and the loss of irreplaceable eco-systems and biodiversity.

United Nations Development Programme–Global Environment Facility Small Grants Programme national co-ordinator Dr. Martin Abraham says:

"When there is a big oil spill, GDP actually goes up because clean-up equipment has to be purchased, temporary workers have to be hired to help clean up the mess."

Often, when the erosion of natural resources and environmental damage are factored in, a country's economic growth may well be reinterpreted as negative growth. For example, according to conventional economic measurements, countries such as the US, Germany, UK, Netherlands and Australia have all enjoyed strong economic growth over the past five decades.

But when an Index of Sustainable Economic Welfare created by green economists, which includes indicators of quality of life and environmental health, is applied it turns out that their per capita well-being has been stagnant or declining for 15 to 30 years….

The most important challenge, say environmentalists and green economists, is to come up with accurate monetary values for environmental resources, because conventional economics does not assign any value to these goods.

Universiti Putra Malaysia forest resource economist Dr. Awang Noor Abd Ghani, for one, notes that resources such as fresh water and air are treated as if they are free because they are not produced or owned by any identifiable individual or organization.

There is no mechanism for fixing a price, as they are not traded in the open market. It is easier to assign monetary values to some resources such as fish or forests because

Source: New Straits Times (Malaysia), April 30, 2000, p. 26.

they are traded, but this price almost always fails to reflect their true value.

Dr Awang says these hidden costs have to be made known. Policy makers can then compare the obvious benefits of, say, obtaining timber and new land for agriculture from felling a forest, and the loss of medicines that can be developed from the forest's biodiversity, income from eco-tourism, livelihoods of Orang Asli living in the forest and ecosystem functions such as water catchment, soil protection or carbon dioxide absorption.

A lot of work has been done on establishing the values of environmental resources but there is as yet no widely accepted standard. One of the methods, Damage Cost, calculates the cost of the damage caused if the activity is continued.

On a small scale this can be used to reduce pollution: a charge based on the cost of cleaning up and dealing with health impact can be imposed as a fine or a per unit charge. It also includes costs which include displacement of whole populations and changes in agricultural production patterns.

It is obviously a lot harder to attach a price to the continued existence of global diversity or a stable climate. This is where Option Value can be of great use.

When possible future use of a resource can be foreseen but its monetary value can-not be estimated precisely, an "option value" can be put on it. It can then be considered in any decision about whether or not to conserve the resource for the future. This value may be uncertain and depend on a number of different factors. For instance, a tropical forest may be a potential source of new drugs, but fulfillment of this potential depends to a large extent on how much the pharmaceutical industry is prepared to invest in research.

Willingness To Pay is another method. It involves asking people who will be affected by the loss or preservation of the resource how much they would be willing to pay to keep it, whether they value it for aesthetic, leisure, religious, or other reasons. The problem is that the results would depend on whose opinion is sought.

Poor people, for example, are unlikely to be willing to pay as much as richer people.

Centre for Environment, Technology and Development Malaysia executive-director Gurmit Singh says local efforts to establish accurate monetary values for environmental resources are hamstrung by lack of data.

"One of the problems is that it depends on how much data you have. If, say, air pollution in the form of sulfur dioxide is causing cancer, how many million ringgit is it going to cost in healthcare? The problem with Malaysia is we often do not have data. We have to look at data in the US and try to extrapolate to the Malaysian case. But some people will question whether this is accurate. If the data base is already wrong, it's going to be impossible to be accurate"…

Use Your Economic Reasoning

1. Why do environmentalists believe that GDP provides an inaccurate record of economic performance?
2. According to the article, a big oil spill will tend to increase GDP. Is that true? Explain.
3. Green economists want to assign monetary values to environmental resources so that we can estimate the cost (price) of using them. We have prices for labor and coal and other resources; why don't we know the price of using environmental resources? How does the absence of these prices lead to the abuse of the environment?
4. Why have environmentalists found it difficult to attach monetary values to the environment? Do you think approaches such as the "Willingness to Pay" method can provide us with useful estimates? Defend your conclusion.

with their profits: (a) *corporate profits tax liability*—profits used to pay federal and state taxes, (b) *dividends*—profits paid out to stockholders, and (c) *retained earnings*—profits kept by businesses for reinvestment (also called *undistributed corporate profits*).

5. *Proprietors' income.* This category includes the income earned by unincorporated businesses, such as proprietorships, partnerships, and cooperatives.

6. *Indirect business taxes.* Indirect business taxes include sales taxes and excise taxes. The important thing about such taxes is that they are collected *by* businesses *for* government. Therefore, a portion of the money received by businesses must be passed on directly to government; it is not available as a payment to the owners of economic resources. Such taxes are described as *nonincome payments.*

7. *Capital consumption allowances.* Also called *allowances for depreciation*, these are funds set aside for the eventual replacement of worn-out factories and equipment. Like indirect business taxes, they represent a nonincome payment.

To measure gross domestic product by the income approach, we add the five types of income and the two nonincome payments. As you can see in Exh. 10.8, the answer we get is the same as the one generated earlier by the expenditures approach.[8] Again, that result is necessary because every dollar spent on output must be received by someone as income or as a nonincome payment.

Interpreting GDP Statistics

Now that we know what gross domestic product means and how it is measured, we need to note two facts before interpreting GDP statistics. An increase in GDP does not always mean that we're better off. Similarly, a decrease in GDP is not always a cause for concern and corrective action.

Real GDP versus Money GDP

From 1990 to 2000, gross domestic product in the United States increased from $5,803.2 billion to $9,963.1 billion (from $5.8 trillion to $10 trillion), an increase of 72 percent in 10 years. On the surface that seems like a pretty good performance, particularly when you realize that our population increased only about 10 percent in that period. It looks as though the average American had a lot more goods and services at his or her disposal in 2000 than in 1990.

---

[8] In fact, the GDP calculated by the income approach never turns out to be exactly the same as the GDP calculated by the expenditures approach. The difference is what the Department of Commerce calls the *statistical discrepancy*. In Exh. 10.8 the entry for indirect business taxes has been adjusted to incorporate the statistical discrepancy.

But numbers can be misleading. Because GDP is the physical output of a given year valued at the prices that prevailed in that year, it can increase from one year to another because of increased output, increased prices, or a combination of the two. (To underscore that GDP can change simply in response to a change in prices, economists often refer to GDP as *money* GDP or *nominal* GDP.) Therefore, if we want to know how much *physical* output has increased, we have to calculate the **real gross domestic product**—that is, the GDP that has been adjusted to eliminate the impact of changes in the price level.

To eliminate the impact of changing prices from our GDP comparison, we need to value the output produced in these two different time periods at some common sets of prices. For example, we could value both the 2000 output and the 1990 output at 1990 prices or at 2000 prices or at the prices that prevailed in some intermediate time period. The Bureau of Economic Analysis (BEA) uses the third approach; it values both years' outputs at the prices that prevailed in some base year, currently 1996. According to the BEA, when 1990 and 2000 outputs are valued at 1996 prices, we find that real GDP increased from $6,683.5 billion in 1990 to $9,318.6 billion in 2000, an increase of 39 percent.

As you can see, the increase in the real GDP (39%) was much smaller than the increase in nominal GDP (72%); much of the increase in money GDP was due to inflation. This is why economists insist on comparing real GDPs rather than nominal GDPs. Comparison of real GDPs gives us a much better picture of what's actually happening to the economy's output and the population's standard of living.

What GDP Does Not Measure

Even real GDP figures should be interpreted with caution. They don't measure all of our society's production, and they certainly don't provide a perfect measure of welfare, or well-being. Some of the things that GDP does not consider are as follows:

1. *Nonmarketed goods and services.* GDP does not measure all production or output but only production that is intended to be sold through markets. This means that GDP excludes the production of homemakers and do-it-yourselfers, as well as all barter transactions, in which one person directly exchanges goods or services with another.

2. *Illegal activities.* GDP does not include illegal goods and services, such as illicit drugs, illegal gambling, and prostitution. It also excludes otherwise legal transactions that are unreported in order to avoid paying taxes—the sale of firewood for cash, for example.

3. *Leisure.* GDP does not measure increases in leisure, but such increases clearly have an impact on our well-being. Even if real gross domestic

product didn't increase, if we could produce a constant real GDP with shorter and shorter workweeks, most of us would agree that our lives had improved.

4. *Population.* GDP statistics tell us nothing about the size of the population that must share a given output. A GDP of $2 trillion means one thing in an economy of 100 million people and something completely different in an economy of 500 million people. (It's like the difference between an income of $20,000 for a single person and an income of $20,000 for a family of five.) Economists generally attempt to adjust for this problem by talking about GDP per capita, or per person—that is, GDP divided by the population of the country.

5. *Externalities.* We have a very sophisticated accounting system to keep track of all the goods and services we produce, but we have not established a method of subtracting from GDP when the production process yields negative externalities—air and water pollution, for example. (See Chapter 9 for a review of this concept.)

While all of these are important limitations, concerns about environmental damage have gained particular attention. "Green" economists have called for modifications in our GDP accounts to reflect environmental degradation. (Read "What Price for the Environment" on page 316, to see the kinds of changes that are being called for.) And we've made some slight progress in that direction. In 1994, the Commerce Department published a series of supplementary, or "satellite," GDP accounts to record changes in our stocks of natural resources. But these efforts are still in their infancy and largely experimental. For now, we'll have to be satisfied with our imperfect GDP statistics, along with an understanding of their limitations.

SUMMARY

To keep track of the economy's performance, people watch *economic indicators*—signals or measures that tell us how well the economy is performing. Three major economic indicators are the *unemployment rate*, price indexes (the Consumer Price Index, the Producer Price Index, and the Implicit Price Deflator), and the gross domestic product. Each of these indicators looks at a different dimension of the economy's performance.

The *civilian unemployment rate* is the percentage of the civilian labor force that is unemployed. (The *civilian labor force* is made up of all persons over the age of sixteen who are not in the armed forces and who are either employed or actively seeking employment.) Each month, the Bureau of Labor Statistics surveys some 60,000 households to determine the employment status of the residents. It then uses the results from this sample to estimate the size of the labor force and the rate of unemployment for the nation as a whole.

We attempt to measure inflation with something called a *price index*. A price index is a ratio of two prices: a price in some base period that serves as a reference point divided into the price in whatever period we wish to compare with the base period. For example, if tennis shoes sold for $50 in 1990 and $80 in 2000, the price index for tennis shoes would be 160 if 1990 were used as the base year:

$$\text{Price index} = \frac{\text{Price in a given period}}{\text{Price in the base period}}$$
$$= \frac{\$80.00}{\$50.00}$$
$$= 1.60 \text{ or } 160 \text{ percent}$$

Since the price index in the base period is always 100, an index of 160 means that price has increased by 60 percent since the base period. By the same logic, an index of 75 would indicate that price has decreased by 25 percent since the base period.

The other major indicator, the *gross domestic product* (GDP), is the total monetary value of all final goods and services produced in one year. In other words, it is a measure of the economy's annual production or output. GDP can be estimated by the expenditures approach or by the income approach. The expenditures approach sums the categories of expenditures made for final goods and services. The income approach looks at the forms of income that are created when final goods are produced and adds to those income figures certain nonincome payments.

Since GDP is measured in monetary units (dollars), it is possible to add apples and oranges (that is, to sum the economy's output of eggs, stereos, houses, tractors, and so on) and arrive at a meaningful measure of the economy's total output. GDP figures must be interpreted with caution, however. When we compare the GDPs for two different years, we must be sure to correct for the impact of changing prices—to compare *real GDPs*, not money GDPs. We must also recognize that GDP is not a complete measure of our economy's production because it excludes the work of homemakers and do-it-yourselfers as well as other nonmarket transactions. Nor is it a complete measure of welfare, or well-being; it doesn't take into account the value of leisure, for example, or the negative externalities associated with the production of some goods and services.

KEY TERMS

Annual inflation rate	Frictional unemployment	Price index
Business cycle	Full employment	Real gross domestic product
Civilian labor force	Gross domestic product	Real income
Civilian unemployment rate	Inflation	Structural unemployment
Cyclical unemployment	Macroeconomics	Unemployment rate
Economic indicators	Natural rate of unemployment	

STUDY QUESTIONS

Fill in the Blanks

1. The study of the economy's overall performance and the factors that influence that performance is called _Macroeconomics_ .

2. Clauses that provide for automatic wage and salary adjustments to compensate for inflation are called _COLA_ clauses.

3. _Economic indicators_ are signals, or measures, that tell us how well the economy is performing.

4. The price index that is used to adjust union wage contracts and Social Security payments for inflation is the _Consumer price index_ .

5. Unemployment caused by a reduction in the economy's total demand for goods and services is called _Cyclical_ unemployment.

6. A common estimate for the natural rate of unemployment is _5_ percent.

7. People who stop looking for jobs because they are convinced that none are available are called _discourage Workers_.

8. The two approaches to measuring GDP are the _Expenditure_ _Income_ approach and the _Income_ approach.

9. GDP that has been adjusted to eliminate the impact of changes in the price level is called _Real_ GDP.

10. The largest component of spending in GDP is _consumption_ spending.

Multiple Choice

1. The civilian labor force is made up of
   a) all persons over the age of sixteen.
   b) all persons over the age of eighteen who are not in the armed forces.
   c) all persons over the age of sixteen who are not in the armed forces and who are either employed or actively seeking employment.
   d) all persons over the age of eighteen who are not in the armed forces and who are either employed or actively seeking employment.

2. If you are out of work because you are in the process of looking for a better job, economists would say that you are
   a) frictionally unemployed.
   b) cyclically unemployed.
   c) structurally unemployed.
   d) None of the above

3. People who are unemployed because they have no marketable skills are said to be
   a) frictionally unemployed.
   b) cyclically unemployed.
   c) structurally unemployed.
   d) None of the above

4. The unemployment rate for blacks is about
   a) three times the rate for whites.
   b) twice the rate for whites.
   c) 2 percent higher than the rate for whites.
   d) the same as the rate for whites.

5. Which of the following is false?
   a) Inflation tends to redistribute income.
   b) Inflation is particularly hard on people with fixed incomes.
   c) No one benefits from inflation.
   d) COLA clauses help protect workers from inflation.

6. If the Consumer Price Index is 250, that means that
   a) the average price of a product is $2.50.
   b) prices are two times as high as they were in the base year.
   c) prices have risen 150 percent since the base year.
   d) Both b and c are correct.

7. The natural rate of unemployment is the rate that would exist in the absence of
   a) frictional unemployment.
   b) structural unemployment.
   c) cyclical unemployment.
   d) frictional and structural unemployment.

8. Which of the following items would be counted in GDP?
   a) The work of a homemaker
   b) The sale of a used car
   c) A soda you buy at your local drive-in
   d) The firewood you cut for your home last winter

9. Suppose that Susan received a 3 percent raise last year, but her rent and the other prices she had to pay rose 5 percent. An economist would say that Susan's
   a) real income rose, but her nominal income fell.
   b) nominal income rose, but her money income fell.
   c) money income rose, but her nominal income fell.
   d) nominal income rose, but her real income fell.

10. If both output and prices are higher in year 2 than they were in year 1, which of the following is true?
    a) Real GDP declined from year 1 to year 2.
    b) GDP declined from year 1 to year 2.
    c) GDP increased from year 1 to year 2, but real GDP declined.
    d) Both GDP and real GDP increased from year 1 to year 2.

11. The Consumer Price Index was 130.7 in 1990 and 136.2 in 1991. Therefore, the rate of inflation between 1990 and 1991 was
    a) 30.7 percent.
    b) 5.5 percent.
    c) 4.2 percent.
    d) about 136 percent.

12. In comparison to other major industrialized nations,
    a) the U.S. unemployment rate is higher than average.
    b) the U.S. inflation rate is lower than average.
    c) the U.S. inflation rate has been higher than average over the past decade.
    d) the U.S. unemployment rate has been about average over the past decade.

13. Which of the following would *not* be considered in computing GDP by the *expenditures approach*?
    a) Personal consumption expenditures
    b) Gross private domestic investment
    c) Compensation of employees
    d) Net exports

14. Which of the following would *not* be considered in computing GDP by the *income approach*?
    a) Rental income
    b) Corporate profits
    c) Indirect business taxes
    d) Government purchases of goods and services

15. If nominal GDP is increasing but real GDP is not, then
    a) the economy must be experiencing inflation.
    b) output must be falling.
    c) the price level must be falling.
    d) population must be increasing.

Problems and Questions for Discussion

1. What is the purpose of economic indicators? Can they be of any value to you?

2. A student could be counted as employed, unemployed, or "not participating" in the labor market. Explain.

3. An increase in the unemployment rate is not always a sign of growing weakness in the economy. Explain.

4. Some frictional and structural unemployment is probably a sign of a healthy economy. Why is that true?

5. How does inflation redistribute income?

6. How can savers be hurt by inflation?

7. Why is it true that "the people who are most hurt by inflation are those who have the least bargaining power in the marketplace"?

8. Some workers are convinced that they are worse off today than they were ten years ago, even though they have received annual raises. Is this possible, or must their perceptions be incorrect?

9. Use the following information to compute GDP by the income approach. (Some figures are not required for solving the problem.)

Employee compensation	$400
Proprietors' income	70
Rental income	25
Indirect business taxes	20
Personal consumption	450
Gross investment	250
Net interest	40
Capital consumption allowance	75
Corporate profits	55

10. Use the following information to compute GDP by the expenditures approach. (Some figures are not required for solving the problem.)

Personal consumption	$500
Exports	10
Gross investment	200
Imports	12
Proprietors' income	450
Government purchases	250
Corporate profits	50

11. Why must total income always equal total output?

ANSWER KEY

Fill in the Blanks

1. macroeconomics
2. cost-of-living adjustment (COLA)
3. Economic indicators
4. Consumer Price Index
5. cyclical
6. 5
7. discouraged workers
8. expenditures, income
9. real
10. consumption

Multiple Choice

1. c	4. b	7. c	10. d	13. c
2. a	5. c	8. c	11. c	14. d
3. c	6. c	9. d	12. c	15. a

CHAPTER ELEVEN

Aggregate Demand and Supply:
The Model of the Self-Correcting Economy

1. Identify three factors that are responsible for the downward slope of the aggregate demand curve.
2. Understand why the short-run aggregate supply curve slopes upward.
3. Review how the economy's equilibrium output and price level are determined and how this process is represented graphically.
4. Discuss the factors that will shift the aggregate demand and supply curves to new positions.
5. Predict the impact of changes in aggregate demand or supply on the economy's equilibrium output and the price level.
6. Explain how the economy will tend to automatically eliminate unemployment in the long run.
7. Understand why the long-run aggregate supply curve is vertical.

Chapter 10 identified some important dimensions of the economy's overall performance and examined techniques used to measure those aspects of its performance. Now, in Chapter 11, we will begin to explore why the aggregate economy behaves as it does and how its performance changes. The model most commonly used to examine the economy's overall performance is the model of aggregate demand and aggregate supply. Just as demand and supply are important tools in microeconomics, aggregate demand and aggregate supply are important in macroeconomics. In this chapter we will examine how aggregate demand and supply interact to determine the levels of output, employment, and prices, and how unemployment and inflation arise. We conclude by exploring the possibility that the economy contains a self-correcting mechanism: that it will ultimately return to full employment and potential GDP. We begin our consideration of the aggregate demand–aggregate supply model by introducing the concept of aggregate demand.

AGGREGATE DEMAND

Aggregate demand is the total quantity of output demanded by all sectors in the economy together at various price levels in a given period of time. Thus, aggregate demand (*AD*) is the sum of consumption spending by households (*C*), investment spending by businesses (*I*), government purchases of goods and services (*G*), and net exports (*NX*) to foreign countries. In short, $AD = C + I + G + NX$.

Because the quantity of output demanded by these sectors depends in part on the price level, the *AD* curve slopes downward and to the right (see Exhibit 11.1) like the demand curve for a single product. But the demand curve and the aggregate demand curve are very different concepts. The demand curve shows the relationship between the price of a *particular* product and the quantity of that product demanded. The aggregate demand curve relates the *overall* price level in the economy (as measured by a price index, such as the CPI) to the total quantity of real output that consumers, businesses, governments, and foreigners want to buy.

There are three reasons for the aggregate demand curve's downward slope: the real balance effect, the interest rate effect, and the international trade effect.[1] Let's consider each of these reasons in turn, beginning with the real balance effect.

The Real Balance Effect

When the price level falls, the real value, or purchasing power, of the public's financial assets—savings accounts, retirement funds, and other financial assets with fixed money values—tends to increase. This makes people feel wealthier, and they tend to demand more goods and services—more real output. The **real balance effect** is the increase in the amount of aggregate output demanded that results from the increased real value of the public's financial assets.

As an example, suppose that you work each summer to help pay for college. This summer you managed to save $2,000, your share of the year's anticipated expenses. Now, assume that the overall price level falls to half of what it was when you established your $2,000 objective. In essence, that means that all prices have been cut in half; so your $2,000 will now stretch twice as far as before. How

---

[1] The demand curve and the aggregate demand curve slope downward for very different reasons. Recall from Chapter 3 that the demand curve is downward sloping, in part, because of the *substitution effect*. When the price of a product is reduced, consumers respond by substituting more of this relatively cheaper product in the place of other products for which it is deemed a substitute. This substitution effect cannot explain the downward slope of the *AD* curve because a reduction in the price *level* means that the average price of *all* goods and services has fallen. For instance, there is no incentive to substitute tennis shoes for jogging shoes if both have fallen in price.

EXHIBIT 11.1

| EXHIBIT 11.1
| An Overview of Aggregate Demand and Supply

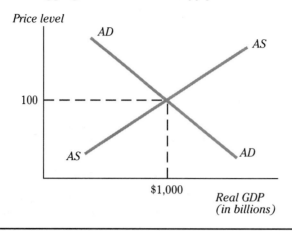

The intersection of the aggregate demand and supply curves determines the equilibrium level of real GDP and the equilibrium price level in the economy.

will you react? You will probably start buying things you don't normally purchase because you have $1,000 in your savings account that won't be needed for anticipated college expenses. That's the real balance effect in action; the real value, or purchasing power, of the money balance in your savings account has increased, and this increase in wealth is spurring you to purchase more goods and services. Of course, if the price level increases, everything will work in reverse; your savings will be worth less, so that you feel less wealthy and demand fewer goods and services than before. Either way we describe it, the price level and spending on real output are moving in opposite directions, and so the aggregate demand curve must slope downward. Exhibit 11.2 depicts the aggregate demand curve for a hypothetical economy.

The Interest Rate Effect

In addition to its impact on real balances, a change in the price level also has an effect on the prevailing interest rate. The interest rate is determined by the demand and supply of money. When the price level falls, consumers and businesses will require less money for their day-to-day transactions because a given amount of money will buy more goods and services than before. In other words, a reduction in the price level will reduce the demand for money. Since each aggregate demand curve assumes a fixed supply of money in the economy, a reduction in the demand for money will tend to reduce the price of money—the interest rate. When the interest rate falls, the lower cost of

EXHIBIT 11.2
The Aggregate Demand Curve

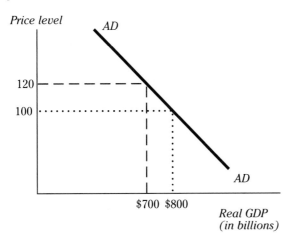

The aggregate demand curve shows an inverse relationship between the overall price level and the quantity of real output demanded. For instance, when the price level decreases from 120 to 100, the quantity of real GDP demanded increases from $700 billion to $800 billion.

borrowing money tends to stimulate investment spending and some types of consumer spending. The **interest rate effect** is the increase in the amount of aggregate output demanded that results when a reduction in the overall price level causes interest rates to fall.[2]

To illustrate, let's suppose that the price level—the average price of goods and services—fell to half of what it is today. Homes that had been selling for $200,000 would cost $100,000; automobiles that had been priced at $20,000 would be available for $10,000. As a consequence, consumers would need to borrow only half as much money as before to finance their new homes and automobiles and other credit purchases. This reduced demand for money would tend to lower interest rates and stimulate spending. Thus, more real output would be demanded at the lower price level. Of course, if the price level increased (which may seem a more realistic possibility), the demand for money would tend to increase, pushing up interest rates and depressing spending on real GDP.

---

[2] The interest rate effect actually has to do with the impact of a price level change on the "real" interest rate—the interest rate after adjustment for inflation. If the nominal interest rate (the interest rate before adjustment) is 15 percent a year and the expected rate of inflation is 5 percent, the real interest rate is 10 percent.

Business investment decisions are influenced by real interest rates, not nominal rates. A higher nominal interest rate (resulting from a higher expected rate of inflation) would not necessarily discourage businesses from borrowing since they would also anticipate receiving higher prices for their products (and thus a higher nominal rate of return). The proof that a higher price level causes a higher real interest rate is beyond the scope of this text.

The International Trade Effect

The third way in which price level changes can affect the amount of aggregate output demanded is through international trade. The two basic transactions in international trade are the importing and exporting of products. **Imports** are goods and services that are purchased from foreign producers. Americans' purchases of German automobiles, French wines, and Japanese electronics are examples of U.S. imports. **Exports** are goods and services that are produced domestically and sold to customers in other countries. The Ford automobiles, California wines, and IBM computers that are sold to customers in Germany, France, and elsewhere are examples of U.S. exports.

How would U.S. imports and exports be affected if the overall price level in the United States fell by, say, 10 percent and everything else (including prices in other countries)[3] remained constant? Since U.S. products would become more attractive in price, we'd expect fewer Americans to buy imported products (because they'd buy domestic products instead) and more foreigners to buy U.S. exports. To illustrate, suppose that the prices of U.S. automobiles fell by 10 percent and the prices of comparable foreign cars remained unchanged. Under these conditions, we'd expect to see more Americans buying cars made in the United States (and fewer buying imports) and increased auto exports as well. In short, at the lower U.S. price level, a larger quantity of U.S. automobiles would be demanded. The **international trade effect** is the increase in the amount of aggregate output demanded that results when a reduction in the price level makes domestic products less expensive relative to foreign products. It provides us with a third reason for the downward slope of the aggregate demand curve.

CHANGES IN AGGREGATE DEMAND

As with the demand curve for a single product, we need to distinguish between *movement along* an *AD* curve and a *shift* of the *AD* curve. We've seen that changes in the price level will cause movement up or down along a stationary curve. *Any change in the spending plans of households, businesses, governments, or foreigners that results from something other than a change in the price level will shift the AD curve.* Factors that will shift the aggregate demand curve include changes in the expectations of households and businesses, changes in aggregate wealth, changes in government policies, and changes in foreign income and price levels.

---

[3] Another factor that is assumed constant is the foreign exchange rate, the rate at which one country's currency exchanges for that of another.

Household and Business Expectations

Suppose that households and businesses become more upbeat about the future, perhaps because the unemployment rate has been dropping and business has been strong. What impact will these optimistic expectations have on aggregate demand? Households may be expected to increase their consumption spending (since they are more confident of continued employment in the future), whereas businesses may increase their investment spending for factories and machinery in anticipation of future business. Because total spending at any price level is greater, the AD curve will shift to the right (from AD_1 to AD_2 in Exh. 11.3), an increase in aggregate demand. More pessimistic expectations have the opposite effect: The AD curve will shift to the left, reflecting a reduction in aggregate demand.

Aggregate Wealth

An increase in the overall wealth of the society also tends to shift the aggregate demand curve to the right. Consider, for example, the impact of a stock market boom that increases the value of households' stock holdings. Since households can finance spending by selling shares of stock and other forms of wealth, this increase in stock values tends to spur consumption spending; households may be expected to demand more real output than before at any price level. A reduction in wealth—due, perhaps, to a decline in the stock

---

EXHIBIT 11.3
Shifts of the Aggregate Demand Curve

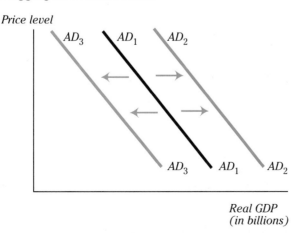

Any change in the spending plans of households, businesses, or government that results from something other than a change in the price level will shift the AD curve. A shift to the right is an increase in aggregate demand; a shift to the left is a decrease.

USE YOUR ECONOMIC REASONING

Recession Worries Rise as Key Stock Market Indexes Fall

By Thomas S. Mulligan and
Walter Hamilton

WALL STREET suffered another major rout Thursday, driving key stock indexes down sharply in some of the heaviest trading volume ever. The market's deepening losses now are raising a question whose impact goes far beyond the ranks of share owners: Are stocks foretelling a full-blown recession in the economy in 2001?

Some analysts turn that around, and ask the question this way: With a record number of Americans owning stocks, will a continuing market slide help cause the next recession by frightening many consumers into paring their spending plans?

Historically, the stock market's predictive power when it comes to the economy has been mixed. Nonetheless, the sell-off Thursday—on a day when fresh economic data gave unmistakable signs of widespread weakness—triggered new concerns that many investors are fleeing because they fear the first recession in 10 years may be imminent....

Typically, many investors who expect a sharp economic slowdown, or an outright recession, seek to sell stocks because they anticipate that companies' sales and earnings will dwindle or fall....

The stock market's trend could be both cause and effect of the next economic turn, experts say. Concern is growing on Wall Street that a worsening market drop could have a dire impact on the economy if consumers suddenly reduce their spending to offset stock losses, just as many boosted their buying when stocks shot up in recent years.

Indeed, it is widely acknowledged that the late-1990s economy was aided by a "wealth effect" in which consumers spent more freely because the swelling values of their stock portfolios made them feel richer.

Fed Chairman Alan Greenspan has said that the wealth effect was responsible for 1 percentage point of the 4% annualized growth in gross domestic product since 1996.

Economists say that for every $1 increase in personal wealth, Americans spend 3 to

Source: Los Angeles Times, Dec. 1, 2000, p. 1.

market—will shift the *AD* curve to the left. (In December of 2000, a plunging stock market was causing some economy watchers to worry about a recession. In fact, some were calling the stock market downturn both the cause and the effect of an impending recession. Read "Recession Worries Rise as Key Stock Market Indexes Fall," on page 332, to discover why.)

5 cents extra—which adds up to billions of dollars in spending nationwide.

Stephen Roach, chief economist at Morgan Stanley Dean Witter in New York, estimates that real consumption growth has risen an average of 4.4% a year from 1996 through this year. But real disposable personal income has risen only 3.3% a year in that period.

The difference came from people dipping into their market gains—or borrowing more, thanks in part to those gains—to buy cars, big-screen televisions and a host of other consumer goods, he said....

Roach and other economists fret that the opposite scenario could occur if stock prices keep falling. That could create a vicious cycle in which a slowing economy hurts stock prices, and, in turn, a weak stock market exacerbates the economic downturn because it discourages spending.

"What the stock market giveth, it can taketh," Roach said. "This wealth effect could be sharper on the downside than on the upside." A falling market may have a greater impact on the economy because of what Roach terms Americans' rising "wealth dependency." More Americans than ever before—an estimated one of every two people—have money in the stock market and are therefore more sensitive than ever to a falling market, he said.

Also, the population is getting older and closer to retirement—and depending more than ever on their stock holdings to finance their lifestyles, he said.

Still, economists say it normally takes six to 12 months for Americans to adjust their spending habits to a rising or falling market. And the urge to downshift spending is muted somewhat by the fact that people who have been in the market for many years still have sizable gains despite this year's sell-off.

Even Roach concedes that broad market indexes would have to fall by an additional 15%—and stay down for an extended period—for Americans to dramatically slash their spending. So far, the blue-chip S&P 500 index is down 13.9% from its March peak, far less than Nasdaq's drop.

Some economists, in fact, dispute that the reverse wealth effect would be that powerful. They say Americans have far more of their wealth tied up in their homes than in the stock market, and that home prices remain strong. What's more, unemployment is low and wages are rising—two forces that determine Americans' outlook far more than the stock market....

Use Your Economic Reasoning

1. Consumers tend to spend less when there is a decline in the value of their stock portfolios. Explain this behavior.
2. What do the authors mean when they say that the stock market's trend could be both the cause and the effect of the next turn in the economy?
3. Studies suggest that each $1 increase in wealth leads to an additional 3 to 5 cents of spending. How would this affect the aggregate demand curve? Would you expect a reduction in wealth to have the opposite effect?
4. Suppose the stock market stays depressed, and this causes the AD curve to shift leftward. If the AS curve remains stationary, what will happen to the equilibrium level of real GDP? Is this result consistent with the concerns voiced in the article?

Government Policy

Government can also influence aggregate demand through its policies. For instance, a reduction in government spending for goods and services will cause the AD curve to shift to the left, as will an increase in personal income taxes (since consumers have less to spend at each price level). A reduction in the money supply will also cause aggregate demand to fall. The size of the economy's money supply is determined by the Federal Reserve, or Fed. If the Fed decreases the money supply, the interest rate that businesses and others have to pay to borrow money will tend to increase. This, in turn, will tend to depress investment spending by businesses and some forms of consumption spending by households, shifting the aggregate demand curve to the left.

Consider an increase in military spending by the federal government. What impact will that have on aggregate demand? It will increase the amount of real GDP demanded at any price level, and so it will shift the AD curve to the right (from AD_1 to AD_2 in Exh. 11.3). A tax reduction or an increase in the money supply also tends to increase aggregate demand.

Foreign Incomes and Prices

When foreign incomes grow, foreign households increase their consumption spending. Some of this increased spending will be for U.S. products, causing U.S. exports to increase and shifting the aggregate demand curve to the right. Increased foreign prices would also stimulate spending for U.S. products. An increase in foreign price levels would, ceteris paribus, cause U.S. products to appear more attractive and cause foreign consumers to substitute them for those produced domestically. At the same time, Americans would find foreign products less attractive in price, decreasing our imports. Thus, an increase in foreign incomes or price levels would stimulate the demand for U.S. products and shift the AD curve to the right.[4] Reductions in foreign incomes or price levels would shift the aggregate demand curve for U.S. products to the left.

In summary, the aggregate demand curve will shift in response to changes in the expectations of households or businesses, wealth, government policy, foreign incomes, or foreign price levels. These are the major causes of shifts in aggregate demand, but the list is not exhaustive; other changes may have a similar impact. The important point is that any change in spending plans that stems from something other than a change in the price level will shift the AD curve; changes in the price level will cause movement *along* a stationary curve. (Instructors wishing to explore the role of aggregate demand in greater detail may want to consider a supplemental chapter, "The Keynesian Total Expenditures Model," which can be accessed from the textbook web page at www.aw.com/rohlf.)

---

[4] This assumes that the foreign exchange rate does not change. Chapter 17 will discuss exchange rates in some detail.

AGGREGATE SUPPLY

Aggregate demand is only half of the model; the other half is aggregate supply. **Aggregate supply** refers to the total quantity of output supplied by all producers in the economy together at various price levels in a given time period.

In the short run, the aggregate supply (*AS*) curve slopes upward, as represented in Exh. 11.4. This upward slope indicates that businesses tend to supply more aggregate output at higher price levels than at lower price levels. Businesses behave in this manner because increases in the overall price level make it profitable for them to produce more goods and services. This increased profitability results from a fact of life in the business world: Some wages and other resource prices are rigid, or inflexible, in the short run. If aggregate demand increases and pushes up the prices that firms can charge for their *products*, the rigidity of these *resource* prices makes it profitable for those businesses to expand output. The result: Higher price levels lead to higher output, so the short-run *AS* curve slopes upward.

As you can see, the rigidity of resource (or input) prices is a critical element in explaining the upward slope of the short-run *AS* curve. But why are some input prices inflexible in the short run? A major reason for such rigidity is long-term contracts. Contracts with labor unions, for example, are commonly renegotiated every three years. During the term of the agreement, wage rates

EXHIBIT 11.4
The Short-Run Aggregate Supply Curve

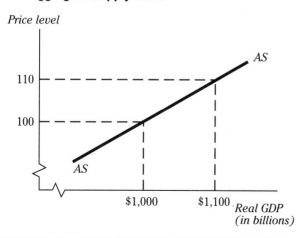

The short-run aggregate supply curve slopes upward because businesses tend to supply more real output at higher price levels than at lower price levels.

are at least partially fixed. The prices paid for raw materials and manufactured inputs may also be governed by long-term contracts. Because wage rates and other input prices are commonly fixed in the short run, businesses find it profitable to expand output when the selling prices of their products rise. This positive relationship between the overall price level and the economy's real GDP is reflected in the upward slope of the *AS* curve depicted in Exh. 11.4.

The Short-run *AS* Curve: A Closer Look

An example from microeconomics may help to illustrate why the short-run *AS* curve slopes upward. Consider the behavior of the competitive firm. Recall that in the model of pure competition, the individual firm is a price taker; it must charge the price dictated by the market. But the firm can sell as much output as it chooses at that price. The firm will continue to expand output so long as the additional (marginal) revenue it will receive from selling an additional unit of output is greater than the additional (marginal) cost of producing that unit. When marginal cost is exactly equal to marginal revenue, the firm will be maximizing its profit (or minimizing its loss). This situation is represented in Exh. 11.5, which shows a firm that is initially maximizing its profit by producing an output of 1,000 units, the output dictated by the intersection of MR_1 and MC_1.

EXHIBIT 11.5
Price Level Adjustments and the Individual Firm

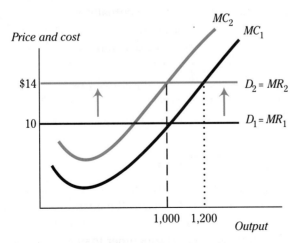

When the price of its product rises and input prices remain unchanged, the competitive firm responds by expanding output. Here output is increased from 1,000 to 1,200 units when the selling price rises from $10 to $14. However, if input prices rise by the same percent as the product price, *MC* will shift up from MC_1 to MC_2, and the profit-maximizing output will be unchanged.

Now, suppose that the market price of the firm's product increases from \$10 to \$14. This would be represented by shifting the demand curve upward from D_1 to D_2. Note what happens to the firm's profit-maximizing output: It increases from 1,000 units to 1,200 units! The higher price provides incentive for the firm to expand output because the firm can earn a marginal profit on the additional units.

Note that it is not profitable for the firm to expand output indefinitely. Because the marginal cost curve slopes upward, marginal cost will eventually increase enough to match the new price. Of course, production beyond that point will not be profitable. Why does MC increase as the firm expands its output? Why does the MC curve slope upward? Think back to Chapter 6. In the short run, if the firm wants to produce more output, it has to squeeze that production from its fixed factory. It does this by hiring more labor and using its factory and equipment more intensively. But this leads to more and more crowding of the fixed facility. Workers have to wait to use equipment; machines are subject to more frequent breakdowns; workers begin to get in one another's way; and so on. As a consequence, successive units of output become more costly to produce; that is, marginal cost rises. Eventually the cost of producing another unit will have increased enough to match the new product price. At that point the output expansion will cease; the firm will have achieved its new profit-maximizing level of production.

It is essential to note that the firm would not have expanded output if wage rates and other resource prices had increased along with the price of the firm's product. Proportionally higher wages and other input prices would have shifted the marginal cost curve up from MC_1 to MC_2. Note that MC_2 intersects MR_2 (the new, higher product price) at 1,000 units of output, the original profit-maximizing output. The higher input prices have completely offset the higher product price, eliminating any incentive to expand output. In the long run, this is precisely what we expect to happen, since contracts eventually expire and wage rates and other input prices are able to adjust upward. As a consequence, the long-run aggregate supply curve is vertical, not upward sloping. We'll discuss the long-run AS curve later in the chapter. For now, the important point is that wage contracts and other rigidities provide a gap between product prices and production costs that makes it profitable for firms to expand output in the short run.

CHANGES IN AGGREGATE SUPPLY

The short-run aggregate supply curve slopes upward because there is a positive relationship between the price level and the quantity of aggregate output supplied. This relationship assumes that the other factors influencing the amount of real GDP supplied—the factors other than the price level—remain constant. These nonprice determinants of aggregate supply include resource prices, the level of technology, and the stock of economic resources. Changes in any of these factors will cause a change in the aggregate supply curve; the entire *AS* curve will shift to a new position. Let's consider each of these factors, beginning with resource prices.

Wage Rates and Other Resource Prices

Suppose that the average wage rate paid by firms in the economy increases. What will that do to the *AS* curve? If it costs more to produce a given level of output, firms will require higher prices in order to produce that output; thus, the *AS* curve must shift upward (to the left). This is represented in Exh. 11.6 by the movement of the aggregate supply curve from AS_1 to AS_2. Lower wages would have the opposite effect; they would tend to shift the *AS* curve downward (to the right), from AS_1 to AS_3. Remember that wage rates tend to be fixed by contract in the short term. But when these labor contracts expire, wage rates may be renegotiated up or down, causing the short-run *AS* curve to shift.

Labor is only one of the resources required to produce output. Businesses also need capital equipment, raw materials, manufactured inputs, and managerial talent. Changes in the price of any of these inputs will tend to shift the position of the short-run *AS* curve; increases will shift it upward, whereas decreases will shift it downward.

EXHIBIT 11.6
Shifts of the Short-Run *AS* Curve

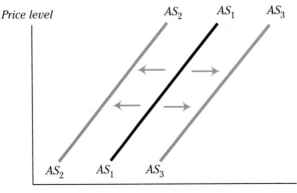

The short-run *AS* curve will shift upward (to the left) if there is a hike in wage rates, an increase in the prices of nonlabor inputs, or a reduction in labor productivity. It will shift downward (to the right) if wages or other input prices fall or if labor productivity rises.

Consider, for instance, the impact of the increase in the price of gasoline and other petroleum products resulting from OPEC's decision to restrict production in 1999–2000. When the prices of petroleum-based inputs increased, the cost of producing a given level of output rose; thus, the *AS* curve shifted upward. Bad weather that reduces agricultural output may have a similar impact, since it tends to increase the price of wheat, corn, and other agricultural products that are inputs in the production of breakfast cereals and other food items.

Technology and the Productivity of Labor

The cost of producing output is influenced not only by wage rates and other input prices but also by the productivity of labor—by how efficient labor is at transforming inputs into finished products. If the productivity of labor increases, the cost of producing the finished product tends to fall. Suppose that labor is paid $8 per hour and that the average worker is able to produce ten units of output per hour. The average labor cost of producing each unit of output is $.80 ($8 per hour divided by ten units per hour). Now, suppose that because of improved training or new technology, the average worker could produce twenty units of output per hour. The labor cost per unit of output would fall to $.40 ($8 per hour divided by twenty units of output per hour). As you can see, an increase in labor productivity reduces the cost of producing a given level of output.

A variety of factors can influence the productivity of labor. For example, if the labor force became more highly educated, we would expect its productivity to rise. A technological change that improved the quality of the capital equipment used by labor could also raise productivity. For instance, a faster computer would allow more work to be done per hour. Regardless of the source of higher productivity, its impact is to reduce the cost of producing the goods and services that make up GDP. We represent this impact by shifting the short-run *AS* curve down and to the right, because producers can now offer a given level of output at a lower price than before (or more output than before at the prevailing price).

Supplies of Labor and Capital

Finally, the position of the economy's aggregate supply curve is influenced by the economy's supplies of labor and capital. The larger the labor supply and the stock of capital equipment, the more output the economy is capable of supplying at any price level. Increases in either the labor force or the capital stock will cause the aggregate supply curve to shift to the right. Decreases would have the opposite effect.

Before continuing, let's review. We've seen that the aggregate demand curve shows the quantity of real GDP that will be demanded at each price level, whereas the aggregate supply curve shows the quantity of real GDP that will be supplied at each price level. The aggregate demand curve will shift to a new position if there is a change in the expectations of households or businesses, the level of aggregate wealth, government policy, foreign incomes, or foreign price levels. The short-run aggregate supply curve will shift in response to a change in resource prices, labor productivity, or the supplies of capital or labor.

THE EQUILIBRIUM OUTPUT AND PRICE LEVEL

The interaction of aggregate demand and aggregate supply simultaneously determines the equilibrium price level and real GDP in the economy. This process is illustrated in Exh. 11.7, which shows the intersection of *AS* and *AD* resulting in an equilibrium price level of 100 and an equilibrium real GDP of $1,000 billion.

As you can see in the graph, if the price level was initially above equilibrium (120, for example), the amount of real GDP supplied would exceed the amount of real GDP demanded. This would mean unsold merchandise and pressure to cut prices. The price level would decline until the amount of aggregate output demanded was equal to the amount supplied. If the price level was initially below equilibrium (80, for instance), the result would be a shortage that would put upward pressure on prices until the equilibrium price level was achieved and the shortage eliminated.

EXHIBIT 11.7
Equilibrium GDP and Price Level

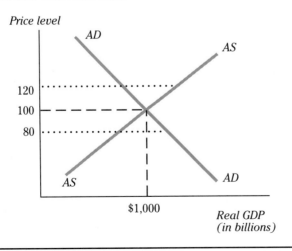

The intersection of the aggregate demand and supply curves determines the price level and the level of output in the economy. Here the equilibrium real GDP is $1,000 billion, and the equilibrium price level is 100.

In summary, only at the equilibrium price level is the amount of real GDP demanded equal to the amount supplied. At any other price level, there will be an overall surplus or shortage, which will tend to alter the prevailing price level.

THE IMPACT OF CHANGES IN AGGREGATE DEMAND OR SUPPLY

In a dynamic economy, aggregate demand and supply change frequently. As these changes occur, the equilibrium price and output levels are disturbed and new levels are established. Suppose, for example, that less optimistic expectations caused businesses to cut back on investment spending. Since this would result in less output being demanded at any given price level, the aggregate demand curve would shift to the left. What impact would this have on the economy? As you can see in Exh. 11.8, when aggregate demand declines from AD_1 to AD_2, the level of real GDP in the economy contracts from $1,000 billion to $850 billion, and the overall price level falls from 100

EXHIBIT 11.8
The Effects of Changes in Aggregate Demand on Real Output and Prices

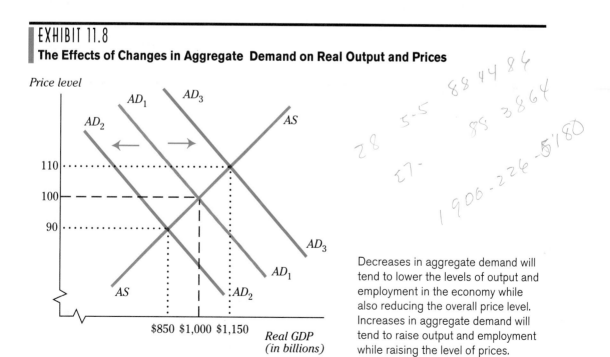

Decreases in aggregate demand will tend to lower the levels of output and employment in the economy while also reducing the overall price level. Increases in aggregate demand will tend to raise output and employment while raising the level of prices.

to 90. Since the economy's ability to provide jobs is tied to the level of production, employment in the economy will also tend to fall (which means that, ceteris paribus, unemployment will rise).

If aggregate demand increased as a result of increased government spending, a tax cut, or some other spur to aggregate demand, the *AD* curve would shift to the right, from AD_1 to AD_3. This would result in higher output and employment, but would also push the price level upward; that is, it would generate inflation. Economists describe this as **demand-pull inflation** because it is caused by increased aggregate demand.

The economy's equilibrium can also be disturbed by changes in aggregate supply. Suppose that aggregate supply decreased as a result of a supply shock, such as an increase in the price of imported oil or a drought that raised grain prices. Exhibit 11.9 shows that when aggregate supply falls from AS_1 to AS_2, the overall price level is driven up and the equilibrium level of real GDP is reduced.

In this instance the economy is experiencing supply-side, or **cost-push inflation**; higher production costs are pushing up prices. Although both demand-pull and cost-push inflation mean higher prices for consumers, cost-push inflation is doubly destructive because it is associated with falling real output.

EXHIBIT 11.9
The Effects of Changes in Aggregate Supply on Real Output and Prices

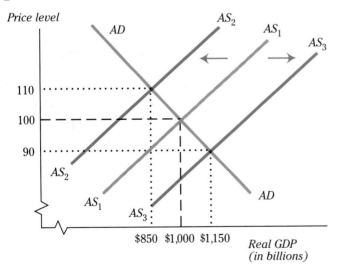

Decreases in aggregate supply will tend to lower the levels of output and employment in the economy while raising the overall price level. Increases in aggregate supply will tend to raise output and employment while lowering the level of prices.

As you can see from Exh. 11.9, when the aggregate supply curve shifts to the left, the level of equilibrium real GDP falls from $1,000 billion to $850 billion. In short, cost-push inflation raises prices while lowering output and employment. This provides us with one possible explanation for the problem of **stagflation,** high unemployment combined with high inflation.

If reductions in aggregate supply are particularly harmful, increases in aggregate supply appear most beneficial. Suppose that aggregate supply expands in response to an increase in labor productivity. As the AS curve shifts to the right (from AS_1 to AS_3 in Exh. 11.9), the price level is driven down *and* output and employment are expanded. It is these obviously desirable outcomes that led to a surge of interest in supply-side economics in the 1980s. Supply-siders promoted a variety of policies designed to enhance labor productivity and otherwise lower production costs in an attempt to increase aggregate supply. Chapter 15 will have much more to say about policies to stimulate aggregate supply.

As the preceding discussion indicates, changes in aggregate demand or supply can lead to unemployment, inflation, or even stagflation. The next section examines the economy's response to these problems and considers the possibility that the economy contains a self-correcting mechanism. (Before proceeding, take a moment to read "Price of Natural Gas Hits Boiling Point," on page 344. It will test your understanding of the *AD–AS* framework.)

THE MODEL OF THE SELF-CORRECTING ECONOMY

As you've seen, the economy is buffeted about by all sorts of demand and supply shocks. Sometimes these shocks result in higher output and employment; sometimes they lead to lower output and unemployment. You learned in Chapter 10 that these ups and downs in the level of economic activity are known as the *business cycle*.[5] A period of rising output and employment is called an *expansion;* a period of declining output and employment is called a contraction or *recession.*

Expansions and recessions are short-run phenomena. In the long run, the economy tends to operate at full employment and potential GDP. That's because the economy contains a self-correcting mechanism that tends to ul-

---

[5] Economists disagree about the relative importance of demand and supply shocks in explaining business cycles. Some emphasize demand shocks; others emphasize shocks occurring on the supply side.

USE YOUR ECONOMIC REASONING

| Price of Natural Gas Hits Boiling Point

By Susan Warren

DALLAS—For the past year, industrial companies have complained loud and long about rising oil prices. But like the old joke about curing a headache by dropping a brick on your foot, some companies that have been pinched by high oil prices are now facing a far more painful reality: skyrocketing natural-gas prices.

Indeed, oil prices have eased in recent weeks, with prices falling from about $35 a barrel to about $28 a barrel. On Friday, spot oil prices were quoted at about $28.88 a barrel.

Fourfold Price Jump in a Year

But prices for natural gas, which is used to heat 61 million households and is a major source of energy for makers of chemicals, plastics and electricity, have jumped more than fourfold in the past year and are approach-

ing $10 a million BTU. In California, prices have shot up to astronomical levels, with spot prices as high as $17 or $19 a million BTU. That's the equivalent of paying $120 a barrel of oil.

For consumers, the price increases could translate into winter heating bills that jump 50% or more. Consumers also will notice the impact of high natural-gas prices from the hardware store to the grocery store as natural-gas costs jack up the price of plastic products and packaging materials.

To some economists, the potential shock from escalating natural-gas prices could be bigger than anything the economy has seen in decades. During past energy shocks, says economist David Resler at Nomura Securities International in New York, "oil prices rose and most other energy prices remained low." But now, he says, consumers are facing a

market where oil prices are high and natural-gas prices are even higher. In addition, he says, the rise in natural-gas prices "will have a much bigger impact on households than the rise in oil prices, because six times as many households use natural gas as use oil," says Mr. Resler.

Vulnerable to Cheap Imports

Meantime, the price explosion has exposed just how vulnerable American manufacturers are to cheaper imports. "Eight dollar natural gas has turned U.S. petrochemical producers into the most expensive producers in the world," observes Gary Adams, president of consulting group Chemical Market Associates Inc.

Natural-gas prices that are running three and four times year-ago rates will cut even more deeply into industry profits than oil prices, which merely doubled over a year's time. The steep, sudden rise

Source: Wall Street Journal, Dec. 18, 2000, p. A2.

timately return the economy to potential GDP whenever it is disturbed from that equilibrium.[6] To illustrate that mechanism, let's consider an econ-

[6] This self-correcting mechanism is part of the model presented in this chapter, a model that represents reality as many economists see it. Some economists would undoubtedly dispute at least portions of this model.

has forced companies to shut down some operations that have grown too expensive and has thrown hedging programs, designed to deal with fluctuating prices, into havoc.

For industries such as chemicals that have been obsessed with managing costs to boost profits, the wild card of soaring natural-gas prices came as a shock. "This is hurting more than the oil for one major reason: It's just been so volatile," says Gary Pfeiffer, chief financial officer of chemicals giant DuPont Co.

Higher oil and natural-gas prices boosted DuPont's costs by more than $1 billion this year over last year. If natural gas stays close to current rates, that would pile an additional $400 million onto DuPont's expenses in 2001, says Mr. Pfeiffer....

Ammonia Makers' Woes

Hardest hit are makers of ammonia and methanol, products derived directly from natural gas. Those businesses have seen widespread shutdowns in recent months, and more are expected, industry experts say. "Just do the math," says J.P. Morgan analyst Don Carson. With natural gas at $8 a million BTUs, ammonia costs about $300 a ton to make. The current market price for ammonia ranges from $200 to $225 a ton.

Although most ammonia makers have hedged at least part of their natural-gas needs at lower prices, it can be cheaper to shut down, says Mr. Carson.

A big part of the problem is that natural gas remains relatively cheap outside North America, where demand is lower and supplies are more robust. That means cheap imports have been able to snatch away market share as U.S. producers find themselves unable to compete on price....

Gauging how much the higher production costs may trickle down to consumers is tricky.

A cooling economy means demand growth is weakening, and could be only about half of last year's healthy 6% to 8% rate, says

CMAI's Mr. Adams. That makes it tougher to pass along rising costs through price increases.

If natural-gas prices stay high, though, chemical prices eventually will have to rise.

"First, we'll start seeing it in construction products, PVC pipe, wire and cable, and ultimately in packaging materials, which means consumers are going to see it in the costs they pay for consumables that are in plastics packaging," says Mr. Adams.

Farmers in need of fertilizer for their spring crops will feel the pinch much earlier. With about 30% of the North American ammonia production shut down, supplies will be short, and fertilizer prices will be rising just as demand peaks in February and March....

Use Your Economic Reasoning

1. Natural gas is an input used in producing many products. What examples does the author provide?
2. How would you represent the impact of increases in natural-gas prices using the *AD–AS* model?
3. At the time this article appeared (December 2000), the U.S. economy was operating at, or perhaps beyond, potential GDP. But some analysts were voicing concern that increases in oil and natural gas prices could propel the economy into a recession. Is that possibility consistent with the *AD–AS* model?
4. How is it possible for an increase in natural-gas prices to lead to both a higher price level *and* lower real GDP? Try to explain this in a step-by-step manner.

omy that is currently operating at full employment and potential GDP and examine its short-run and long-run reactions to a change in aggregate demand. We will begin with an increase in aggregate demand and then consider a decrease.

Adjustments to an Increase in Aggregate Demand

Suppose that aggregate demand expands because the federal government reduces personal income taxes. Households now have more to spend, and so they tend to demand more goods and services at each price level—the aggregate demand curve shifts to the right, from AD_1 to AD_2 in Exh. 11.10.

When aggregate demand increases, the resulting higher price level creates incentive for businesses to expand output. This incentive is provided by the fact that many of a business's costs—particularly wage rates—are fixed by long-term contracts. When product prices rise, these costs do not; thus, firms stand to profit by expanding output. In our example, output will be increased up to the point at which AS_1 is intersected by AD_2 (point B in Exh. 11.10), well beyond potential GDP.

It may seem contradictory to suggest that the economy can operate beyond its potential. The term "potential" is commonly interpreted to mean "maximum." But the meaning of potential is somewhat different in this context. Potential GDP is not the maximum output the economy is capable of producing but rather the maximum *sustainable* level of production. Businesses can run factories beyond their designed or intended capacities for some period of time, and workers may

EXHIBIT 11.10
Adjusting to Higher Aggregate Demand

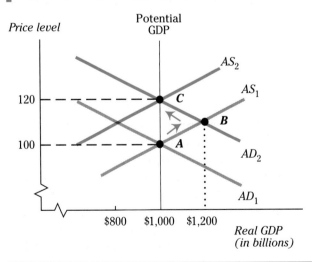

When aggregate demand increases, businesses initially find it profitable to expand output because wage rates and certain other costs are fixed by long-term contracts. Thus, equilibrium real GDP expands beyond potential. But when these contracts expire and costs rise, the short-run *AS* curve shifts upward and eventually reduces equilibrium output to the level of potential GDP.

be willing to work overtime. However, neither of these practices is sustainable; ultimately equipment breaks down and employees become disgruntled and unproductive. But in the short run, these actions permit the economy to operate beyond its potential; that is, they allow actual GDP to exceed potential GDP.

As we've seen, businesses expand output beyond potential GDP because higher prices make it profitable for them to do so. But the higher prices that are attractive to businesses are bad news for employees. Workers find that they must pay more for the goods and services they buy, even though their wage rates are unchanged; thus, their *real* wages—the purchasing power of their money wages—have declined.

Eventually firms will have to renegotiate their labor contracts. When that happens, workers will demand higher wages. Other input suppliers, also pressed by higher prices, will demand more for their resources. The result of the higher renegotiated input prices will be an upward shift of the short-run aggregate supply curve. (Remember that a change in input prices will shift the *AS* curve.) Tight markets for labor and other inputs will put continuing upward pressure on wages and other input prices. The short-run *AS* curve will continue to shift upward until workers and other input suppliers have regained their original purchasing power. This is represented in Exh. 11.10 by the shift from AS_1 to AS_2. Note that when contracts have been renegotiated, the incentive that originally motivated businesses to expand real output to $1,200 billion will have evaporated. Equilibrium real GDP will return to $1,000 billion (point *C* in the exhibit), the level of GDP consistent with the economy's potential output. The self-correcting forces have returned the economy to its potential GDP. As you can see, the long-run impact of the increase in aggregate demand is simply a higher price level since the increase in production cannot be sustained.

Adjustments to a Decrease in Aggregate Demand

The economy's response to a reduction in aggregate demand is similar to its adjustments to an increase, but in the opposite direction. To illustrate, let's again assume that the economy is operating at its potential GDP (at point *A* in Exh. 11.11). If aggregate demand fell from AD_1 to AD_2, firms would initially find their prices falling while some of their costs were fixed by long-term contracts. This would cause them to cut back on output (since output levels that had been profitable at a higher price level are no longer profitable) and to reduce equilibrium GDP below potential. This is represented in Exh. 11.11 by the movement along AS_1 from *A* to *B*. Of course, when actual GDP falls below potential, the rate of unemployment rises above the full employment level.

Adjusting to Lower Aggregate Demand

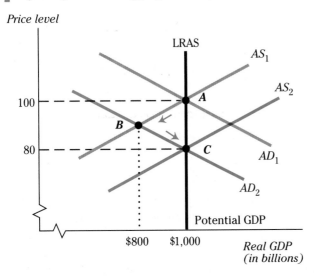

Price level

When aggregate demand declines, businesses initially find it necessary to reduce output because certain costs are fixed by long-term contracts. But when those contracts expire and costs fall, the *AS* curve shifts downward, returning the economy to potential GDP.

   If we connect the points of long-run equilibrium (*A* and *C*) we find that the long run aggregate supply (LRAS) curve is a vertical line at potential GDP.

Eventually labor and other contracts will be renegotiated. At that point, the high unemployment rates and unused productive capacity of input suppliers will cause wages and other resource prices to fall. As that occurs, the short-run *AS* curve will begin shifting to the right, eventually shifting from AS_1 to AS_2 (from *B* to *C*) and returning the economy to potential GDP and full employment. The long-run impact of the reduction in aggregate demand is a lower price level; output and employment have returned to their initial levels.

The preceding examples suggest that although the economy can deviate from potential GDP in the short run, these deviations are ultimately corrected. In the long run, the economy tends to operate at potential GDP and full employment. This implies that in the long run the economy's aggregate supply curve is vertical, since the economy ultimately returns to the same level of output, but at a higher or lower price level. If that point is unclear, return to Exh. 11.11 for a moment. Recall that the economy began at point *A*. The demand shock temporarily pushed it to *B*, but it ultimately came to rest at *C*. If we connect the initial and final equilibrium points, we arrive at a vertical line through points *A* and *C*; the long-run aggregate supply (LRAS) curve is a vertical line at potential GDP. (To test your understanding, review Exh. 11.10; you will discover that a similar result holds true.)

Shifts in the Long-Run Aggregate Supply Curve

Although the economy tends to return to potential GDP in the long run, potential GDP is not a static concept. The economy's productive capacity can increase over time if the stock of economic resources increases or if those resources become more productive (for instance, if the workforce becomes more skilled or if a technological advance provides workers with better capital equipment). Changes such as these would be represented by shifting the long-run aggregate supply (LRAS) curve to the right, as depicted in Exh. 11.12. Of course, the LRAS curve can also shift to the left, as it would if there was a reduction in the economy's labor supply or in its stock of capital.

As you can see from this chapter, there are two kinds of changes that occur in the macro economy: short-run changes and long-run changes. Short-run changes involve deviations from potential GDP. Long-run changes involve adjustments back to potential GDP, and they may also involve changes in the level of potential GDP itself. Both types of changes are important, and both are explored in this textbook. For instance, the next chapter, "Fiscal Policy," examines the short-run impact of the federal government's tax and spending decisions and considers the possibility that government action may sometimes be needed to speed the economy's return to full employment. Chapter 15, "Economic

EXHIBIT 11.12

Shifts in the Long-Run Aggregate Supply Curve

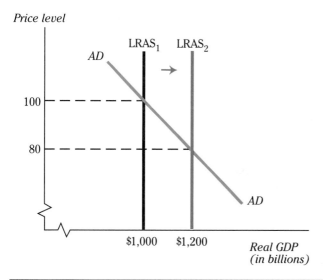

Increases in the stock of economic resources or the productivity of those resources will tend to shift the long-run aggregate supply (LRAS) curve to the right.

Growth: The Importance of the Long Run," examines the factors that determine the level of potential GDP and whether government can influence those factors through economic policy.

SUMMARY

Economists use the concepts of aggregate demand and aggregate supply to represent the forces that determine the economy's equilibrium GDP and price level. *Aggregate demand* (*AD*) is the total quantity of output demanded by all sectors in the economy together at various price levels in a given period of time. The *aggregate demand curve* slopes downward and to the right, indicating that more real output will be demanded at a lower price level than at a higher price level. There are three reasons for the downward slope of the aggregate demand curve: the *real balance effect*, the *interest rate effect*, and the *international trade effect*. The factors that will shift the aggregate demand curve include changes in the expectations of households and businesses, aggregate wealth, government policy, foreign incomes, and foreign price levels.

Aggregate supply (*AS*) refers to the quantity of output supplied by all producers in the economy together at various price levels in a given period of time. The short-run *aggregate supply curve* slopes upward because higher price levels stimulate businesses to expand output. Since wage rates and some other input prices are commonly fixed by contracts, an increase in the price level provides incentive for firms to expand output. A given short-run *AS* curve assumes the prevailing level of resource prices, the current level of technology and labor productivity, and the existing supplies of labor and capital. If one or more of these factors change, the short-run *AS* curve will shift to a new position.

The intersection of the aggregate demand and supply curves simultaneously determines the level of equilibrium real GDP and the equilibrium price level in the economy. Shifts in aggregate demand or supply will tend to alter these equilibrium values. If aggregate demand increases, both real GDP and the price level will tend to increase. The economy enjoys higher levels of output and employment, but it experiences *demand-pull inflation*. If aggregate demand declines, the levels of output, employment, and prices decline.

Changes in equilibrium can also be caused by changes in aggregate supply. A supply shock, such as an increase in the price of imported oil, will tend to reduce aggregate supply. This will cause *cost-push inflation* since the higher cost of oil pushes up prices. When aggregate supply is reduced, the levels of output and employment in the economy also decline. Supply shocks provide one possible explanation for *stagflation*, high unemployment combined with high inflation. If aggregate supply increases, the results will be doubly beneficial; the levels of output and employment in the economy will tend to increase, whereas the overall price level will decline.

Most modern economists agree that, to some extent, the economy contains a self-correcting mechanism. In the short run, the economy can deviate from potential GDP because certain wages and prices are rigid. In the long run, however, all wages and prices become flexible. As a consequence, reductions in aggregate demand are ultimately met by falling wages and input prices, which cause short-run aggregate supply to expand and return the economy to potential GDP. Increases in aggregate demand eventually lead to higher wages and input prices, which cause short-run aggregate supply to contract and output and employment to fall. Thus, wage and price adjustments ultimately return the economy to potential GDP and full employment. These adjustments imply that the long-run aggregate supply curve is vertical, not upward sloping like the short-run *AS* curve.

KEY TERMS

Aggregate demand
Aggregate supply
Cost-push inflation
Demand-pull inflation

Exports
Imports
Interest rate effect
International trade effect

Real balance effect
Stagflation

STUDY QUESTIONS

Fill in the Blanks

1. The _Aggregate demand_ curve shows the amount of real output that will be demanded at various price levels.

2. According to the _Real Balance_ effect, an increase in the price level will reduce the purchasing power of financial assets and cause society to demand less real output.

3. Any change in the spending plans of consumers, businesses, or government that results from something other than a change in the _Price Level_ will shift the aggregate demand curve.

4. A broad-based technological advance will tend to shift the aggregate _supply_ curve to the _right_.

5. The aggregate supply curve is upward sloping in the short run but _vertical_ in the long run.

6. According to the interest rate effect, a reduction in the price level will tend to (increase/decrease)

decrease, the demand for money, which in turn will (increase/decrease) _decrease_ the rate of interest and lead to (an increase/a reduction) _an increase_ in the quantity of real output demanded.

7. Increases in the price level cause businesses to _increase_ output in the short-run because some wages and other input prices are fixed by _contracts_.

8. An increase in government spending will tend to shift the aggregate _demand_ curve to the _right_.

9. Cost-push inflation is caused by the aggregate _supply_ curve shifting to the (right/left) _left_.

10. The term _stagflation_ is used to describe high inflation combined with high unemployment.

11. If the economy is initially in equilibrium at potential GDP, an increase in aggregate demand will tend to raise both output and prices in the short run, but will only raise _prices_ in the long run.

Multiple Choice

1. The type of inflation caused by increased spending for goods and services is
   a) demand-pull inflation.
   b) cost-push inflation.
   c) structural inflation.
   d) expenditure inflation.

2. If a reduction in the price level causes more real output to be demanded,
   a) the aggregate demand curve will shift to the right.
   b) the aggregate demand curve is downward sloping.
   c) the short-run aggregate supply curve will shift to the right.
   d) the short-run aggregate supply curve is downward sloping.

3. Which of the following will shift the aggregate demand curve to the left?
   a) An increase in government spending
   b) A reduction in labor productivity
   c) An increase in personal income taxes
   d) An increase in society's aggregate wealth

4. Which of the following will increase both the price level and real GDP?
   a) A nationwide drought that drives up the prices of agricultural products
   b) A reduction in government spending for goods and services
   c) A reduction in the money supply
   d) Greater optimism among business executives

5. In 1974 disease killed many anchovies and raised anchovy prices. Anchovies are used in cattle feed as a source of protein. The likely short-run impact of this event would be to
   a) raise both the price level and real GDP.
   b) lower both the price level and real GDP.
   c) raise the price level but lower real GDP.
   d) lower the price level but raise real GDP.

6. According to the real balance effect,
   a) a reduction in the price level stimulates spending by lowering interest rates.
   b) an increase in the money supply will shift the aggregate demand curve to the right.

c) an increase in the price level reduces spending by lowering the real value of society's financial assets.

d) an increase in society's aggregate wealth will shift the aggregate demand curve to the right.

7. An increase in the productivity of the labor force would be likely to shift
   a) the aggregate supply curve to the right.
   b) the aggregate supply curve to the left.
   c) the aggregate demand curve to the right.
   d) the aggregate demand curve to the left.

8. A decrease in foreign income levels would, ceteris paribus, tend to shift the aggregate _Demand_ curve for U.S. products to the _left_ .
   a) demand, right
   b) demand, left
   c) supply, right
   d) supply, left

9. The international trade effect provides a rationale for
   a) shifts in the aggregate demand curve.
   b) shifts in the aggregate supply curve.
   c) the slope of the aggregate demand curve.
   d) the slope of the aggregate supply curve.

10. In the short run, an increase in the money supply will
    a) reduce both real GDP and the price level.
    b) reduce real GDP and increase the price level.
    c) increase both real GDP and the price level.
    d) increase real GDP and reduce the price level.

11. If the prevailing price level was initially below equilibrium,
    a) there would be a surplus of output.
    b) the price level would tend to fall.
    c) the amount of real GDP supplied would exceed the amount demanded.
    d) there would be a shortage of output.

12. Suppose that Congress increased government spending at the same time that the price of imported oil (which is used to manufacture gasoline and heating oil) increased. In the short run, this would clearly
    a) increase both the price level and real GDP.
    b) reduce both the price level and real GDP.
    c) increase the price level, but the impact on real GDP is uncertain.
    d) increase real GDP, but the impact on the price level is uncertain.

13. The short-run aggregate supply curve slopes upward
    a) as a result of the real balance effect and the interest rate effect.
    b) if all wages and input prices are flexible in the short run.
    c) because increases in the overall price level result in enhanced labor productivity and higher real output.
    d) because input price rigidities make it profitable for firms to expand output when product prices rise.

14. Suppose that the economy is operating below potential GDP. According to the self-correcting model, the economy will ultimately return to potential because
    a) the Fed will expand the money supply.
    b) wages and resource prices will fall as contracts expire and are renegotiated.
    c) workers will eventually demand higher wages, and resource suppliers will demand higher input prices.
    d) aggregate demand will automatically increase enough to push the economy back to potential GDP.

15. When the overall price level rises,
    a) businesses tend to reduce output because production becomes less profitable.
    b) wage rates and other input prices tend to increase immediately, forcing businesses to cut back on production.
    c) businesses have incentive to expand output because many costs are fixed by long-term contracts.
    d) businesses may either increase or decrease output, depending on the magnitude of the hike in the price level.

16. According to the self-correcting model, if the economy is producing a level of output in excess of potential GDP,
    a) potential GDP will automatically expand to match the actual level of production.
    b) workers and input suppliers will eventually negotiate higher wages and prices, which will return the economy to potential GDP.
    c) wages and input prices will ultimately fall, which will return the economy to potential GDP.
    d) None of the above; the economy cannot operate beyond potential GDP.

17. According to the self-correcting model,
    a) unemployment can exist indefinitely.
    b) the economy can never operate beyond potential GDP.
    c) unemployment is eventually eliminated by falling wages and prices.
    d) the economy always operates at potential GDP.

18. Which of the following would *not* shift the *long-run AS* curve to the right?
    a) An increase in the stock of capital
    b) A technological advance
    c) A reduction in the average wage rate
    d) An increase in worker training

Problems and Questions for Discussion

1. Explain in detail why the aggregate demand curve slopes downward .

2. Any change that shifts the long-run *AS* curve will also shift the short-run *AS* curve. But the converse is not true. Try to explain why.

3. What role do contracts play in explaining the upward slope of the aggregate supply curve?

4. Suppose that, on average, wage rates increase less than the increase in labor productivity. What will happen to the overall price level and real GDP? Explain how you arrived at your conclusion.

5. Whenever the stock market threatens to tumble (bringing down stock prices), economy watchers worry about its potential impact on the economy. Is there any justification for this concern—could a large decline in the stock market harm the economy? Defend your answer.

6. Explain the difference between demand-pull and cost-push inflation. Use aggregate demand and supply curves to show how each problem would be represented graphically.

7. Suppose that the economy is in equilibrium at potential GDP and that policymakers increase aggregate demand (perhaps because they do not recognize that the economy is operating at potential). Discuss the short-run

and long-run impact of this change. Supplement your answer with graphs.

8. Consider the short-run impact of the changes listed below. Which changes would cause the economy's price level and real GDP to move in the same direction (both increase, both decrease), and which would cause the price level and real GDP to move in opposite directions (increasing the price level but reducing real output, for example)? After you have worked through the list, see if you can draw any general conclusions.
   a) An increase in government spending
   b) A severe frost that destroys crops
   c) A large decline in the stock market
   d) An increase in labor productivity
   e) An increase in consumer optimism
   f) Higher prices for imported raw materials

9. Suppose that government spending in support of education was increased. Would this action shift the aggregate demand curve, the aggregate supply curve, or both curves? What would happen to the price level and real GDP?

10. Assume that the economy is in short-run equilibrium at less than full employment. Describe the forces that will ultimately return the economy to potential GDP.

ANSWER KEY

Fill in the Blanks

1. aggregate demand
2. real balance
3. price level
4. supply, right

5. vertical
6. decrease, decrease, an increase
7. increase, contracts

8. demand, right
9. supply, left
10. stagflation
11. prices

Multiple Choice

1. a
2. b
3. c
4. d

5. c
6. c
7. a
8. b

9. c
10. c
11. d
12. c

13. d
14. b
15. c

16. b
17. c
18. c

Fiscal Policy

We discovered in the last chapter that the government's spending and taxing decisions affect the level of aggregate demand. In this chapter we will take a closer look at those decisions. What does the federal government do with our tax dollars? What do people mean when they say the federal government is projecting a budget surplus or a budget deficit? Should government deliberately alter its tax and spending plans in an attempt to guide the economy's performance? And what is the public debt? These are some of the questions we will attempt to answer in this chapter. We'll begin with a brief look at the federal budget. Then we'll use the *AD–AS* model from Chapter 11 to examine the cause of unemployment and inflation and to consider the possibility that government might use its tax and spending powers to combat these problems. The chapter will conclude with a look at the public debt and concerns about the debt.

THE FEDERAL BUDGET

The **federal budget** is a statement of the federal government's planned expenditures and anticipated receipts for the coming year. The budget is the result of interaction between the president and Congress. Each February, the president proposes a budget, which is then debated and amended by Congress. Because there are diverse views about the proper functions of government, this process can be protracted. However, it is usually completed before October 1, the start of the federal government's *fiscal* year. (According to Webster, the word fiscal means "pertaining to financial matters." So, in essence, a fiscal year is an accounting year. The federal government's fiscal year runs from October 1 to September 30.)

The budgetary process is not over after Congress enacts a budget. If the economy does not perform as expected, the government's expenditures and tax revenues will be different from those anticipated. As a consequence, Congress is commonly required to pass supplemental budgets to accommodate these changes. With this background, we turn now to a consideration of the federal government's budget for the 2001 fiscal year, as represented in Exh. 12.1.

Tax Revenues

As you can see from the exhibit, $2,019 billion in tax revenue was projected for fiscal 2001. The major source of federal tax receipts is personal income taxes, which were expected to bring in $972 billion in 2001, about 48 percent of the federal government's revenues. Social insurance taxes, such as Social Security taxes and Medicare taxes, were the second most important source of revenue, accounting for an anticipated $682 billion, or about 34 percent of the total. The remaining revenue sources are much less important. In 2001, corporate income taxes were projected to bring in approximately $195 billion (10 percent), while the remaining categories—excise taxes (such as the taxes on alcoholic beverages and tobacco products), estate and gift taxes (taxes on inheritances and gifts), and customs duties (taxes on imported products)—together account for only $170 billion, a little more than 8 percent of total revenue.

Social insurance taxes have become increasingly important as a source of government tax revenue. In the 1960s, social insurance taxes generated about 16 percent of federal tax revenues. By 1980, that figure had expanded to 30 percent. And, as we saw earlier, social insurance taxes are projected to account for more than 33 percent of federal revenues in 2001. Over the 1960–2001 period, personal income taxes provided a relatively constant share of federal revenues, but corporate income taxes declined in relative importance (from roughly 23 percent of

EXHIBIT 12.1
Federal Budget for 2001 (billions of dollars)

TAX RECEIPTS	$2,019	
Personal income taxes		$972
Social insurance taxes		682
Corporate income taxes		195
Excise taxes		77
Estate and gift taxes		32
Customs duties, etc.		61
EXPENDITURE	**$1,835**	
Transfer payments		$993
Purchases of goods and services		634
Debt interest		208
Surplus	**$184**	

Source: *Budget of the United States Government, Fiscal Year 2001,* U.S. Government Printing Office, Washington, 2000. For an accessible source, see *The Citizen's Guide to the Federal Budget,* which accompanies the more detailed volumes of the budget.

total revenue in 1960 to about 10 percent in 2001). Excise taxes, estate and gift taxes, and customs duties have also declined in importance.[1]

Government Expenditures

How does the federal government spend our tax dollars? Returning to Exh. 12.1, you can see that there are three major categories of expenditures: transfer payments, purchases of goods and services, and debt interest.

The largest category of government expenditures is transfer payments. **Transfer payments** are expenditures for which government receives no goods or services in return. Examples of transfer payments include Social Security benefits, Medicare and Medicaid expenditures, unemployment compensation, and farm subsidies. In 2001, the federal government projected expenditures of $993 billion for transfer payments, more than half of total federal outlays.

---

[1] Comparisons are based on statistics drawn from *Historic Tables: Budget of the United States Government, Fiscal Year 2000.*

The fraction of the federal budget going to transfer payments has been rising for a number of years. Consider Social Security, for example. In 1970, Social Security accounted for about 15 percent of federal expenditures. By 1990 it had grown to almost 20 percent. And in 2001, it is projected to account for 24 percent of spending. An even more dramatic pattern appears if we look at Medicare and Medicaid. In 1970, these two programs accounted for about 4 percent of federal spending. By 1990, the Medicare and Medicaid programs had grown to more than 10 percent of total expenditures. And in 2001, they are expected to absorb almost 19 percent of total spending. As you can see, the growth of transfer payments has been striking. In fact, the persistent growth of transfer payments has become a significant source of concern and heated debate among politicians and others.

The second largest category of government expenditures is government purchases of goods and services. This category includes government spending for national defense—outlays for submarines, the services of military personnel, and so on—and nondefense purchases—expenditures for roads, parks, schools, the services of legislators and bureaucrats, and so on. In 2001, the federal government anticipated spending $634 billion on goods and services. That represents approximately 35 percent of total expenditures, down dramatically from 50 percent in 1970.

The final category of government expenditures is interest on the national debt. As you probably recognize, the federal government sometimes spends more than it earns in tax revenue. In fact, that was commonplace until very recently. This is accomplished by borrowing money, just like you might borrow money to buy a home or finance a vacation. Of course, whenever you borrow money you create a debt. This entry reflects the interest payments that the federal government must make annually to the owners of that debt. In 2001, the federal government projected approximately $208 billion in debt interest, about 11 percent of total expenditures. That percentage is significantly higher than it was in 1970 (7 percent), but has fallen somewhat since 1990 (15 percent).

If you compare the government's projected revenues and expenditures for 2001, you can see that the government was anticipating a budget surplus in fiscal 2001. A **budget surplus** exists if the federal government collects more in taxes than it spends. According to Exh. 12.1, the federal government is projecting a surplus of $184 billion for the 2001 fiscal year. The federal government has run surpluses for the last few years; in fact, they are a major reason for the smaller debt interest payments described earlier. These budget surpluses, however, are a relatively new phenomenon. For most of the last three decades, budget deficits have been norm. **Budget deficits** occur when government expenditures exceed revenues. If government expenditures equal tax revenues, the federal government has a **balanced budget.** We'll have more to say about the causes and consequences of deficits and surpluses later in the chapter.

CLASSICAL ECONOMICS, THE GREAT DEPRESSION, AND JOHN MAYNARD KEYNES

Although the primary objective of the federal budget is to pay for the activities of the federal government, there is a secondary objective as well. The federal budget may also be used as a tool for influencing the performance of the aggregate economy, for helping to combat unemployment or inflation. Before we discuss this function we need to review and expand on some concepts introduced in the previous chapter. Let's begin by revisiting the model of a self-correcting economy.

Chapter 11 concluded that a self-correcting mechanism tends to restore the economy to full employment and potential GDP whenever it deviates from those standards. Prior to the 1930s, economists thought that the economy's self-correcting mechanism not only worked, but worked quickly. The economists of this period are known as **classical economists**, and they believed that any reduction in aggregate demand would quickly be met by falling wages and prices, which would tend to restore full employment. This belief held up reasonably well until the Great Depression, which began in 1929. By 1933, the economy's real GDP had declined by almost one-third, and the unemployment rate had reached 25 percent. Although the economy began to recover after 1933, it was a slow and weak recovery. In 1937, the unemployment rate still hovered around 14 percent.

The Great Depression called into question the classical economists' belief in a quickly adjusting economy. In 1936, John Maynard Keynes, a British economist, offered an alternative view of how market economies work. According to Keynes, if pessimism causes businesses and consumers to reduce their spending, an economy could find itself in an unemployment "equilibrium"—a situation in which output and employment are stuck at low levels for some time. In terms of the AD–AS model, Keynes was saying that the self-correcting mechanism may operate slowly. Moreover, Keynes didn't think we should wait for this automatic adjustment to occur. "In the long-run we're all dead" was his comforting way of putting it. Instead, he argued that government should take an active part in trying to stimulate a recovery.

What should governments do? According to Keynes, the federal government should increase its spending or reduce taxes in order to stimulate private spending. In other words, it should use the federal budget to get the economy moving again. We'll have more to say about these policies in just a moment. For now, the important point is that Keynes saw the federal budget as more than an accounting device; he saw it as a tool for influencing economic performance.

Because of his belief in government intervention, Keynes is regarded as one of the first **activist economists**—economists who see an important role for government in guiding the economy's performance. On the other hand, the classical economists were **non-activists**. Because they had faith in the economy's ability to heal itself, they did not believe that government intervention was necessary.[2]

Today, most economists appear to believe that there is a self-correcting mechanism operative in the economy. But there is continuing disagreement about how rapidly that mechanism operates and whether government policy can be used to speed the process. Modern non-activists tend to believe that the economy's self-correcting mechanism works relatively quickly and that government action is either ineffective or counterproductive. Modern activists see the self-correcting mechanism as working slowly and view government intervention—at least in the case of significant deviations from potential GDP—as advisable.

THE EXISTENCE OF UNEMPLOYMENT OR INFLATION

The aggregate demand–aggregate supply model can be used to illustrate the unemployment problem that was the focus of Keynes's analysis of the Great Depression. In Exh. 12.2 (a), we find the economy in equilibrium at an output of $800 billion, an output less than the economy's potential GDP of $1,000 billion. Of course, whenever the economy is operating below its potential, the rate of unemployment in the economy exceeds the natural rate. As we learned in Chapter 10, this situation is commonly described as a recession (the term *depression* is reserved for severe downturns like the Great Depression), and the amount by which the equilibrium GDP falls short of potential GDP is known as the **recessionary gap**. In this example, the recessionary gap is equal to $200 billion, the difference between the potential output of $1,000 billion and the actual output of $800 billion.

While Keynes was primarily concerned with recessionary gaps, he recognized that economies can also be in equilibrium beyond potential GDP. Exhibit 12.2 (b) illustrates that situation. Here we find the economy in equilibrium at an output of $1,250 billion, well beyond the economy's potential GDP. Because the economy is operating beyond potential, the unemployment rate is less than the natural rate, and strong demand for labor puts upward pressure on wages and prices. Because operating beyond potential GDP creates inflationary pressures, we describe the excess in equilibrium GDP as the inflationary gap. More precisely, the **inflationary gap** is the amount by which the equilibrium level of real GDP exceeds potential GDP. In this instance the inflationary gap is equal to $250 billion, the difference between the actual output of $1,250 billion and the potential output of $1,000 billion.

---

[2] Students wishing to explore the debate between Keynes and the classical economists in greater detail, can do so by reading "Keynes and the Classical Economists: The Early Debate on Policy Activism," which can be accessed on the textbook web page.

EXHIBIT 12.2
Recessionary and Inflationary Gaps

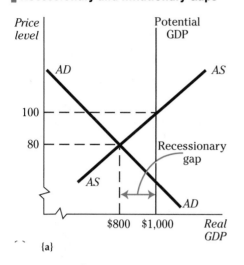

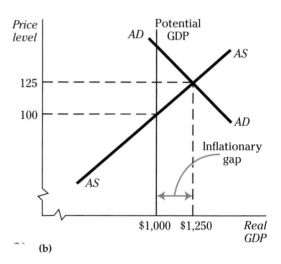

{a}   (b)

A *recessionary gap* exists whenever equilibrium GDP falls short of potential GDP. Part (a) shows a recessionary gap of $200 billion, the difference between the potential GDP of $1,000 billion and the equilibrium output of $800 billion.

   An *inflationary gap* exists whenever the equilibrium GDP exceeds potential GDP. Part (b) shows an inflationary gap of $250 billion, the difference between the potential GDP of $1,000 billion and the equilibrium GDP of $1250 billion.

DISCRETIONARY FISCAL POLICY: COMBATING UNEMPLOYMENT OR INFLATION

Since the time of Keynes, activist economists have argued that government policies should be used to eliminate recessionary or inflationary gaps rather than waiting for the economy to self-correct. One form of policy activism involves discretionary fiscal policy. **Discretionary fiscal policy** is the deliberate changing of the level of government spending or taxation in order to guide the economy's performance. Discretionary fiscal policy attempts to influence an economy's performance by altering the level of spending or aggregate demand. When a recessionary gap exists and unemployment is above the natural rate, an *expansionary fiscal policy* is called for: Increase government spending, reduce taxes, or do both. Increasing government spending for goods and services directly increases aggregate demand since it means more spending at any price level. Tax reductions work indirectly; by reducing taxes, they leave households with more take-home pay, which in turn tends to stimulate the demand for fur-

EXHIBIT 12.3
Using Discretionary Fiscal Policy

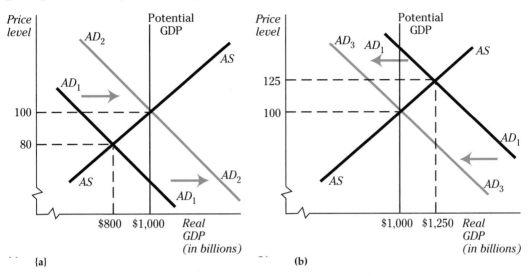

{a}

(b)

According to activist economists, unemployment can be attacked by using an *expansionary fiscal policy:* increasing government spending or reducing taxes. (a) An expansionary fiscal policy shifts the aggregate demand curve from AD_1 to AD_2, thereby eliminating the recessionary gap and the accompanying unemployment.

Inflationary pressures can be eliminated by employing a *contractionary fiscal policy:* reducing government spending or increasing taxes. (b) A contractionary fiscal policy shifts the aggregate demand curve from AD_1 to AD_3, thereby eliminating the inflationary gap and the accompanying inflationary pressures.

niture and other consumer items.[3] Either policy would tend to expand the economy to a higher level of equilibrium GDP and lower the unemployment rate.[4] For instance, in Exh. 12.3(a), we can see that an increase in government spending (or a reduction in taxes) has shifted the AD curve from AD_1 to AD_2, raising the economy's equilibrium GDP from $800 billion to $1,000 billion and the price level from 80 to 100. In short, discretionary fiscal policy has eliminated the recessionary gap and lowered unemployment to the natural rate.

---

[3] While increases in government purchases of goods and services directly increase aggregate demand, increases in government spending for transfer payments act indirectly, like a tax reduction. By providing households with additional income, increases in transfer payments tend to increase the demand for goods and services.

[4] An increase in government spending for goods and services would actually shift the AD curve farther than an equal-sized increase in transfer payments or an equal-sized reduction in taxes. That's because households would tend to save a portion of the tax reduction or increase in transfer payments.

The existence of an inflationary gap would call for a *contractionary fiscal policy*: Government spending should be cut, or taxes should be increased in order to reduce private spending. By reducing aggregate demand, these policies would tend to contract the level of equilibrium GDP and reduce or eliminate inflationary pressures. For instance, Exh. 12.3(b) shows that by cutting government spending (or increasing taxes), we can reduce aggregate demand from AD_1 to AD_3. This would reduce the equilibrium level of real GDP from $1,250 billion to $1,000 billion (the economy's potential output) and thereby eliminate the inflationary pressures that had existed.

AUTOMATIC FISCAL POLICY: THE ECONOMY'S AUTOMATIC STABILIZERS

Discretionary fiscal policy, as the term implies, requires Congress to deliberately change the level of government spending and/or taxation. But not all fiscal policy is discretionary; some is automatic. **Automatic stabilizers** are changes in the level of government spending or taxation that occur automatically whenever the level of aggregate income (GDP) changes. This automatic fiscal policy tends to reduce the magnitude of fluctuations in total spending and thereby help prevent wide swings in the level of output and employment.

The federal income tax is one powerful automatic stabilizer. To see how it works, imagine a family earning $50,000 a year and paying $10,000 a year in taxes. (Its average tax rate would be 20 percent since $10,000 is 20 percent of $50,000.) After taxes, our hypothetical family will have $40,000 to spend on food, housing, and whatever else it chooses to purchase.

Now, suppose the economy enters a recession and the family sees its income shrink by $10,000 as a result of reduced hours of work. This will cause the family's tax bill to fall to $8,000, leaving it with $32,000 to spend. The family's ability to purchase goods and services has fallen, but only by $8,000, not by the full $10,000 reduction in income. Other families with falling incomes will have a similar experience; they will receive automatic tax reductions that will cushion the impact of the reductions in income. Because taxes automatically decline with income, the tax system prevents spending from falling as much as it would have if taxes remained constant. This helps to retard the weakening of the economy and prevents unemployment from becoming as severe as it otherwise would.

When the economy strengthens, the tax system operates to dampen inflationary pressures. Increases in income mean higher taxes; consumers are left with less income to spend than they would have if taxes had remained constant. If the higher incomes push families into higher tax brackets (the 30 percent bracket, for example), the increase in after-tax income will be even less.[5] Thus, the income tax helps to dampen spending increases and reduce inflationary pressures.

Federal unemployment compensation and state welfare benefits also operate as built-in stabilizers. When the level of economic activity declines and the jobless rate begins to rise, the total amount paid out in the form of unemployment compensation and welfare benefits increases automatically. These transfer payments compensate somewhat for the declining incomes of the unemployed, and in so doing, they prevent a steeper drop in consumption spending by households. This action retards the downward spiral of spending and slows the deterioration of the economy.

When the economy begins to recover and the unemployment rate drops, these transfer payments automatically decrease, which helps prevent inflation by slowing the growth of spending.

Although automatic stabilizers reduce the magnitude of fluctuations in economic activity, they do not ensure full employment and stable prices. They cannot stop a severe inflation once it is under way, and they cannot pull the economy out of a deep recession. In fact, the same fiscal features that tend to stabilize the economy can also retard the economy's recovery from a recession. As the recovery begins, personal income starts to rise, but higher taxes reduce the growth of spending and therefore slow the recovery. For these reasons, activist economists believe that automatic stabilizers must be supplemented by the kinds of discretionary (deliberate) fiscal policies we examined earlier.

FISCAL POLICY AND THE FEDERAL BUDGET

When we resort to fiscal policy to combat unemployment or inflation, we are deliberately tampering with the federal budget. That's what discretionary fiscal policy really is—budget policy.

According to activists, whenever unemployment exists (whenever the unemployment rate is above the natural rate), the federal government should plan a *deficit budget*; that is, it should plan to spend more than it expects to collect in taxes. By taking this action, the government injects the economy with additional spending, or aggregate demand, that should help drive it toward full employment. Inflationary times call for the opposite approach, a *surplus budget*, which expresses the government's intention to spend less than it expects to collect in taxes. A surplus budget helps reduce the amount of aggregate demand in the economy and thereby moderates inflationary pressures. According to the

---

[5] Existing tax law is somewhat progressive; that is, those with higher incomes pay a higher fraction of those incomes in the form of taxes.

activist (or Keynesian) model, a *balanced budget*—a plan to match government expenditures and tax revenues—is appropriate only when the economy is operating at full employment, when it has achieved a satisfactory equilibrium and needs neither stimulus nor restraint.

Planned and Unplanned Deficits and Surpluses

While discretionary fiscal policy calls for deliberate deficits and surpluses, not all federal deficits or surpluses are the result of deliberate action. In fact, even the most carefully planned budget will be inaccurate if the economy performs in unexpected ways. That's true because changes in the level of national income and employment will mean automatic changes in tax revenues and government expenditures. The same automatic stabilizers that help to reduce the magnitude of economic swings lead to deficits when the economy experiences a downturn, and to unexpected surpluses during periods of expansion.

To illustrate, consider an experience from the Reagan administration. Early in 1981 President Reagan recommended to Congress a budget with a projected deficit of $45 billion for the 1982 fiscal year. This budget assumed that the economy's real gross domestic product would grow at a rate of 4.2 percent in 1982 and that the unemployment rate would average 7.2 percent for that year. Both assumptions turned out to be incorrect. Real GDP *declined* by 2.1 percent in 1982, and the unemployment rate averaged 9.5 percent. As a result of this unexpectedly weak performance, the federal government's outlay for unemployment compensation and welfare was higher than anticipated, and tax revenues were lower. This produced a budget deficit of approximately $128 billion, a far cry from the administration's $45 billion projection.

In contrast, sometimes the economy outperforms the projections of planners. When that happens, the automatic stabilizers have the opposite effect on the government's receipts and expenditures. As the economy expands, tax revenues rise, and expenditures for unemployment compensation decline. This tends to decrease the size of the deficit or increase the size of the surplus. The Clinton administration's experience in 1997 illustrates the point. Prior to the start of the year, the administration estimated a budget deficit of $125 billion. But a booming economy lowered the unemployment rate (and the accompanying payments to the unemployed) and ballooned tax receipts. The result was a deficit of only $22 billion, a much lower figure than anyone anticipated.

Unemployment and the Federal Budget

As the foregoing examples show, when the economy performs in unexpected ways, budget planners are likely to miss their target. Moreover, efforts to get the budget back on track can harm the economy. To illustrate, suppose the economy is initially operating at full employment and that the federal government projects a balanced budget. What will happen to the budget if the economy suddenly weakens and unemployment begins to rise? As you know, the fiscal system's automatic stabilizers will work automatically to retard the downturn. But what will this do to the balanced federal budget? It will push it into deficit!

Suppose that Congress insists on restoring a balanced budget. What should be done to accomplish this objective? The logical response would be to increase taxes and reduce government spending. But wait—this response is clearly inconsistent with the activist remedy for unemployment. The reduced level of government spending and concomitant higher taxes will mean less aggregate demand, which will cause the downturn to worsen. Moreover, because this effort to balance the budget prolongs the recession, it may result in a larger cumulative deficit.

According to the activist model, whenever the economy is in recession, the preferred route to a balanced budget entails a deliberate increase in government spending or a reduction in taxes. Obviously, either measure would increase the short-term deficit, but by stimulating output and employment, either action could help pull the economy out of its depressed state. When the economy improves, tax revenues will rise automatically, and government spending for transfer payments will decline automatically. Thus, expansionary fiscal policy may create a larger deficit in the short run. But by restoring the health of the economy, it can lead to a balanced budget.

We can see how this process works if we look at the tax cut instituted by President Johnson in the mid-1960s. In 1964 the federal budget was already in deficit when Congress finally approved an $11 billion tax reduction (originally requested by President Kennedy in 1963) designed to push the economy closer to full employment. The stimulus provided by this tax cut helped increase GDP by some $36 billion and lower the unemployment rate from 6 percent to 4.7 percent. According to Arthur Okun, chairman of the Council of Economic Advisors under President Johnson, the higher tax revenues that resulted from the improved economy brought the federal budget into surplus in the first half of 1965.[6]

---

[6] Arthur N. Okun, *The Political Economy of Prosperity* (New York: W.W. Norton, 1967), pp. 47–48.

ISSUES RELATED TO FISCAL POLICY

The foregoing discussion seems to suggest that discretionary fiscal policy is easily used to combat the problems of unemployment and inflation. It's time to dispel that impression. As we noted earlier, not all economists are activists. And even activists recognize that implementing discretionary fiscal policy is tougher in reality than it is on the chalkboard (or in the textbook). Let's examine why.

Crowding Out

According to activists, unemployment should be combated by increasing government spending (or reducing taxes). This is supposed to increase aggregate demand, pushing the economy back to full employment. But the beneficial impact of higher government spending may be partially offset by a phenomenon known as crowding out.

When the federal government borrows money to finance additional spending, it must compete with private borrowers for funds. Under certain circumstances this increased demand for funds will drive up interest rates, which will discourage private businesses from borrowing for investment purposes. This phenomenon is known as **crowding out**: Government borrowing pushes aside, or crowds out, private borrowing.

Crowding out has two important consequences that we need to consider. First, crowding out tends to reduce the expansionary impact of any increase in government spending. To illustrate, suppose that a deficit-financed increase in government spending would (in the absence of crowding out) increase the economy's equilibrium GDP by $200 billion. If the higher interest rates associated with government's borrowing reduce investment spending, that reduction will partially offset the expansionary impact of the government's fiscal policy. As a result, the economy's equilibrium output will expand by less than $200 billion, perhaps substantially less.

Second, crowding out can affect the economy's rate of economic growth. Unlike consumption spending, investment spending allows businesses to expand their productive capacity and produce more output in the future. In other words, investment spending permits the economy to grow and, by making more goods and services available, increases the society's standard of living. To the extent that crowding out reduces the level of investment spending, it hinders economic growth and thereby harms future generations. (To the extent that the increased government spending is for roads, schools, and other "investment-like" purchases, this portion of the crowding-out argument is invalidated.)

Crowding out is unlikely to be a significant problem when the economy is in a severely depressed state with substantial excess capacity. Under those conditions, businesses are reluctant to invest, even in the face of low interest rates. Crowding out is more likely to be a problem when the economy is expanding, as it was throughout the late 1990s. Under those conditions, higher interest rates may indeed choke off some private investment spending. That's why economists have generally been pleased to see recent budget surpluses, instead of the deficits that had become so commonplace. We'll have more to say about those surpluses in Chapter 15.

The Expansionary Bias

Activists call for expansionary fiscal policy to combat unemployment and for contractionary fiscal policy to combat inflation. But expansionary policies are more attractive politically than contractionary policies. Incumbent politicians don't want to sacrifice votes, and voters don't want to pay higher taxes—nor do they want to lose government programs that benefit them. The result is a bias in favor of expansionary fiscal policies. It may be relatively easy for Congress to pass measures to stimulate the economy, but it's quite difficult to muster the votes necessary to trim government spending or increase taxes. This bias has led to ongoing deficits in good times and bad and has significantly tarnished the image of discretionary fiscal policy. (Prior to 1998, the last budget surplus experienced by the federal government was in 1969. That's almost thirty years of uninterrupted deficits. Clearly, the expansionary bias was a problem not envisioned by Keynes.)

Time Lags

Many critics argue that the most significant problem associated with the use of discretionary fiscal policy is time lags. Often a substantial interlude passes between the time when a policy change is needed and time when the economic impact of any change actually takes place. This lag may reduce the effectiveness of the remedial fiscal policy; in some instances, it may even make the change counterproductive.

   The time lag associated with fiscal policy has three elements. First, the economy does not always provide clear signals as to what the future will bring. As a consequence, there is commonly a *recognition lag*; that is, some time elapses before policymakers recognize the need for a policy change. Second, even after the need is acknowledged, action is historically slow to take place. It can take a substantial amount of time to draft legislation and get it through Congress. Even if lawmakers are in general agreement that action is needed, there may be heated disagreements about the form that action should take. Many economists argue that this *implementation lag* is unacceptably long and is the real downfall of fiscal policy. The final lag is the

USE YOUR ECONOMIC REASONING

Too Late for the Tax-Cut Cure? Economists Prefer Fed Action, Doubt Bush Plan Would Avert Slump

By John M. Berry

PRESIDENT-ELECT Bush, continuing to worry out loud about signs that U.S. economic growth has slowed sharply and a recession could be on the way, said last week that one way to improve consumer confidence and encourage more spending "would be to let the people have some of their own money back."

"There are clear warning signs, warning signs which will require action in the halls of Congress," Bush said in urging passage of his $1.6 trillion, 10-year tax cut.

But a number of economists, including both conservatives and liberals, have expressed serious doubt that any tax cut could be passed and implemented quickly enough to help the economy avoid an imminent slump. Several also said it is not yet clear that the economy needs any such stimulus, and if it does, they say it would be better to let the Federal Reserve provide it through monetary policy with a fast series of interest-rate cuts.

Moreover, as proposed during the campaign, Bush's tax cut would not take effect until 2002 and would then be phased in over several years— a timetable that would give the economy little if any boost next year, the economists said. The slow beginning and gradual implementation was designed to hold down its cost in terms of lost government revenue over a decade, the period of estimation required by congressional budget procedures.

While at various times Bush, Vice President-elect

Source: Washington Post, Dec. 29, 2000, p. 33A.

---

impact lag. Even after legislation is passed and put into effect, more time is required for policy to have its full effect on aggregate demand.

The existence of these time lags clearly limits the effectiveness of discretionary fiscal policy as a vehicle for guiding the economy's performance. Today, even activists agree that policymakers should not attempt to use discretionary fiscal policy to eliminate every minor increase in unemployment or inflation. Instead, discretionary policies should be reserved for major downturns or inflationary episodes, situations in which the lag will be of less critical importance. Fortunately, automatic stabilizers respond mechanically to changes in the economy's performance, so they are not subject to the recognition or implementation lags. (The Use Your Economic Reasoning selection

Cheney and some of their advisers said the tax proposal could be useful in warding off a possible economic slump, the president-elect also has stressed other rationales. The one most frequently mentioned was the need to reduce the federal tax burden so families would be allowed to keep more of what they earn to meet their differing needs.

A Bush spokeswoman said the president-elect is committed to sending a legislative proposal to Capital Hill with exactly the same provisions he promised in the campaign. But unnamed groups of Bush advisers are already working with some members of Congress to speed passage of the tax cut, which could well be modified in the process, the spokeswoman said.

Speeding up the tax cuts could raise the 10-year cost dramatically, however, and several analysts said quick passage is highly unlikely unless the distribution of the tax cuts by income groups is modified to attract Democratic support. Under the current proposal, a large share of the tax relief flows to upper-bracket taxpayers.

"The jury is still out on whether the [economic] weakness will turn into a problem or whether it is just the medicine the doctor—[Fed Chairman Alan] Greenspan, of course—ordered to dampen the fires of inflation. When we do know, it will be too late" for a timely tax cut, said Robert Reischauer of the Urban Institute, a Democrat and former director of the Congressional Budget Office.

Reischauer said that in the past when government policymakers tried to cut taxes or increase spending to give the economy a short-term fiscal boost, the actions usually came too late to do much good.

"There are long lags before monetary policy kicks in, but even longer for fiscal policy," Reischauer said. "It's hard to imagine any impact before late fall, because it will take the new administration some time to get its policy formulated and sent up to Capitol Hill. It will take Congress several months to pass a budget resolution and deal with the policy proposals, and then it will take several months to get the cuts implemented."

If a recession similar in length to that of 1990–91 were to begin next month—which virtually no forecaster is predicting—then it would be over by the end of the summer. By Reischauer's timetable, it would be over before any taxpayer likely would have received any benefit from a tax cut....

John B. Taylor, a Stanford University economist who has been mentioned as a possible chairman of the Council of Economic Advisers in the Bush administration, as recently as summer was sharply critical of "discretionary countercyclical" fiscal policy—using changes in taxes or government spending to counter the peaks and valleys of economic cycles.

Writing in the *Journal of Economic Perspectives*, Taylor said, "Much has happened in macroeconomics since the 1960s and 1970s when discretionary countercyclical fiscal

(Continued)

on page 370, "Too Late for the Tax-Cut Cure?", reiterates the concern about the lags associated with fiscal policy. Test your understanding of fiscal policy by reading the article and answering the accompanying questions.)

THE PUBLIC DEBT

No discussion of the federal budget and fiscal policy would be complete without at least some attention to the topic of the **public debt**—the accumulated borrowings of the federal government. The public debt is not grabbing headlines the way it once did (for reasons that will be made clear in a moment), but

(Too Late for the Tax-Cut Cure? Economists Prefer Fed Action, Doubt Bush Plan Would Avert Slump *Continued*)

policy was last considered a serious option in the United States."

The biggest change, Taylor said, has been in the way the Fed has conducted monetary policy, with the result that "inflation has been low since the early 1980s and the real economy has been more stable."

"If the countercyclical goals of fiscal and monetary policy are the same, then why not simply let monetary policy do the job?... In recent years, the Fed appears to be making the needed adjustments more successfully than ever before, so the role for fiscal policy seems to have diminished…. It is also likely that the use of discretionary fiscal policy could make the Fed's job more difficult.

"In the current context of the U.S. economy, it seems best to let fiscal policy have its main countercyclical impact through the automatic stabilizers," Taylor concluded….

Taylor argued that the automatic stabilizers "represent such a predictable and systematic response" to short-term changes in the economy that "it would be appropriate in the present American context for discretionary fiscal policy to be saved explicitly for longer-term issues."

In an interview yesterday, Taylor said the Bush tax proposal is not an example of the type of "discretionary" fiscal policy whose value he questioned in his article. Instead, the plan addresses longer-term issues, such as reducing marginal income tax rates and reducing the overall tax burden relative to the size of the economy, both of which, he said, will improve economic efficiency.

As for speeding up the cuts, Taylor said, "I don't think it's essential. If that's the timing that's most acceptable to the Congress, that's okay." And there would be some limited impact on the economy from "expectational effects" once the cuts were enacted even if they didn't go into effect immediately, he added. In other words, consumers might spend more now if they know a tax cut is coming later….

Use Your Economic Reasoning

1. In the article, the primary argument against tax cuts is the existence of lags. Why do lags create problems for discretionary fiscal policy?
2. How many types of lags are illustrated in the article? Identify each.
3. Professor Taylor argues that we should rely on monetary policy (the subject of the next chapter) and automatic stabilizers to preserve full employment. What are automatic stabilizers? Provide examples.
4. In a different article, economist Paul Krugman also argues against a tax cut in this situation. But he adds the following: "Fiscal pump-priming has its place; it's appropriate in the face of deep and persistent slumps." Why would it be appropriate then but not today? ("Reckonings: Cheney Gets Vulgar," *New York Times,* Dec. 6, 2000, p. A33)

---

it is still a part of most policy debates, and every student should have some familiarity with the topic.

Whenever the federal government incurs a deficit—be it planned or unplanned—it must finance that deficit by borrowing. This is accomplished by instructing the U.S. Treasury to sell government bonds to individuals, businesses, financial institutions, and government agencies. Each of these transactions increases the public, or national, debt. At the end of 2000, the national debt stood at $3.4 trillion, a figure so large that it is beyond the comprehension of most of us. That amount represents all the borrowing it took to finance several wars, numerous economic downturns, and a variety of government projects and programs.

Concerns About the Public Debt

The size of the public debt troubles many Americans. Some of their concerns are justified, and some are not. In this section we want to lay to rest some myths and examine the real burden of the debt.

Can We Ever Pay Off the Debt?

A common misconception about the public debt is that it must be paid off at some time in the future. In reality, there is no requirement that the federal government ever pay off the debt. In recent years, budget surpluses have allowed the federal government to reduce the size of the public debt, but that is not because it was required to do so. Instead, government may choose to simply refinance the debt year after year with new borrowing. As government bonds become due, the Treasury sells new bonds to take their place. So long as there is a market for government bonds, the government can keep issuing them. And because U.S. bonds are probably the most secure investment in the world today, that market is not likely to disappear.

Does the Public Debt Impose a Burden on Future Generations?

Some critics of the debt suggest that it imposes an unfair burden on future generations, who will be forced to pay higher taxes in order to make the interest payments on the debt.

What this logic overlooks is that one person's debt is another person's asset. Future generations will inherit not only the public debt but also the bonds and other securities that make up the debt. When a future generation pays taxes to service the debt, its members will also be the recipients of the interest payments made by the government. In a sense, this future generation will be paying itself. Of course, some members of the generation will pay more in additional taxes than they receive in interest, while others will receive more in interest than they pay in additional taxes. This will lead to some income redistribution among the members of the generation; some will be better off, and others will be worse off. If this results in greater inequality, we may not like the result. But it's certainly a far cry from the claim that the debt is burdening an entire generation.

Isn't the Foreign-Owned Debt Particularly Burdensome?

It is true that some of our public debt is owed to foreigners, and this portion does threaten to burden future generations. You and your children will pay taxes in order to provide interest payments to foreign investors, whose dollars thus acquired will permit them to claim a share of the goods and services that might otherwise go to other Americans. Consequently, our standard of living may be lowered somewhat.

The percentage of the debt owned by foreigners has been increasing since 1984, when foreign interests owned about 13 percent of the debt. The rate of increase was gradual until 1995, but has been dramatic since then. In 1999, foreigners owned 35 percent of the debt, and received almost 40 percent of all interest payments on the debt. These percentages are well above what we have come to expect, and they are a source of concern for the reason noted above. The next section will clarify the significance of those changes.

Can Americans Afford the Interest Payments on the Public Debt?

Even if the federal government never has to pay off the national debt, it must continue to make interest payments on what it owes. After all, that's why people buy securities—to earn interest.

The ease with which Americans can pay the interest on the debt depends on how rapidly their incomes are growing. As long as incomes are growing at the same rate as interest payments, those interest payments will continue to absorb the same fraction of the average taxpayer's paycheck. But if interest payments grow more rapidly than income, they will begin to absorb a larger share.

If we all owned equal shares of the public debt, paying higher taxes would be offset by receiving interest payments on our shares. But whereas most people pay taxes, only some hold bonds and receive interest on the national debt. To the extent that bondholders have higher incomes to begin with, this process tends to produce greater inequality. This effect is at least partially modified by our progressive income-tax system. Those with higher incomes may receive more in interest payments, but they also pay more in taxes.

The higher tax rates needed to service the debt (that is, to make interest payments on it) may also have a negative effect on the incentive to work and earn taxable income. If individuals are allowed to keep less of what they earn, some may choose to work less. Others may attempt to avoid taxation by performing work that is not reported to taxing authorities—work for friends and barter transactions, for example.

Until about 1975, the burden imposed on taxpayers by the interest charges on the public debt was relatively stable. Exhibit 12.4 shows that although the interest payments were growing, so was our GDP—our measure of the economy's income and output. Thus, our ability to make those interest payments was growing also. The last column in Exh. 12.4 shows that from World War II until 1975, interest payments on the debt represented a relatively constant fraction of GDP—between 1.3 and 1.8 percent. Then, in the late 1970s and early 1980s, the interest cost of the debt began to grow much more rapidly

EXHIBIT 12.4
The Public Debt and Interest Payments in Relation to Gross Domestic Product

YEAR	PUBLIC DEBT (billions)	INTEREST PAYMENT ON DEBT (billions)	GROSS DOMESTIC PRODUCT (billions)	INTEREST AS A PERCENTAGE OF GDP
1930	$ 16.2	$ 0.7	$ 90.7	0.8%
1935	28.7	0.8	68.7	1.2
1940	42.7	0.9	95.4	0.9
1945	235.2	3.1	212.0	1.5
1950	219.0	4.8	265.8	1.8
1955	226.6	4.9	384.7	1.3
1960	236.8	6.9	504.6	1.4
1965	260.8	8.6	671.0	1.3
1970	283.2	14.4	985.4	1.5
1975	394.7	23.2	1,509.8	1.5
1980	709.8	52.5	2,644.1	2.0
1985	1,499.9	129.5	3,967.7	3.3
1990	2,410.7	184.2	5,481.5	3.4
1995	3,603.4	232.2	7,265.4	3.2
2000	3,410.2	222.8	9,962.6	2.2

source: *Economic Report of the President,* 2001.

than GDP, primarily as a result of the record budget deficits that characterized this period. (Note that interest payments on the debt climbed to 2.0 percent of GDP in 1980 and to 3.4 percent in 1990.) This trend has been a major concern for economists and politicians. Fortunately, in 1993 interest payments began to decline as a percentage of GDP. By 1995 they had dropped to 3.2 percent of GDP, and by 2000 to 2.2 percent of GDP, the lowest fraction since 1984. This new trend reflects the surpluses of the last several years, surpluses that have arisen in part because of budget restraint but largely because of the strong performance of the economy. For the present at least, interest payments represent a manageable fraction of GDP.

Concluding Comments on the Public Debt

So what can we conclude about the national debt? Is it something we should stay awake worrying about? Or can we safely ignore it and go about our business? As you've probably guessed, neither of these responses is justified. Given the debt's present size, making the interest payments on the debt does not appear to represent a crushing burden on American taxpayers. Moreover, we can take comfort in the fact that the debt appears to be shrinking, not expanding. On the other hand, the debt is probably larger than it needs to be. Much of the debt was accumulated due to a lack of political restraint in the last two decades, not in response to automatic stabilizers or the use of discretionary policy. The deficit spending that characterized those decades probably caused interest rates to be somewhat higher than they would otherwise have been, with the result that investment spending was probably somewhat lower. Neither of these outcomes has destroyed our economy, but they have likely resulted in somewhat slower economic growth than would have been the case with smaller deficits. Of course, economic growth is not the only goal worth pursuing. But it appears to be a worthy goal. As you will learn later, a fraction of a percent faster growth each year can ultimately make a significant difference in your standard of living. That may make it easier for you to pay the higher Social Security taxes that are probably in store for your generation. Or it may make it possible for you to buy your first home somewhat sooner. So, while you needn't lose any sleep over the size of the national debt, it's not something you should ignore either. Today, the national debt is very manageable. We should urge our congressional representatives to keep it that way.

SUMMARY

The *federal budget* is a statement of the federal government's planned expenditures and anticipated receipts for the coming year. The major source of federal tax revenues is the personal income tax, which is projected to bring in 48 percent of federal tax revenues in 2001. This is followed by social insurance taxes, which are expected to contribute 34 percent of tax revenue. The remaining sources of revenue (excise taxes, estate and gift taxes, and customs duties) are much less important.

The largest category of government expenditures is transfer payments. *Transfer payments* are expenditures for which the government receives no goods or services in return. In 2001, the federal government is expected to spend $993 billion for transfer payments. The fraction of the federal budget consumed by transfer payments has been rising for a number of years. It has increased from approximately 15 percent of federal expenditures in 1970 to more than 50 percent of anticipated outlays for 2001.

The second largest category of federal expenditures is purchases of goods and services. This category includes government spending for national defense and non-defense purchases. In 2001, the federal government anticipated spending $634 billion on goods and services. That represents about 35 percent of total expenditures, down from 50 percent in 1970.

The final category of government expenditures is interest on the debt. In 2001, the federal government projected spending $208 billion on debt interest, down somewhat from 1990.

Although the primary objective of the federal budget is to pay for the activities of the federal government, there is a secondary objective as well. The federal budget may also be used as a tool for influencing the performance of the aggregate economy.

Prior to the 1930s, economists thought that the economy's self-correcting mechanism worked quickly to restore deviations from full employment. The *classical economists* of this time period believed that any reduction in aggregate demand would soon be met by falling wages and prices that would restore full employment. Because of their faith in the economy's ability to heal itself, these classical economists can be described as *nonactivist economists,* economists who do not believe that government should play an active role in attempting to guide the economy's performance.

The Great Depression called this belief into question. In 1936, John Maynard Keynes, a British economist, contended that an economy could find itself in an unemployment equilibrium—a situation in which output and employment are stuck at low levels for some time. Today, we would say that whenever the economy is in equilibrium below potential, a *recessionary gap* exists. Alternatively, if the level of equilibrium GDP exceeds potential, an *inflationary gap* is present.

Activist economists (like Keynes) argue that government policies should be used to eliminate recessionary or inflationary gaps whenever they exist. One form of policy activism involves the use of *discretionary fiscal policy*. Discretionary fiscal policy is the deliberate changing of the level of government spending or taxation in order to guide the economy's performance. According to activists, when a recessionary gap exists, the appropriate fiscal policy would involve increasing government spending or reducing taxes. Either of these policies would tend to increase aggregate demand and close the recessionary gap. When an inflationary gap exists, government spending should be reduced or taxes should be increased. These policies would reduce aggregate demand and thereby reduce inflationary pressures.

In addition to discretionary fiscal policy, the economy contains *automatic stabilizers* that help to improve its performance. Automatic stabilizers are the changes in the level of government spending or taxation that occur automatically whenever the level of aggregate income (GDP) changes. The federal income tax and unemployment compensation are examples of automatic stabilizers. These features of the fiscal system help to reduce the magnitude of fluctuations in total spending and thereby help prevent wide swings in the levels of output and employment.

When we resort to fiscal policy to combat unemployment or inflation, we are deliberately tampering with the federal budget. When unemployment exists, the activist model suggests that government should plan a *deficit budget* in order to stimulate the economy. When inflation is a problem, a *surplus budget* is called for. Only when the economy is operating at full employment is a *balanced budget* appropriate.

Critics of discretionary fiscal policy argue that deficit-financed government spending can be harmful to economic growth because it tends to crowd out private investment spending. *Crowding out* occurs when government borrowing pushes up interest rates and the higher interest rates reduce, or crowd out, investment spending. Because crowding out reduces investment spending, it offsets, at least partially, the expansionary effect of activist fiscal policy. And because investment spending plays a major role in expanding the economy's productive capacity, this reduction in the rate of investment spending will tend to reduce economic growth.

The possibility of crowding out is one criticism of discretionary fiscal policy, but there are others. Another major criticism stems from the substantial time lags that occur between the appearance of a problem (a recessionary or inflationary gap) and the economic impact of the remedial policy. As a consequence, by the time the policy is felt, it may no longer be appropriate to the state of the economy. This criticism has caused many economists, including activists, to argue that discretionary policies should be reserved for combating major downturns or inflationary episodes, not minor fluctuations.

A final limitation of discretionary fiscal policy is its *expansionary bias*: Expansionary fiscal policy is more attractive politically than contractionary policy. This makes it easy to incur deficits, but difficult to incur surpluses.

When the federal government incurs a deficit, it finances that deficit by borrowing. This results in an increase in the *public debt*—the accumulated borrowing of the federal government. The public debt is a source of concern to many Americans and does impose some burdens on our society. That the government must make interest payments on the debt means that taxes will be higher than would otherwise be necessary. Since not all taxpayers are bondholders, this results in some income redistribution from taxpayers in general to bondholders in particular. In addition, the dollars that foreign investors acquire as interest payments permit them to claim a share of the goods and services produced in our economy.

The burden of the debt is perhaps best represented by interest payments (on the debt) as a fraction of GDP. Although this ratio increased in the 1980s, it has been declining since 1993. This decline represents, in large part, the impact of a strong economy. The economy's strength has provided the federal government with budget surpluses—surpluses that have allowed the federal government to reduce the size of the national debt and the interest payments that accompany it.

KEY TERMS

Activist economists
Automatic stabilizers
Balanced budget
Budget deficit
Budget surplus

Classical economists
Crowding out
Discretionary fiscal policy
Federal budget
Inflationary gap

Nonactivist economists
Public debt
Recessionary gap
Transfer payments

STUDY QUESTIONS

Fill in the Blanks

1. Government expenditures for which no goods or services are received in exchange are known as _Transfer payments_.

2. In the period from 1960 to 2001, the fraction of government receipts coming from _Social Insurance_ taxes increased dramatically.

3. Economists who see a role for government in guiding the economy's performance are described as _activist_.

4. According to the activist (or Keynesian) model, if an economy is experiencing unemployment, the federal government should _Increase Government G/P_ or _reduce taxes_ or do both.

5. If the federal government spends more than it takes in from tax revenues, we say that it is incurring a _deficits_; if it takes in more in taxes than it spends, it has a _surpluses_.

6. The amount by which the equilibrium GDP falls short of potential GDP is known as the _recessionary_ gap.

7. The deliberate changing of government spending or taxation in order to guide the economy's performance is referred to as _discretionary fiscal policy_.

8. _Automatic Stabilizers_ tend to reduce the magnitude of fluctuations in total spending without any action by policymakers.

9. According to the activist model, the appropriate fiscal policy to combat inflation

would be to _reduce Your Expending_ or _Increase Taxes_ or do both.

10. If the economy is operating at full employment and Congress decides to engage in deficit spending, the result would probably be _Inflaction_.

11. According to activists, a _Balance_ budget would be appropriate if the economy was operating at full employment.

12. The accumulated borrowings of the federal government are called the _National debt_.

13. Examples of automatic stabilizers include unemployment compensation and the _Federal Income Tax Fitor_.

14. Political considerations may make it particularly difficult to use fiscal policy in combating _Inflaction_.

15. The time that elapses before policymakers recognize the need for a policy change is known as the _recognition_ lag.

Multiple Choice

1. In the period from 1960 to 2001,
   a) personal income taxes have grown as a fraction of federal tax revenue.
   b) corporate income taxes have grown as a fraction of federal tax revenue.
   c) social insurance taxes have grown as a fraction of federal tax revenue.
   d) excise taxes have grown as a fraction of federal tax revenue.

2. The largest category of federal government expenditures is
   a) interest on the national debt.
   b) transfer payments.
   c) purchases of goods and services.
   d) military spending.

3. According to activists, when the economy is experiencing unemployment, the federal government should
   a) increase taxes.
   b) reduce government spending.
   c) deliberately incur a surplus budget.
   d) reduce taxes.

4. When an inflationary gap exists, activists would recommend a
   a) tax reduction.
   b) surplus budget.
   c) increase in government spending.
   d) deficit budget.

Use the following exhibit in answering questions 5–8:

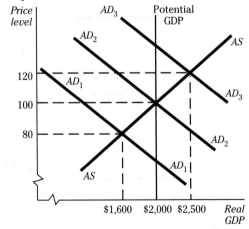

5. If the economy is in equilibrium at the intersection of AD_1 and AS, then
   a) a recessionary gap exists; the gap is equal to $400 billion.
   b) a recessionary gap exists; the gap is equal to $900 billion.
   c) an inflationary gap exists; the gap is equal to $400 billion.
   d) an inflationary gap exists; the gap is equal to $900 billion.

6. If the economy is in equilibrium at the intersection of the AS curve and
   a) AD_1, activists would recommend a surplus budget.
   b) AD_2, activists would recommend a balanced budget.
   c) AD_3, activists would recommend a deficit budget.
   d) AD_2, activists would recommend a deficit budget.

7. **Review Question:** Suppose the economy is in short-run equilibrium at an output of $1,600 billion. If activist policies are not used, the economy will
   a) eventually return to an output of $2,000 billion but at a price level less than 80.
   b) eventually return to an output of $2,000 billion but at a price level of 120.
   c) remain at an output of $1,600 billion indefinitely.
   d) eventually return to an output of $2,000 billion but at a price level of 100.

8. **Review Question.** Suppose the economy is in short-run equilibrium at an output of $2,500 billion. If activist policies are not used, the economy will
   a) return to an output of $2,000 billion when wage contracts expire and the aggregate demand curve shifts to the left.
   b) remain at an output of $2,500 billion indefinitely.
   c) return to an output of $2,000 billion when wage contracts are renegotiated and the aggregate supply curve shifts left.
   d) return to an output of $2,000 billion when the aggregate demand curve automatically shifts back to AD_2.

9. Which of the following is *not* an advantage of automatic stabilizers?
   a) They do not involve the political hassle associated with discretionary fiscal policy.
   b) They help speed recovery from a recession.
   c) They go to work automatically, so that lags are minimal.
   d) They help prevent a minor downturn from becoming a major recession.

10. Because of automatic stabilizers, the budget will
    a) tend toward surplus during a recession.
    b) tend toward deficit during an economic expansion.
    c) tend toward deficit during a recession.
    d) always remain in balance.

11. According to the activist model, when the economy is in a recession, the shortest route to a balanced budget may entail
    a) higher taxes.
    b) less government spending.
    c) lower taxes and more government spending.
    d) Both a and b

12. Which of the following statements is false?
    a) If the economy is operating at full unemployment, a reduction in taxes may increase inflationary pressures.
    b) If the economy is experiencing unemployment, increased government spending may help combat the problem.
    c) Deficit spending is desirable only when the economy is experiencing inflation.
    d) If we attempt to balance the budget during a period of unemployment, we may aggravate the unemployment problem.

13. A legitimate concern regarding the national debt relates to
    a) the higher taxes that are necessary to make the interest payments on the debt.
    b) our inability to pay off such a large sum.
    c) the fraction of the debt owed to foreign factions.
    d) Both a and c

14. "Crowding out" occurs when
    a) U.S. producers lose sales to foreign competition.
    b) an increase in taxes results in a lower level of consumption spending.
    c) foreign interests buy government securities.
    d) government borrowing forces up interest rates and reduces the level of private investment spending.

15. Deficit spending is *least* likely to harm economic growth if it
    a) occurs when the economy is operating at or beyond potential GDP.
    b) is used to finance increases in transfer payments.
    c) crowds out a substantial amount of investment spending.
    d) occurs when there is substantial unemployment.

16. The lags associated with discretionary fiscal policy
    a) make it more effective.
    b) may make it counterproductive.
    c) apply only to changes in government spending, not to changes in tax rates.
    d) apply only to changes in tax rates, not to changes in government spending.

17. The phrase *expansionary bias* refers to the fact that
    a) discretionary fiscal policy works with a lagged effect.
    b) politicians are more willing to lower taxes and increase spending than they are to do the opposite.
    c) policymakers tend to overestimate the size of the recessionary gap.
    d) deficit-financed government spending can lead to crowding out.

Problems and Questions for Discussion

1. When the government increases spending to combat unemployment, why shouldn't it increase taxes to pay for the increased spending? Why run a deficit instead?

2. Deficit spending for education and scientific research may impose less of a tax burden on future generations than deficit-financed increases in transfer payments. Explain.

3. Some experts argue that the ratio of interest payments (on the debt) to GDP is the most reasonable measure of the burden the public debt imposes on society. Explain.

4. Most deficits are not the result of discretionary fiscal policy; they are the result of downturns in the economy. Explain.

5. Why is the fraction of the debt owed to foreigners more troublesome than the fraction we owe to ourselves?

6. What advantages can you see to using tax reductions rather than government spending increases to combat unemployment?

Can your personal values influence which of these approaches you prefer? Explain.

7. George Humphrey, secretary of the treasury during the Eisenhower administration, once declared: "We cannot spend ourselves rich." What do you suppose he meant? Would Keynes agree? Why or why not?

8. List the various types of lags associated with fiscal policy. Why is the existence of lags a serious limitation of such policies?

9. Suppose the federal government decided to pay off the public debt. How would it go about doing it? What do you suppose would be the impact on the economy?

10. Concern over continuing federal deficits once spawned a movement to amend the Constitution of the United States to require the federal government to balance its budget each year. Can you think of any reasons to argue against a balanced budget amendment? Why would it be difficult to carry out such a rule during a recession?

ANSWER KEY

Fill in the Blanks

1. transfer payments
2. social insurance taxes
3. activists
4. increase government spending, reduce taxes
5. deficit, surplus
6. recessionary
7. discretionary fiscal policy
8. Automatic stabilizers
9. reduce government spending, increase taxes
10. inflation
11. balanced
12. public or national debt
13. federal income tax
14. inflation
15. recognition

Multiple Choice

1. c
2. b
3. d
4. b
5. a
6. b
7. a
8. c
9. b
10. c
11. c
12. c
13. d
14. d
15. d
16. b
17. b

CHAPTER **THIRTEEN**

Money, Banking, and Monetary Policy

LEARNING OBJECTIVES

1. State the three basic functions of money and explain each.
2. Distinguish between money and near money.
3. Distinguish between the M-1 and M-2 money-supply definitions.
4. Explain how depository institutions create money.
5. Calculate the deposit multiplier and explain its purpose.
6. Discuss the functions of the Federal Reserve.
7. Define monetary policy.
8. Describe the three major policy tools the Fed uses to control the money supply.
9. Explain how changes in the money supply lead to changes in output, employment, and prices.
10. Discuss the factors that limit the effectiveness of monetary policy.

Everything you've read thus far in the text has implied a monetary system—the existence of some kind of money. Most of us take the use of money for granted. We pay our bills in money and expect to be paid in money. We compare prices, incomes, and even gross domestic products in terms of money. But exactly what is money, and why is it essential to an economic system? What determines the amount of money in existence, and where does it come from? In this chapter we will provide answers to those questions. We begin by considering the functions performed by money and deciding what constitutes money in the U.S. economy. Next, we examine how banks "create" money, and consider why individuals can't do the same. Then we introduce you to the Federal Reserve—the independent government agency responsible for regulating the money supply and performing other duties related to the banking system. You will discover how the Fed attempts to use monetary policy to guide the economy's performance and what the limitations of its policies are. Let's start by examining what is meant by money.

WHAT IS MONEY?

Economists define money in terms of the functions it performs; anything that performs the functions of money *is* money. Money performs three basic functions. First, money serves as a **medium of exchange:** the generally accepted means of payment for goods and services. A medium of exchange enables members of a society to transact their business without resorting to barter. In a barter economy, goods are exchanged for goods. A shoemaker who wants to buy a painting must locate an artist in need of shoes. As you can imagine, this requirement makes trading slow and burdensome. Money facilitates trade by permitting the shoemaker to exchange shoes for money and then use the money to purchase a painting or other goods and services.

The second function of money is to provide a **standard of value,** a unit for expressing the prices of goods and services. In a barter economy, we would need an almost endless list of prices, one for each possible exchange. For example, we might find that one painting equals (exchanges for) one pair of shoes and that one pair of shoes equals four bushels of apples and that four bushels of apples equals two shirts. Which is more expensive: a shirt or a pair of shoes? It may take you a moment to figure out the answer because the absence of a standard of value makes the communication and comparison of prices very difficult. The use of money simplifies this process by enabling us to state all prices in terms of a particular standard of value, such as the dollar. Using the dollar as a standard of value, we can easily determine that if a pair of shoes sells for $50 and a shirt sells for $25, the shoes are twice as expensive as the shirt.

Finally, money is a **store of value,** a vehicle for accumulating or storing wealth to be used at some future date. A tomato farmer would find it difficult to accumulate wealth in the form of tomatoes. They don't keep very well! Money is not a perfect store of value, especially in inflationary times, but clearly it is better than a bushel of perishable tomatoes. By exchanging the tomato crop for money, the farmer can begin to build a nest egg for retirement or to save for some major purchase—a tractor or a new barn, for example. In a sense, the availability of a store of value widens the range of spending choices available to individuals and businesses. Their options are no longer limited to what they can afford to buy (trade for) with a single period's income.

Money and Near Money

What qualifies as money in the U.S. economy? We all know that coins and paper currency are money, and a check is usually as good as cash. Non-interest-bearing checking deposits at commercial banks[1] are known as **demand deposits** since the bank promises to pay at once, or "on demand," the amount specified by the owner of the account. Checks drawn on demand-deposit accounts are an accepted medium of exchange; they are measured in dollars, the standard of value in the United States, and it is certainly possible to accumulate wealth in your checking account. But although it is relatively easy to agree that currency—coins and paper money—and demand deposits are money, some other assets are more difficult to categorize. An **asset** is anything of value owned by an entity—that is, by an individual or an organization, such as a business. Many assets perform some, but not all, of the functions of money. Others perform all the functions of money but do so incompletely.

One debate among economists concerns the proper classification of **savings deposits**—interest-bearing deposits at banks and savings institutions. The traditional passbook savings account cannot be used directly to purchase goods and services; hence, such deposits do not qualify as a medium of exchange. As a consequence, economists have generally classified savings deposits as **near money**—assets that are not money but that can be converted quickly into money. Not everyone has supported this position, however. Some economists argue that savings deposits should be considered money because they can be converted easily into cash or demand deposits and therefore have essentially the same impact on spending as other financial assets do.

Innovations in banking, moreover, have blurred the distinction between savings deposits and demand deposits. Consider, for example, the negotiable order of withdrawal (NOW) account commonly offered by banks and other financial institutions. The **NOW account** is essentially a savings account on which the depositor is permitted to write checks. Here we seem to have the best of both worlds: the convenience of a checking account plus the earning power of a savings account. Banks have also developed automatic transfer service (ATS) accounts, in which funds from savings can be transferred automatically to a checking account. These types of deposits probably should be considered along with demand deposits as a form of money. But we still face the task of categorizing financial assets that do not function as media of ex-

---

[1] Commercial banks are so named because in their early days, they specialized in loans to businesses. Today, commercial banks engage in a much wider range of lending, including home-mortgage loans, automobile loans, and other consumer loans.

change. These include passbook savings accounts, U.S. government savings bonds, and shares in money-market mutual funds.[2] Are such assets money or not? The answer is not clear, even to the Federal Reserve.

Credit Cards and Debit Cards

If you're accustomed to paying for your books (or your pizza) with a credit card, you probably wonder where that "plastic" fits into this classification system. After all, credit cards seem to work as well as cash, and they are often even more convenient. Actually, credit cards are neither money nor near money; they are simply a means of deferring payment. (Said differently, credit cards are a way of obtaining credit—loans; hence the term *credit card*.) When you pay for something with cash or a check, you have completed the transaction. But when you buy something with a credit card, you are incurring a debt that you ultimately will have to settle by sending the credit card company either cash or a check.

The cousin of the credit card is the *debit card*, a card that allows you to withdraw money automatically from your checking account. When you use a debit card to make a purchase, you are, in effect, telling your bank to withdraw money from your account and transfer it to the store owner's account. Since a debit card is simply a way of accessing your checking balance, it does not constitute a different type of money.

Definitions of the Money Supply

As we noted earlier, the Federal Reserve is responsible for controlling the money supply—the total amount of money in the economy. Before the Fed (as the Federal Reserve is often called) can attempt to control the money supply, it must, of course, decide what money is.

Rather than settling on a single definition of money, the Fed has developed several. The narrowest, **M-1,** is composed of currency in the hands of the public *plus* checkable deposits. **Checkable deposits** are all types of deposits on which customers can write checks: demand deposits at commercial banks; NOW accounts; credit union share draft accounts, which are essentially the same as NOW accounts but are provided by credit unions; and ATS accounts. The primary characteristic of all M-1 money is that it can

---

[2] A mutual fund is an organization that pools people's money and invests it in stocks or bonds or other financial assets. A money-market mutual fund invests in short-term securities, such as U.S. Treasury bills. If you own shares in a money-market mutual fund, you can write checks against your account, but generally they must exceed some minimum amount (commonly $500). This makes money-market funds less useful for everyday transactions involving smaller amounts of money.

function easily as a medium of exchange. As you can see from Exh. 13.1, about 49 percent of this readily spendable money is in the form of currency. Demand deposits account for another 29 percent of the M-1 money supply. The remaining 22 percent is in other checkable deposits.

The Federal Reserve also classifies the money supply according to two broader definitions: M-2 and M-3. The **M-2** portion of the money supply includes everything in M-1 *plus* money-market mutual fund balances, money-market deposits at savings institutions, and certain other financial assets that do not function as a medium of exchange but that can be converted easily into currency or checkable deposits—small savings deposits (less than $100,000) at banks and savings institutions, for example.

An even broader measure of the money supply is **M-3**. It includes everything in M-2 *plus* large savings deposits (over $100,000) and other financial assets that are designed essentially to be used as business savings accounts.

Throughout this chapter and the remainder of the text, we will use the M-1 definition of money: We assume that money consists of currency plus checkable deposits. These assets function easily as a medium of exchange, the function that many economists regard as the most important characteristic of money.

EXHIBIT 13.1

M-1, M-2, and M-3 as of January 2001 (billions of dollars)

M-1

Currency (coins and paper money)	$ 534.3
Demand deposits	317.0
Other checkable deposits	249.8
Total M-1	$1,101.1

M-2

M-1 plus small savings accounts and money-market mutual fund balances	$4,998.0

M-3

M-2 plus large savings deposits and other financial assets that provide an outlet for business saving	$7,190.0

Source: *Federal Reserve Statistical Release* "Money Stock and Debt Measures," March 15, 2001.

HOW DEPOSITORY INSTITUTIONS CREATE MONEY

Where does M-1 money come from? The currency component is easy to explain. It comes from the Federal Reserve, which supplies banks with enough coins and paper money to meet the needs of their customers. (Here and throughout the chapter, we use the term *bank* in a general way, to refer to all types of depository institutions—commercial banks and savings, or thrift, institutions.[3]) But the checkable-deposits element of M-1 is more of a mystery. Checkable deposits are actually created by the numerous banks that offer such accounts.

A Bank's Balance Sheet

To demonstrate how banks create checkable-deposit money, we can use a simple accounting concept known as a balance sheet. A **balance sheet** is a statement of a business's assets and liabilities. The assets of a business are, as we saw earlier, the things of value that it owns. **Liabilities** are the debts of the business, what it owes. The difference between the business's assets and liabilities is the **owners' equity,** which represents the interest of the owner or owners of a business in its assets. These accounting statements "balance"; whatever value of the business is not owed to creditors must belong to the owners: assets = liabilities + owners' equity.

We turn now to Exh. 13.2 to examine the balance sheet of a hypothetical bank, the Gainsville National Bank. The left-hand side of the balance sheet lists the bank's assets. The first entry, *reserves,* includes cash in the bank's vault plus funds on deposit with the Federal Reserve. Banks are required by law to hold a certain amount of their assets as required reserves. The **reserve requirement** is stated as a percentage of the bank's checkable deposits and can be met only by cash in its vault and deposits with the Fed. Because reserves earn no interest income, banks understandably try to maintain only the minimum legal requirement. Reserves greater than the minimum requirement are called **excess reserves,** and they play an important role in a bank's ability to create checkable-deposit money.

The next two entries on the left-hand side, *securities* and *loans,* are the interest-earning assets of the bank. Banks usually have substantial holdings of U.S. Treasury bills and other securities that are both safe and highly liquid—that is, easily converted into cash. Loans offer less liquidity but generally have the advantage of earning a higher rate of interest.

---

[3] There are three major types of thrift institutions: savings and loan associations, mutual savings banks, and credit unions.

EXHIBIT 13.2
A Hypothetical Balance Sheet: Gainsville National Bank

ASSETS		LIABILITIES AND OWNERS' EQUITY	
Reserves (vault cash plus deposits with the Federal Reserve)	$ 200,000	Checkable deposits	$1,000,000
		Savings deposits	360,000
Securities	450,000	Owners' equity	240,000
Loans	800,000		
Property	150,000	Total liabilities	
Total assets	$1,600,000	+ owners' equity	$1,600,000

The final entry on the left-hand side of the balance sheet is *property*, the physical assets of the bank: the bank building, its office equipment, and any other nonfinancial holdings of the organization.

The right-hand side of the balance sheet lists liabilities and owners' equity. In our example the only liabilities entered are *checkable deposits* and *savings deposits*. Although both items are assets for customers, they are debts to the bank. If we write a check on our checking account or ask to withdraw money from our savings account, the bank has to pay. That makes each of those accounts a liability to the bank.

The only remaining entry on the right-hand side of Exh. 13.2 is *owners' equity*, the owners' claims on the assets of the business. As you know, the two sides of the statement have to balance, because whatever value of the business is not owed to creditors (the bank's liabilities) must belong to the owners (owners' equity).

The Creation of Checkable Deposits

Earlier we noted that all banks must meet a reserve requirement established by the Federal Reserve. Let's assume that the reserve requirement for our hypothetical bank is 20 percent. Our bank has $1,000,000 in checkable deposits; therefore, it is required by law to maintain $200,000 in reserves ($1,000,000 × 0.20 = $200,000). As you can see from the bank's balance sheet, it has precisely $200,000 in reserves.

Even in the absence of regulation, banks would need to maintain some reserves against their deposits. The bank must have the currency to pay a depositor who walks into the Gainsville Bank and writes a check for "cash." However, the bank does not have to maintain $1 in reserve for every $1 of checkable deposits it accepts, because it is unlikely that all depositors will request their money simultaneously. In fact, while some depositors are writing checks and drawing down their accounts, others are making deposits and thereby increasing their balances.

The key to a bank's ability to create money is this **fractional reserve principle,** the principle that a bank needs to maintain only a fraction of a dollar in reserve for each dollar of its checkable deposits. Once a bank discovers this principle, it can loan out the idle funds and earn interest. That's the name of the game in banking—earning interest by lending money. In the process of making loans, banks create money: specifically, checkable deposits. We can see how this is true by working through the balance sheet entries of the lending bank. In order to simplify things somewhat, we will show only the changes in assets and liabilities for each entry, not the entire balance sheet.

Step One: Accepting Deposits

Let's assume that one of the bank's depositors, Adam Swift, deposits $1,000 in cash in his checking account. We would reflect this change by increasing the bank's checkable deposits by $1,000 and increasing its reserves by the same amount.

The bank now has an additional $1,000 in cash reserves (clearly an asset) and the liability of paying out that same amount if Mr. Swift writes checks totaling $1,000. Because the bank's deposits have increased by $1,000, it must now maintain an additional $200 in required reserves (20 percent of $1,000). The Gainsville Bank now finds itself with excess reserves of $800:

GAINSVILLE NATIONAL BANK

ASSETS			LIABILITIES	
Reserves		+$1,000	Checkable deposits	+$1,000
required	+$200			
excess	+$800			
	-	+$1,000		+$1,000

What will the Gainsville Bank do with those excess reserves? If it simply let them sit in the vault, it would be sacrificing the interest that could be earned on $800. Because the bank wants to show a profit, it will probably use those excess reserves to make loans.

Step Two: Making a Loan

Let's assume that another resident of Gainsville, June Malthus, walks in and asks to borrow $800. How will we record this transaction? On the asset side, we will record a loan for $800. The bank receives this asset in the form of a note, or IOU, agreeing to repay the $800 plus interest. On the liability side of the balance sheet, we increase checkable deposits by $800 (from $1,000 to $1,800):

GAINSVILLE NATIONAL BANK

ASSETS		LIABILITIES		
Reserves	$1,000	Checkable deposits		$1,800
Loans	+$ 800	Adam Swift	$1,000	
		June Malthus	$ 800	
	$1,800			$1,800

This last entry may seem puzzling to you if you have not yet borrowed money. The way you generally receive money borrowed from a bank is in the form of a checking account with your name on it. This is the money-creating transaction of the bank. Ms. Malthus has exchanged a piece of paper (an IOU) that is *not* money for something that *is* money, checkable deposits. If you think about this process, you'll see the logic of it: The Gainsville Bank is now using $1,000 in reserves to support $1,800 of checkable deposits. And because of the fractional reserve principle, bank officials can be confident that this support is adequate; they know that not all the original depositors will withdraw their money simultaneously.

Not everyone can create money through lending. When you lend money to a friend, your friend ends up with more money, but you have less. The total money supply has not increased. However, when you borrow money from a bank, you end up with more money, but no one has any less. And the money supply actually increases.

How do we explain the difference? Your IOU does not circulate as money, whereas the IOU of a bank does. What happens when you deposit cash in your checking account? You do not reduce your personal money supply as you would if you had made a loan to your friend. Instead, you merely exchange cash (a form of money) for an IOU known as a checkable deposit (a different form of money). Your currency then serves as reserves for supporting loans that result in the creation of additional deposits. Someone else ends up with more money, but you don't have any less. Once you understand this process, you can see that the bank has really "created" money.

Step Three: Using the Loan

Now that we have seen how banks create money, we can ask what happens to that money when it is used to buy something. Let's assume that Ms. Malthus uses her newly acquired checking account to buy furniture in the nearby town of Sellmore—at the Sellmore Furniture Store. Let's also assume that she spends the entire amount of her loan. She will write a check on the Gainsville Bank and give it to the owner of the Sellmore Furniture Store, who will deposit it in the firm's account at the First National Bank of Sellmore. The Sellmore Bank will then send the check to the district Federal Reserve Bank for collection. (One function of the Federal Reserve is to provide a check collection and clearing service. We'll discuss this and other functions of the Fed later in the chapter.) After the Federal Reserve Bank receives the check, it will reduce the reserve account of the Gainsville Bank by $800 and increase the reserve account of the Sellmore Bank by $800. It will then forward the check to the Gainsville Bank, where changes in assets and liabilities will be recorded. Ms. Malthus has spent the $800 in her checking account; so checkable deposits will be reduced by that amount (from $1,800 to $1,000). The bank's reserves have also fallen by $800 (from $1,000 to $200), the amount of reserves lost to the Sellmore Bank.

GAINSVILLE NATIONAL BANK

ASSETS			LIABILITIES		
Reserves		$ 200	Checkable deposits		$1,000
($1,000 − $800)			($1,800 − $800)		
required	$200		Adam Swift	$1,000	
excess	0		June Malthus	0	
Loans		+$ 800			
		$1,000			$1,000

Note that the Gainsville Bank no longer has any excess reserves. It has reserves of $200, the exact amount required. If the bank had loaned Ms. Malthus more than $800 (the initial amount of its excess reserves), it would now be in violation of the reserve requirement. But each bank realizes that when it makes a loan, it will probably lose reserves to other banks as the borrower spends the loan. For that reason, *individual banks must limit their loans to the amount of their excess reserves.* That's one of the most important principles in this chapter; so be sure you understand it before reading any further.

The Multiple Expansion of Loans and Deposits

Recall that the money lent in the form of checkable deposits circulates. Thus, the money created when the Gainsville Bank made a loan to Ms. Malthus is not destroyed when she uses the loan but rather is simply transferred from one bank to another. The checkable deposits and reserves originally represented on the balance sheet of the Gainsville Bank may now be found on the balance sheet of the Sellmore Bank. This means that the Sellmore Bank will now be able to expand its loans.

We know that each bank can expand its loans to create checkable deposits equal to the amount of its excess reserves. Assuming that the Sellmore Bank also faces a reserve requirement of 20 percent and that it had no excess reserves to begin with, it will now have excess reserves of $640. How did we arrive at that amount? The Sellmore Bank increased its checkable deposits, and thus its reserves, by $800, the amount deposited by the owner of the Sellmore Furniture Store. With a 20 percent reserve requirement, the increase in required reserves is $160 ($800 × 0.20 = $160). That leaves $640 in excess reserves, which can be used to support new loans and create additional checking deposits.

This expansion of loans and deposits continues as the money created by one bank is deposited in another bank, where it is used to support even more loans. In Exh. 13.3, we see that the banking system as a whole can eventually create $4,000 in new loans and new money (checkable deposits) from the initial $800 increase in excess reserves received by the Gainsville Bank. We also see the difference between the ability of a single bank and the banking system as a whole to create money. Whereas an individual bank must restrict its loans—and consequently its ability to create money—to the amount of its excess reserves, the banking system as a whole can create loans and deposits equal to some multiple of the excess reserves received by the system. In our example that multiple is 5; the banking system was able to create loans and deposits five times greater than the initial increase in excess reserves ($800 × 5 = $4,000).

The Deposit Multiplier

Fortunately we need not work through all the individual transactions to predict the maximum amount of money that the banking system will be able to create. As a general rule, the banking system can alter the money supply by an amount equal to the initial change in excess reserves times the reciprocal of the reserve requirement:

$$\text{Change in excess reserves} \times \frac{1}{\substack{\text{Reserve requirement} \\ \text{(written as a decimal)}}} = \substack{\text{Maximum possible increase in} \\ \text{checkable deposits by the} \\ \text{banking system as a whole}}$$

EXHIBIT 13.3

The Creation of Money by the Banking System

BANK	NEWLY ACQUIRED DEPOSITS AND RESERVES	REQUIRED RESERVES (20 percent of checkable deposits)	POTENTIAL FOR NEW LOANS (creating money)
Gainsville	$1,000.00	$200.00	$ 800.00
Sellmore	800.00	160.00	640.00
Third bank	640.00	128.00	512.00
Fourth bank	512.00	102.40	409.60
Fifth bank	409.60	81.92	327.68
Sixth bank	327.68	65.54	262.14
Seventh bank	262.14	52.43	209.71
All others	1,048.58	209.71	838.87
Total amount of money created by the banking system			$4,000.00*

*This figure represents the *maximum* amount of money that the banking system could create from an initial $800 increase in excess reserves. The example assumes that all banks face a 20 percent reserve requirement and that they are all "loaned up" (have no excess reserves) initially.

The reciprocal of the reserve requirement, 1 divided by the reserve requirement, yields a number called the deposit multiplier. The **deposit multiplier** is the multiple by which checkable deposits (in the entire banking system) increase or decrease in response to an initial change in excess reserves.

The reserve ratio in our hypothetical example is 0.20, and so the deposit multiplier must be 1/.20, or 5. Therefore, an $800 increase in excess reserves will permit the banking system to create up to $4,000 of new demand deposits. This $4,000 figure is really the *maximum* possible expansion in checkable deposits, given the stated change in excess reserves and the existing reserve requirement. The actual amount may, for a variety of reasons, be less than the maximum predicted.

An illustration will help: Suppose that the recipient of Ms. Malthus's check decides not to redeposit the entire amount in a checking account. This event will reduce the amount of money being passed on to the remaining banks in the system and thus reduce the amount the system can create through lending. The expansion in checkable deposits will also be less than the maximum if bankers maintain some excess reserves. For instance, perhaps some bankers anticipate deposit withdrawals and prepare for them by holding, rather than lending, excess reserves. Or banks may be forced to hold excess reserves simply because they cannot find enough loan customers. For all these reasons, the expansion in the checkable-deposit component of the money supply may be substantially less than the maximum predicted by the deposit multiplier.

The Destruction of Checkable Deposits

The deposit multiplier can also work in reverse. Suppose that Adam Swift, our original depositor, withdrew $1,000 in cash from his account at the Gainsville Bank and kept it in his wallet. What would this transaction do to the money supply? The initial transaction merely changes its composition: Mr. Swift is giving up his claim to $1,000 in checkable deposits (a form of money) and is receiving in return $1,000 in cash (another form of money). The size of the money supply remains the same, even though more cash and fewer checkable deposits are in circulation.

What happens next? When Mr. Swift withdraws $1,000 from his checking account, the Gainsville Bank loses $1,000 in deposits and reserves:

GAINSVILLE NATIONAL BANK

ASSETS		LIABILITIES	
Reserves	−$1,000	Checkable deposits	−$1,000

Assuming that the bank had no excess reserves to begin with, it now finds itself with a reserve deficiency; that is, it doesn't have sufficient reserves to meet the 20 percent reserve requirement. What is the amount of the deficiency? It is $800—the difference between the amount that Mr. Swift has withdrawn from his checking account ($1,000) and the reserve that the bank was required to maintain on that deposit ($200). To correct this deficiency, the bank has two choices. One is to sell $800 worth of securities (remember, banks hold securities, particularly government securities, which earn interest and can be converted easily into cash); another is to allow $800 worth of loans to be repaid without making new loans. In either case, the next bank in the sequence is going to lose $800 worth of deposits and reserves as its depositors buy those securities or repay those loans. That bank will then be faced with a reserve deficiency; it too may need to sell securities or reduce the amount of its loans to build up reserves.

As you may suspect, this contractionary process can spread to other banks in the system and result in a multiple contraction of loans and deposits that is similar to the multiple expansion we observed earlier. Once again, the limit to this process is set by the reserve requirement and the deposit multiplier derived from that requirement. To predict the maximum contraction in checkable deposits, we multiply the initial reserve deficiency times the deposit multiplier. In our example that would mean a reduction of $4,000 ($800 × 5 = $4,000).

THE FEDERAL RESERVE SYSTEM

Now we are ready to examine the role of the Federal Reserve, the central bank of the United States. Virtually every industrialized nation in the world has a **central bank**—a government agency responsible for controlling the national money supply. At one time, the size of a nation's money supply was determined largely by its stock of gold. That's because most of a nation's money supply was currency, and virtually all nations "backed" their currency with gold.[4] But things change. Today, nothing backs the U. S. dollar (or any other major currency) except the faith that the currency can be used to make purchases. And currency is no longer the most important component of the money supply in most industrialized nations; that role has been assumed by checkable deposits. As a consequence, the size of a nation's money supply is no longer tied to its gold stock. Instead, it is determined by its central bank. In the United Kingdom the central bank is the Bank of England, in Germany the Bundesbank, in the United States the Federal Reserve System.

The Origin of the Federal Reserve

The Federal Reserve was established in 1913. Its original purpose was to act as a "lender of last resort," to make loans to banks only when all other sources had dried up. It was thought that by performing this function, the Federal Reserve could prevent or stop the financial panics that had characterized this period. A *financial panic* is a situation in which depositors lose confidence in banks and rush to withdraw their money. The panics of this period were usually precipitated by a shortage of cash reserves: Some banks

---

[4] For example, between 1900 and 1933 the United States issued gold certificates that could be redeemed for gold coins. In 1934 the United States stopped *redeeming* currency for gold but continued to maintain 25 percent gold backing for currency. (The Fed could issue $4 of currency for each $1 of gold it held.) Throughout this period, gold continued to be used to pay international debts, and this gradually caused the U.S. gold supply to shrink to low levels. (The reasons for this gradual outflow of gold are discussed in Chapter 17.) In 1968, the requirement that Fed currency be backed by a gold reserve was eliminated, and in 1971 the United States stopped using gold to settle international debts. That few people noticed either of these events is an indication that the value of our currency stems from what it can buy, not from the backing provided by some scarce commodity.

found that they had too little cash to satisfy their customers, and were forced to close their doors. This led to a general distrust of banks and to additional bank closings and business failures. It was felt that by acting as lender of last resort, the Fed could stop any financial panic before it got under way and would thus prevent the bank closings and business failures of previous panics. In addition to this primary function, the Federal Reserve was also authorized to provide an efficient mechanism for collecting and clearing checks throughout the United States and to help supervise banks to ensure the prudence of their investment and lending practices.

Today, the primary responsibility of the Fed is to help stabilize the economy by controlling the money supply. We expect the Federal Reserve to manipulate the money supply in an effort to prevent (or combat) unemployment or inflation, a responsibility much broader than the one envisioned by Congress in 1913. Because the responsibility for controlling the money supply grew as the federal government assumed a greater role in managing the economy, the modern Federal Reserve organization is far more powerful than Congress intended it to be.[5] Some contemporary economists believe that the

[5] Unlike central banks in other nations, the Federal Reserve is an independent organization that is not required to take orders from any other agency or branch of government. This gives the Federal Reserve at least the appearance of somewhat greater independence than other central banks. Members of Congress periodically threaten to revoke this independence when the Fed pursues policies they disagree with.

Alan Greenspan, chairman of the Federal Reserve, has been described as the second most powerful person in the world.

Fed's powers to influence the economy should be sharply curtailed; others argue that a strong Federal Reserve is necessary to combat unemployment and prevent inflation. (We'll look further at this debate in Chapter 14.)

The Organization of the Federal Reserve System

The Federal Reserve System is composed of a board of governors, twelve Federal Reserve banks, and several thousand member banks. The board of governors is the policymaking body of the Federal Reserve. It consists of a chairperson (currently Alan Greenspan) and six members, all appointed by the president of the United States to serve fourteen-year terms. These terms are structured so that only one expires every two years, which helps to provide continuity and to insulate board members somewhat from political pressure. The primary function of the board is to make the major policy decisions that determine how rapidly or slowly the nation's money supply will grow.

To implement these decisions, twelve Federal Reserve banks (plus twenty-four branches) are located strategically throughout the country. Their primary function is to oversee the actions of the member banks and other depository institutions within their districts. Member banks include all nationally chartered commercial banks, which are required to join the Federal Reserve System, as well as any state-chartered banks that have chosen membership.

The Monetary Control Act of 1980

Prior to 1980, the distinction between member and nonmember banks was significant: Only member banks were subject to the direct regulation of the Fed. Nonmember banks were subject only to regulations imposed by the states that chartered them. Because the Fed's reserve requirements were generally higher than those imposed by the states, member banks were forced to sacrifice more interest income. (Remember, reserve dollars don't earn interest.)

In the days of relatively low interest rates (4–5 percent), many banks were willing to forgo this interest income in order to obtain the check-collection services and borrowing privileges provided by the Fed. But as interest rates rose, the opportunity cost of those idle reserves increased, and Federal Reserve membership grew less and less attractive. As a consequence, more than 300 banks withdrew from the Federal Reserve between 1973 and 1979. Faced with declining membership, the Federal Reserve began to search for some way either to stem the loss of member banks or to establish more effective control over the money-creating activities of nonmember banks.

During this time, the Federal Reserve was also concerned about NOW accounts, which enabled savings and loan associations, mutual savings banks, and credit unions (institutions beyond the Fed's control) to create money. The emergence of NOW accounts further threatened the Fed's ability to monitor and control the money supply. To counter this, the Fed pressed for substantial regulatory changes, and Congress responded with the Depository Institutions Deregulation and Monetary Control Act of 1980.

The Monetary Control Act virtually eliminated the distinction between member and nonmember commercial banks and significantly reduced the distinction between commercial banks and other financial institutions. The act required that all depository institutions—member commercial banks, nonmember commercial banks, savings and loan associations, mutual savings banks, and credit unions—meet the same standards with regard to reserve requirements. It lifted many of the regulations that historically had limited competition among various types of financial institutions, and it opened to all such institutions the option to purchase any of the services offered by the Federal Reserve. These changes improved the Fed's ability to monitor and control the money supply and intensified competition among the various types of depository institutions for depositors and loan customers alike. The Riegle–Neal Interstate Banking and Efficiency Act of 1994 further intensified competition by permitting banks in one state to establish branches in another state.

Deregulation, Bank Failures, and Changing Financial Markets

Not all the consequences of the Monetary Control Act and subsequent banking reforms were positive. Many analysts argue that the relaxed regulatory environment contributed to an enormous number of bank and savings and loan failures in the 1980s and early 1990s. In the period from 1980 to 1994, more than 2,900 depository institutions failed—almost 200 a year! That's up from just a handful of bank failures in each of the preceding forty years.

The inordinate number of bank failures led to closer monitoring in the 1990s. But increased supervision brings with it higher costs for the supervised institutions, and that can have unintended consequences. Because today's financial markets are increasingly international, countries that impose costly regulations risk driving businesses to other, less-regulated countries. (This concern has resulted in growing international coordination of banking regulations.) Another consequence is the diversion of money from depository institutions, such as banks and savings and loans, to nondepository institutions, such as mutual funds and insurance companies. Nondepository institutions have been growing very rapidly, in part because they can afford to pay higher interest rates than the more highly regulated depository institutions with which they compete. For instance, the assets of stock and bond mutual funds increased 145 percent between 1995 and 1999, while the assets of commercial banks only increased about 33 percent over that period.[6] Moreover, because these nondepository institutions are largely beyond the Federal Reserve's control, the Fed's policymakers are concerned that this trend is undermining their ability to control the money supply. It remains to be seen how they will address this challenge.

In addition to undermining the Fed's control, the rapid growth of nondepository financial institutions appears to signal a somewhat diminished role for depository institutions. But these depository institutions are not likely to disappear. As we saw a moment ago, commercial bank assets continue to grow, though more slowly than those of some competitors. Threatened by increased competition in the borrowing and lending business, depository institutions have increasingly turned to the provision of financial services—services for which they earn fees, as opposed to the interest they earn from loans—to bolster their income. These services include the preparation of payrolls for businesses, the supervision of company pension funds, assistance in arranging mergers, the buying and selling of foreign exchange, and a host of others. This broadening of the role of depository institutions has helped to ensure their financial viability. In fact, some studies indicate that these institutions are becoming more, not less, important to the economy.[7]

The Functions of the Federal Reserve

The foregoing discussion highlights the dynamic nature of our financial institutions and the difficulty of determining the proper level of supervision. Supervising financial institutions is one of the functions of the Fed, a responsibility it shares with the Federal Deposit Insurance Corporation (FDIC), the primary agency insuring deposits at financial institutions.

The Fed also performs a number of other functions. First, the twelve Federal Reserve Banks hold the reserves (other than vault cash) of all the depository institutions in their districts. Second, as lenders of last resort, the Federal Reserve banks stand ready to make loans to depository institutions in temporary need of funds. Third, the Federal Reserve supplies the economy with coins and paper money. Fourth, as we have seen, the Fed provides a system for collecting and clearing checks throughout the United States, making it possible for checks drawn on out-of-town banks to be returned to the home institution for collection. But all these functions are secondary to the Fed's primary responsibility: the control of the nation's money supply. That is the topic we will examine next.

---

[6] *Federal Reserve Flow of Funds Accounts,* Dec. 2000.
[7] For a discussion, see Mark D. Vaughan, "Bullish on Banking: Surviving in the Information Age," *The Regional Economist,* Federal Reserve Bank of Saint Louis, Jan. 1996.

MONETARY POLICY AND THE FEDERAL RESERVE

Monetary policy is designed to control the supply of money. More precisely, monetary policy is any action intended to alter the supply of money in order to influence the level of total spending and thereby combat unemployment or inflation.

Although the objective of monetary policy is the same as that of fiscal policy (to prevent or combat unemployment and inflation), its methodology is somewhat different. In Chapter 12 you saw how policymakers use the government's spending and taxation powers to alter aggregate demand and thereby eliminate recessionary or inflationary gaps. Likewise, monetary policy works to influence aggregate demand but through a different mechanism: by increasing or decreasing the money supply.

The Fed does not manipulate the amount of money by printing more currency or by removing existing paper money from circulation. Remember, most of our nation's money supply is composed of balances in checking accounts—demand-deposit accounts, NOW accounts, and other forms of checkable deposits. It is this element of the money supply that the Fed's actions are designed to influence. You have seen how depository institutions create checkable deposits when they make loans. Now you will discover how the Federal Reserve can influence the lending ability of depository institutions and thereby alter the supply of money.

The Federal Reserve uses three major policy tools to control the money supply: (1) the buying and selling of government securities, a process known as **open-market operations;** (2) the ability to alter the reserve requirement of depository institutions; and (3) control over the **discount rate**—the interest rate at which banking institutions can borrow from the Federal Reserve. All three policy tools affect the reserve positions of depository institutions. As you have learned, the more excess reserves a bank has, the more loans it can make and the more money (checkable deposits) it can create. By altering the volume of excess reserves, the Fed is able to influence the banking system's ability to make loans. Because making loans means creating more money, the Fed's actions influence the money supply.

Open-Market Operations

The Federal Reserve controls the money supply primarily through its open-market operations: buying and selling government securities on the open market. Whenever the U.S. government runs a deficit, the Treasury finances that deficit by selling government securities to individuals, businesses, financial institutions, and government agencies. Most are marketable, or *negotiable*, meaning that they can be held until maturity or resold to someone else.[8] Banks find such securities an attractive investment. They not only earn interest but also convert easily into cash in the event that additional reserves are needed. The Federal Reserve uses the market for negotiable securities as a vehicle for controlling the money supply. Let's see how open-market operations work.

If the Fed wants to increase the money supply by expanding loans, it can offer to buy government securities at attractive prices in the open market. The Fed pays for securities purchased from a commercial bank, for example, by increasing the bank's reserve account at the district Federal Reserve bank. Because this transaction does not increase the bank's deposit liabilities, the additional reserves are all excess and can be used to expand loans and deposits—up to the maximum predicted by the deposit multiplier. As you know, any change in the excess reserves of one bank will lead eventually to a much larger change in the total system's loans and checkable deposits. As commercial banks and other depository institutions make more loans and create more checkable deposits, the money supply will expand.

If the Fed wishes to reduce the money supply, it can shift its open-market operations into reverse and cut the lending ability of banks by selling them government securities. The purchasing banks will experience a reduction in their reserve accounts at district Federal Reserve banks. As their reserves decline, these institutions will have to contract loans or at least limit their expansion. This will cause the money supply to decline or expand at a slower rate.

Changing the Reserve Requirement

The Fed can also influence the reserve position of banks by changing the reserve requirement. Under existing law, the Federal Reserve has the power to specify reserve requirements between 8 and 14 percent for depository institutions above a specified size. (At present, most banks must satisfy a 10 percent reserve requirement.) This flexibility provides the Federal Reserve with a tool for influencing the money supply by changing the lending ability of depository institutions.

Lowering the reserve requirement would convert some required reserves into excess reserves and thereby expand the lending ability of depository institutions. When these institutions increase their loans, they create checkable deposits, and the money supply expands. Increasing the reserve requirement

---

[8] There are different types of marketable government securities. *Treasury bills* are short-term securities with maturities of ninety-one days to one year. *Government notes* are intermediate-term securities maturing in one to five years. Finally, *government bonds* are long-term securities with maturities of more than five years.

has the opposite effect. As excess reserves are converted into required reserves, lending contracts and the money supply shrinks.

Modifying the reserve requirement is effective but somewhat dangerous. Even changes as small as one-half of one percent can alter by several billion dollars the banking system's ability to make loans. Changes of this magnitude, particularly when they are sudden, can jolt the economy severely. Therefore, the Federal Reserve uses this tool sparingly, adjusting the reserve requirement only infrequently and relying mainly on other tools to control the money supply.

Changing the Discount Rate

Since the passage of the Monetary Control Act of 1980, any depository institution may ask to borrow reserves from its district Federal Reserve bank to avoid reducing the number of loans it can grant or to increase its volume of loans and thereby earn additional interest income.[9]

Recall that the rate of interest charged by the Federal Reserve on loans to depository institutions is called the *discount rate*. In theory, increasing the discount rate should discourage borrowing from the Federal Reserve and thus force banks to limit or even contract the number of loans they grant. We know that if banks contract their loans, the money supply will fall.

Lowering the discount rate should have the opposite effect. By encouraging depository institutions to borrow from the Fed and create additional loans and deposits, the lowered rate should lead to an increase in the money supply.

Note the use of the words "in theory" and "should." In practice, changes in the discount rate have proved to be a very weak policy tool. Bankers tend to equate loans from the Federal Reserve with money borrowed from in-laws; it's something you avoid unless you have no other options. This attitude is not surprising when one considers the Fed's corresponding view that borrowing is a privilege and not a right: If Federal Reserve authorities believe that a bank has overextended itself through poor planning or has borrowed too often or for the wrong purposes, they can refuse to lend the needed reserves. This disciplinary action forces the wayward bank to contract loans, sell securities, or look elsewhere for reserves. Because bankers don't like such restrictions, they prefer to borrow through the **federal funds market,** a market that brings together banks that need reserves and banks that temporarily have excess reserves. The rate charged on such loans is called the **federal funds rate** and usually applies to reserves borrowed on a very short-term basis—often overnight to meet temporary reserve deficiencies.

[9] When depository institutions repay these loans to the Fed, their reserves decline, and they are forced to contract loans or find other sources of reserves.

Because banks borrow from the Federal Reserve only infrequently, changes in the discount rate have little impact on the banking system's lending ability and thus register little effect on the money supply. In fact, many economists tend to view a change in the discount rate more as an indication of the Fed's intentions than as an effective policy move. Increases in the discount rate are thought to indicate the Fed's intention to contract the money supply or slow its rate of growth; decreases signal a desire to expand the money supply or increase its rate of growth.

MONEY, INTEREST RATES, AND THE LEVEL OF ECONOMIC ACTIVITY

Now that we've seen how the Federal Reserve can expand or contract the money supply, let's explore how changes in the money supply affect the economy. Economic theory suggests that changes in the money supply affect output and employment primarily by altering interest rates. Because a significant amount of consumption and investment spending is financed by borrowing, changes in the interest rate can affect the amount of aggregate demand in the economy and thereby alter the level of equilibrium GDP and the price level. This transmission process can be summarized as follows:

$$\text{Money supply} \rightarrow \text{Interest rate} \rightarrow \text{Aggregate demand} \rightarrow \begin{array}{c}\text{Output,}\\\text{employment,}\\\text{and prices}\end{array}$$

Interest Rate Determination

Why would changes in the money supply tend to alter the interest rate? To answer that question, we need to think back to Chapter 3, where we discussed price determination in competitive markets. Like the price of wheat or of cattle, the interest rate—the price of money—is determined by the forces of demand and supply. As a consequence, any change in either the demand for money or its supply will affect the rate of interest.[10]

Consider, first, the demand for money. Like conventional demand curves, the demand curve for money slopes downward. That's because the quantity of money demanded by individuals and businesses is inversely related to the

---

[10] To simplify matters, we will assume a single rate of interest; in fact, there are several. For example, short-term borrowers generally pay a lower interest rate than those who require the money for a longer period. In addition, borrowers with good credit ratings usually pay lower rates than those with poor ratings.

Federal Reserve policies are not always popular. Here, demonstrators protest policies that raised interest rates to slow the economy and prevent inflation.

interest rate: The higher the rate of interest, the less money is demanded. To understand that relationship, remember that the money you hold (cash in your wallet or money in your checking account) generally pays little or no interest. But other assets you could hold instead of money—bonds, for instance, or bank certificates of deposit—do pay interest. The higher the prevailing interest rate, the more attractive it becomes to hold these assets instead of money. As a consequence, less money will be demanded when interest rates are *high* than when they are *low*. The demand curve in Exh. 13.4 shows that $100 billion would be demanded at an interest rate of 10 percent, whereas $300 billion would be demanded at an interest rate of 6 percent.

The supply of money is depicted as a vertical line in Exh. 13.4 to illustrate that the quantity of money supplied does not respond automatically to changes in the interest rate; instead, it remains constant at the level determined by the Federal Reserve. The intersection of the demand curve and the vertical supply curve determines the equilibrium interest rate: the interest rate at which the amount of money that people want to hold is exactly equal to the amount available. In our hypothetical example the

EXHIBIT 13.4

The Equilibrium Interest Rate

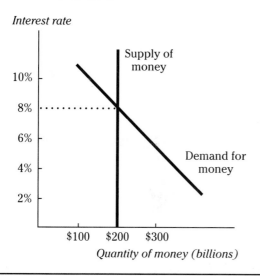

The intersection of the demand curve for money and the supply curve of money determines the equilibrium interest rate—the interest rate at which the amount of money that individuals and businesses want to hold is exactly equal to the amount available. In this example the equilibrium interest rate is 8 percent.

equilibrium interest rate is 8 percent. At that interest rate individuals and businesses are willing to hold $200 billion, exactly the amount being supplied by the Federal Reserve.

Monetary Policy and the Level of Economic Activity

The Fed attempts to guide the economy's performance by adjusting the money supply and thereby pushing the interest rate up or down. As we've seen, changes in the interest rate alter aggregate demand, and changes in the level of aggregate demand lead to changes in equilibrium GDP and the price level.

To illustrate how monetary policy works, let's assume that the economy is suffering from abnormally high unemployment: a recessionary gap exists. The Fed can attack this unemployment problem by increasing the money supply. This could be accomplished by reducing the reserve requirement, buying government securities, or lowering the discount rate. Any of these changes would shift the money supply curve in Exh. 13.5(a) from S_1 to S_2, denoting an increase in the money supply from $200 billion to $300 billion. Since the demand for money is unchanged, the equilibrium interest rate will

EXHIBIT 13.5
Using Monetary Policy to Attack Unemployment

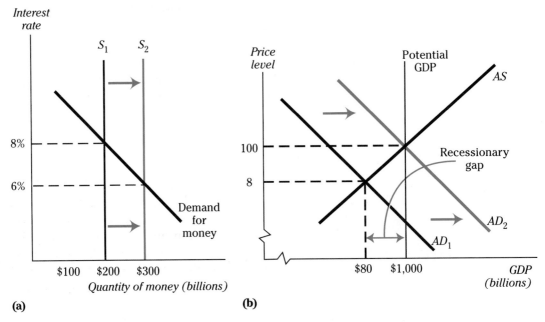

By increasing the money supply from S_1 to S_2, as in (a), the Fed can lower the interest rate from 8 to 6 percent. The lower interest rate stimulates consumption and investment spending, shifting the aggregate demand curve from AD_1 to AD_2, as in (b), and eliminating the recessionary gap.

fall from 8 percent to 6 percent. At this lower interest rate, businesses will find it profitable to borrow additional money to invest in plants and equipment; households will be inclined to borrow and spend more on new homes, automobiles, and other consumer goods. Thus by lowering the interest rate, an increase in the money supply raises aggregate demand. This is represented in Exh. 13.5(b) by a shift of the aggregate demand curve from AD_1 to AD_2. As you can see, this increase in aggregate demand raises the equilibrium level of GDP from $800 billion to $1,000 billion, eliminating the recessionary gap and restoring full employment. (In January of 2001, the Fed cut interest rates to try to head off a recession. Read "The Rate Cut: The Overview..." on page 410 and then test your understanding of monetary policy by answering the accompanying questions.)

To attack inflation, the Federal Reserve must raise interest rates by contracting the money supply. This is accomplished by increasing the reserve requirement, selling government securities, or increasing the discount rate.

What is the effect of the higher rate of interest? Businesses will tend to reduce investment spending, and households will be likely to spend less on new homes, boats, camping trailers, and other items that they buy on credit or through borrowing. Reducing the money supply thus raises the interest rate and lowers aggregate demand in the economy, which helps to reduce inflationary pressures.

As you can see, monetary policy works through its impact on the interest rate. By adjusting the cost of money, the Fed is able to influence the level of aggregate demand in the economy and thereby eliminate recessionary or inflationary gaps.

THE LIMITS TO MONETARY POLICY

The Federal Reserve's independent status gives monetary policy some distinct advantages over fiscal policy. When the Fed's board of governors decides that action should be taken to combat unemployment or inflation, it does not need to wait for Congress to agree. The board can approve the needed policy changes and have them implemented in a very short time. Board members' fourteen-year terms also serve to insulate them from political pressures, although the insulation is not complete in view of the periodic threats to bring the Fed under the direct control of Congress.

But monetary policy has limitations as well. (Recall the limitations of fiscal policy that we examined in Chapter 12.) Here we will look at two problems that may be encountered when monetary policy is used in an attempt to guide the economy's performance.

Time Lags

Like fiscal policy, monetary policy is subject to some time lags. Although Federal Reserve authorities don't need the approval of Congress to implement policy changes (thus eliminating the *implementation lag*), they do need time to recognize that a problem exists. As we learned earlier, our economic indicators sometimes send mixed or unclear messages, so some time may elapse before members of the board of governors identify a problem and agree to take action. Of course, this is what we described in Chapter 12 as the *recognition lag*. Once they take action, additional time passes before their policy change exerts its impact on the economy. If board members decide to stimulate the economy, for example, it will take time for an increase in lending to trigger the associated increase in spending, output, and employment. As before, this is the *impact lag*. If these recognition and impact lags are too long, the added stimulus may hit the economy when it is already on the road to spontaneous recovery. In that event, the Fed's actions may contribute to inflation rather than help to reduce unemployment.

USE YOUR ECONOMIC REASONING

The Rate Cut: The Overview; Federal Reserve, Reacting to Signals of a Slowdown, Cuts Key Rate Half a Point

By Richard W. Stevenson and Louis Uchitelle

CONFRONTED with increased evidence that the economy is stalling, the Federal Reserve slashed its benchmark interest rate by half a percentage point yesterday, stunning investors and sending a powerful signal that the Fed is worried about the prospects for keeping the decade-long expansion alive.

Acting between scheduled meetings, and with barely disguised haste, the central bank cut its federal funds target rate on overnight loans between banks to 6 percent from 6.5 percent. In a statement, it then signaled that it was likely to cut rates further in coming weeks and months.

"There's a simple message," Bruce Steinberg, chief economist at Merrill Lynch, said. "The Fed will do whatever it takes to keep the U.S. economy from going down the tubes."

The action, announced just after 1 P.M., caught most investors flat footed. It set off a strong rally on Wall Street, where lower rates are seen as a powerful antidote to the months-long tumble in stock prices....

The Fed's announcement came two weeks before the inauguration of President-elect George W. Bush, who was meeting with business executives in Austin, Tex., to build support for his $1.6 trillion tax cut proposal. Mr. Bush has been warning of an economic downturn, and in welcoming the Fed's action yesterday he said it in no way reduced the need for a tax cut.

Although the full effects of the rate cut are not likely to be felt for months, the action immediately began putting downward pressure on the rates paid by businesses and consumers to borrow money. Still, it is impossible to know with certainty when credit card rates will be affected.

The rate reduction was an abrupt turnabout for the Fed, which only months ago was far more worried about the prospect of an overheating economy igniting inflation than about the possibility of a recession. Yesterday's move followed six rate increases between June 1999 and May of last year....

The Fed had hinted last month that a rate cut was in the cards. But in taking its action four weeks ahead of its next scheduled meeting on Jan. 30–31, and in opting to cut rates by half a point rather than by a quarter point, its more normal increment, the Fed conveyed the clear impression that it saw economic conditions deteriorating faster than it or most analysts had anticipated....

Clearly, the economy has weakened since the Fed policy makers last met, on Dec. 19, and left interest rates unchanged. "Consumers are retrenching, business is pulling back, manufacturing is in recession, and banks have become more cautious," said Mark Zandi, chief economist of Economy.com, a forecasting and consulting service.

The Fed move came a day after the National Association of Purchasing Management released the December results for an index that measures activity in the manufac-

Source: New York Times, Jan. 4, 2001, p. 1A.

turing sector. The index fell to 43.7 last month from 47.7 in November, leaving the measure at its lowest level since the end of the last recession nearly a decade ago.

"They saw the N.A.P.M., and it scared the pants off them," said Ian Shepherdson, an economist at High Frequency Economics, a consulting firm in Valhalla, N.Y.

The downward spiral in the stock market is also likely to have concerned Mr. Greenspan, who in recent years has made much of the tight links between what happens in the financial markets and the health of the economy in general. Investors have become increasingly convinced that Mr. Greenspan will step in with a rate cut whenever the market shows signs of deep trouble.

Yet for months, Fed officials have insisted that interest rate policy has been aimed at controlling inflation, and not the stock market. The half-point cut yesterday, however, was clear recognition of the stock market's enormous power to make the economy boom or bust.

"The data for the real economy is not yet that frightening," said Peter Hooper, chief domestic economist for Deutsche Bank North America. "But if the markets continued down on the basis of fear feeding on fear, that could push us into recession. And that got the Fed acting today."

The Fed's rate cuts are traditionally aimed at stimulating economic growth by making credit less expensive, thus encouraging people to borrow and spend, particu-

larly for homes, cars and appliances, three pillars of the economy.

But weeks or months can pass before a Fed rate cut actually lowers borrowing costs for individual Americans. This time, the Fed, in cutting rates in such a highly noticeable way, seemed to seek faster action, economists said. The rate cut may lift the spirits of investors, with the hope that a rising market will raise the confidence of consumers everywhere.

"Consumers had become concerned because they thought the economy was slowing down too fast, and that would affect their job prospects and security," said Richard T. Curtin, director of consumer surveys at the University of Michigan.

It also appeared that Mr. Greenspan had concluded that the release of unemployment figures for December on Friday would show further signs that what started as a modest slowdown was threatening to deteriorate

into a downturn in which the economy would actually shrink. The Fed usually has one component of the unemployment report a few days in advance, providing a sense of employment trends among manufacturers. But the full employment report is not disclosed to the Fed until the afternoon before it is released.

"If the employment report came out even moderately negative without a response from the Fed, you could have a tremendous sell-off in the stock market," Mr. Hooper said....

The Fed made clear that yesterday's action was likely to be the first step in a series of rate cuts intended to prolong an expansion that became the longest on record last February. The economy has been growing without interruption since March 1991.

In its statement yesterday, the Fed signaled that the central bankers believed that further rate cuts would probably be necessary, perhaps as soon as the regularly scheduled meeting on Jan. 30–31....

Use Your Economic Reasoning

1. What evidence did the Fed have to indicate that the economy was weakening? Do you think the factors mentioned in the article affect aggregate demand or aggregate supply? Try to represent the Fed's concerns graphically.

2. If the Fed wants to lower interest rates, does it need to increase the money supply or decrease the money supply?

3. The Fed generally uses open-market operations to alter the money supply and thereby change interest rates. In this case, did the Fed need to buy government securities or sell government securities?

4. Explain in a step-by-step manner how the Fed's policies are supposed to help the economy. Start with the Fed's open-market operations and continue from there.

Uneven Effectiveness

Monetary policy may be less effective in combating unemployment than in combating inflation. When the Fed reduces banks' reserves to combat inflation, banks are forced to restrict (or even contract) lending. However, when it implements an easy-money policy to combat unemployment and makes more reserves available to depository institutions, bankers may not choose to use those reserves to support loans. If bankers doubt the ability of customers to repay loans, they refuse to lend; if households and businesses are pessimistic about the future, they may decide not to borrow. Without greater lending and borrowing, spending will not increase; thus, the economy will not receive the stimulus needed to pull it from its depressed state.

How significant are the monetary policy limitations noted here? As with fiscal policy, the issue is open to debate. But the performance of the Federal Reserve in the last two decades seems to provide evidence that discretionary policy can be successful in guiding the economy's performance. After halting inflation in the early 1980s, the Fed has managed to maintain high unemployment without allowing significant inflation. Moreover, in 2000 the unemployment rate dipped to a mere 4 percent, the lowest in thirty years, with little or no increase in the "core" rate of inflation. (The core rate of inflation is the rate that remains after subtracting out the impact of special factors such as bad agricultural harvests or OPEC price increases.) Many economists argue that this experience demonstrates the wisdom of activist monetary policy. If fact, as we mentioned in the last chapter, most activists appear to prefer monetary policy to discretionary fiscal policy as a vehicle for guiding the economy's performance. This preference appears to reflect, in large part, the belief that the lags associated with monetary policy are shorter than those associated with fiscal policy.

But all do not agree with this assessment. Monetarists believe that the lags in monetary policy are long and unpredictable. Consequently, they contend, attempts to use monetary policy to guide the economy's performance can result in worse rather than better economic performance. New classical economists also argue against discretionary monetary policy, believing that, as with fiscal policy, the actions of policymakers will be anticipated and neutralized. They argue that an expansionary monetary policy will have no beneficial impact on the economy; it will only lead to inflation. The views of the monetarists and the new classical economists will be considered in detail in Chapter 14.

SUMMARY

Economists define *money* as anything that serves as a *medium of exchange*, a *standard of value*, and a *store of value*. Currency (coins and paper money) and *checkable deposits* (checking accounts at banks and savings institutions) clearly perform all the functions of money. Other *assets*—passbook savings accounts, for example—perform some, but not all, of the functions of money or perform those functions incompletely. Assets that are not money but that can be quickly converted into money are termed *near money*.

In its role as controller of the U.S. money supply, the Federal Reserve defines that supply according to three classifications. The narrowest is *M-1*, composed of currency in the hands of the public plus all checkable deposits. A somewhat broader definition of the nation's money supply, *M-2* includes everything in M-1 plus money-market mutual fund balances, money-market deposits at savings or thrift institutions, and small *savings deposits*. The broadest definition of the money supply, *M-3*, includes everything in M-2 plus savings deposits in excess of $100,000.

Approximately 51 percent of the M-1 money supply is in the form of checkable deposits; the remainder is currency. The Federal Reserve provides depository institutions (commercial banks and thrift institutions) with the coins and paper currency they need in order to serve their customers. Checkable deposits, on the other hand, are actually created by the depository institutions themselves when they make loans.

According to the *fractional reserve principle*, a bank must maintain only a given fraction of a dollar in *required reserves* for each dollar in checkable deposits; the balance of those funds can be loaned out to earn interest. In the process of making these loans, banks create checkable deposit money. For example, when a person borrows money from a bank, he or she exchanges something that is not money (an IOU) for something that is money (a checking account balance). This increases the money supply by the amount of the loan.

Each depository institution must limit its loans to the amount of its *excess reserves*—reserves in excess of the sum it is legally required to maintain in the form of vault cash and deposits with the Federal Reserve. This limitation is necessary because as loans are spent, reserves are likely to be lost to other depository institutions. Thus, each institution can expand the money supply by an amount equal to its excess reserves but no more than that.

The banking system (including all depository institutions) does not have to worry about losing reserves. Reserves lost by one depository institution must be deposited in some other bank in the system. The banking system as a whole, then, can create loans and deposits equal to some multiple of its excess reserves. To be precise, it can expand loans and deposits by an amount equal to the initial change in excess reserves times the reciprocal of the reserve requirement (the *deposit multiplier*).

The Federal Reserve, our nation's *central bank,* influences the ability of depository institutions to expand or contract deposits and thereby regulates the size of the nation's money supply. The Fed's board of governors makes all major policy decisions and communicates them to the twelve Federal Reserve banks that oversee the actions of all depository institutions in their districts.

The Federal Reserve has three major tools with which to control the money supply: (1) the buying and selling of government securities, a process known as *open-market operations;* (2) the ability to alter the reserve requirement; and (3) control over the *discount rate*—the interest rate at which commercial banks and other depository institutions can borrow from the Federal Reserve.

All these policy tools affect the reserve position of banks. By influencing the volume of excess reserves, the Fed is able to affect the banking system's ability to make loans and is thereby able to influence the money supply. This control over the money supply enables the Federal Reserve to alter the interest rate, which in turn influences the level of aggregate demand in the economy.

Monetary policy has some distinct advantages over fiscal policy. The lags in monetary policy may be shorter than those in fiscal policy, and because the Fed tends to be somewhat insulated from political pressures, it may have more freedom to pursue long-run goals than Congress does.

Monetary policy is also subject to limitations: (1) The lags in monetary policy have the potential to make Fed action counterproductive. (2) Monetary policy may be more effective in combating inflation than in dealing with unemployment.

KEY TERMS

Asset	Federal funds rate	NOW account
Balance sheet	Fractional reserve principle	Open-market operations
Central bank	Liabilities	Owners' equity
Checkable deposits	M-1	Required reserves
Demand deposits	M-2	Reserve requirement
Deposit multiplier	M-3	Savings deposits
Discount rate	Medium of exchange	Standard of value
Excess reserves	Monetary policy	Store of value
Federal funds market	Near money	

STUDY QUESTIONS

Fill in the Blanks

1. Money functions as a _Medium of Exchange,_ _Standard of value_, and a _store value_

2. Demand deposits, NOW accounts, and ATS accounts are all examples of _Checkable deposits_.

3. The primary characteristic of all M-1 money is that it can easily function as a

   Medium of Exchange

4. A bank must maintain reserves equal to a specified fraction of its

   checkable deposits .

5. Banks create money when they

   make loans ; the amount of money that a bank can create is

   equal to its _Excess reserves_

6. Today, the primary purpose of the Federal Reserve is to regulate or control the

   The money supply in order to combat unemployment and inflation.

7. According to economic theory, an increase in the money supply would tend to

   (increase/decrease) _decrease_

   the interest rate, which would tend to

   (increase/decrease) _increase_ ag-

   gregate demand, which, in turn, would

   (increase/decrease) _increase_ GDP.

8. The primary policy tool used by the Federal Reserve to control the money supply is

   Open market operations.

9. The rate charged by the Federal Reserve on loans to depository institutions is called the

   discount Rate

10. Monetary policy may be less effective in

    combating _unemployment_

    than _inflation_

Multiple Choice

1. Which of the following is the largest component of the M-1 money supply?
   a) Currency
   b) Passbook savings accounts
   c) Checkable deposits
   d) Money-market accounts

2. Which of the following is *not* an example of near money?
   a) A savings account
   b) A government bond
   c) A piece of prime real estate
   d) An account with a money-market fund

3. Which of the following does *not* appear as an asset on the balance sheet of a bank?
   a) Demand deposits
   b) Reserves
   c) Securities
   d) Loans

4. Assuming that the reserve requirement is 30 percent, how much additional money can the bank represented below create? (All figures are in millions of dollars.)

ASSETS		LIABILITIES	
Reserves	$23	Checkable	$50
Securities	25	deposits	
Loans	17	Owner equity	40
Property	25		
	90		90

   a) $ 8 million
   b) $12 million
   c) $15 million
   d) $25 million

5. Assuming a reserve requirement of 25 percent, how much additional money can the bank represented below create? (All figures are in millions.)

ASSETS		LIABILITIES	
Reserves	$35	Checkable	$80
Securities	30	deposits	
Loans	25	Owner equity	20
Property	10		
	100		100

a) $20 million
b) $15 million
c) $10 million
d) $ 5 million

6. If the reserve requirement is 25 percent, the deposit multiplier would be equal to
   a) 4.
   b) 5.
   c) 1/4.
   d) 10.

7. If the balance sheet represented in question 5 were for the banking *system* rather than for a single bank, the system could expand the money supply by an additional
   a) $15 billion.
   b) $30 billion.
   c) $60 billion.
   d) $80 billion.

8. Which of the following was *not* accomplished by the Monetary Control Act of 1980?
   a) It virtually eliminated the distinction between member and nonmember commercial banks.
   b) It enhanced competition between the various types of financial institutions.
   c) It established uniform reserve requirements for all depository institutions.
   d) It eliminated the "lender of last resort" function of the Federal Reserve.

9. If banks hold checkable deposits of $200 million and reserves of $50 million and if the reserve requirement is 20 percent, how much additional money can the banking *system* create?
   a) $20 million
   b) $50 million
   c) $100 million
   d) $200 million

10. Which of the following is *not* a function of the Federal Reserve?
    a) To control the money supply
    b) To make loans to depository institutions

c) To insure the deposits of customers
d) To provide a check-collection service

11. If the Federal Reserve wants to reduce the equilibrium interest rate, it should
    a) increase the reserve requirement in order to expand the money supply.
    b) sell securities on the open market in order to expand the money supply.
    c) buy government securities in order to expand the money supply.
    d) increase the discount rate in order to expand the money supply.

12. When the Federal Reserve sells government securities on the open market, the lending ability of banks
    a) tends to decline; the money supply shrinks, and the interest rate tends to decline.
    b) tends to decline; the money supply expands, and the interest rate tends to rise.
    c) increases; the money supply expands, and the interest rate tends to fall.
    d) tends to decline; the money supply shrinks, and the interest rate tends to rise.

13. Let's assume that all banks in the system are "loaned up" (have no excess reserves) and that they all face a reserve ratio of 20 percent. If the Federal Reserve buys a $100,000 security from Bank A, how much new money can the banking *system* create? (*Hint:* Remember that the Fed will pay for the security by increasing the reserve account of Bank A.)
    a) $100,000
    b) $1,000,000
    c) $400,000
    d) $500,000

14. If the Federal Reserve wanted to reduce inflationary pressures, what would be the proper combination of policies?
    a) Increase the reserve ratio, decrease the discount rate, and sell securities.
    b) Increase the reserve ratio, increase the discount rate, and sell securities.

c) Increase the reserve ratio, increase the discount rate, and buy securities.

d) Decrease the reserve ratio, decrease the discount rate, and buy securities.

15. To combat unemployment, the Federal Reserve should

a) reduce the money supply by selling government securities.

b) reduce the money supply by lowering the reserve requirement.

c) increase the money supply by raising the discount rate.

d) increase the money supply by buying government securities.

Problems and Questions for Discussion

1. Explain each of the functions of money. Which of these functions does a traditional savings account perform? A NOW account?

2. Explain what is meant by the fractional reserve principle. How is it related to a bank's ability to create money?

3. Why must individual banks limit their loans to the amount of their excess reserves?

4. If a bank can create money, why can't you?

5. What is the deposit multiplier, and how is it calculated?

6. If you asked for your loan in cash rather than accepting a checking account, what impact would this action have on the money-creating ability of your bank? What about the banking system as a whole?

7. Suppose that you have a credit card with a $1,000 limit (you cannot charge more than $1,000). Should that $1,000 be considered part of the money supply? Why or why not?

8. Why might monetary policy be less effective in combating unemployment than in combating inflation?

9. Discuss the reasons for the passage of the Monetary Control Act of 1980.

10. According to Keynesians, monetary policy works through the rate of interest. Explain.

11. Suppose that the Federal Reserve increases the reserve requirement. Explain the step-by-step impact of that change on the economy.

12. Why is the discount rate often described as a weak policy tool?

13. What are the advantages of open-market operations over changes in the reserve requirement?

14. Suppose that the housing industry is depressed. What monetary policy actions would you recommend to help the housing industry? Why do you think they would help?

15. If the Fed buys a government security from a private individual, the money supply will immediately be increased. If the Fed buys a government security from a bank, this action will not affect the money supply until a loan is made. Explain the difference. That is, why does one transaction have an immediate impact while the other does not?

ANSWER KEY

Fill in the Blanks

1. medium of exchange, standard of value, store of value

2. checkable deposits

3. medium of exchange

4. checkable deposits

5. make loans, excess reserves

6. money supply

7. decrease, increase, increase

8. open-market operations

9. discount rate

10. unemployment, inflation

Multiple Choice

1. c
2. c
3. a
4. a
5. b
6. a
7. c
8. d
9. b
10. c
11. c
12. d
13. d
14. b
15. d

CHAPTER FOURTEEN

The Activist–Nonactivist Debate

LEARNING OBJECTIVES

1. Discuss the views held by monetarist economists.
2. Explain the monetary rule and why monetarists support it.
3. Discuss the views of the new classical economists.
4. Explain the theory of rational expectations.
5. Discuss the policy ineffectiveness theorem.
6. Discuss the views held by supply-side economists.
7. Describe the policies that supply-side economists advocate.

In theory, monetary and fiscal policies can be used to maintain full employment and stable prices. But each of these demand-management policies is subject to limitations. Activists argue that in spite of their limitations, these policies can still play an important role in guiding the economy's performance. Nonactivists find the limitations so severe as to make the policies ineffective or counterproductive. This is the controversy that concerns us in this chapter.

As you can see, we have returned to the activist–nonactivist debate that we first encountered in Chapter 12. Just as Keynes and the classical economists disagreed about the advisability of government intervention to guide our economy, modern Keynesians disagree with monetarists and new classical economists (also known as rational-expectations theorists). This chapter introduces you to the views of these competing schools of thought and examines the debate about demand-management policies. It also takes a brief look at supply-side economics. We turn first to a short review of the Keynesian, or activist, position.

THE ACTIVIST POSITION: KEYNES REVISITED

As you learned in Chapter 12, Keynes did not believe that capitalist economies necessarily tend to full employment. Rather, he argued that because of the volatility of spending, particularly investment spending, they could be in equilibrium at a level of output either less or greater than potential GDP. If business executives were pessimistic, they might choose to cut back on investment spending, sending the economy into a tailspin and causing unemployment. If they were optimistic about the future, they might choose to expand investment spending, pushing GDP above potential and causing inflation.

Keynes was an activist economist in the sense that he advocated government action to prevent outbreaks of unemployment or inflation and to combat these problems when they occur. According to Keynes, the central government should use fiscal and monetary policies to ensure sufficient aggregate demand to achieve full employment without inflation.

Fiscal policy, you will recall, is the manipulation of government spending or taxation in order to guide the economy's performance. The appropriate Keynesian fiscal policy for a period of unemployment would be to increase government spending for goods and services or to reduce taxes. These policies would expand aggregate demand, raise the equilibrium GDP, and lower unemployment. Inflation calls for reductions in government spending or higher taxes. By reducing aggregate demand, these policies will reduce inflationary pressures.

Monetary policy—deliberately changing the money supply to influence the level of economic activity—can also be used to combat unemployment or inflation. If unemployment exists, the Federal Reserve (the government agency that regulates the money supply) can increase the money supply in order to drive down the market rate of interest. The lower interest rate will tend to stimulate investment spending and certain forms of consumption spending. By stimulating aggregate demand in this manner, monetary policy can raise equilibrium GDP and lower unemployment. Inflation can be attacked by reducing the money supply and thereby raising the prevailing rate of interest. A higher interest rate will cause businesses and consumers to cut back on their borrowing (and spending) and reduce inflationary pressures.

Even if fiscal and monetary policies work in the manner Keynesians suggest, why would anyone consider using them? If the economy is self-correcting in the long run, why not let it take care of itself? According to Keynesians, waiting for the self-correcting mechanism to work may be too painful. The adjustment process described in Chapter 11 takes time, perhaps a substantial period of time. If the economy is experiencing a recession, society loses output that will never be regained, individuals suffer the humiliation of being without work, and families deplete their savings or are forced to rely on charity or government assistance. In short, unemployment is costly, and the losses incurred as we wait for self-correction may be unacceptable.

Production above potential also imposes costs on society. As we saw in Chapter 11, when equilibrium GDP exceeds potential, the price level is pushed up, generating inflation. Although society benefits from the additional output and employment, unanticipated inflation tends to redistribute income in an arbitrary way. Moreover, the long-run adjustment process will ultimately eliminate the short-term gain in output and leave the economy with a still higher price level.

In summary, Keynesians believe that capitalist economies are inherently unstable, so that they are always in danger of operating either above or below potential GDP. Although the economy will ultimately return to potential GDP, waiting for this long-run adjustment to occur is needlessly costly to society. Instead, fiscal and monetary policies should be used to prevent deviations from potential GDP or to minimize their duration if they occur.

THE NONACTIVIST POSITION: THE MONETARISTS

Not all economists agree with the activist, or Keynesian, position. The two major groups, or schools, of nonactivist economists are the monetarists and the new classical economists (rational-expectations theorists). We will begin by examining the monetarist position.

Monetarism is the belief that changes in the money supply play the primary role in determining the level of aggregate output and prices in the economy. Economists who hold this belief are called *monetarists.*

According to monetarists, an increase in the money supply will tend to stimulate consumption and investment spending, raising equilibrium output and the price level; a reduction in the money supply will have the opposite effect. Keynesians agree that changes in the money supply can alter output and prices, but they emphasize that other factors—changes in investment or government spending, for instance—can also influence the economy. Monetarists tend to see these other factors as decidedly secondary; changes in the money supply are what really matter.

Fiscal Policy and Crowding Out

The paramount importance that monetarists attach to the money supply is illustrated by their criticism of Keynesian fiscal policy. According to monetarists, fiscal policy is ineffective unless it is accompanied by monetary policy.

To illustrate this view, let's suppose that the economy is suffering from unemployment and that Congress decides to increase government spending to combat the problem. What will happen? The monetarists believe that if the money supply is not increased, government borrowing to finance the larger deficit will drive up the interest rate and discourage, or crowd out, investment spending. In an economy with more government spending but less investment spending, the net effect will be no stimulus to the economy. However, if the Federal Reserve allowed the money supply to expand while the government borrowed, it *would* be possible to provide some net stimulus to the economy. The interest rate would not be bid up, and so investment spending would not be discouraged; thus, total spending would actually expand. Monetarists are quick to point out that the stimulus in this situation results from the increase in the money supply, not from the added government spending.

Monetary Policy and the Monetary Rule

Because monetarism focuses attention on the money supply, eager students sometimes conclude that monetarists must favor the use of discretionary monetary policy to guide the economy's performance. But that's not the case. Monetarists believe that changes in the money supply are too important to be left to the discretion of policymakers. Instead, they support a **monetary rule** that would require the Federal Reserve to expand the money supply at a constant rate, something like 3 percent a year.[1]

If the Fed were required to increase the money supply at a constant annual rate, it would no longer be free to use changes in the money supply as a policy tool; it could not increase the money supply more rapidly to combat unemployment or slow the growth of the money supply to combat inflation. In other words, a monetary rule would eliminate the possibility of the activist monetary policies described in Chapter 13. In a sense, the Fed would be put on autopilot. Monetarists favor this approach because they are convinced that the Fed's attempts to combat unemployment or inflation have often made things worse rather than better.

---

[1] Monetarists believe that the money supply should be expanded at 3 percent a year because they think that potential GDP expands at about that rate. If sustainable output is growing at 3 percent a year, a 3 percent larger money supply is needed in order to facilitate this greater volume of transactions. But whether we choose to increase the money supply at 3 percent or 4 percent or 6 percent is not too important, so long as we pick *some* rate and stick with it. If the money supply is growing more rapidly than the economy's ability to produce output, inflation will result. But because it will be a reasonably constant rate of inflation, we will know what to expect and will be able to build it into our wage agreements and other contracts. Thus, it will not tend to redistribute income the way unanticipated inflation does.

Milton Friedman, shown here accepting his Nobel Prize in economics, would like to see the Federal Reserve adhere to a monetary rule.

Policy Lags and the Self-Correcting Economy

According to the monetarists, it is time lags that tend to make discretionary monetary policies counterproductive. Obviously, Fed policymakers cannot take action until they recognize that a problem exists. Unfortunately, the economy commonly sends mixed signals about its performance. As we learned in the previous chapter, this results in a *recognition lag* before agreement is reached that a problem exists. Even after the problem is recognized and policymakers take action, there will be an *impact lag* before the economy feels the effect of the policy.

The existence of lags would not be a major argument against discretionary monetary policy if the economy tended to remain in an unemployment or inflationary equilibrium indefinitely. But that's not what happens. As our discussion of the self-correcting mechanism indicates, the economy ultimately begins to solve its own problems. When we recognize this self-correcting tendency, lags can mean trouble for policymakers. To illustrate, suppose that the economy gradually weakens and begins to experience a recession. Fed policymakers eventually recognize the problem and take action to expand the money supply. But if the recognition and impact lags are long enough, the economy may begin to recover on its own before these policies start to take effect. Thus, monetary policy may begin to stimulate spending when such stimulus is no longer welcome. Of course, too much spending can lead to inflation, which is precisely what monetarists believe has happened on several occasions. (There is some evidence that the lags associated with monetary policy are changing. Read "Lag Time is a Variable to Watch in Fed Rate Cuts," on page 426, to see why.)

In summary, monetarists shun discretionary monetary policy because they believe that it often has a destabilizing effect on the economy—creates additional problems—rather than the stabilizing effect that Keynesians predict. In fact, monetarists believe that government tinkering with the money supply may be the major destabilizing force in the economy. For example, Milton Friedman—who is sometimes referred to as the father of monetarist economics—argues that it was inept monetary policy that caused the Great Depression. According to Friedman, the Fed turned what could have been a serious downturn into a major catastrophe by allowing the money supply to fall substantially in the early 1930s. He contends that a policy of stable money growth would have been vastly superior.[2]

Monetarism: Concluding Points

Perhaps the major source of disagreement between Keynesians and monetarists is about the nature of the economy. Keynesians tend to see the economy as inherently unstable and relatively slow to recover from demand and supply shocks. Monetarists, on the other hand, believe that the economy is fundamentally stable and returns fairly rapidly to potential GDP whenever deviations occur. If it persists in deviating from potential GDP, it is due to government tinkering, not to the nature of the economy.

Monetarists emphasize that eliminating the Fed's ability to tinker with the money supply would not completely eliminate unemployment or inflation. Fluctuations in spending would still occur, and some unemployment or inflation would result. But the adoption of a monetary rule would eliminate the major source of fluctuations in spending—fluctuations in the growth of the money supply—and would therefore tend to minimize any unemployment or inflation.

Criticisms of Monetarism

Keynesian economists disagree with monetarists on several basic points. First, they believe that monetarists attach too much importance to the money

---

[2] Milton Friedman, "The Case for a Monetary Rule," *Newsweek,* Feb. 7, 1972. Reprinted in Milton Friedman, *Bright Promises, Dismal Performance: An Economist's Protest* (Sun Lakes, Ariz.: Thomas Horton and Daughters, 1983).

supply. Keynesians agree that changes in the money supply can alter GDP, but they argue that other factors are also important—perhaps even more important. These factors include changes in the level of investment or government spending. Keynesians believe that such autonomous changes can lead to inflation or unemployment even if the money supply expands at a constant rate. For instance, Keynesians argue that pessimism about the future might cause businesses to cut back on investment and that this might lead to unemployment even if the money supply continues to expand at a steady rate.

Second, although virtually all Keynesians agree with monetarists that crowding out reduces the effectiveness of fiscal policy, Keynesians believe that only a small amount of investment spending will normally be crowded out, so that expansionary fiscal policy can still have a significant impact on equilibrium GDP.

But many modern Keynesians are quite critical of the long lags involved in implementing changes in taxation and government spending. Since the lags in implementing monetary policy are generally shorter than the lags in implementing fiscal policy (though pro-rule monetarists argue that they are still too long), monetary policy is seen as the primary technique for stabilizing the economy.

Third, Keynesians are critical of the monetary rule because they believe that it could contribute to greater, rather than less, unemployment and inflation. Because Keynesians believe that the economy is *inherently* unstable (due to the volatility of investment spending), they argue that Fed policymakers need discretion to be able to offset fluctuations in spending and thereby maintain full employment without inflation.

THE NONACTIVIST POSITION:
THE NEW CLASSICAL ECONOMISTS

As you probably noted, monetarists have much in common with the classical economists we discussed briefly in Chapter 12. Both groups see the economy as fundamentally stable and believe in laissez-faire policies. But another school of modern economists has even more in common with the original classical theorists, so much so that this school has been dubbed the "new" classical school of economics.

The new classical economics is based on two fundamental beliefs: (1) wages and prices are highly flexible, and (2) expectations about the future are formed "rationally." The remainder of this section investigates the implications of those beliefs.

USE YOUR ECONOMIC REASONING

Lag Time Is a Variable to Watch in Fed Rate Cut

By Jon E. Hilsenrath

NEW YORK—Here is a New Economy paradox: Thanks to the increasingly free flow of information, it takes less time than ever for companies and individuals to adjust to changes in the economy. Yet shifts in monetary policy, while perhaps having a faster impact than in the past, can still take between six and 12 months to make their presence really felt.

"We're not going to see growth any stronger tomorrow than it was yesterday," says Bruce Steinberg, chief economist at Merrill Lynch & Co. In fact, he says, "It is going to be the second half of the year at the soonest," before the economy feels the full impact of the half percentage-point decline in interest rates that the Federal Reserve pushed through on Wednesday.

Why such a long lag? Economists say that markets and information may be traveling at supercharged speeds, but simple decisions about how to invest in stocks, whether to buy a new home and when's the right time to upgrade business equipment, travel at very human speeds—and can take months to play out.

"Individuals, in their consumption behavior, are not forward-looking at all," says Alan Blinder, a Princeton University economist and vice chairman of the Fed between mid-1994 and early 1996. As a result, individuals may hear that interest rates will fall, but it isn't until they actually believe that the economy is improving—and thus their own lives might be more secure—that they make decisions to spend.

"People reasonably want to wait and see if [Wednesday's stock-market rally] is going to be durable," says Mr. Blinder. When it comes to consumer spending, he says, "I don't see any reason to abandon the previous historical patterns of lags. This gradually will affect spending."

That is true when interest rates are rising as well as falling. "It will take a year before the direct impact of the rate cut is felt by many companies, but you get some initial impact through expectations. Consumers will start to feel better. They will make more positive plans than negative plans. They won't cancel orders and those orders create production down the line. We will see impact, but it will take a while," says Wynn Van Bussman, chief economist at DaimlerChrysler.

Norm Wesley expects to see a quick payoff from the rate cut; nevertheless, he doesn't expect to ramp up his company's spending plans anytime soon. "We'll get an immediate reduction in our borrowing cost," said the chairman and chief executive

Source: Wall Street Journal, Jan. 5, 2001, p. A2.

Wage/Price Flexibility and Full Employment

Like the classical theorists of old, the economists of the new classical school (of which the most prominent members are Robert Lucas of Chicago, Thomas Sargent of Stanford, and Robert Barro of Harvard) believe that wages and

of Fortune Brands Inc., a Lincolnshire, Ill., company that makes consumer products ranging from Moen faucets to Titleist golf balls and Jim Beam bourbon. But when it comes to his own investment decisions for the company, Mr. Wesley is singing a slightly different tune. "At this point, we would continue to take a cautious view of capital spending until we get a better idea of what impact this is going to have on the economy," he says.

Consider as evidence of lag times these quirks from the latest cycle of Fed movements: The Federal Reserve started tightening interest rates in June 1999, and the Nasdaq peaked in March 2000. Yet the Conference Board's consumer-confidence index hit an all-time high in May 2000. And the business-spending plans of many corporations didn't slip until the final months of the year.

According to Bill Dudley, a Goldman Sachs economist, the wealth effect—in which consumers increase their spending in response to increases in stock-market holdings or home values—takes as many as 18 months to play out. First, investors take stock of their gains or losses. That suggests that after the drubbing many investors took in 2000, they could be hesitant, at least at first, to respond to a stock-market recovery with the

kind of spending binges they exhibited in late 1999 and early 2000.

In other respects, however, both Mr. Blinder and Mr. Dudley say that old rules are indeed changing for a variety of reasons. First, the Federal Reserve has become more transparent, tipping off the market to its inclinations well before it changes policy and to the data that it is watching closely. This allows investors to anticipate Fed actions long before they happen.

That, says Diane Swonk, an economist with Bank One in Chicago, has been happening in the mortgage market. In the past, lenders have followed the Fed's lead, cutting mortgage rates only after the Fed began an easing cycle. This time around, however, mortgage rates began falling months before the Fed's move. Mortgage servicer Freddie Mac said that average rates on 30-year fixed-rate mortgages dipped to

7.07%, down from 7.13% last week and a five-year high of 8.64% in mid-May.

"The lags are becoming shorter," says Mr. Dudley. Yet he doesn't see a pickup in economic growth until the second half of this year. Mr. Blinder also says the lags are becoming shorter, but he adds that the full impact of the round of easing that has just started might not be felt until the spring of 2002.

Some people, however, argue that the economy may have been more responsive to the Federal Reserve Board 30 years ago. Mr. Steinberg at Merrill Lynch notes that back then, a rule known as Regulation Q fixed bank-interest rates, putting the Fed in the position to shut down lending overnight by raising the cost of bank funds above the fixed lending rates. Today, however, the Fed is operating in global financial markets that are much more difficult to manage single-handedly.

Use Your Economic Reasoning

1. Why do the lags associated with monetary policy create problems for policymakers?
2. If the Fed is becoming more "transparent" in its monetary policy—if it is communicating more clearly its inclinations— this may tend to reduce

the impact lag. Why? What evidence does the article provide that this is occurring?
3. If the lags associated with monetary policy become shorter, does this strengthen or weaken the monetarist case against discretionary policy?

prices are highly flexible. This flexibility permits markets to adjust quickly to changes in supply or demand, so that shortages or surpluses are prevented. In short, highly flexible prices ensure that the quantity of the good or service demanded will equal the quantity supplied; markets will "clear."

New classical economists believe that the market-clearing principle applies not only to individual markets—the markets for shoes or cars or accountants, for instance—but also to the aggregate economy. Its implications for the overall labor market are particularly important. To illustrate, let's suppose that the economy experiences a decline in aggregate demand. Of course, when the overall demand for products declines, the demand for labor must also fall. But the new classical economists do not believe that this reduction in labor demand will result in unemployment. Because wages are highly flexible, the reduced level of labor demand will cause wages to drop. Lower wage rates will both encourage employers to hire more workers and reduce the amount of labor supplied (at the lower wage, some workers will prefer leisure to work). The reduction in wages will thus restore equilibrium in the labor market; everyone who is willing to work at the new, lower wage will find employment, and every employer who is willing to pay that wage will find workers.[3] Any unemployment must be voluntary.

The Importance of Expectations

The belief in highly flexible wages and prices and the voluntary nature of unemployment is not new; this view was held by the original classical economists. But the new classical economists are not clones of the originals; they have made their own distinctive contribution to economic thinking. The distinctive feature of the new classical economics is its focus on expectations and the way that expectations influence people's behavior.

These economists remind us that different expectations about the future can lead to different decisions today. For instance, if consumers expect new-car prices to be lower in a few months, they will probably wait to buy; if they expect prices to be higher, they will buy now. These are commonsense observations that few of us would challenge. But the new classical economists go well beyond these observations. They are interested in how expectations are formed; in other words, they want to know how individuals come to expect whatever they expect—higher car prices, lower interest rates, or more rapid inflation, for instance.

Keynesians and monetarists disagree about many things, but both groups have assumed that individuals base their expectations only on experience—by looking backward at past events. The new classical economists argue that this assumption implies that individuals are irrational because it presumes that they ignore current events that they know will influence the future. As an alternative, the new classical economists have proposed the theory of rational expectations.

---

[3] The new classical economists do not believe that labor contracts make wages so inflexible as to prevent these adjustments.

The **theory of rational expectations** suggests that people use all available information to develop realistic (rational) expectations about the future. According to this theory, the public is quite perceptive in forming its expectations. Households and businesses do not merely project past trends into the future; they also take current economic developments quickly into account.

For instance, when forecasting inflation, people will consider the inflation of recent years, but they will also consider the potential impact of upcoming labor negotiations, the rate of productivity growth, the anticipated quality of agricultural harvests (and their impact on food prices), developments in the Middle East (and their impact on oil prices), and—perhaps most important of all—the expected government response to inflation. (Just how rational are human beings? Read "Stock Market Mind Games…," on page 432, and see what behavioral economists have to say.)

Rational Expectations and Discretionary Policy

The belief that wages and prices are highly flexible and that expectations are formed "rationally" leads the members of the new classical school to some interesting policy conclusions. According to the new classical economists, *systematic* monetary and fiscal policies cannot alter the level of output or employment in the economy; they can change only the price level. This belief is known as the **policy ineffectiveness theorem.** The implications of the policy ineffectiveness theorem are clear: Government attempts to reduce unemployment are doomed to failure; they will result only in inflation.

The problem, according to the new classical theorists, is that systematic policies whereby the government always responds to a particular set of economic conditions in a given way are *predictable.* But if discretionary policies are predictable, individuals will anticipate those policies and alter their behavior in ways that make the policies ineffective. Thus, individuals, *acting on rational expectations,* make government stabilization policies ineffective.

To illustrate, let's suppose that historically the Fed has expanded the money supply whenever the measured unemployment rate reached 6 percent.[4] Now, let's assume that the unemployment rate reaches that magic

---

[4] How can the unemployment rate reach 6 percent if wages and prices are highly flexible? According to the new classical economists, this can occur as a result of *unexpected* shocks in aggregate demand or supply—reductions in planned investment, the outbreak of war, or significant crop failures, for instance. Because these events are unexpected, they may be misperceived by workers. For instance, if the economy experiences a reduction in aggregate demand, some workers may mistakenly assume that the downturn has affected only their industry. Equally important, they may fail to recognize that the overall price level has also fallen, so that the real wage—the purchasing power of their money wage—is unchanged. Suffering from these misperceptions, they are unhappy with their lower money wage. Thus, workers quit their jobs and set out in search of positions that pay as much as they are accustomed to earning. In this way an unexpected shock may lead to unemployment.

number and the Fed feels compelled to take action. Of course, when the money supply is expanded, the aggregate demand curve will shift to the right, as depicted in Exh. 14.1 by the movement from AD_1 to AD_2. This increase in aggregate demand would, ceteris paribus, tend to raise the level of output in the economy. In our example, output would be expanded from the original equilibrium of $900 billion to $1,000 billion (the intersection of AS_1 and AD_2). Because increased output normally means additional jobs, employment would also tend to expand.

But supporters of the theory of rational expectations believe that the assumption of ceteris paribus is unreasonable in this situation. They argue that workers and businesses have learned to anticipate the Fed's policy response to unemployment. Moreover, they have discovered that when the money supply is increased, inflation inevitably follows. (Note that the increase in aggregate demand pushes up the price level along with the level

---

EXHIBIT 14.1

Rational Expectations and Economic Policy

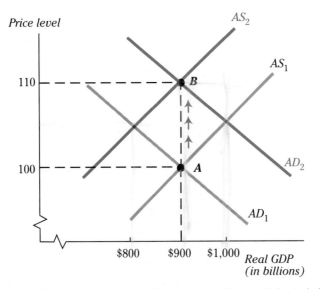

According to the theory of rational expectations, anticipated changes in monetary or fiscal policies cannot alter the level of output or employment; they can change only prices. In this example the expansionary monetary policy that shifts the aggregate demand curve from AD_1 to AD_2 is anticipated, causing workers to ask for higher wages and suppliers to ask for higher input prices. These changes cause the AS curve to shift upward from AS_1 to AS_2, neutralizing the output effect of the monetary expansion and raising the overall price level.

of output.) So when the public perceives that the Fed is likely to increase the money supply, it takes actions to protect itself from the anticipated inflation. Workers ask for higher wages, suppliers raise their input prices, and businesses push up product prices. Because prices and wages are assumed to be highly flexible, these adjustments occur immediately, the moment the public anticipates higher prices. Of course, if wage rates and other costs rise, the aggregate supply curve will tend to shift upward (from AS_1 to AS_2 in Exh. 14.1), and so less real output will be supplied at any given price level. Since the government-mandated increase in aggregate demand has been immediately offset by a *reduction* in aggregate supply, the net effect is to leave output and employment unchanged. The only impact of the expansionary monetary policy has been an increase in the price level from 100 to 110.

The preceding example focused on efforts to combat unemployment, but the theory of rational expectations has equally interesting implications for the the battle against inflation. To illustrate, let's suppose that the inflation rate rises to some level that Fed policymakers have openly designated as unacceptable. According to the theory of rational expectations, if the public is convinced of the Fed's commitment to reducing inflation, it will expect lower inflation; workers will therefore immediately accept wage cuts, and input suppliers will accept lower prices. As a consequence, the AS curve will quickly shift downward, lowering the price level but preserving the same level of output and employment. Once again, discretionary policy alters only the price level; it has no impact on real output or the level of employment. (Note that this result is quite different from the effect predicted by Keynesians. Keynesians would argue that because *some* wages and prices are rigid due to contracts, a reduction in aggregate demand would lower *both* the overall price level and the levels of output and employment. In fact, a major concern of Keynesians has been the unemployment "cost" of combating inflation.) Although these examples have dealt with monetary policy, the same conclusions would hold for systematic applications of fiscal policy.

The Need for Policy Rules

What conclusions can we reach from the preceding examples? The primary conclusion is that systematic monetary and fiscal policies affect only the price level; they do not alter either the level of output or employment. Of course, for discretionary policies to have the effect intended by Keynesians, they must be systematic; it wouldn't make sense to expand the money supply or to cut taxes at random time intervals. So, in effect, the new classical economists are arguing that discretionary monetary and fiscal policies cannot be used to reduce unemployment.

USE YOUR ECONOMIC REASONING

Stock Market Mind Games: Investors More Lucky than Clever and Rational Thinking Doesn't Rule, Economics Professors Say

By Al Lewis

UNIVERSITY of Chicago economics professor Richard Thaler... is among a small but growing clique of economists that is challenging the most fundamental assumptions of financial economics: That people are rational, and that rational minds reign on Wall Street.

Last week, Thaler and his colleagues discussed results of their studies with members of the Colorado Society of Certified Public Accountants. Their consensus: The average American has far more confidence than ability when it comes to investing, and that easy gains in a bull market [a market where investors expect rising stock prices] are setting the stage for a future disaster....

Shoddy Records

In the bull market of the late 1990s, stories of huge gains—particularly with technology and Internet stocks—are everywhere. Tales of loss are simply not heralded. In that sense, investing has become even more like gambling. Participants boast of gains but quietly walk away when their chips are gone.

Additionally, many investors do not keep track of the actual gains and losses.... Consequently, they are able to believe in their investing prowess when a basic audit would show them under-performing the market....

Hindsight bias is another human condition that lends itself to irrational investment decisions. To demonstrate hindsight bias, Thaler once asked his students to forecast the Dow Jones industrial average at the beginning of a school year. At the end of the semester, he asked the same students to recall their predictions. Most recalled accurately forecasting the index's rise, even though they hadn't....[According to Thaler,] "We all remember being brilliant and omniscient when we weren't."

What Investors Really Do

At the University of California, professor Terrance Odean has analyzed tens of thousands of records from individual investor accounts. In summarizing his conclusions at the Executive Conference Center at Inverness last week he quoted Benjamin Graham, father of modern securities analysis.

"The investor's chief problem—and even his worst enemy—appears to be himself," Graham said. Odean's research shows that individual investors trade too often. They sell their winning stocks and hang on to their losers. And they spend too much time chasing hot tips and news.

"People who are successful take too much credit for their successes, and this leads to overconfidence," Odean said. "It's the old Wall Street adage, 'Don't confuse brains with a bull market.' "

Overconfidence, which can overcome the best and worst of investors, often

---

Source: Denver Rocky Mountain News, Sept. 26, 1999, p. 1G.

leads to too much [stock] trading. Odean said he's conducted several studies of individual accounts, all of which show that those who trade more actively will under-perform investors who buy and hold....

In other studies, Odean showed that, on average, women do better than men in the stock market because they are less likely to be overconfident.

Overconfidence is exacerbated in the electronic age. Investors have unprecedented access to information, but Odean said many investors make the mistake of confusing information with knowledge.

"Suppose I told you everything there was to know about a roulette wheel," he said. "Who manufactured it, where it was manufactured, what materials were used to make it. And then I gave you the history of where the ball had landed for the last 10,000 spins of the wheel. Are you now able to predict where the ball is going to land next time?"

This, he says, is no different in the stock market. Investors have incredible access to information, which gives them the illusion of knowledge, but predicting the future remains impossible.

Why Americans Don't Save

Harvard University professor David Laibson believes economists have made all the wrong assumptions about Americans as both investors and consumers. "Mainstream economists believe that consumers are highly sophisti-

cated and rational," he said at the Colorado CPA conference last week. "But behavioral economists believe that consumers have a lot to learn."

He points to the sagging U.S. savings rate, and postulates that Americans suffer from limited rationality, limited self-control and unbounded optimism. "By any measure, the vast majority of U.S. households are not saving enough to maintain their standard of living after retirement," Laibson said.

The median U.S. household retires with liquid

wealth of $10,000 and net worth of $100,000, most of which is home equity and automobiles. Also, the median U.S. household experiences a 33 percent drop in per capita consumption during retirement.

This scenario isn't likely to change. Laibson said his research shows consumers and investors begin with the best of intentions. Like dieters or people wishing to quit smoking, they devise long-term goals but fail to meet them through their actions in the present....

Use Your Economic Reasoning

1. What is "hindsight bias"? How can hindsight bias contribute to irrational investing?
2. Odean's studies (and others) suggest that people who buy and hold stocks do better than people who trade (buy and sell) stocks more frequently. Individuals have access to these studies, but many continue to trade stocks frequently. Why? What possible reasons does the article provide?
3. New classical economists assume that individuals are rational in the sense that they use all available information and use it intelligently. This means, for instance, that they can see the relationship between observed variables—like Fed policy actions—and variables they are trying to predict—like the rate of

inflation. Does the work of Thaler and his colleagues lend support to that assumption? What evidence do you find most compelling?
4. The theory of rational expectations suggests that people learn from their mistakes. So, for instance, if the Fed's policies drive up the price level, individuals may not learn that immediately, but they will eventually; they won't continue to misjudge the Fed's impact. Does the research of Thaler and his colleagues suggest that stock market investors learn from their mistakes? Might their research be inconclusive? (*Hint:* Do any of the studies mentioned in the article track the performance of *particular* investors over time?)

Because the new classical economists are convinced that government policies cannot be used to alter employment, they believe that policymakers should concentrate on achieving and maintaining a low rate of inflation. This, they suggest, can be best accomplished by permitting a slow, steady growth of the money supply and avoiding large budget deficits. Thus, the new classical economists favor rules much like the monetarists': Increase the money supply at a constant rate, and balance the federal budget over some agreed-on period (not necessarily on an annual basis but over some predictable time frame). These rules will prevent government policymakers from aggravating inflation in their well-intentioned but futile attempts to lower unemployment.

Criticisms of the New Classical Economics

The new classical economics is quite controversial. Both the assumption of wage/price flexibility and the assumption of rational expectations have been criticized. Few economists seem willing to accept the assertion that wages are sufficiently flexible to ensure that labor markets are continually in equilibrium. These economists point to the prolonged unemployment of the Great Depression and periods in the 1970s and 1980s as evidence that wages adjust slowly, not rapidly as the new classical model implies.

The belief that expectations are formed rationally has also been met with skepticism, both by Keynesians and by many monetarists. Critics argue that the public does not gather and analyze information as intelligently as the theory suggests; nor does it always make fully rational decisions based on that information. Studies of the theory of rational expectations have produced mixed results. Although some early evidence supported the theory, its performance on more recent tests has not upheld its initial promise.

If either of the basic assumptions is incorrect, the policy ineffectiveness theorem of the new classical economists is invalidated. In other words, monetary and fiscal policies would be capable of generating short-run changes in the levels of output and employment. This seems to be the view held by most economists. Of course, whether such policies should be used to change output and employment still depends on the length of the lags involved in policy implementation—the issue raised by the monetarists.

A NEW FORM OF ACTIVISM: MANAGING AGGREGATE SUPPLY

The debate about the desirability of government efforts to manage aggregate demand has been with us for a long time. Given that it is very difficult to prove statistically which of the schools of thought has the most accurate model of the economy, the debate is likely to continue. We'll indicate a few areas of consensus among macroeconomists after we take a brief look at supply-side economics.

Even if monetary and fiscal policies work as Keynesians suggest (which is certainly not the conclusion of the monetarists or the new classical economists), they produce mixed results. As we saw in Chapter 12, efforts to reduce unemployment tend to aggravate inflation, whereas policies to reduce inflation lead to greater unemployment. In addition, demand-management policies are incapable of offsetting supply shocks—unexpected reductions in aggregate supply. Since supply shocks lead to stagflation, they put pressure on policymakers to combat the two problems instead of one. But once again policymakers are confronted by trade-offs. If they choose to combat inflation, they make the unemployment problem even worse; if they decide to attack unemployment, the inflation rate escalates. In the late 1970s these limitations led to an intense interest in policies to increase aggregate supply.

Supply-Side Economics

The attraction of increasing aggregate supply is probably obvious. Anything that causes the *AS* curve to shift to the right will raise output and employment, while also lowering the overall price level. As you consider Exh.14.2, suppose that the economy is operating at point *A*, at the intersection of *AD* and AS_1. If policymakers can increase aggregate supply from AS_1 to AS_2, they can move the economy to point *B*; they will have increased equilibrium output (and employment) in the economy while also reducing the overall price level. Policymakers will have succeeded in simultaneously reducing unemployment and inflation.[5]

Theory suggests a variety of policies for increasing aggregate supply. The phrase **supply-side economics** is commonly used to refer to a branch of economics that focuses on stimulating aggregate supply through policies that involve minimal government intervention. Supply-side economists advocate policies such as the following:

1. *Encourage saving and investment through tax policies.* By encouraging saving through a reduction in taxes on interest income, for example, the government can make more funds available for investment purposes. Various techniques can then be used to encourage businesses to borrow this money and invest it. *Investment tax credits* would allow firms to deduct a certain percentage of their investment outlays from their tax liabilities. To

---

[5] Policymakers are aiming to increase both short-run and long-run aggregate supply. For continuity, this chapter focuses on the short-run *AS* curve. The next chapter, which explores policies to increase aggregate supply in greater depth, will focus on the long-run *AS* curve.

EXHIBIT 14.2
The Impact of Supply-Side Remedies

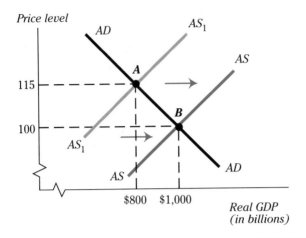

The purpose of supply-side remedies is to shift the aggregate supply curve to the right, thereby reducing the overall price level while increasing output and employment.

the extent that such policies encourage business to borrow and invest in new factories and equipment, they help to increase the economy's productive capacity so that more output is supplied at any given price level. Of course, if more output is produced at each price level, the aggregate supply curve shifts to the right, as depicted in Exh. 14.2.

2. *Reduce government regulations that drive up the cost of doing business.* We all recognize that government regulations are necessary to protect consumers, the environment, and the health and safety of workers. In some instances, however, regulations may add substantially to the cost of producing goods and services yet may provide little real benefit for the society. For example, the Food and Drug Administration has been accused of driving up the cost of developing new drugs by needlessly prolonging the testing that is required to gain FDA approval. Reducing such costs should free resources to produce other goods and services; thus, more output can be supplied at each price level.

3. *Encourage individuals to work harder and longer by reducing marginal tax rates.* Marginal tax rates are the tax rates paid on the last increment of income. For example, under a progressive income tax system, an individual earning $15,000 might be required to pay a tax of 15 percent on the first

$10,000 and 20 percent on the remaining $5,000. Supply-siders insist that high marginal tax rates discourage work. The way to get people to work more (and thereby increase aggregate supply) is to reduce marginal tax rates and let them keep more of what they earn.

Unlike monetary and fiscal policies, supply-side remedies have the very desirable feature of being able to combat unemployment and inflation at the same time. As you consider Exh. 14.2, suppose that the economy is operating at point A, the intersection of AD and AS_1. If policymakers can increase aggregate supply from AS_1 to AS_2, they can move the economy to point B; they will have increased equilibrium output (and employment) in the economy while reducing the overall price level. Policymakers will have succeeded in simultaneously reducing unemployment and inflation.

The Reagan Supply-Side Experiment

When President Reagan took office, he presented several supply-side features in his Program for Economic Recovery (announced in February 1981). The cornerstone of Reagan's program was the Economic Recovery Tax Act (ERTA) of 1981. ERTA called for a 5 percent reduction in tax rates in 1981 and a 10 percent reduction in 1982 and 1983. ERTA also contained provisions to encourage saving and to stimulate business investment. According to its supporters, the reduction in tax rates would cause the economy to grow rapidly as the lower tax rates stimulated saving and investment and convinced Americans to work harder.

What actually happened? Initially, the effects of the Reagan administration's tax cuts were more than offset by a restrictive monetary policy engineered by the Federal Reserve to combat inflation (which was running at more than 12 percent a year in 1980). While these policies helped to quell inflation, they also pushed the economy into the deepest recession since the Great Depression.

The recession ended in December 1982, and output and employment expanded rapidly through 1984. For the remainder of the 1980s, however, economic growth was unspectacular (President Reagan's term ended in 1988). Overall, the rate of economic growth experienced in the decade of the 1980s was identical to the experience of the previous decade; in both decades the average annual growth rate of real GDP was 2.7 percent. Clearly, the supply-side measures did not lead to the spectacular economic growth that some supporters expected.

Judged by what some supply-siders initially promised—an explosion in work effort, investment, and saving—the Economic Recovery Tax Act was clearly a disappointment. Moreover, Keynesian economists attributed most of

President Reagan's Program for Economic Recovery contained several supply-side features.

the economic expansion of the Reagan years not to the supply-side policies but to the demand-side stimulus provided by the substantial budget deficits.

These economists argue that tax cuts shift both the aggregate demand curve (the traditional Keynesian impact) and the aggregate supply curve (the supply-side impact). However, they believe that in the short run, the supply-side impact tends to be minor in comparison with the demand-side effect.

Even if Keynesians are correct about the short-run impact of supply-side policies, we should not conclude that measures to enhance aggregate supply are to be ignored. On the contrary, virtually all economists agree that expanding aggregate supply is crucial to the long-run well-being of Americans. The next chapter, "Economic Growth: The Importance of the Long Run," examines this issue in much more detail.

SUMMING UP: FINAL THOUGHTS ON POLICY ACTIVISM

Economists obviously disagree about the role of government in attempting to maintain full employment and about the possible benefits of supply-side remedies. This section is the author's interpretation of current thinking.

1. Virtually all economists agree that the economy contains, to one degree or another, a self-correcting mechanism. The economy tends to return to potential GDP and full employment in the long run. Economists disagree about how long this adjustment process takes.

2. Economists disagree about the ability of demand-management policies to speed up the adjustment to potential GDP and full employment. Keynesians support such measures; monetarists and new classical economists do not.

   The differences between activists and nonactivists may not, however, be quite as great as they first appear. Even Keynesians recognize that discretionary policies are subject to lags. Thus, modern Keynesians believe that it is undesirable to attempt to fine-tune the economy—to try to correct every minor increase in unemployment or in the overall price level. Instead, they believe that policymakers should confine their efforts to combating major downturns or inflationary threats.

3. The new classical economics has clearly shaken up macroeconomic thinking but hasn't gained very many converts. Most economists do not appear to believe that expectations are formed in a totally "rational" manner. Even fewer economists are willing to accept the classical contention that wages are highly flexible and that markets are continuously in equilibrium. If economists reject these arguments, they must reject the policy ineffectiveness theorem that grows from them.

   Although few economists seem willing to embrace the entire new classical model, most tend to agree that the theory of rational expectations is an improvement on the expectations models previously applied by Keynesians and monetarists. Moreover, there appears to be support for a weaker version of the policy ineffectiveness theory: Fully anticipated policy changes have *smaller* effects than unanticipated changes.

4. Virtually all economists support measures to stimulate aggregate supply. But evidence suggests that supply-side measures do little in the short run to stimulate GDP or to lower the price level. The major impact of supply-side policies comes in the long run, when their benefits can be substantial.

SUMMARY

Although economists generally agree about the existence of a self-correcting mechanism, they disagree about the speed with which this adjustment process occurs and about the desirability of government efforts to enhance these naturally occurring forces.

Keynesians believe that the economy's self-correcting mechanism works quite slowly. Thus, they support an active role for government in speeding the adjustment process through discretionary monetary and fiscal policies.

Monetarists believe that the economy's self-adjustment mechanism works reasonably quickly and that government efforts to aid this process are either ineffective or counterproductive.

According to monetarists, changes in the money supply play the primary role in determining the level of aggregate output and prices in the economy. Government efforts to stimulate the economy through fiscal policy are futile because they lead to the crowding out of investment spending.

The monetarists also argue against the use of discretionary monetary policy. Because of the recognition lag and the impact lag, the effect of a monetary policy change may be felt when it is no longer appropriate. Thus, discretionary monetary policy has a destabilizing effect on the economy: It contributes to greater unemployment and inflation.

Because monetarists believe that discretionary monetary policy tends to intensify the economy's problems rather than to lessen them, they support a *monetary rule* that would require the Fed to expand the money supply at a constant annual rate.

Monetarists are not alone in opposing the use of discretionary policies to guide the economy's performance; *new classical economists* also argue against such intervention. The new classical economics is founded on two basic tenets: (1) wages and prices are highly flexible, and (2) expectations about the future are formed rationally.

Because new classical economists believe that wages and prices are highly flexible, they believe that the economy quickly tends toward full employment. Reductions in aggregate demand are met by falling wages and prices, which quickly restore equilibrium. Any unemployment is voluntary.

New classical economists emphasize the impact of expectations on behavior; different expectations about the future can lead to different decisions today. The *theory of rational expectations* suggests that people use all available information to develop realistic expectations about the future.

The new classical economists' belief in highly flexible wages and prices and rational expectations led to the *policy ineffectiveness theorem*. According to this theorem, systematic monetary and fiscal policies cannot alter the level of output or employment in the economy; they can change only the price level.

Because the new classical economists are convinced that government policies cannot be used to alter output or employment, they believe that policy-makers should concentrate on achieving and maintaining a low rate of inflation. The new classical economists, like the monetarists, favor rules to achieve this objective.

The activist–nonactivist debate has focused on the desirability of demand-management policies. But in the late 1970s, supply-side remedies—policies to increase aggregate supply—attracted a great deal of attention. The desirable feature of such policies is that they can reduce unemployment and inflation at the same time. Available evidence suggests that supply-side measures have a relatively modest impact on aggregate supply in the short run; most of the impact comes in the long run.

KEY TERMS

Monetarism
Monetary rule

Policy ineffectiveness theorem
Supply-side economics

Theory of rational expectations

STUDY QUESTIONS

Fill in the Blanks

1. Keynesian economists who advocate government intervention to guide the economy's performance are also known as _activest_ .

2. The two modern schools of thought that oppose the use of demand-management techniques are the _Clasieal_ and the _Monetarst Economst_

3. The primary reason that monetarists oppose the use of discretionary monetary policy is because such policy is subject to _Lags_ .

4. According to the _Monetarist_ and the _new classical economist_ , the Fed should be required to expand the money supply at a constant rate.

5. _Milton Friedman_ is often called the father of monetarism.

6. According to the _new classical economist_ , expectations are formed rationally.

7. The belief that systematic monetary and fiscal policies cannot alter the level of output or employment is known as the _Policy ineffectiveness_ theorem.

8. The requirement that the Fed expand the money supply at a constant rate is known as the _Monetary Rule_ .

9. The use of monetary or fiscal policy in an attempt to eliminate even minor increases in unemployment or inflation is known as

~~Fine Tunning~~ the economy and is opposed by virtually all modern economists.

10. Unlike monetary and fiscal policies,

~~supply side~~ remedies can be used to reduce unemployment and inflation at the same time.

Multiple Choice

1. Which of the following schools of economists would be described as "activists"?
   a) Classical economists
   b) Keynesian economists
   c) Monetarist economists
   d) New classical economists

2. Which of the following statements about the activist–nonactivist debate is true?
   a) Monetarists advocate the use of discretionary monetary policy to manage aggregate demand and to ensure full employment.
   b) New classical economists support the use of fiscal policy to guide the economy but believe that monetary policy is ineffective.
   c) Keynesians advocate government intervention because they believe that the self-correcting mechanism works too slowly.
   d) All of the above

3. According to the monetarists,
   a) fiscal policy is ineffective because of crowding out.
   b) fiscal policy is more effective than monetary policy.
   c) increases in government spending tend to lower interest rates, thus stimulating investment spending.
   d) increases in government spending tend to stimulate investment spending by making business leaders more optimistic.

4. Which of the following is a true statement about the monetarists?
   a) They favor the use of discretionary monetary policy to guide the economy's performance.
   b) They believe that the money supply should be increased at a constant rate.
   c) They favor legislation to provide Fed policymakers with more power to guide the economy's performance.
   d) a and c

5. When monetarists call for a "monetary rule," what they really want is
   a) greater reliance on discretionary monetary policy and less reliance on discretionary fiscal policy.
   b) legislation to provide Fed policymakers with more power to guide the economy's performance.
   c) legislation that would require the Fed to increase the money supply at a constant rate.
   d) bigger paychecks for monetarist economists.

6. The two types of lags in monetary policy are the
   a) policy lag and the implementation lag.
   b) recognition lag and the impact lag.
   c) recognition lag and the policy lag.
   d) identification lag and the implementation lag.

7. The major reason monetarists oppose the use of discretionary monetary policy to guide the economy's performance is that they
   a) do not believe that changes in the money supply have any impact on output or employment.
   b) believe that lags cause monetary policy to have a destabilizing effect on the economy.
   c) believe that monetary policy is not as effective as fiscal policy.

d) believe that rational expectations make monetary policy changes ineffective.

8. Keynesians believe that the economy is inherently unstable because of
   a) the instability created by government fiscal policy.
   b) fluctuations in the level of government spending.
   c) the volatility of investment spending.
   d) Federal Reserve monetary policies.

9. Which of the following is *not* a belief of the new classical economists?
   a) Wages and prices are highly flexible.
   b) Expectations are formed rationally.
   c) Unemployment is voluntary.
   d) Labor markets adjust very slowly to changes in demand.

10. According to the theory of rational expectations,
    a) households and businesses base their expectations only on past experience.
    b) people use all available information in developing their expectations about the future.
    c) it is reasonable for households and businesses to ignore the actions of policymakers.
    d) only policymakers have sufficient knowledge to develop accurate estimates of future price levels.

11. According to the policy ineffectiveness theorem,
    a) anticipated changes in monetary or fiscal policy will alter only the price level.
    b) fiscal policy is ineffective unless it is accompanied by monetary policy.
    c) monetary policy is ineffective unless it is accompanied by fiscal policy.
    d) unanticipated changes in monetary or fiscal policy will alter only the price level.

12. The new classical economists believe that any anticipated increase in the money supply will
    a) expand output and employment.

b) be immediately offset by a reduction in aggregate supply.
   c) immediately cause potential GDP to expand.
   d) lead to an immediate reduction in the price level, with no change in output or employment.

13. According to Keynesians, which of the following is true?
    a) When unemployment is caused by inadequate aggregate demand, expanding the money supply will reduce unemployment but intensify inflation.
    b) When inflation is caused by a supply shock, reducing the money supply will lower the rate of inflation but aggravate unemployment.
    c) When unemployment is caused by a reduction in aggregate supply, increasing the money supply will reduce unemployment but aggravate inflation.
    d) All of the above
    e) None of the above

14. Which of the following is *not* a supply-side policy?
    a) Use tax credits to encourage investment.
    b) Reduce marginal tax rates to encourage people to work longer and harder.
    c) Increase tax rates on interest income in order to discourage saving and stimulate consumption spending.
    d) Eliminate government regulations that do not serve a valid purpose.

15. In the short run, reductions in marginal tax rates probably increase
    a) only aggregate demand.
    b) only aggregate supply.
    c) both aggregate demand and aggregate supply but have a greater impact on demand.
    d) both aggregate demand and aggregate supply but have a greater impact on supply.

Problems and Questions for Discussion

1. Given that the economy has a self-correcting mechanism, what is the essence of the Keynesian argument for government intervention to combat unemployment?

2. Why do the monetarists believe that fiscal policy cannot be used to stimulate the economy?

3. Discuss the lags involved in the implementation of monetary policy.

4. Keynesians blame the inherent instability of capitalist economies on the volatility of investment spending. Why do you suppose investment spending by businesses is more volatile than consumption spending by households?

5. What is the nature of the *monetarist* argument for a monetary rule?

6. The new classical economists sometimes argue that only random monetary policy can alter output and employment. Use their model to explain this conclusion. Does this mean that policymakers should replace Keynesian demand-management policies with random policies?

7. Explain the logic behind the policy ineffectiveness theorem of the new classical economists. Supplement your explanation with a graph.

8. Discuss the similarities and differences between the monetarists and the new classical economists with regard to the issue of demand-management policy.

9. List as many supply-side remedies as you can remember, and discuss the rationale for each.

10. Critics of the Reagan experiment with supply-side economics often argue that it was "oversold." What do they mean? What evidence might they summon to support their position?

ANSWER KEY

Fill in the Blanks

1. activists

2. monetarists, new classical economists

3. lags

4. monetarists, new classical economists

5. Milton Friedman

6. new classical economists

7. policy ineffectiveness

8. monetary rule

9. fine-tuning

10. supply-side

Multiple Choice

1. b
2. c
3. a

4. b
5. c
6. b

7. b
8. c
9. d

10. b
11. a
12. b

13. d
14. c
15. c

CHAPTER FIFTEEN

Economic Growth: The Importance of the Long Run

Will you live as well as your parents? Will you be able to buy your dream house, send your kids to college, and retire while you're still young enough to enjoy it? These are important questions! The answers depend in part on individual decisions—on how hard you work and the career choices you make, for instance. But they also depend on something largely beyond your personal control; they depend on the long-run performance of the economy—on how rapidly it grows. In this chapter we explain what is meant by economic growth and examine how it affects our material standard of living. Then we explore the determinants of economic growth and the policies that promote growth. We conclude by examining some debates and concerns about economic growth.

ECONOMIC GROWTH AND WHY IT MATTERS

Thus far, we've spent very little time discussing economic growth. Instead we've focused on the short run and the factors that cause the economy's output to deviate from potential GDP. You've discovered that actual GDP sometimes falls short of potential, creating a "recessionary gap," and that the economy's GDP sometimes surges ahead of potential, creating an "inflationary gap." You've also learned that activists and non-activists disagree about whether discretionary policy can speed the return to potential. What may not have been evident in the preceding chapters, however, is that potential GDP can change; it is not a static concept. **Economic growth** is defined as an increase in an economy's production capacity or potential GDP. As we will see in a moment, it is this expansion in potential GDP that is responsible for long-run increases in a society's standard of living.

Economic Growth and the Standard of Living

How do we know when we're better off, when our standard of living has increased? The most common measure of a society's standard of living is GDP per capita—output per person. This measure of well-being is relatively easy to calculate. We simply divide an economy's GDP in a given year by its population in that year. For example, the United States' GDP was $9,248.4 billion in 1999, while the U.S. population was 273.1 million. We can conclude that GDP per capita was

$$1999 \text{ GDP per capita } = \frac{\$9,248.4 \text{ billion in GDP}}{273.1 \text{ million people}} = \$33,863.42$$

This figure compares favorably with other developed nations of the world. For example, 1999 per capita GDP was $22,700 in Germany, $23,300 in France, and $23,400 in Japan. These figures dwarf those for less-developed nations such as Bangladesh ($1,470) and Ethiopia ($560).[1] Exhibit 15.1 displays figures for additional nations.

Of course, if we want to make comparisons over time—for instance, if we want to determine whether we in the United States are better off today than we were in 1990—we have to base those comparisons on real GDP rather than nominal GDP. As you learned in Chapter 10, GDP can increase either because of rising output or because of rising prices. We need to eliminate the impact of rising prices to find out if we really are better off. If real GDP per capita is increasing, we can conclude that our material standard of living has increased because we have more goods and services per person. Of course, that doesn't ensure happiness and it doesn't indicate that *everyone* in our society is sharing in the increased output. But it does suggest that the average person's standard of *material* well-being has increased.

---

[1] Data are from Central Intelligence Agency, *The World Factbook, 2000,* Washington D.C.

EXHIBIT 15.1
Per Capita Gross Domestic Product, 1999

COUNTRY	GDP per Capita	COUNTRY	GDP per Capita
Afghanistan	$800	Japan	$23,400
Argentina	$10,000	Malaysia	$10,700
Australia	$22,200	Mexico	$8,500
Bangladesh	$1,470	Nicaragua	$2,650
Botswana	$3,900	Pakistan	$2,000
Brazil	$6,150	Puerto Rico	$9,800
Canada	$23,300	Russia	$4,200
China	$3,800	Saudi Arabia	$9,000
Cuba	$1,700	Singapore	$27,800
Denmark	$23,800	South Africa	$6,900
Egypt	$3,000	South Korea	$13,300
Ethiopia	$560	Sweden	$20,700
France	$23,300	Switzerland	$27,100
Germany	$22,700	Taiwan	$16,100
Ghana	$1,900	Turkey	$6,200
Haiti	$1,340	United Arab Emirates	$17,700
Hong Kong	$23,100	United Kingdom	$21,800
India	$1,800	United States	$33,900
Iran	$5,300	Vietnam	$1,850

Source: Central Intelligence Agency, *The World Factbook, 2000.*

Per Capita GDP: The United States' Experience

Americans have enjoyed a rising standard of living for about as long as they have kept records. Consider the progress that has been made in the last forty years (about the length of a person's working life). Per capita real GDP was $12,934 in 1959 (measured in 1996 dollars). By 1979 it had climbed to $21,640, and by 1999 it had risen to $33,863. In a little more than a generation, output per person increased more than 160 percent, an impressive increase in the standard of living.

How do we explain this increase in the standard of living? Let's begin with the basics. In order for a nation's standard of living to rise, real GDP must increase more rapidly than population. That may be obvious, but let's take a moment to consider the logic behind that statement. Suppose a nation's population increases by 1 percent a year. Under those circumstances, real GDP (output) must increase by 1 percent a year to provide the population with the same amount of goods and services, the same standard of living. If real GDP increases more rapidly than population, the standard of living (per capita GDP) increases; if population increases more rapidly than GDP, the standard of living declines. In recent decades, the U.S. population has been increasing at a rate of about 1 percent a year, so, for example, when real GDP increases by 3 percent, per capita GDP increases by 2 percent. Many less-developed nations are not so fortunate. For instance, the population of Ethiopia is increasing at a rate in excess of 2 percent, so a 3 percent increase in Ethiopia's real GDP would increase the standard of living by less than 1 percent.

Exhibit 15.2 plots the growth of real GDP in the United States since 1970. As you can see from the exhibit, the trend in real GDP (the green wavy line in the exhibit) clearly has been upward. But while real GDP has grown over time, the expansion has not been steady or regular. Sometimes, output has grown rapidly. At other times, output has grown slowly or even declined. As you discovered in Chapter 10, we call these recurring ups and downs in the level of economic activity the *business cycle.* A period of rising output is called an *expansion;* a period of declining real output is called a *recession.* In the short run, the business cycle can have a significant impact on real GDP, lowering it during recessions and raising it rapidly during expansions. But over the long run, it is the behavior of *potential* GDP that really matters, because actual GDP tends toward potential GDP.

The smooth black curve in Exhibit 15.2 represents potential GDP. This curve shows potential GDP increasing at a rate of 3 percent a year, about the average rate at which real GDP has increased over the last thirty-year period. As you can see, actual GDP was sometimes above potential, sometimes below. But the self-correcting model tells us that in the long run, actual GDP returns to potential. That's why it is the growth rate of potential GDP that is important in determining our standard of living: because it is the behavior of potential GDP that dictates the path that actual GDP will *ultimately* follow.

The Rule of Seventy-Two:
Why the Growth Rate Matters

There's no reason to believe that potential GDP must always increase at the 3 percent rate we've experienced over the last thirty years. In fact, there is substantial evidence that potential GDP increased at something like 4 ½ percent a

EXHIBIT 15.2
The Trend of Real GDP in the United States

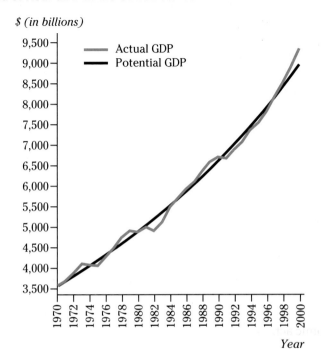

$ (in billions)

In the period from 1970 to 2000, potential GDP (represented by the smooth black curve) increased by approximately 3% a year. Actual GDP (the green wavy line) diverged from potential, sometimes growing more rapidly, sometimes more slowly.

year in the 1960s, and many economists believe that the growth rate of potential GDP accelerated in the last half of the 1990s. But why should we care about the growth rate of potential GDP? For example, suppose that the growth path of potential GDP was steeper; suppose, for instance, that potential GDP was growing at 4 percent a year instead of 3 percent. What impact would this have on our lives?

Small differences in the growth rate don't matter very much in the short run, but they matter a great deal in the long run. To illustrate, let's look at something you have a personal stake in—your income. Suppose you graduate from college at twenty-two and take a job paying $30,000 a year. How long will it take for your income to double—to increase to $60,000 a year? Obviously, it depends on how big your raises are! If your raises average 2 percent a year, it will take thirty-six years for your salary to reach $60,000. (You'll be fifty-eight years old!) If your raises average 3 percent, the time drops to twenty-four years (so you'll make it by the time you're forty-six). If you're fortunate enough to receive 4 percent raises, your income will double in only eighteen years. You'll be earning $60,000 by the time you turn forty, and your income will be $120,000 at fifty-eight. A percentage point or two may not seem like much, but in the long run it matters a great deal.

We base the preceding predictions on the **rule of seventy-two**, which states that a variable's doubling time equals seventy-two divided by the growth rate. (So, for instance, at a 4 percent growth rate, income would double in 72 / 4 = 18 years.) The mathematics behind the rule of seventy-two need not concern us here. The important point is that seemingly small changes in the growth rate make a big difference in the long run. The rule of seventy-two applies to any numeric value, including potential GDP—the source of rising living standards. If potential GDP is expanding at a rate of 3 percent a year, then potential GDP doubles every twenty-four years. At a 4 percent rate, GDP will take eighteen years to double. That one percentage point difference in the rate of growth has a substantial impact on our standard of living. It gives us more of the "fun stuff" like sports cars, vacations, and computer games. And it also provides more of the important things like housing, education, and health care. In summary, the rate of economic growth can have a significant impact on our lives. But what determines the rate of economic growth? We now turn to that question.

SOURCES OF ECONOMIC GROWTH

We've defined economic growth as an increase in potential GDP. Because the long-run aggregate supply (LRAS) curve is a vertical line at potential GDP, we can represent economic growth by shifting the long-run aggregate supply curve to the right, as represented in Exh. 15.3.[2] The question, then, is what factors can cause the LRAS curve to shift to the right? These factors are the sources of economic growth.

There are basically two sets of factors that can shift the LRAS curve to the right: increases in the stock of economic resources (land, labor, or capital) and increases in technology; that is, technological advance. Let's explore these possibilities.

Growth in the Stock of Natural Resources

We discovered in Chapter 1 that economists use the term "land" to refer to society's stock of natural resources. The term encompasses surface land, but it also includes timber, mineral deposits, oil, water, and so on.

---

[2] Recall from Chapter 1 that economic growth can also be represented by shifting the economy's production possibilities curve to the right. A rightward shift in the production possibilities curve indicates that the economy's production capabilities have increased. This is simply another way of saying that potential output has expanded.

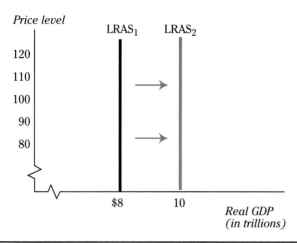

EXHIBIT 15.3
Graphing Economic Growth

We define economic growth as an increase in an economy's productive capacity, or potential GDP. It is represented graphically by a rightward shift in the economy's long run aggregate supply curve.

The discovery of additional supplies of natural resources does not appear to play a major role in the economic growth of modern economies. On the one hand, Japan developed into a major world power with very little in the way of a natural-resource base. And the Asian tigers—South Korea, Taiwan, and Singapore—appear to be on a similar path. On the other hand, some resource-rich nations—Brazil and Argentina, for instance—have experienced relatively slow rates of economic growth.

While at this time the availability of natural resources does not appear to be a make-or-break factor for a nation's economic growth, that could some day change. Land is the only economic resource on the planet that is truly in fixed supply. Because greater output requires more natural resources, the earth's fixed supply of natural resources may eventually mean an end to rising per capita incomes. Many economists argue that with technological advances (which we will discuss later) we can postpone that day for centuries—perhaps indefinitely. Others argue that, one way or another, natural-resource constraints—including those imposed by the ozone layer and available supplies of clean air and water—will eventually bring an end to rising living standards. We'll have more to say about this issue in the last section of this chapter.

Growth in the Labor Supply

Another possible source of increases in potential GDP is increases in the labor force—the supply of labor. Recall from Chapter 10 that we define the U.S.

labor force to include all persons over the age of sixteen who are working or actively seeking work. The labor force can increase for two reasons: because of more rapid growth in the (working-age) population or because a larger fraction of that population chooses to work.

By itself, population increase does not appear to be a very promising avenue for increasing living standards. Think about our definition of the standard of living—GDP per capita. While an increase in population can help to raise potential GDP—the size of the pie we have to divide—it also raises the number of people who want shares of that output—the number of slices of pie. This dual effect limits the benefit to be derived from an increase in population. In fact, less-developed countries like China and India devote their efforts to limiting population, not to stimulating its growth.

An increase in the labor-force participation rate—the fraction of the population that chooses to enter the labor force—is more promising. In 1950, only about one-third of women sixteen and over were in the labor force. Today, the fraction is approaching two-thirds.[3] This increase allows the economy to increase potential GDP without adding to the number of mouths to be fed. Of course, this avenue of growth is not free. Working moms or dads are not home raising kids, doing their own home repairs, or learning to play tennis. As you already know, every choice involves an opportunity cost.

Growth in the Capital Stock

An increase in the labor supply may have little impact on the rate of economic growth unless the additional workers are provided with capital to supplement their efforts. As we discovered in Chapter 1, the term *capital* is most commonly used to refer to **physical capital**—physical aids to production such as machines, tools, and factories. Computers are an example of physical capital, as are delivery trucks, robots, and hand tools (hammers, saws, etc.). Imagine a business hiring an additional secretary without providing the employee with a computer. That worker would be required to share someone's existing computer, using it only when it was vacant. Although this new employee would probably make a contribution to the firm, the contribution would clearly be less than if the business had been willing to provide additional capital to enhance the new worker's productivity.

The addition of **human capital**—the knowledge and skills that are embodied in labor—can also enhance worker productivity. Human capital is acquired through education and training. You're acquiring human capital right

---

[3] As the labor-force participation rate for women has risen, the rate for men has fallen (from about 86 percent in 1950 to roughly 75 percent today). The overall rate (the rate for men plus women) has continued to rise.

now, as you work on your college degree! A person with a college degree generally has more human capital than a person with only a high-school education. And a person with a graduate degree generally has more human capital than a person with an undergraduate degree. The more education and training, the more human capital you possess.

Consider our secretary again. Once we have provided this secretary with a computer, we will need to provide training programs on how to use particular types of software, how to troubleshoot for computer problems, and so on. The more knowledgeable this secretary becomes—the more human capital he or she acquires—the more productive this person will be. Of course, as workers become more productive, the economy's ability to produce output increases, so the economy's long-run aggregate supply curve shifts to the right.

The acquisition of additional capital—either physical capital or human capital—requires an investment on the part of society. There are basically two ways that a nation can acquire the money needed to finance investment expenditures: saving and borrowing. Neither option is painless. A decision to increase saving requires that we consume less now, lowering our current enjoyment. Borrowing requires that we eventually repay what we have borrowed, lowering future pleasure.

The pain associated with investment helps to explain why many less-developed countries have remained so. Because incomes in these nations are often extremely low, savings rates tend to be low—in some instances, virtually zero. The average citizen simply cannot forgo current consumption in order to save. That's why these nations try to attract foreign investment as a way of breaking out of this cycle.

Technological Advances

Technology is our state of knowledge about how to produce products. It dictates the ease with which the economy can convert resources into goods and services. **Technological advances** are discoveries that make it possible to produce more or better products from the same resources. For instance, technological breakthroughs in the area of genetics have provided farmers with hybrid seeds that allow them to obtain much higher corn and wheat yields from their fields. Advances in information technology, in turn, have made it possible to use the Internet and e-mail to communicate instantaneously, avoiding the need for more costly (and slower) forms of communication.

Technological change is generally regarded as the most important source of economic growth. It is also the least understood. Why does technological change occur more rapidly in some countries than in others? And why does it occur more rapidly at some times than at others? Unfortunately, we cannot answer these questions conclusively. The following factors may, however, provide some clues.

One factor that appears to influence the rate at which technological advances are made is the level of education. The more educated the workforce, the greater its ability to make technological breakthroughs. The rate of technological change also seems to depend on the availability of funding for research and development. Developing new products and new ways of doing things is not free, so success depends in part on how much money is spent in the search.

The profit potential associated with new technologies is also important. Private enterprises exist to make profits, so businesses are more interested in advancing technology when they can see its impact on their profit–loss statements. Consider, for example, genome research—the attempt to map human DNA. An important factor driving this research is the immense profit potential that better medicines might bring. According to George Scanos, president and CEO of Exelixis, Inc., a genetic-information company in San Francisco, California, "In a few years all the genes that are useful for treating diabetes, Alzheimer's and cancer will be known…. Whoever gets them first will get significant intellectual property rights and a significant competitive advantage."[4]

Finally, competition plays a role in promoting technological advance. When competitive pressures are present, firms have incentive to innovate to avoid being outperformed by their rivals. For example, many of the advances in U.S. automobiles—both in design and reliability—have been made in response to competitive pressures from foreign car makers, particularly the Japanese car makers.

As you can see, a variety of factors appear to influence the rate of technological advance, including everything from the education level of workers to the degree of competitive pressure felt by producers. Given this complexity, is there anything that government policymakers can do to promote technological change? We turn now to a discussion of policies to promote economic growth.

POLICIES TO PROMOTE GROWTH

Until recently, economists questioned whether a government's economic policy could influence an economy's long-run growth rate. Today, both economic theory and empirical evidence suggest that government policy does affect long-term growth, though not always in a positive way.[5] In this section, we explore the role of government policy in promoting economic growth. We will

---

[4] Scott Hensley, "New Race Heats Up to Turn Gene Information into Drug Discoveries," *Wall Street Journal,* June 26, 2000, p. B1.
[5] Federal Reserve Bank of Kansas City, *Policies for Long-Run Growth,* 1992. See the "Symposium Summary," by George A. Kahn.

concentrate our attention on policies designed to increase the capital stock (including both physical and human capital) and the rate of technological advance. These policies are all intended to enhance the **productivity of labor**: the amount of output the average worker can produce. For instance, if we provide workers with more or better capital equipment, we enable them to produce more output. Enhancing their skill level through education or training has a similar impact. We begin by examining policies designed to increase the capital stock. Then we turn to policies to promote technological advance.

Promoting Capital Investment

If we want workers to become more productive, one approach is to provide them with more capital, either more physical capital (tools, machinery, etc.) or more human capital (education and skill). As we've already seen, increasing the capital stock requires investment spending.

To understand investment decisions, we need to become familiar with the **loanable funds market,** the market in which businesses and households borrow funds to make investments. The price that borrowers must pay to obtain funds is the interest rate. As you can see from Exh. 15.4, the demand curve for loanable funds slopes downward. This indicates that businesses and others are willing to borrow more funds at lower interest rates than at higher interest

---

EXHIBIT 15.4
The Loanable Funds Market

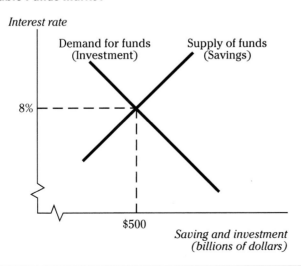

Interest rate

Demand for funds
(Investment)

Supply of funds
(Savings)

8%

$500

*Saving and investment
(billions of dollars)*

In the long run, the interest rate is determined by the demand and supply of loanable funds. The demand for loanable funds comes from borrowers seeking to finance investment projects. The supply of loanable funds comes from saving. The equilibrium interest rate balances demand and supply.

rates. The supply of loanable funds comes from saving. The upward-sloping supply curve indicates that more will be saved at higher interest rates than at lower interest rates. In our hypothetical example, the interaction of demand and supply results in an equilibrium interest rate of 8 percent. At that rate, $500 billion is saved and invested.[6]

Policies to Encourage Saving

If a nation wants to increase its investment spending, it must consume less in order to provide the saving necessary to finance that investment. In short, increased investment requires increased saving.

There are two sources of saving, private saving and public saving. **Private saving** is done by households. It is the amount of income that households have left over after subtracting taxes and consumption spending for goods and services. **Public saving** is done by government. It is the amount of tax revenue that is left over after government pays for its spending. The sum of private saving and public saving is called **national saving** (private saving + public saving = national saving); it represents the total amount of saving occurring in the economy. If policymakers want to increase national saving, they can target private saving, public saving, or both. Let's consider these possibilities.

Spurring Private Saving

How do we encourage households to save more? Some economists are convinced that private saving can be increased by providing tax incentives to households. For instance, the federal government could eliminate the tax on interest income—the income earned from savings accounts. Or it might allow households to make larger tax-deductible contributions to Individual Retirement Accounts (IRAs), accounts intended to promote saving for retirement. A more far-reaching proposal would replace the federal income tax with a **consumption tax,** also called an **expenditure tax.** A consumption tax is like a national sales tax; individuals are taxed on what they spend (consume) rather than on what they earn. Because spending is taxed and saving is not, this proposal should encourage saving.

Each of these proposed changes would cause households to save more at any given interest rate, shifting the supply curve of saving to the right as illustrated in Exh. 15.5. The rightward shift in the supply curve would, in turn, reduce the equilibrium interest rate. This would encourage businesses to borrow and invest in physical capital, and it would encourage workers to increase their investment in human capital.

---

[6] If you think we've discussed interest-rate determination before, you're right! Chapter 13 examined how interest rates are determined in the *short run*, by the supply and demand for money. The loanable funds model shown here looks instead at how interest rates are determined in the *long run*, by the supply and demand for savings.

EXHIBIT 15.5

Tax Incentives To Increase Saving

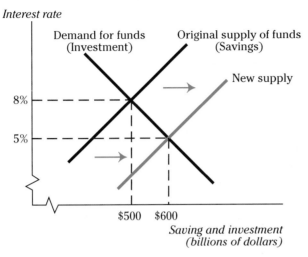

Tax incentives can be used to increase saving. These policies, by lowering the interest rate, can increase the amount of investment spending.

Increasing Public Saving

We discovered earlier that public saving is the amount of government tax revenue that is *not* spent. Alternatively, we could say that whenever government runs a budget surplus (takes in more tax revenue than it spends), it is engaging in "public" saving.

To clarify why economists call budget surpluses *public saving*, consider what happens when the federal government runs a surplus. What does it do with the surplus? It can't spend it; if it did there would be no surplus. Instead, it must somehow save the surplus. One approach that has been followed in recent years is to use the surplus to buy back some of the government bonds that make up the national debt. This provides the former bondholders with funds that they can make available to investors. Alternatively, the government could use its surplus to purchase the stocks and bonds of private companies, providing them with the funds they need to make investments. Either way, the federal government is supplying additional funds to the loanable funds market. Of course, this shifts the supply curve of loanable funds to the right, lowering the interest rate and thereby encouraging investment. This process is depicted in Exh. 15.6 by the rightward shift of the supply curve from S_1 to S_2. (Saving the budget surplus may be the best way to preserve Social Security and protect you from substantially higher Social Security taxes. To understand why, read "Saving the Surplus Will Save Social Security" on page 460.)

Budget surpluses are a relatively new phenomenon for Americans. Until 1998, budget *deficits* were the norm. Budget deficits mean that the federal government is spending more than its tax revenue, so public saving must be negative. In effect, government is borrowing money rather than saving money. As a consequence, budget deficits represent a reduction in national saving; they shift the supply curve of saving back to the left as represented by the shift from S_1 to S_3 in Exh. 15.6.

Why do deficits have this impact—why do they reduce national saving? When the federal government incurs a deficit, it must borrow the money to finance that deficit. This government borrowing reduces the supply of funds available to finance private investment spending by businesses and households. Of course, this drives up the interest rate, reducing the willingness to borrow and invest. Note that by using the loanable funds model we arrive at the same answer we obtained in Chapter 14; budget deficits *crowd out* private investment spending.

EXHIBIT 15.6
Budget Policy And Saving

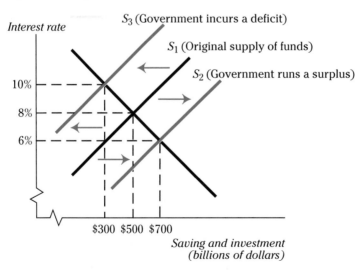

Budget deficits tend to reduce the supply of saving, driving up interest rates and reducing investment spending. Budget surpluses have the opposite effect; they increase the supply of saving, lowering interest rates and increasing investment spending.

The foregoing analysis suggests that budget deficits are always undesirable since, by crowding out investment spending, they slow economic growth. But long-run growth is not our only performance objective. We're also interested in short-run goals, including full employment and stable prices. And, as we learned earlier in the text, activists regard budget deficits as a tool for combating short-term unemployment. This conflict points out the necessity of evaluating policies in terms of both their short-run and long-run effects. There's no free lunch, not even for policymakers![7]

Policies to Encourage Investment

The preceding proposals attempt to stimulate investment indirectly, by lowering the prevailing interest rate. Other policies attempt to stimulate investment more directly. For example, **investment tax credits** reduce taxes for firms that invest in eligible equipment. By increasing the potential profitability of investments, this policy encourages businesses to undertake additional investment, shifting the demand curve for loanable funds to the right as represented in Exh. 15.7.

---

[7] The conflict in objectives may be more apparent than real. Keynesians argue that crowding out is less likely to be a problem during periods of unemployment because business borrowing tends to be depressed under these conditions anyway. Rather than replacing or crowding out business borrowing, government borrowing tends to absorb funds that would otherwise have been unused.

EXHIBIT 15.7
Tax Incentives To Stimulate Investment

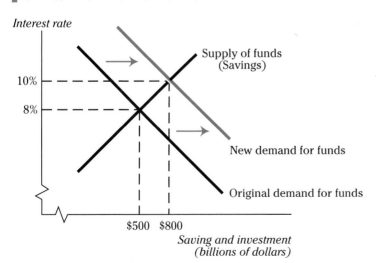

By increasing profit potential, tax incentives (such as an investment tax credit) can increase investment spending.

USE YOUR ECONOMIC REASONING

Saving the Surplus Will Save Social Security

*By Alan S. Blinder and Frank N. Newman**

THIS YEAR'S budget battle will likely present the proverbial mix of good and bad news for Social Security. The bad news is obvious: Social Security isn't likely to be reformed in this election year. The good news is that another government stalemate will produce the desired outcome: The federal budget surplus will be maintained, and thus a sizable chunk of the national debt will be retired.

Why is this good for Social Security? Because one of the primary ways we can provide for retirement is to increase U.S. productivity growth—as the report released yesterday by the Social Security trustees illustrates. In part because of faster productivity growth, the trustees estimated that

the trust fund will remain solvent until 2037—three years later than expected. And one way to keep productivity up is by maintaining a budget surplus.

The first step in understanding these economics involves realizing that unlike pension funds, Social Security does not own independent assets (other than the government's own debt) that can be sold to pay off beneficiaries. Rather, retired Americans can consume more of our gross domestic product only if other segments of society—including working people and children—consume less. And the harsh reality is that the work force of the future will have to support a larger number of retirees.

Most of the reasons why are pleasant. First, Americans are living longer. Second, as the nation grows wealthier, more Americans can contem-

plate a lengthy retirement. Third, policy changes in Medicare, 401(k) plans and individual retirement accounts have made early retirement more attractive. These developments are a plus for society, but they do increase the financial burden on Social Security.

Just how heavy that burden will be depends on several factors, including the level of retirement benefits and the rate of population growth. But one factor stands out as particularly important: the rate of productivity growth.

If people live longer and retire earlier, the working population must consume a smaller share of the nation's GDP. That's inevitable. But productivity growth offers a potent offset. Here's a simple example:

The U.S. now has about three workers for every

Source: Wall Street Journal, March 31, 2000, p. A18.

Tax incentives for education and training have the same impact. For instance, the **Lifetime Learning Tax Credit** targets adults who want to go back to school to prepare for new careers or upgrade their skills. It provides a tax deduction equal to 20 percent of the cost of qualified educational expenses.

460

retiree, so if retirees and workers enjoy the same consumption standard, the working population gets to keep about 75% of the economic pie. Thirty years from now, there will be closer to 1.5 workers for every retiree, so the working population will get to keep only about 60% of the GDP. If the GDP pie does not grow in the interim, living standards will fall—by about 20% in this example.

But the pie will grow. If productivity increases by just 1.4% a year, as it did from 1973 to 1995, workers in 2030 will produce 1.52 times as much GDP as today's workers. That bigger pie will leave the working population better off than they are today (21% better off, precisely), even though they will have to fork over a bigger share to retirees. If productivity growth averages 2.6% a year, as it did from 1995 through 1999, workers of 2030 will be 73% better off than today's workers.

In brief, with zero productivity growth, living standards fall 20%. With 1.4% productivity growth, they rise 21%. With 2.6% productivity growth, they rise 73%—even though there are more retirees to support. While this is just one example, it serves to illustrate the point: Faster productivity growth is by far the best way to provide for retirement.

How best to encourage productivity growth is a matter of debate. Some argue for more spending on research and development; others stress the importance of education or tax policy. Social Security policy has little to do with any of these.

But it does have a quite a bit to do with how much our nation saves. Most economists argue that running budget surpluses to pay down the national debt is the surest route to higher national savings. Higher national savings will lead to more investment, which in turn will boost productivity. For all this to work, the Federal Reserve must help make sure that full employment is

maintained despite an increase in government saving.

It may sound like abstract theory, but think about the U.S. in recent years. Our federal budget deficit has melted away and turned into a surplus. Business investment has boomed. The Fed has promoted full employment. And both productivity and real wages, after years of sluggish growth, have accelerated. The theory appears to be working....

Mr. Blinder is former vice chairman of the Fed and a professor of economics at Princeton. Mr. Newman is former deputy secretary of the Treasury and a director of Dow Jones, publisher of the *Wall Street Journal.*

Use Your Economic Reasoning

Social Security is a "pay-as-you-go" system: Workers pay Social Security *taxes* that are used to provide Social Security benefits to retirees. The following questions are designed to illustrate how additional retirees can burden such a system and how productivity growth can help.

1. Imagine an economy composed of thirty workers and ten retirees. If each worker produces $20,000 worth of output each year, what is the economy's GDP? What is GDP per capita?

2. Suppose that the number of workers remains at thirty, but the number of retirees increases to twenty. If labor productivity (output per person) remains the same, what will happen to GDP per capita? Why is this happening?

3. How much must labor productivity increase to keep the society's standard of living (GDP per capita) from declining?

4. Carefully explain how saving the surplus can help to "boost productivity."

Note that the impact of investment incentives is different from that of saving incentives. Because these policies tend to increase the *demand* for loanable funds rather than the supply, they result in higher interest rates. These higher interest rates help to ensure that funds are available to finance the expanded level of investment spending. As interest rates rise, households move along their supply curve of saving, supplying the higher quantity of loanable funds now being demanded.

Promoting Technological Progress

Growth in the capital stock, both in the stock of physical and human capital, is an important source of economic growth. The other major source of growth is technological progress—discoveries that make it possible to produce more or better products from the same resources.

To make sense out of technology policy—policy to promote technological development—we need to recognize that technological progress proceeds in stages. The initial stage generally involves **research**, the process of gaining new knowledge. Research is sometimes categorized as *basic research* (research conducted to gain knowledge for its own sake) and *applied research* (research conducted with a commercial purpose in mind). The distinction is far from clear-cut, however, because even basic-research agendas tend to be influenced by the practical concerns of the day.

Research can lead to **invention**—the discovery of new products or processes that might have practical applications. Inventions are ideas in their formative stages, before we really know if they have practical value. The final stage is **innovation**, the process of converting an invention into something marketable. This is the stage where firms try to get the kinks out of new products and processes, so that they will gain commercial value.

Taken together, the three stages that lead to technological advances are often referred to as **research and development**. To illustrate these stages, consider research and development efforts in the drug industry. As AIDS research has provided insights into how the AIDS disease progresses, researchers have invented drugs that they believe might be successful in combating the disease. But there is still much that is not known about AIDS, so the researchers' models are incomplete. It takes additional research and clinical trials to discover which of these drugs have real medical value. This is the innovation stage. Unfortunately, many of these drugs have not turned out to have practical benefits, so relatively few have made it to the market. The same is true of many other inventions; they can't be converted into marketable products.

Policymakers generally attempt to promote technological progress by trying to stimulate one or more of the stages in the research and development process. Consider, for example, the following policies.

Direct Support for Basic Research

Most of the basic research conducted in the United States is supported by the federal government and is carried out either in federal laboratories or by universities receiving government grants. The justification for government support of basic research is similar to that for public goods.[8] Basic research seldom produces discoveries of direct economic benefit to the researchers. Hence private firms will tend to ignore such research. But even though they do not benefit the researchers, such projects may have a significant payoff to the economy as a whole. In fact, economist Edwin Mansfield estimates that some basic research discoveries represent returns on investment in the neighborhood of 30 percent.[9]

Tax Policies to Promote Research and Development

Private firms tend to concentrate on applied research and innovation, projects that are more likely to return a profit. Like investment, these activities can be encouraged through tax policy. For instance, government can increase the incentive to invest by providing tax credits for research and development. Likewise, policies that increase the supply of saving (through tax incentives or increasing the federal budget surplus) can stimulate research and development by driving down the interest rate and thereby reducing the cost of financing research and development projects.

Policies to Protect Intellectual Property

One area where technological progress may require unique forms of government policy is in the protection of intellectual property rights—the ownership rights to new ideas. The development of new products and processes is an expensive proposition, and success is never assured. In many instances, firms invest millions of dollars in research and development without producing commercially viable products. Firms are unlikely to invest in these inherently risky projects unless they believe that successful products will allow them to recoup their investment, including their investment in unsuccessful projects. But if rivals can easily copy successful new products or processes, any profits will be quickly competed away, destroying the incentive to invest in the research and development necessary to make them possible.

To encourage research and development, economists support the granting of patents—exclusive rights to control a new product or process—to temporarily shield innovating firms from competition. It can be argued that technological progress would be enhanced by lengthening the period for which patents are granted (currently, twenty years) or by increasing the variety of discoveries that may be patented. Of course, the growth-enhancing benefits of these changes must be weighed against the resulting reduction in competition. This

---

[8] Recall from Chapter 9 that public goods convey their benefits equally to payers and nonpayers. This creates a *free-rider problem* which makes it difficult for private businesses to earn a profit by providing such products.
[9] Martin Baily, Gary Burtless and Robert Litan, *Growth with Equity,* (The Brookings Institution, Washington D.C. 1993), p. 89.

cost–benefit comparison will be increasingly difficult in the New Economy, where patents are requested for more and more intangible innovations. For instance, Amazon.com Inc. recently patented its "1-Click" purchasing method. And CyberGold has received a patent on using incentives to reward customers for reading Internet ads. Do these patents protect legitimate innovations, or do they merely stifle competition in electronic commerce? And what about the patents on human genes? While some argue that it is wrong to issue patents for elements of nature, advocates counter that drug research is expensive, and that without patents firms would be unwilling to engage in such research. These questions illustrate the complexity of the patent question and why patent policy is the subject of much current debate.[10]

Antitrust Policy to Foster Innovation

The nature of competition is changing, particularly for firms in the information-intensive sector of our economy. Rather than competing on price, these firms tend to compete on innovation, developing new products and new processes. It is important that our antitrust laws keep pace with this trend. For example, some economists argue that firms should have greater leeway to engage in **joint research ventures**—research projects in which firms pool their resources and share the costs of research and development—rather than having those joint ventures blocked by antitrust policy. Joint ventures can potentially cut the cost of developing new products while also reducing each firm's risk of failure.

Some critics of antitrust support more far-reaching changes. They argue that antitrust is poorly suited to the fast-paced world of the Internet and e-commerce. In their view, antitrust enforcers are always behind; they are looking at markets as they once were and at rivalries that no longer exist. By the time they spot a potential problem, the situation has changed and their proposed remedies are unnecessary or counterproductive. In short, these critics view antitrust as an antiquated doctrine that needs to be scrapped or enforced very sparingly. Not surprisingly, Joel Klein, assistant attorney general for antitrust during the Clinton administration, disagrees. According to Klein, "While technology changes, human nature does not." The anticompetitive techniques "used to protect and extend monopoly power in the New Economy are essentially no different from those used throughout history." It remains to be seen how this controversy will be resolved.

---

[10]Another interesting area of debate is the granting of patents for "pure" medical procedures. For instance, a patent was granted for a particular type of incision that is used in cataract surgery. Critics of such medical method patents argue that, unlike new drugs, new medical methods are often discovered during the normal course of medical practice, and do not require substantial capital investment. Therefore these patents do little to encourage new procedures. Instead, they allow patent owners to charge monopoly prices without providing any offsetting gain to society. In fact, by hindering doctors from sharing information, they may actually slow the use of such new procedures.

Industrial Policy: Can Government Pick the Winners?

A minority of economists argue that government should do more than provide general incentives and support for research and development. They believe that policymakers should single out specific industries and technologies for targeted support (either through grants or tax incentives). For instance, if genetic engineering is deemed to be a particularly promising avenue for stimulating economic growth, the federal government could make tax credits available for research in this area, or it could provide grants to firms with expertise in genetic engineering. Note that this is a variation of the *industrial policy* used by Japan and South Korea to guide the growth of their economies.

As you can see, promoting technological progress is a complex task. It involves everything from providing government grants for basic research to carefully designing the patent system. As you might expect, these policies have varying degrees of support. In fact, not everyone agrees that economic growth is an objective worth pursuing. The last section considers these issues.

DEBATES ABOUT GROWTH POLICY

Before closing this chapter, we need to explore two ongoing debates about growth policy. The first debate is about details, about the specific policies that should be pursued to promote growth. The second debate is more fundamental; it voices concerns about the impact of economic growth on the earth's environment and questions the wisdom of economic growth as an objective. This final section of Chapter 15 examines the basic elements of these two debates.

The Devil Is in the Details: Debates about How to Stimulate Growth

Economists *generally* support the goal of economic growth. They disagree, however, about the role that government should play in this process and about the specific policies that should be employed to promote growth. In part, this disagreement stems from philosophical differences regarding the proper role of government in the economy. As we learned in Chapter 14, **supply-side economics** refers to a branch of economics that focuses on stimulating aggregate supply through policies that involve minimal government intervention. Supply-side economists were particularly visible and vocal during the Reagan administration, when they advocated cuts in marginal tax rates to stimulate work effort (and increase the labor supply), tax incentives to increase saving and investment, and reductions in government regulation to reduce the cost of doing business. While supply-siders deserve credit for calling attention to the importance of aggregate supply, they are not the only economists interested in stimulating economic growth. Keynesians also support policies to stimulate long-run growth, but are often willing to accept more direct government involvement than supply-siders would find palatable.

While the disagreement between these groups is partly philosophical, it also stems from different interpretations of empirical evidence. The different policies these groups propose to stimulate saving illustrate their disagreement. Keynesians see little evidence that tax policy has been effective in stimulating saving, and they therefore prefer deliberate budget surpluses as a more promising route. Supply-side economists disagree. They believe that tax policy has proved effective in stimulating saving. Moreover, supply-side economists are philosophically opposed to government surpluses, preferring to cut taxes (and tax revenues) as a method of limiting the size of government. As you can see, even economists who agree on the need to stimulate growth often disagree about the policies used to pursue that goal.

Will Economic Growth Harm the Environment?

As we mentioned earlier, not everyone supports economic growth as a goal. Although economists see economic growth as largely beneficial, environmentalists do not. They tend to see economic growth exhausting our nonrenewable resources and generating ever-increasing amounts of pollution. There are basically two sources of this problem: rising population and rising GDP per capita. People use resources, so as population expands there are increased demands placed on the earth, both as a source of resources and as a waste receptor. Rising incomes intensify these demands because increased affluence causes people to consume more resources per person.

Environmentalists see a limit to this process. Eventually, we either run out of resources or we generate enough pollution to destroy life as we know it. A study published in 1972 (and updated in 1992) under the title **The Limits to Growth** illustrates these concerns. Researchers, using a computer model to simulate likely future outcomes, reached the following conclusion:

> If present growth trends in world population, industrialization, pollution, food production, and resource depletion continue unchanged, the limits to growth on this planet will be reached sometime within the next one hundred years. The most probable result will be a rather sudden and uncontrollable decline in both population and industrial capacity.[11]

Although this computer model raises very serious concerns, most economists would be quick to criticize its assumptions—that present trends in population, food production, resource depletion, and so on will continue. As

---

[11] Donella Meadows, Dennis Meadows, Jorgen Randers, and William Behrens III, *The Limits to Growth* (New York: Universe Books, 1972, p. 23).

we've seen throughout this textbook, market participants respond to economic incentives. When incentives change, their behavior changes. As nonrenewable resources becomes scarcer and therefore more expensive, one response is to switch to other resources—including renewable resources. Another response is to develop technologies that use less of that resource (and to develop completely new alternatives to that resource). The point is that markets are not static, so the assumption that the future holds more of the same is almost certainly incorrect.

To illustrate, consider just one of the trends mentioned in the quotation, the trend in food production. While there was once substantial concern about our ability to feed the world, that concern has now largely evaporated. Hybrid seeds and other technological advances have dramatically increased agricultural output, even though the amount of land under cultivation continues to shrink in response to increased land prices. Unfortunately, there are still people starving. But this is not because of insufficient food production. These instances stem from inequality, from natural disasters (such as droughts), and from human tragedies (such as war).

Economists anticipate similar changes in other areas. For instance, we know from past experience that as incomes and education levels rise, population growth rates tend to fall and concern for the environment tends to increase in importance. Of course, slowing population growth would reduce one source of pollution and resource depletion. And increased concern for the environment would magnify those adjustments. In short, the process of economic growth unleashes all sorts of changes—changes that tend to modify the trends in population, food production, and so on that are incorporated in the *Limits to Growth* forecast.

While the preceding explanation provides some reason for optimism, too much optimism could be a mistake. One element that we have left out of this debate is the timing of these adjustments. We can be confident that population growth will slow; that we will develop less-polluting technologies; and so forth. The critical issue is when, on what timetable. We need to make these adjustments before we destroy our ozone layer, before global warming makes parts of the world uninhabitable, and before biological diversity decreases in ways that critically damage the ecosystem. Can we count on market forces and the invisible hand to do this? Robert Solow, Nobel Laureate in Economics, believes that the answer is no! He argues that markets do not adequately consider the future, at least not the distant future. So policies to stimulate growth must be combined with policies to direct that growth toward less-polluting technologies.

Solow's position is a controversial one. It takes us to another form of the activist–nonactivist debate. Some economists agree with Solow that, by themselves, markets are not up to the task. Others are convinced that government "help" will only make matters worse. These are legitimate issues for debate. It is a debate we can't afford to postpone; it is a debate we need to have now.

SUMMARY

Economic growth is defined as an increase in an economy's production capacity or potential GDP. The rate of economic growth is the key determinant of changes in a society's standard of living, which is commonly measured by GDP per capita. When potential GDP is growing more rapidly than population, a society's standard of living is increasing. When potential GDP is growing more slowly than population, the standard of living is decreasing.

Relatively small differences in the growth rate of potential GDP ultimately translate into large differences in the standard of living. According to the *rule of seventy-two*, a variable's doubling time roughly equals seventy-two divided by the growth rate. So, for example, if potential GDP is growing at 4 percent a year, it will double in approximately eighteen years. But if potential GDP is growing at only 2 percent a year, it will require thirty-six years to double.

There are two sources of economic growth: increases in the stock of economic resources (land, labor, and capital), and increases in technology. The most important of these are increases in the capital stock and *technological advances*. The capital stock includes both *physical capital*—physical aids to production such as machines, tools, and factories—and *human capital*—the knowledge and skills embodied in labor.

Policymakers can influence the rate of capital investment in a variety of ways. For instance, *investment tax credits* can be used to increase the potential profitability of investments and to encourage businesses to undertake additional investment. Alternatively, policymakers can drive down the interest rate as a way of encouraging investment. This can be accomplished through tax policies that encourage households to save more (by eliminating the tax on interest income, for instance, or replacing the federal income tax with a *consumption tax*), or by deliberately incurring a budget surplus.

Policymakers can also attempt to stimulate economic growth by spurring the rate of technological progress. Technological progress generally proceeds in stages. The first stage, *research*, is the process of gaining new knowledge. The second stage, *invention*, is the discovery of new products or processes that have practical applications. The final stage, *innovation*, is the process of converting inventions into something marketable.

Attempts to promote technological progress generally do so by stimulating one or more stages in the *research and development* process. For instance, basic research can be promoted by increasing the size of government grants to universities. And applied research and innovation can be encouraged through tax policy—for instance, by providing tax credits for research and development. Some economists believe that government policymakers should single out critical industries or technologies to be the recipients of this support, though this *industrial policy* approach is controversial.

Technological progress may also require government policies to protect intellectual property. Firms are unlikely to invest in risky research and development projects unless they can protect their results through patents and copyrights. In addition, government may need to modify antitrust laws to promote research and development.

Although economists generally endorse the goal of economic growth, they disagree about the role that government should play in that process and about the specific policies that should be employed to promote growth. Supply-side economists generally prefer policies that will stimulate aggregate supply with minimal government intervention. Keynesians are often willing to accept more direct government involvement.

Environmentalists generally oppose economic growth because they see it exhausting our nonrenewable resources and generating ever-increasing amounts of pollution. While some economists are confident that market forces will provide the incentives necessary to avoid these catastrophic outcomes, others believe that government intervention will be needed.

KEY TERMS

Applied research	Investment tax credit	Public saving
Basic research	Joint research venture	Research
Consumption tax	Lifetime Learning Tax Credit	Research and development
Economic growth	Loanable funds market	Rule of seventy-two
Expenditure tax	National saving	Supply-side economics
Human capital	Physical capital	Technological advances
Innovation	Private saving	
Invention	Productivity of labor	

STUDY QUESTIONS

Fill in the Blanks

1. A common measure of a society's standard of living is _Per Capita GDP_.

2. The term _Human Capital_ refers to the knowledge and skills embodied in labor.

3. The market where businesses and households borrow funds to make investments is called the _loanable fund_ market.

4. One policy for encouraging saving would be to replace the federal income tax with a _Consumption_ tax.

5. National saving is the sum of _Private public_ saving (by households) and _public_ saving (by government).

6. The process of converting an invention into something marketable is referred to as

   Innovation .

7. To encourage research and development, economists support the granting of

   Patents to temporarily shield innovating firms from competition.

8. Investment *tax credits* reduce taxes for firms that invest in eligible equipment.

9. The term *industrial policy* is used to describe a program of targeted government support for research and development in specific industries or technologies.

10. The discovery of new products or processes that *might* have practical applications is known as *invention*.

Multiple Choice

1 Economic growth is defined as
   a) an increase in GDP per capita.
   b) an increase in real GDP.
   c) an increase in potential GDP.
   d) an increase in GDP.

2. According to the *rule of seventy-two*, if potential GDP is expanding at a rate of 3 percent a year, then potential GDP doubles in approximately
   a) 72 years.
   b) 18 years.
   c) 24 years.
   d) 36 years.

3. The most common measure of an economy's standard of living is
   a) median family income.
   b) per capita income.
   c) GDP per capita.
   d) average household income.

4. In 1999, the United States' GDP per capita was approximately
   a) $10,000.
   b) $35,000.
   c) $ 2,000.
   d) $17,000.

5. The country with the standard of living most closely approximating the United States is
   a) Argentina.
   b) France.

   c) Switzerland.
   d) United Arab Emirates.

6. If a country's population is increasing at 2 percent a year and its real GDP is increasing at 5 percent a year, then per capita real GDP will be
   a) rising at a rate of 7 percent a year.
   b) falling at a rate of 2 percent a year.
   c) rising at a rate of 3 percent a year.
   d) falling

7. Population growth, by itself, may do little to raise the standard of living because
   a) any increase in real GDP must be divided among a larger population.
   b) without additional capital, there can be no increase in real GDP.
   c) people are not an economic resource.
   d) population growth inevitably leads to inflation.

8. The term *human capital* refers to
   a) machines, tools, and factories.
   b) money.
   c) the knowledge and skills of workers.
   d) None of the above

9. Which of the following would tend to increase the supply of loanable funds?
   a) Providing investment tax credits to firms that invest in eligible equipment
   b) Increasing the size of the federal budget deficit

c) Reducing the size of the tax-deductible contributions that households are allowed to make to Individual Retirement Accounts

d) Replacing the federal income tax with a consumption tax

10. Policies that increase the supply of loanable funds lead to more investment spending because they
   a) reduce the taxes of firms that increase their investment spending.
   b) lower the interest rate and thereby encourage borrowing.
   c) make firms more optimistic about the future.
   d) lower the price level in the economy.

11. Which of the following would tend to increase private investment spending?
   a) An increase in the size of the federal budget deficit
   b) An increase in the tax on interest income
   c) A reduction in the size of tax-deductible contributions to IRAs
   d) A surplus in the federal budget

12. Investment tax credits tend to
   a) increase the supply of loanable funds and reduce interest rates.
   b) increase the supply of loanable funds and raise interest rates.
   c) increase the demand for loanable funds and reduce interest rates.
   d) increase the demand for loanable funds and raise interest rates.

13. Which of the following policies would a supply-side economist be *least* likely to support?
   a) Cuts in marginal tax rates designed to spur work effort
   b) Investment tax credits designed to stimulate investment spending
   c) An industrial policy intended to promote technological advances
   d) Tax incentives to spur saving by households

14. Suppose households are saving $500 billion a year, all state and local governments together have a budget surplus of $300 billion, and the federal government has a $150 billion deficit. How much is national saving?
   a) $350 billion
   b) $500 billion
   c) $650 billion
   d) $950 billion

15. Deficit spending may slow the rate of economic growth
   a) by raising interest rates and lowering investment spending.
   b) by increasing the level of national saving.
   c) by reducing aggregate demand.
   d) by lowering consumption spending by households.

16. Which of the following would *not* tend to promote more rapid technological advance?
   a) An increase in government funding for federal research laboratories
   b) A reduction in the rate of interest on loanable funds
   c) A reduction in the period for which patents are granted
   d) More liberal tax credits for research and development

17. Under an industrial policy,
   a) all businesses would receive substantial tax breaks to encourage research and development.
   b) corporate income taxes would be reduced to provide additional funds for research and development.
   c) government policymakers would select critical industries to receive tax incentives and other support for research and development.
   d) tax incentives would be used to encourage saving, lower interest rates, and spending for research and development.

18. Rising incomes may pose a threat to the environment because
   a) this trend generally leads to less-rapid population growth.
   b) this trend generally leads to more-rapid population growth.
   c) rich people tend to care less about the environment.
   d) rich people consume more resources per capita.

19. Economists argue that present trends in population, food production, and resource depletion will probably not continue because
    a) as resources become scarcer, prices will rise and this increase will lead to conservation.
    b) new technologies will be developed to conserve scarce resources and augment food supplies.
    c) as incomes rise, population growth rates tend to slow.
    d) All of the above

20. Robert Solow argues that government may need to supplement market forces to avoid the eventual destruction of the environment. He bases this recommendation on the fact that
    a) resource scarcity does not appear to alter the behavior of consumers or businesses.
    b) government policymakers always have better foresight than markets.
    c) markets do not adequately consider the distant future.
    d) population growth rates appear to be independent of economic variables such as income.

Problems and Questions for Discussion

1. When we compare the per capita GDP of a less-developed country like Ethiopia with that of a more-developed country like the United States, the differential may somewhat exaggerate the true difference in the standards of living. Can you think of any reasons why this comparison may be unfair to the less-developed country? (*Hint:* What is included in a nation's GDP?)

2. Why is an increase in the labor-force participation rate a more promising avenue for increasing the standard of living than is population growth?

3. Less-developed countries tend to have much lower rates of capital investment than more-developed countries. Why?

4. Technological progress and increases in the labor-force participation rate are both avenues to a higher standard of living. Which would you prefer and why?

5. Explain in step-by-step fashion how an increase in the supply of loanable funds leads to an increase in capital investment.

6. Why do budget surpluses represent increases in national saving? How do they promote investment spending?

7. Suppose that households are saving $600 billion a year and that the federal government is running a surplus of $200 billion. Ignoring the budgets of state and local governments, how much is national saving?

8. Starting from the information provided in question 7, suppose that the federal government reduces personal income taxes by $100 billion. If households consume (spend) 75 percent of each additional dollar they receive—including dollars from tax cuts—what will be the new levels of public, private, and national saving?

9. Economists argue that increases in per capita GDP indicate a rising standard of living. Environmentalists view rising per capita GDP as a source of pollution. Discuss.

10. Keynesians see deliberate budget deficits as desirable during periods of unemployment. But budget deficits can soak up savings, reducing the pool of funds available for private investment and slowing growth. Can these two outcomes be reconciled?

11. Robert Solow argues that markets and the invisible hand may not be capable of avoiding irreparable and catastrophic environmental damage. What does Solow see as the critical shortcoming in the market mechanism?

ANSWER KEY

Fill in the Blanks

1. per capita GDP

2. human capital

3. loanable funds

4. consumption or expenditure

5. private, public

6. innovation

7. patents

8. tax credits

9. industrial policy

10. invention

Multiple Choice

1. c	5. c	9. d	13. c	17. c
2. c	6. c	10. b	14. c	18. d
3. c	7. a	11. d	15. a	19. d
4. b	8. c	12. d	16. c	20. c

PART FOUR

International Economics: Trade, Exchange Rates, and the Balance of Payments

Chapter 16 introduces the economic rationale for international trade and considers the consequences of barriers to free trade. You will learn the meaning of such concepts as "comparative advantage" and "absolute advantage" and see why these concepts are used to summon support for free trade. Arguments for and against free trade will be presented, and we will look closely at the impact of foreign competition. Chapter 17 considers the financial dimension of international trade and the role of exchange rates. You will see how exchange rates are determined and how changes in exchange rates influence international trade. You will also learn about the balance of payments accounts that nations use to keep track of their international transactions, and why a nation's balance of payments always balances.

CHAPTER SIXTEEN

International Trade

The first fifteen chapters of the text have included numerous examples involving our economic relationships with other nations. We've previewed the benefits of international trade, and we've considered the impact of trade on our GDP. We've seen how international influences can dominate the process of price determination in competitive markets and how a recession in Europe or some other part of the world can affect the U.S. economy. We've included these examples because, like it or not, the U.S. economy is increasingly an **open economy**— an economy that exchanges goods and services with other nations. (A **closed economy**, by contrast, does not exchange goods and services with other nations.)

The increased openness of the U.S. economy is a matter of some controversy. Many Americans see foreign competition as a destructive force that threatens their jobs and their way of life. Others view foreign competition as a blessing that provides quality products at prices lower than domestic producers charge. Economic policymakers must weigh these costs and benefits as they develop policies to promote or retard international trade. In this chapter we'll explore the theoretical basis for free, or unrestricted, international trade, and we'll take a closer look at the costs and benefits associated with it.

INTERDEPENDENT ECONOMIES AND U.S. TRADE

Statistics show that the economies of the world are becoming more interdependent. Consumers in the United States are buying more foreign products, and foreign consumers are buying more U.S. goods. Producers around the world are using more imported parts and raw materials in the products they manufacture. In short, foreign trade is already more important than most Americans realize, and current signs indicate that it will gain even more importance in the future.

Import and Export Patterns

The Sony television sets, Nike tennis shoes, and Raleigh bicycles we see in U.S. stores are all **imports**—goods or services purchased from foreign producers.[1] In the last two decades, trade between the United States and other nations has expanded significantly. More Americans are driving Saabs, Nissans, Peugeots, and Isuzus; are listening to CD players made in Japan; are drinking wine from France and Italy; and are wearing clothes made in Korea, Romania, Taiwan, and other countries. As you can see from Exh. 16.1, imports more than tripled as a fraction of GDP between 1960 and 2000.

U.S. exports are expanding as well. **Exports** are goods and services produced domestically and sold to customers in other countries. For example, U.S. farmers export wheat and rice and a variety of other agricultural products, while U.S. manufacturing firms export products such as earth-moving equipment, laptop computers, and jet airplanes. Exports of goods and services accounted for less than 5 percent of our gross domestic product in 1960; by 2000 that figure had climbed to 11 percent of GDP. That percentage is low compared with Canada (38 percent of GDP), Sweden (47 percent of GDP), and Ireland (90 percent of GDP), but it is a significant fraction of GDP and one that undoubtedly will increase in the future.[2]

---

[1] The services component of imports includes such items as transportation charges for moving goods and passengers between nations and expenditures made by tourists while traveling in foreign countries.
[2] The percentage figures are for 1999 and are based on information from Central Intelligence Agency, *The World Factbook, 2000,* Washington D.C.

EXHIBIT 16.1
Trends in U.S. Imports and Exports

	1960	1980	2000
Exports of goods and services	$25.3 billion (4.9% of) GDP	$279.2 billion (10.3% of GDP)	$1,097.6 billion (11% of GDP)
Imports of goods and services	$22.8 billion (4.4% of GDP)	$293.9 billion (10.9% of GDP)	$1,468.6 billion (14.7% of GDP)

Source: Developed from data in *The Economic Report of the President,* 1998 and the *Survey of Current Business,* April 2001.

Interdependence and Attitudes Toward Trade

We are constantly reminded of the many ways in which national economies are linked to one another. When there is a poor harvest in Brazil, we all pay higher prices for coffee. If the United States undergoes a recession, European businesses suffer a loss of customers. When workers at a German auto-parts manufacturer slow down production to pressure for a wage increase, a Spanish automobile assembly plant is hurt. Like a game of dominoes, events in one part of the world reverberate elsewhere.

Countries often react strongly, almost resentfully, to the actions of foreign nations with whom they trade. When Japanese automobile producers step up production, U.S. producers cry foul. When Federal Reserve policies drive up interest rates in the United States and attract investment funds, complaints ring out from other nations. With increasing frequency, economic events in one part of the world have global repercussions—repercussions that affect each of us.

How should Americans react to this growing interdependence? Does the availability of Japanese automobiles and Taiwanese shoes and other foreign products make Americans better off? Or does the inflow of foreign products simply mean less demand for American products and fewer jobs in domestic manufacturing industries? Should we support U.S. steel and automobile producers and shoe manufacturers when they appeal to our government for protection from "cheap foreign labor"? To respond intelligently to these questions, it is necessary to have some understanding of international economics. We need to understand why countries trade. What are the benefits of trade? Does trade help one country at the expense of another, or is it mutually beneficial? What are the arguments for and against trade barriers? These are the questions we now take up.

Domestic workers often protest against imported products.

THE BASIS FOR INTERNATIONAL TRADE

Why do countries trade? The various nations of the world are not all equally blessed in terms of either natural resources or capital and labor endowments. Therefore, different nations have different production abilities. Great Britain may be self-sufficient in petroleum products because of oil discoveries in the North Sea. If the British want oranges and grapefruit, however, they will probably have to trade for them because Britain's climate is ill-suited to growing citrus fruits. Americans, by contrast, have no trouble buying domestically grown fruits and vegetables but must rely on other nations for such items as tin, tea, and teakwood furniture. One reason why countries trade, then, is to acquire the products they cannot produce themselves. But that is not the sole—or even the most important—reason for trade.

The Opportunity Cost of Domestic Production

Virtually every country is capable of producing almost any product its citizens desire—if it is willing to expend the necessary resources. Lacking alternative sources of supply, the British probably could grow hothouse oranges and grapefruit, and Americans probably would find some way to produce tea domestically. The important point is that neither country chooses to expend its resources this way because other countries can produce these products so much less expensively.

Think of the resources the British would need to use to produce hothouse oranges. More important, think of the other products that Britain could produce with those same resources. Whenever economists talk about the true cost of producing something, they mean the *opportunity cost.* As you will recall, the opportunity cost of anything is what you have to give up to obtain it. The opportunity cost of hothouse oranges would be whatever products the British would sacrifice to produce those oranges. By the same token, the cost of tea or coffee produced in the United States would be whatever other domestic products we could have produced with the same resources.

By making comparisons based on opportunity cost, we can determine which country is the low-cost producer of a particular product without becoming confused or misled as we would if we made comparisons in dollars or some other currency. Economic logic dictates that each country should specialize in the products it can produce at a relatively low opportunity cost and trade for the items that other countries can produce more cheaply. This logic is called the principle of **comparative advantage,** and it is the key to understanding how countries can benefit from trade.

The Principle of Comparative Advantage

The classic example of comparative advantage doesn't involve foreign countries; it has to do with a lawyer and the lawyer's secretary. The lawyer, Ms. Legal Wizard, not only is the best legal mind in the country but also types better than anyone else around. We could say that she has an **absolute advantage** over her secretary (and everyone else in the community) in both jobs. That means that the lawyer is more efficient at those jobs; she can accomplish more work in a given amount of time. If that is the case, why does the lawyer have her secretary, Mr. Average Typist, do the typing? By having the secretary do the typing, the lawyer frees her own time to do legal work.

Consider the high opportunity cost of having the lawyer do her own typing. It would mean the loss of the additional income she could have generated by handling more cases. The secretary, who has almost no talent for legal work, has a comparative advantage in typing because the amount of legal work he gives up to perform the typing duties is insignificant. The secretary does the typing not because he is a better typist than the lawyer (absolute advantage) but because he is better at typing than at legal work (comparative advantage). By allowing individuals to concentrate on the jobs they do best— the jobs in which their absolute advantage is the greatest or their disadvantage the least—the firm is able to handle more clients, earn more money, and thereby raise the standard of living of all its members.

Comparative Advantage as a Basis for Trade

Countries can benefit from specialization and trade in much the same way that the lawyer and the secretary benefit from their relationship. Consider the possibility of trade between the United States and France. Even if the United States were more efficient than France in the production of everything, specialization and trade along the lines of comparative advantage would allow each country to achieve a higher standard of living than it could possibly attain if it remained self-sufficient.

To illustrate that conclusion as simply as possible, let's assume that the United States and France are the only two countries in the world and that they produce only two products: microcomputers and champagne. Exhibit 16.2 summarizes the production abilities of these two nations in terms of a hypothetical unit of resources, with each unit representing some combination of land, labor, capital, and entrepreneurship, some set amount of those resources. For instance, each resource unit might contain 10,000 hours of labor, 1,000 units of raw materials, the use of 10 machines for a year, and 500 hours of entrepreneurial talent. Although each unit contains the same quantities of these resources, the quality of these inputs would vary from nation to nation, giving rise to differences in productive abilities.

With each unit of resources, the United States can produce either 50 microcomputers or 100 cases of champagne. With the same unit, France can produce either 20 microcomputers or 80 cases of champagne. Because the United States can produce more microcomputers and more champagne per unit of resources, we know that it has an absolute advantage over France in the production of both products, just as the lawyer had an absolute advantage over her secretary in both typing and legal work. How is it possible for both countries to benefit from trade when one of them is more efficient, or has an absolute advantage, in producing both products? To answer this question, we must explore the concept of comparative advantage.

In our example the United States has a comparative advantage in the production of microcomputers because the opportunity cost of producing that

---

EXHIBIT 16.2

Production Possibilities per Unit of Economic Resources

	MICROCOMPUTERS	CASES OF CHAMPAGNE
United States	50	100
France	20	80

product is lower in the United States than in France. The United States must sacrifice two cases of champagne in order to free the resources necessary to produce one additional microcomputer. (Each resource unit can produce either 50 microcomputers or 100 cases of champagne, so that each additional computer costs us two cases of champagne.) In France, however, the opportunity cost of each additional microcomputer is four cases of champagne because each unit of French resources can produce either 80 cases of champagne or 20 microcomputers. The United States can produce microcomputers at a lower opportunity cost and therefore has a comparative advantage in that product.

If we switch our attention to champagne production, we note that the French have a comparative advantage in this area. In the United States the production of one additional microcomputer forces the society to sacrifice two cases of champagne. The opportunity cost of producing one more case of champagne is therefore half a computer. In France the cost is lower. Each additional microcomputer requires the sacrifice of four cases of champagne. Therefore the opportunity cost of each case of champagne is one-fourth of a computer. The French do indeed have a comparative advantage in the production of champagne.

THE BENEFITS OF TRADE

Now that you understand how to determine a nation's comparative advantage, let's see how trade based on the principle of comparative advantage can result in a higher standard of living for both trading partners. In the absence of product specialization and trade, both France and the United States would produce some microcomputers and some champagne, with the exact amounts of each depending on the strength of demand for the two products. Prior to trade, we can't say with precision what those amounts would be, but we know that one microcomputer would exchange for two cases of champagne in the United States and for four cases of champagne in France.

Suppose that the United States decides to specialize in the production of microcomputers and offers to trade one microcomputer to France for three cases of champagne. Would the French agree? Of course they would agree! Through trade they can acquire a microcomputer for three cases of champagne, whereas they would have to sacrifice four cases of champagne to produce one domestically. Under such circumstances they are better off to specialize in producing champagne and to trade for the microcomputers they desire.

As U.S. citizens, would we be better off with this arrangement? We certainly would be. We would be getting three cases of champagne for each microcomputer we traded, whereas we would be able to manufacture only two cases of champagne from the resources we used to produce each microcomputer. Clearly, trade based on the principle of comparative advantage will allow both countries to enjoy a higher standard of living.

The Production Possibilities Curve and the Gains from Trade

We can see the gains from trade more clearly by using the production possibilities curve introduced in Chapter 1. A production possibilities curve (PPC) shows the combinations of goods that an economy is capable of producing with its present stock of economic resources and existing techniques of production.

Let's assume that the United States and France have 100 units of economic resources each to use in producing either microcomputers or champagne and that these resources are equally suited to the production of either product. When resources are assumed to be equally productive, the production possibilities curve appears as a straight rather than a bowed-out line (recall Chapter 1). In the United States these 100 resource units can be used to produce either 10,000 cases of champagne or 5,000 microcomputers or any other combination of champagne and microcomputers found on its production possibilities curve [see Exh. 16.3(a)]. In France the 100 resource units can be used to produce either 8,000 cases of champagne or 2,000 microcomputers or any other combination of champagne and microcomputers found on France's production possibilities curve [see Exh. 16.3(b)]. Recall that any combination of products we can plot either on or within the production possibilities curve (PPC) is available to the society. Combinations falling outside the PPC are beyond the economy's production capability and therefore unattainable unless we can trade for them.

Suppose that prior to trade, the United States chooses to produce and consume 2,000 cases of champagne and 4,000 microcomputers, whereas France chooses a combination of 5,000 cases of champagne and 750 computers. Total world production would then be 7,000 cases of champagne (2,000 produced by the United States and 5,000 by France) and 4,750 microcomputers (4,000 produced by the United States and 750 by France).

Next, suppose that the two countries decide to specialize along the lines of comparative advantage, agreeing to trade with each other at our hypothetical exchange ratio: 1 microcomputer = 3 cases of champagne. The United States has a comparative advantage in microcomputers, so it will use all its 100 resource units to produce microcomputers and will trade for champagne. The French will produce champagne, their product of comparative advantage, and will trade for microcomputers.

We know that the United States is producing 5,000 microcomputers and that France is producing 8,000 cases of champagne. What will be the result if the United States trades 1,000 microcomputers for some champagne? With an exchange ratio of one microcomputer to three cases of champagne, the United States will receive 3,000 cases of champagne in return for its 1,000 microcomputers and will still have 4,000 microcomputers left over. France will have 5,000 cases of champagne left over plus 1,000 microcomputers. The United

EXHIBIT 16.3

Production Possibilities Curves and the Gains from Trade

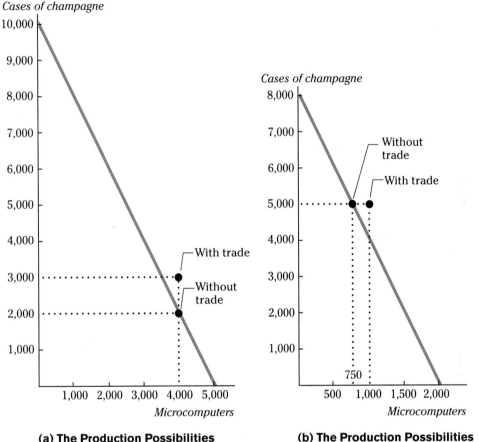

(a) The Production Possibilities of the United States

(b) The Production Possibilities of France

The two production possibilities curves show the combinations of champagne and microcomputers that the United States (a) and France (b) can produce. Without trade, each nation is forced to select a combination of the two products that lies either on the production possibilities curve or inside it. For example, the United States might choose to produce and consume 2,000 cases of champagne and 4,000 microcomputers, whereas France might select a combination of 5,000 cases of champagne and 750 microcomputers. Through specialization and trade, each of these nations can enjoy a higher standard of living. If the United States specializes in producing microcomputers and France specializes in champagne, each of these nations can move to a point beyond its production possibilities curve. For example, if the two countries agree on an exchange ratio of one microcomputer for three cases of champagne, the United States can exchange 1,000 microcomputers for 3,000 cases of champagne. That will leave the United States with 4,000 microcomputers and 3,000 cases of champagne, whereas France will have 1,000 microcomputers and 5,000 cases of champagne; both countries will be better off than they were without trade.

States will have 1,000 more cases of champagne than it had prior to trade, and France will have 250 more microcomputers.

Trade and specialization have made it possible for each country to move beyond its PPC and to enjoy a combination of products that it could not obtain on its own. Moreover, total world production has increased from 7,000 to 8,000 cases of champagne and from 4,750 to 5,000 microcomputers. The principle of comparative advantage has allowed each of the trading partners to obtain more goods from each resource unit and to enjoy a higher standard of living.

The Transition to Greater Specialization: Winners and Losers

Trade based on comparative advantage clearly makes sense. And in the absence of **trade barriers**—legal restrictions on trade—we can be confident that the pursuit of self-interest will automatically lead producers to specialize in the products in which their country has a comparative advantage. Consider again our hypothetical world economy. Prior to trade, microcomputers were selling for twice as much as a case of champagne in the United States but four times as much as a case of champagne in France. Enterprising French and U.S. businesses would take advantage of these international price differentials to increase their profits. For instance, suppose that microcomputers were selling for $1,000 in the United States and that a case of champagne was selling for $500. In France, on the other hand, microcomputers were selling for 4,000 francs and a case of champagne for 1,000 francs. U.S. businesses could make a substantial profit by selling microcomputers in France and using the money to buy champagne for resale in the United States. French businesses could do the reverse; they could sell champagne in the United States and use the proceeds to buy computers for resale in France. Because French producers can sell champagne for less, ultimately they would force U.S. champagne producers out of business. The same fate would befall French computer manufacturers: They would be eliminated by competition from the United States.[3]

What would happen to the workers displaced from the French computer industry and the U.S. champagne industry? Our model assumes that all resources

---

[3] Even in the absence of trade barriers, specialization may be less than complete. The United States might continue to produce some champagne, and France might continue to produce some microcomputers.

To conclude that foreign trade along the lines of comparative advantage will lead to complete specialization, we have to assume that (1) the products offered by French and U.S. manufacturers are identical—that French champagne is the same as U.S. champagne; (2) all economic resources are equally productive in both uses; (3) economic resources can move freely from one industry to the other but not between countries; (4) transportation costs are not large enough to outweigh the differences in production costs in the two nations; and (5) the computer and champagne industries are purely competitive. To the extent that these assumptions are not met, specialization will be less than complete.

are equally suited for champagne production or computer manufacturing and that they move freely between those industries within each country but not between countries. Thus, the economic resources—workers, factories, and equipment—no longer needed by the U.S. champagne industry would flow to the U.S. computer industry, and the resources released by the French computer industry would flow to the French champagne industry. With greater specialization, workers in both countries would become more productive, and they would be paid higher wages by their employers. In this way the benefits of trade would be shared by all members of the society; everyone would benefit from specialization and trade based on comparative advantage.

The transition to greater international specialization, however, is never painless. When a domestic industry is eliminated or reduced in size by foreign competition, difficult adjustments follow. Unemployed workers need time to find other jobs, and factories must be put to other uses. Some of these resources will never be reemployed because firms are reluctant to invest money to retrain a fifty-five-year-old winemaker, for example, or remodel a thirty-year-old computer plant. Even though the total output of both countries will be greater than before trade (see Exh. 16.3), not every individual or group will be better off. Thus, specialization has costs as well as benefits.

Lower Prices through International Competition

Even when specialization is incomplete and several countries continue to produce the same products, international trade can benefit consumers by providing them with a wider variety of products from which to choose. Furthermore the availability of foreign products limits the pricing discretion of domestic producers and forces them to be more responsive to consumer demands.

Consider the U.S. automobile market. Foreign competition has not only given U.S. consumers more brands from which to choose but has also spurred domestic manufacturers to develop small, fuel-efficient cars. In addition, competition from foreign producers has helped to keep automobile prices in the United States lower than they would be otherwise. A study by the Council of Economic Advisers concluded that if automobile imports were limited to 10 percent of the U.S. market, new-car prices would increase between 13 and 17 percent. Studies by the Federal Trade Commission and the International Automobile Dealers Association also predicted significant price hikes—up to $3,000 a car.[4] As you can see, international competition can be a powerful force in restraining the market power of domestic oligopolists and promoting a higher standard of living for consumers.

---

[4] Murray L. Weidenbaum, with Michael C. Munger and Ronald J. Penoyer, *Toward a More Open Trade Policy* (Center for the Study of American Business, Formal Publication 53, Jan. 1983), p. 5.

Competition from foreign automobile manufacturers has helped to hold down new-car prices in the United States.

When we consider the benefits of trade in permitting greater specialization along the lines of comparative advantage and fostering greater competition, we can understand why economists generally agree on the desirability of **free trade**—trade that is not hindered by artificial restrictions or trade barriers of any type.

TYPES OF BARRIERS TO TRADE

We have seen that free trade benefits consumers but often imposes substantial costs on particular groups in a society. Moreover, the benefits of free trade are widely diffused across a large number of people, each of whom is made a little better off, whereas the losses tend to be concentrated in a relatively small segment of the society. Workers who are forced out of jobs by foreign competition provide the best example.

Not surprisingly, the segment that is significantly harmed by foreign competition is likely to be more vocal than the group whose welfare is slightly improved. That's why politicians in the United States and elsewhere hear more often about the costs of free trade than about its benefits. As Michael Oldfather, former chairman of the Kansas Council on Economic Education, has noted,

> [R]emoving import barriers on cars . . . might save every car-buying family a few hundred dollars a year. On the other hand, several thousand families would lose a great deal each (the families of U.S. automobile workers). Even though the total gains of car buyers would far exceed the total losses of car makers, it's not hard to guess whose voice will be the loudest.[5]

Virtually all the nations of the world impose trade barriers of one sort or another, partly in response to political pressure. These trade barriers are designed primarily to limit competition from imports, although export restrictions are sometimes established. The most common devices for limiting import competition are protective tariffs and import quotas.

Tariffs

A **tariff** is a tax on imported goods. Its purpose is either to generate revenue for the taxing country through a *revenue tariff* or to protect domestic producers from foreign competition by means of a *protective tariff*. Historically, revenue tariffs were the major tool for financing government expenditures. Such tariffs served as the principal source of revenue for the U.S. government through the nineteenth century and remain the principal source in some less-developed countries.

Today, most developed countries rely on other forms of taxation for revenue—income and sales taxes, for example. When developed countries, such as the United States, employ tariffs, their main purpose is to protect domestic producers. A tariff on a foreign product increases its price and makes it less competitive in the marketplace, thereby encouraging consumers to buy domestic products instead. For instance, the United States imposes tariffs of up to 20 percent on imported luggage, and imports of some synthetic apparel are subject to tariffs of more than 30 percent. Of course, these tariffs make the imported items less attractive relative to domestic products, thereby helping to insulate U.S. producers from foreign competition. We'll have more to say about the impact of tariffs a little later in the chapter.

Quotas

Quotas restrict trade in a different way. An **import quota** specifies the maximum amount of a particular product that can be imported. The volume of

---

[5] Michael Oldfather, "Cost of Any Import Ban Outweighs Gain," *Springfield* (Mo.) *News-Leader,* March 9, 1983, p. 7E.

imported wine, for example, might be limited to 50 million gallons per year, or the quantity of imported steel could be limited to 100,000 tons each year.

Import quotas can be either global or selective. A *global quota* limits the amount of a product that can be imported from the rest of the world. When the limit is reached, all further imports of that item are prohibited. A *selective quota* specifies the maximum amount of a product that can be imported from a particular country. For example, the United States might set a global quota of 500,000 imported automobiles per year and further specify selective quotas: 250,000 cars from Japan and 50,000 from France, perhaps, and the remaining 200,000 from other countries.

Domestic producers generally support import quotas over tariffs. Both trade barriers reduce competition from imported goods, but quotas are considered more effective. If consumers prefer foreign products to those offered by domestic producers, they can continue to buy relatively large amounts of those products in spite of the higher prices caused by the tariff. On the other hand, a quota will completely prohibit imports once the limit has been met.

The impact of quotas can be substantial. For example, the Government Accounting Office estimated that sugar quotas cost American consumers $1.9 billion in higher prices in 1998. (Because of import quotas, sugar sold for 22 cents a pound in the United States but only 11 cents a pound in the world market. That meant higher U.S. prices for soft drinks, candy, and numerous other products.)[6] And import quotas on clothing are estimated to cost U.S. consumers something in the neighborhood of $20 billion a year in higher prices for everything from sweatshirts and swimsuits to neckties and dresses.[7] In short, the existence of quotas is not merely of academic interest; it's a pocketbook issue for each of us.

Other Restrictions

Trade agreements (which are discussed later in the chapter) have helped to discourage the use of quotas and have reduced tariff rates significantly. But other forms of trade protection are more subtle and more difficult to legislate against. For example, health and safety laws are sometimes invoked to prevent or complicate the importation of certain products. The acquisition of import licenses can be made difficult or expensive, and government agencies can be required to purchase domestic products. New York requires that state agencies buy American-made steel, for example, and New Jersey requires that all state cars be produced in the United States.[8]

---

[6] Robert E. Robertson, *Sugar Program: Supporting Sugar Prices Has Increased Users' Costs While Benefiting Producers* (Government Accounting Office, Report Number RCED-00-126, June 9, 2000).
[7] Marcy Burstiner, "Foot-Dragging on Trade Treaty Socks Levi's GAP," *San Francisco Business Times,* March 17, 1995, p.3.
[8] Murray Weidenbaum, *Confessions of a One-Armed Economist* (Center for the Study of American Business, Formal Publication 56, Aug. 1983), p. 25.

In addition, new forms of trade interference have emerged, largely to by-pass, or take advantage of, the rules in existing trade agreements. Among the most troubling is the **voluntary export restraint (VER),** an agreement under which an exporting country "voluntarily" limits its exports to a particular country, often under threat of the imposition of a quota. For example, in 1981 Japan signed a VER that limited its auto exports to the United States to 1.68 million units annually through 1984. And in 1995 Canada agreed to a five-year pact limiting its lumber exports to the United States. Voluntary export restraints have also been used to influence trade in textiles, steel, footwear, motorcycles, machine tools, and consumer electronics.[9] Although VERs have essentially the same effect as quotas, they are not expressly prohibited by existing trade agreements, which discourage the use of *unilaterally imposed* quotas.[10]

Another method of discouraging imports is to accuse foreign firms of dumping. **Dumping** occurs when a product is sold to foreign consumers at a price that is less than the cost of producing that good or service. The United States has long held that dumping is an unfair form of competition, perhaps because (in *rare* circumstances) it might be used to drive a competitor out of business. As a consequence, U.S. laws prohibit dumping and call for additional tariffs to be imposed on products dumped in the U.S. market. Existing trade laws permit such "antidumping duties," in large part due to the insistence of the United States.

Because it is difficult for trade courts to determine the true cost of producing a product, the mere fact that a firm is selling its product in foreign markets for less than it charges in its own domestic market is often taken as evidence of dumping. Economists find this logic flawed. As you discovered in Chapter 7, selling to different markets at different prices may make perfect economic sense. In fact, profit maximization *requires* that firms charge higher prices in markets where consumers are less price-sensitive (where demand is less elastic) and lower prices in markets where consumers are more price-sensitive (where demand is more elastic). Economic logic notwithstanding, dumping remains illegal in the United States. The U.S. Department of Commerce judges cases involving dumping in the United States and generally finds in favor of American companies. As a consequence, the mere threat of a dumping case is often enough to convince foreign firms to raise their prices. As with VERs, the real loser is the consumer. (Recently, some foreign firms have begun to turn the tables on their U.S. rivals. Read "Payback Time as Countries Protest U.S. Trade Policies," on page 492, to learn how.)

---

[9] Jagdish Bhagsati, *Protectionism* (Cambridge, Mass: The MIT Press, 1988), p. 44.
[10] As a result of the Uruguay Round of GATT (The General Agreement on Tariffs and Trade), countries agreed to eliminate the use of VERs by the year 2005. GATT will be discussed later in the chapter.

USE YOUR ECONOMIC REASONING

Payback Time as Countries Protest U.S. Trade Policies

By Evelyn Iritani

AS FREE-TRADER George W. Bush settles into the White House, the United States—the world's most vocal and prosperous open-market advocate—is increasingly being called to account for its own protectionist policies.

Even as it pushes for ever-greater access to foreign markets for U.S. banana, telecommunications and pharmaceutical firms, the United States has lost several key cases recently before the World Trade Organization. And more and more countries, tired of the nearly constant U.S. application of anti-dumping laws to protect American corporations and workers, are retaliating with dumping cases against Uncle Sam.

Suddenly, American cattle ranchers and corn syrup producers are being hit with dumping penalties in Mexico, farmers are accused of flooding the Canadian market with cheap corn, poultry producers face 200% duties in South Africa, and a U.S. newsprint producer is fighting dumping charges in China.

U.S. markets, of course, are more open than most. But the United States "talks out of both sides of its mouth," Australian Ambassador Michael Thawley complained last month, echoing the views of a growing number of nations.

This growing antipathy from some of America's closest allies, coming amid a U.S. economic slowdown, doesn't bode well for the free-trade initiatives expected from a Bush administration. Warning of trouble ahead, Charlene Barshefsky, the outgoing U.S. trade representative, acknowledges that the U.S. needs to tackle some of its own "Achilles' heels, such as textiles and sugar," if it is serious about launching another round of trade talks....

Increasingly,...complaints are finding their way to the Geneva-based WTO, where the U.S. has been on the losing end of several recent decisions. Last month, a WTO dispute panel ruled that U.S. import duties on New Zealand and Australian lamb, South Korean steel and European wheat gluten violated global trade rules.

On Dec. 22, Europe, Japan and seven other countries filed a WTO challenge to what they consider a particularly outrageous new law that awards U.S. firms the proceeds of anti-dumping tariffs. That followed a WTO ruling against the U.S. on an export tax subsidy program challenged by the Europeans.

"I think Japan, Europe and others see the WTO as a great leveler," said Greg Mastel, a trade expert who recently left the New America Foundation, a Washington think tank, to work on Capitol Hill. "After years of feeling they're on the defensive against U.S. companies, they see the WTO as a forum where they can turn the tables."...

While the overall U.S. economy is quite open to foreigners, sectors such as sugar, peanuts and tobacco are protected by a wall of restrictive quotas and high tariffs. Industries such as steel have staved off aggressive foreign firms through the use

Source: Los Angeles Times, Jan. 25, 2001, p. A1.

of anti-dumping laws designed to prevent foreign goods from being sold below cost in the U.S. market. And U.S. farmers, while blaming foreign agricultural subsidies for excess global production, themselves received a record $28 billion in government support last year....

Particularly reprehensible, according to World Bank research manager Bernard Hoekman, is the heavy U.S. reliance on anti-dumping laws to protect domestic firms from low-cost producers often found in the poorest countries.

"We regard this as a very inefficient and dishonest instrument of protection," he said.

Anti-dumping laws are one of the most globally inflammatory and domestically sensitive issues in the U.S. trade realm. The U.S. refused to even include dumping on the agenda for the ill-fated Seattle WTO summit meeting in November 1999, angering Japan and much of the developing world.

As a result, U.S. multinationals are feeling the heat. A decade ago, the U.S. and Europe filed the lion's share of dumping complaints. But in recent years, foreign governments such as Mexico and South Africa have turned the tables, according to a new analysis of trade policy by the Institute for International Economics.

Gary Horlick, a Washington trade attorney who specializes in these cases, said foreign officials have told him, "It's payback time."...

"American agriculture exports 40% of its production, and it is being hit with cases all over the world," he said. "It used to be that the U.S., Europe, Canada and Australia filed 95% of the dumping cases. Now they file less than half."

Jeffrey Schott, a senior fellow with the Institute for International Economics, doubts Congress would give up the controversial trade measures because they provide an "escape clause" by offering fearful domestic producers temporary protection against globalization's dark side.

"Anti-dumping is a sacred cow on Capitol Hill," he said.

But former Trade Representative Barshefsky believes the U.S. needs to reconsider its position on dumping, given the global upsurge in cases aimed at U.S. firms. She pointed out that these complaints are often filed in developing countries where the judicial system is weak or corrupt and U.S. firms might not get a fair hearing....

Use Your Economic Reasoning

1. What behavior do anti-dumping laws prohibit?
2. Suppose that Korean steel producers face less competition in their domestic market than they do in the U.S. market. Would you expect them to charge the same price in both markets? If not, where would you expect them to charge the higher price? Would this behavior harm U.S. consumers?
3. Imagine the following situation: A U.S. filmmaker has been renting its most recent film, *Bride of King Kong,* to U.S. movie theaters for $100,000 a week plus 40 percent of ticket revenues. The movie has been a huge success and the company has already recovered its $30 million production costs, but would like to enlarge its profits by distributing the film in Japan. Japanese theater owners are not convinced the movie will catch on in their country. The U.S. filmmaker agrees to rent the Japanese rights to the film for $25,000 a week, plus 20 percent of ticket revenues. Japanese film producers file antidumping charges against the U.S. filmmaker. Should these charges be sustained?
4. World Bank research manager Bernard Hoekman argues that antidumping laws are merely a "dishonest instrument of protection." Explain this description: Why might the laws be seen as dishonest? Why might they be seen as an instrument of protection?
5. Former Trade Representative Charlene Barshefsky points out that U.S. firms might not get a fair hearing in some foreign courts. Do you think foreign firms believe that they are receiving a fair hearing when their cases are heard by the U.S. Department of Commerce?

TRADE BARRIERS AND CONSUMER WELFARE

Economists generally condemn all forms of trade barriers. By reducing competitive pressures on domestic producers, such barriers allow firms with market power to charge higher prices yet be less responsive to the demands of consumers. Moreover, trade barriers interfere with the principle of comparative advantage: They prevent countries from concentrating on the things they do best and enjoying the best products produced by other countries.

Consider the impact of tariffs imposed by the United States on luggage imported from China and the Dominican Republic. These tariffs not only increase the prices consumers have to pay for imported luggage but also permit U.S. producers to charge more for their luggage. If imported luggage were not taxed, it would sell for less, and U.S. producers would be forced to reduce their prices in order to compete. Therefore, U.S. producers desire tariffs even though tariffs are harmful to U.S. consumers.

Tariffs are less damaging to consumer welfare than quotas are, however. When increased demand causes the prices of domestic products to rise, comparable tariff-bearing foreign products become more competitive because the price differential between the foreign and domestic products is reduced. Because foreign products are now a more viable alternative for consumers, domestic producers may be restrained from raising prices further, lest they lose sales to foreign rivals. This is not the case with import quotas. When domestic producers are protected by quotas rather than tariffs, rising domestic prices cannot call forth additional units from foreign suppliers once the quotas have been met. As a consequence, domestic producers have more freedom under a quota system to increase prices without fear of losing their market share to foreign firms. (For example, the voluntary export restraint—in effect, a "voluntary" quota—negotiated with Japan in the 1980s is estimated to have cost U.S. consumers $2,000 more for their foreign *and domestic* automobiles. By restricting imports, the VER not only drove up the prices of imports, it also increased the pricing discretion of domestic producers.)[11]

Another point in favor of import tariffs is that they provide governments with additional revenue, whereas quotas do not. This additional revenue can be used to reduce personal taxes or provide additional government services. Suppose, for example, that instead of using a voluntary export restraint (in effect, a "voluntary" quota) to restrain Japanese automobile exports, we chose to impose a tariff of $1,000 on each imported Japanese car. If 2 million cars were imported annually, that would amount to an additional $2 *billion* in revenue,

---

[11] Anne O. Krueger, *American Trade Policy: A Tragedy in the Making* (Washington D.C.: American Enterprise Institute, 1995), p. 3.

not an insignificant sum. None of this is meant to suggest that tariffs are desirable, only that they are preferable to quotas.

The impact of trade barriers on the prices that consumers pay is only part of the story. When the United States erects trade barriers to keep out Japanese steel, Mexican avocados, or South Korean clothing, it interferes with the pursuit of comparative advantage. Not only do U.S. consumers get less from their dollars, but the United States and the other nations of the world also get less from their scarce resources. When we establish import quotas to protect our old, inefficient steel mills, for example, we allow those firms to stay in business and use labor and other resources that could be better employed producing aircraft or farm equipment or something in which the United States has a comparative advantage.[12] We can acquire more steel by producing aircraft and trading for steel than by producing the steel U.S. firms demand. If the United States insists on protecting its steel manufacturers and Japan insists on protecting its aircraft manufacturers, both societies will lose. The people will have to settle for fewer goods and services than free trade could produce. The price tag for this kind of protection is a lower standard of living for the average citizen.

COMMON ARGUMENTS FOR PROTECTION

In spite of the costs they impose, trade barriers continue to exist. They exist because they serve the interests of certain powerful groups, even though they penalize society as a whole. Anyone who reads the newspaper or watches television is aware of the ongoing efforts of U.S. shoe manufacturers to maintain import protection against cheaper products from Taiwan and South Korea and Italy. Steel producers, clothing manufacturers, and farmers also lobby for protection. They argue that removing import restrictions would mean eliminating some producers and shrinking the output of others. The workers in these industries would have to look for new jobs, learn new skills, and perhaps even relocate to other parts of the country. These adjustments would be easy for some but difficult for others, particularly older workers. For these reasons, employers and employees in industries that suffer from foreign competition have a strong personal interest in appealing to Congress for protection. Invariably the arguments that are used to justify protection mix some truth with at least an equal amount of misunderstanding or distortion. Let's consider three of the most popular arguments.

---

[12] While old-line steel companies, such as Bethlehem, USX, and Inland, have had a difficult time competing with foreign firms, American "minimill" companies (which use scrap steel to produce new steel) have proved to be highly efficient and are expanding rapidly.

1. *Infant industries need protection from foreign competition.* The infant-industry argument suggests that new industries need protection until they become firmly established and able to compete with foreign producers. This argument makes little sense in a diversified and sophisticated economy like that of the United States but may have some relevance in less-developed countries. Even in that setting, there are dangers. There is no assurance that the new industry will ever be able to compete internationally, and once protection has been granted, it is difficult to take away.

2. *Defense-related industries must be protected to ensure our military self-sufficiency.* This argument suggests that we must protect certain critical industries so that the United States will not be dependent on foreign countries for the things it needs to defend itself in time of war. The national-defense argument is commonly used to summon support for the protection of a long list of industries, including steel, munitions, rubber, and petrochemicals. There is no way to decide which industries are critical to our national defense and which are not. The longer the list, the more expensive protection becomes for U.S. consumers.

3. *U.S. workers need protection from cheap foreign labor.* The cheap-labor argument is heard often today. It claims that U.S. producers and their workers need protection from firms operating in countries with much lower wage rates than the United States, wage rates that constitute an unfair advantage that protection should offset. (A variation of this argument suggests that we need to prohibit or limit imports from low-wage countries, not only to protect U.S. workers but also to protect foreign workers from sweatshop conditions.)

   There are two major flaws in this argument. First, low wages do not necessarily mean cheap labor. Labor is cheap only if the value of the output it produces is high relative to the wage rate. In many industries the United States is very competitive internationally despite its high wage rates. Workers produce more output per hour than their foreign counterparts because U.S. workers tend to work with more and better machinery and tend to be better trained than workers in many other countries.

   Second, we must remember that no country can have a comparative advantage in everything. The United States has a comparative disadvantage in the production of products whose manufacture requires large amounts of unskilled labor. On the other hand, we tend to have a comparative advantage in goods that are produced using highly skilled labor or large quantities of land or capital.

If we insist on protecting our labor-intensive industries, other nations have every right to protect their capital-intensive industries. Of course, such protectionism will deprive everyone of the benefits of comparative advantage, and we'll all be poorer for having resorted to protectionist measures.

REDUCING BARRIERS: THE ROLE OF TRADE AGREEMENTS

Arguments in favor of protecting domestic businesses and workers have been with us always. They were heard when our nation was in its infancy, and they are widely heard today. Protectionist sentiments ran particularly high during the Great Depression. The job losses and business failures of that period led to pleas for protection from foreign competition. In 1930 Congress responded by passing the Smoot–Hawley Act, which raised import tariffs to an average of roughly 50 percent. Other countries retaliated, and the result was a lessening of trade, which may have contributed to a deepening of the Depression. Fortunately the remainder of the twentieth century has seen significant, though halting, progress toward eliminating trade barriers.

The Reciprocal Trade Agreements Act of 1934 began the work of undoing Smoot–Hawley. The 1934 act permitted the president to engage in negotiations with individual trading partners of the United States to reduce tariffs. Because negotiations were on an item-by-item basis, progress was slow. But by the end of World War II, substantial progress had been made: U.S. tariff rates had been reduced from the 50 percent range to about half that level.

International Trade Agreements: GATT

Following World War II, the United States led efforts to reduce trade barriers still further. In 1947 twenty-three countries signed the General Agreement on Tariffs and Trade (GATT), which established some basic rules for trade and created an organization to oversee trade negotiations. Under GATT rules, countries are discouraged from using import quotas. Instead, they are expected to use tariffs as their means of import protection. And although tariffs are viewed as the preferable form of import protection, the primary objective of GATT has been to reduce tariff rates. This has been accomplished through periodic negotiations known as "rounds."

The most recent round of GATT negotiations, the Uruguay Round (so-named because it was held in Punta del Este, Uruguay), concluded in 1993. The Uruguay Round succeeded in reducing tariffs by about one-third. As a consequence, the average tariff applied by industrial nations is now less than 3 percent, a far cry from the 50 percent rates of the Depression era. The Uruguay Round also resulted in an agreement to end the use of voluntary export restraints (VERs) by 2005 and made some modest progress toward reducing agricultural subsidies. These talks also resulted in the formation of the

World Trade Organization (WTO) to replace GATT and to arbitrate trade disputes between nations.

In its short existence, the WTO has had both successes and failures. The WTO's dispute settlement body, which is like a court for resolving trade disputes, seems to work reasonably well. Unlike those of its predecessor, the WTO's decisions are binding on members; if members fail to comply, they may face trade sanctions. This puts some teeth, something that was lacking under GATT, into efforts to solve trade disputes. But the organization has had little success in moving trade negotiations forward to tackle the tough issues that continue to impede free trade. How do we eliminate agricultural subsidies—subsidies that may unfairly advantage a country's producers? Can the United States and the other major powers be convinced to curtail their use of antidumping laws as a tool for discouraging imports? And what can be done to eliminate subtle forms of protectionism—such as the use of health and safety laws to discourage imports? As Laura D'Andrea Tyson, chief economic advisor under President Clinton, notes, "The easy issues in multilateral trade negotiations have largely been resolved. Tariffs have been slashed and quotas eliminated for most manufactured goods. Future negotiations will focus on... politically sensitive sectors."[13]

With 140 member countries—some rich, some poor, some in-between—the WTO has found it difficult to even agree on an agenda for talks. In 1999, talks collapsed at the WTO meeting in Seattle, partly because of protests by labor unionists, environmentalists, and others who see a dark side to globalization, but primarily because the membership could not agree about what issues would be "on the table" for discussion. (Read "Troubled Trade Group Sees Slight Chance for Progress," on page 500, to learn about the issues that divide the WTO membership.)

As this text goes to press, the next round of talks is scheduled to be held in Qatar, a small, oil-rich country in the Persian Gulf, in November of 2001. But whether these talks will be any more productive than those held in Seattle remains to be seen. Some critics argue that the WTO is simply too large and diverse a body to make any headway on the complex issues that remain to be resolved. These critics suggest that the future lies in bilateral trade agreements—agreements between two countries—and regional trade accords that generally involve a handful of countries. As you'll see in a moment, economists have a mixed reaction to these bilateral and regional trading agreements. But if the WTO remains in a state of gridlock, these bilateral and regional agreements may be the best we can hope for.

---

[13] Laura D'Andrea Tyson, "What Really Sabotaged the Seattle Trade Talks," *Business Week,* February 7, 2000, p. 26.

Regional Trade Agreements: NAFTA

The GATT agreements and the WTO have as their objective the reduction of trade barriers worldwide. Recently, however, we have seen the emergence of regional trade agreements that attempt to eliminate or reduce trade barriers only among countries in a particular region or trading block. Trading barriers are removed or reduced for members of the trading block but not for nonmembers. For example, the European Union (a trading block composed of fifteen European countries) has eliminated most tariff barriers among member nations while continuing to impose tariffs on imports from nonmembers. The North American Free Trade Agreement (NAFTA) created a similar trading block involving the United States, Canada, and Mexico. Under the agreement (signed by the United States and Canada in 1989 and joined by Mexico in 1993), tariffs among the countries are to be eliminated in steps over a ten-year period.

The NAFTA agreement, and particularly its extension to Mexico, has been the subject of much heated debate. Supporters find evidence of significant benefits; detractors point to costs—businesses and workers that have been hurt, and damage that has been imposed on the environment, for example. Economists find some evidence that NAFTA has increased the total volume of trade (rather than simply diverting or redirecting trade), but so far there is little data available and the results are inconclusive.[14] But while observers in Mexico, Canada, and the United States may be uncertain about the impact of NAFTA, many political leaders outside the agreement are not. They want in—into NAFTA or whatever regional trading block is available! While Chile is lobbying to become a member of NAFTA, Japan is considering agreements with Singapore and Korea. The European Union meanwhile, hopes to establish a Euro-Mediterranean free-trade area by 2010 and the United States recently signed trading accords with China, Jordan, and Vietnam. The list goes on.

Are these bilateral and regional trade agreements a good thing? Economists aren't so sure. Although both the GATT and NAFTA agreements appear to be steps in the direction of more-open, or less-restricted, trade, economists are generally more supportive of GATT (and now of the WTO) than of NAFTA. If the world moves toward trading blocks rather than open trade among all nations, the principle of comparative advantage may be compromised. For example, the United States may find itself buying shoes

---

[14] Anne O. Krueger, "NAFTA's Effects: A Preliminary Assessment," *World Economy,* (June 2000), p. 761.

USE YOUR ECONOMIC REASONING

Troubled Trade Group Sees Slight Chance for Progress: World Trade Organization Is House Divided Among Squabbling Members

By James Cox

GENEVA—"Seattle" is synonymous with failure inside the somber 18th century estate that houses the World Trade Organization. The word is loaded with unhappy imagery: protesters trashing Starbucks and Niketown; riot police firing off tear gas and plastic bullets; the world's trade ministers cowering in hotel lobbies.

The global trade summit in Seattle a year ago this week will be remembered for its mayhem, but street clashes only obscured the obvious. The gathering was doomed—protests or not—

because the WTO is deadlocked over its future.

A year later, the institution is still struggling to regain its footing. And unless things change soon, the ill will and inertia that plague the 138-nation trade body will burst into public view this spring. That's when the WTO will try again to launch a new round of global talks aimed at wiping out barriers to trade in services and farm products and setting rules for e-commerce and other areas.

Close observers of the WTO rate chances for the launch of a new round in 2001 at no better than 50–50…. Before that can hap-

pen…, the WTO must recover from its malaise. It was created in 1995 to act as a forum for trade negotiations and serve as an impartial international court to resolve trade disputes. Lately, it's had trouble with both roles because:

* The big boys can't agree. The U.S. and 15-nation European Union (EU) still haven't bridged the gaps that split them in Seattle. Unlike the U.S., Europe wants a wide-open playing field in a new round. It wants to set global antitrust standards and foreign investment rules. It sides with Japan in wanting to challenge U.S. anti-dumping laws, used by the Clinton

Source: USA TODAY, Nov. 29, 2000, p. 1B.

from Mexico (because Mexico can produce shoes at a lower opportunity cost than the United States) but forgoing shoe imports from Taiwan (which may be able to produce shoes at a lower opportunity cost than Mexico) because Taiwan is outside our trading block and thus faces higher U.S. tariffs. If this occurs, the U.S. standard of living will be somewhat lower than it would have been under a system that provided equal access to all produc-

administration to punish foreign steelmakers.

The world's two biggest trading entities remain stalemated over how to trim farm subsidies. U.S. negotiators are hellbent on slashing the EU's elaborate system of export subsidies and farm price supports. That would let U.S. farmers boost poultry and beef sales in Eastern Europe, wheat shipments to North Africa, pork exports to Japan.

The Europeans are just as determined to cut certain U.S. supports—food-aid programs, export credits and emergency farm bailouts. Government payments average about $19,000 a year per farmer in the EU and the USA. The difference is that payments are about 45% of European farm income vs. 22% of U.S. farm income. And farmers in Europe have much more to lose: A bigger chunk of their payments falls into categories likely to be targeted by new WTO rules in agriculture.

Agriculture is so politically sensitive, it has defied most efforts at trade liberalization for 50 years. But the pressure is on: WTO members have been restricted by a "peace clause" from using the Geneva dispute court to target each other's farm programs. The truce expires in 2003.

U.S.–EU trade friction is running especially high these days. The two parties are locked in high-profile disputes that threaten to undermine confidence in the system. The EU has chosen to absorb penalties imposed by Washington rather than change its beef and banana import regulations to comply with WTO rules.... The U.S. faces the possibility next year of $4 billion in EU trade sanctions—the trade equivalent of nuclear war—if the WTO declares a revised system of tax breaks for American exporters violates global trade rules.

* The little guys feel cheated. Countries in the Caribbean, sub-Saharan Africa, Central America and Southeast Asia don't see the WTO working for them. They lack the resources to mount legal challenges against other countries in Geneva. As respondents, they are sitting ducks in the WTO dispute court, because they are short on the expertise needed to bring their tariffs, customs procedures and import laws into line with WTO rules.

At the same time, poor countries haven't been able to capitalize on their strengths—agriculture and textile manufacturing—because those areas have gone largely unliberalized in past trade negotiations. The result is that the USA, Europe, Japan and other wealthy nations have been able to use the WTO as a bludgeon to open markets in the poorest of nations while protecting their farmers and textile makers from poor-country exports.

"It was the issue that brought us to our knees before Seattle and in Seattle," [says Michael Moore, the WTO's director-general]. "It has put the least developed countries in a shameful position. They represent half of 1% of all trade, but in the areas of their excellence, they can't get product into (richer) markets."...

* The 'tweeners are flexing their muscles. Largely on the sidelines in the past, Brazil, India, Egypt, South Africa, Mexico and a handful of others have realized how much they stand to gain from trade.

(Continued)

ers—the kind of system the WTO is designed to promote. On the other hand, if membership in regional trading blocks like NAFTA increases the willingness of nations to negotiate in a larger forum like the WTO, then NAFTA will ultimately lead to a more-efficient trading system. At this point, it is too early to determine the impact that these bilateral and regional trading agreements are likely to have.

(Troubled Trade Group Sees Slight Chance for Progress: World Trade Organization Is House Divided Among Squabbling Members, continued)

Many 'tweeners are walking both sides of the street. On one hand, they oppose giving the poorest countries greater market access and more time to implement WTO rules. On the other hand, they vow that they will never go along with desires by the U.S. and EU to introduce minimum labor and environmental standards into trade rules.

Unions and environmentalists want standards to keep poor countries from exploiting workers and pillaging resources to achieve economic growth. Poor countries fear an attempt to erase their advantage as low-cost suppliers.

The [labor and environmental] standards issue is so explosive that it could ultimately destroy the WTO. Proposals to form a no-strings-attached "working party" to discuss it in parallel with new trade negotiations are headed for a dead end....

Even if member countries resolve the impasse over labor and the environment, there is no guarantee they will agree to open new trade talks. The negotiators in Geneva "realize that there are people back home... who don't really want to see this go anywhere," says David Woods, editor of *World Trade Agenda*. "They're all very nervous about setting the WTO bull running again. They're going to have to have good reason to let the wrath of the protesters come down on their heads again by agreeing to a new round."...

Use Your Economic Reasoning

1. The United States and the European Union both seem intent on slashing subsidies to agriculture. If that's true, why aren't they willing to sign an agreement to eliminate the subsidies?
2. Some of the smaller and poorer countries believe that the WTO has failed them. What are their grievances?
3. Labor unions and environmentalists in richer countries want the WTO to require that member trading nations uphold certain standards for wages, working conditions, and environmental protection. Why do poor countries generally oppose these standards?
4. The 'tweeners (countries that are neither rich nor poor, but in between) have their gripes as well. Like rich countries, they oppose giving poor countries more access to their markets. But, like poor countries, they oppose the adoption of labor and environmental standards. What countries belong in the 'tweeners category? Explain why they are "walking [on] both sides of the street."

THE CASE FOR TRADE ADJUSTMENT ASSISTANCE

Although it is too early to fully assess the impact of NAFTA, there is no doubt that it has benefited some parties and harmed others. Economists argue that more-open trade is beneficial because it results in a higher standard of living in each of the trading nations. But as we learned earlier, that doesn't mean that *everyone* in each of these countries is made better off. When trade barriers are reduced, there are winners and losers. Unfortunately, the losers are often those who can least afford to lose. For this reason many economists believe that efforts to reduce trade barriers should be accompanied by programs to retrain workers and otherwise assist those harmed by foreign competition.

The Trade Expansion Act of 1962 took an important first step in this direction. Under this act, workers losing their jobs because of increased competition from imports become eligible for **trade adjustment assistance** in the form of higher unemployment compensation and funds for retraining. Businesses receive grants to modernize and better prepare to compete with foreign producers. The Trade Act of 1974 enhanced the benefits provided by the 1962 Trade Expansion Act. Later, in 1993, Congress created the NAFTA Transitional Adjustment Assistance Program to target workers harmed by the reduced trade barriers between the United States, Canada, and Mexico. Congress is now considering merging these two programs and increasing funding for job training.

The number of workers certified for trade adjustment assistance reached a high of 228,000 in 1999. Program services and benefit payments for the five years from 1995 to 1999 totaled $1.3 billion, about 70 percent of which was used to pay for extended income support and about 30 percent for job training. While the trade adjustment programs have clearly helped to reduce the hardship caused by job loss, the programs have not been without their critics. In particular, delays in processing applications for assistance have proved to be a problem, in part because they make it difficult for workers to make plans for retraining and career changes.[15]

Even with government programs, the process of retraining and relocating workers is much more complicated than it appears. In some cases displaced workers have very poor educational backgrounds, which make retraining difficult and expensive. Sometimes there are no additional industries in the area for which the workers can be retrained. Additional factors, such as age, family ties, and limited personal savings, often mean that relocation can be accomplished only at the cost of considerable personal hardship.

All these problems complicate the transfer of labor to other industries and increase the human suffering associated with the removal of trade barriers. In fact, some critics argue that the case for free trade is commonly overstated because economists forget that the assumptions of the model—that resources can shift easily from one industry to another, for example—seldom hold true in reality. This important criticism reinforces what we learned earlier in the chapter: Free trade tends to benefit consumers in general, but it usually imposes substantial costs on particular groups in the society. Such criticisms point to the need for adjustment assistance and programs and policies designed to improve

---

[15] Susan S. Westin, *Trade Adjustment Assistance: Trends, Outcomes, and Management Issues in Dislocated Worker Programs* (United States General Accounting Office, October, 2000).

the mobility of the workforce—better general education for high school students, for example—so that there will be a greater likelihood that workers released by one industry can find employment elsewhere without an unbearable delay. By approaching the problem this way, we can move closer to the ideal of free trade while minimizing the distress of workers who are displaced by foreign competition.

SUMMARY

The economies of the world are becoming more interdependent. Americans are buying more *imports*—goods or services purchased from foreigners—and foreign consumers are buying more of our *exports*—products produced domestically and sold in other countries. Furthermore, many American-made products have foreign-made components. To know how to react to this growing interdependence, it is necessary to have some understanding of international economics—of why nations trade and how countries can benefit from trade.

One reason why nations trade is to acquire products that they cannot produce domestically. However, this is not the most important reason. Most countries can produce any product their citizens desire, *if* they are willing to expend the necessary resources. But trade may permit countries to import products much more cheaply—at a lower opportunity cost—than they can produce them domestically. This is the major benefit of international trade.

According to the theory of *comparative advantage,* each country should specialize in the products it can produce at a relatively low opportunity cost and trade for the items that other countries can produce more efficiently. This principle will permit each nation to achieve a higher standard of living than it could possibly attain if it remained self-sufficient.

Even when specialization is incomplete, trade can benefit consumers by providing them with a wider variety of products, limiting the pricing discretion of domestic producers, and forcing domestic producers to be more responsive to consumer demands.

Although free, or unrestricted, trade generally benefits consumers, it often imposes substantial costs on particular groups in any society—workers forced out of jobs by foreign competition, for instance. At least partly in response to pressure from these groups, countries erect *trade barriers*—legal restrictions on trade—to protect their domestic industries.

The most common devices for restricting imports are protective tariffs and import quotas. A *tariff* is a tax on imported products. A tariff on a foreign product increases its price and makes it less competitive in the marketplace, thereby encouraging consumers to buy domestic products instead. An *import quota* specifies the maximum amount of a particular product that can be imported.

Nations also employ a variety of other measures to limit import competition. For instance, stringent safety inspections may be imposed on foreign products to deter their importation, and government agencies may be required to purchase domestic products whenever possible. In addition, countries may negotiate *voluntary export restraints*—agreements under which a country voluntarily limits its exports to a particular country—or may accuse foreign firms of illegal *dumping*—selling to foreign consumers at a lower price than they charge domestic buyers.

Economists tend to condemn all forms of trade barriers. Such barriers allow domestic producers to charge higher prices and to be less responsive to consumers. They also prevent countries from concentrating on the things they do best and trading for the best products produced by other countries.

In spite of the costs they impose, trade barriers continue to exist. Three common arguments are used to support trade barriers: (1) Infant industries need protection from foreign competition; (2) defense-related industries must be protected to ensure our military self-sufficiency; and (3) U.S. workers need protection from cheap foreign labor.

In the 1930s the U.S. government was particularly receptive to protectionist arguments. Since that time, tariff and quota barriers to trade have been reduced substantially. The General Agreement on Tariffs and Trade (GATT) has produced seven rounds of negotiations, which have reduced the average tariff applied by industrial countries to less than 3 percent. The most recent round, completed in 1993, led to the formation of the World Trade Organization, a body intended to replace the GATT organization and extend its trade liberalization efforts.

In addition to the GATT agreements, a number of regional trade agreements have been negotiated between particular countries or trading blocks. The North American Free Trade Agreement (NAFTA) and the European Union (EU) are examples of regional trade agreements. Because these agreements reduce trade barriers within the trading block only, economists view them as less desirable than worldwide trade agreements such as GATT.

Although consumers benefit from more open trade, removal of trade barriers often imposes substantial costs on particular groups in society. When businesses are subjected to foreign competition, they may be forced to close their doors and lay off workers, who may have a difficult time finding employment elsewhere. Therefore, efforts to reduce trade barriers should be accompanied by programs to retrain workers and otherwise assist those harmed by foreign competition.

KEY TERMS

Absolute advantage
Closed economy
Comparative advantage
Dumping
Exports

Free trade
Import quota
Imports
Open economy
Tariff

Trade adjustment assistance
Trade barriers
Voluntary export restraint
  (VER)

STUDY QUESTIONS

Fill in the Blanks

1. Economists advocate that countries specialize in the products they can produce

   at a lower _____ than other countries.

2. If country A can produce all products more efficiently than country B, country

   A is said to have a(n) _____

   _____ in the production of everything.

3. If country A can produce a given product at a lower opportunity cost than country B, country A is said to have a(n)

   _____

   in the production of that product.

4. A _____ is a tax on imported products.

5. A(n) _____ specifies the maximum amount of a particular product that can be imported.

6. The _____ argument suggests that new industries need protection until they are firmly established.

7. A _____ quota simply limits the amount of a product that can be imported from the rest of the world, whereas a

   _____ quota specifies the

maximum amount of a product that can be imported from each country.

8. Aid to workers who have been harmed by foreign competition is called

   _____ .

9. In most situations the (benefits/costs)

   _____ of free trade are widely diffused, whereas the (benefits/costs)

   _____ tend to be concentrated.

10. Most economists would like to see trade barriers eliminated. However, if they are forced to choose between tariffs and quotas, they would probably

    agree that _____ are less damaging to consumer welfare.

11. In 1930 Congress passed the _____

    _____ Act, which raised U.S. import tariffs to roughly 50 percent.

12. Nations may attempt to negotiate voluntary export restraints because the use of import quotas is discouraged by the

    _____ (trade agreement).

13. The _____ replaced GATT as the organization for settling international trade disputes.

Multiple Choice

Use the following table in answering questions 1–4:

Production Possibilities per Unit of Economic Resources

	FOOD	CLOTHING
Country A	60	240
Country B	100	300

1. Which of the following statements is true?
   a) Country A has an absolute advantage in the production of both food and clothing.
   b) Country B has an absolute advantage in the production of both food and clothing.
   c) Country A has an absolute advantage in food, and country B has an absolute advantage in clothing.
   d) Country B has an absolute advantage in food, and country A has an absolute advantage in clothing.

2. In country A, the opportunity cost of a unit of food is
   a) 4 units of clothing.
   b) 60 units of clothing.
   c) 240 units of clothing.
   d) 1 unit of clothing.

3. According to the table,
   a) country A has a comparative advantage in food.
   b) country B has a comparative advantage in clothing.
   c) country A has a comparative advantage in clothing.
   d) country B has a comparative advantage in both food and clothing.

4. According to the principle of comparative advantage,
   a) country A should specialize in food, and country B should specialize in clothing.
   b) countries A and B should each continue to produce both food and clothing.

   c) country A should specialize in clothing, and country B should specialize in food.
   d) country B should specialize in clothing, and country A should specialize in food.

5. Which of the following is *not* a correct statement about trade barriers?
   a) Import tariffs are taxes on imports.
   b) Tariffs encourage consumers to buy domestic products.
   c) Quotas specify the maximum amount of a product that can be imported.
   d) Tariffs are probably more harmful to consumer welfare than quotas.

6. Which of the following is a true statement about trade barriers?
   a) They tend to enhance competition and benefit consumers.
   b) They benefit society as a whole but penalize small groups.
   c) They are needed to protect U.S. workers from cheap foreign labor.
   d) They serve the interests of certain powerful groups, even though they penalize society as a whole.

7. The purpose of trade adjustment assistance is to
   a) assist foreign countries when a tariff or quota is used to reduce imports from that country.
   b) assist domestic workers who are harmed when a quota is levied.
   c) assist domestic workers who are harmed when a tariff is reduced or a quota is eliminated.
   d) both a and c

8. Which of the following is an accurate description of the impact of tariffs?
   a) They tend to raise the prices of imported products that are subject to the tariff.
   b) They tend to raise the prices of domestically produced products that are comparable to those being taxed.
   c) They permit inefficient industries to continue to exist.
   d) All of the above

9. Suppose that Italy can produce either 20 bicycles or 100 calculators with a unit of resources and that Taiwan can produce either 10 bicycles or 80 calculators. Which of the following statements is true?
   a) Taiwan has a comparative advantage in calculators.
   b) Taiwan has an absolute advantage in bicycles.
   c) Italy has a comparative advantage in calculators.
   d) Taiwan has an absolute advantage in calculators.

10. Why do economists prefer tariffs to quotas?
   a) Consumers may continue to buy imported products in spite of the tariff.
   b) Tariffs do not really hinder trade; in fact, they may enhance trade.

   c) As domestic products increase in price, foreign products become more competitive.
   d) Both a and c

11. Neither GATT nor the WTO has been very successful in
   a) reducing tariff rates.
   b) reducing the use of import quotas.
   c) discouraging the filing of dumping cases.
   d) All of the above

12. Dumping occurs whenever a firm
   a) charges a lower price in foreign markets than it charges in its home market.
   b) sells a lower-quality product in foreign markets than it sells in its home market.
   c) earns economic profits on its sales to foreign markets.
   d) disposes of wastes by shipping them to disposal sites in foreign countries.

Problems and Questions for Discussion

1. Suppose that your roommate can make a bed in three minutes, whereas it takes you six minutes. Suppose also that your roommate can polish a pair of shoes in ten minutes, whereas it takes you fifteen minutes to do the same chore. What can we say about comparative advantage and absolute advantage in this example? How could the principle of comparative advantage be used to make you both better off? Does it make any difference how often each of these tasks must be performed?

2. Explain the difference between comparative advantage and absolute advantage. Why do economists emphasize the concept of comparative advantage (rather than absolute advantage) as the basis for trade?

3. How is the concept of opportunity cost related to the principle of comparative advantage?

4. The chapter mentions that politicians in the United States and elsewhere often hear more about the costs of free trade than the benefits. Why is that the case?

5. How can specialization and trade allow countries to consume beyond their own respective production possibilities curves?

6. How do trade barriers contribute to the inefficient use of a society's scarce resources?

7. Some economists have suggested that interference with free trade may be legitimate if it is used as a bargaining chip to convince another country to lower its trade barriers. Economist Robert Lawrence has criticized this approach, likening it to a nuclear deterrent—something that is effective only if it isn't used. Explain Mr. Lawrence's position.

8. If resources (including labor) could move freely from one industry to the next, there would be less opposition to the removal of trade barriers. Explain.

9. As Wisconsin University economist John Culbertson once suggested, "There is little comparative advantage in today's manufacturing industries, since they produce

the same goods in the same ways in all parts of the world."("'Free Trade' Is Impoverishing the West," *New York Times*, July 28, 1985, p. F3.) How could less-developed countries gain access to the same type of capital equipment employed by the United States? Could they operate it if they could obtain it? What are the implications of Mr. Culbertson's statement?

10. State the three most common arguments for trade protection. What are the limitations of each of these arguments?

11. Why are regional trade agreements, such as NAFTA, sometimes viewed as inferior to international agreements, such as GATT?

12. How can domestic firms use antidumping laws to stifle foreign competition?

ANSWER KEY

Fill in the Blanks

1. opportunity cost
2. absolute advantage
3. comparative advantage
4. tariff
5. import quota

6. infant-industry
7. global, selective
8. trade adjustment assistance
9. benefits, costs

10. tariffs
11. Smoot–Hawley
12. GATT
13. World Trade Organization (WTO)

Multiple Choice

1. b
2. a
3. c

4. c
5. d
6. d

7. c
8. d

9. a
10. d

11. c
12. a

CHAPTER SEVENTEEN

International Finance

What are exchange rates, and how do they influence the prices we pay for imported products and even for travel? What do news commentators mean when they say that the dollar has "appreciated in value" or that the "depreciation of the yen" has made Japanese cars less expensive for Americans?

In Chapter 16 our simplified trade model assumed an arrangement whereby two countries exchanged their products directly. In reality, however, international transactions almost always involve money. Indeed, they usually involve two different types of money—the currencies of the two nations participating in the exchange. As we examine the financial dimension of international transactions, we'll learn how the dollars we spend on imported products are converted into the currencies desired by foreign producers, and we'll explore the systems used to determine exchange rates. We'll consider the factors that can cause the exchange value of a nation's currency to change and the impact of those changes on the nation's economy. Finally, we will examine the U.S. balance of payments accounts and learn what it means to have a "current account deficit" and a "capital account surplus." In short, this chapter extends the analysis of Chapter 16, allowing us to gain a more complete understanding of international trade and our economic relationships with other nations.

THE MEANING OF EXCHANGE RATES

If you want to buy a Japanese radio, you can pay for your purchase with cash, check, or credit card. Ultimately, however, Japanese producers want to receive payment in yen, their domestic currency, because their workers and domestic suppliers expect to be paid in yen. That's why Mexican avocado growers seek payment in pesos and Swiss watchmakers expect payment in Swiss francs. The need to convert dollars into foreign currency (or foreign currency into dollars) is the distinguishing feature of our trade with other nations.

The rate at which one currency can be exchanged for another currency is called the **exchange rate;** it is simply the price of one nation's currency stated in terms of another nation's currency. If you have traveled abroad, you know that the exchange rate is of more than passing interest. Suppose that you are having

Because manufacturers desire payment in their domestic currency, U.S. importers must convert dollars into Japanese yen, South Korean won, and other currencies in order to purchase foreign televisions.

dinner at a quaint London restaurant where steak and kidney pie costs ten pounds (£10). How much is that in U.S. money? If the exchange rate is £1 to $3, you'll be spending $30; if it's £1 to $1.50, the same meal will cost you only $15.

U.S. importers also want to know the dollar cost of British goods. A wool sweater that sells for £25 will cost the importer $75 if the exchange rate is £1 to $3, but it will cost $100 if the exchange rate is £1 to $4. Whenever the pound is cheaper (whenever it takes fewer dollars to purchase each pound), U.S. tourists and importers will find British goods more attractive. If the pound becomes more expensive, fewer tourists will opt for British vacations, and fewer British products will be imported into the United States.

EXCHANGE RATE SYSTEMS: FLEXIBLE EXCHANGE RATES

Today, exchange rates are determined primarily by market forces, by the interaction of the demand and supply of the various currencies. This is described as a system of **flexible**, or **floating**, **exchange rates**, since rates are free to move up or down with market forces.

To illustrate how the system works, assume that the United States and Britain are the only two countries in the world, so that we need to determine only one exchange rate, that between the U.S. dollar and the British pound. As you can see from Exh. 17.1, the demand curve for pounds slopes downward because, ceteris paribus, as the price of the pound falls, Americans will tend to buy more British products. For example, if the dollar price of the pound fell from $2.00 per pound ($2.00 = £1) to $1.50 per pound ($1.50 = £1), U.S. consumers would tend to buy more wool fashions, Scotch whiskey, and London vacations. And of course, to buy these products, they would demand more British pounds. This assumes that the other factors affecting the demand for British pounds remain unchanged. The factors that are assumed to be constant include the tastes and preferences of U.S. consumers, interest rates in the United States and Britain, and the overall price levels in the two countries. If any of these factors changes, the entire demand curve will shift to a new position.

The British supply pounds when they want to purchase dollars. If British residents want to buy U.S. products or to visit Disneyland or to invest in California real estate, they exchange their pounds to buy dollars. The supply curve of pounds slopes upward because, other things being constant, as the value of the pound increases (which means that the dollar becomes less expensive), the British want to buy more U.S. products and will therefore supply more pounds. This assumes that the tastes and incomes of British consumers remain unchanged, that British and U.S. interest rates remain constant, and that the price levels in the United States and Britain are unchanged.

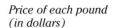

EXHIBIT 17.1
The Equilibrium Exchange Rate

*Price of each pound
(in dollars)*

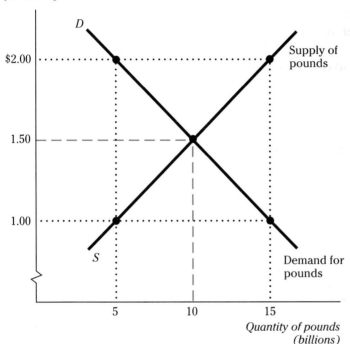

At the equilibrium exchange rate ($1.50 = £1), the quantity of pounds demanded is exactly equal to the quantity supplied. If the dollar price of the pound is too high for equilibrium, the resulting surplus will tend to reduce the price of the pound. If the price is too low for equilibrium, the shortage of pounds will tend to increase its price.

The Equilibrium Exchange Rate

The intersection of the supply and demand curves for British pounds determines the **equilibrium exchange rate**—the exchange rate at which the quantity of pounds demanded is exactly equal to the quantity supplied. In our example these market forces will lead to an equilibrium exchange rate of $1.50 = £1. At that rate 10 billion pounds are demanded and supplied.

If the exchange rate in our example were temporarily above or below the equilibrium level, pressures would exist to push it toward the equilibrium rate. For instance, if the exchange rate were $2.00 = £1, 15 billion pounds would be supplied, but only 5 billion would be demanded. This surplus of pounds would drive down the dollar price of the pound, just as a surplus drives down the price of wheat or cattle or anything else sold in a competitive market. At an exchange rate of $1.00 = £1, 15 billion pounds would be demanded but only 5 billion supplied, and the resulting shortage would tend to push the price of the pound upward. These pressures would exist until the equilibrium exchange rate had been established.

Changes in the Equilibrium Exchange Rate

Exchange rates can change frequently and sometimes quite dramatically. Any change that results in a shift of either the demand or the supply curve for a currency will cause the exchange rate to change. The factors that can shift the demand and supply curves include changes in tastes or income levels, changes in relative interest rates, and changes in price levels.

Changes in Tastes or Income Levels

Suppose that the average income in the United States increased. This would cause U.S. consumers to demand more goods and services, including British goods and services. The result would be an increase in the demand for British pounds: The demand curve for pounds would shift to the right, as depicted in Exh. 17.2. The same thing would happen if Americans suddenly found British fashions more appealing or decided to switch from American beers to those imported from Britain.

EXHIBIT 17.2
An Increase in the Demand for Pounds

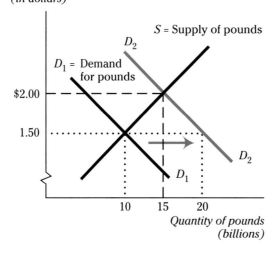

Price of each pound (in dollars)

S = Supply of pounds

D_2

D_1 = Demand for pounds

$2.00

1.50

D_1

D_2

10   15   20

Quantity of pounds (billions)

An increase in U.S. incomes or an increased preference for British products would tend to increase the demand for pounds. This would cause the pound to appreciate in value; each pound would buy more U.S. dollars than before. When the pound appreciates, the dollar depreciates; it takes more dollars to buy each pound.

When the demand curve for pounds shifts to the right, the dollar price of the pound is driven up. For example, in Exh. 17.2 you can see that the dollar price of the pound has risen from $1.50 per pound to $2.00 per pound. The dollar has **depreciated** (lost value against the pound) because it now takes more dollars to buy each pound. Conversely, the pound has **appreciated** (gained value) against the dollar because each pound now buys more dollars than before.

How would we represent the impact of an increase in British incomes or an increased desire to buy American fashions—Levi's blue jeans, for example? Either of these changes would increase the demand for U.S. products and consequently would increase the demand for U.S. dollars. And the British acquire more dollars by supplying more pounds. Remember that! To acquire more dollars, the British must supply more pounds! As a consequence, the supply curve of pounds will shift to the right, as depicted in Exh. 17.3. Would these changes cause the dollar to appreciate or to depreciate? What about the pound? Take a moment and try to answer these questions before reading further.

The correct answer is that an increase in the supply of pounds would cause the dollar to appreciate in value. As you can see from Exh. 17.3, the dollar price of the pound has declined from $1.50 to only $1.00. The dollar must be more valuable—must have appreciated—because it now takes fewer dollars to buy a pound. Conversely, the pound has depreciated in value because each pound now buys fewer dollars than before.

EXHIBIT 17.3
An Increase in the Supply of Pounds

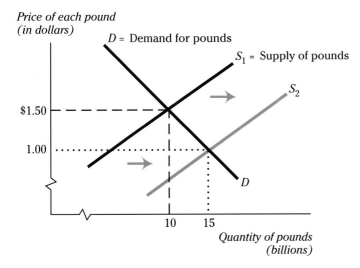

Price of each pound (in dollars)

D = Demand for pounds

S_1 = Supply of pounds

S_2

$1.50

1.00

D

10   15

Quantity of pounds (billions)

An increase in British incomes or an increased preference for U.S. products would lead to an increase in the supply of pounds. This would cause the pound to depreciate and the dollar to appreciate.

Changes in Relative Interest Rates

In the short run, one of the most important sources of changes in exchange rates is changes in relative interest rates. If British interest rates increased relative to those in the United States (as shown in Exh. 17.4), we could expect U.S. households and businesses to buy more British securities in order to earn the higher interest rates. This would shift the demand curve for pounds to the right. At the same time, fewer British investors would be willing to buy U.S. securities, and so the supply curve of pounds would shift to the left. As the exhibit shows, these changes would cause the dollar price of the pound to rise from $1.50 to $2.00; the pound would appreciate, and the dollar would depreciate.

Changes in Relative Price Levels

Changes in relative price levels also influence exchange rates. To illustrate, imagine a U.S.-made automobile that sells for $30,000 in the United States and a comparable British auto that sells for £20,000 in Britain. At an exchange rate

EXHIBIT 17.4
The Impact of Higher British Interest Rates

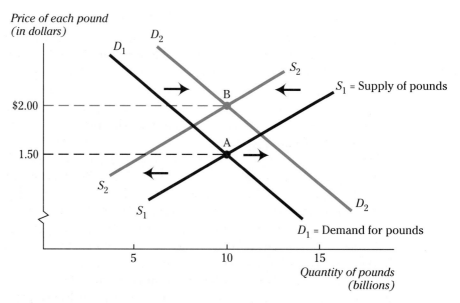

If British interest rates increase in relation to those in the United States, British securities become relatively more attractive. U.S. investors will demand more pounds in order to buy British securities, whereas British investors will reduce their purchases of U.S. securities and thus supply fewer pounds. These changes will tend to appreciate the pound and depreciate the dollar. (We move from equilibrium point *A* to point *B*.)

of $1.50 = £1, these vehicles will have the same sticker prices; the U.S. auto will sell for £20,000 in Britain and the British auto for $30,000 in the United States. Consumers in each country will choose between these vehicles on the basis of design features, available options, and other nonprice characteristics.

Now, suppose that Britain experiences 20 percent inflation while inflation in the United States is only 10 percent. On average, prices in Britain will increase by 20 percent, so that the price of the British auto will be pushed up to £24,000. U.S. prices, including automobile prices, will rise by only 10 percent, and so the U.S.-made automobile will now sell for $33,000. At an exchange rate of $1.50 = £1, U.S. automobiles now cost British consumers £22,000, whereas British automobiles will be available for $36,000 in the United States. The same thing will happen to the prices of the other products traded by the two countries. Since U.S. products have become more attractive in price, the result will be an increase in the supply of pounds (as British consumers demand more U.S. products) and a reduction in the demand for pounds (as U.S. consumers demand fewer British products). As you can see from Exh. 17.5, these changes will cause the dollar price of the pound to fall from $1.50 to $1.37. The pound has depreciated in value, whereas the dollar has appreciated.

The Impact of Changes in Exchange Rates

How will Americans react when the dollar appreciates relative to the pound; will they be happy about the stronger dollar or unhappy? (When the dollar appreciates relative to another currency, it is described as getting stronger, whereas the other currency has weakened.) In truth, it depends on which Americans we are talking about. Consider U.S. exporting firms, for example. If the dollar appreciates as it did in Exh. 17.5, U.S. products will become more expensive for British consumers and thus less attractive. To illustrate, consider a computer that is selling for $1,500 in the United States. When the exchange rate is $1.50 = £1, that computer will cost British consumers £1,000. But if the dollar appreciates so that it takes only $1.00 to buy each pound, that same computer will cost British consumers £1,500. Predictably, fewer British consumers will buy U.S. computers at the higher price, and U.S. exporters will find their sales suffering as a result of the appreciation of the dollar. And if U.S. exports suffer, some U.S. workers lose their jobs.

The other side of the story has to do with U.S. importers of British products. A stronger dollar means a weaker pound. And a weaker pound means that British products will be cheaper for Americans. Consider a bottle of premium Scotch whiskey that sells for £40 in Britain. When the exchange rate is $2.00 = £1, that bottle of whiskey will cost a U.S. importer $80. But if the pound depreciates so that the exchange rate is $1.50 = £1, that same bottle of whiskey will cost a U.S. importer only $60. So the strong dollar will be welcomed by U.S.

EXHIBIT 17.5

The Effect of a Rise in the British Price Level

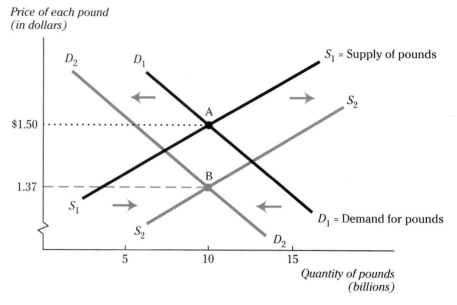

If prices in Britain rise in relation to those in the United States, U.S. products will become more attractive. British consumers will supply more pounds as they demand more U.S. products, and U.S. consumers will demand fewer pounds as they demand fewer British products. The dollar price of the pound will fall from $1.50 to $1.37 (we move from equilibrium point *A* to point *B*).

businesses that import foreign products and by U.S. consumers who buy those products. The point is that whenever the exchange rate changes, there are winners and losers; some individuals and businesses will like the change, and others will not. (The article on page 519, "Sagging Euro, Pound Raise Pressure on U.S. Exporters," looks at the dual impact of a stronger *euro*—the common currency unit used by twelve of the fifteen countries that make up the European Union. Great Britain, the country we've used to illustrate exchange rate determination, is a member of the European Union that thus far has chosen to retain its own currency rather than adopt the euro. We'll have more to say about the euro later in the chapter.)

Although changes in exchange rates are always unpopular with some groups, wide swings in exchange rates—whereby the currency appreciates or depreciates substantially in a relatively short period of time—are particularly

USE YOUR ECONOMIC REASONING

Sagging Euro, Pound Raise Pressure on U.S. Exporters

By James Cox

THE FEEBLE euro and British pound are worrying U.S. exporters, even as U.S. tourists and business travelers ride the mighty dollar to Europe in record numbers. The euro, common currency for [twelve] European countries, continues to sag near its all-time low of 88.45 cents on May 4.

Wednesday, it fell to 88.75 cents in European trading before closing in the USA at 89.24 cents. Also Wednesday, the British pound touched a seven-year low of $1.44 against the dollar in European trading.

The euro has slid steadily since its introduction at $1.17 on Jan. 4, 1999. That's worrisome to U.S. manufacturers, whose products have become more expensive in Europe and less competitive with European imports at home and in other countries.

U.S. paper, wood products and chemical companies are already feeling the impact, says Frank Vargo, trade chief at the National Association of Manufacturers. "It's slowing down exports to Europe and boosting imports from Europe. U.S. companies are going to be reluctant to lose market share, so it'll mean pressure on profits."

The strong dollar is partly behind a likely record year for travel to Europe. The European Travel Commission forecasts 12.2 million departures to Europe by U.S. citizens this year. That would be the eighth consecutive annual record and a 4.3% increase over 1999....

The euro is not expected to strengthen much in the short term, despite attempts by the European Central Bank to prop it up. The ECB meets today and is expected to raise a key interest rate from 4.25% to 4.75%, a move aimed at stemming inflation and halting the euro's slide.

Use Your Economic Reasoning

1. In the period from Jan. 4, 1999 until this article's publication, the euro declined in value from $1.17 to approximately $ .89. Did the euro appreciate or depreciate relative to the dollar? Did the dollar appreciate or depreciate relative to the euro?

2. According to the article, the "feeble euro and British pound" are worrying U.S. exporters but helping U.S. tourists who are visiting Europe. Explain this dual effect.

3. Can you imagine any U.S. companies that might be benefiting from the weak euro? What kinds of companies would they be?

4. The European Central Bank apparently thinks that it can strengthen the euro—cause it to appreciate somewhat—by pushing up interest rates in European countries. Is that expectation consistent with our model of exchange rate determination? (*Hint*: Draw a graph showing the demand and supply of euros. Measure the dollar price of the euro on the vertical axis. What impact will higher interest rates in Europe have on these demand and supply curves and on the equilibrium exchange rate?)

Source: USA Today, Aug. 31, 2000, p. 3B

disruptive. For example, from the late 1970s to the mid-1980s, the dollar appreciated an average of approximately 80 percent against foreign currencies. Then, over the next half-dozen years, the dollar fell about as much as it had risen. Some Asian nations have experienced even more volatile swings in exchange rates. For example, in 1997 Indonesia, Malaysia, and South Korea saw the value of their currencies fall more than 50 percent against the dollar in a period of less than six months. This much volatility creates a great deal of risk for firms trading internationally because they cannot know how much imports will cost (in their own country's currency) or how much they will receive for their exports.[1] In addition, wide swings in exchange rates can have a major impact on the competitiveness of exporting firms and firms facing import competition. This, in turn, can translate into undesirable volatility in the levels of domestic employment. These problems have caused some critics to argue for government intervention to "fix" or at least "manage" exchange rates. We will consider those possibilities next.

EXCHANGE RATE SYSTEMS: FIXED EXCHANGE RATES

Prior to the emergence of flexible exchange rates, the international monetary system was characterized by one form or another of **fixed exchange rates**—rates established by central governments rather than by market forces.

From the early 1800s to the end of the Great Depression, the international fixed exchange rate system was the **gold standard**; each country's currency was linked to gold. A central government agreed to buy and sell gold to anyone and everyone at a specified price stated in terms of that country's currency. For example, if the United States agreed to buy gold for $20 an ounce, and Britain agreed to pay £10 an ounce, the exchange rate of dollar to pound was $20 = £10, or $2 = £1. That rate would prevail until either the United States or Britain changed the price it was willing to pay for gold.

The gold standard fell apart following World War I for reasons that are beyond the scope of this chapter. From the end of World War I until after World War II, the international community experimented with a variety of temporary exchange rate systems, none of which gained acceptance. Then an international monetary conference held in 1944 at Bretton Woods, New Hampshire, devel-

---

[1] Many exporters and importers protect themselves against exchange rate changes by buying and selling foreign currency in the "futures market." For example, if an importer wanted to protect itself against a change in the exchange rate, it would buy forward foreign exchange of the country whose products it was importing. This means that the importer buys foreign currency to be received in the future at an exchange rate agreed on now. This service is not free, and so it increases the cost of foreign trade. And since most futures contracts cover only a few months, long-term importing and exporting agreements remain risky.

In 1944, a conference at Bretton Woods, New Hampshire, led to a new fixed exchange rate system. The British economist John Maynard Keynes (seated at the far left) represented Great Britain.

oped a new fixed exchange rate system in which the U.S. dollar played a prominent role. Under what became known as the **Bretton Woods system**, most governments agreed to maintain a fixed value for their currency in terms of the dollar; the United States agreed to redeem dollars (from foreign central banks) for gold at $35 an ounce. This linked all major currencies directly to the dollar and indirectly to one another. For example, if Britain and the United States agreed that £1 would exchange for $2, and the United States and Japan agreed that $1 would exchange for 100 yen, then one pound would exchange for 200 yen (£1 = 200 yen). Each government would then be committed to maintaining that exchange rate, even if market forces wanted to push the exchange rate elsewhere.

Fixed Exchange Rates and the Balance of Payments

To illustrate the consequences of fixed exchange rates, consider the demand and supply curves for pounds represented in Exh. 17.6. Suppose that the governments of Britain and the United States have fixed the exchange rate at $2 = £1 (or one dollar equals half a pound), and that this initially represents the equilibrium exchange rate. Now, suppose that an increase in U.S. incomes causes the demand for pounds to increase from D_1 to D_2. Under a system of flexible exchange rates, the dollar price of the pound would increase to $2.50. But that can't happen under a system of fixed exchange rates because the governments are committed to maintaining an exchange rate of $2 = £1. At the fixed exchange rate of $2 = £1, 15 billion pounds will be demanded but only 10 billion supplied; there will be a shortage of 5 billion pounds.

This shortage of pounds represents a balance of payments deficit for the United States. A **balance of payments deficit** exists when a nation's foreign expenditures exceed its foreign receipts in a given year. In our hypothetical example, the U.S. deficit is 5 billion pounds (or $10 billion at an equilibrium exchange rate of $2 per pound). Of course, if the United States has a balance of payments deficit, Britain enjoys a **balance of payments surplus**; its foreign receipts exceed its foreign expenditures.

As we've already noted, with flexible exchange rates the shortage of pounds would push the price of the pound up to $2.50. This would eliminate Britain's balance of payments surplus (and the U.S. balance of payments

---

EXHIBIT 17.6
Fixed Exchange Rates and the Balance of Payments

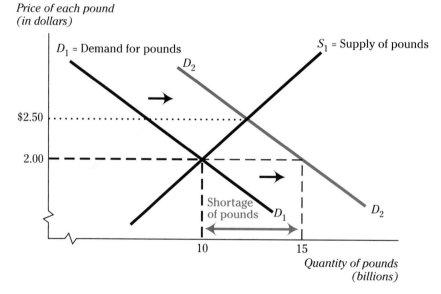

If the exchange rate is fixed at $2.00 = £1, an increase in the demand for pounds would lead to a shortage of the British currency. This shortage of pounds represents a balance of payments deficit for the United States and a balance of payments surplus for Britain.

deficit). That's one of the desirable features of flexible exchange rates; they automatically eliminate balance of payments deficits and surpluses. But because the United States and Britain are committed to maintaining an exchange rate of $2.00 = £1, that can't be allowed to happen. Instead, something must be done to maintain the agreed-on rate.

Intervention in Foreign Exchange Markets

One approach to maintaining the fixed exchange rate would be for the Federal Reserve, the U.S. central bank, to use its accumulated reserves of pounds to supply pounds to the foreign exchange market. This would tend to shift the supply curve of pounds to the right, as represented in Exh. 17.7, and allow the exchange rate to be maintained at $2.00 = £1. Alternatively, the British central bank could directly demand dollars. (Remember, in order to buy dollars, the central bank would need to supply pounds.)

EXHIBIT 17.7

Intervention in Exchange Markets

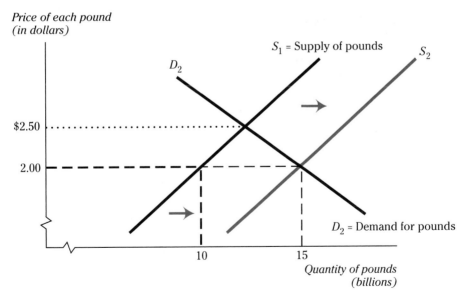

To maintain the exchange rate at $2.00 = £1, the Federal Reserve must be willing to use its reserves of pounds to buy dollars. By supplying pounds to buy dollars, the Fed can shift the supply curve of pounds to the right and maintain the fixed exchange rate.

As long as the equilibrium exchange rate is sometimes above and sometimes below the fixed exchange rate (and relatively close to it), this type of intervention can go on indefinitely. Central banks will sometimes be required to use their reserves of foreign currencies, but during other periods they will be accumulating reserves. But when a more or less permanent change in demand or supply causes the equilibrium exchange rate to remain consistently above or below the fixed rate, something has to give. In our example the Federal Reserve cannot intervene forever; eventually its reserves of pounds will run out. And the British central bank won't be willing to buy dollars forever. After all, the British are accumulating dollars without any guarantee that they will ever want to use them.

Intervention in the Domestic Economy

When persistent balance of payments problems exist, they can be eliminated by using fiscal and monetary policy to alter the demand and supply of foreign exchange. For example, the United States could eliminate its balance of payments deficit with Britain by increasing income taxes. This would reduce the disposable incomes of U.S. consumers and cause them to buy fewer British imports, shifting the demand curve for pounds back to D_1 in Exh. 17.6. Reducing government spending in the United States could accomplish the same objective, since it would also tend to reduce income levels in the United States. Alternatively, the country with a surplus (Britain) could employ an expansionary fiscal policy, cutting taxes and increasing government spending. This would tend to increase income levels and cause Britain to import more U.S. products, reducing the U.S. balance of payments deficit.

Monetary policy could be used in a similar manner. By reducing the money supply, the Fed could push up interest rates in the United States and slow spending for goods and services, including imported products. This would tend to reduce the demand for pounds. In addition, the higher interest rates available in the United States would tend to attract money from British investors, who would need to buy dollars (supply pounds) for that purpose. This would also help to reduce the U.S. balance of payments deficit. The alternative would be for Britain to expand its money supply. By driving down British interest rates, the British central bank would cause spending to increase, including spending for U.S. products. And the lower British interest rates would cause British investors to buy more U.S. securities.

Curing balance of payments problems by using monetary and fiscal policies can be tough medicine. In effect, the country with the deficit is forced to reduce employment and income as the price it must pay to eliminate the deficit. Alternatively, the country with the surplus is asked to accept the inflation that results as it expands its economy to eliminate the surplus. It was the unwillingness of either party to accept this harsh medicine that led to the breakdown of the Bretton Woods system, the fixed exchange rate system that prevailed from World War II until 1971.

THE CURRENT SYSTEM:
THE MANAGED FLOAT

As we've seen, neither fixed exchange rates nor flexible exchange rates provide nations with everything they want. Flexible exchange rates can lead to undesirable fluctuations in exchange rates, but fixed rates force countries to sacrifice domestic employment (or price stability) in order to stabilize exchange rates. Perhaps because neither of these systems is fully satisfactory, the system that has emerged for major industrialized countries can best be described as a system of managed exchange rates.

Managed exchange rates combine the flexible exchange rate system we described earlier in the chapter with intervention by central banks. Rather than completely fixing exchange rates (as in the fixed rate system), the purpose of central bank intervention is to limit or narrow exchange rate movements. In some instances they may even attempt to reverse exchange rate changes they consider inappropriate or to hasten exchange rate changes they see as desirable. This system of quasiflexible exchange rates is sometimes described as **managed float.**

Like flexible exchange rates and fixed exchange rates, the managed float has also been subject to criticism. Even with intervention, exchange rates have proved to be quite volatile. This is not surprising when you recognize that the amounts central banks can spend to intervene in foreign exchange markets are small in comparison with the total amounts traded. For example, when central banks intervene, they spend something on the order of $1 or $2 billion a day. That compares with approximately $200 billion in foreign currency trading taking place on the average day. So while central banks may be effective in offsetting minor changes in supply and demand conditions or in slowing the pace of more fundamental changes, it is unlikely that central banks can preserve exchange rates that are significantly out of line with prevailing demand and supply conditions for the currencies in question. As a consequence, exchange rates have remained quite volatile, and the search continues for an exchange rate system that can provide greater stability in exchange rates without the problems posed by the fixed exchange rate systems of the past. (Some of the countries in the European Union have agreed on a novel solution to the problem of exchange rate volatility and the associated **exchange rate risk**—the risk of losing income or wealth when the exchange rate changes unexpectedly. As you have learned earlier in this chapter, these countries have chosen to adopt a common currency, the euro, to replace their individual national currencies.[2] (Read "The Euro: A Dismal Failure, a Ringing Success," on page 528, to learn about the impact of this change.)

THE U.S. BALANCE OF PAYMENTS ACCOUNTS

Regardless of the exchange rate system adopted, countries will always want to keep track of their transactions with other nations. They want to know how dependent they are on imported products and how well their own exports are selling. And they're interested in where their residents are investing and in how much foreign money is being invested in their land. The answers to these questions and others are contained in a nation's balance of payments statement.

The U.S. **balance of payments (BOP) statement** is a record of all economic transactions between the United States and the rest of the world during a given year. Like other accounting statements, the BOP statement records credits and debits. Transactions that provide us with foreign exchange (the sale of exports, for example) are recorded as credits and are entered with a plus sign. Transactions that require us to use foreign exchange (such as the purchase of imports) are recorded as debits and are entered with a minus sign.

To simplify the recording of these debits and credits, the BOP statement is divided into four main sections: the current account, the capital account, the statistical discrepancy, and official reserve transactions. These categories are clearly indicated in Exh. 17.8, which depicts the U.S. balance of payments statement for 2000.

The Current Account

The first entries listed under the **current account** are merchandise exports and imports. The exports figure (a credit) reflects the value of the computers, airplanes, agricultural products, and other merchandise sold by U.S. firms to buyers in other countries. The figure for imports (a debit) reflects our purchases of Japanese automobiles, Brazilian coffee, Canadian lumber, and any other merchandise purchased from foreign sellers. As you can see

---

[2] At present, twelve of the fifteen member countries of the European Union have adopted the euro as their common currency. The countries in the "euro zone" are Austria, Belgium, Finland, France, Germany, Greece, Ireland, Italy, Luxembourg, the Netherlands, Portugal, and Spain. At the time of this writing, Britain, Denmark, and Sweden are also members of the European Union, but have not adopted the euro.

EXHIBIT 17.8

The U.S. Balance of Payments Accounts: 2000 (Billions of Dollars)

Current Account

Merchandise exports*	+ 773.3	
Merchandise imports	– 1,222.7	
Merchandise balance	– 449.4	
Service exports	+ 296.2	
Service imports	– 215.2	
Service balance	+ 81.0	
Receipts of investment income	+ 345.3	
Payments of investment income**	– 351.2	
Balance on investment income	-5.9	
Balance on current account		– 374.3

Capital Account

Capital inflows	+ 916.5	
Capital outflows	– 552.3	
Balance on capital account		+ 364.2
Statistical Discrepancy		– 25.5

Official Reserve Transactions

Increase (–) in U.S. reserve assets abroad	– .3	
Increase (+) in foreign reserve assets in the United States	+ 35.9	
Official reserve balance		+ 35.6

*The figures for exports and imports will differ slightly from those presented in earlier chapters.

**This entry includes unilateral transfers such as gifts and charitable contributions made to people and organizations in other countries and aid provided to foreign governments.

Source: U.S. Department of Commerce, Bureau of Economic Analysis News Release, "U.S. International Transactions: Fourth Quarter and Year 2000" (March 15, 2001).

from Exh. 17.8, in 2000 U.S. merchandise imports exceeded exports by $449.4 billion. This means that the United States experienced a **trade deficit** in 2000. If merchandise exports had exceeded merchandise imports, the United States would have enjoyed a **trade surplus.**

The next entries in the current account are the exports and imports of services. This category includes such items as shipping and banking services,

USE YOUR ECONOMIC REASONING

The Euro: A Dismal Failure, a Ringing Success

By G. Thomas Sims and
David Wessel

FRANKFURT—The euro has been a surprise in two ways: It has dropped nearly 30% against the dollar in its first 22 months. And it has changed European financial markets, businesses and the economy faster than its founders dared to hope.

The first fact steals the headlines, prompts European Central Bank intervention and makes the common-currency experiment look like a failure. The second likely will have more lasting and profound effects, and will help sustain the euro during troubled times....

The euro is—as some of its proponents had hoped, and some of its detractors had feared— eroding national economic boundaries, prompting national stock and bond markets to consolidate and pressuring European governments, which now have a common monetary policy, to harmonize other economic policies....

Apart from the currency's alarming decline, the ramifications of its use are big, and will be unsettling. "The speed of these changes has been breathtaking, their implications far-reaching," says Barry Eichengreen, an international economist at the University of California at Berkeley. "This revolution in European finance implies that the European economy will be market-driven to a far greater extent in the future than in the past. It implies the decline of the national champions on which European industrial policy has long been based." The speed with which national bond markets have evolved into a much larger European market has been a "deep surprise," Mr. Eichengreen says....

"It's extremely unfortunate the euro is weak for its maiden flight," says Charles Wyplosz, a professor at the University of Geneva. "The fact is, monetary union is doing pretty well."

One instant benefit of the euro is that exchange rates among the 11 member countries—soon to be 12, when Greece joins in January—are fixed, eliminating what had been one major business risk in Europe. So for all the criticism the ECB gets these days, Ernst Welteke, president of the German central bank and, in that role, one of the 17 members of the ECB's governing council, is greeted as a hero when he visits Bosch GmbH in Stuttgart. He says senior managers at the German auto-parts maker praise the euro because it has permanently locked exchange rates with many of the company's most important export destinations.

In the past, for example, Bosch was susceptible to frequent changes in the Italian government, which would

Source: Wall Street Journal, Nov. 6, 2000. p. A29.

play havoc with the lira and lead to lower revenue. Bosch's profit in 1999 was 64% higher than in 1995, a time of volatile exchange rates throughout Europe. "Business in Euroland is certainly made easier through the euro," Bosch spokesman Helmut Krause says. "Two-thirds of Bosch's 1999 sales came from outside Germany; two-thirds of Bosch's 1999 sales revenue came from outside Germany; 39% of sales revenues came from other European countries."

"The disappearance of currency risk has been one of the most important factors behind the deepening and harmonization of European markets," says the ECB's Ms. [Sirkka] Haemaelaeinen. "Even though we are still lagging behind, we are gradually coming to a situation similar to that in the U.S."

Of course, importers are struggling…. It was "difficult to cope" with currency fluctuations in the mid-1990s, says Karsten Pomaska, controller for Vivanco AG, a German manufacturer and importer of accessories for consumer electronics. "Today it's much easier. The idea behind the euro is still very good, and there is no real alternative to this thing." But the euro's weakness against the dollar is a big problem, because Vivanco buys 70% of its goods in dollars from Asia, leading the company to raise prices. "The disadvan-

tages due to weakness of the euro nearly counter the advantages of fixed exchange rates within the euro area," Mr. Pomaska says.

By removing the risk that smaller, inflation-prone economies, such as Italy and Spain, will be forced to devalue their currencies against the mighty German mark, the euro clearly means interest rates are lower than they would otherwise be in some places….

The euro also is helping to create a larger and more liquid stock market, because investors are more willing to buy and trade shares in euros rather than just in lire or Portuguese escudos….

Grapes Communications—the Dutch telecom company that has operations in Italy, Spain, Portugal and Greece—already has tapped the junk bond market for 200 million euros to finance ac-

quisitions and build a fiber-optic network in Italy. Mr. Lucciola, the finance director, is now courting big-name investors in anticipation of an initial public offering of its shares as soon as stock-market conditions improve….

Not everyone is a winner. Companies used to rely on local banks to secure funding but now step right over them and pay an investment bank, which can quickly put together a bond for financing. This has put banks in stiff competition and further increased consolidation in the sector….

Mr. Lucciola of Grapes, a former banker himself, says it is becoming "tougher for local banks to be competitive." Grapes can do most of its business with places like J.P. Morgan & Co. and Chase Manhattan Corp. Four years ago, local banks had a monopoly….

Use Your Economic Reasoning

1. What is exchange rate risk? Does the existence of the euro eliminate all exchange rate risks for European firms in the euro zone? What if the transactions involve French and German firms? What if German and U.S. firms are involved?
2. The European Central Bank's Ms. Haemaelaeinen says that Europe is "gradu-

ally coming to a situation similar to that in the U.S." What situation is she talking about? How does that situation benefit U.S. firms?
3. Karsten Pomaska, the controller for the German firm Vivanco AG, says that the weak euro has been a big problem for them. Why? What types of firms would you expect to benefit from a weak euro?

insurance, and tourist expenditures. For example, if Colombian rose growers decide to use U.S. air carriers to ship their flowers to market, the transportation charge will be recorded as a credit in the services category of our balance of payments statement. On the other hand, when U.S. citizens vacation in Paris, their expenditures are recorded as a debit under services. Exhibit 17.8 reveals that in 2000 the value of service exports exceeded the value of service imports by $81.0 billion.

The final entries in the current account record investment income paid to and received from foreigners. This includes interest and dividend income earned by U.S. residents on investments in other countries (a credit) and interest and dividend income earned by foreign residents on investments in the United States (a debit). If you're earning interest on money in a Swiss bank account, that interest payment will be recorded as a credit in the U.S. balance of payments. On the other hand, when General Motors makes dividend payments to British stockholders, that payment will be recorded as a debit. According to the exhibit, in 2000 U.S. interest and dividend payments exceeded receipts by almost $6 billion.

The current account balance gives us the net result of all transactions involving merchandise, services, and payments of investment income. In 2000, the United States spent $374.3 billion more for these purposes than it received, and so it had a current account deficit of that amount. (If it had earned more than it spent, it would have enjoyed a current account surplus.)

The Capital Account

Like individuals, nations can spend more than they earn either by selling assets to raise money or by borrowing. For example, one of the ways that the United States can pay for a current account deficit is by selling some of its capital assets—real estate or factories or entire businesses—to foreigners. So if a group of Japanese businesspeople buys a quaint San Francisco hotel or a small midwestern brewery, that transaction will be recorded as a credit under our **capital account.** The United States can also finance its current account deficit by borrowing money. This is accomplished when foreigners purchase U.S. stocks and bonds and bank accounts. Since these transactions also provide us with foreign funds, they too are recorded as credits under the capital account. Of course, while some U.S. residents are selling assets and borrowing money, others may be buying foreign assets and lending abroad. If a U.S. resident purchases an Italian winery or buys stock in a new Canadian company or opens a bank account in Japan, these transactions are recorded as debits under the capital account.

As you can see, the United States enjoyed a large capital account surplus in 2000. The $364.2 billion surplus was almost enough to finance the substantial current account deficit it experienced that year.

Statistical Discrepancy

If we compare the balance on current account and the balance on capital account, it appears that the United States experienced a balance of payments deficit of $10.1 billion in 2000. That is, the country's foreign spending exceeded its foreign earnings by $10.1 billion. But that figure misrepresents the true situation. When information is collected for the balance of payments accounts, some transactions are missed or improperly recorded. The entry entitled **statistical discrepancy** reflects an adjustment to compensate for these transactions. After adjustment for the statistical discrepancy ($25.5 billion), we find that the U.S. actually had a balance of payments deficit of $35.6 billion in 2000.[3]

Official Reserve Transactions

Whenever a balance of payments deficit exists, it must be financed in some way. The primary method is through **official reserve transactions** by central banks.

The Federal Reserve and foreign central banks maintain reserves of foreign currencies that they can use to intervene in exchange markets. The Fed maintains reserves of Japanese yen and euros, for example, whereas the European Central Bank maintains reserves of yen and dollars. Exhibit 17.8 indicates that in 2000 the Fed increased its holdings of reserve assets by $.3 billion. (It was using dollars to buy foreign currencies.) This entry is recorded as a debit because, like U.S. imports, it increases the demand for foreign currency. Over the same period, foreign central banks increased their holdings of reserve assets (dollars) held in the United States by $35.9 billion. By buying dollars (and supplying foreign currencies), these central banks, in effect, loaned U.S. residents another $35.9 billion to finance their expenditures abroad. The net effect of these two official reserve transactions is to provide a credit of $35.6 billion, exactly enough to finance the U.S. balance of payments deficit.

As you can see from this example, a nation's balance of payments statement always balances. The only question is *how* it will balance. If a country experiences a current account deficit, it must be offset by a capital account surplus or by official reserve transactions or by some combination of the two. If a country experiences a current account surplus, the surplus must be offset either by a capital account deficit or by official reserve transactions or by some combination of the two.

The common wisdom is that a nation cannot run current account deficits indefinitely; ultimately it must learn to "live within its means." But the United States has recorded such deficits for more than a decade. Clearly our

---

[3] Recall that before adjusting for the statistical discrepancy the U.S. had a BOP deficit of $10.1 billion. If we add the statistical discrepancy of $25.5 billion, the result is a deficit of $35.6 billion.

capacity to spend more than we earn depends on our ability to attract foreign investment funds (to generate a surplus in the capital account). When foreigners no longer see the United States as an attractive place to invest, the dollar will tend to depreciate, and the current account deficit will shrink. But as long as foreign residents and central banks are willing to loan us the foreign exchange we need to finance our present spending habits, our current account deficits can continue.

SUMMARY

The feature that distinguishes international trade from trade within a nation is the need to convert the currency of one nation to the currency of some other nation. The rate at which one currency is exchanged for some other currency is called the *exchange rate.* The exchange rate plays a critical role in determining each country's level of imports and exports. Whenever the dollar is cheaper—that is, whenever it takes fewer pounds or yen or pesos to purchase each dollar—importers find U.S. goods more attractive, and Americans will find British and Japanese and Mexican goods more expensive. On the other hand, if the dollar becomes more expensive, U.S. goods will become less attractive and foreign goods a better buy.

Under a system of *flexible,* or *floating, exchange rates,* exchange rates are determined by market forces, by the interaction of demand and supply. At the *equilibrium exchange rate,* the quantity demanded of a currency is equal to the quantity supplied, and there is neither a shortage nor a surplus of the currency.

The equilibrium exchange rate will change in response to changes in the demand or supply of the currency being exchanged. When the exchange value of a nation's currency increases relative to other currencies, the currency has *appreciated* in value; when its exchange value declines, it has *depreciated* in value. Factors that will shift the demand and supply curves of currencies include changes in the tastes and income levels in the trading countries, changes in relative income levels in the trading countries, and changes in relative prices in the trading countries.

The alternative to flexible exchange rates is a system of fixed exchange rates. *Fixed exchange rates* are established by central governments rather than by market forces. Under a system of fixed exchange rates, nations are expected to use central bank intervention or monetary and fiscal policies to maintain the established rate. The *gold standard* and the *Bretton Woods system* are examples of fixed exchange rate systems.

Neither fixed nor flexible exchange rates provide nations with everything they desire. Flexible exchange rates can lead to undesirable fluctuations in exchange rates, whereas fixed rates may force countries to sacrifice domestic employment or price stability in order to stabilize exchange rates. Because neither system is fully satisfactory, most nations have turned to a system of managed exchange rates. *Managed exchange rates* combine the flexible exchange rate system with occasional intervention by central banks.

Regardless of the exchange rate system, countries want to keep track of their transactions with other nations. This is facilitated through a balance of payments statement. A *balance of payments statement* is a record of all economic transactions between a given country and the rest of the world.

Each country's balance of payments statement is divided into four parts: the current account, the capital account, the statistical discrepancy, and official reserve transactions. The *current account* is the portion of the balance of payments statement that records the exports and imports of goods and services. The *capital account* records the purchase and sale of capital assets, including factories and businesses, as well as stocks, bonds, and bank accounts. The *statistical discrepancy* adjusts for missing or improperly recorded transactions. The *official reserve transactions* entry is a record of the purchase or sale of reserve assets—including reserve currencies—by central banks. These reserve transactions commonly reflect central bank intervention in exchange markets.

When all transactions have been completed, each country's balance of payments statement must balance. If a country has a deficit on current account, that deficit (after adjustment for any statistical discrepancy) must be offset by a surplus on capital account or official reserve transactions.

KEY TERMS

Appreciation of currency
Balance of payments deficit
Balance of payments (BOP) statement
Balance of payments surplus
Bretton Woods system
Capital account
Current account

Depreciation of currency
Equilibrium exchange rate
Exchange rate
Exchange rate risk
Fixed exchange rate
Flexible exchange rate
Floating exchange rate
Gold standard

Managed exchange rates
Managed float
Official reserve transactions
Statistical discrepancy
Trade deficit
Trade surplus

STUDY QUESTIONS

Fill in the Blanks

1. The price of one currency in terms of another currency is called the

   _____ .

2. Another term for foreign currency is

   _____ .

3. When imports exceed exports, a country is

   experiencing a _____ ;
   when exports exceed imports, a country is ex-

   periencing a _____ .

4. The _____ refers
   to merchandise imports and exports, whereas

   the _____ refers to all economic transactions between nations.

5. There are essentially two types of exchange rate systems: those involving

   _____ exchange rates and those

   involving _____ exchange
   rates.

6. Under a system of flexible exchange rates,
   if it takes more British pounds than before
   to buy a U.S. dollar, we can say that the dol-

   lar has _____ and that the

   pound has _____ .

7. If per capita incomes increased in the
   United States as a result of an economic expansion, U.S. imports of foreign products
   would probably (increase/decrease)

   _____ .

8. If a country's exports of goods and services
   exceeded its imports of goods
   and services, it would experience a

   _____ account

   _____
   (deficit/surplus).

9. If interest rates are higher in the United
   States than they are abroad, foreign investors will tend to invest more money
   in the United States, and the dollar will
   tend to (appreciate/depreciate)

   _____ in value.

10. If the dollar appreciates in value, it will

    be (harder/easier) _____
    for U.S. producers to sell their products
    abroad.

Multiple Choice

1. If total merchandise exports by the United
   States exceed total merchandise imports,
   the United States is experiencing a
   a) balance of payments deficit.
   b) balance of payments surplus.
   c) trade deficit.
   d) trade surplus.

2. Which of the following is not a source of
   foreign exchange for the United States?
   a) Foreign tourists visiting the United
      States
   b) U.S. exports to France
   c) U.S. imports from Japan
   d) German investments in the United States

3. For which of the following transactions must the United States acquire foreign exchange?
   a) Buying Japanese automobiles
   b) Investing in French companies
   c) Paying dividends to Arabs on their U.S. investments
   d) All of the above

4. If Americans decide to buy more Japanese automobiles,
   a) the demand curve for Japanese yen will shift to the left.
   b) the demand curve for American dollars will shift to the right.
   c) the demand curve for Japanese yen will shift to the right.
   d) the supply curve of Japanese yen will shift to the right.

5. The Bretton Woods system
   a) preceded the gold standard.
   b) was identical to the gold standard.
   c) was established after World War II.
   d) lasted until 1982.

6. If interest rates in the euro zone increased relative to those in the United States,
   a) Americans would tend to demand fewer euros.
   b) Europeans would tend to supply more euros.
   c) the euro would tend to appreciate relative to the dollar.
   d) the dollar would tend to appreciate relative to the euro.

7. If the price level in Japan increases more rapidly than the price level in the United States,
   a) the Japanese will tend to supply more yen, appreciating the dollar relative to the yen.
   b) the Japanese will tend to supply fewer yen, appreciating the dollar relative to the yen.
   c) U.S. consumers will tend to demand more yen, depreciating the dollar relative to the yen.
   d) U.S. consumers will tend to demand more yen, appreciating the dollar relative to the yen.

8. If the European central bank intervenes in the foreign exchange market by buying dollars for euros, the intervention would tend to
   a) depreciate the dollar relative to the euro.
   b) appreciate the euro relative to the dollar.
   c) depreciate both the euro and the dollar.
   d) appreciate the dollar.

9. The purchase of a French company by a U.S. business would be recorded in the U.S. balance of payments accounts as a
   a) credit in the current account.
   b) debit in the current account.
   c) credit in the capital account.
   d) debit in the capital account.

10. Interest payments to foreign residents would be recorded in the U.S. balance of payments accounts as a
    a) credit in the current account.
    b) debit in the current account.
    c) credit in the capital account.
    d) debit in the capital account.

11. If the British decide to purchase more U.S. products,
    a) the demand curve for the British pound will shift to the right.
    b) the supply curve of the British pound will shift to the right.
    c) the supply curve of the American dollar will shift to the right.
    d) the supply curve of the American dollar will shift to the left.

12. If a $40,000 U.S. computer costs a Mexican importer 400,000 pesos, the exchange rate must be
    a) 1 peso to 10 dollars.
    b) 1 peso to 1 dollar.
    c) 1 dollar to 100 pesos.
    d) 1 dollar to 10 pesos.

13. Under a system of flexible exchange rates, if U.S. citizens started buying more British goods,
    a) the dollar would tend to appreciate relative to the pound.
    b) the price of the pound (in dollars) would begin to fall.

c) the dollar would tend to depreciate relative to the pound.

d) the price of the dollar (in pounds) would begin to rise.

14. If the yen price of the dollar (the price of a dollar stated in terms of Japanese yen) declined,

a) Japanese cars would cost Americans fewer dollars.

b) Japanese tourists would find American meals less expensive.

c) American cars would cost Japanese consumers more yen.

d) American tourists would be encouraged to tour Japan.

15. The existing exchange rate system is best described as a

a) gold standard.

b) system of fixed exchange rates.

c) system of flexible exchange rates.

d) managed float.

Problems and Questions for Discussion

1. If you were visiting London, which exchange rate would you prefer: $4 to £1 or $3 to £1? Why?

2. Suppose that we are operating under a system of flexible exchange rates. If Americans demand more British automobiles, will the dollar tend to appreciate or depreciate? Show this result graphically. What about the pound?

3. How was the Bretton Woods system different from the gold standard? What did the two systems have in common?

4. We sometimes read about balance of payments deficits or surpluses, but a nation's balance of payments statement must always balance. Clarify this apparent contradiction.

5. Japan's central bank has often intervened to buy dollars and prevent the dollar from depreciating relative to the yen. What is the rationale for such intervention?

6. Japan's central bank is in a better position to keep the dollar from depreciating than is the U.S. central bank (the Fed). Why? (*Hint:*

How would the Fed go about trying to appreciate the dollar?)

7. If a nation is experiencing persistent balance of payments deficits, how could monetary and fiscal policies be used to remedy this problem? Why might a nation be reluctant to use such remedies?

8. Suppose that the Fed pursues a restrictive monetary policy to combat inflation in the United States. What impact would these policies be likely to have on the current account balance, the capital account balance, and the exchange value of the dollar relative to other currencies?

9. Federal government deficits are thought to drive up domestic interest rates. How could this indirectly hurt our merchandise exports?

10. If Europe's economy entered a recession, what impact would this have on the exchange rate between the euro and the U.S. dollar? Why would it have this impact?

ANSWER KEY

Fill in the Blanks

1. exchange rate
2. foreign exchange
3. trade deficit; trade surplus
4. balance of trade, balance of payments
5. fixed, flexible
6. appreciated, depreciated
7. increase
8. current, surplus
9. appreciate
10. harder

Multiple Choice

1. d	4. c	7. a	10. b	13. c
2. c	5. c	8. d	11. b	14. b
3. d	6. c	9. d	12. d	15. d

GLOSSARY

Absolute advantage. One nation's ability to produce a product more efficiently–with fewer resources–than another nation.

Activist economists. Economists who see an important role for government in guiding the economy's performance.

Aggregate demand. The total quantity of output demanded by all sectors in the economy together at various price levels in a given time period.

Aggregate supply. The total quantity of output supplied by all producers in the economy together at various price levels in a given time period.

Allocative efficiency. Using society's scarce resources to produce in the proper quantities the products that consumers value most.

Annual inflation rate. The percent change in a price index from one year to the next.

Antitrust laws. Laws that have as their objective the maintenance and promotion of competition.

Applied research. Research conducted with a commercial purpose in mind.

Appreciation of currency. An increase in the exchange value of a currency relative to other currencies.

Asset. Anything of value owned by an entity.

Automatic stabilizers. Changes in the level of government spending or taxation that occur automatically whenever the level of aggregate income (GDP) changes.

Average fixed cost (AFC). Total fixed cost divided by the number of units being produced.

Average total cost (ATC). Total cost divided by the number of units being produced.

Average variable cost (AVC). Total variable cost divided by the number of units being produced.

Balance of payments (BOP) statement. A record of all economic transactions between a particular country and the rest of the world during some specified period of time.

Balance of payments deficit. Total payments to other countries exceed total receipts from other countries for an unfavorable balance of payments.

Balance of payments surplus. Total receipts from other countries exceed total payments to other countries for a favorable balance of payments.

Balance sheet. A statement of a business's assets and liabilities.

Balanced budget. A situation in which government tax revenue is exactly equal to government expenditures.

Barriers to entry. Obstacles that discourage or prevent firms from entering an industry; examples include patent restrictions, large investment requirements, and restrictive licensing regulations.

Basic research. Research conducted to gain knowledge for its own sake.

Bretton Woods system. A fixed exchange rate system whereby nations agreed to fix a value on their currency in terms of the dollar, and the United States agreed to redeem dollars from other central banks for gold.

Budget deficit. The situation that exists when government expenditures exceed tax revenues.

Budget surplus. The situation that exists when government tax receipts exceed government expenditures.

Business cycle. The recurring ups and downs in the level of economic activity.

Capital. Physical aids to the production process; for example, factories, machinery, and tools.

Capital account. The portion of a nation's balance of payments statement that records the purchase and sale of capital assets.

Capitalism. An economic system in which the means of production are privately owned and fundamental economic choices are made by individual buyers and sellers interacting in markets.

Cartel. A group of producers acting together to control output and the price of their product.

Central bank. A government agency responsible for controlling a nation's money supply.

Ceteris paribus. "Other things being equal"; the assumption that other variables remain constant.

Change in demand. An increase or decrease in the quantity demanded at each possible price, caused by a change in the determinants of demand; represented graphically by a shift of the entire demand curve to a new position.

Change in quantity demanded. An increase or decrease in the amount of a product demanded as a result of a change in its price, with factors other than price held constant; represented graphically by movement along a stationary demand curve.

Change in quantity supplied. An increase or decrease in the amount of a product supplied as a result of a change in its price, with factors other than price held constant; represented graphically by movement along a stationary supply curve.

Change in supply. An increase or decrease in the amount of a product supplied at each and every price, caused by a change in the determinants of supply; represented graphically by a shift of the entire supply curve.

Checkable deposits. All types of deposits on which customers can write checks.

Civilian labor force. All persons over the age of sixteen who are not in the armed forces and who are either employed or actively seeking employment.

Civilian unemployment rate. The percentage of the civilian labor force that is unemployed.

Classical economists. A school of eighteenth- and nineteenth-century economists who believed that market economies automatically tend toward full employment.

Closed economy. An economy that does not exchange goods and services with other nations.

Coefficient of demand elasticity. A value that indicates the degree to which quantity demanded will change in response to a price change.

Coefficient of supply elasticity. A value that indicates the degree to which the quantity supplied will change in response to a price change.

Collusion. Agreement among sellers to fix prices or in some other way restrict competition.

Command socialism. An economic system in which the means of production are publicly owned and the fundamental economic choices are made by a central authority.

Common-property resources. Resources that belong to society as a whole rather than to particular individuals.

Comparative advantage. One nation's ability to produce a product at a lower opportunity cost than other nations.

Complement. A product that is normally purchased along with another good or in conjunction with another good.

Conscious parallelism. A situation in which firms adopt similar policies even though they have had no communication whatsoever.

Consumer sovereignty. An economic condition in which consumers dictate which goods and services will be produced by businesses.

Consumption tax. A tax assessed on the amount spent. Also called an *expenditure tax.*

Cost–benefit analysis. A systematic comparison of costs and benefits.

Cost-push inflation. Inflation caused by rising costs of production.

Crowding out. The phenomenon that occurs when increased government borrowing drives up interest rates and thereby reduces the level of investment spending.

Current account. The portion of a nation's balance of payments statement that records the exports and imports of goods and services.

Cyclical unemployment. Joblessness caused by a reduction in the economy's total demand for goods and services.

Deficiency payment. A payment made to farmers on a price-support program; equal to the difference between the market price and the support price times the number of bushels sold.

Demand. A schedule showing the quantities of a good or service that consumers are willing and able to purchase at various prices during a given time period, when all factors other than the product's price remain unchanged.

Demand curve. A graphical representation of demand, showing the quantities of a good or service that consumers are willing and able to purchase at various prices during a given time period, ceteris paribus.

Demand deposits. Non-interest-bearing checking accounts at commercial banks.

Demand-pull inflation. Inflation caused by increases in aggregate demand.

Deposit multiplier. The multiple by which checkable deposits (in the entire banking system) increase or decrease in response to an initial change in excess reserves.

Depreciation of currency. A decrease in the exchange value of a currency relative to other currencies.

Determinants of demand. The factors that underlie the demand schedule and determine the precise position of the demand curve: income, tastes and preferences, expectations regarding prices, the prices of related goods, and the number of consumers in the market.

Determinants of supply. The factors that underlie the supply schedule and determine the precise position of the supply curve: technology, resource prices, and number of producers in the market.

Discount rate. The rate of interest charged by the Federal Reserve on loans to depository institutions.

Discretionary fiscal policy. The deliberate changing of the level of government spending or taxation in order to guide the economy's performance.

Diseconomies of scale. Increases in the average cost of production caused by larger plant size and scale of output.

Dominant strategy. A strategy that should be pursued regardless of the strategy selected by a firm's rivals.

Dumping. The sale of a product to foreign consumers at a price that is less than the cost of producing that good or service.

Economic growth. An increase in an economy's production capacity or potential GDP.

Economic indicators. Signals or measures that tell us how well the economy is performing.

Economic loss. The amount by which total cost, including all opportunity costs, exceeds total revenue.

Economic profit. The amount by which total revenue exceeds total cost, including the opportunity cost of owner-supplied resources; also called an *above-normal profit*.

Economic resources. The scarce inputs used in the process of creating a good or providing a service; specifically, land, labor, capital, and entrepreneurship.

Economic system. The set of institutions and mechanisms by which a society provides answers to the three fundamental questions.

Economic theories. Generalizations about causal relationships between economic facts, or variables.

Economics. The study of how to use our limited resources to satisfy our unlimited wants as fully as possible.

Economies of scale. Reductions in the average cost of production caused by larger plant size and scale of output.

Entrepreneurship. The managerial function that combines land, labor, and capital in a cost-effective way and uncovers new opportunities to earn profit; includes willingness to take the risks associated with a business venture.

Equilibrium exchange rate. The exchange rate at which the quantity of a currency demanded is equal to the quantity supplied.

Equilibrium price. The price that brings about an equality between the quantity demanded and the quantity supplied.

Equilibrium quantity. The quantity demanded and supplied at the equilibrium price.

Excess reserves. Bank reserves in excess of the amount required by law.

Exchange rate. The price of one nation's currency stated in terms of another nation's currency.

Exchange rate risk. The risk of losing income or wealth when the exchange rate changes unexpectedly.

Expenditure tax. A tax assessed on the amount spent. Also called a *consumption tax*.

Exports. Goods and services produced domestically and sold to customers in other countries.

External benefits. Benefits paid for by one party or group that spill over to other parties or groups; also referred to as *spillover benefits*.

External costs. Costs created by one party or group and imposed on other (unconsenting) parties or groups; also referred to as *spillover costs*.

Externalities. Costs or benefits that are not borne by either buyers or sellers but that spill over onto third parties.

Federal budget. A statement of the federal government's planned expenditures and anticipated receipts for the upcoming year.

Federal funds market. A market that brings together banks in need of reserves and banks that temporarily have excess reserves.

Federal funds rate. The rate of interest charged by banks for lending reserves to other banks.

Firm. The basic producing unit in a market economy. Firms buy economic resources and combine them to produce goods and services.

Fixed costs. Costs that do not vary with the level of the activity in which the individual or business is engaged and that cannot be avoided; for businesses, costs that do not change with the level of output.

Fixed exchange rate. An exchange rate established by central governments rather than by market forces.

Flexible exchange rate. An exchange rate that is determined by market forces, by the supply and demand for the currency. Also described as a *floating exchange rate*.

Floating exchange rate. See *flexible exchange rate*.

Fractional reserve principle. The principle that a bank needs to maintain only a fraction of a dollar in reserve for each dollar of its demand deposits.

Free trade. Trade that is not hindered by artificial restrictions or trade barriers of any type.

Frictional unemployment. People who are out of work because they are in the process of changing jobs or are searching for their first job.

Full employment. When the actual rate of unemployment is equal to the natural rate of unemployment.

Game theory. The study of the strategies employed by interdependent firms.

Gold standard. A fixed exchange rate system whereby the value of each country's currency is directly tied to gold.

Government failure. The enactment of government policies that produce inefficient and/or inequitable results.

Government franchise. An exclusive license to provide some product or service.

Gross domestic product. The total monetary value of all final goods and services produced within a nation in one year.

Gross national product. The total monetary value of all final goods and services produced by domestically owned factors of production in one year.

Household. A living unit that also functions as an economic unit. Whether it consists of a single person or a large family, each household has a source of income and responsibility for spending that income.

Human capital. The knowledge and skills that are embodied in labor. Human capital is acquired through education and training.

Import quota. A law that specifies the maximum amount of a particular product that can be imported.

Imports. Goods and services that are purchased from foreign producers.

Income effect. Consumer ability to purchase greater quantities of a product that has declined in price.

Industry. A group of firms that produce identical or similar products.

Industry structure. The makeup of an industry: its number of sellers and their size distribution, the nature of the product, and the extent of barriers to entry.

Inferior good. A product for which demand decreases as income increases and increases as income decreases.

Inflation. A rise in the general level of prices.

Inflationary gap. The amount by which the equilibrium level of real GDP exceeds potential GDP.

Interest rate effect. The increase in the amount of aggregate output demanded that results from the lower interest rates that accompany a reduction in the overall price level.

Internal benefits. The benefits accruing to the person or persons purchasing a good or service; also referred to as *private benefits*.

Internal costs. The costs borne by the firm that produces the good or service; also referred to as *private costs*.

Internalize costs. Consider external costs as if they were private costs.

International economics. The study of international trade and finance: why nations trade and how their transactions are financed.

International trade effect. The increase in the amount of aggregate output demanded that results when a reduction in the price level makes domestic products less expensive in relation to foreign products.

Investment tax credit. A tax reduction available to firms that invest in eligible equipment.

Invisible hand. A doctrine introduced by Adam Smith in 1776 holding that individuals pursuing their self-interest will be guided (as if by an invisible hand) to achieve objectives that are also in the best interest of society as a whole.

Joint research venture. Research projects in which firms pool their resources and share the costs of research and development.

Labor. The mental and physical work of those employed in the production process.

Laissez-faire economy. An economy in which the degree of government intervention is minimal.

Land. All the natural resources or raw materials used in production; for example, acreage, timber, water, iron ore.

Law of demand. The quantity demanded of a product is negatively, or inversely, related to its price. Consumers will purchase more of a product at lower prices than at higher prices.

Law of increasing costs. As more of a particular product is produced, the opportunity cost per unit will increase.

Law of supply. The quantity supplied of a product is positively, or directly, related to its price. Producers will supply a larger quantity at higher prices than at lower prices.

Liabilities. The debts of an entity, or what it owes.

Lifetime Learning Tax Credit. A federal program that provides a tax deduction equal to 20 percent of the cost of qualified educational expenses.

Loanable funds market. The market in which businesses and households borrow funds to make investments.

Logrolling. The trading of votes to gain support for a proposal.

Long run. The period of time during which all a business's inputs, including plant and equipment, can be changed.

Long-run equilibrium. A situation in which the size of an industry is stable: There is no incentive for additional firms to enter the industry and no pressure for established firms to leave it.

Loss. The excess of total cost over total revenue.

M-1. Federal Reserve definition of the money supply that includes currency in the hands of the public plus all checkable deposits; the narrowest definition of the money supply.

M-2. Federal Reserve definition of the money supply that includes all of M-1 plus money-market mutual fund balances, money-market deposits at savings institutions, and small savings deposits.

M-3. Federal Reserve definition of the money supply that includes all of M-2 plus large savings deposits.

Macroeconomics. The study of the economy as a whole and the factors that influence the economy's overall performance.

Managed exchange rates. Exchange rates that are determined by market forces with some intervention by central banks. Also described as a *managed float*.

Managed float. See *managed exchange rates*.

Marginal. Additional or extra.

Marginal cost (MC). The additional cost of producing one more unit of output.

Marginal revenue (MR). The additional revenue to be gained by selling one more unit of output.

Marginal social benefit. The benefit that the consumption of another unit of output conveys to society.

Marginal social cost. The cost that the production of another unit of output imposes on society.

Market. All actual or potential buyers and sellers of a particular item. Markets can be international, national, regional, or local.

Market failure. Situations in which a market economy produces too much or too little of certain products and thus does not make the most efficient use of society's limited resources.

Market power. Pricing discretion; the ability of a firm to influence the market price of its product.

Means of production. The raw materials, factories, farms, and other economic resources used to produce goods and services.

Medium of exchange. A generally accepted means of payment for goods and services; one of the three basic functions of money.

Merger. The union of two or more companies into a single firm.

Microeconomics. The study of the behavior of individual economic units.

Mixed economies. Economies that represent a blending of capitalism and socialism. All real-world economies are mixed economies.

Monetarism. The belief that changes in the money supply play the primary role in determining the level of aggregate output and prices in the economy.

Monetary policy. Any action intended to alter the supply of money in order to influence the level of total spending and thereby combat unemployment or inflation.

Monetary rule. A rule that would require the Federal Reserve to increase the money supply at a constant rate.

Monopolistic competition. An industry structure characterized by a large number of small sellers of slightly differentiated products and by modest barriers to entry.

Monopoly. An industry structure characterized by a single firm selling a product for which there are no close substitutes and by substantial barriers to entry.

Motivating. The function of providing incentives to supply the proper quantities of demanded products.

Nash equilibrium. A situation in which each firm's strategy is the best it can choose, given the strategies chosen by the other firms in the industry.

National saving. The sum of private saving and public saving; the total amount of saving taking place in an economy.

Natural monopoly. A situation in which a single firm can supply the entire market at a lower average cost than two or more firms could.

Natural rate of unemployment. The minimum level of unemployment that an economy can achieve in normal times. The rate of unemployment that would exist in the absence of cyclical unemployment.

Near money. Assets that are not money but that can be converted quickly to money.

Nonactivist economists. Economists who do not believe that government should play an active role in attempting to guide the economy's performance.

Normal good. A product for which demand increases as income increases and decreases as income decreases.

Normal profit. An amount equal to what the owners of a business could have earned if their resources had been employed elsewhere; the opportunity cost of owner-supplied resources.

Normative issue. A question that calls for a value judgment about how things ought to be.

NOW account. A savings account on which the depositor can write checks; NOW stands for negotiable order of withdrawal.

Official reserve transactions. The purchase and sale of reserve assets by central banks.

Oligopoly. An industry structure characterized by a few relatively large sellers and substantial barriers to entry.

Open economy. An economy that exchanges goods and services with other nations.

Open-market operations. The buying and selling of government securities by the Federal Reserve as a means of influencing the money supply.

Opportunity cost. The best, or most valued, alternative that is sacrificed when a particular action is taken.

Owners' equity. The owners' claims on the assets of the business; it is equal to assets minus liabilities.

Physical capital. Physical aids to production. Examples include machines, tools, and factories.

Policy ineffectiveness theorem. The theory that systematic monetary and fiscal policies cannot alter the level of output or employment in the economy; they can change only the price level.

Price ceiling. A legally established maximum price below the equilibrium price.

Price discrimination. The practice of charging different consumers different prices for the same product.

Price elasticity of demand. A measure of the responsiveness of the quantity demanded of a product to a change in its price.

Price elasticity of supply. A measure of the responsiveness of the quantity supplied of a product to a change in its price.

Price index. A measure of changes in the general level of prices. Three basic price indexes are used in the United States: the Consumer Price Index, the Producer Price Index, and the Implicit Price Deflator.

Price leadership. An informal arrangement whereby a single firm takes the lead in all price changes in the industry.

Price searcher. A firm that possesses pricing discretion.

Price support. A legally established minimum price above the equilibrium price.

Price taker. A firm that must accept price as a given that is beyond its control.

Private benefits. The benefits accruing to the person or persons purchasing a good or service; also referred to as *internal benefits*.

Private costs. The costs borne by the firm that produces the good or service; also referred to as *internal costs*.

Private goods that yield significant external benefits. Products that convey most of their benefits to the person making the purchase but also create substantial external benefits for other individuals or groups.

Private saving. The amount of income that households have left over after subtracting taxes and consumption spending.

Product differentiation. Distinguishing a product from similar products offered by other sellers in the industry through advertising, packaging, or physical product differences.

Production efficiency. Producing a product at the lowest possible average total cost. The essence of production efficiency is that each product is produced with the fewest possible scarce resources .

Production possibilities curve. A curve that shows the combinations of goods that an economy is capable of producing with its present stock of economic resources and existing techniques of production.

Productivity of labor. The amount of output the average worker is able to produce. A common measure of the productivity of labor is output per hour.

Profit. The excess of a business's total revenue over its total cost.

Profit maximizer. A business that attempts to earn as much profit as possible.

Property rights. The legal rights to use goods, services, or resources.

Public choice. The study of how government makes economic decisions.

Public debt. The accumulated borrowings of the federal government; also known as the *national debt*.

Public goods. Products that convey their benefits equally to paying and nonpaying members of society.

Public saving. The amount of tax revenue that is left over after the government pays for its spending.

Pure competition. A situation in which a large number of relatively small buyers and sellers interact.

Pure private goods. Products that convey their benefits only to the purchaser.

Rationing. The function of dividing up or allocating a society's scarce items among those who want them.

Real balance effect. The increase in the amount of aggregate output demanded that results from an increase in the real value of the public's financial assets.

Real gross domestic product. Gross domestic product that has been adjusted to eliminate the impact of changes in the price level.

Real income. The purchasing power of your income; the amount of goods and services it will buy.

Recessionary gap. The amount by which the equilibrium level of real GDP falls short of potential GDP.

Rent ceiling. A legally established maximum rent below the equilibrium rent.

Rent control. A legally established maximum rent below the equilibrium rent.

Required reserves. The amount of reserves a depository institution is required by law to maintain. These reserves must be in the form of vault cash or deposits with the Federal Reserve.

Research. The process of gaining new knowledge. Research is sometimes characterized as *basic research* or *applied research.*

Research and development. The term used to describe the three stages leading to technological advances: research, invention, and innovation.

Reserve requirement. The fraction of a bank's checkable deposits that must be held as required reserves.

Rule of seventy-two. The mathematical principle that a variable's doubling time roughly equals seventy-two divided by the growth rate.

Savings deposits. Interest-bearing deposits at commercial banks and savings institutions.

Secondary rationing device. A nonprice condition that supplements the primary rationing device, which is price.

Short run. The period of time during which at least one of a business's inputs (usually plant and equipment) is fixed—that is, incapable of being changed.

Shortage. An excess of quantity demanded over quantity supplied.

Social benefit. The full benefit received by all the members of society; the sum of private benefits and external benefits.

Social cost. The full cost to a society of the production and/or consumption of a product; the sum of private, or internal, costs and external costs.

Stagflation. High unemployment combined with high inflation.

Standard of value. A unit in which the prices of goods and services can be expressed; one of the three basic functions of money.

Statistical discrepancy. The entry in a nation's balance of payments statement that adjusts for missing or improperly recorded transactions.

Store of value. A vehicle for accumulating or storing wealth to be used at a future date; one of the three basic functions of money.

Structural unemployment. Unemployment caused by changes in the makeup, or structure, of the economy, whereby some skills become obsolete or in less demand.

Substitute. A product that can be used in place of some other product because, to a greater or lesser extent, it satisfies the same consumer wants.

Substitution effect. Consumers' willingness to substitute for other products the product that has declined in price.

Sunk cost. Costs that cannot be avoided. See *Fixed costs.*

Supply. A schedule showing the quantities of a good or service that producers are willing and able to offer for sale at various prices during a given time period, when all factors other than the product's price remain unchanged.

Supply curve. A graphical representation of supply.

Supply-side economics. The branch of economics that focuses on stimulating aggregate supply through policies that involve minimal government intervention.

Surplus. An excess of quantity supplied over quantity demanded.

Tariff. A tax on imported goods.

Technological advances. Discoveries that make it possible to produce more or better products from the same resources.

Technology. The state of knowledge about how to produce products.

Theories. Generalizations about causal relationships between facts, or variables.

Theory of rational expectations. The theory that people use all available information to develop realistic expectations about the future.

Total cost (TC). Total fixed cost plus total variable cost.

Total revenue (TR). The total receipts of a business from the sale of its product. Total revenue is calculated by multiplying the selling price of the product times the number of units sold.

Trade adjustment assistance. Aid to workers and firms that have been harmed by import competition.

Trade barriers. Legal restrictions on trade.

Trade deficit. Merchandise imports exceed merchandise exports for an unfavorable balance of trade.

Trade surplus. Merchandise exports exceed merchandise imports for a favorable balance of trade.

Transfer payments. Expenditures for which no goods and services are received in exchange.

Trusts. Combinations of firms organized for the purpose of restraining competition and thereby gaining economic profit.

Tying contract. An agreement specifying that the purchaser will, as a condition of sale for some product, also buy some other product offered by the seller.

Unemployment rate. See *Civilian unemployment rate.*

Utility. Personal satisfaction.

Variable costs. Costs that change with the level of output, tending to increase when output increases and to decrease when output declines.

Voluntary export restraint (VER). An agreement under which an exporting country voluntarily limits its exports to a particular country, often under threat of the imposition of a quota.

PHOTO CREDITS

Chapter 1
p. 13 Peter Southwick/Stock, Boston
p. 16 Tony Freeman/Photo Edit

Chapter 2
p. 42 AP/Wide World Photos
p. 50 Ron Chapple/FPG International

Chapter 5
p. 129 Adam Fernandez/The Image
          Works
p.147 A. Ramey/Unicorn Stock Photos,
          LLC

Chapter 6
p. 161 Spencer Grant/Stock, Boston

Chapter 7
p. 194 Spencer Grant/Stock, Boston

Chapter 8
p. 238 John Wilkes/Superstock
p. 247 © Reuters NewMedia Inc./Corbis

Chapter 9
p. 263 Alan Oddie/Photo Edit

Chapter 10
p. 298 Steven Rubin/The Image Works
p. 312 N.R. Rowan/Stock, Boston

Chapter 13
p. 398 John Ficara/Woodfin Camp &
          Associates, Inc.
p. 406 P. Hosefros/NYT Pictures

Chapter 14
p. 423 © Bettmann/Corbis
p. 438 © Bettmann/Corbis

Chapter 16
p. 480 Corbis
p. 488 Michael Hirsch/Gamma Liaison

Chapter 17
p. 511 David R. Austen/Stock, Boston
p. 521 Brown Brothers

INDEX